Criminal Justice

Criminal Justice

Andrew Sanders   LLB, MA

Deputy Director, Centre for Criminological
Research, University of Oxford,
Fellow in Law, Pembroke College, Oxford

Richard Young   LLB, PhD

Lecturer in Law, Birmingham University

Butterworths
London, Dublin, Edinburgh
1994

United Kingdom	Butterworth a Division of Reed Elsevier (UK) Ltd, Halsbury House, 35 Chancery Lane, LONDON WC2A 1EL and 4 Hill Street, EDINBURGH EH2 3JZ
Australia	Butterworths, SYDNEY, MELBOURNE, BRISBANE, ADELAIDE, PERTH, CANBERRA and HOBART
Canada	Butterworths Canada Ltd, TORONTO and VANCOUVER
Ireland	Butterworth (Ireland) Ltd, DUBLIN
Malaysia	Malyan Law Journal Sdn Bhd, KUALA LUMPUR
New Zealand	Butterworths of New Zealand Ltd, WELLINGTON and AUCKLAND
Puerto Rico	Butterworth of Puerto Rico, Inc, SAN JUAN
Singapore	Reed Elsevier (Singapore) Pte Ltd, SINGAPORE
South Africa	Butterworths Publishers (Pty) Ltd, DURBAN
USA	Butterworth Legal Publishers, CARLSBAD, California and SELEM, New Hampshire

A CIP Catalogue record for this book is available from the British Library.

ISBN 0 406 51660 X

Typeset in Sabon by M Rules
Printed by Redwood Books, Trowbridge, Wiltshire

This book is dedicated to the memory of:

Michael Young (1948–1993)

and Sylvia Sanders (1921–1983)

Preface

This is a book written for students of criminal justice at undergraduate and postgraduate level. It examines the various stages of the criminal process from the exercise of police powers on the street (stop-search and arrest), through to the final determination of the guilt or innocence of defendants in the criminal courts. We do not extend our analysis to post-conviction matters other than appeals against conviction. Sentencing and penal policy raise a number of related yet distinctive issues which merit separate treatment. Sentencing patterns are discussed within these pages only in relation to their effect on pre-trial and trial processes.

The approach taken throughout is legal (in that we analyse the law), socio-legal (in that we consider how legal rules operate in practice) and sociological (in that we discuss why the police and courts operate in the way that they do). Since this approach differs from that taken in traditional textbooks and courses, it is worth saying a little about the genesis of, and justification for, what follows.

The book has grown out of a compulsory first year undergraduate course on criminal justice which we both taught (and which one of us still teaches) at Birmingham University. Some readers might regard our approach as an interesting but marginal adjunct to a standard criminal justice course in which the exposition of rules of law is bound to take centre stage. Our experience of teaching is, to the contrary, that such an approach distorts the nature of the issues studied. The traditional positivist approach, with its claim to be focusing on law, begs the question of what is meant by law. This book tries to show that the way legal rules are operated, and their effects, are central to understanding what those rules actually are.

One consequence of this is that this book contains more critical comment and explicit value judgments than most legal texts. Readers will have to assess what we say in the light of those judgments. But what distinguishes this book from many other texts is not that we make value judgments, but that we do so openly. In our view, traditional texts are as value-laden as our own work, but maintain a spurious air of objectivity and even-handedness which can mislead the reader.

We have chosen to concentrate on 'traditional' law enforcement as practised by the police and courts. We do so not because we fail to recognise the importance of alternative strategies of law enforcement, as seen in the regulation of white collar crimes like fraud, tax evasion and pollution. Rather, our twin aims of providing a thorough analysis of the law in books and the law in action, and of producing an affordable textbook that impoverished students might think it worth buying, led us to confine our attention to what are generally regarded as mainstream concerns. We have, nonetheless, woven in broader issues of criminal justice where this seemed appropriate. We hope that this might stimulate students to rush to their overcrowded law library and harass the staff by demanding back copies of obscure journals. Who knows, perhaps such a flurry of activity might even persuade law libraries not to cancel their subscriptions to inter-disciplinary periodicals. Legal rules cannot sensibly be studied in a vacuum, but, in the current economic climate, librarians cannot be blamed for cutting back in areas which are under-utilised by staff and students.

We have not attempted to cover anywhere near all important criminal justice topics. There is no chapter on powers of entry, search and seizure, for example, and discussion of other important issues such as identification evidence and sex discrimination is limited. What we have attempted to do is provide a framework of analysis, particularly in chapter 1, within which such issues could be explored by students on their own, thus allowing them to develop research skills. This works at Birmingham, and it might even catch on in Oxford. Why not elsewhere too ?

The book was written at a time of apparently great change within the criminal justice system. The government is currently pushing two major Bills through Parliament. These are the Criminal Justice and Public Order Bill, and the Police and Magistrates' Courts Bill. Some of the provisions of these Bills were derived from the report of the Royal Commission on Criminal Justice, some were not, and some directly contradicted the position taken by the Royal Commission. The recommendations of the Royal Commission are discussed within the body of the book, as are the main elements of the two Bills insofar as that is possible. The Bills are becoming so heavily amended, however, that by the time they receive the Royal Assent they could be very different from their original versions. However, despite the great number of changes of detail taking place in the early 1990s, and the controversy that some of them have aroused, it is arguable that the government's legislative programme represents historical continuity rather than a sudden break with tradition. In many ways, this book is an argument precisely to that effect. This is why we consider that it is more important to grasp the sociological context within which the system operates than the minutiae of its legal rules. If we allow ourselves to be mesmerised by the ever changing minutiae we are in danger of failing to see the nature and shape of the picture as a whole.

We do not believe that 'the law' can be pinned down in the precise way that law students would like and many lawyers would claim. It also means that we believe that taking a snapshot of the law at any one time is less instructive than assessing the way it is developing. The best thing about these intellectual arguments is that they let us off the hook of having to claim that the law is stated as at a certain date. (If we were honest, we would have to give a different date for each chapter.) Generally speaking, major developments up to the end of 1993 are covered, and our bibliomania has extended to a few 1994 publications and cases as well.

Finally, we thank everyone who has helped us in this enterprise, in particular Niki Lacey for looking at some of our draft chapters. Jan knows what her contributions to this book were but we will not embarrass her by spelling them out in public. Rosalind in no way wishes to be associated with this book, although she has expressed an interest in any royalties.

Andrew Sanders, Oxford   May 1994
Richard Young, Birmingham

Contents

Table of Statutes

References in this Table to *Statutes* are to Halsbury's Statutes of England (Fourth Edition) showing the volume and page at which the annotated text of the Act will be found.

List of Cases

Chapter 1

Evaluating Criminal Justice

1. INTRODUCTION

In 1981, the Royal Commission on Criminal Procedure (the Philips Commission), originally set up because of the wrongful conviction of three youths for the murder of Maxwell Confait,[1] published its blueprint for a 'fair, open, workable and efficient' system.[2] It recommended that there should be a fundamental balance in criminal justice between the rights of suspects and the powers of the police.[3] Although not all of its proposals were accepted, the report of the Philips Commission led to the passing of the Police and Criminal Evidence Act 1984 (PACE) and the Prosecution of Offences Act 1985.

PACE, together with its associated codes of practice, provided, for the first time, a detailed legislative framework for the operation of police powers and suspects' rights. The 1985 Act created the Crown Prosecution Service to take over the prosecution function from the police. Lawyers, rather than the police, now have the final say on how cases should be brought to court. The aim was, in part, to try to ensure that a number of defects in criminal procedure exposed by the 'Confait Affair'—such as undue pressure on suspects to confess, the unavailability of legal advice for suspects in police stations and the absence of an independent check on police decisions—would be eliminated, thereby reducing the risk of further miscarriages of justice. However, in the late 1980s and early 1990s, a string of similar cases came to light, including the 'Guildford Four', the Maguires, Stefan Kiszko, Judith

---

[1] See the official inquiry into what became known as the 'Confait Affair', Report of an Inquiry into the Circumstances leading to the Trial of Three Persons on Charges arising out of the Death of Maxwell Confait and the Fire at 27 Doggett Road, London SE6 (HCP 90) (HMSO, 1977).

[2] Royal Commission on Criminal Procedure, Report (Cmnd 8092) (HMSO, 1981) para 10.1.

[3] Ibid paras 1.11–1.35.

Ward, the 'Cardiff Three', the 'Tottenham Three' and the Taylor sisters. The most dramatic of all was the 'Birmingham Six', who in 1991, their convictions quashed after spending 16 years in prison, emerged into the daylight punching the air in triumph.

Many of the people involved in these cases were tried before the changes in the law ushered in by the Philips Commission, but some (such as the 'Cardiff Three', where three young men were wrongly accused of murdering a prostitute) were convicted under the new regime. Also, by July 1993, the convictions of as many as 14 people had been quashed because of irregularities by one particular group of police officers (the West Midlands Serious Crime Squad), most of these being post-PACE cases.[4] The pressure created by these spectacular miscarriages of justice led to the establishment of the Royal Commission on Criminal Justice (the Runciman Commission), which reported in 1993.[5] Never before had the due process protections for suspects against wrongful conviction appeared to require such urgent repair work. In this book we shall consider whether the new framework established by the 1984 and 1985 Acts is basically sound, there simply being a need for the existing safeguards to be operated properly. Another view is that something more than mere tinkering is needed if suspects are to be adequately protected. An opposite view is that the pendulum has already swung so far in favour of safeguards for suspects that the ability of the police to bring criminals to justice has been unduly hampered.

A first step in evaluating the criminal justice system must be to establish what it is supposed to be achieving. The government has stated that it is wholly committed to the following aims:[6]

- to prevent and reduce crime, especially violent crime, and help victims;
- to ensure that those suspected, accused or convicted of crimes are dealt with fairly, justly and with the minimum of delay;
- to convict the guilty and acquit the innocent;
- to punish those found guilty in a suitable manner, and where possible, discourage further offending;
- to achieve these aims as economically, efficiently and effectively as possible.

The problem is that these aims may come into conflict with one another and so decisions need to be made as to which should take priority.

---

[4] Many of these cases are discussed in T Kaye, 'Unsafe and Unsatisfactory?' Report of the Independent Inquiry into the Working Practices of the West Midlands Police Serious Crime Squad (Civil Liberties Trust, 1991).

[5] Royal Commission on Criminal Justice, Report (Cm 2263) (HMSO, 1993).

[6] See Home Office Report for 1992 (Cm 1909).

There is also the difficulty of knowing which methods to adopt to achieve these aims. How, for example, is the criminal system reliably to distinguish between the factually innocent and the factually guilty? Guilt that is established to the satisfaction of the criminal courts is not the same as actual guilt. In any system there must always be the probability that some people who are found legally guilty will not be actually guilty, and that some people who are legally innocent will in fact be guilty.

The rhetoric of English criminal justice is that priority is given to protecting the actually innocent from wrongful conviction over bringing the actually guilty to justice. In the *Hobson* case,[7] Holroyd J declared that 'it is a maxim of English law that ten guilty men should escape rather than one innocent man should suffer'. But even at this rhetorical level the system can claim no more than to afford priority to protecting the innocent. It cannot offer any guarantee against miscarriages of justice occurring. The only way to guarantee this would be not to prosecute anybody at all. But this cannot be countenanced. The detection and prosecution of at least some suspected criminals is vital to punish and deter criminal behaviour, to declare and uphold important social values and, ideally, to encourage people to lead more law-abiding lives. Therefore, a compromise has to be struck between procedures which allow the effective prosecution of suspected offenders whilst reducing the risk of wrongful conviction to an acceptable level. Holroyd J, it will be noted, did not suggest that it was better that 100, or 1000 guilty persons went free in the effort to avoid a solitary conviction of an innocent. Acquitting the innocent may be a priority but it is not the overriding consideration. The Court of Appeal judgment in the Judith Ward case acknowledges this in asserting that the task of judges is

'to ensure that the law, practice and methods of trial should be developed so as to reduce the risk of conviction of the innocent to an absolute minimum. At the same time we are very much alive to the fact that, although the avoidance of the conviction of the innocent must unquestionably be the primary consideration, the public interest would not be served by a multiplicity of rules which merely impede effective law enforcement.'[8]

Not all are prepared to pay even lip service to such rhetoric, however. A differently constituted Court of Appeal, giving judgment in the 'Birmingham Six' case, merely observed that 'justice is as much concerned with the conviction of the guilty as the acquittal of the

---

[7] (1823) 1 Lew CC 261.
[8] (1993) 96 Cr App Rep 1 at 52.

innocent.'[9] Similarly, just as no priority is afforded to the protection of
the innocent in the list of government objectives quoted above, neither
the Philips Commission nor the Runciman Commission was directed by
their terms of reference to prioritise the acquittal of the innocent. We
shall see that this lack of commitment to a supposedly hallowed maxim
of English law is reflected in the detailed rules and practices of the legal
system itself.

As the United Kingdom lacks a written constitution, and still clings
to the notion of the supremacy of the legislature, there are no
entrenched rights or principles governing the operation of the criminal
justice system.[10] Common law rights created by the judges and rights
created by statute can be whittled away, amended, or removed altogether by the courts or by Parliament. Admittedly, the United Kingdom
is bound by the European Convention on Human Rights at an international level (on which more later) but this is not binding within our
domestic legal system. The fundamental rights set out in the
Convention can only be enforced before our national courts if legislation has been passed giving effect to our international obligations.
Great care must be exercised, therefore, in analysing the English criminal justice system. Rather than be taken in by rhetorical flourishes
concerning the 'right to a fair trial', or 'the right to silence', one must
consider in detail the actual rules and their operation. To what extent
is the acquittal of the innocent a priority of English criminal justice in
fact?

The main theoretical safeguard offered to suspects in the English system of criminal justice is the presumption of innocence. This
presumption finds expression in the principle that guilt must be proved
beyond reasonable doubt. There are two aspects to this principle;
firstly, it stipulates a high standard of proof, and, secondly, it places the
burden of proof on the prosecution. The standard of proof required
acknowledges the importance of guarding against wrongful conviction,
although the evidential threshold is not as high as it might be. If a court
was allowed to find a person guilty on the balance of probabilities (the
standard of proof applied in civil cases) then many more factually guilty
persons could be successfully prosecuted, but so too could many more
who were factually innocent. If, on the other hand, it was required that
guilt be proven beyond any doubt at all, whether reasonable or not,
then few successful prosecutions could be brought. This would protect

---

[9]   *McIlkenny* (1991) 93 Cr App Rep 287 at 311.

[10]   Note, however, that the operation of criminal justice in this country is now subject in
a growing number of areas to EC law and, therefore, to judicial supervision from the
European Court of Justice. See J Dine, 'European Community Criminal Law?' [1993]
Crim LR 246.

people who were actually innocent, but such a system would allow the vast majority of suspects who came to the notice of the police (and who were in fact guilty) to escape conviction. The standard of proof required amounts to a compromise between two conflicting aims: to convict all of the guilty and to acquit all of the innocent.

Turning to the burden of proof, it follows from the presumption of innocence that the prosecution must bear the burden of making out its accusation that the defendant is in fact guilty. The defendant need say nothing, either to the police or in court, and no adverse inferences should be drawn concerning the defendant's guilt in consequence of such silence. It is not for the defendant to establish his or her innocence but for the authorities to establish guilt.

That it is for the prosecution to prove guilt beyond reasonable doubt was described by Viscount Sankey LC in *Woolmington v DPP* as the 'golden thread' which ran throughout criminal law.[11]

'No matter what the charge or where the trial, the principle that the prosecution must prove the guilt of the prisoner is part of the common law of England and no attempt to whittle it down can be entertained.'[12]

In fact, however, the principle has been made subject to so many exceptions that one may question whether it is better thought of as a rule which applies only in certain residual situations.[13] One of the many statutory offences which reverses the burden of proof is s 5 of the Public Order Act 1986. This provides that it is an offence to use threatening, abusive or insulting words or behaviour within the hearing or sight of a person likely to be caused harassment, alarm or distress thereby. If the prosecution proves these conduct elements (ie that the defendant did do as alleged) accused persons may escape liability only if they can prove that their conduct was reasonable. Thus the prosecution does not have to prove that the defendant's behaviour was unreasonable to secure a conviction; the burden of proof is placed on the defendant.

It is not only specific statutory exceptions which have tarnished the golden thread. Section 101 of the Magistrates' Courts Act 1980 (re-enacting earlier provisions which date back to 1848) provides that wherever a defence rests upon 'any exception, exemption, proviso, excuse or qualification' (regardless of whether the exemption appears in a clause creating the offence or elsewhere) the burden of proving the

---

11 [1935] AC 462 at 481.
12 Ibid at 481–482.
13 See A Ashworth, 'A Threadbare Principle' [1978] Crim LR 385 and 'Public Order and the Principles of English Criminal Law' [1987] Crim LR 153 and D McBarnet, *Conviction* (Macmillan, 1983) pp 102–110.

excusing condition shall lie on the defendant.[14] To illustrate, in *Flood*[15] the defendant was charged with statutory offences relating to the use of dumper trucks to move waste from a building site to a tip 860 metres away by road. The relevant statute would have exempted the defendant from liability if the building site and tip were in the 'immediate vicinity' of one another, but was silent on the question of whether it was for the prosecution to prove that the required degree of proximity was missing or for the defence to prove that such proximity was present. The Court of Appeal ruled that the effect of s 101 was to place the burden of proof on the defendant. One would have thought, given the constitutional supremacy of Parliament over the courts, that the latter would always be bound to apply s 101 in this manner. On occasion, however, the courts have simply overlooked or ignored this statutory provision. In the case of *Hill*[16], for example, the Court of Appeal took it for granted that, on a charge of criminal damage, it was for the prosecution to prove an absence of lawful excuse rather than for the defence to establish the presence of the excusing state of affairs. The due process adherent (see below) would no doubt see this decision as a welcome reaffirmation of the golden thread. However, the inconsistent approach of the courts makes it difficult to determine what the legal position is or to predict which of two conflicting norms (one a common law principle, the other a statutory rule) will be applied in any given case.[17]

As for the defendant's so-called right of silence, later chapters will demonstrate how contingent this right has always been, and how the appellate courts have allowed adverse comments to be made by trial judges in a whole range of situations.[18] At the time of writing, the government, ignoring the recommendations of the Runciman Commission on this point, is pressing ahead with its plans to abolish the right of silence completely. Whether the relevant clauses of the Criminal Justice and Public Order Bill (cll 27–31) will survive the parliamentary process is uncertain. It also remains to be seen whether these reforms will fall foul of the European Convention on Human Rights, which declares a right to a 'fair and public hearing' (art 6(1)) and that everyone 'shall be

---

14   The case of *Edwards* [1975] QB 27 decided that the same rule should be applied to trials in the Crown Court. See also the House of Lords decision in *Hunt* [1987] 1 All ER 1. For discussion, see P Healy, 'Proof and Policy: No Golden Threads' [1987] Crim LR 355 and P Mirfield, 'The Legacy of *Hunt*' [1988] Crim LR 19.

15   [1992] Crim LR 509.

16   [1989] Crim LR 136, with accompanying commentary by J C Smith.

17   For further discussion, see D Birch, 'Hunting the Snark: the Elusive Statutory Exception' [1988] Crim LR 221, and the response from P Mirfield, 'An Ungrateful Reply' [1988] Crim LR 233.

18   See eg *Martinez-Tobon* [1994] 1 WLR 388.

presumed innocent until proved guilty according to law' (art 6(2)).[19] It is sufficient for our purposes here to draw attention to the controversial nature of criminal justice and the lack of consensus concerning such fundamentals as the proper aims and priorities for the system and the principles which should govern its operation.

2. ADVERSARIAL VERSUS INQUISITORIAL THEORIES OF CRIMINAL JUSTICE

The principles underlying different criminal justice systems vary according to history, culture and underlying ideology. There are important differences even between Scotland, Northern Ireland and England and Wales, for instance. The adversary principle that it is for the prosecution to bring a case to court and prove guilt is an important characteristic of the English system and of other common law systems such as Australia, Canada and the United States. The major alternative to adversarial systems is that posed by civil law systems, such as France or Germany, based on inquisitorial principles. When the Runciman Commission was set up, interest was expressed in inquisitorial systems as offering superior protection against miscarriages of justice. Let us consider this possibility by examining briefly the main differences between adversarial and inquisitorial models of criminal justice.

In an inquisitorial system, the dominant role in conducting a criminal inquiry is played, at least in theory, by the court. A dossier is prepared to enable the judge taking the case to master its details. The judge then makes decisions about which witnesses to call and examines them in person, with the prosecution and defence lawyers consigned to a subsidiary role. In some inquisitorial systems the dossier is prepared (in serious cases) by an examining magistrate (*juge d'instruction*) with wide investigative powers, but more frequently this preparatory task is carried out by the prosecutor and police.[20]

In the 'pure' adversarial system, by contrast, the burden of preparing the case for court falls on the parties themselves. The judge acts as an umpire, listening to the evidence produced by the parties, ensuring that the proceedings are conducted with procedural propriety, and announcing a decision at the conclusion of the case. If the parties choose not to call a certain witness, then however relevant that

---

[19] See further A Ashworth, 'Plea, Venue and Discontinuance' [1993] Crim LR 830.
[20] There are considerable differences between systems which are labelled 'inquisitorial'. See eg the review by L H Leigh and L Zedner, A Report on the Administration of Criminal Justice in the Pre-Trial phase in England and Germany (Royal Commission on Criminal Justice, Research Study no 1) (HMSO, 1992).

person's evidence might have been, there is nothing the court can do about it.

The adversarial contest in court thus resembles a game in which truth might appear to be the loser.[1] Indeed, it is sometimes said that adversarial systems focus on proof, and inquisitorial systems on truth. But this is too simplistic. Both systems are concerned with establishing the truth, but they differ on the best way of achieving that end. As an eminent English judge put it:

'In the system of trial which we have evolved in this country, the judge sits to hear and determine the issues raised by the parties, not to conduct an investigation or examination on behalf of society at large, as happens, we believe, in some foreign countries. Even in England, however, a judge is not a mere umpire to answer the question "How's that?". His object, above all, is to find out the truth . . .'[2]

The traditional English view has been that 'truth is best discovered by powerful statements on both sides of the question'[3] which are then evaluated by a passive and impartial adjudicator. This recognises that the events leading up to a criminal offence, and the intentions or knowledge of the parties involved, are always open to interpretation and dispute. The danger in an inquisitorial system is that whoever conducts the investigation (whether the police, a prosecutor or an examining magistrate) will come to favour one particular view of the matter and that this will lead to bias creeping in. In this connection, it has been observed of inquisitorial systems that it 'is difficult for the defence to be sure that the dossier actually includes all that it should—and especially all the material potentially helpful to the accused.'[4] There is also the danger that a trial judge, having formed an initial view of the case based on a reading of the dossier, will give too much weight to evidence adduced at the trial which is consistent with the pre-existing theory, and too little to that which conflicts with it.[5] Fuller is one writer who doubted the wisdom of adjudicators actively conducting inquiries in court:

'What starts as a preliminary diagnosis designed to direct the inquiry tends, quickly and imperceptibly, to become a fixed conclusion, as all that confirms this diagnosis makes a strong imprint on the mind,

---

[1]   See M E Frankel, 'The Search for the Truth: An Umpireal View' (1975) 123 U Penn LR 1031.

[2]   *Jones v National Coal Board* [1957] 2 QB 55, per Lord Denning.

[3]   *Ex p Lloyd* (1822) Mont 70 at 72n.

[4]   M Zander, *Cases and Materials on the English Legal System* (Weidenfeld and Nicolson, 1992) p 332.

[5]   See the account of one inquisitorial trial by C Johnston, 'Trial by Dossier' (1992) 142 NLJ 249.

while all that runs counter to it is received with diverted attention.'[6]

Far better, according to the adversarial theory, that the judge remain impartial throughout and allow the parties to put forward their interpretations of the facts and law in the way most favourable to them.[7] By opening up a range of possible views, it is more likely that the 'real truth' will emerge. As Fuller put it:

'The arguments of counsel hold the case, as it were, in suspension between two opposing interpretations of it. While the proper classification of the case is thus kept unresolved, there is time to explore all of its peculiarities and nuances.'[8]

So, while inquisitorial systems are rightly portrayed as involving searches for the truth, the way in which that search is conducted can shape the 'truth' that is proclaimed in court. Adversarial systems, by contrast, with their emphasis on the parties proving their case, can lose sight of the truth for different reasons: one or both of the parties might deliberately suppress relevant evidence for tactical reasons, or one party (almost invariably the defendant) might lack adequate access to the resources or expertise needed to counter-balance the arguments of their opponent.

It might seem, from this discussion, that neither system, at the theoretical level, is demonstrably superior in establishing the truth or at avoiding miscarriages of justice. But the differences between adversarial and inquisitorial models extend beyond the question of the best method to arrive at the truth. The adversarial model asserts that the reality of any criminal matter is that the state is trying to prove a case against a suspect. It is important, therefore, that guarantees are provided against the state abusing its investigative powers and that the means are provided to suspects to challenge the prosecution case. Thus, for example, defence lawyers are meant to play a central part in the adversarial system and there are limits on the length of time suspects can be held by the police for questioning. The importance attached in an adversarial system to the integrity of the procedures followed in collecting evidence and proving guilt can also be seen in the development of a complex web of rules of evidence.[9] Such rules are often lacking in the inquisitorial setting precisely because they may hamper the search for the truth.[10]

---

[6] L L Fuller, 'The Forms and Limits of Adjudication' (1978) 92 Har L R 353 at 383.

[7] See the discussion by J Sprack, 'The Trial Process' in E Stockdale and S Casale (eds), *Criminal Justice Under Stress* (Blackstone, 1992) pp 67–70.

[8] Op cit.

[9] For a full discussion see J McEwan, *Evidence and the Adversarial Process* (Basil Blackwell, 1992).

[10] See the classic article by M Damaska, 'Evidentiary Barriers to Conviction and Two Models of Criminal Procedure: A Comparative Study' (1973) 121 U Penn LR 506 at 513–525.

Thus the government's aim of ensuring that those suspected or accused of crimes be dealt with 'fairly, justly and with the minimum of delay' may conflict with the aim of finding the truth in order that the guilty may be convicted and the innocent acquitted. Indeed, because of its concern for civil liberties, the adversarial model appears less committed than the inquisitorial model to ascertaining the truth.[11] It is that very concern, however, which has resulted in continuing support for the adversarial model: 'The current ideology extols the adversary system primarily as the best system for protecting individual dignity and autonomy.'[12]

In the inquisitorial system, of course, the theory is that the state is conducting a neutral investigation into the truth and therefore the need for safeguards such as rules of evidence and defence lawyers is seen as much reduced.[13] It is not uncommon for suspects to be subjected to lengthy periods of pre-charge incarceration without access to legal advice.[14] Leigh and Zedner have noted that

'while nothing in French law requires the over-use of detention, a tendency to do so seems deeply ingrained in the legal culture and doubtless derives from a desire not to release a suspect until the truth has been ascertained.'[15]

Closer examination of how inquisitorial systems operate in practice reveals that all too often the supposed safeguard offered by judicial control of the investigation process is a chimera. As Leigh and Zedner observe of the French system:

'by the time a suspect has been brought before the *juge d'instruction* he has already been in the hands of the police for forty-eight hours during which time he has been questioned vigorously . . . We do not believe that the examining magistrate is a real protection against overbearing police practices save in rare cases where physical brutality is involved. Furthermore, despite the fact that only ten per cent of cases go before the *juge d'instruction*, the system is overburdened and works slowly.'[16]

---

[11] Ibid at 580.

[12] E E Sward, 'Values, Ideology, and the Evolution of the Adversary System' (1989) 64 Ind L J 301 at 302.

[13] They are not absent altogether, however. See ibid at 314.

[14] It remains to be seen whether recent moves in France towards allowing suspects held by the police access to legal advice will make any difference in practice: see further J Hodgson and G Riche, 'A Criminal Defence for the French?' (1993) 143 NLJ 414.

[15] L H Leigh and L Zedner, A Report on the Administration of Criminal Justice in the Pre-Trial phase in England and Germany Royal Commission on Criminal Justice, Research Study no 1) (HMSO, 1992) p 53.

[16] Ibid p 68.

The problem of abuse in the inquisitorial system has been further highlighted by the controversial way in which the broadly drawn powers of the *juge d'instruction* have been exercised. In Germany this role was abolished in 1975 and in Italy in 1988 (as part of a general jettisoning of inquisitorial procedures in favour of the adversarial model)[17] and there have been calls for France to follow this trend.[18]

The Philips Commission considered that 'change to a fully-fledged inquisitorial system, even if it could be shown to be desirable, would be so fundamental in its effect upon institutions that had taken centuries to build as to be impossible on political and practical grounds.'[19]

The Runciman Commission lingered a little longer over this question and went so far as to commission a research study of French and German pre-trial procedures.[20] The authors advised against any attempt to adopt these procedures wholesale, arguing that a more effective reform might be achieved 'by an intelligent adaptation of the existing English system.'[1] The Runciman Commission adopted this position itself, arguing that it was too dangerous to attempt a transplant of a continental legal system into the very different setting of England and Wales.[2] But having rejected a move to a thoroughgoing inquisitorial system, the Runciman Commission acknowledged that a number of its recommendations could 'fairly be interpreted as seeking to move the system in an inquisitorial direction, or at least as seeking to minimise the danger of adversarial practices being taken too far.'[3] One such recommendation was that judges should regard themselves as in charge of the trial and should intervene

'to expedite the proceedings, to see that witnesses are treated by counsel as they should be, to curtail prolix or irrelevant questioning, to prevent the jury from being confused or misled, and to order the payment of costs when they have been wastefully or unnecessarily incurred.'[4]

---

[17] See M Zander, 'From Inquisitorial to Adversarial—the Italian System' (1991) 141 NLJ 678.

[18] Commission Justice Penale Et Droits De L'Homme 'Rapport Sur La Mise En Etat Des Affaires Penales' (1990). For recent developments see J Bell, 'The French Pre-Trial System' in C Walker and K Starmer (eds), *Justice in Error* (Blackstone, 1993).

[19] Royal Commission on Criminal Procedure, Report (Cmnd 8092) (HMSO, 1981) para 1.8.

[20] Leigh and Zedner, op cit.

[1] Ibid p 67.

[2] Royal Commission on Criminal Justice, Report (Cm 2263) (HMSO, 1993) p 4.

[3] Ibid p 3.

[4] Ibid p 119.

All of this seems far removed from the adversarial theory that it is for the parties to control the production and presentation of evidence and for the judge to adopt a passive and impartial role.

It might be thought that the danger of a transplant failing is actually less than the risks attendant in grafting such inquisitorial features onto an adversarial body. None the less, the recommendations of the Runciman Commission should not be regarded as a threat to the theoretical purity of English criminal justice. Because of a recognition that the adversarial system, in its undiluted form, may not serve the goal of finding the truth, certain mechanisms and accommodations have long been incorporated within it in the English context.[5] Thus, for example, a criminal court has the power to call a witness of its own volition and can override any objections to this action. This is because there will occasionally be cases where there are such glaring gaps in the evidence that the interest in finding the truth will outweigh the interest in preserving the appearance of strict impartiality.[6] But this power is rarely used. In *Grafton*,[7] the judge tried to stop the prosecution dropping its case and he himself called their remaining witnesses, for the evidence was, in his opinion, capable of being weighed fairly by the jury. The Court of Appeal, while sympathetic to the judge, refused to allow this. It stated that this power should never be used to pursue a prosecution role, should only be used to achieve 'justice and fairness', and in any event should always be used 'most sparingly'.[8]

Walking the tightrope separating one value, truth, from the competing value of procedural fairness is clearly difficult. Other values also come into play, such as economy and efficiency. The result is accommodation and compromise. Non-adversarial, as well as adversarial, values shape the procedures and operations of the criminal justice system, and these different values often conflict with each other.

3.   CRIME CONTROL AND DUE PROCESS

Over twenty years ago, an American writer, Packer, developed two models of the criminal process: due process and crime control.[9] These models illuminate the major conflicts in values at the heart of the

---

[5]   As is also true of the American system see Sward, op cit. It is a commonplace to observe that no system of justice conforms exactly to an idealised adversarial or inquisitorial theory.

[6]   See *Chapman* (1838) 8 C & P 558 and *Holden* (1838) 8 C & P 606.

[7]   [1992] 3 WLR 532.

[8]   Ibid at 536.

[9]   H L Packer, *The Limits of the Criminal Sanction* (Stanford University Press, 1968) ch 8.

English criminal justice system. They are not the only way of thinking about criminal justice,[10] but they are widely recognised as useful tools of analysis.[11] Indeed, the Chief Inspector of Police for England and Wales (Sir John Woodcock) in October 1992 gave these models wider currency in well-publicised comments that included the observation that the 'police working environment is one in which some procedures actually compete with others—the impetus of investigation versus the rights of suspects—so that crime control is in conflict with due process.'[12] In order to make sense of the criminal system, reference will be made to these theoretical models throughout this book.

Packer developed the two models of crime control and due process in 'an attempt to abstract two separate value systems that compete for priority in the operation of the criminal process.'[13] The models describe two normative positions at opposite ends of a spectrum. Neither model is meant to be taken as according with reality or as being prescriptive. Rather, as Packer puts it:

'The two models merely afford a convenient way to talk about the operation of a process whose day-to-day functioning involves a constant series of minute adjustments between the competing demands of two value systems and whose normative future likewise involves a series of resolutions of the tensions between competing claims.'[14]

(a) Crime control

In this model, the repression of criminal conduct is viewed as by far the most important function to be performed by the criminal process. In the absence of such repression, a general disregard for the criminal law would develop, public order would break down and law-abiding citizens would live in constant fear. In order to uphold social freedom successfully, the model must achieve a high rate of detection and conviction. But because resources are limited, the model depends for success on speed and on minimising the opportunities for challenge. Formal fact finding through examination and cross-examination in court is slow and wasteful. Speed can best be achieved by allowing the

---

[10] For refinements and other approaches, see eg A E Bottoms and J D McClean, *Defendants in the Criminal Process* (Routledge & Kegan Paul, 1976) pp 226–232 and M King, *The Framework of Criminal Justice* (Croom Helm, 1981) ch 2.

[11] See eg M McConville and J Baldwin, *Courts, Prosecution, and Conviction* (Oxford University Press, 1981) pp 3–7 and S H Bailey and M J Gunn, *Smith and Bailey on the English Legal System* (1991) pp 680–695.

[12] See (1992) Guardian, 14 October.

[13] Op cit p 153.

[14] Ibid.

police to establish the facts through interrogation. To guarantee speed further, procedures must be uniform and routine, so that the model as a whole resembles a conveyor belt in its operation.

The quality control in this system is entrusted in large measure to the police. By the application of their expertise, the probably innocent are quickly screened out of the process while the probably guilty are passed quickly through the remaining stages of the process. As Packer puts it

'If there is confidence in the reliability of informal administrative fact-finding activities that take place in the early stages of the criminal process, the remaining stages of the process can be relatively perfunctory without any loss in operating efficiency.'[15]

Indeed, the model goes further in claiming that the pre-trial administrative processes are more likely to produce reliable evidence of guilt than formal court procedures.

The ideal mechanism for truncating the judicial stage of the process is the guilty plea, as then the need for lengthy and expensive trials is eliminated. The police will thus seek to extract confessions from those whom they presume to be guilty as this makes it very difficult for the suspect to do other than admit guilt at court. For, as Packer concludes of the crime control model,

'when reduced to its barest essentials and operating at its most successful pitch, it offers two possibilities: an administrative fact-finding process leading (1) to exoneration of the suspect or (2) to the plea of guilty.'[16]

The crime control model accepts that some (but not many) mistakes will be made in identifying the probably guilty and the probably innocent, but is prepared to tolerate such mistakes for the sake of the overall goal of repressing crime. But if too many guilty people were shown to be escaping liability, or the system was perceived to be generally unreliable (as would be the case if it was shown that innocent people were being prosecuted on a large scale), then the deterrent efficacy of the criminal law would be weakened. The crime control model seeks to avoid this in a number of ways. Its first line of attack is to ensure a high rate of guilty pleas, as then police and prosecutor judgments will not be challenged and the possibility of error will not be examined. Its fallback position is to characterise most acquittals as perverse or achieved 'on a technicality', rather than as reflecting failures of police (or prosecutor) judgment.

15 Ibid pp 160–161.
16 Ibid pp 162–163.

It is only when these tactics fail (in the sense that so many clear-cut miscarriages of justice come to light that the system is perceived to be unreliable) that the crime control model comes to its last ditch and accepts the need for safeguards to be built into the system to improve the reliability of informal fact-finding processes. It will, however, fight to keep such measures to the minimum necessary to achieve renewed public confidence in the system. To accept more than this would be inconsistent with speed and informality and thus with the overall goal of repressing crime.

Similarly, while crime control can tolerate rules forbidding illegal arrests or coercive interrogations (since such rules might promote reliability) it strongly objects to those rules being vindicated through the criminal process itself, through the exclusion of illegally obtained evidence or the quashing of convictions where the rules have been breached. From this perspective it is intolerable that perfectly credible evidence is ruled inadmissible merely because the methods used to obtain it were improper. To let the guilty go free on such a 'technicality' undermines crime control. In the 'Dirty Harry' films, the eponymous hero (played by Clint Eastwood) is spurred into law-breaking action by the operation of just such a due process mechanism. For Harry, the ends—getting the bad guys—always justify the means. The means used by the good and bad guys end up being identical and only the different ends sought enable us to tell which is which. 'Dirty Harry' is the personification of crime control ideology.

(b) Due process

Due process ideology is composed of a number of ideas and values. At its most straightforward the model lacks confidence in informal pre-trial fact-finding processes. The police will naturally hold a genuine belief that they have correctly apprehended the right suspect, but only in the movies are they invariably correct. Many factors may contribute to a mistaken belief in guilt, which itself may become a force in the production of unreliable evidence against the suspect. For example, witnesses to disturbing events tend to make errors in recollecting details, or may be animated by a bias that the police will not seek to discover, and confessions by suspects in police custody are as likely to be an indicator of the exertion of psychological coercion as they are to be of guilt. This leads to an insistence on formal, adjudicative, adversary fact-finding processes in which the case against the accused is tested before a public and impartial court.

Because of this concern with error, the due process model also rejects the crime control obsession with finality. There must always be a possibility of a case being reopened to take account of some new fact that has come to light since the last public hearing. Thus, unlike crime control, the due process model insists on the prevention and elimination of errors to the greatest extent possible as an end in itself: 'The aim of the process is at least as much to protect the factually innocent as it is to convict the factually guilty.'[17]

As important as is its concern with reliability, the due process model upholds other values of more far-reaching effect. Chief amongst these is the primacy of the individual citizen, and thus the need for limits on official power. Those enforcing the criminal law are endowed with extremely coercive powers and controls are needed to prevent them exercising these powers in an oppressive manner. That such controls might impair the overall efficiency of the system is of minor concern to the due process model. The presumption of innocence can be seen as one such control, since it places the burden on the state to prove legal guilt affirmatively in a procedurally proper manner. Thus, it is not open to the police in a due process model to arrest on a hunch and then demand that suspects prove their innocence or else face conviction.

In certain situations, the concern with abuse of power in the due process model takes precedence over reliability. Suppose, for example, that the police had illegally obtained evidence that established beyond doubt that a suspect had committed a murder. The due process model would none the less insist that the suspect walk free because of the procedural irregularity. To do otherwise would be to encourage such abuses to take place which, in the long run, would be more harmful to society than releasing one murderer. It is only by demonstrating to officials that there is nothing to be gained by abusing power and breaking rules that adherence to them can be guaranteed.

The due process model is also concerned with the upholding of moral standards for their own sake. In the belief that the best way to encourage law-abiding behaviour is by example, due process adherents insist that the legal system does not benefit from its own illegalities. This provides another reason for refusing to use unlawfully obtained evidence.

An example of this kind of thinking is contained in Professor Michael Zander's note of dissent to the report of the Runciman Commission.[18] The dissent covered three points, one of which concerned the powers of the Court of Appeal when reviewing a conviction.[19] The majority view as expressed in the report proper was that, where there was sufficient reliable evidence of guilt, even the most

---

[17] Ibid p 165.
[18] Royal Commission on Criminal Justice, Report (Cm 2263) (HMSO, 1993) p 221.
[19] One other commissioner lent her support to this aspect of Zander's dissent.

serious misconduct by the prosecution should not result in the conviction being quashed. Zander's disagreement was fundamental:

'The majority's position would I believe encourage serious wrongdoing from some police officers who might be tempted to exert force or fabricate or suppress evidence in the hope of establishing the guilt of the suspect, especially in a serious case where they believe him to be guilty . . . If the behaviour of the prosecution agencies has deprived a guilty verdict of its moral legitimacy the Court of Appeal must have a residual power to quash the verdict no matter how strong the evidence of guilt. The integrity of the criminal justice system is a higher objective than the conviction of any individual.'[20]

The due process model also upholds the ideal of equality—that everyone should be placed in the same position as regards the resources at their disposal to conduct an effective defence of a criminal charge. It would be unjust for defendants to be left at a disadvantage merely because they were too poverty-stricken to secure adequate advice and representation. Thus, whenever the system affords a theoretical right for a lawyer to advise or represent a client, the due process model insists that substance be given to that right by providing public funds to those who cannot afford the costs of a lawyer unaided. Lawyers play a much more central part in this model, since they are needed to bring into play the remedies and sanctions which due process offers as checks against the operation of the system.

Finally, the due process model is sceptical about the morality and utility of such an extreme sanction as the criminal law for the wide variety of uses common in modern societies. As well as the activities covered by the criminal law which spring readily to mind (such as theft, vandalism and violence) criminal law also covers pollution, tax evasion, obscene publications, traffic violations, litter, cruelty to animals, neglect of children, public drunkenness and health and safety at work, to name but a few. The model also points out that in practice the criminal law is used most frequently against the poor and disadvantaged and that to seek to punish or deter these groups in the name of justice smacks of cruel hypocrisy. 'In short', as Packer puts it, 'doubts about the ends for which power is being exercised create pressure to limit the discretion with which that power is exercised.'[1]

At the risk of oversimplification, one can summarise the different positions of the two models in the following way: crime control values prioritise the conviction of the guilty, even at the risk of the conviction

---

[20] Ibid pp 234–235.
[1] Op cit p 171.

of some (fewer) innocents, and with the cost of infringing the liberties of the citizen to achieve its goals, while due process values prioritise the acquittal of the innocent, even if risking the frequent acquittal of the guilty, and giving high priority to the protection of civil liberties as an end in itself. Both models employ powerful arguments and Packer himself suggested that anyone who supported one model to the complete exclusion of the other 'would be rightly viewed as a fanatic'.[2]

In Packer's models it is common ground that the system has the potential to become an adversarial struggle. But whereas due process seeks to maximise this potential by introducing obstacles and hurdles for the prosecution to surmount at every stage, crime control seeks ways of ensuring that the adversarial contest never gets beyond round one (ie the encounter between the police and the suspect in the police station). Due process and adversarial ideology thus can work harmoniously together, whereas crime control values tend to subvert adversarial procedures.

(c)   English criminal justice: due process or crime control?

The English criminal system, just like the that of the United States, is usually characterised as one which emphasises adversarial procedures and due process safeguards. In terms of the formal structure, we can observe these safeguards intensifying as a person's liberty is progressively constrained. The least constraining exercise of police power is simple questioning on the street of someone who is merely a citizen, not a suspect. The police officer here is not acting in an adversarial manner. Since the questions are not aimed at incriminating the individual, no due process protections are needed, but no compulsion can be exercised either. The police are here in a fact-finding or inquisitorial mode.

As soon as the police have any reason to suspect the individual, an adversarial relationship is formed. The citizen becomes a suspect. The police now have the task of proving what they believe the suspect has done to the satisfaction of the courts. To assist them in this task the law provides them with various powers and, in order to guard against the misuse of these powers, due process protections begin. Suspects should be cautioned that they need not say anything. The privilege against self-incrimination (ie right of silence) entails that the prosecution must prove guilt and the suspect need not co-operate in this process. Only if there is 'reasonable suspicion' can coercive powers be exercised to search or to arrest a suspect. On arrest, the suspect is generally taken to a police station and detained. This requires further due process justification, because civil liberties are further eroded by lengthy detention

---

[2]   Ibid p 154.

and its associated procedures, such as interrogation, search of the suspect's home and fingerprinting. Further forms of due process protection become appropriate. The right of silence continues, bolstered by a right to legal advice, a right not to be held incommunicado and other procedural safeguards. In order to charge a detainee, further evidence is required and further protections are provided—vetting of the case by the Crown Prosecution Service and a grant of legal aid to prepare a defence. In order to convict, there must be yet more evidence (proof beyond a reasonable doubt).

And so, at each stage, as a citizen becomes in turn a suspect, a detainee, an accused and a defendant, the due process requirements become more stringent. This is in accordance with Packer's portrayal of due process as an obstacle course, with each successive stage presenting formidable impediments to carrying the citizen any further along the process. This should mean that few factually innocent persons are found legally guilty, but it will also mean that many factually guilty persons will be ejected from the system for lack of the required standard of evidence.

If we look at the way the system actually operates, however, it displays certain features characteristic of a crime control model. In particular, in both England and America, the great majority of defendants plead guilty and forego their right to an adversarial trial. The prosecution evidence is never tested, witnesses are not cross-examined and the case is not proved beyond reasonable doubt. The probability in such a system is that many more factually innocent persons will be found legally guilty and that many more factually guilty persons will be convicted. In Packer's imagery, the system operates as a conveyor belt, moving suspects through a series of routinised procedures which lead, in the vast majority of cases, to conviction.

Packer's conclusion in the American context was that the actual operation of the criminal process conformed closely to crime control, but that the law governing that process (as developed, in particular, by the Supreme Court) expressed due process ideology.[3] He identified a gap, in other words, between the law in books and the law in action. This is in line with the popular belief that the police are forced to break the rules in order to 'get results', and is what Sir John Woodcock meant in speaking of the impetus of investigation versus the rights of suspects. But, as Packer himself pointed out, it was perfectly possible for the Supreme Court to change tack and develop case law which expressed crime control values.[4] If the rules themselves were in harmony with the crime control model, then there would be no need for the police to

---

[3] Ibid p 239.
[4] Ibid p 240.

break them in order to achieve their central goal (if such it is) of repressing crime efficiently. The only gap that would then exist would be between the law in books and due process ideology. McBarnet argues that this is precisely the situation in Britain:

'the law governing the production, preparation and presentation of evidence does not live up to its own rhetoric . . . Police and court officials need not abuse the law to subvert the principles of justice; they need only use it.'[5]

McBarnet developed this view of the English criminal justice system at the end of the 1970s. McConville and Baldwin, whose examination of the criminal process was conducted at around the same time, also concluded that the crime control model described well the English system. In their view, however, McBarnet failed to give sufficient emphasis to those due process rights that were enshrined in law, but that in practice were unenforceable (because, for example, the suspect was denied access to a lawyer who could have guaranteed those rights) or were not enforced by the courts when presented with opportunities so to do. As McConville and Baldwin argued:

'Although this means that, for practical purposes, suspects do not have rights in these respects, it is the organisation and operation of the criminal process which produces this situation, not the formal law.'[6]

The question of where on the spectrum between crime control and due process the English system of criminal justice is today to be located must, therefore, take account of both the formal law, as laid down in statutes and case law, and the organisational practices of officials operating within that legal framework. And because due process rights without remedies to back them up can become meaningless, we must also examine the nature of the remedies provided for breaches by officials of the rules. Have the acknowledged deficiencies of the 1970s been rectified by PACE and the Prosecution of Offences Act 1985? Let us examine the nature of the rules that were introduced by this legislation.

4.   A TYPOLOGY OF LEGAL RULES

We have suggested that the police stand in an adversarial relationship to the suspect. In a crime control system the police would be given extensive powers so that they could repress crime effectively. They would be

---

[5] D McBarnet, *Conviction* (MacMillan, 1983) pp 154 and 156.

[6] M McConville and J Baldwin, *Courts, Prosecution and Conviction* (Oxford University Press, 1981) p 200.

allowed to act upon their instincts, hunches or working assumptions in stopping, searching, arresting, detaining, questioning and charging suspects. This would be sanctioned because of faith in the ability of the police to distinguish reliably between the innocent and the guilty, and because priority was given to the repression of crime over the protection of civil liberties.

The Philips Commission advocated giving more powers to the police so that they could repress crime more effectively, and this recommendation was implemented by PACE. Thus a large number of legal rules now correspond with police working assumptions. In many instances, the law was brought into line with police practice or police aspirations. Legal rules which respond to police aspirations may be termed 'enabling rules'. As we shall see, stop and search laws were extended by PACE from certain localities to the country as a whole. This enabled the police to operationalise their working assumptions more extensively than hitherto. When the law is brought into line with pre-existing police practice the rules are 'legitimising'. As chapter 4 will show, before 1984 many suspects used to 'help the police with their inquiries' before charge without being formally arrested; PACE now allows pre-charge detention, legitimising their former practices.

These examples demonstrate that many of the rules in PACE were not intended to control the police but rather were introduced to allow them more leeway. Bridges and Bunyan show that much of PACE was a product of 'the highly assertive evidence presented to the Royal Commission by various police spokesmen and pressure groups'.[7] It is no surprise to find that rules resulting from the initiative of the police generally embody more crime control values than due process values.

The Philips Commission recommended, however, that new due process safeguards be introduced to 'balance' the additional powers it proposed the police should be given. This recommendation too was, in large measure, implemented by PACE. Some of the legal rules to be analysed thus have a due process character. They are intended to inhibit the police from following their working assumptions (or are intended to give that impression), especially where those working assumptions embody crime control values. If they succeed in this ostensible aim they are 'inhibitory rules'. If they do not (whether or not they were really intended to do so) they are 'presentational rules', which allow the police to follow their working assumptions (see Fig 1.1, below). Presentational rules can thus be defined as those which appear to be inhibitory but in fact are not.

---

[7] L Bridges and T Bunyan, 'Britain's New Urban Policing Strategy—the Police and Criminal Evidence Bill in Context' (1983) 10 JLS 85 at 86. See also M McConville, A Sanders and R Leng, *The Case for the Prosecution* (Routledge, 1991) pp 173–178.

Fig 1.1: Types of legal rule and effect on police behaviour

	Crime control value	*Due process value*
Influence police	Enabling	Inhibitory
Do not influence the police	Legitimising	Presentational

That the 1980s legislation which followed in the wake of the Philips Commission exhibits a basic tension or compromise between due process and crime control is to be expected. Neither the Philips Commission nor the government of the time were comprised of fanatics. Few legal rules are entirely one-dimensional in reality, originating, as they do, from mixed motives and/or messy compromises.[8] But one of our concerns in this book will be to see the extent to which the law in general is inhibitory as distinct from presentational, and how and why some rules are, on balance, enabling or legitimising. In other words, we shall be attempting to assess whether the criminal system inclines more towards due process or crime control in appearance and in substance. We shall also develop a view of what the likely effect would be of implementing the recommendations of the Runciman Commission and assessing the government's own agenda for reform as announced in the Criminal Justice and Public Order Bill and the closely related Police and Magistrates' Courts Bill.

In order to make such assessments, we will need to look not just at the law in books but also at the law in action. It is impossible to judge, for example, whether a law providing a due process safeguard is inhibitory or merely presentational unless police practices are examined. Both the Philips Commission and the Runciman Commission recognised this. They commissioned a large amount of research on the actual operation of criminal justice because they knew that it was not enough to produce a set of proposals for legal reform which would look fair on the statute book but which were not fair in action. Laws providing safeguards, for example, should be capable of enforcement by citizens and should be adhered to by the police. Criminal justice is about the reality of procedures and practices as well as about the rules in the books, and both Royal Commissions provided an important lead in this understanding.

---

[8] Section 78 of PACE (discussed in ch 9, below), which provides a discretionary exclusionary power for judges at trial when evidence is 'unfair', is a good example.

5. THE RIGHTS OF VICTIMS

The due process and crime control models have little to say about the place of the victim within criminal justice. At the time Packer was writing in the late 1960s, the dominant concern of criminology concerned the treatment of suspected and convicted offenders. Subsequently, there has been a rediscovery of the importance of victims to criminal justice. Surveys demonstrate their importance in reporting crime to the police, providing information on likely suspects and acting as witnesses in prosecutions.[9] Research also suggests that where victims perceive that the values and goals of the criminal process are insensitive or inimical to their interests, they are correspondingly less likely to come forward and participate in criminal justice.[10] This realisation has led to calls for reform in police practices, pre-trial procedures and in sentencing, but should such reforms aim for more crime control or more due process? And how are the interests of victims to be reconciled with those of defendants?

At a theoretical level, we may observe that it is the crime control model that appears to embody a greater concern for the victim. It offers a higher prospect of conviction of those accused of crime and, by aiming to dispose of cases expeditiously through encouraging defendants to plead guilty, it obviates the need for victims to come to court and give evidence. This latter feature is particularly important in cases involving child abuse, serious violence or sexual offences, where the giving of evidence and the ordeal of cross-examination may prove highly distressing. A clear example is rape, where the previous sexual history of the victim is still often treated by the courts as relevant to the issue of consent.[11] As McEwan puts it:

'There is little incentive for rape victims to come forward when the system which is supposed to protect the public from crime serves them up in court like laboratory specimens on a microscope slide.'[12]

In such areas, one finds inroads being made into the due process rights of the defendant in order to protect the vulnerable victim better. For example, the law now allows the admission of documentary (which

---

[9] See eg M Hough and P Mayhew, *Taking Account of Crime* (Home Office Research Study no 111) (HMSO, 1985).

[10] See the cross-national study by M Joutsen, *The Role of the Victim of Crime in European Criminal Justice Systems* (Helsinki Institute for Crime Prevention and Control, 1987).

[11] See J Temkin, 'Sexual History Evidence—the Ravishment of Section 2' [1993] Crim LR 3.

[12] J McEwan, 'Documentary Hearsay Evidence—Refuge for the Vulnerable Witness' [1989] Crim LR 629.

includes videotaped) evidence in a limited range of cases, including those where the statement is made to a police officer and the maker does not give oral evidence through fear.[13] But, like a seesaw, as trial procedures become more just or bearable for victims, the defendant's ability to contest the prosecution case is increasingly undermined. When evidence is admitted in documentary form, it is not given on oath, the defence is given no opportunity to cross-examine the maker of the statement and the magistrates or jury are denied the chance to assess demeanour. This makes it less likely that defendants can win in court, and thus less likely that they will contest the matter in the first place. Crime control and concern for victims can thus be made to walk hand in hand.[14]

The benefits that the due process model offers victims are more subtle than those tendered by crime control. How, it may be asked, could more due process protection for the defendant be of any possible benefit to the victim? Typical crime control techniques employed to secure guilty pleas are offers of reduced charges or reduced sentences, as we shall explore in chapters 6 and 7. To take the example of rape again, charge bargaining may result in victims learning to their horror that the legal process has labelled the act in question as some lesser wrong, such as indecent assault. Of a sample of incidents recorded as rape in 1985 which resulted in conviction, the proportion that were convicted of a less serious offence than rape or attempted rape was as high as 42%, and there was strong evidence that the motor for this downgrading of cases was charge bargaining.[15] Similarly, sentence discounts for pleas of guilty may result in convicted offenders receiving a more lenient penalty than victims consider just. Due process, by contrast, opposes such strategies, which means that, where a conviction occurs, it is likely that the offence proved and the sentence imposed will more accurately reflect the victim's suffering.

More fundamentally, due process offers individual victims greater certainty that 'their' offenders have been correctly identified and convicted. With the model's insistence on proof of (rather than belief in) guilt, it offers superior protection to that achieved by crime control against miscarriages of justice occurring. This is important in this context, because a wrongful conviction represents an injury to the victim as

---

[13] See s 23 of the Criminal Justice Act 1988 and the analysis by D Birch, 'Documentary Evidence' [1989] Crim LR 15. For an early indication of the treatment of this section by the courts, see *R v Acton Justices, ex p McMullen* (1990) 92 Cr App Rep 98.

[14] See D Miers, 'The Responsibilities and the Rights of Victims of Crime' (1992) 55 MLR 482 at 496.

[15] S Grace, C Lloyd and L J F Smith, Rape: from Recording to Conviction (Home Office Research and Planning Unit Paper no 71) (Home Office, 1992) pp 5 and 8.

well as to the defendant. When Stefan Kiszko was cleared of the murder of Lesley Molseed after spending 16 years in prison, her father summed up the family's feelings: 'For us, it is just like Lesley had been murdered last week.' As counsel for Mr Kiszko put it:

'We acknowledge their pain in having to listen to some of the details surrounding their daughter's death and the new pain of learning that her killer has not, after all, been caught.'[16]

But while crime control may convict more factually innocent persons in proportional terms than due process, the former model is also capable of convicting far more factually guilty persons than the latter. Overall, more victims will be able to see their offenders brought to justice, albeit of a flawed kind, in a system which rejects due process in favour of crime control. Thus, the dilemma that Packer highlighted through the use of his two models of criminal justice exists also in relation to arguments about the treatment of victims. The claims of victims must be weighed against the competing claims of efficiency, defendants and the need to preserve the moral integrity of the criminal process. What must be recognised is that, in weighing the social costs of wrongful convictions and wrongful acquittals against each other, the interests of victims do not fall solely onto one side of the scales.

It must not be forgotten that people who report alleged crimes to the police are not always victims. Shopowners have been known to burn down their own premises in order to cash in on their insurance policies. Businesspeople have sometimes staged robberies and burglaries for the same reason, or in order to cover up earlier asset losses through their own fraud or thieving. False allegations of rape are undoubtedly rare, but the risk of them occurring cannot be discounted. Our natural sympathy for victims of crime should not blind us to the fact that one of the objects of the system is to discover whether prosecution witnesses, including the 'victim', are telling the truth or not. A system in which 'victims' were treated with kid gloves would be as indefensible as one which ritually humiliated them.[17]

There are interests of victims which are furthered by neither the due process model nor the crime control model. Some vulnerable victims find that, despite the types of protection discussed above, they cannot face continuing with proceedings. Many trials of rape and domestic violence collapse for this reason, and there are other examples too, such as

---

[16] (1992) Guardian, 18 February.
[17] It is none the less true that there is much that can and is being done for victims without prejudicing the rights of defendants, such as providing them with counselling services, better information on the progress of prosecutions and improved procedures for obtaining compensation. See generally Miers, op cit.

a blackmail victim who found to his consternation that his identity was going to be revealed in the trial. He preferred to let the alleged blackmailers go free than let this happen.[18] A crime control model would force such victims to give evidence, and even the most rudimentary due process considerations would insist on such evidence being tested in court in the normal way. There is a public interest in crime being prosecuted and there is nothing in either model which would prioritise the views of the victim over that public interest. Only a 'victim centred' model would prioritise the interests of victims at the expense of the public interest. No-one has yet managed to develop a victim centred model which is also consistent with due process or crime control. Given these unresolved dilemmas of principle, it will not be surprising to find that the rules and practices of the criminal justice system are similarly confused.

6. CONCLUSION

Value judgments permeate every argument about particular laws or particular police practices. This is reflected in the fact that the two Royal Commissions were split on a number of issues. There was some disagreement over facts, but basically the disagreement was over principles—how much power the police should have, how much value should be attached to the presumption of innocence and how much trust should be reposed in government agencies if given more power. This is not to say that it is all just a matter of opinion, however. It is possible to make some evaluation of whether there is a need for more due process or more crime control to achieve a particular objective. For example, crime control assumes that the police are reliable fact finders, whereas due process rests, in part, on quite the contrary assumption. If it could be established that the police were not particularly reliable fact finders, or, indeed, that fact finding was not always their goal, the argument in favour of more due process would be strengthened. We begin to examine this issue in the next chapter, where we look at the first of the array of powers that PACE provides to police officers, the power to stop and search suspects. It should be remembered, however, that ultimately a preference for more crime control or more due process rests upon a value judgment rather than upon empirical evidence. All that analysis of the law in books and the law in action can provide is material to assist in the process of moral reasoning.

---

[18] See (1993) Guardian, 12 August.

Chapter 2

Stop and Search

1. STREET POLICING IN CONTEXT

In a legal text book on criminal justice, it is natural to concentrate on the law enforcement role of the police. Thirty years ago, however, Banton made the point that:

'The policeman on patrol is primarily a "peace officer" rather than a law officer. Relatively little of his time is spent enforcing the law in the sense of arresting offenders; far more is spent "keeping the peace".'[1]

Not only do patrolling police officers (whether on foot or in patrol cars) spend little time exercising their legal powers, but not much police time is spent patrolling or investigating crime. Lest the impression be given that policing primarily revolves around classic detection methods such as fingerprinting, forensic science and the use of stop-search and arrest powers, something needs to be said about the nature of modern policing.

(a) Proactive and reactive policing

In the decade or so following publication of Banton's book, policing became more technologically sophisticated. It was thought to be more efficient if, instead of officers patrolling the streets on foot looking for evidence of crime (a 'proactive' role in the police jargon), the police were able to react swiftly to reports of crime. The greater use of cars and personal radios in the late 1960s and 1970s switched the emphasis from 'proactive' to 'reactive' policing. Like the fire brigade, police officers (excluding the increasing numbers in support roles and in specialist sections such as juvenile liaison, fingerprints, and so forth) spent much

---

[1] M Banton, *The Policeman in the Community* (Tavistock, 1964) p 127.

of their time reacting to emergencies. This entailed visiting the scenes of crimes and interviewing victims (and witnesses, if any) and dealing with the subsequent paperwork. The volume of crime was such that little time was left actually to investigate, in the classical sense, except in very serious crimes.

'Fire brigade policing', as it became known, appeared to reduce the scope for the exercise of discretion by officers because they went where they were directed. Not only did this entail the public (usually the victim) deciding with what offences the police were to be concerned, but the public often identified the offender too. In one recent study, civilians were found to have initiated police action or identified the suspect in well over half of all arrests.[2] Even those officers who act as 'detectives' rarely employ the classic detection methods we are all familiar with from television dramas and 'cop movies'.[3] Detectives actually spend most of their time

'. . . gathering information from the public; locating suspects; interviewing and, on the basis of information derived from both the public and suspects, preparing cases for the prosecution.'[4]

This has led some writers to argue that police discretion to stop-search or arrest is unimportant and that most policing is done, in reality, by the public.[5] Although this body of work is a useful corrective to the view that the police do what they want, when they want, and in any way they want, it is just as one-sided. Policing is continuing to evolve and, in many ways, is reverting to the style which Banton described. 'Community policing' is now supplanting 'fire brigade' policing, at least in the superficial sense of getting 'more bobbies back on the beat'. Most policing is still 'reactive', but, as a result of skilful advocacy on the part of 'community policing' lobbyists, less so than was the case in the 1970s.[6]

Regardless of changes in policing style, just because much policing is

---

[2]   M McConville, A Sanders and R Leng, *The Case for the Prosecution* (Routledge, 1991) p 19.

[3]   See the studies discussed by R Reiner, *The Politics of the Police* (Harvester Wheatsheaf, 1992).

[4]   P Morris and K Heal, Crime Control and the Police (Home Office Research Study no 67) (HMSO, 1981).

[5]   See, in particular, J Shapland and J Vagg, *Policing by the Public* (Routledge, 1988) and D Steer, Uncovering Crime: The Police Role (Royal Commission on Criminal Procedure Research Study no 7) (HMSO, 1980).

[6]   Often police, or ex-police, officers themselves. For the most influential example, see J Alderson, *Policing Freedom* (Macdonald and Evans, 1979). There is now much scepticism about what 'community policing' really involves. See, for instance, M McConville and D Shepherd, *Watching Police, Watching Communities* (Routledge, 1992).

a response to the public, it does not follow that the nature of that response is predetermined. The police have to sift and interpret what they are told by the public, and they do so on the basis of their own views, experiences and priorities. This is acknowledged even by the 'policing by the public' school.[7] Indeed, officers responding to a call often have to decide there and then whether or not to classify the incident as a crime; and, if so, which specific crime. A process of 'construction' by the officer then takes place which categorises the incident. Sometimes the officer will discuss or negotiate an appropriate response with the people involved in the incident. The outcome, however, whether arrest, a warning or no action at all, is largely in the hands of the officer.[8]

Although most police officers have apparently reactive roles, some groups of officers are established precisely to spend much of their time 'proactively'. For example, specialist drug, vice and serious crime squads are expected to take the lead in tackling particular spheres of criminal activity, and therefore stop-search and arrest very much on their own initiative.[9] Also, it is precisely because many police officers get few opportunities to act on their own initiative, or even to make any arrests at all, that when they get the chance to make 'quality' arrests they grasp it enthusiastically. Indeed, promotion and the securing and retention of 'plum' jobs (such as the CID) still depend partly on 'activity', as measured by stops and quality arrests.[10] Yet most incidents to which the police are called generally concern scuffles, domestic assaults, disputes between neighbours and landlord-tenant disputes, none of which is regarded by the police as offering 'quality' work.[11]

Another way of looking at the nature of police work is to see what percentage of the population has an encounter with the police in a given year, and what percentage of these encounters is 'adversarial', ie where the police suspect someone of something. Southgate and Ekblom estimate that around half of all adults have some contact with the police, over 30% of that (ie around 16% of all adults) being adversarial. Most

[7] See Shapland and Vagg, op cit p 35.
[8] R Ericson, Reproducing Order: A Study of Police Patrol Work (University of Toronto Press, 1982); C Kemp, C Norris and N Fielding, 'Legal Manoeuvres in Police Handling of Disputes' in D Farrington and S Walklate (eds), *Offenders and Victims, Theory and Policy* (British Society of Criminology, 1992).
[9] See M Maguire and C Norris, The Conduct and Supervision of Criminal Investigations (Royal Commission on Criminal Justice Research Study no 5) (HMSO, 1992).
[10] Ibid ch 9; McConville and Shepherd, op cit ch 7 and M Young, *An Inside Job* (OUP, 1991). This is implicitly criticised by the Royal Commission on Criminal Justice: 'We believe that police performance should be assessed on the basis of other factors besides arrest and conviction rates . . .', Report (Cm 2263) (HMSO, 1993) p 21.
[11] Kemp et al, op cit.

adversarial encounters are stops of individuals either on foot or in vehicles.[12] So although there were many more neutral contacts than adversarial ones, a large proportion of people none the less are made aware of police suspicions about them. For some sections of the population this is particularly true: Southgate and Ekblom found that half of all 16–24-year-olds had adversarial encounters, as did over one third of the unemployed of all ages.

(b)   Factors influencing the exercise of discretion

When officers see crimes, or suspected crimes, whether they exercise their discretion to stop-search or arrest depends partly on whether they 'need' to increase their tally of 'nickings' at that time. But there are other factors to be taken into account. Firstly, the degree of likelihood that a crime has been committed. Secondly, the strength of the probability that the suspect in the immediate vicinity is responsible for that crime. Thirdly, whether something is worth investigating or whether a person is worth arresting for that crime. To use the language of economics, the cost of investigating one crime is the opportunity lost to investigate others. Smith and Gray's study of the Metropolitan Police illustrates this well. A typical beat officer in London, they say:

'Walks past many illegally parked vehicles, drives behind speeding cars, walks past traders openly selling hard-core pornography, sees prostitutes soliciting, knows of many clubs selling liquor and providing gaming facilities without a licence, goes past unlicensed street traders, and so on, usually without taking any immediate action. Where he does take action over any one of these matters, this will usually occupy him for a considerable period, so that in the meantime he can do nothing about the others.'[13]

The myriad of crimes facing the police are not solely the relatively minor victimless crimes to which Smith and Gray refer. Every year there are nearly three million offences of robbery, theft, burglary, violence and vandalism reported to the police. As if this were not staggering enough, the 1992 British Crime Survey revealed that there is twice as much burglary, four times as much wounding, seven times as much vandalism, and eight times as much robbery and theft from the

---

[12]   P Southgate and P Ekblom, Contacts Between Police and Public (Home Office Research Study no 77) (HMSO, 1984) p 6.
[13]   D Smith and J Gray, *Police and People in London* (Policy Studies Institute) (Gower, 1983) vol 4, 'The Police in Action' p 14.

person as these official figures record.[14] Although crimes abound almost everywhere, some are more easier to detect than others, and the amount and type of criminal activity varies with time and from place to place.

It follows that the police necessarily exercise discretion when deciding who to stop and who to arrest. Other things being equal, given the volume of crime, only the apparently most serious offences and offenders will be selected. In this context, however, other things are rarely equal and a number of other important criteria govern the exercise of police discretion. In consequence, the police devote a large amount of resources to mundane crime and turn their backs on much serious crime. The most important criteria can be listed briefly:[15]

- personal: where officers feel under pressure to make arrests in order to justify themselves and enhance promotion prospects, they may target simple cases (such as drunkenness and motoring offences);
- procedural: offenders who have the protection of the privacy of their home or office, for instance, are less vulnerable than people on the street or in public places, where no warrants are needed. This allows 'white collar' (ie business) crimes to be particularly well hidden. Tax evasion, pollution, unsafe working conditions and so forth—all as criminal as theft, assault and criminal damage—are conducted in private and are therefore protected by procedural safeguards;
- interpretational latitude: many substantive laws (eg offences against public order) are ambiguous, as are many police powers (eg arrest).[16] Such ambiguities may deter a police officer from acting or may, conversely, allow officers to act much as they wish;
- organisational constraints: some police forces adopt particular policies in relation to certain offences (eg a drive against drunken driving, vice or domestic violence; or a tolerance policy concerning the possession of 'soft' drugs);

---

[14] P Mayhew, N Maung and C Mirrlees-Black, The 1992 British Crime Survey (Home Office Research Study no 132) (HMSO, 1993). This was a survey, relating in fact to 1991, of around 10,000 randomly selected people aged 16 or over aimed at assessing the 'true' rate of victimisation in Britain. Previous surveys took place in 1982, 1984 and 1988. The discrepancy between actual rates of crime and the official figures stems largely from failure to report crimes to the police, but also some failure on the part of the police to record reported offences. For discussion of reporting and recording problems, see A Bottomley and K Pease, *Crime and Punishment: Interpreting the Data* (Open University Press, 1986). See also ch 5, section 3(a), below.

[15] The following list is based loosely on A Bottomley, *Decisions in the Penal Process* (Martin Robertson, 1973) pp 37–43.

[16] See later in this chapter and ch 3 below.

- societal pressures: s 106 of PACE requires individual police forces to consult the community in relation to policing, thus envisaging the shaping of policing by forces outside the police. Wider societal pressures occur from time to time in relation to particular offences such as robbery or, again, domestic violence.[17] It may be societal pressures, of course, which shape police organisational policies. In the United States, two towns with widely differing juvenile arrest rates were found to have similar juvenile crime rates. In the town with the low arrest rate, residents had exerted pressure on the police to avoid arrest wherever possible;[18]

- political pressures: as part of a campaign to secure more resources or powers for the police, police forces may deliberately allow the detection rate to fall.

The way in which some of these factors work is illustrated by a study by Walmsley of offences of indecency between males between 1946 and 1976.[19] The Sexual Offences Act 1967 legalised many offences of indecency between males. If the level of homosexual activity remained constant, one would have expected the number of offences recorded by the police to decline, for a considerable amount of that homosexual behaviour would have been illegal before 1967 but legal afterwards. But Walmsley found the reverse. In 1967 there were 840 indecencies between males recorded by the police as offences, while between 1973 and 1976 the figure averaged just under 1,660—twice as much as in 1967. Walmsley also found the prosecution rate very much higher after 1967 than it was before.

It is most unlikely that there really were more crimes of this sort committed after 1967 than before. The more likely explanation is that the police were prosecuting in a higher proportion of suspected indecency cases than they had hitherto. It seems that the police, aware of society's ambivalent attitude to the criminalisation of homosexuality, had previously exercised discretion not to arrest and prosecute. When they sensed that clear lines had been drawn, in social attitudes as well as in the letter of the law, they responded by changing the way they exercised their discretion.[20] There are two general lessons here: firstly, that, whether the police act reactively or proactively, discretion still

---

[17] See, for instance, S Hall, C Critcher, T Jefferson, J Clarke and B Roberts, *Policing the Crisis* (MacMillan, 1978), an analysis of, among other things, the 'mugging' scare of the 1970s.

[18] See A Meehan, 'Internal Police Records and the Control of Juveniles' (1993) 33 BJ Crim 504.

[19] R Walmsley, 'Indecencies Between Males' [1978] Crim LR 400.

[20] Ibid at 405.

needs to be exercised and, secondly, that shifts in the way that discretion is operated can bring about dramatic changes in the apparent levels of crime.

(c) Cop culture

It is important to appreciate that factors such as community pressures, and concepts such as 'seriousness', all require interpretation by the police. The desires of local or wider communities (which are rarely expressed with one voice) need to be sifted and interpreted by the police. Similarly, offence 'seriousness' is not an objective category; what is or is not 'insulting' will depend in part on one's view of the world. The police world outlook does not simply encapsulate that of society at large. It is moulded by 'cop culture'. This is

'rooted in constant problems which officers face in carrying out the role they are mandated to perform . . . Cop culture has developed as a patterned set of understandings which help to cope with and adjust to the pressures and tensions which confront the police.'[1]

Cop culture comprises a number of related elements. The most important are 'danger', which is the officers' sense of the unpredictability of interactions with members of the public; 'authority', the upholding of which is needed to maintain order; the need, as we saw earlier, to produce 'results'; and a sense of mission to prevent 'them' from ruining things for 'us'. This is a dichotomous view of society which sees a relatively small section of society perpetually on the verge of revolt against the respectable majority. The sense of impending chaos and the importance of the 'thin blue line' holding it at bay permeates cop culture. Only the police know what it is really like 'out there'. If the naive, well-meaning, respectable majority knew what it was like, they would not make police officers work with one hand tied behind their backs. Thus, though the police see their interests and values as being those of the majority, cop culture is impatient with that majority for not realising how much it needs the police and how impractical its due process values are.[2] The social isolation of officers from 'civilians' (both 'rough' and 'respectable') and the social solidarity among officers minimises the extent to which this view of the world is challenged. The negative effects of cop culture were recognised by the Runciman Commission, as in this reference to the effect of police solidarity on 'cover ups': 'There is a real risk that police

---

[1] R Reiner, *The Politics of the Police* (Harvester Wheatsheaf, 1992) p 109.
[2] Reiner, op cit ch 3, summarises the voluminous research literature. An interesting and critical view from a former police superintendent is provided by M Young, op cit.

officers and the civilian staff employed by police forces may be deterred by the prevailing culture from complaining openly about malpractice.'[3]

Cop culture leads to such descriptions of the police as being 'a race apart',[4] and a considerable body of research has tried to ascertain whether the intolerance and authoritarianism characteristic of the police is a product of socialisation after joining the service or a characteristic of the type of people who wish to become police officers.[5] One result is, as the rest of this chapter and later chapters will show, a very particular view of what constitutes 'suspicious' behaviour and impatience with any rules which get in the way of the 'fight against crime'. As Goldsmith points out, this means that legality is often sacrificed for efficiency.[6] Thus, cop culture acts as a powerful crime control engine at the heart of the machinery of criminal justice.

The criminal process can be likened to a series of canal locks or gates with the police being the most important gatekeepers. Since there is too much crime for the police to handle, they have to prioritise, and in doing so they are guided by the informal norms which comprise cop culture. If an officer is confronted with an offence or suspect which is too uncertain or too trivial (however these evaluations are made) it is unlikely that any formal action will be taken but, as we shall see, there are many other factors which police officers consider, notwithstanding the efforts of legislators to reduce their influence.

2.   STOP AND SEARCH PRIOR TO PACE

The first power to which a police officer might wish to resort on the street is that of stopping and searching suspects. At the time of the Royal Commission on Criminal Procedure (Philips Commission) report, the law was confused and often arbitrary, having developed in an ad hoc manner. For example, whereas various pieces of legislation concerning such matters as controlled drugs, firearms, and protected animals allowed stop and search for related crimes, there were no national stop and search powers for stolen goods or offensive

---

[3] Royal Commission on Criminal Justice, Report (Cm 2263) (HMSO, 1993) p 22.
[4] See Banton, op cit.
[5] The research, which is inconclusive, is discussed by Reiner, op cit pp 125–128. Also see M Young, op cit.
[6] A Goldsmith, 'Taking Police Culture Seriously: Police Discretion and the Limits of the Law' (1990) 1 Policing and Society 91.

weapons. On the other hand, local legislation for many big cities including London and Birmingham allowed stop and search for stolen goods.[7] It was plainly irrational that the police had greater enforcement powers for some relatively minor offences than for some more important offences and that powers varied according to locality.

All these powers had one feature in common, however. The police could only stop and search if they 'reasonably suspected' a person of the offence in question. That the police were constrained in this way is not surprising: even in the crime control model, some restrictions would be placed on police powers.[8] A major issue of concern in the 1970s and early 1980s, however, was how far the police really were inhibited by the reasonable suspicion requirement. The early 1980s saw a number of riots in several inner-city areas where poverty and ethnic minority conflict with the police was (and still is) commonplace.[9] A massive stop-search operation, 'Swamp 81', in particular, was identified as one of the 'triggers' of the Brixton riot of 1981.[10] Described by some as 'saturation policing', stop-search on this scale was manifestly not on a 'reasonable suspicion' basis.[11]

There is no doubt that in some urban areas stop and search powers were used extensively: in 1981 there were over 700,000 recorded stops in London alone. Only 67,275 of these (that is, less than 10%) led to arrest, casting some doubt on the level of suspicion in many of these cases. A survey in Moss Side (in Manchester) by Tuck and Southgate found that one third of males aged 16–35 reported being stopped, searched or arrested in 1979–80, although the proportions were the same for blacks as for whites.[12] If minorities or the inhabitants of particular localities were disproportionately the subject of these powers, it is not surprising that resentment arose. Study after study in the 1970s, 1980s and 1990s has discovered hostility to the

---

[7] See Royal Commission on Criminal Procedure, The Investigation and Prosecution of Criminal Offences in England and Wales: The Law and Procedure (Cmnd 8092–1, app 1 or PACE Code of Practice A, Annex A, for a comprehensive list of stop and search powers.

[8] H L Packer, *The Limits of the Criminal Sanction* (Stanford University Press, 1968) p 156.

[9] For discussion, see E Cashmore and E McLaughlin (eds), *Out of Order?* (Routledge, 1991) p 113.

[10] See further section 4 below. This was not the only civil disturbance 'triggered' by street confrontation: See Cashmore and McLaughlin (eds), op cit p 149.

[11] Sir L Scarman, The Brixton Disorders: 10–12 April 1981 (Cmnd 8427) (HMSO, 1981).

[12] M Tuck and P Southgate, Ethnic Minorities, Crime and Policing (Home Office Research Study no 70) (HMSO, 1981).

police among young black people.[13] As Rex has noted more generally:

'While most white people in Britain feel that they can ultimately rely on the police to defend them, for many young blacks they seem an alien force or an occupying army.'[14]

The perception of unfairness, however, is not the same as actual unfairness. Whether or not the legal rules and police working assumptions were congruent, and whether or not police working assumptions were explicitly or implicitly racist, was a factual question which only empirical research could determine.

The most important pieces of research, by Willis (for the Home Office) and by Smith and Gray (for the Policy Studies Institute), were carried out in the early 1980s with the co-operation of the Metropolitan Police in London. The officers who Willis interviewed made a note of all the stops they made, and their reasons for them, during the research. She found that relatively few officers stopped and searched suspects for specific offences like theft or drugs. The most important single category of stops, according to police records was 'movements'. This constituted the reason for 60% of the stops in Watford, 58% of the stops in Luton, 57% of the stops in Kensington and 26% of the stops in Peckham. Yet 'movements' does not constitute a valid reason for stopping. Indeed, when Willis interviewed police officers, she found that they all gave different interpretations of what this category of stop covered. She concluded 'that this category covered stops made on grounds which police officers find it hard to specify.'[15]

If police officers find it hard to specify why they make a particular stop, it is difficult to say that their suspicion was 'reasonable'. The arrest rates for these 'movements' stops also suggest the absence of reasonable suspicion in most of them. Whilst there were relatively many arrests of those stopped for offensive weapons and controlled drugs (between 30% and 100% per cent of these stops), for 'movements' the arrest rates varied by police station from 1% to 6%. In other words, stops on grounds of movements were much less successful, which is not surprising if the police had little reason for making these stops in the

---

[13] See eg M McConville, 'Search of Persons and Premises: New Data from London' [1983] Crim LR 605; A Brogden, 'Sus is dead: what about "SaS"?' (1981) 9 New Community 44; G Gaskell, 'Black youths and the Police' (1986)2 Policing 26; T Jefferson, M Walker and M Seneviratne in D Downes (ed), *Unravelling Criminal Justice* (Routledge, 1992) and P Southgate and D Crisp, Public Satisfaction with Police Services (Home Office Research and Planning Unit Paper no 73) (Home Office, 1993). The study by Tuck and Southgate, op cit, is the only exception.

[14] See J Rex, *The Ghetto and the Underclass* (Avebury, 1988) p 116.

[15] C Willis, The Use, Effectiveness and Impact of Police Stop and Search Powers (Home Office Research and Planning Unit Paper no 15) (Home Office, 1983) p 15.

first place. One must conclude that, in many—perhaps most—of these stops, there was no reasonable suspicion.

Willis' conclusions were bolstered by the PSI research. Smith and Gray categorised stops as follows: traffic offences (18%), reasonable suspicion of other offences (49%), and no good reason to stop (33%). Even these statistics flatter the police because the 'reasonable suspicion' criteria adopted by the PSI included 'running or moving quickly', 'hanging about, moving very slowly, especially at night' and 'being out on foot in the small hours of the morning'. Arguably such criteria artificially inflate the proportion of stops made on the basis of 'reasonable' suspicion, as the low arrest rate (similar to Willis') suggests. However, the PSI report did not conclude that stops were usually arbitrary. Rather, a distinct pattern of policing emerged:

'[Officers] strongly tend to choose young males, especially young black males. Other groups that they tend to single out are people who look scruffy or poor ("slag"), people who have long hair or unconventional dress (who, they think, may use drugs) and homosexuals. We observed two cases where men were stopped purely because they appeared to be homosexual. In a few cases there appeared to be no criteria at all and the stop is completely random; this happens especially in the early hours of the morning when police officers tend to be bored.'[16]

A similar point was made, in relation to stop and search for drugs of 'unconventional-looking' youths, by the Advisory Committee on Drug Dependence,[17] and large numbers of stops observed by Southgate also appeared to be without reasonable suspicion.[18] Like the PSI, Willis also found that young black males were more likely to be stopped than whites, as did other studies such as the Islington Crime Survey where over half of the former had been stopped the previous year, as compared to less than one third of the latter.[19] The claims of many young people, especially young black people, that the police picked on them disproportionately seemed incontrovertible.

3.   STOP AND SEARCH AFTER PACE

The Philips Commission, which reported in 1981, knew that stop and search was difficult to control, and was aware of the damage which

---

[16]   D Smith and J Gray, *Police and People in London* (Policy Studies Institute) (Gower, 1983) vol 4, 'The Police in Action', p 233.

[17]   Report (1970) para 111.

[18]   P. Southgate, Police-Public Encounters (Home Office Research Study no 90) (HMSO, 1986) app 1.

[19]   T Jones, B McLean and J Young, *The Islington Crime Survey* (Gower, 1986).

these powers did, or could do, to the relationship between police and black youth in particular. It recommended extending stop-search powers to all police officers, but it also believed that 'the exercise of the powers must be subject to strict safeguards.'[20]

The Philips Commission therefore recommended a single uniform power for the police to stop and search for stolen goods or 'articles which it is a criminal offence to possess'.[1] Along with many other of the Philips Commission's proposals, this was enacted in PACE. The bundle of laws and controls that resulted contained elements of all four of the types of rule we identified in chapter 1: the extension of the powers nationwide legitimised pre-existing police working practices and, by cloaking officers with legal authority, enabled more intensive stop and search strategies in future. At the same time, inhibitory elements were incorporated (with limited success) in the form of 'safeguards'.

Section 1 of PACE is headed 'Power of constable to stop and search persons, vehicles, etc'. This power can best be understood as comprising three main elements: the 'reasonable suspicion' criterion, the offences to which stop and search is applicable, and the power itself. The safeguards which the Philips Commission thought were vital, now contained in ss 2 and 3, are a fourth element. A fifth element limits where stop and search may take place to any public place or any non-dwelling place to which the public have access.[2]

(a) Reasonable suspicion

'Reasonable suspicion' is a widely used standard in English criminal justice: we shall see in later chapters that it governs many police powers, such as arrest, and entry, search and seizure. If the criminal justice system applied 'due process' norms rigidly the police would not be allowed to exercise any powers of this kind without sufficient evidence to prosecute. On the other hand, if extreme 'crime control' values were applied the police would be allowed to apply coercive power if they had any suspicion. 'Reasonable suspicion' is an attempt to steer something of a middle course between these two polarities. It is aimed at inhibiting the police from stopping and searching indiscriminately—or, indeed, in discriminatory ways—without unduly fettering their ability to detect crime. It is a problematic standard by which to control and judge the police, as the Philips Commission recognised:

---

[20]   Royal Commission on Criminal Procedure, Report (Cmnd 8092) (HMSO, 1981) para 3.17.

[1]   Ibid.

[2]   For a more detailed account of the spatial limitation of the power to stop and search see V Bevan and K Lidstone, *The Investigation of Crime: A Guide to Police Powers* (Butterworths, 1991) pp 63–68.

'We acknowledge the risk that the criterion could be loosely interpreted and have considered the possibility of trying to find some agreed standards which could form the grounds of reasonable suspicion and could be set out in a statute or in a code of practice. Like others before us we have concluded that the variety of circumstances that would have to be covered makes this impracticable. We have therefore looked for other means of ensuring that the criterion of reasonable suspicion is not devalued.'[3]

The Philips Commission thus recommended the retention of 'reasonable suspicion', despite its elasticity, and the government accepted this. Under s 1(3) of PACE, police officers may only stop and search if they have 'reasonable grounds for suspecting' that evidence of relevant offences will be found; and seizure may take place only of articles which, under s 1(7), the officer 'has reasonable grounds for suspecting' to be relevant.

The few cases on reasonable suspicion do little to define it. According to the House of Lords in *Shaaban Bin Hussien v Chong Fook Kam*,[4] reasonable cause (which is synonymous with reasonable suspicion) is a lower standard than information sufficient to prove a prima facie case. Reasonable cause may take into account matters that could not be put in evidence at all, such as hearsay evidence,[5] or matters which although admissible would not on their own prove the case. Lord Devlin declared that:

'Suspicion arises at or near the starting point of an investigation of which the obtaining of *prima facie* proof is the end . . . *Prima facie* proof consists of admissible evidence. Suspicion can take into account matters that could not be put in evidence at all.'[6]

This definition, if such it is, fails to specify the nature of the threshold between mere suspicion, reasonable suspicion and prima facie proof. Other cases are of little more help. In *King v Gardner*,[7] an officer heard a description over his radio of a suspect of a crime. Someone who was loitering nearby fitted this rather vague description so the officer asked for permission to search the large bag he was carrying. The suspect refused, assaulted the officer in an attempt to prevent the search and was arrested for assault in the execution of the officer's duty. The arrest could only be justifiable if the officer was right to

[3] Report, op cit para 3.25.
[4] [1970] AC 942.
[5] See eg *Erskine v Hollin* [1971] RTR 199.
[6] [1970] AC 942 at 948–94.
[7] (1979) 71 Cr App Rep 13.

carry out the search. This depended on him having reasonable suspicion (the Metropolitan Police byelaw in force at the time being similar to what is now PACE, s 1). It was held that the magistrates' court which heard the original case was entitled to conclude that there was no reasonable suspicion, as the description of the suspect was not sufficiently clear to create reasonable suspicion in relation to the person arrested, and his lingering around with a large bag did not create any additional suspicion.

This suggests a fairly high threshold of suspicion. However, in *Lodwick v Sanders*[8] a police officer stopped a lorry because it had no brake lights or tax disc. There was no initial suspicion of theft, but during discussion the officer asked the suspect if he owned the lorry, to which he answered: 'Maybe I do, maybe I don't. If you are going to do me, do me. If you're going to bollock me, bollock me and let me go. I'm in a hurry.' After further discussion the suspect tried to drive off, the officer tried to stop him, and the suspect assaulted the officer. As in *King v Gardner*, he was arrested for assaulting an officer in the execution of his duty. The question for the Divisional Court was whether the officer was acting in the execution of his duty in detaining the lorry driver in order to find out who owned the lorry. The suspect argued that there was no reasonable suspicion of theft, for the officer had found nothing out after making the stop that he did not know at the time of the stop. The Divisional Court, however, upheld the officer's decision.

Was it right to do so? At the time of the initial stop, all the officer reasonably suspected was that the lorry driver was committing various road traffic offences. All he found out following the stop was that the lorry driver refused to answer his questions about the possible theft of the lorry directly. Very little—if anything—was added to the officer's knowledge or understanding of the situation. Yet, for the Divisional Court, that very little seemed enough to create a reasonable suspicion. *King v Gardner* and *Lodwick v Sanders* are not easily reconcilable but this is as much a product of the vagueness of 'reasonable suspicion' as a concept than it is a criticism of the courts.[9]

The 'reasonable suspicion' rule is not unique in its elasticity. Hart has identified two elements in legal rules: a 'core' of settled meaning and a 'penumbra' of uncertainty.[10] All legal rules have both, he argues,

---

[8]   [1985] 1 WLR 382 (no relation).
[9]   See S H Bailey and D Birch, 'Recent Developments in the Law of Police Powers' [1982] Crim LR 475 for discussion of the few other cases prior to *Lodwick v Sanders*. These suggest that the courts have not applied their minds to this issue as rigorously as they might. Judging by *Castorina* (see ch 3 below), it seems that *Lodwick v Sanders* is more representative of the courts' thinking than is *King v Gardner*.
[10] See H Hart, *The Concept of Law* (OUP, 1961).

but some have more extensive penumbras than others. Reasonable suspicion, then, has a core meaning, encompassing such situations as someone trying to climb through a window at night (the fact that it could be a householder locked out does not affect the reasonableness of the suspicion). People hanging around with large bags, or people who answer questions evasively, lie in the penumbra of uncertainty. An alternative analysis is offered by Dworkin, who argues, in opposition to the legal positivists such as Hart, that law is not exclusively constituted by rules.[11] Underlying (and filling in the gaps between) the rules are principles which require continual interpretation and reinterpretation. Thus, the question of what constitutes reasonable suspicion is inevitably one that must be left to the courts to examine in an ethical and principled manner, since it is impossible for Parliament to lay down rigid rules in such a sensitive area. More radical accounts are offered by 'legal realists' and 'critical theorists' who come near to questioning the existence of legal rules altogether and who argue that courts interpret the wording of legal rules in the light of many factors (social, political, economic and so forth) rather than simply seeking their literal and grammatical meaning.[12] On this analysis, the court in *Lodwick v Sanders* may have been as much influenced by a desire to back police judgments and maintain police morale as by any canon of statutory interpretation.

These varied jurisprudential perspectives serve as warnings about the ability or willingness of courts and legislators to control the police (or any other agencies) through legal rules. On any of these analyses we should not be surprised by the impossibility of pinning down the meaning of 'reasonable suspicion'. We shall see the importance of the open-textured nature of much law, to use Hart's language, throughout the criminal justice system.[13]

An attempt to clarify the concept of 'reasonable suspicion' is contained in the PACE Code of Practice A (para 1.6) as follows:

'Whether reasonable grounds for suspicion exist will depend on the circumstances in each case, but there must be some objective basis for it. An officer will need to consider the nature of the article suspected of being carried in the context of other factors such as the time and the place and the behaviour of the person concerned or those with him.'

---

[11] R Dworkin, *Taking Rights Seriously* (Duckworth, 1977).

[12] See R Cotterrell, *The Politics of Jurisprudence* (Butterworths, 1989) ch 7 (also chs 4 and 6 on Hart, Dworkin and other theorists).

[13] Even apparently precise concepts such as the 'necessity' principle (s 37 of PACE), which governs the lawfulness of detaining suspects in police custody between arrest and charge, can be seen to lose certainty in the light of practice. See further ch 4, below.

This still leaves scope to identify certain groups as more suspicious than others (as Willis and the PSI study showed the police do). This was acknowledged in the Code of Practice (para 1.7) in the following terms:

'Reasonable suspicion can never be supported on the basis of personal factors alone. For example, a person's colour, age, hairstyle or manner of dress, or the fact that he is known to have a previous conviction for possession of an unlawful article, cannot be used alone or in combination with each other as the sole basis on which to search that person. Nor may it be founded on the basis of stereotyped images of certain persons or groups as more likely to be committing offences.'

It is remarkable that a legislative code of practice directs, in effect, that people should not be stopped just because they are black. The provision is a rare example of the law attempting to take into account the social reality of policing on the streets.

The Code of Practice, however, raises as many questions as it answers. What, for instance, if a suspect does not simply refuse to answer questions put to him by an officer,[14] but refuses rudely and aggressively? Would this constitute 'behaviour of the person' creating reasonable suspicion?[15]

Lodwick v Sanders is the only post-PACE appeal known at the time of writing which turned upon the meaning of 'reasonable suspicion'. The paucity of cases is significant. If legal rules are, because of their due process content, in conflict with police working assumptions, the extent to which they are inhibitory will depend in part on their enforceability in the courts. The lack of reported court cases suggests that either the police are now adhering faithfully to the law or that the law is unenforceable. The vagueness of the reasonable suspicion test virtually rules out the possibility of strict adherence, and the evidence of research suggests that the paucity of legal cases is not due to the inhibitory qualities of the law.

Taking the race issue first, Norris et al, in research carried out in 1986–87, observed police stops by accompanying police officers on patrol duty. In one London borough they observed 272 stops, of which 28% were of black people, even though black people constituted only

---

[14] Stated by the code of practice not to constitute reasonable suspicion (para 2.3).

[15] See the arrest case of *Ricketts v Cox* (1981) 74 Cr App Rep 298, discussed in ch 3, below. There is evidence from some research that the demeanour of suspects influences police officers in this way (see Southgate, op cit) but other research suggests that this is not universally so: see C Norris, N Fielding, C Kemp and J Fielding, 'Black and Blue: An Analysis of the Influence of Race on Being Stopped by the Police' (1992) 43 BJ Soc 207.

10% of the local population.[16] Each black person was stopped four times as often as each white person (Asians, incidentally, were stopped disproportionately infrequently).[17] As expected from the pre-PACE research, young males were also stopped disproportionately often. This meant that, in that area, between one-quarter and one-third of white males under 35 would be stopped in one year, while for black males under 35 the figure would be a remarkable nine out of ten. This would be justifiable if black people were actually behaving disproportionately more criminally to this extent. Norris et al did not attempt to assess the justifiability of these stops under s 1, but they did divide the reasons for stops into 'tangible' and 'intangible' reasons. It is telling that black people were more frequently stopped for 'intangible' reasons than were white people.

Just as, it would seem, race remains as significant now as it was before PACE, so police working practices based on 'instinct' remain as important as ever. In one of many similar cases discussed by McConville et al, the police checked the occupants of a parked car. Asked why, they said: 'it was just a matter of instinct . . . something indefinable.'[18] In another, an officer was asked how he decided which cars to stop; he simply laughed, replying:

'We check cars when we see people just sitting inside them for a period. We stop them when we see three men in a car. Basically it's impossible to say, we just use our instincts.'[19]

Clearly the legal understanding of 'reasonable suspicion' plays little part in police officers' thought processes or decision making. This is not just because this concept is so hard to define. It is, more fundamentally, because it does not chime with the experience of police officers. Experience is valued, whereas 'books' or theory are not.[20] The reality of the streets, not a legal text, is what police officers respond to, although it is possible that PACE may slowly be bringing about a degree of cultural change, as shown by this officer's remarks to McConville et al:

---

[16] Norris et al, op cit. The analysis of British Crime Survey data by W Skogan, The Police and Public in England and Wales (HMSO, 1990) also reveals disproportionate stops among young people and black people, and especially people who are both young and black.

[17] Recent Home Office research has produced similar findings: P Southgate and D Crisp, Public Satisfaction with Police Services (Home Office Research and Planning Unit Paper no 73) (Home Office, 1993).

[18] M McConville, A Sanders and R Leng, *The Case for the Prosecution* (Routledge, 1991) p 27.

[19] Ibid p 28.

[20] N Fielding, *Joining Forces* (Routledge, 1988) and M Young, op cit.

'The officer said that he had been a police officer for 10 years and any experienced copper would back him up. He had to use his instincts most of the time otherwise his job would not get done. He said that he was worried that a lot of young coppers were being taught to act by the book and having instinctive policing trained out of them . . . "When you get to know an area and see a villain about at two in the morning you will always stop him to see what he is about."'[1]

Spotting a 'villain' in the middle of the night does not qualify as 'reasonable suspicion' in law, but it is enough for many police officers. Dixon et al, for instance, report photographs of drug offenders being posted on police parade room walls with the note 'well worth a stop and search'.[2]

Being where one does not belong—incongruity—is particularly important: a scruffily dressed young male in a 'posh' area, for instance, or for that matter someone dressed in a dinner jacket driving around a decaying inner-city area. There is an even-handedness here which is more apparent than real. The rich are equally at risk of having police power exercised against them if they spend time in poor areas as are the poor in wealthy areas. But wealthy people are less likely to be in such areas, will not be offended if the police suggest that they do not 'belong', and generally possess fewer traits (race, previous convictions and so forth) which would, when added to incongruity, lead to suspiciousness. It is also far easier for the wealthy to avoid incongruity when out of their own area (by dressing scruffily) than it is for the poor.

As with the pre-PACE findings and numerous English and American studies[3] the research of Dixon et al identifies a process of stereotyping, whereby quick judgments are made about people on the basis of visible signs. Thus Jefferson and Walker found that black people were disproportionately stopped only in predominantly white areas: areas where they did not 'belong'.[4] The instinctive decisions the police make are illustrated in an example given by Southgate, whereby a well-dressed black youth was carrying a bag but doing nothing suspicious. 'Let's give him a look. I want to see what's in that bag', said the officer.[5]

---

[1] McConville, Sanders and Leng, op cit p 24.
[2] D Dixon, A K Bottomley, C A Coleman, M Gill and D Wall, 'Reality and Rules in the Construction and Regulation of Police Suspicion' (1989) 17 IJ Sociology of Law 185 at 194.
[3] For an American example, see I Piliavin and S Briar, 'Police Encounters with Juveniles' (1964) 70 AJS 206, discussed in ch 3, below.
[4] T Jefferson and M Walker, 'Ethnic Minorities in the Criminal Justice System' [1992] Crim LR 83.
[5] P Southgate, Police-Public Encounters (Home Office Research Study no 90) (HMSO, 1986) app 1.

Taking all the research together, the pattern which emerges is not of racism or prejudice per se,[6] but continued use of crude stereotypes, focusing on age, gender, class and race. The police generally stop those who they perceive to threaten order and authority, those who appear 'suspicious' to them, and those known to have previous convictions.

(b) The offences

Under s 1(3) of PACE, a police officer may stop and search only if 'he has reasonable grounds for suspecting that he will find stolen or prohibited articles or any article to which subsection (8A) below applies.' 'Stolen articles' clearly include those stolen in contravention of s 1 of the Theft Act 1968. Whether they also include goods obtained by deception (s 15 Theft Act) or blackmail (s 21) is less clear. Bevan and Lidstone argue that since s 24 of the Theft Act defines such articles as stolen goods, 'it is inconceivable that the courts would exclude such other forms of dishonesty from the scope of a s 1 stop and search.'[7]

However, Levenson and Fairweather point out that s 24 specifically applies to the Theft Act alone. Arguing that it should apply to s 1 of PACE would not necessarily succeed in a criminal context, as the 'general rule of interpretation is that penal statutes are to be interpreted restrictively and therefore "stolen" in the 1984 Act should have the narrower meaning.'[8]

Since both views have theoretical merit and there are no cases on the point, there can be no answer to the question (or, if one adopts an extreme positivist or Dworkinian position, the answer which exists has not yet been revealed to us). It is perhaps no wonder that the police pay so little attention to legal niceties when the law is so uncertain.

One case that has a bearing on what may be seized using the s 1 power is *DPP v Gomez*[9] where the House of Lords decided that 'appropriation' in theft could occur even when goods were taken with the fraudulently obtained consent of the owner. In making most offences of obtaining goods by deception also offences of theft, 'stolen' goods now undoubtedly include most goods obtained by deception. This is a good

---

6 Police research unanimously reports the widespread expression of racist views by police officers (see eg Southgate, op cit; McConville and Shepherd, op cit). But such views do not necessarily influence police actions. Thus, although Norris et al, op cit, found disproportionate stopping of black youths, the attitudes displayed to black suspects were no more hostile or provocative, on average, than those displayed to white suspects.

7 Bevan and Lidstone, op cit p 56.

8 H Levenson and F Fairweather, *Police Powers, A Practitioner's Guide* (LAG, 1990) p 15.

9 [1993] AC 442.

example of the way in which decisions which increase the scope of the substantive law may also increase police powers.

Here, however, the increase is more apparent than real. Even if the law were interpreted as not allowing searches for fraudulently obtained goods, it would make no difference to the reality of the police stop and search power. In the unlikely event of officers suspecting a person of carrying goods obtained by deception, as distinct from goods obtained by theft, they could simply not specify the exact offence in relation to which suspicion was held, or could (untruthfully) claim suspicion of theft. If fraudulently obtained goods were discovered, they could still be seized and the suspect arrested, for the fact that something was discovered other than that which was purportedly suspected does not preclude arrest and prosecution. Further, if the officers' suspicions were that precise, they would undoubtedly have sufficient evidence on which to arrest (for the two powers have identical 'reasonable suspicion' thresholds).[10] The suspect could be searched and questioned when in custody without the need for prior stop and search. The significance of there being no cases on the point is not that no one has thought to litigate; it is that in the real world outside legal treatises there is no issue to litigate: the police can do as they wish in this respect regardless of the exact legal position. From this perspective we may say that, as far as stop and search powers are concerned, *Gomez* is not an enabling rule but merely a legitimising one.

What are 'prohibited articles'? They are defined in s 1(7) and (8) as being either (i) an offensive weapon or (ii) articles intended for use in burglary, theft, taking vehicles or obtaining property by deception. Section 1(8A) was added by the Criminal Justice Act 1988. It allows searches for articles which, under s 139 of that Act, are unlawful if carried without a good excuse. Such articles include anything with blades or sharp points, including penknives if the blade is over three inches long. This broadens the notion of the offensive weapon, which is actually very broad anyway. Any item can be classed as an offensive weapon so long as it can be shown that the person possessed it with intention to cause injury. Thus a stone[11] and a pepperpot[12] have been held to be offensive weapons, and such articles as steel combs, shoes with stiletto heels[13] or even pens might be considered offensive. Again we can see that the broadness of substantive criminal law impinges on the procedural power of the police. The Philips Commission recognised this but, by a majority, rejected the argument that the vagueness

---

[10]   See ch 3, below, for discussion of arrest powers.
[11]   *Harrison v Thornton* [1966] Crim LR 388.
[12]   *Parkins* (1956) 120 JP 250, report of a first instance decision.
[13]   (1964) Times, 25 September.

surrounding the offence of carrying an offensive weapon made it too dangerous to give the police a power to stop and search: 'If there is imprecision in the definition of the offence, the remedy for the difficulty . . . lies in removing that imprecision rather than in refusing the police the power to search.'[14] Similarly, a very wide range of articles could be intended for use in committing crimes of dishonesty. The purpose of a jemmy or set of skeleton keys may be fairly obvious, but one's own cheque book would be such an article if one set out intending to purchase goods with it, knowing or suspecting that it would 'bounce'.[15]

To sum up, the police may stop and search for offensive weapons or for goods which either are stolen or would be used to commit offences of dishonesty. Broad as these powers are, they represent additions to (rather than replacements for) the miscellaneous powers to which we referred earlier. Thus, powers to search for narcotics under drugs legislation are still important. Section 159 of the Road Traffic Act 1972 (now s 163, Road Traffic Act 1988) is also important. This provides police officers with the power to stop vehicles if they are believed (whether reasonably or not in this case)[16] to be committing road traffic offences, such as having faulty lights or no tax disc. If the police stop a car under this section, they do not have the right per se to search for stolen goods or prohibited articles. However, if in the course of the stop under s 159 police suspicion relating to, for instance, theft is aroused, then the police will be able to continue the stop and search for that second purpose, as in *Lodwick v Sanders*, discussed earlier. In fact, after observing 1,000 encounters between police and public, Southgate states that: 'It was sometimes unclear whether, when stopping a vehicle, it was a criminal or a traffic law violation the officer suspected.'[17]

New powers to stop and search vehicles and pedestrians are included in the Criminal Justice and Public Order Bill, introduced into Parliament in late 1993. According to cl 62(4), police officers will be enabled to stop any vehicle or person and make any 'search he thinks fit whether or not he has any grounds for suspecting that the vehicle or person is carrying articles [which could be used in terrorist activities]'. This is an enabling rule par excellence, lacking in any of the due process elements one usually finds provided when police powers are extended by statute. Although these powers are directed at suspected terrorists, in the light of the above discussion it may be predicted that

---

14 Royal Commission on Criminal Procedure, Report (Cmnd 8092 (HMSO, 1981) para 3.21.
15 *Metropolitan Police Comr v Charles* [1976] 3 All ER 112.
16 *Chief Constable of Gwent v Dash* [1986] RTR 41.
17 Southgate, op cit p 13.

they will be put to more general use in the fulfilment of the policing mandate.

Although the Divisional Court decided that there was reasonable suspicion of theft on the facts in *Lodwick v Sanders*, it is hard to see what produced the officer's suspicion other than the suspect's obstructiveness and hostility. But many people are, regrettably, obstructive and hostile to the police. Even if it signifies likely criminality (which it does not) it is as likely to be criminality for which stop and search cannot be used (such as being wanted for assault) as, say, theft. If this is true of someone with whom the police are already in conversation, how much more true it must be of most people who the police simply observe in the street or in their cars. If someone is acting 'suspiciously', how can a police officer tell if that person is about to commit a burglary or to threaten someone with a weapon? In one of McConville et al's cases, a youth ran away when he saw the police, so he was chased and searched.[18] A Krugerrand was found, so he was arrested. It turned out that he had this lawfully, but that hardly matters. The police often stop, search and arrest people who run away when they see police officers. This is, by any standards, suspicious behaviour. But of what can one reasonably suspect such people? In this particular case, was it really reasonable suspicion of theft? The arrests which resulted from stops in this study were often unrelated to the reasons for the stops: when the occupants of the parked car discussed earlier were searched, drugs were found. But the occupants were a young couple whose lengthy period alone in a discreetly parked car had a far more obvious, and entirely legal, explanation.[19]

The way police-public encounters begin in relation to one issue and end in completely unrelated ways has been observed by others, before and after PACE.[20] Smith, though, suggests not just that unsuspected offences come to light following legitimate stops, but also that suspicion of an offence to which s 1 applies is sometimes used as a pretext when other offences are suspected:

'. . . observations at police stations suggest that police may often find illegal immigrants by carrying out stops and searches of black people in vehicles or on foot. There is no power to detain or search a person in the street on suspicion of immigration offences, but some other justification can be found for the original stop.'[1]

---

[18]   M. McConville, A Sanders and R Leng, *The Case for the Prosecution* (Routledge, 1991) p 28.

[19]   Ibid p 27.

[20]   See eg Southgate, op cit p 8.

[1]   D Smith, 'Origins of Black Hostility to the Police' (1991) 2(1) Policing and Society 6.

In some areas and in some contexts, there are simply numerous crimes waiting to be discovered. The fact that there is no specific reason to stop those particular individuals or cars does not alter the fact that statistically the officer is more likely to notch up a successful 'collar' by stopping them than by stopping people randomly, or by stopping respectable-looking people in affluent suburbs. Most stops are in inner-city areas, largely because they *are* inner-city areas. These areas are not necessarily more criminogenic than others, but the crimes which predominate in them (drugs, car theft, burglary and street violence) are more amenable than most to discovery by stop and search. Not surprisingly, the attempt of legislators through s 1 to require specific suspicion of specific offences as a condition of using stop and search powers is proving unsuccessful.

(c)   The power

This is in fact a bundle of powers. Section 1(2)(b) states that a police officer 'may detain a person or vehicle for the purpose of . . . a search', and s 1(6) provides a power to seize certain property discovered in the course of this search. In addition, the police have an implicit power to question.[2] As we shall see, police officers may question any persons they wish prior to arrest, and this is true whether or not they are exercising these s 1 powers.[3] However, there is no obligation to answer these questions and so the power of an officer to question is slightly different to the other powers contained in s 1. Suspects must submit to search and detention, but they need not answer questions.

A police officer acting under s 1 thus has the power to stop, detain, question, search and seize. The section provides no time limits on the length of detention, nor does it specify how intimate a search may be. The only guidance is provided in the PACE Code of Practice A and is as follows:

'The length of time for which a person or vehicle may be detained will depend on the circumstances, but must in all circumstances be reasonable and not extend beyond the time taken for the search. The thoroughness and extent of a search must depend on what is suspected of being carried, and by whom.'[4]

---

[2] *Daniel v Morrison* (1979) 70 Cr App Rep 142.
[3] As Note 1B of the PACE Code of Practice A states: 'This Code does not affect the ability of an officer to speak to or question a person in the ordinary course of his duties (and in the absence of reasonable suspicion) without detaining him or exercising any element of compulsion.'
[4] See para 3.3. Limitations on searches involving the removal of outer clothing are made in para 3.5.

Section 1 provides the power to require citizens to stop and submit to searches. It provides no power to ask this of citizens. This is because no such power is needed. Legally, anyone can ask anything of anyone else, whether they be police officers or ordinary citizens. Of course, it would be remarkable if ordinary citizens did go around asking people to agree to be stopped and searched, and few people would assent to such an odd request. Police officers, however, often do ask people if they will consent to be stopped and searched, and consent is often given. The Code of Practice A (in Note 1D(b)) amplifies that stop and search with consent is lawful: 'Nothing in this Code affects . . . the ability of an officer to search a person in the street on a voluntary basis . . .' Such consensual searches do not require the exercise of s 1 powers, and, as a corollary, the restrictions outlined earlier—reasonable suspicion of specific offences—do not apply; nor do the other controls to be discussed in the next section.

The research by both Dixon et al and McConville et al shows that most stops are 'consensual'.[5] Most officers carry out 'consensual' stops, and few exercise their statutory powers. As one officer explained to Dixon et al 'I have never had any problems with anyone refusing to be searched . . . so I have never had to fall back on proving my reasonable suspicion.'[6] Similarly, an officer told McConville et al that 'I've always got their consent . . . I tell people, "Why make life difficult on yourself."'[7]

Thus the official figures provide no true indication of the level of stops carried out, because of 'consent' searches.[8] But what is consent in this context? As Dixon et al point out, when an officer asks someone on the street whether they would mind answering questions, this is usually perceived not to be a genuine request, admitting either 'yes' or 'no' as an answer, but a polite way of insisting. Officers rarely disabuse suspects of that perception. As one officer interviewed admitted, 'a lot of people are not quite certain that they have the right to say no and then we sort of bamboozle them into allowing us to search.'[9]

Dixon et al go on to say that many people assume that an officer who says 'what have you got in your pocket?' or 'let's have a look in your bag' has a power to search. When police officers were asked how

---

[5] D Dixon, C Coleman and K Bottomley, 'Consent and the Legal Regulation of Policing' (1990) 17 Journal of Law and Society 345 at 348; McConville, Sanders and Leng, op cit p 94.

[6] Dixon et al, 'Consent and the Legal Regulation of Policing', op cit at 349.

[7] McConville, Sanders and Leng, op cit p 94.

[8] See the discussion in section 4, below, based on the British Crime Survey.

[9] Dixon et al, 'Consent and the Legal Regulation of Policing', op cit at 348.

often people who were stopped and searched knew their rights, 79% said rarely or never. The researchers concluded that 'such lack of knowledge must mean that their "consent" has little substance.'[10]

Thus the formal equivalence between consensual stops by officers and consensual stops by citizens is completely unreal. Most people do as officers ask, but not as other strangers ask. The identical treatment by the law of dissimilar social situations allows police officers to avoid the legal constraints. The legal sanctioning of 'consensual' searches by police officers is an enabling rule which renders the safeguards of s 1 largely presentational.

The failure of the law to address the reality of policing is evident in another way too. Breaking stop and search down into discrete actions, as we did at the start of this section, takes no account of the social processes involved. In an encounter which begins with a consensual and innocuous conversation, suspicion may develop and the suspect may get impatient. The point at which consent is no longer present and s 1 powers are, or should be, invoked cannot be identified with precision. This allows the police to manipulate the rules and, equally important, makes those rules irrelevant to policing and thus marginal to the basis for police decision making. Their potentially inhibitory effects are reduced almost to vanishing point.

(d) Constraints and controls on police discretion

The Philips Commission were aware that the criterion of reasonable suspicion could become devalued in practice, and that random stops had to be guarded against. Its solution was to introduce a battery of secondary controls:

'We consider that the notification of the reason for the search to the person who has been stopped, the recording of searches by officers, and the monitoring of the records by supervising officers would be the most effective and practical ways of reducing the risk.'[11]

Section 2 of PACE accordingly stipulates that a police officer must provide certain information to suspects before searching them, including the officer's name and police station, the object of the proposed search and the grounds for proposing to make it.[12] The officer must also tell the suspect, unless this is not practical, that he is making a

---

[10] Ibid.

[11] Royal Commission on Criminal Procedure, Report (Cmnd 8092) (HMSO, 1981) para 3.25.

[12] Section 2(1) provides that this provision, and those in s 3, apply to searches under all legislation, not just PACE.

record of the circumstances of the search and that the suspect is entitled to a copy of it.[13]

Officers must make the record of the search as soon as practical unless it is not practical to make one at all (s 3(1) and (2)). But why should it ever be entirely impractical to make a record? It is obviously not practical for an officer to make a record in the context of a violent arrest, but it can be made afterwards. Only if a large number of people is being searched could the making of records at some point be imprac- tical. But, as Bevan and Lidstone ask, how can there be reasonable suspicion in the context of mass searches?[14] Bevan and Lidstone are right to conclude that this shows that routine searches with minimal suspicion are not merely common, but are endorsed by the government and the senior officers who pressed for these provisions. The 'practi- cality' provision is an enabling and legitimating provision which undermines the inhibitory content of ss 2 and 3 and which underwrites the crime control-based working assumptions of the police.

Sub-section (6) provides that the record must state:

(1) the object of the search (ie stolen goods or prohibited articles);
(2) the grounds for making it (ie what has given rise to the suspicion);
(3) the time and date when it was made;
(4) the place where it was made;
(5) whether anything (and if so what) was found;
(6) whether any (and if so what) injury to a person or damage to property appears to the officer to have resulted from the search.

As we have said, suspects are entitled to copies of these records if they request them. The purpose of providing information before search, committing it to writing afterwards and providing suspects with those records is to enable suspects to hold police officers to account if they misuse their s 1 powers. This is intended to provide a remedy for those who are wrongly stopped, and the fear of complaints should produce more compliance in the first place.

There are a number of reasons to question the realism of this. Firstly, it only applies to searches. Many stops do not go this far, and remain unrecorded.[15] Secondly, it is no use having a right not to be stopped and

---

13 PACE Code of Practice A, para 2.6.
14 V Bevan and K Lidstone, *The Investigation of Crime: A Guide to Police Powers* (Butterworths, 1991) p 72. In situations where there is thought to be a pressing social need for mass searches, such as at a particular football ground where there are grounds for fearing an outbreak of violence, submitting to a search can be made a condition of entry, in which case it will be a consensual search to which ss 2 and 3 will not apply.
15 Prior to PACE, Willis, op cit p 22 found that searches took place in only around a quarter of all stops.

searched unlawfully if people do not know what that right entails. The difficulties discussed above in defining reasonable suspicion mean that it is virtually impossible to know what a right not to be stopped and searched unlawfully means. Thirdly, it is no use having a record made if people do not know of its existence. This is why the police are obliged to inform suspects that they may see the record. Not to do so is a breach of PACE. However, if the officer fails to inform the suspect, then the suspect will remain unaware of the entitlement to see the record so will not know that the officer breached the legal duty to explain this. As Dixon et al point out, one major reform which is needed if PACE is to be at all effective in relation to powers on the street is for citizens to be fully educated about their rights and, by implication, not to have to rely on the police for this knowledge.[16]

Sections 2 and 3 apply only to non-consensual searches, for when there is consent no statutory powers need be invoked and, therefore, the search is not subject to any statutory controls. Since there are more 'consensual' searches than there are compulsory searches, most searches will not have records.[17] A further problem is the dubious nature of the 'consent' given in many searches. If the 'consensual' nature of a stop were to be disputed, it would usually be only the suspect's word against the officer's. The written record which—if completed accurately— would show what really happened will not have been made, precisely because the police officer designated the stop as consensual for official purposes. Some police forces have sought to resolve this impasse by urging their officers to make records for all stops where there was reasonable suspicion regardless of whether or not there was consent. This is not a complete solution to the problem since in situations where there was no reasonable suspicion no record would be expected, and the legality or otherwise of the stop would turn on whether or not consent was given, which cannot be determined without witnesses.

Whether consensual or not, the fact remains that most searches are not recorded. The police force researched by Dixon et al had 2,000 officers, yet in 1986–8 less than 700 searches per annum, on average, were recorded. This force is probably not unusual, for in 1987 there were fewer recorded searches for the whole country than there were officers. Contrast this with the fact that the officers interviewed by Dixon et al revealed that on the average patrol they would expect to carry out four or five searches. Recording of searches is so rare that

---

[16] D Dixon, A Bottomley, C Coleman, M Gill and D Wall, 'Reality and Rules in the Construction and Regulation of Police Suspicion' (1989) 17 IJ Sociology of Law, 185 at 203.

[17] Dixon et al, 'Consent and the Legal Regulation of Policing' (1990) at 348. See the discussion based on the British Crime Survey in section 4, below.

many officers do not even bother to carry the stop and search forms with them.[18]

The most obvious problem with written records is that police officers may write accounts designed more to fit the statutory criteria than the actual events. This is not to suggest that this is usual, but stops which fail to satisfy the statutory criteria are probably not usual anyway. The problem arises with unlawful stops. Only the bravest (or most foolish) officers would complete written records in such ways as to reveal this. So if there were a challenge to a particular stop, it would again be the suspect's word against the officer's, just as if there were no written record. The record therefore may be more of a protection for the officer than it is for the suspect. Many officers told Dixon and his colleagues that they made a record only if they feared that there would be some sort of 'comeback'. If, for example, a middle class person who was aware of the law happened to be stopped 'you would probably revert to the standard opening speech procedure and complete a form.'[19]

One function of a written record is to allow supervision: to allow a supervisory officer to examine an officer's work without having to observe it at first hand. In many jobs, written records of work do form a basic supervision. This is fine when the essence of one's work is actual writing—such as a university lecturer whose product is supposed to be work in the form of books or articles. A police officer's job is different. It is not to write things down but to act in accordance with the law. When a supervisory officer scrutinises an officer's record of an event, the scrutiny is not of what the officer did or whether it was within the law but of the officer's account of what was done. It is rather like a university lecturer's output being assessed on the basis of the author's own account of its academic value. The lecturer is as unlikely to give a poor self-assessment as a police officer is to portray a stop search as anything other than lawful.

In any event, records are generally treated by officers as 'mere paperwork'. Dixon et al report that some forms were completed tautologically (grounds for search being stated as 'suspicious behaviour'), while most officers were 'concerned about saving on paperwork'. Only a quarter of police supervisory officers questioned by Dixon et al mentioned checking paperwork as a form of supervision. Over three quarters of the constables and sergeants interviewed said that their stops were not generally supervised.[20]

---

[18]   Ibid.

[19]   Ibid p 349.

[20]   Dixon et al, 'Reality and Rules in the Construction and Regulation of Police Suspicion' (1989) at 200–1.

Police stop and search is a classic example of low visibility work. It is no criticism of the law or of the police hierarchy to say that stop and search cannot, for this reason, be adequately supervised. What is open to criticism is the pretence that effective supervision is possible and that requiring officers to make written records of stop searches amounts to an adequate check on the legality of their actions. One may also censure the police hierarchy for failing to encourage supervisory officers to take their responsibilities seriously. Adequate supervision may not be possible, but better supervision certainly is: senior officers can hardly be unaware of photographs of criminals on parade room walls with notes urging stops simply because of their criminal records.[1] The problems inherent in attempts to control low visibility and discretionary police work are compounded by laxity in the law and by a policing culture which emphasises 'results' rather than procedural propriety.

(e)   Remedies

Where a stop is legally questionable, what is the probability and likely consequence of a successful challenge? If a stop is unsuccessful, both officers and suspects are usually happy to forget the whole incident, and the absence of reasonable suspicion will rarely be an issue. If the stop is successful, in the sense of a crime being discovered, it will rarely be questioned because the initial illegality becomes overshadowed by the crime itself. In the unlikely event of a challenge being made to a stop and search, what actions or remedies are available?

It is striking that PACE itself is silent on this point, neither making it a crime nor a tort to stop and search someone unlawfully, to fail to provide information before search, or to make a record of it afterwards.[2] At common law, a failure to provide information prior to search renders the stop and search unlawful.[3] However, the consequences of

---

[1] See pre-penultimate paragraph in section 3(a), p 44, above. For discussion of the lax supervisory arrangements generally in police investigations, see J Baldwin and T Moloney, Supervision of Police Investigations in Serious Criminal Cases (Royal Commission on Criminal Justice Research Study no 4) (HMSO, 1992); and M Maguire and C Norris, The Conduct and Supervision of Criminal Investigations (Royal Commission on Criminal Justice Research Study no 5) (HMSO, 1992).

[2] Section 67(10) provides that a failure on the part of a police officer to comply with the provisions of Code of Practice A 'shall not of itself render him liable to any criminal or civil proceedings'.

[3] The pre-Act case of *Pedro v Diss* [1981] 2 All ER 59 held, following *Christie v Leachinsky* [1947] AC 573, that detention was unlawful if the reason for it was not provided.

unlawfulness are not always clear. In *Pedro v Diss*[4] the suspect concerned (D) was charged with assaulting an officer in the execution of his duty after D used force to free himself from detention. The unlawfulness of the detention meant that the officer was not acting in the execution of his duty, and so the assault was not criminal. But a violent response to the exercise of police power is still fairly unusual. A stop and search which was unlawful—whether because inadequate reasons were provided or because inadequate reasons existed (such as no reasonable suspicion)—would be more likely to give rise to the possibility of an action in tort or, if charges followed the discovery of stolen or prohibited articles, a motion to exclude from court evidence discovered as a result of the stop and search.

If stops are challenged in court (in either of these ways), and the officers' accounts differ from those of the suspect what would or could the court do? If defining the absence of reasonable suspicion is difficult, proving it is virtually impossible: these are low visibility decisions where there are seldom other civilian witnesses and where—because those stopped are so often people with previous convictions and so forth—suspects are easily 'discredited'.[5]

If a stop were to be successfully challenged in a criminal case, there is the possibility of the evidence obtained as a result of the search being excluded from trial, as happened in *Fennelley*.[6] However, as a Crown Court case, this is a weak authority and, as chapter 9 will show, it is not consistent with the courts' normal interpretation of the exclusionary provisions of PACE. The decision of the trial judge in *Fenneley* would be a logical response within a system committed to due process but amounts to something of an aberration within the system as it normally operates in this country.

An action in tort might lie on grounds of wrongful arrest or even assault.[7] However, there have been no reported cases of this, partly because such an action would be speculative, and partly, no doubt, because the loss or damages suffered as a result of an unlawful stop and search is limited. It is not clear whether not making a record renders a stop and search unlawful and thus an assault. There is no case law or statutory provision on this, although the government, in reply to an MP's question, did express the view when PACE was passing through Parliament that not doing so would not render a stop and search unlawful.

---

[4] [1981] 2 All ER 59.
[5] See the discussion of discrediting in the context of complaints against the police in ch 9, below.
[6] [1989] Crim LR 142.
[7] See further ch 3, section 5, below.

One other possible remedy is the making of a complaint against the police officer concerned. Section 67(8) of PACE makes it a disciplinary offence to breach any of the provisions in the PACE Code of Practice A. The chances of having a complaint upheld are low, however; this is partly because of the difficulty of establishing that an officer lacked reasonable suspicion or failed to give information prior to search, and partly because of the failings or inadequacies of the police complaints machinery.[8]

4.   THE IMPACT OF PACE

(a)   Changes in the numbers of stops and searches

One effect of the combination of ss 1–3 of PACE should have been more discriminating (ie reduced) use of stop and search in areas where it had previously been used extensively (such as inner London), but more overall use in those (relatively thinly populated) areas where these powers were previously not available. A measure of the inhibitory effectiveness of PACE is whether there are now fewer stops than there were in the early 1980s.

In 1981, it will be recalled, there were over 700,000 recorded stops in London alone. Post-PACE figures for the whole of England and Wales are as follows:

Table 2.1: Recorded searches and 'success rates'[9]

Year	Stop/Searches	Arrests	% leading to arrests
1986	109,800	18,900	17.2%
1987	118,300	19,600	16.6%
1988	149,600	23,700	15.8%
1989	202,800	32,800	16.2%
1990	256,900	39,200	15.3%
1991	303,800	46,200	15.2%
1992	351,700	48,700	13.8%

[8]   See ch 9, below on remedies.
[9]   Source: Home Office Statistical Bulletin 21/93, Table A. Note that these figures relate to stop-searches under PACE only.

There certainly are considerably fewer recorded stops now than there were in the early 1980s. On the face of it, this suggests that, at the time that Willis and the PSI did their research, the police in London used stop and search powers much more extensively than they or any other police force do now. However, these figures could be misleading. Firstly, there is no requirement to record simple stops. Only searches need be recorded (s 3), and in only 10% of vehicle stops and 22% of pedestrian stops do searches take place.[10] Secondly, even searches need not be recorded if they are 'consensual'. Thirdly, officers are known to be reluctant to record searches of any kind. Finally, there is enormous variation in recorded stop-searches between police force areas; Norfolk and Greater Manchester, for instance, have some eight times as many searches per head of population than do Suffolk and West Yorkshire. Significantly, the 1992 arrest rates for the high stop-search forces (Norfolk: 14.8%; Manchester: 10.9%) are lower than for the low stop-search forces (Suffolk: 18.7%; West Yorkshire: 20.9%).[11] This might be because some forces simply record unsuccessful stop-searches less often than do others. Or it might simply be that Manchester really does do eight times as many stops as West Yorkshire and the lower arrest rate reflects the fact that the more often you perform a task, the less discriminating you tend to be.

These recording problems render the absolute figures of little value. A more accurate estimate of the level of stops is provided by the 1988 British Crime Survey.[12] It appears from this that 15% of all adults (ie several million people) were stopped in 1987–8—which is remarkably similar to the estimate made by Southgate and Ekblom pre-PACE some years earlier.[13] Of these 15%, 12% were traffic stops and 3% were pedestrian stops (with a few people experiencing both). Traffic stops would generally be Road Traffic Act 1974, not 'PACE', stops, but if even only half of the pedestrian stops were PACE stops this would still total some half a million, in a year when less than 150,000 were recorded. As always, black people were found to be disproportionately stopped.

Skogan compared data from the 1982 British Crime Survey with that of the 1988 Survey and concluded that there had probably been little change.[14] It is unlikely that there has been a real fall in stop-

[10]   W Skogan, The Police and Public in England and Wales (Home Office Research Study no 117) (HMSO, 1990) p 33.
[11]   All these figures are derived from the Home Office Statistical Bulletin 21/93, Fig 2 and Table 1.
[12]   Skogan, op cit Table 6.
[13]   P Southgate and P Ekblom, Contacts Between Police and Public (Home Office Research Study no 77) (HMSO, 1984). See discussion in section 1, above.
[14]   Skogan, op cit pp 41–42.

search since PACE was introduced. If there has been a fall, this is not necessarily because of general adherence to ss 1–3 of PACE. Table 2.1 shows that recorded stops more than tripled between 1986 and 1992. If we discount the possibility of 'reasonably suspicious' incidents or the number of police patrols tripling in that time, we are left with one or more of three explanations: initial underuse of what to many officers would have been the unfamiliar s 1 powers, increasing overuse of PACE, or a greater willingness to record searches. Since it is likely, in the light of the post-PACE research evidence discussed earlier, that all three explanations are accurate, the failure of these rules and controls to constrain the police significantly is obvious. Thus in one study (not in London) 71% of police officers with pre-PACE experience said that PACE had not affected the way they carried out stop and search.[15] Public reaction to the excess use of stop and search in the early 1980s could have been as influential as was PACE in producing dramatic reductions in recorded stops; we might speculate that increased police confidence in more recent years lies behind the upward trend. If so, it is possible in the 1993–4 period, when the police are being scrutinised more critically, that the use of stops will decline slightly.

(b) 'Success' rates and crime control

How valuable are stop-search powers for the police? Table 2.1 (above) shows that less than 14% of recorded stops now lead to arrest. The reality is even less impressive: according to the 1988 British Crime Survey, only about 4% of pedestrian stops and 10% of car stops led to arrest or prosecution (car stops would normally lead, if anything, to a summons for a Road Traffic Act 1974 offence rather than an arrest).[16] This may seem ineffective, especially when only half of all arrests lead to prosecution.[17] And one has to question whether it is worth providing such powers when most 'catches' are for relatively minor traffic matters.

Overall, arrests following stops constitute a small percentage of all arrests: Steer found that they accounted for less than 3% of arrests.[18] Moreover, there is little reason to believe that, in the absence of stop-search powers, most of these crimes would remain undetected. Firstly,

---

[15] D Dixon, C Coleman and K Bottomley, 'Consent and the Legal Regulation of Policing' (1990) 17 Journal of Law and Society, 345 at 347.

[16] Skogan, op cit p 32.

[17] M McConville, A Sanders and R Leng, *The Case for the Prosecution* (Routledge, 1991) ch 6.

[18] D Steer, *Police Cautions* (Blackwell, 1972). This was, of course, a pre-PACE study.

there is the opportunity to search with consent. Without the power to compel lying behind requests, of course, fewer people would consent than they do now, but less coercive policing could indirectly produce more co-operation rather than less over time.[19] Secondly, the police could arrest where they genuinely have reasonable suspicion. Again, they would do so less often than they currently stop and search, but since we could expect a more selective policy to be based on more evidence, the fall in the detection rate is unlikely to be as extensive as one might otherwise expect.

None the less, there is little escaping the probability that the more stop-searches carried out, the more detections there will be. Forces which carry out a large number of stop-searches, like Norfolk and Manchester, may have a lower arrest rate than do forces like West Yorkshire and Suffolk, but they do make more arrests. From the crime control perspective, the loss of liberty involved for suspects (whether innocent or not) is a price worth paying for increased detections. From a due process perspective, the marginal utility of each extra arrest would not outweigh the loss of liberty involved. However, crime control adherents place considerable stress on the fact-finding ability of professionals. Low arrest rates tend both to undermine that confidence in relation to stop-search and to strengthen the argument for more due process.

That, however, is not the end of the matter, for the widespread use of stop-search powers may be effective in deterring potential offenders. Thus David Powis, in a book written as a manual for police officers when he was a deputy assistant commissioner in the Metropolitan Police, argues that 'young officers' should never be disappointed if stopping an innocent person leads to no arrest: 'who is to say that an apparently unsuccessful stop is not a crime prevented? Real effort will give your police area a reputation that it is a hot place . . .'[20]

The police service as a whole, in its evidence to the Philips Commission, stressed the role of stop and search as part of a wide array of powers to combat crime.[1] This classic crime control argument gets perilously close to arguing for stop-search without reasonable suspicion on deterrent grounds. Even leaving aside the due process objections, one may doubt the effectiveness of such a policy. The

---

[19]   This is the argument of advocates of 'community policing'. See discussion in section 1, above.

[20]   D Powis, *The Signs of Crime* (McGraw-Hill, 1977) p 104.

[1]   See M Brogden, 'Stopping the People' in J Baxter and L Koffman (eds), *Police—The Constitution and the Community* (Professional Books, 1985).

problem was highlighted by Swamp 81.[2] This massive operation, in which the police made 943 stops, saturated the streets of Brixton for several days and triggered a riot. Scarman observed that:

'. . . the evidence is not clear that a street saturation operation does diminish street crime: it may well only drive it elsewhere. And, after the operation has ended, street crime returns.'[3]

So stop and search may impact upon crime at one time and in one place, but otherwise allows crime to flourish. This 'displacement' phenomenon is common in relation to other areas of crime and policing, such as prostitution and crime prevention measures,[4] and can only be countered by consistent, widespread and powerful street policing antithetical to the 'community policing' styles also being encouraged in the 1980s and 1990s.

Another way in which stop and search contributes to crime control is in augmenting 'criminal intelligence'. Police collators, for instance, build up computer databases of information about suspects and witnesses based on information derived from stops.[5] Written records in particular—ostensibly introduced as protections for suspects—provide the basis for systematic collation of information about suspects.[6] In some areas, more stops lead to fewer arrests, precisely because the criminal intelligence normally gathered after arrest is collected on the street instead. Sometimes complex systems of data storage are thereby created, allowing certain target populations to be monitored.[7]

Stop and search, then, has a limited impact in terms of specific arrests, but could have a wider impact in general crime control. Brogden goes further and argues that this is actually part of a wider social control function: that historically the police have been more concerned with social control of the streets than with detecting crime.[8] From medieval times, such laws

---

[2] Sir L Scarman, The Brixton Disorders: 10–12 April 1981 (Cmnd 8427) (HMSO, 1981) para 3.27, discussed in section 2, above.

[3] Ibid para 4.78.

[4] See eg R Leng and A Sanders, 'The CLRC Report on Prostitution' [1983] Crim LR 644.

[5] D Dixon, A Bottomley, C Coleman, M Gill and D Wall, 'Reality and Rules in the Construction and Regulation of Police Suspicion' (1989) 17 IJ Sociology of Law, 185 at 189.

[6] C Willis, The Use, Effectiveness and Impact of Police Stop and Search Powers (Home Office Research and Planning Unit Paper no 15) (Home Office, 1983) p 15 and see L Bridges and T Bunyan, 'Britain's New Urban Policing Strategy—the Police and Criminal Evidence Bill in Context' (1983) 10 Journal of Law and Society 85.

[7] See A Meehan, 'Internal Police Records and the Control of Juveniles' (1993) 33 BJ Crim 504.

[8] M Brogden, op cit; and see also M Brogden and A Brogden, 'From Henry III to Liverpool 8' (1984) 12 IJ Sociology of Law 37.

'to keep in order the unruly' or to apprehend 'rogues, vagabonds and other disorderly persons' were common. The Head Constable of Liverpool instructed his men in 1878, for instance, to watch 'vigilantly the movements of all suspected persons . . . For the purposes of seeing whether his suspicions are well founded, he may stop any person . . .'[9] Reasonable suspicion, as found in modern legislation, was an afterthought. PACE, far from providing a new power for the police armoury, represents historical continuity (in its substance). It is the attempt to impose due process on street policing which is the novelty. Stop and search, and the street policing which stop and search facilitates, is precisely about monitoring and controlling groups of 'suspicious' people, rather than about detecting specific crimes and specific criminals. If certain groups feel they are special targets it is because they are. They, or other groups which used to occupy their place in society, always have been.

This is where we see the importance of the stop and search power being limited to public places. For it is those at the bottom of the socio-economic heap who tend to gather in such places and are thus, as a group, subjected to the stop and search power most frequently. As Lord Scarman observed in his report on the Brixton disorders of 1981, young unemployed black people had little alternative but to make their lives on the streets:

'And living much of their lives on the streets, they are brought into contact with the police who appear to them as the visible symbols of the authority of a society which has failed to bring them its benefits or do them justice.'[10]

In this tense situation, it is easy to see how the power to stop and search could become employed by the police as much to assert their own authority on the streets (which we have seen is a key element in 'cop culture') as to detect specific crimes.

(c) Police and community relations

We have made reference before to the notions of 'policing by consent' and 'community policing'. These concepts are not as straightforward as they may sound, and the assumptions on which they are based are questionable.[11] However, in so far as these notions are tenable and

[9] Brogden, 'Stopping the People' in J Baxter and L Koffman (eds), op cit pp 106–107.
[10] Sir L Scarman, op cit para 2.23.
[11] There is a contradiction between the aspiration to foster community solidarity and the encouragement of an informant culture: M McConville and D Shepherd, *Watching Police, Watching Communities* (Routledge, 1992). Also see P Gordon, 'Community Policing: Towards the Local Police State' in P Scraton (ed), *Law, Order and the Authoritarian State* (Open University Press, 1987).

desirable, the negative impact on them of extensive use of stop and search needs to be considered.

There is no doubt that many local communities get intensely angry and feel harassed as a result of stop and search, especially when they perceive these powers to be exercised in a discriminatory way. Whether or not the police actually behave in a discriminatory way, it is clear from many studies that many black communities certainly believe them to do so. Thus Scarman blamed 'unimaginative and inflexible' tactics (culminating in stop and search sweeps such as Swamp 81) for the fact that relations in Brixton had 'been a tale of failure'.[12] The Conservative MP John Wheeler warned that 'the principal casualty [of PACE's stop and search powers] is likely to be a worsening of police community relations',[13] a view which is supported by Home Office research.[14] As Norris et al say, the perception by many black communities of 'police behaviour will remain unfavourable because blacks feel, for understandable reasons, that they are subject to excessive levels of police surveillance.'[15]

The perception of discrimination is given substance by the enormous variation in recorded stop rates from police force to police force and, within a given force, from one locality to another. In 1987 in London, there were approximately 7.6 stops per 1,000 people, while in West Yorkshire there were only 0.8. But over half of the stops in the six subdivisions in Leeds were in just one subdivision, bringing the stops per 1,000 people in that subdivision much nearer to that of London. Significantly, that subdivision is an ethnically mixed inner-city area, and two thirds of the stops were for drugs (something of which black people are disproportionately suspected).[16]

If people believe the police to be against them—whether or not this belief is justified—then they are far less likely to participate in community policing. Jefferson et al found that hostility to the police in the black community was unrelated to the specific number of times individuals were stopped: hostility to the police had become a feature of the whole community.[17] Moreover, it seems from the 1988 British Crime

---

12 Sir L Scarman, op cit para 4.43.
13 Quoted in Brogden, 'Stopping the People', op cit pp 99–100.
14 R Clarke and M Hough, *Crime and Police Effectiveness* (Home Office Research Study no 79) (HMSO, 1984).
15 C Norris, N Fielding, C Kemp and J Fielding, 'Black and Blue: An Analysis of the Influence of Race on Being Stopped by the Police' (1992) 43 BJ Sociology 207.
16 T Jefferson, M Walker and D Seneviratne in D Downes (ed), *Unravelling Criminal Justice* (Routledge, 1992).
17 This point has been made countless times. See, for example, Brogden, 'Stopping the People', op cit. People who are young, black or male have far less confidence in the police than do older, white females: McConville and Shepherd, op cit pp 16–19.

Survey that things are getting worse rather than better, as policing methods 'seem to have widened the gulf between ethnic minorities and the police'.[18] One such method is the differential use of search after stop: blacks are searched four times as often as whites following traffic stops.[19]

What the police gain from stop and search, on the one hand, they may lose through lack of public co-operation, on the other. This may be a problem if they seek to detect crime through public co-operation. However, just as cop culture divides individuals into 'rough' and 'respectable', so it divides areas similarly. McConville and Shepherd were discussing with an officer a 'Neighbourhood Watch' scheme in a middle class area which was surrounded by working class communities. Asked whether the new scheme would spread into the surrounding areas the officer replied, 'No, it's them that the scheme is protecting members from.'[20] Loss of co-operation from those areas would not worry the police, who have low expectations of them in the first place. If policing against black people is the main objective of the police, then the absence of a cooperative relationship and of information that might lead to a detection is a subsidiary matter.

5.   CONCLUSION

We have seen that ss 1–3 of PACE are not of great inhibitory effect and a number of reasons for this have been identified. Firstly, the main legal constraint—reasonable suspicion—is too vague to act as a standard by which most police actions can be judged. Secondly, the provisions for providing information and recording of searches are difficult to enforce. Thirdly, many stops—probably most—are in formal terms done with consent, enabling the legal constraints and controls to be evaded. Fourthly, these due process provisions envisage a model of policing which does not accord with 'cop culture', the modern reality of street policing, or its history. Fifthly, the remedies for unlawful stop and search are uncertain in scope, inadequate in operation and insufficiently stringent in effect.

Despite PACE, the police still primarily act according to working assumptions based on 'suspiciousness', ie hunch, incongruity and stereotyping on the basis of types of people, previous records and so forth. These are all crime control norms, rooted as they are in the

---

[18] W Skogan, The Police and Public in England and Wales (Home Office Research Study no 117) (HMSO, 1990) p 43.

[19] Ibid p 34.

[20] McConville and Shepherd, op cit p 140.

world of professional experience and generalised suspicion. The police sometimes discover crime when acting upon their instincts, but such suspicion as they have is seldom in relation to any particular offence, and therefore rarely is it 'reasonable' in terms of the due process norms of s 1 of PACE. Stop and search in operation corresponds far more closely to the crime control model than to the due process model to which the law is purportedly oriented, which means that s 1 of PACE is primarily presentational, legitimising and enabling. One important consequence of this is the over-representation of black people in stop-search (and hence arrest and prosecution) statistics.

It is clear that much police work around stop and search fails to satisfy due process ideals. Sometimes this is because the law itself is constituted by enabling and legitimising rules, such as that which allows consensual stops in the absence of reasonable suspicion. The police need not subvert such a law to breach due process, they need only use it.[1] Sometimes, however, the police breach due process rules which are in conflict with their working assumptions.

It might be argued that to require the police to claim that they have 'reasonable suspicion' in relation to a particular offence when in fact they are simply generally suspicious is to encourage them to treat the provisions of the law with contempt (while pretending otherwise to suspects and courts). This cannot be healthy either for the law in general or for the regard in which the police are held. It might be better either to allow stops on grounds of general suspicion or not to allow stops at all. The former option is not attractive from a due process perspective. Laws such as these could be seen, like speed limits, as broadly inhibitory, whereby no one expects precise compliance, but blatant transgression is rare. Relaxing the limits might only encourage the police to overstep the mark once again. Policing on the streets might then be based on random stops rather than, as now, on general suspicion.

On the other hand, not only may attempting to 'firm up' the law and make it more inhibitory be undesirable (since it would reduce police crime control effectiveness) it may not even be possible. Police behaviour on the street is inherently fact finding—ie inquisitorial—and the skilful finding of facts requires streetwise knowledge, technique, and experience. Imposing an adversarial due process structure onto this craft is an attempt to deny one of the key elements of what policing is about. And if policing is more about general social control than detection of specific crimes, then this is all the more true.

---

[1] D McBarnet, *Conviction* (MacMillan, 1983) p 157.

The Philips Commission recommended a national stop and search power because:

'. . . people in the street who have committed property offences or have in their possession articles which it is a criminal offence to possess should not be entirely protected from the possibility of being searched. The availability of powers to search is of use in the detection of crime and the arrest of offenders.'[2]

Although this statement has a beguiling quality, on closer analysis it may be seen to contain a trite and misleading argument. It is like saying that known offenders should not be entirely protected from the process of law enforcement. Of course they should not. But the important question does not relate to known offenders, for if the police knew who all the offenders were, our crime problems would be minimal. In reality, the identities of most actual offenders are unknown and many suspects are not actual offenders. To say that actual criminals should not be protected from the possibility of search is to miss the point. The real issue is whether people suspected of being criminals (many of whom will in fact be innocent) should be so protected.

The confusion arises from a false dichotomy in the Philips Commission's terms of reference, which enjoined it to have 'regard both to the interests of the community in bringing offenders to justice and to the rights and liberties of persons suspected or accused of crime . . .'[3] In reality, persons 'suspected or accused' have as much interest as anyone else in bringing actual offenders to justice, and all members of the 'community' are potential suspects. The question which requires consideration is whether the community as a whole should be subject to the interference with liberty which these powers involve, especially bearing in mind that they are not exercised against all sections of the community equally.

Who is to weigh up the competing demands of detection versus liberty? Those in positions of power in this debate (the two Royal Commissions, members of Parliament and the government, Home Office officials, senior police officers etc) are not a representative cross-section of society. The law is reviewed, made and implemented primarily by the white, middle aged, middle classes, while those who are stopped and searched are primarily black, young and poor. One section of society shapes the law (both in books and in action) which bears down on the other. It is easy for the decision making community to decide that it is in 'society's' interests for suspects to have their liberty

---

[2] Report, op cit para 3.17.
[3] Ibid p vi.

compromised, when those suspects are mainly drawn from the non-decision-making community. Indeed, if it is true that stop and search is part of a wider policing strategy of policing against certain communities, then the apparent dichotomy in the Philips Commission's terms of reference was not false: the question raised by stop and search in a divided society is just how far police powers are used to help perpetuate existing structures of inequality.

Chapter 3

Arrest

1. INTRODUCTION

The act of taking persons into custody and exerting physical control over their movements is commonly thought of as an arrest. Suspects are under arrest when they are no longer at liberty to go where they choose. The police typically want to arrest suspects to facilitate investigation and prosecution, but to what extent should they be allowed to infringe the freedom of the individual in this way?

(a) Due process

Under this model, no one should be arrested unless it is clear that they probably committed a specific offence. Normally such a determination should be made by a magistrate who would then issue a warrant authorising the police to arrest. In situations of necessity the model would accept that the police may act without prior authority, but only on hard evidence which would be subject to subsequent judicial scrutiny.

These standards would impair police efficiency, but this is the price to be paid 'for a regime that fosters personal privacy and champions the dignity and inviolability of the individual.'[1] If the police were to be given wider powers to arrest suspects for questioning, it is unlikely that all classes of society would suffer greater interference, since the outcry would be too great. Rather, police powers would 'be applied in a discriminatory fashion to precisely those elements in the population—the poor, the ignorant, the illiterate, the unpopular—who are least able to draw attention to their plight and to whose sufferings the vast majority of the population are the least responsive.'[2]

---

[1] H Packer, *The Limits of the Criminal Sanction* (Stanford University Press, 1969) p 179.

[2] Ibid p 180.

The model accepts that police practice may not meet due process standards, but rejects the argument that this demonstrates the necessity of broader arrest powers. Rather than bringing the law into line with practice (by introducing legitimising rules), attempts must be made to secure conformity with the law; for a 'society that covertly tolerates indiscriminate arrest is hypocritical; but one that approves its legality is well on the way to becoming totalitarian in nature.'[3] There must, therefore, be strong sanctions to penalise and condemn unlawful behaviour, such as a rule excluding evidence obtained as a result of a wrongful arrest and independent scrutiny of citizens' complaints of illegal police actions.

(b)   Crime control

To make reasonable suspicion the pre-condition for arrest is nonsensical. The police need much broader powers. They need to be able to round up known offenders from time to time to see if they are responsible for crimes occurring in the locality. They need the power to act on their instincts by stopping suspicious looking characters. It may be that no crime has been committed, but the very fact of arresting such persons may prevent a planned crime. Periodic infringements of the liberty of known criminals may be enough to persuade them to leave the area or desist from their illegal activities. Efficient crime control demands that the police be allowed to use the arrest power in this repressive manner. The law should reflect that essential fact rather than setting up unrealistic due process norms which the police are then forced to subvert.

The innocent have nothing to fear from broad arrest powers. In the rare case where they are arrested by mistake, release will quickly follow. The police should therefore be given powers to arrest citizens irrespective of whether they are reasonably suspected of committing a particular crime. The standard should be no more than that a police officer honestly thinks that an arrest will serve the goal of crime control. Alternatively, the substantive laws must be so broadly defined that the reasonable suspicion hurdle can be easily overcome. A combination of vague laws and lax standards is ideal. Of course it is still possible that a police officer will arrest in bad faith, perhaps because of a private grudge harboured against some person. Even under lax standards, wrongful arrests are possible and some remedies must therefore be devised. But these should be aimed at promoting police efficiency. Corrective discipline by a superior officer meets this requirement,

[3] Ibid p 179.

whereas excluding evidence obtained as a result of an unlawful arrest does not. As Packer puts it, the latter 'simply gives the criminal a windfall without affecting the conduct of the erring police officer.'[4]

2.   THE PLACE OF ARREST IN THE CRIMINAL PROCESS

In this chapter, we consider where on the spectrum of possibilities between these two models our laws on arrest lie. There is no satisfactory definition of arrest in the case law and none at all in PACE. Blackstone said that arrest is 'the apprehending or restraining of one's person in order to be forthcoming to answer an alleged or suspected crime.'[5] This definition implies prosecution for a specific crime and suggests conformity with the due process model. To understand why Blackstone's account is no longer satisfactory, we need briefly to examine how arrest and prosecution have changed in the last 150 years.

(a)   Historical development of arrest

Up until the early part of the nineteenth century, it was for magistrates to determine whether or not to prosecute someone. They usually made their decisions on the basis of information provided to them by police officers, other enforcement agencies or private citizens. If they were satisfied by this evidence, they could issue a warrant for arrest or a summons to appear in court at a later time. Some people were arrested first and then immediately brought before the magistrates, who, again, decided whether or not to prosecute.[6]

So arrest used simply to be a mechanism for bringing offenders to court. This is no longer so. Arrest and prosecution are now entirely separate in theory, in practice and in PACE. Anything can follow arrest: no action at all, an official warning, charge or, indeed, release followed by a summons to appear at court. In one study, for instance, less than 50% of all arrests led to prosecution.[7] Arrest is now simply an exercise of police power which does not, in itself, determine the next stage in the process.

The place of arrest in the investigative process has changed over the years. At one time, the police or any other law enforcer used to investigate an offence and then arrest (or not) at the end of that investigation.

---

[4] Ibid p 178.
[5] Bl Com (1830) p 289, quoted in V Bevan and K Lidstone, *The Investigation of Crime: A Guide to Police Powers* (Butterworths, 1991).
[6] See A Sanders, 'Arrest, Charge and Prosecution' (1986) 6 LS 257.
[7] M McConville, A Sanders and R Leng, *The Case for the Prosecution* (Routledge, 1991).

This means that the investigation took place (in theory) before the police exercised coercive powers. In reality, certainly in more recent years, many people 'helped the police with their inquiries' in the police station, which means that they were not arrested but in an undefined state of detention. If, as a result of this 'help', the police secured enough evidence to prosecute, they would arrest and bring the suspect before the magistrates; if they did not have enough evidence, the suspect was (eventually) released. Gradually, being in detention came to be seen as being under arrest, and so arrest moved nearer to the beginning of the investigative process. This was formalised by the Criminal Law Act 1967, which created a wide range of 'arrestable offences', ie offences for which the police could arrest without obtaining a warrant from the magistrates.

(b) The purpose of arrest

Arrest and subsequent detention is now frequently used as part of the investigation, not as the culmination of it. Its purpose is often to secure the evidence which used to be secured before the arrest took place. In a study of over 1,000 arrests, McConville found that the evidence in over three-quarters of them was 'weak' at the point of arrest. There was, in other words, insufficient evidence to charge and prosecute. By the time these arrested suspects were interviewed by the police, further investigation (eg interviews with witnesses, searches of property and collection of forensic evidence) substantially reduced the number of weak cases, which was reduced yet again as a result of the interviews.[8]

This is all possible only because of a relaxation of legal controls on police questioning which took place in the latter half of this century. Whereas at one time pre-charge detention was something which could only be authorised by the magistrates, pre-charge detention and questioning is now authorised by the police themselves. In this way, we can see the development of crime control methods. Thus in 1969 the House of Lords found itself in *Shaaban Bin Hussien v Chong Fook Kam* criticising the police for making:

'a premature arrest rather than one that was unjustifiable from first to last. The police made the mistake of arresting before questioning; if they had questioned first and arrested afterwards, there would have been no case against them.'[9]

---

[8] M McConville, Corroboration and Confessions: The Impact of a Rule Requiring that no Conviction can be Sustained on the Basis of Confession Evidence Alone (Royal Commission on Criminal Justice Research Study no 13) (HMSO, 1993) pp 24–36.

[9] [1970] AC 942 at 949, per Lord Devlin.

We shall see in chapter 4 that the law has changed since then to allow the police to arrest first and then to ask questions. In fact, the law now virtually always requires them to do so, as a result of restrictions on police questioning outside the police station.[10] Questioning away from the police station has been almost prohibited in order to protect suspects, but with the ironic result that many arrests are 'premature' (in the *Shaaban* sense), thus infringing due process values.

Another way of looking at these changes is to see the position of suspects detained in custody as being regularised. In the 1960s and 1970s, pre-trial detention was secured unlawfully or quasi-lawfully through the mechanism of 'helping the police with their inquiries', but now it is secured openly and lawfully through the mechanism of arrest and detention. The legal rules which we shall be discussing are therefore legitimising rules (legitimising the 'helping the police with their inquiries' syndrome) and enabling rules (enabling the police to act as they wish to do without fear of legal repercussions). The extent to which they are also inhibitory, preventing abuse of power through restrictions on their use, will be a key issue in this chapter and the next one.

By contrast, the United States has largely adhered to the original idea of arrest as the culmination of investigation and a prelude to prosecution. Thus pre-charge detention is very limited and release without charge is (as it used to be in Britain) rare. Moreover, the threshold for arrest—'probable cause'—is more stringent than 'reasonable suspicion'. Stop and search is allowed for 'reasonable suspicion', and so unlike in Britain the American police can stop and search in situations where they cannot arrest. The result is relatively more sparing use of arrest and formal detention in the United States. However, de facto arrest and detention is used instead, police officers persuading suspects to attend the station voluntarily in a similar fashion to our 'helping with inquiries'.[11]

The Royal Commission on Criminal Procedure (Philips Commission) wanted to restrict the wide arrest powers introduced by the Criminal Law Act 1967 in Britain.[12] This is because it sought to restrict the exercise of coercive power to circumstances where it was necessary. The Philips Commission believed that coercive powers like arrest were often used unnecessarily, relying on a study by Gemmill and Morgan-Giles which showed great regional variations between police

---

[10] This is particularly so under the 1991 version of the PACE Code of Practice C.

[11] Practice varies considerably, however, from locality to locality. See A Meehan, 'Internal Police Records and the Control of Juveniles' (1993) 33 BJ Crim 504.

[12] Royal Commission on Criminal Procedure, Report (Cmnd 8092) (HMSO, 1981) paras 3.75–3.79.

forces in the use of arrest, on the one hand, and summons, on the other.[13] In other words, it seemed that similar offences in similar circumstances were subject to arrest, detention and charge in some areas, where in other areas they would be subject to a summons to appear in court on a specified date.

The Philips Commission accordingly advocated a 'necessity principle'. Arrest and detention would only have been allowed if one of the following conditions applied:

(a) the person concerned refused to reveal his or her identity so that a summons could be served;
(b) there was a need to prevent the continual repetition of the offence;
(c) there was a need to protect the arrested person or property;
(d) there was a need to secure or preserve evidence, or it was likely that the person would fail to appear at court to answer the summons.

If none of these conditions applied, suspects should be interviewed, processed and brought to court in a less coercive manner than arrest and detention.

In this way, the Philips Commission attempted to balance due process with crime control by allowing the police to exercise coercive powers only when they needed to for prosecution purposes, and to impose due process norms on them at other times. The Commission's approach to this issue rests upon a legalistic and myopic view of police activity. It assumes that arrests are always geared to initiating specific prosecutions, ignoring the role of arrest and detention as an investigative tool. As with stop and search, we will argue that police power to coerce through arrest and detention is more important than specific police powers to deal with specific cases.

(c) Relationship between arrest and stop-search

We have established that arrest cannot be defined in terms of its function in the prosecution system. Instead, as Robbilliard and McEwan observe: 'An arrest is the major way by which a citizen may and without recourse to judicial process, albeit temporarily, be deprived of his liberty . . .'[14] In *Lewis v Chief Constable for South Wales*[15] it was stated that:

---

13 R Gemmill and R Morgan-Giles, Arrest, Charge and Summons: Arrest Practice and Resource Implications (Royal Commission on Criminal Procedure, Research Study no 9) (HMSO, 1981).
14 J Robbilliard and J McEwan, *Police Powers and the Individual* (Blackwell, 1986) p 107.
15 [1991] 1 All ER 206 at 209–10, confirming *Spicer v Holt* [1977] AC 987.

'Arrest is a matter of fact; it is not a legal concept . . . Arrest is a situation . . . Whether a person has been arrested depends not on the legality of his arrest but on whether he has been deprived of his liberty to go where he pleases.'

Further, as was made clear in *Shaaban Bin Hussien v Chong Fook Kam*,[16] there need be no explicit statement of arrest or detention; arrest occurs if it is made clear that the arrestee would be prevented from leaving.

If we can only define arrest by reference to a temporary deprivation of liberty whereby one is not free to go as one pleases, there is no distinction between arrest and stop-search, especially as the offences for which suspects may be stopped and searched are also offences for which suspects may be arrested. If in every circumstance that a suspect may be lawfully stopped and searched he or she may also be arrested—if, indeed, the stop is in essence an arrest—the need for stop and search powers which we queried in chapter 2 is brought further into question. Instead of 'stopping', the police could 'arrest'. The argument that more arrest (instead of stop-search) would involve too much bureaucracy is false. The law need not require someone to be taken to a police station immediately on arrest. As we have seen, the definition of arrest merely involves the temporary deprivation of liberty. The police can, perfectly lawfully, arrest, search and question and then release that person. Perhaps the reason for not doing so is that an arrest simply sounds more dramatic and would make people more reluctant than they are now to accept such treatment on the streets.

As the police may always arrest lawfully when they can lawfully stop and search, it is difficult to understand why so few recorded stop-searches (around 15%)[17] lead to arrest. The act of stop and search will sometimes dispel reasonable suspicion, rendering any subsequent arrest unlawful. But this is unlikely to account for the majority of stop-searches which do not lead to arrest, for beliefs which are so easily and so frequently dispelled can hardly be regarded as 'reasonable'. It is likely that in many cases, where there are inadequate grounds for reasonable suspicion, the police will be prepared to stop and search but reluctant to take the major step of arrest instead.

What would happen if stop-search were abolished and this led to more suspects being taken to the police station? There is no reason why the police should be afraid of this if indeed they have reasonable suspicion. Arrest and detention instead of stop-search would take up time and resources, for both suspect and police officer, it is true, but

[16] [1970] AC 942.
[17] See ch 2, section 4(a), Table 2.1, above.

that might be a fair price to pay for the increased protection which suspects would have as a result of being taken to a police station and documented by a custody officer. In so far as this occurred, and to the extent that some arrests would be deterred (ie those where no reasonable suspicion existed), the system would correspond with due process values far more than it does now.

3. THE LEGAL BASIS FOR ARREST

(a) With warrant

At one time, arrest was only lawful if backed by a judicial warrant. Now it is rare for the police to seek prior approval for an arrest. This is because the Criminal Law Act 1967 created the concept of the 'arrestable offence' for which the police may arrest without warrant.

The move away from arrest warrants, which is part of the general move away from judicial supervision of police powers, means that most arrests are now made by the police acting on their own knowledge and initiative rather than acting under the supervision of magistrates. It mirrors the decline in the use of summonses (issued by magistrates) and search warrants (also issued by magistrates). Nowadays, the police themselves generally decide what powers they will exercise and when. The withering away of external supervision of their work marks a shift within the system towards greater crime control.

Warrants are nowadays mainly used when a suspect fails to appear in court to answer a summons or to answer bail. In these circumstances, the police or prosecutor would apply to the magistrates for a warrant,[18] which would usually be granted straight away, authorising the arrest of that suspect. The suspect can be kept in custody if the warrant so provides, and then made to appear before the magistrates, who will decide whether or not that person should be bailed.

(b) Arrestable offences

The police may arrest anyone, subject to certain conditions, for an 'arrestable offence' without a prior warrant. This is by far the most common basis for arrest, although there are no national figures for arrests as a whole or for the different types of arrest. Any offence punishable by a jail term of five years or more is arrestable (PACE, s 24(1)) as are miscellaneous other offences (PACE, s 24(2) and (3)). This broadly re-enacts the pre-PACE law as created by the 1967 Act. It

---

[18] Under the Magistrates Court Act 1980, s 125, as amended by PACE, s 33.

covers a very wide range of offences, because most English legislation provides for maximum punishments much heavier than the normal punishments. Thus theft is punishable by seven years in jail even though very few people get jailed at all for theft, and certainly very rarely for five years or more. Most offences of dishonesty and violence are therefore arrestable.

Section 24(4)—(7) sets out when a person may be summarily arrested for an arrestable offence in the following terms:

'(4) Any person may arrest without a warrant—
   (a) anyone who is in the act of committing an arrestable offence;
   (b) anyone whom he has reasonable grounds for suspecting to be committing such an offence.
(5) Where an arrestable offence has been committed, any person may arrest without a warrant—
   (a) anyone who is guilty of the offence;
   (b) anyone whom he has reasonable grounds for suspecting to be guilty of it.
(6) Where a constable has reasonable grounds for suspecting that an arrestable offence has been committed, he may arrest without a warrant anyone whom he has reasonable grounds for suspecting to be guilty of the offence.
(7) A constable may arrest without a warrant—
   (a) anyone who is about to commit an arrestable offence;
   (b) anyone whom he has reasonable grounds for suspecting to be about to commit an arrestable offence.'

Broadly speaking, the police may make arrests for offences (whether actual or reasonably suspected) in the past, in the present or in the future. A valid arrest can thus occur even if there is no offence if the police 'reasonably suspect' that there is (sub-s 6). They may also arrest a suspect for an offence, whether or not he or she committed it, if they 'reasonably suspect' that person committed it (see para (b) in each of the subsections). Conversely, the police may arrest even when they have no reasonable suspicion, and the arrest will be lawful so long as the arrested person had in fact committed an arrestable offence, or was in the course of doing so, or was about to do so (sub-ss 5(a), 4(a) and 7(a) respectively.) This is a classic crime control norm since the ends are regarded as justifying the means. It does not matter that the arrest was arbitrarily made, so long as the suspect turns out to have been engaged in a crime. We saw in chapter 2 that the police frequently stop people who appear to be generally 'suspicious' without necessarily having a specific offence in mind. This provision allows them to arrest on this basis and, if their suspicions turn out to be justified, the arrest is lawful.

The effect of these provisions is to give the police broad arrest powers. Indeed, the breadth of these powers is such that it gives rise to some unresolved dilemmas. For instance, the police are entitled to arrest someone who is about to commit an arrestable offence (sub-s 7) but they are also entitled to arrest someone who is attempting to commit an arrestable offence, since under s 4(1) of the Criminal Attempts Act 1981 an attempt carries the same punishment as the full offence. It seems, therefore, that they may arrest people who are about to commit attempts, since the attempt would itself qualify as an arrestable offence. This is rather a long way away from the actual crime. Moreover, an 'attempt' is only criminal if it is 'more than merely preparatory' in relation to the completed offence (Criminal Attempt Act 1981, s 1). Persons who are 'about to' commit a crime may have performed acts which are merely preparatory.[19] What is to be done with those people if the police exercise the arrest power? There may be no crime with which they could be charged (being about to commit a crime would sometimes be conduct liable to cause a breach of the peace, but this need not always be so). It is therefore difficult to conceive of any detention, however momentary, which would be lawful. This use of the arrest power might prevent a crime taking place, but the police would not be able to take the matter any further than that and, strictly speaking, would have to release the suspect almost immediately (with the danger that the suspect might seek to resume the course of action interrupted by the arrest). This may tempt the police to do one of two things: either they could wait until the suspect 'embarks on the crime proper'[20] before intervening, which carries the risk that the intervention will come too late to prevent harm being caused; or they might arrest and detain the suspect on the pretext that an offence such as threatening behaviour or conduct liable to cause a breach of the peace had been committed. In the unlikely event that the police actions were challenged, the breadth of these offences may provide a shield for the officers to hide behind.[1]

(c) Non-arrestable offences

According to s 24, the police may only arrest without a warrant if the offence is arrestable, implying that all other offences are not summarily arrestable. However, s 25 (and certain other sections) make non-arrestable offences arrestable under certain circumstances. Section 25 requires the police to show that special circumstances exist to justify

---

[19] For an example of a case where the police arrested before an attempt had been committed, see *Campbell* [1991] Crim LR 268.

[20] To adopt the language of the leading case on the *actus reus* of an attempt: *Gullefer* [1990] 3 All ER 882.

[1] See section 3(e), below.

summary arrest without warrant in these cases. As with arrestable offences covered by s 24, the police may arrest when they have reasonable suspicion, and they may arrest in relation to an offence which has been committed or is being committed. However, they may not arrest someone who is about to commit a non-arrestable offence. A police officer may only arrest for such an offence if 'it appears to him that service of a summons is impractical or inappropriate because any of the general arrest conditions is satisfied' (s 25(1)). The general arrest conditions are set out in sub-section (3) as follows:

'(3) The general arrest conditions are—
  (a) that the name of the relevant person is unknown to, and cannot readily be ascertained by, the constable;
  (b) that the constable has reasonable grounds for doubting whether a name furnished by the relevant person as his name is his real name;
  (c) that—
      (i) the relevant person has failed to furnish a satisfactory address for service; or
      (ii) the constable has reasonable grounds for doubting whether an address furnished by the relevant person is a satisfactory address for service;
  (d) that the constable has reasonable grounds for believing that arrest is necessary to prevent the relevant person—
      (i) causing physical damage to himself or any other person;
      (ii) suffering physical injury;
      (iii) causing loss of or damage to property;
      (iv) committing an offence against public decency; or
      (v) causing an unlawful obstruction of the highway;
  (e) that the constable has reasonable grounds for believing that arrest is necessary to protect a child or other vulnerable person from the relevant person . . .'

What all these conditions are concerned with is the probability of a suspect answering a summons and being traced if he or she does not do so, for summons is the only way to proceed against someone who is not arrested. Section 25 allows the police to arrest, even for minor offences (such as motoring or litter offences), if this is the only way of getting an offender to court. It is not enough for the police to consider that it would be more convenient or efficient to arrest rather than summons.

An arrest is only lawful if, as s 25(1) implies, the officers believe that one of the general arrest conditions is met. If they do not so believe, the arrest will be unlawful.[2] In addition to this subjective element, the

---

[2] See *Edwards v DPP* [1993] Crim LR 854.

officers must have 'reasonable grounds' for considering that a specific arrest condition applies. In *G v DPP*,[3] an officer arrested G for a non-arrestable offence even though G had readily given his name and address to that officer shortly before committing the offence. The officer considered that the general arrest condition in s 25(3)(b) was satisfied because, in his experience, people who committed offences did not give their correct names and addresses. Such reasoning should have been condemned by the Divisional Court in reviewing the legality of the arrest, since its logic is such that the police would always be able to arrest for non-arrestable offences. Unfortunately, the court appears to have overlooked this point, although the arrest was held to be unlawful on other grounds.[4] An opportunity to affirm the importance of the general arrest conditions as a due process hurdle for the police to overcome was thereby missed.

These conditions, and the principle on which they are based, will be familiar as being similar to the necessity principle which the Philips Commission wanted to provide in relation to all arrests. What PACE has provided is that the necessity principle applies not in relation to all offences (which would have been an inhibitory rule), but in relation to non-arrestable offences only. As an extension of the law of arrest, this is an enabling rule. Had the Divisional Court in *G v DPP* upheld the arrest, the arrest conditions would have been rendered entirely presentational, for since all arrests are of suspected offenders the proposition of the police in that case would have justified the arrest of any and every suspect. As it is, there remains at least some potential inhibitory element in s 25, preventing it from being limitlessly enabling.

If the police may only arrest for non-arrestable offences when it is necessary for them to do so, it seems that the police may arrest for arrestable offences even when it is not necessary for them to do so. Were this not so, the distinction between arrestable and non-arrestable offences would be redundant. We shall see in the next chapter that the absence of a necessity principle in relation to arrestable offences is difficult to reconcile with the rules of detention, causing practical problems for the police and making some of the rules designed to safeguard suspects more presentational than inhibitory.

(d) Other statutory powers of arrest

Section 26 and Sch 2 of PACE preserve the summary arrest powers provided by 21 existing statutes. As in relation to stop and search, PACE

---

[3] [1989] Crim LR 150. The spare details given in this report are fleshed out by A Lawson, 'Whither the "General Arrest Conditions"?' [1993] Crim LR 567.

[4] See ibid for a critique of the Divisional Court's reasoning.

adds to, but rarely takes away, police powers.[5] Thus, police power is continually being extended. There are a large number of statutes providing arrest powers for specific offences, including the Bail Act 1976 (s 7) allowing arrest of persons who breach bail conditions, the Street Offences Act 1959, allowing arrest for soliciting and loitering for prostitution and various statutory drunkenness and vagrancy offences; and, perhaps most importantly of all, the Public Order Act (originally 1936, now 1986). The police may arrest for these offences on the same basis that they may arrest for arrestable offences under s 24.[6]

(e)   Common law breach of the peace

The only common law power of arrest was for breach of the peace. Since this was not abolished by PACE, it has been held to have been preserved.[7] Police may arrest if a breach of the peace is occurring, is imminent, or has recently happened or is likely to recur.[8] This means that the powers of arrest for breach of the peace are rather more restricted than the powers of arrest for arrestable offences. Judgment is required, not only in relation to whether the breach of the peace is occurring, but also in relation to the question of imminence and whether it is likely to occur again. The police have

'the right to take reasonable steps to make the person who is breaking or threatening to break the peace refrain from doing so; and those reasonable steps in appropriate cases will include detaining him against his will.'[9]

What constitutes a breach of the peace is not always obvious. In *Howell*[10] the Court of Appeal confirmed the view that a breach of the peace must be related to violence: a breach of the peace occurs when harm is done is likely to be done, or if someone fears that violence may occur. Thus threatening, abusive or insulting behaviour does not in itself constitute a breach of the peace, although it would if a police officer reasonably regarded it as likely to cause imminent violence. Demonstrations, picketing, disputes between neighbours, street brawls and so forth are the usual context for this type of problem, although this does not mean that most demonstrations—any more than most

---

[5]   Although s 26 did abolish summary arrest powers for those offences which are not specified in Sch 2.

[6]   Under s 27 of PACE, the police may also arrest convicted people who have not already been fingerprinted, but only in very circumscribed circumstances.

[7]   *DPP v Orum* [1989] 1 WLR 88.

[8]   *Howell* [1981] 3 All ER 383.

[9]   *Albert v Lavin* [1981] 3 All ER 878 at 880.

[10]   [1981] 3 All ER 383.

disputes between neighbours —actually end in breach of the peace.

Belief in the imminence of a breach of the peace is necessarily diffi-cult to pin down. This was particularly evident in the miners' strike of the mid-1980s where there was a number of violent confrontations at pits where miners refused to strike. In *Moss v McLachlan*,[11] 60 miners were stopped by a police roadblock on the M1 motorway while on their way to picket some pits a few miles away. They carried banners and shouted abuse at a lorry driver who was passing the road block to break the strike. The men could only be arrested if it was suspected that a breach of the peace was likely to occur. Skinner J stated that, pro-vided the police officers

'honestly and reasonably form the opinion that there is a real risk of a breach of the peace in the sense that it is in close proximity both in place and time then the conditions exist for reasonable preventive action including if necessary the measures taken in this case [that is to say arrest] . . . The possibility of a breach must be real to justify any pre-ventive action. The imminence or immediacy of the threat to the peace determines what action is reasonable.'[12]

In this particular case, the miners were abusive and the pits to which they were travelling were nearby, so it may be that the police were jus-tified in the roadblock and the arrest of the men on those grounds. However, in another miners' strike incident, the police established a roadblock at the Dartford Tunnel near London, over 100 miles from the area which some miners intended to picket. The miners were turned back on the same basis as in *Moss v McLachlan*, even though it could hardly be said that a breach of the peace was imminent or proximate in these circumstances.[13]

There were many other incidents where striking miners were stopped by the police and were told when and how they could travel in the vicinity of working mines. Sometimes these miners were on their way to picket, and arguably there was a risk of a breach of the peace. However, police invocation of the breach of the peace law against strik-ing miners spilled over into general restrictions on the liberty of working miners and other members of mining communities. As one present put it, 'There were no justifications, just the threat of arrest if we failed to comply.'[14] It seems that a lot of police action was aimed at

---

[11] [1985] IRLR 76.
[12] Ibid at 78–79.
[13] R East and P Thomas, 'Freedom of Movement: *Moss v McLachlan*' (1985) 12 JLS 77.
[14] P Green, *The Enemy Without: Policing and Class Consciousness in the Miners' Strike* (Open University Press, 1990) p 63.

using breach of the peace arrest powers to prevent picketing, regardless of whether there was an imminent risk of breaches of the peace. At times, such as these, of crises of law and order, legalistic models of policing simply collapse.[15] Police powers are stretched to enable the police to fulfil wider functions than would be possible if due process principles prevailed.

(f) Citizen's arrest

Before 1829, there was no organised professional police force in England and Wales, and it was many years before the police operated across the whole country. Before the establishment of the police, all citizens had the power to arrest suspects, and police powers were originally no greater than those of ordinary citizens. Little or no distinction was made, in theory, between the two, and arrestees had to be taken before the magistrates immediately, no matter who arrested them. Thus we find the Royal Commission on Police Powers and Procedure of 1929 saying:

'The principle remains that a policeman, in the view of the common law, is only "a person paid to perform, as a matter of duty, acts which if he was so minded he might have done voluntarily."'[16]

However true this might once have been, the police are now in a quite different position to that of a citizen. In this century in particular, police officers have been given considerably more power than ordinary citizens. Regarding arrest, PACE, s 24, only partially applies to citizens. The powers of arrest in sub-ss (4) and (5) apply to citizens and police officers (they refer to 'any person') but sub-ss (6) and (7) refer to police officers alone.

Under sub-ss (4) and (5), citizens may arrest without warrant persons who are committing an arrestable offence or where they have reasonable grounds for suspecting them to be committing such an offence (sub-s 4); or someone who is guilty of an offence or where there are reasonable grounds for suspecting that person to be guilty of the arrestable offence (sub-section 5). This means that citizen's arrests may take place for past and present but not future offences; the offence must have been, or be in the process of being, committed. It is not enough that there be reasonable suspicion of an offence. It is lawful to

---

[15] See I Balbus, *The Dialectics of Legal Repression* (Russell Sage, 1973); and R Vogler, 'Magistrates and Civil Disorder' (1982) LAG Bull, November p 12.

[16] (Cmd 3297). Quoted in Royal Commission on Criminal Procedure, The Investigation and Prosecution of Criminal Offences in England and Wales: The Law and Procedure (Cmnd 8092–1) (HMSO, 1981) p 2.

arrest a person of whom one has reasonable suspicion, even if that person turns out not to be guilty, but the offence must be a fact.

This reflects the common law as stated in *Walters v W H Smith,*[17] where it was reasonably suspected that the defendant (D) had stolen a particular book and so he was arrested under what is now s 24(5) of PACE. In fact, other books had been stolen by D but not that particular book. The offence for which D had been arrested had not been committed, so the arrest was wrongful. Had an officer arrested in those circumstances, the arrest would not have been wrongful (had s 24(6) of PACE been in force). Broadly speaking, PACE has not altered the law on citizen's arrest. This may be briefly illustrated. In *Brosch,*[18] D was in the toilets of a restaurant holding a syringe, appearing to be under the influence of drugs. The manager of the restaurant questioned D about drugs, which led to a struggle and a citizen's arrest. At trial and on appeal, the arrest was upheld, as drugs offences were clearly being committed by D, about whom the manager had reasonable suspicion. But in *Self,*[19] the defendant was seen taking a box of chocolates out of a shop. He was arrested for theft and for 'assault with intent to resist lawful arrest' (he hit the shop assistant who carried out the citizen's arrest). He was acquitted of theft but convicted of assault. On appeal, it was held that if he had not committed theft the arrest was unlawful, and therefore the conviction for assault must be quashed, since it is not a crime to resist unlawful arrest.

A large number of arrests, especially for shoplifting, are made by citizens. In most of these cases, the initial arrest is carried out by a shop employee; either a store detective employed for that purpose, or a member of the management. These are ordinary citizens for the purposes of the law, so when they detain people until the police arrive, they make citizen's arrests.

The subject of a citizen's arrest must be placed in lawful custody as soon as is practicable. This is generally understood to mean either the custody of the police or (as used to be usual) that of a magistrate, but in some circumstances it might be better to take the defendant briefly elsewhere. This is not covered by PACE, and the common law is confused. In *John Lewis & Co Ltd v Tims,*[20] the defendant (D) was arrested by a store detective and brought before the store manager for questioning. Even though D was not brought before the police or magistrates, this was held to be valid on the grounds that the arrestor was acting for someone else. This is an artificial argument; after all, most

---

[17] [1914] 1 KB 595.
[18] [1988] Crim LR 743.
[19] [1992] 3 All ER 476.
[20] [1952] AC 676.

police arrests are really on behalf of other people, namely the victims. But it would be far from helpful to arrestees had the law been decided otherwise; for the consequence of citizen's arrest would usually then be that the police be contacted immediately without the victim (or, more usually, a shop manager) considering whether such drastic action was desirable. Large stores often require their store detectives or employees to bring alleged thieves before the management to decide what should be done, and this can hardly be criticised.

A similar situation arose in *Brewin*,[1] where a child was arrested by an ordinary person, who brought him before his father. This was held to be an unlawful arrest, since the arrest was not made on behalf of the father and there was no firm intention to take the child to the police. As a Crown Court decision, this is not authoritative, but it does illustrate the problem. Perhaps legislation should provide a similar provision for citizen's arrest as for police officers under PACE, s 30(10): this states that officers may delay taking an arrested person to a police station if it is necessary to take the person elsewhere in order to carry out further investigation. The danger is that something close to kidnapping could be thereby legitimised. What is clear, though, is that the current uncertainty and convoluted reasoning regulating the law on citizen's arrest is in no one's interest.

(g) Non-police agencies

There is a considerable body of criminal law which is enforced by non-police agencies. For example, health and safety laws are enforced by the Factory Inspectorate, tax laws by Customs and Excise and the Inland Revenue and pollution laws by the Pollution Inspectorate. These are commonly regarded as 'regulatory offences' rather than as 'real crimes'. They are not, however, always less serious than police-enforced laws. Tax frauds involve at least as much money as dishonesty offences enforced by the police. More people die through the negligence of employers in breach of health and safety laws than die as a result of pub brawls, muggings and street fights, and pollution is more of a threat to the public's safety than is drunkenness, prostitution and criminal damage.[2]

The criminal justice system does not seem to treat these offences with the seriousness one would expect in view of the harm they cause. Non-police agencies do not have the arrest powers possessed by the police, so are in the position of private citizens in this respect; and these offences are rarely arrestable. Very few are subject to maximum

---

[1] [1976] Crim LR 742.
[2] See generally S Box, *Power, Crime and Mystification* (Tavistock, 1983) chs 1 and 2.

custodial sentences of five years or more (and so fail to qualify as arrestable under s 24(1) of PACE) and neither do they have specific arrest powers attached to them. Nor do stop and search powers apply. There is therefore no equivalent of 'street policing' for these offences. Investigation is either reactive, in response to a major incident, or routine, in which case appointments are made with the potential 'criminal' to inspect the premises concerned.[3] The result is that these offences have a low profile in the criminal justice system and society at large, creating a vicious circle, whereby because they are little known, there is little concern about them, ensuring that maximum penalties remain low, ensuring that little remains known, and so on.

4.   ARREST DISCRETION AND REASONABLE SUSPICION

(a)   Reasonable suspicion

Reasonable suspicion (or reasonable cause) for arrest is the same as for stop and search. Reasonable cause is a lower standard than information sufficient to establish a prima facie case. To quote Lord Devlin in *Shaaban Bin Hussien v Chong Fook Kam*:

'Suspicion arises at or near the starting point of an investigation of which the obtaining of prima facie proof is the end . . . *Prima facie* proof consists of admissible evidence. Suspicion can take into account matters that could not be put in evidence at all.'[4]

This means that it is very difficult to control police discretion, although the courts have shown little inclination to exert such control. In *Castorina v Chief Constable of Surrey*,[5] for example, the police arrested a middle aged woman for burgling the firm from which she had previously been dismissed. The grounds of suspicion were that the burglary appeared to be 'an inside job', and she was presumed by the police to have a grudge. Against this, she had no criminal record, and even the victim thought that she was an unlikely culprit. None the less, the evidence was held sufficient to warrant reasonable suspicion. The court emphasised that it was not a pre-condition of a lawful arrest that the police believe a suspect to be guilty. The issue was whether, given the information the police had at the time of the arrest, their suspicion

---

[3]   K Lidstone, R Hogg and F Sutcliffe, Prosecutions by Private Individuals and Non-Police Agencies (Royal Commission on Criminal Procedure, Research Study no 10) (HMSO, 1980).

[4]   [1970] AC 942 at 948–949. See ch 2 for a related discussion in the context of stop and search powers.

[5]   [1988] NLJR 180.

could be regarded as reasonable. The decision gives the police considerable freedom to follow crime control norms, in that it allows them to arrest on little hard evidence. As Clayton and Tomlinson put it:

'If the police are justified in arresting a middle aged woman of good character on such flimsy grounds, without even questioning her as to her alibi or possible motives, then the law provides very scant protection for those suspected of crime.'[6]

It is not just police powers such as those in s 24 of PACE which give the police discretion, but also the substantive law itself. If the law is vague, then the police have to decide for themselves what behaviour is or is not criminal and, therefore, arrestable. Indeed, Lustgarten argues that many of our laws would be held to be unconstitutional on the grounds of vagueness were they to be passed by a state legislature in the United States. He notes that in 1972 the Supreme Court invalidated a vagrancy law on these very grounds. He quotes the Supreme Court as follows:

'where as here there are no standards governing the exercise of discretion [this] permits and encourages an arbitrary and discriminatory enforcement of the law. It furnishes a convenient tool for "harsh and discriminatory enforcement by local prosecuting officials against particular groups deemed to merit their displeasure".'[7]

Both he and Ashworth single out the Public Order Act 1986 for particular criticism. Ashworth points out that the essence of a public order offence might be thought to be that public order crimes engender fear of violence and disorder among bystanders. Yet, as he says, the 1986 Act

'goes so far as to include an expressed dispensation from proof that any member of the public was even at the scene, let alone put in fear—a dispensation which virtually undermines the rationale of the offence. These dispensations undoubtedly smooth the path of the prosecutor and make it correspondingly more difficult for defendants to obtain an acquittal . . . does it seem right to convict a person of a serious public order offence without the need to hear the evidence from a member of the public?'[8]

Ashworth's point here is that the police are enabled to prove that a public order offence occurred by virtue of what they alone saw and

---

[6] R Clayton and H Tomlinson, 'Arrest and Reasonable Grounds for Suspicion' (1988) LS Gaz, 7 September, p 22 at 26.

[7] See L Lustgarten, 'The Police and the Substantive Criminal Law' (1987) 27 BJ Crim 24 at 26.

[8] A Ashworth, 'Defining Offences Without Harm' in P Smith (ed), *Criminal Law: Essays in Honour of JC Smith* (Butterworths, 1987) p 17.

what they infer from what they saw. This gives the police enormous discretion in deciding what is a crime and therefore in deciding when they should or should not, and can or cannot, arrest.

In principle, there is a clear distinction between evidence justifying arrest and evidence justifying conviction, but many Public Order Act offences and many other similar offences (like common law breach of the peace) conflate the two. Take s 139 of the Criminal Justice Act 1988, for example. It makes it an offence to carry a bladed or pointed article unless the arrestee can demonstrate a reasonable excuse for carrying it. If the arrestee cannot provide such an excuse to the arresting officer so as to prevent arrest, that failure will also suffice to convict him.[9] This conflation of substantive law with police powers gives even more power to the police than they would otherwise have. In a recent study of 60 disputes to which the police were called, there were six arrests. There was evidence to justify arrest on the grounds of the victims' complaints, such as criminal damage or assault, but the arrests were actually for breach of the peace, drunkenness or possession of an offensive weapon. This was because these public order charges

'only required police evidence and, therefore, did not require the production of independent evidence from witnesses or victim statements ... because of the permissiveness of public order legislation, they can figure out precisely how to charge a person after they have made the arrest.'[10]

The result is that police officers on the street can arrest in such a way as virtually to guarantee conviction. In selecting an 'appropriate' offence from the range of possibilities open to them they are acting in a quasi-judicial manner. Their choice reduces the possibility that suspects will be able to challenge their actions and minimises their accountability to the judiciary. This is consistent with the developing arrest practices of the police, but inconsistent with the due process rhetoric with which PACE was ushered in.

There is a parallel here with some non-police agencies. Health and safety and pollution laws require all 'practical' steps to be taken to prevent accidents, pollution and so forth. The enforcement agency decides what is, and what is not, 'practical'. This has the potential for working like public order laws, whereby evidence justifying enforcement action (failure to take practical steps to prevent the accident) also constitutes

---

[9] For a discussion of the implications of this particular law, see G Broadbent, 'Offensive Weapons and the CJA' (1989) LS Gaz, 12 July, p 23.

[10] C Kemp, C Norris and N Fielding, 'Legal Manoeuvres in Police Handling of Disputes' in D Farrington and S Walklate (eds), *Offenders and Victims: Theory and Policy* (British Society of Criminology, 1992) p 73.

evidence of guilt, just as public order laws enable arrest and conviction when an officer regards action as likely to engender fear in others. Despite the theoretical parallel there is a practical difference. Non-police agencies work out what is 'practical' with the firms against whom they are enforcing the law. This is like the police negotiating with Saturday night pub rowdies how many bottles they will be allowed to smash on the way home. Law enforcement is partly dictated by the law (in so far as, for instance, pollution inspectors have no arrest powers) but also partly by policies formulated by those agencies.[11]

(b)   Working rules

The imprecision of public order laws enable them to be used as a resource for the police. Enabling rules are contained within the law itself, allowing—but not requiring—arrest in a very wide spectrum of circumstances. But if the law does not dictate when and who the police arrest, what does? We saw in relation to stop-search that, in deciding when and how to exercise their powers, the police draw on their experience and institutional objectives, as mediated by cop culture. On this basis, McConville et al identified various 'working rules' which, they argued, structure police decision making.[12] These apply to arrest just as they do to stop and search. What are these working rules, and how far are they consistent with the reasonable suspicion criterion?

Disorder and police authority

Ever since the creation of the modern police in the early nineteenth century, the maintenance of public order has been its prime concern.[13] With no national riot squads and with very sparing use of armed forces in situations of disorder, the police have the lead role in these matters. Consequently, the maintenance of order is always a concern of the police, in general policy terms and at the street policing level.

The maintenance of police authority is linked to this. Since the police usually have little if anything by way of weapons, they rely on numbers and their sheer authority (as distinct from fear) to persuade people to do as they are told. This is particularly important when disorder is imminent (eg street fights and pub brawls) but also in 'straightforward'

---

[11] See eg B Hutter, *The Reasonable Arm of the Law?* (Oxford University Press, 1988) particularly at pp 132–133.

[12] M McConville, A Sanders and R Leng, *The Case for the Prosecution* (Routledge, 1991) p 27. R Ericson uses the similar formulation of 'recipe rules' in *Making Crime: A Study of Detective Work* (Butterworths, 1981).

[13] R Reiner, *The Politics of the Police* (Harvester Wheatsheaf, 1992).

criminal situations such as theft and burglary. In order to maintain the authority of the police, people must believe that when police officers make requests or give orders they can enforce compliance. Thus, as we saw in relation to 'consent' searches, the police secure co-operation because people believe that they will have to do as requested anyway.

It follows that when there are challenges to police authority or outbreaks of disorder, the police feel the need to get on top of the situation quickly, preferably by securing voluntary submission. If this is secured, and if no serious offences have been committed, the police usually take no further action. Thus Shapland and Hobbs found that only 19–25% of 'disturbances' attended by the police led to arrest.[14] Kemp, Norris and Fielding found the police taking 'immediate authoritative action' (which includes arrest, but also removing suspects, reporting the incident and so forth) in just one-third of criminal disputes.[15] However, if submission is not voluntary, the police will enforce it. Now that violence is unacceptable,[16] arrest is all that is left to the police. Arrests for 'contempt of cop' are fairly common. Thus McConville et al give examples of cases where the police arrested because, as the police told them in one case, 'you come to the point like a parent with a child where if you don't do something the others will all join in.'[17] In another case, the police officer explained that it 'would have been all right if he'd just gone away but he had to be Jack the Lad . . . I grabbed him and arrested him.'[18] Regarding a dispute over a restaurant bill, the arresting officer said:

'Had their attitude towards the police been different we could have dealt with it in a different way . . . but there were another five, perhaps six, customers in the restaurant . . . So far as I was concerned it had got to be taken away from there.'[19]

These examples shed light on both the general questions asked earlier: how far arrest is based on 'reasonable suspicion', and what are the consequent patterns of class, race and so forth. Firstly, the 'reasonable suspicion' element is often missing from public order arrests. The

---

[14] J Shapland and R Hobbs, 'Policing Priorities on the Ground' in R Morgan and D Smith (eds), *Coming to Terms with Policing* (Routledge, 1989).

[15] Op cit. Also see C Clarkson, A Cretney, G Davis and J Shepherd, 'Assaults: the Relationship between Seriousness, Criminalisation and Punishment' [1994] Crim LR 4.

[16] That officers would habitually mete out 'street justice' in times gone by is well documented. See eg M Brogden, *On the Mersey Beat* (Oxford University Press, 1991) pp 96–100.

[17] Op cit p 25.

[18] Ibid.

[19] Ibid p 22.

restaurant case was really a civil debt matter, and when asked the basis for the arrest of 'Jack the Lad', all the officer could say was 'it's Ways and Means, just to get him away, control the situation . . .'[20] As has frequently been pointed out,[1] where order or authority are jeopardised, arrest is a resource for the police. It is not so much a means of getting someone to court as a means of control. Not only is prosecution not the main concern, but sometimes it is not envisaged at all, and persons arrested in this way are frequently released without charge.[2]

In most situations, the flexibility of public order-type laws discussed earlier makes it difficult to say that there was insufficient evidence to arrest, for little evidence is required by them. Thus Kemp et al found that the police took action in a lower proportion of disturbances where criminal laws were being broken than where they were being observed.[3] As we have already noted, the few arrests that did occur were for public order offences, even though arrests for criminal damage or assault would have been equally or more appropriate.

Secondly, at the everyday level of policing, since arrestees tend to be those with an 'attitude problem', this falls disproportionately on those who dislike the police—particularly young, black, working class males—whose dislike is thus compounded, increasing the probability of 'attitude problems' next time round. In the more politically charged atmosphere of major strikes, riots, confrontations with 'alternative' movements and so forth, the police—as upholders of order and the status quo—arrest any who challenge their authority.[4] Again this tends to be young or working class males.

There is another parallel here with non-police agencies. Just as suspects are arrested or not in part on the basis of their perceived moral character (as displayed by their attitude to the police) so this is also true of regulatory offences. Carson, for instance, found that factory inspectors only took action against those who appeared to be cavalier and disrespectful.[5] It is not just the police, then, who insist on the upholding of order and authority. However, the fact that the 'clients' of non-police agencies are generally companies or middle class individuals who

---

[20] McConville, Sanders and Leng, op cit pp 25–26. The wryly named (and fictitious) 'Ways and Means Act' is frequently invoked in the absence of more helpful legislation.

[1] M Chatterton, 'Police in Social Control' in J King (ed), *Control Without Custody* (Cambridge Cropwood Papers, 1976); A Sanders, 'Prosecution Decisions and the Attorney-General's Guidelines' [1985] Crim LR 4.

[2] Kemp et al, op cit.

[3] Ibid.

[4] See, on the miners' strike, P Green, op cit ch 3 and B Fine and R Millar (eds), *Policing the Miners' Strike* (Lawrence and Wishart, 1985).

[5] W G Carson, 'White Collar Crime and the Enforcement of Factory Legislation' (1970) 10 BJ Crim 383.

are respectful of authority may partly account for the lower level of enforcement of their crimes than of the crimes with which the police are concerned. And, of course, non-police agencies, unlike the police, do not deal with people who threaten political authority or the established social order.

Suspiciousness and previous convictions

There is a line in the classic film 'Casablanca' when, following a serious crime, the police chief instructs his officers to 'round up the usual suspects'. These are, of course, people with relevant previous convictions. It does not usually happen quite like this, although it can if the police decide to mount a major investigation.[6] Indeed, such investigations provide a good excuse for arresting local 'villains' to see what else they will 'cough' to. Many people are arrested for serious offences because they are known to favour the modus operandi employed,[7] and many police officers spend time with arrestees in order to get to know their criminal character traits for future reference.[8]

'Previous' triggers arrest in three common ways. It is sometimes the first lead in a reported crime, the police arresting someone known to do this kind of thing or to have previously pestered the victim in question. Thus McConville et al cite examples where this was the totality of evidence; no further police action, not surprisingly, was the frequent result.[9] Sometimes knowledge of someone's previous convictions leads to that person being followed, thus allowing the officer sometimes to watch the suspect until he commits a crime.[10] Finally, as we saw in the previous chapter, sometimes just being a known criminal is enough to prompt a stop and search; if this reveals, say, drugs then arrest will follow. The point in these second and third situations is not that arrest is per se wrong (although frequently there will be no reasonable suspicion for the stop, where it occurs, which preceded it), but that if such people had no 'previous', their offences would probably not have been discovered. Again, the pattern created is one which excludes 'respectable' people from the criminal justice net and repeatedly enmeshes those without status.

Being 'known to the police' is only a special case of appearing 'suspicious', which we saw was a key working rule in relation to stop-

---

[6] McConville, Sanders and Leng, op cit p 24.
[7] See D Smith and J Gray, *Police and People in London* (Policy Studies Institute) (Gower, 1983) vol 4, 'The Police in Action', p 345 and A Sanders and L Bridges, 'Access to Legal Advice and Police Malpractice' [1990] Crim LR 494.
[8] McConville et al, op cit p 23.
[9] Ibid ch 2.
[10] Ibid p 24.

search. Association with other criminals, such as sharing a house where drugs are dealt or being seen in public together, is particularly important. Some associates are arrested even when the police have no evidence at all of their guilt; here, arrest is used to secure witness statements and is, of course, entirely without reasonable suspicion.[11] Other 'suspicious' characteristics include appearance and attitude to the police. Attitude is related to the question of authority, discussed above. Suspects who are unco-operative when apprehended are often arrested without more ado, allowing further investigation to determine whether or not they are likely to be the culprits. In cases like this, it is clear that arrest has moved to the start of the investigative stage—too early in many instances for reasonable suspicion to be formed, and much earlier in any event than used to be common.

Even where there is reasonable suspicion, whether arrest takes place depends on a combination—all other things being equal—of offence seriousness and offender seriousness. The police judge the latter, in the absence of information about 'previous', by the attitude displayed by the suspect. In a classic American study, Piliavin and Briar observed police decisions whether or not to arrest or warn juvenile offenders on the street: 25 juveniles were arrested or given official reprimands and 41 juveniles were released with no official action at all. These different dispositions had little to do with the juveniles' alleged offences, but had a lot to do with their demeanour. Most of the co-operative juveniles were released with no official action, while most of the uncooperative juveniles were arrested or given official reprimands. As Piliavin and Briar put it:

'Assessment of character—the distinction between serious delinquents, "good" boys, misguided youths, and so on—and the dispositions which followed . . . were based on youths' personal characteristics, and not their offences.'[12]

In other words, the police attempted to avoid rigidity by taking action only in 'deserving' cases, but they based that judgment on rather superficial personal characteristics. More recently in Britain, Southgate reported similar findings:

'Observers noticed cases where officers enforced the law "by the book" in response to difficult or hostile people, whereas they applied discretion to offenders of a similar kind who were more amenable.'[13]

---

[11] These specific examples are taken from several others discussed by R Leng, The Right to Silence in Police Interrogation: A Study of Some of the Issues Underlying the Debate (Royal Commission on Criminal Justice Research Study no 10) (HMSO, 1993) p 25.

[12] I Piliavin and S Briar 'Police Encounters with Juveniles' (1964) 70 AJ Sociology 206.

[13] P Southgate, Police-Public Encounters (Home Office Research Study no 90) (HMSO, 1986) p 47.

The result was that official action (including arrest) was taken against 45% of 'rude, hostile' suspects, 22% of 'civil' suspects, 11% of 'friendly' suspects, and 5% of those who displayed 'particular deference'. As one officer said to the researcher, after finding that one driver had no car tax disc: 'If he had not been so unhelpful I might not have been so determined to prosecute him.'[14]

Taking account of the victim

The wishes of the victim are thought to be important, but not overriding, by everyone. Subject to other factors then, a decision to arrest will in part depend on whether formal police action is desired by the victim. If the victim's evidence is essential to any consequent prosecution (which is by no means always the case) then there will be little point making an arrest without his or her agreement.

Reality is not, however, so straightforward. Firstly, the police themselves are able to influence the wishes of the victim, especially in 'domestics'. When the police attend an alleged domestic assault, they are expected to use their judgment to decide whether, if they believe there has been an assault, it would be better for the victim to take official action, to conciliate or just to warn the offender. They will often discuss these alternatives with the victim, who may have a preference but who will usually be open to advice. Officers who do not wish to arrest can easily make this appear to be an unattractive option, which it may indeed be.[15]

Secondly, the police always pursue grave offences. McConville et al report a serious rape case which led to mass arrests of a broad category of suspect, largely for purposes of elimination.[16] Clarkson et al examined nearly 100 assault cases. The police pursued five of the most serious cases (all meriting charges of inflicting grievous bodily harm) despite the reluctance and unreliability of the victims.[17]

Thirdly, some victims are more influential than others. Ignoring the views of some—local businessmen and politicians, for instance—would cause more trouble for the police than ignoring others. So Kemp et al

---

[14] Ibid p 101.
[15] S Edwards, *Policing Domestic Violence* (Sage, 1989); C Kemp, C Norris and N Fielding, 'Legal Manoeuvres in Police Handling of Disputes' in D Farrington and S Walklate (eds), *Offenders and Victims: Theory and Policy* (British Society of Criminology, 1992).
[16] Op cit ch 2.
[17] C Clarkson, A Cretney, G Davis and J Shepherd, 'Assaults: the Relationship between Seriousness, Criminalisation and Punishment' [1994] Crim LR 4.

comment that in civil disputes, such as trespass, where no criminality is involved:

'the police often take immediate action . . . to end the dispute, generally by ensuring the physical removal of the "offender" from the scene. For instance, all 11 requests made by publicans, security guards, shop/office managers, and private landlords in our 60 disputes were supported by the police.'[18]

They point out that the police have no power to force individuals to leave, and that they could simply explain to the complainants their civil law rights. The important point for us, apart from demonstrating the willingness of the police to exercise authority even where they have no power to back it up, is that police authority is generally exercised in favour of powerful high status victims, rather than victims of low status. The 'explain the position and do nothing' option, on the other hand, is quite often the strategy adopted in 'domestics'. Here the situation is potentially dangerous, but the victim is of low status. Thus Kemp et al discuss one 'domestic' where theft as well as assault was alleged but to no avail. They say in relation to this case, though it serves equally well as a general statement, that '. . . throughout the incident the wishes of the complainant become secondary to those of the officer.'[19] When the police did arrest:

'Victims' views were basically ignored and the offence and the offender became police property to be disposed of in the manner which most suited police rather than victim priorities.'[20]

Victims of domestic violence are in a weak position, so the police have little incentive to arrest unless there is a public order element or threat to their authority.[1] The police are acting entirely within the law in these examples, for there are no laws establishing locus standi for victims and no laws establishing which criteria should or should not be used by the police in exercising their discretion. Exactly the same findings have been made in the United States, showing that this is not a local or temporary phenomenon, but a basic feature of modern Western society.[2] As with many aspects of the operation of police powers, it is not what was done, but who did it or who was the victim of it that matters most.

---

[18] Op cit p 65.
[19] Ibid p 72.
[20] Ibid p 73.
[1] A Sanders, 'Personal Violence and Public Order' (1988) 16 IJ Sociology of Law 359.
[2] See E Buzawa and C Buzawa, 'The Impact of Arrest on Domestic Assault' (1993) 36 American Behavioural Scientist 558.

Other factors

The other main working rules give primacy to organisational factors, 'information received' from informants or co-suspects and workload. We examined the impact of organisational and societal factors on police discretion in general in the previous chapter.[3] Arrests are as subject to such influences as any other aspect of policing. Periodic panics over vice, drugs, 'mugging' and so forth lead to surges in arrests for these offences. Sometimes individual communities or police forces adopt particular arrest policies, especially in the United States where there is more local control of policing than in the United Kingdom. In one study, the arrest rate in town A was over three times as high as in town B, giving the impression of a much lower crime rate in the latter. In reality, though, the crime rates were very similar. The true difference was that the affluent middle class residents of town B put enormous pressure on the police not to arrest their offspring.[4]

The police frequently arrest suspects purely on the strength of an allegation, or 'information received'. If the allegation coincides with 'previous', so much the better, as in a case cited by McConville et al: '. . . you have to react on what you hear initially . . . when we checked his form we thought there might be a chance; the name even rang a bell to the lads . . .'[5] Since this arrestee did not fit the description and absolutely nothing connected him with the offence, it would have been difficult for the police to claim that they had 'reasonable suspicion'.

Workload can have all sorts of effects. Police officers avoid arresting when they have too much to do, and look for arrests when they have too little to do. The weather can also be important (when it is cold and wet, almost any excuse to get back to the station will do), as can a host of other trivial factors. Overriding it all, however, is the drive for 'figures' and 'quality figures' in particular. As Young says:

'In this [CID] world the detection rate is of vital concern, and a succession of poor returns in the monthly or quarterly detection figures can break the ambitious detective inspector . . . As a result, those calls for a change of emphasis to such matters as "crime prevention" have little or no chance of obtaining prominence . . .'[6]

Exactly the same point is made by Maguire and Norris who observe that arrest and detection rates are still important promotion criteria.[7]

---

[3] See ch 2, section 1(b), above.
[4] A Meehan, 'Internal Police Records and the Control of Juveniles' (1993) 33 BJ Crim 504.
[5] Op cit p 30.
[6] M Young, *An Inside Job* (Oxford University Press, 1991) p 255.
[7] M Maguire and C Norris, The Conduct and Supervision of Criminal Investigations (Royal Commission on Criminal Justice, Research Study no 5) (HMSO, 1992) ch 5.

Since a charge (or a caution) counts as a detection regardless of the outcome (hence regardless of the evidence) the pressures to treat 'reasonable suspicion' lightly are difficult to resist.

(c) Race, class and arrest

It is clear from the above that police working rules do not impact equally upon all sections of society. People who are young, black, male or working class more often exhibit 'suspicious' characteristics than do other people, and are less influential when they are victims. In 'cop culture'[8] some social and racial groups are simply regarded as more criminogenic than others. This viewpoint finds no support in the research literature. But since the police act upon their cultural assumptions, the result is a pattern of unjustified discrimination. For example, Stevens and Willis found that black people in deprived socio-economic conditions were no more likely to commit crimes than were white people in those conditions.[9] Yet both this study (pre-PACE) and post-PACE studies such as that by Jefferson and Walker,[10] found disproportionate arrest rates among black people. Much of this is a product of proactive policing. Stevens and Willis found that black people were particularly liable to be arrested for offences such as preparatory and public order offences where 'there is considerable scope for selective perception of potential or actual offenders.'[11]

That PACE has made little or no difference is evident from the recent study by Norris et al. This found disproportionate stopping (and disproportionate formal action[12] after stopping, of black people, even though their demeanour was similar to that of whites. The result is that, over one year:

'. . . approximately one in three of the black male population under 35 would be involved in a stop resulting in formal police action in contrast to only one in ten of white males under 35.'[13]

It seems that just being black makes one suspicious and thus more

---

8   See ch 2, section 1(c), above.

9   P Stevens and CF Willis, Race, Crime and Arrests (Home Office Research Study no 58) (HMSO, 1979).

10   T Jefferson and M Walker, 'Ethnic Minorities in the Criminal Justice System' [1992] Crim LR 83.

11   Op cit p 41.

12   This includes reports for summons and requirements to produce vehicle documents. There were too few arrests to make meaningful comparison of arrests alone.

13   C Norris et al, 'Black and Blue: An Analysis of the Influence of Race on being Stopped by the Police' (1992) 43 BJ Sociology 207 at 222.

liable to being arrested.[14] Being young and male, as well as black, is even more risky.[15]

Working class people are also massively over-represented in the arrest statistics, even taking into account socio-economic conditions.[16] In addition to community pressures and to 'attitude' problems, working class people are simply more vulnerable to being arrested. In 'Operation Major' in 1982, 283 people were arrested in one day and in one place on suspicion of fraud. Over 104 people were held for up to ten hours before being released without charge. The suspiciousness which triggered their arrest was constituted by walking into a particular unemployment benefit office in Oxford. All people who walked into that office that day were, without exception, arrested. Some were accompanying claimants and not making a claim themselves, but were held anyway. This was not so much because they were disbelieved, for in some cases their innocence was obvious, but in order to prevent warnings being given to claimants due to arrive later in the day.[17] Clearly a large number of these arrests were made without 'reasonable suspicion'. Due process was completely sacrificed to crime control because of the nature of the suspects (claimants) and the victim (the government).

How can we explain the fact that many people are arrested on little or no evidence, in defiance of 'reasonable suspicion' laws, and that black people disproportionately suffer from this? We need to ask what the police want, and what they might fear, when they arrest. They either want to punish, by arrest and detention, those who fail to display respect, or they want evidence leading to prosecution and conviction; they fear adverse come back if they 'mess up'. Arresting people on 'fishing expeditions' who may provide information, arresting people for the purpose of elimination, or arresting people to enforce order is therefore viable for the police if the arrestee is unlikely to sue, make a plausible complaint, or otherwise challenge their actions. This is true largely of low status people: those who are young, black or working class (and especially of those who possess all three characteristics).

14 The overall disproportionate arrest rates of blacks, as compared to whites, can only partially be explained in this way. The difference appears also to be due to the greater social deprivation of blacks and reporting and recording differences: Jefferson and Walker, op cit. Note that all these studies found that Asians were arrested disproportionately infrequently.

15 M Fitzgerald, Ethnic Minorities and the Criminal Justice System (Royal Commission on Criminal Justice, Research Study no 20) (HMSO, 1993) p 16. This is all consistent with the American research. See R Reiner, *The Politics of the Police* (Harvester Wheatsheaf, 1992) pp 156–170 for a discussion of research findings from the UK and the USA.

16 R Reiner, op cit; A Meehan, op cit; A Sanders, 'Class Bias in Prosecutions' (1985) 24 Howard J Crim Justice 76.

17 R Franey, *Poor Law* (NCCL, 1983).

Hence the pattern observed in relation to stop-search is repeated and amplified at the arrest stage. Patterns of bias are created through the following of police working rules which dictate who to select for arrest out of a much larger group of arrestable suspects. The rule that the police must act only when they have 'reasonable suspicion' is sometimes ignored in this process, but the flexibility of this requirement means that breach is often not necessary. It is therefore in part an enabling rule, allowing the police to use informal norms, and in part a presentational rule with little inhibitory effect.

5. REMEDIES FOR WRONGFUL ARREST

What happens if the police arrest when they should not? We have seen in relation to stop-search that the main problem suspects face in challenging police action is credibility. There are rarely independent witnesses to encounters on the street, and proving an absence of reasonable suspicion or reasonable belief is very difficult anyway. To these problems we can add the way the courts have interpreted the requirements of the law in such cases as *Castorina v Chief Constable of Surrey*[18] and those which we shall be examining later in this section.

Leaving such problems aside, what specific remedies are available? A complaint can be made to the Police Complaints Authority. This will be examined in chapter 9. Exclusion in court of evidence obtained following wrongful arrest is another possibility, although this is a discretionary matter for the court even if the arrest is proved to be unlawful. The advantage of this remedy in relation to arrest is that it might deter the police from breaking the rules. However, it only operates when the police prosecute and would otherwise win the case. In other words, exclusion of evidence on the grounds of wrongful arrest only assists defendants if they are legally guilty, ie if the offences with which they are charged can be proved. However, arrest is lawful if the defendant 'is guilty of the offence', regardless of whether the police officer had reasonable suspicion or not.[19] This means that exclusion of evidence would be most unlikely.

The main remedy available is to sue for wrongful arrest in the civil courts. Wrongful arrest is part of the general tort of false imprisonment, and damages can be awarded to compensate for loss. Like unlawful stop-search, it is difficult to demonstrate significant tangible loss, thus making civil actions difficult.[20] Wrongful arrest occurs when the

---

[18] [1988] NLJR 180, discussed in section 4(a), above.
[19] See s 24(5)(a) of PACE, set out in section 3(b), above.
[20] This topic is covered more fully in ch 9.

powers discussed in this chapter are exceeded. It also occurs when an arrest is 'unreasonable', even if no specific power is exceeded. This is because under administrative law principles of judicial review (known as *Wednesbury* principles) all arms of the Executive are accountable to the courts for any unreasonable action. When using arrest powers, police officers must act in good faith, use the arrest powers for the purpose they were given, take into account relevant matters and disregard the irrelevant, and must not act in a way so unreasonable that no reasonable police officer could have so acted.[1] These principles, by their very nature, are capable of flexible application. It is thus crucial to examine the use the courts have made of them in this context.

Should an unnecessary arrest be treated as unreasonable? In a due process system, this would certainly be regarded as a wrongful arrest, but a crime control system would allow it if it enhanced police efficiency. We have seen that arrests need only be necessary if they are for non-arrestable offences (under s 25 of PACE) so it seems that, where arrestable offences are concerned, PACE gives priority to crime control considerations.

That this was also the pre-PACE common law position is demonstrated by the House of Lords decision in *Holgate-Mohammed v Duke*.[2] Stolen jewellery was sold to a shop by someone fitting the description of the suspect. There was therefore reasonable suspicion against the suspect. She was arrested and taken to the police station and questioned but not charged. She sued the police for wrongful arrest on the grounds that there was no need to arrest and detain her because she could have been questioned equally well at home or at work. The police conceded that she could have been questioned elsewhere and that she was not unco-operative, but they decided that she was more likely to confess if held in the police station. The arrest was not necessary, but from the police point of view it was desirable. The House of Lords declared that the question was whether the police had exercised their discretionary power to arrest in accordance with the *Wednesbury* principles. Their decision to arrest could be impugned only if they had taken into account some irrelevant factor that they should have excluded from their consideration. Since, the House of Lords decided, the greater likelihood of the suspect confessing if taken to the police station was a factor the police were entitled to take into account, it followed that they acted lawfully in exercising their power of arrest. This decision legitimised a police working rule which was then cemented into the fabric of PACE itself. The judges and Parliament

[1] These principles derive from *Associated Provincial Picture Houses Ltd v Wednesbury Corpn* [1948] 1 KB 223.
[2] [1984] 1 All ER 1054.

thus seem to be agreed that the police should be encouraged to arrest whenever this would promote efficient crime control.

 Similar considerations arise when considering whether the police have a duty to check a suspect's story on, or prior to, arrest. In *Madden*'s case, a youth, who the police believed had been stealing, was stopped on the street.[3] They found on him a model car. Madden claimed that he had bought the car, telling the officers the name of the shop. Disbelieving him, the officers did not check the story. In the police station, he confessed to the crime but subsequently pleaded not guilty at his trial. He was acquitted, in part because he had a receipt to which the police had paid no attention. Given that his story could have been, but was not, checked, was this wrongful arrest? In other words, is there a duty on the police to seek evidence to dispel the suspicion which they may otherwise reasonably have, as one would expect if due process principles were applied? Or may the police do as they wish once a minimum threshold is reached, as in a crime control system ?

In *Dumbell v Roberts*,[4] a man was arrested for allegedly handling stolen goods. He suggested that if the police accompanied him to his place of work then he would be exonerated, but the police refused to do so. Scott LJ said (obiter) that the police

'. . . should make all presently practicable enquiries from persons present or immediately accessible who are likely to be able to answer their enquiries forthwith. I am not suggesting a duty on the police to try to prove innocence; that is not their function; but they should act on the assumption that their prima facie suspicions may be ill founded.'[5]

This suggests that officers should check suspect's stories when it is reasonable to do so, and that it is wrongful arrest when they do not. As Scott LJ succinctly put it: '. . . to shut your eyes to the obvious is not to act reasonably . . .'[6]

On the other hand, in *McCarrick v Oxford*,[7] where the officer wrongly believed he was dealing with a disqualified driver, it was held that the officer did not need to go to the suspect's home to check the story of the latter. This is difficult to reconcile with Scott LJ's dicta in *Dumbell and Roberts*, although when the driver protested his innocence the police did call their police station to see if the dispute could be resolved; thus they had checked the driver's story, up to a point. The question is whether there is no obligation to check, a major obligation or (reconciling the cases) a limited obligation.

---

[3] See (1981) Guardian, 9 March.
[4] [1944] 1 All ER 326.
[5] Ibid at 329.
[6] Ibid.
[7] [1983] RTR 117.

In *Ward v Chief Constable of Avon and Somerset*,[8] a police officer searched a house into which people had been seen carrying a television set soon after a riot. Property looted in the course of the riot included a large quantity of Easter eggs. He searched the house and found 11 Easter eggs. He asked about them, and was told that they were for the defendant (D's) children and that they cost 37p. The officer thought this sounded too cheap and arrested D for theft. His suspicion could have been dispelled if he had enquired where they had been bought and how many children she had: he wrongly assumed that she had only one child and that, therefore, she would not have bought so many eggs. Briefly recalling the cases of *Dumbell* and *McCarrick*, Croom-Johnson LJ simply stated, without reasons, that 'it is unnecessary for the police to probe every explanation.' Although this begs the question of whether it is acceptable for the police to fail to probe any explanation, the court did not hesitate to reject the claim of wrongful arrest. In *Castorina v Chief Constable of Surrey*,[9] however, the Court of Appeal faced the issue more squarely, Purchas LJ stating that:

'There is ample authority for the proposition that courses of inquiry which may or may not be taken by an investigating police officer before arrest are not relevant to the consideration whether, on the information available to him at the time of the arrest, he had reasonable cause for suspicion. Of course, failure to follow an obvious course in exceptional circumstances may well be grounds for attacking the executive exercise of that power under *Wednesbury* principles.'[10]

Under this approach, the courts may only hold the exercise of the discretionary power to arrest unlawful in 'exceptional circumstances' and when the course of inquiry which was not pursued was 'obvious'. Note too that when these two conditions are satisfied, the arrest is not automatically unlawful since Purchas LJ went no further than saying that in such situations there 'may well be grounds' for challenging the exercise of the arrest power. The obligation to pursue a line of inquiry which might exculpate a suspect (so avoiding an unnecessary arrest) is clearly very limited. It is therefore debatable whether either Madden or, in the 'Confait Affair',[11] Latimore (who had a very strong alibi which was not checked by the police initially) were wrongfully arrested.

The judges have complete freedom to decide issues arising under

---

[8] (1986) Times, 26 June, CA.
[9] [1988] NLJR 180.
[10] Ibid at 181.
[11] See Report of an Inquiry into the Circumstances leading to the Trial of Three Persons on Charges arising out of the Death of Maxwell Confait and the Fire at 27 Doggett Road, London SE6 (HCP 90) (HMSO, 1977).

the *Wednesbury* principles as they like. The cases show that they are in fact increasingly taking a crime control approach. Judges are interpreting arrest rules in ways that enable the police to 'get on with the job', rather than seeking to inject inhibitory elements which would promote civil liberties. This may be contrasted with a much more robust attitude to the actions of some other arms of the Executive, where crime control considerations do not arise.[12]

It is a clear case of wrongful arrest when an arrestee is not informed of the fact of his or her arrest as soon as it is reasonably practicable to do so. This has long been the case, according to the common law (see, for example, *Christie v Leachinsky*[13]), and the requirement to inform is now set out in PACE, s 28. This is also consistent with the law on stop and search which requires that suspects be told why they are being stopped (see chapter 2). Under the common law, this information could be communicated by either words or action. In *Brosch*,[14] a citizen's arrest case discussed earlier, the manager had not told the arrestee that he was under arrest, but since this was obvious it did not matter. PACE now obliges the police (but not other arrestors) to give the reason for arrest explicitly, however obvious it may appear to be, as soon as practicable.[15] This imposes greater due process obligations on the police than did the common law.

Despite this, the police are not subject to the degree of due process rigour that one might think from reading s 28. The problem arises in relation to what is practicable. In *Murray v Minister of Defence*[16] (a Northern Ireland case), soldiers went to the defendant (M's) house at 7 am, detained everyone and searched the premises. The soldier in charge remained with M. At 7.30 am, he formally informed M of her arrest and took her to an army detention centre acting under a statute giving summary arrest powers similar to those in PACE, s 24. M's de facto arrest between 7 am and 7.30 am would appear to breach the common law and the equivalent of s 28.

Following *Shaaban Bin Hussien v Chong Fook Kam*[17] (that, as in M's case, one is arrested if one is not allowed to leave the place in which one is kept) Lord Griffiths held that M was arrested at 7 am

---

[12]   The patterns of judicial control of discretionary powers are charted by J Griffiths, *The Politics of the Judiciary* (Fontana, 1991) ch 4.

[13]   [1947] AC 573.

[14]   [1988] Crim LR 743.

[15]   The reason(s) need not be a precise formulation of the law, however. See *Abbassy v Metropolitan Police Comr* [1990] 1 All ER 193, where the defendants were arrested for 'unlawful possession' of a car. There is no such offence, but as this encompassed all the criminal possibilities the officers had in mind, the Court of Appeal said that this was satisfactory.

[16]   [1988] 2 All ER 521.

[17]   [1970] AC 942.

(when her detention began) rather than at 7.30 am when she was told that she was arrested. However, according to Lord Griffiths, 'If words of arrest are spoken as soon as the house is entered . . . there is a real risk that the alarm may be raised.'[18] It was therefore not practicable to inform M of the fact of, and reasons for, her arrest immediately, and the arrest was therefore not unlawful. This seems to assume that the alarm was not raised when the group of armed soldiers entered the house, rounded everyone up, gave it a thorough search and did not even tell the occupants what was going to happen to them. The decision in this case does not alter the principle at stake but—unless 'terrorist' cases are being treated as special cases (for which there is no legal justification, but which might be understandable in other ways)—it does suggest that drawing the line about when something is reasonably practicable is not easy.

The less demanding the judiciary is in interpreting statutory controls on the police, the greater the play allowed to crime control principles. Even when the legislature, as in s 28 of PACE, appears to be creating strong inhibitory rules, the judiciary still manages to draw their due process sting by rendering them largely presentational.

6. CONCLUSION

The law of arrest has evolved to accommodate changes in police practice. This has entailed the police using arrest to facilitate investigation rather than just as a mechanism to bring alleged offenders before the courts. The courts, and now PACE, have allowed policing considerations instead of due process considerations to dictate the shape and content of the law. Crime control values underlie the law of arrest in several respects. Firstly, although the Philips Commission saw arrest as intrinsically coercive and wanted to restrict it to situations where this was necessary, no such restriction is placed on the police in s 24 of PACE. Secondly, where the law was changed by PACE it was largely by providing arrest powers where they had not previously existed (allowing summary arrest, where 'necessary', in non-arrestable offences in s 25). Thirdly, whereas most executive agencies are increasingly subject to judicial review along *Wednesbury* lines, this remains exceptional in respect of arrest. Finally, the substantive law in most public order offences and in common law breach of the peace is so vague that the police have even more freedom to arrest according to their own priorities than they would otherwise have.

The main due process element in arrest law is 'reasonable suspicion',

---

[18] *Ibid* at p 527.

but arrests are still lawful even when there are no reasonable grounds for them if arrestable offences had actually been committed. The ends may lawfully justify the means. Further, 'reasonable suspicion' is such a low threshold that most arrests are based on weak evidence. More investigation would be possible prior to most arrests, but this is not required by the law. The law offers little due process protection and, instead, provides wide boundaries within which the police operate according to their own working rules. Offence seriousness, the probability that the suspect has committed an arrestable offence and the views of the victim all influence police decisions whether or not to arrest, but police working rules are equally important. These are based on criteria of 'suspiciousness' and 'disorder' that—like stop and search—bear more heavily on some sections of society than others. Patterns of bias result which are a product only in part of police rule breaking. Some people who are arrested, as a punishment or enforcement mechanism in itself, should not be arrested. But the greater problem is that some sections of the population are constantly singled out when others are equally likely to be guilty of criminal offences. A skewed suspect population is constructed, which distorts the whole criminal process thereafter.

This problem can be observed on the broader socio-legal canvas when we consider non-police agencies. Though some of the criteria operated by these agencies are those used by the police (such as disrespect) the offenders are generally more 'respectable' and so application of identical criteria produces different results. In fields of employment and housing, this would be regarded as indirect and unacceptable discrimination.

However, it should not be thought that it is necessarily possible, or even desirable, to create due process-based arrest laws. As with stop-search, police-suspect interactions leading to arrest are fluid and unpredictable. As with stop-search, arrest is sometimes used in order to gather information, rather than as a prelude to court processes (thus limiting the accountability of the police to the law). Different arrest (and stop-search) patterns may not reflect different crime rates so much as different ways of securing criminal intelligence information.[19]

Social situations such as domestic disputes and street brawls rarely fall neatly into legalistic categories. Whilst the police are finding facts, they must necessarily use their initiative and imagination. This is not compatible with *Wednesbury*-style objective reasoning. We must provide the police with discretion and therefore with some of our freedom. But we should also recognise this for the crime control-based process

---

[19] A Meehan, 'Internal Police Records and the Control of Juveniles' (1993) 33 BJ Crim 504.

that it is. For those of us who instinctively lean towards due process the response should not necessarily be to demand tighter definitions of 'reasonable suspicion', for this strategy is unlikely to work. Instead, we might take a leaf out of the book of the non-police agencies and require the police to arrest less and use summons more, as the Philips Commission recommended.

If we are to accept the necessity of crime control techniques, we might none the less seek a greater say in the crimes to be controlled. We might, for example, seek more public control over the types of situation for which arrest is and is not to be regarded as appropriate.[20] For example, during the miners' strike the police operated on the basis of political and social values not shared by many of the police authorities to which the police are nominally accountable.[1] By contrast, a stronger response to domestic violence might be sought. In the United States, mandatory arrest laws are common now in response to the way the police neglected these offences when operating with discretion.[2] We might consider similar laws here too, although the impact of mandatory arrest laws on domestic violence is, at best, limited.[3] Moreover, the police are adept at avoiding action—in this case, domestic violence arrests—which they do not favour.[4]

Finally, if we do accept the necessity of the methods of crime control, it does not follow that we should accept that model's assumptions about the reliability of administrative fact finding. Instead, we should treat with scepticism police claims that, as professionals, they can be trusted not to make mistakes. No one with the amount of power the police possess should ever be trusted to that extent.

---

[20] This raises broad issues concerning police accountability. See further, R Reiner, *The Politics of the Police* (Harvester Wheatsheaf, 1992) pp 236–249 and R Reiner and S Spencer (eds), *Accountable Policing* (IPPR, 1993).

[1] M Brake and C Hale, *Public Order and Private Lives* (Routledge, 1992) pp 44–58.

[2] See E Buzawa and C Buzawa, 'The Impact of Arrest on Domestic Assault' (1993) 36 American Behavioural Scientist 558.

[3] R Morley and A Mullender, 'Hype or Hope? The Importation of Pro-Arrest Policies and Batterers' Programmes from North America to Britain as Key Measures for Preventing Violence against Women in the Home' (1992) 6 IJ Law and the Family 265.

[4] L Sherman, 'The Influence of Criminology on Criminal Law: Evaluating Arrests for Misdemeanour Domestic Violence' (1992) 83 Jo Crim Law and Criminology 1.

Chapter 4

In the Police Station

1. INTRODUCTION

In a crime control system, the police would have discretion to deal with arrested suspects as they thought fit in order to ascertain the truth. Suspects are most likely to co-operate with the police and reveal the truth if denied the opportunity to consult with friends, family or, in particular, a lawyer. Outside interference with the police-suspect encounter in the police station cannot be tolerated. The length of detention should be governed by considerations of efficiency alone. Suspects should be held for as long as it is thought that further interrogation may provide useful information, but no longer. Any reliable statement obtained from a suspect through interrogation should be admissible in evidence regardless of whether it was obtained through coercive methods. A confession should only be ruled inadmissible if shown by the defence to be obtained in such coercive circumstances that it was probably untrue.

In a due process system, the detention of suspects in police custody would be very tightly controlled, if it was allowed at all. Since the police should not arrest unless they first have sufficient information to provide a case that will result in conviction, it follows that there is no necessity to secure a confession from the suspect. Arrest should be followed by charge and judicial proceedings, not by administrative investigation.[1] Some interval of time must elapse between arresting suspects and bringing them before the courts, however. It may be in the suspect's interests to talk to the police during this period since the information provided may dispel suspicion and lead to earlier release. But this opportunity for dialogue may be abused, so safeguards must be provided. Suspects must be told that they are under no obligation to

---

[1] See ch 3, section 1, above, for discussion of the place of arrest in due process and crime control systems.

106

answer questions, that it will not be held against them at court if they maintain silence, that anything said may be used in evidence and that they are free to consult with a lawyer before answering questions. Any confession should be ruled inadmissible if suspects were not told of their rights, were questioned in any situation other than where the right to silence and to consult a lawyer had been expressly waived, if the period of detention exceeded that necessary to bring them before the courts or if the confession was obtained through coercion. Such an exclusionary rule deprives the police of any incentive to obtain a confession in an unethical manner. For, as Packer concludes:

'The rationale of exclusion is not that the confession is untrustworthy, but that it is at odds with the postulates of an accusatory system of criminal justice in which it is up to the state to make its case against a defendant without forcing him to cooperate in the process, and without capitalizing on his ignorance of his legal rights.'[2]

The right of silence is, from this perspective, part and parcel of the presumption of innocence. The state has accused the citizen of a crime and must therefore bear the responsibility of proving its case. Punishment is only justified if this burden is discharged in a proper manner.

We will see that, based on the approach of the Royal Commission on Criminal Procedure (the Philips Commission), PACE steers something of a middle course between the polarities of crime control and due process. The Act allows detention for the purpose of interrogation, but seeks to regulate the conditions under which questioning may take place. Police officers do not have complete discretion, but what they do is largely under the control or supervision of other (senior) police officers.

Prior to PACE, the rights of suspects and powers of the police in the police station were governed largely by the Judges' Rules.[3] Because of important gaps, their unclear status and their inconsistent enforcement by the courts, the situation had by the 1970s and 1980s become very confused. The Judges' Rules were virtually silent on the crucial question of the permissible length of detention prior to charge. This led to the police routinely consigning suspects into the unsatisfactory limbo of 'helping the police with their inquiries'. The need to reform the law was

---

[2] H Packer, *The Limits of the Criminal Sanction* (Stanford University Press, 1968) p 191.

[3] The final version, last revised in 1964, was appended to Home Office circular 89/1978. The circular, the Rules themselves, and the administrative directions (which served as an appendix to the Rules) are reproduced by the Royal Commission on Criminal Procedure, The Law and Procedure, (Cmnd 8092–1) (HMSO, 1981) Appendix 12.

clear to everyone, but the direction which reform should take was controversial. In the event, the government implemented the Philips Commission's proposals on the detention of suspects, unlike its proposals on arrest, very closely. The approach of both the Philips Commission and of the government was not so much to balance the rights of defendants with the rights of the police, or indeed to give priority to one over the other; rather, the philosophy was both to give the police more powers and also to provide more checks and controls on the use of those powers and to provide more safeguards for suspects.

2. THE POWERS AND DUTIES OF THE CUSTODY OFFICER

We saw in chapter 3 that the police station has become the primary site of criminal investigation through changes in police practice. Changes in the law did not keep pace for most of the twentieth century, and institutions such as arrest changed their function without altering their form. It was the scandal of the 'Confait Affair'[4] which showed incontestably how important it was to recognise the power of the police over suspects in police stations. This led to the acceptance, via the Philips Commission, that clear legal regulation of what goes on in the police station was necessary. The question of what rights were to be provided to suspects, and who was going to ensure that they were made available to them, was settled by PACE.

(a) The custody officer

PACE created a new type of police officer named the 'custody officer'. Every 'designated' police station—that is, a police station which has the facilities to hold suspects for significant lengths of time—must have a custody officer available at all times.[5] Custody officers must be at least of the rank of sergeant,[6] but need have no particular training in order to carry out their duties. Any other officer may carry out their functions when they are not available.[7] The post is of great importance, however, as it is on this officer that the main responsibility rests for the maintenance of the rights of suspects.

---

[4] Sir Henry Fisher, Report of an Inquiry into the Circumstances leading to the Trial of Three Persons on Charges arising out of the Death of Maxwell Confait and the Fire at 27 Doggett Road, London SE6 (HCP 90) (HMSO, 1977). See J Baxter and L Koffman, 'The Confait Inheritance—Forgotten Lessons?' [1983] Cambrian LR 14.

[5] PACE, s 36.

[6] PACE, s 36(3).

[7] PACE, s 36(4).

Custody officers are meant to be independent of any investigation in which a detained suspect is involved.[8] So, whilst acting as a custody officer, that individual must not be involved in the process of securing evidence from or about suspects. Although in some areas custody officers do that job and no other for lengthy periods, in others it is common to alternate this job with other duties. Brown et al found that these differing arrangements made no difference to the way in which custody officers performed their duties.[9] At root, a custody officer is still a police officer involved in normal policing. This creates role conflict for custody officers, requiring them to wear different hats, if not at the same time, then at least in close proximity to each other.

Arrested suspects are generally brought straight to a police station and immediately brought before the custody officer. The principle is that nothing may happen to that suspect after arrest prior to being 'logged in' by the custody officer. The custody officer fills in a 'custody record' form for each suspect brought before him. Custody records vary from force to force but they all contain the same basic information. After some personal details (name, address and so forth) are taken down, the custody officer has to decide whether or not to detain the suspect and, if so, on what grounds, and whether or not to charge the suspect (and, again, on what grounds).

(b)   The rights of suspects[10]

Custody officers should immediately inform those suspects who are to be detained of their rights, both orally and by giving them a notice in writing. The most important rights are: to consult a lawyer privately, not to be kept incommunicado, to consult a copy of the PACE Code of Practice C (which sets out their rights and those of the police) and to make a telephone call to anyone of their choice. These functions are similar to, though more detailed than, those which the old station sergeant (sometimes known as the charge sergeant) used to perform.

The right to have someone informed when arrested—otherwise known as 'intimation'—is described in the PACE Code of Practice C as

---

[8] PACE, s 36(5). See, for discussion, V Bevan and K Lidstone, *The Investigation of Crime* (Butterworths, 1991) p 287.

[9] D Brown, T Ellis and K Larcombe, Changing the Code: Police Detention under the Revised PACE Codes of Practice (Home Office Research Study no 129) (HMSO, 1992) p 34.

[10] The outline provided here will not attempt to discuss comprehensively the rights of suspects. Good reference texts are Bevan and Lidstone, op cit and H Levenson and F Fairweather, *Police Powers, A Practitioner's Guide* (LAG, 1990). The right to legal advice, generally regarded as the most important right prior to charge, is dealt with separately in section 4, below.

the 'right not to be held incommunicado'.[11] Under s 56(1) of PACE, a suspect may have:

'One friend or relative or a person who is known to him or is likely to take an interest in his welfare told, as soon as is practicable except to the extent that delay is permitted by this section, that he has been arrested and is being detained . . .'

The police may not stop suspects exercising this right. They may delay its exercise, but only under strict conditions which can rarely be satisfied.[12] The police applied their delaying power to around 1% of requests in 1988 but only 0.2% of requests in 1991, although requests were made in fewer than one in five cases in the first place.[13] However, Note D to Code of Practice C provides that 'In some circumstances it may not be appropriate to use the telephone' in compliance with s 56. This means that the custody officer can require that intimation be made in a written form only.

The exercise by suspects of the separate right to a telephone call or to contact someone by letter[14] may be delayed on a similar basis to the right of intimation, except that here the power to delay is not restricted to serious arrestable offences. Suspects may also 'receive visits at the custody officer's discretion'.[15] Discretion is to be exercised in the light of the availability of sufficient manpower to supervise visits 'and any possible hinderance to the investigation'.[16] These last two 'rights' need not be communicated orally to suspects by custody officers on reception, or indeed at any other time. The only way in which suspects who do not already know of these rights can find them out is by consulting Code of Practice C and (in the case of the phone call) the written notice. Not surprisingly, very few people ask for visits, and less than 10% of suspects ask for a phone call.[17] This may well be fewer than before PACE.[18]

Although intimation is formally delayed rarely, informal delay is much more common. According to Dixon et al, informal delay in intimation 'may be deliberate, for example, when officers who wish to

[11] Code of Practice C: The Detention, Treatment and Questioning of Persons by Police Officers (HMSO, 1991) s 5.
[12] The conditions are similar to those which apply to the delaying of a suspect's access to legal advice, discussed below, section 4(a).
[13] Brown et al, op cit pp 54–56.
[14] Code of Practice C, op cit para 5.6.
[15] Ibid para 5.4.
[16] Ibid Note 5B.
[17] Brown et al, op cit p 55.
[18] D Dixon, K Bottomley, C Coleman, M Gill and D Wall, 'Safeguarding the Rights of Suspects in Police Custody' (1990) 1 Policing and Society at 118.

search premises wait to inform a suspect's family of arrest until they arrive to search his/her house'.[19] Dixon et al point out that informal delay is also often an unintentional product of pressure of work. It takes time for officers to get around to informing a relative or friend of someone's arrest. The result is that the provisions on intimation, while embodying due process values, are not fully adhered to. However, since s 56(1) merely provides that intimation should be done 'as soon as is practicable', it is difficult for suspects to demonstrate that the law has been broken. Thus there are no reported cases on delay of intimation or refusal to intimate. Requests for phone calls also frequently appear to be informally delayed or ignored. Brown et al found that custody records recorded requests in 7–8% of cases, but they observed requests being made in 10–12% of cases.[20]

(c) Vulnerable suspects

Some people have very specific vulnerabilities, such as deafness or an inability to understand English. The custody officer must locate inter-preters for such people.[1] Suspects who are 'generally' vulnerable—ie juveniles, the mentally handicapped and the mentally disordered—have special protections, in recognition of their greater welfare needs and susceptibility to coercion or suggestion. It is no accident that in the 'Confait Affair' two of the wrongly convicted youths were juveniles, while the 18 year old had a mental age of 13.[2] The police must inform a 'responsible adult' of their detention and ask that person—usually a parent, guardian or social worker—to attend the station.[3] That respon-sible adult has several responsibilities: to see and advise the detainee in private, to request (if appropriate) a solicitor on the detainee's behalf and to attend interviews, offering advice as appropriate, ensuring fair-ness and facilitating communication. Interviews cannot take place without an appropriate adult except in the most extreme circumstances. Although there is some overlap with the role of a legal advisor (and in the early days of PACE, lawyers were frequently asked to fulfil the dual role) the securing of an appropriate adult in no way diminishes the suspect's legal right to separate legal advice. However, in practice the police are reluctant to call a lawyer until the appropriate adult arrives, even though such a delay is a clear breach of Code of Practice C.[4] An

[19] Ibid at 118.
[20] Brown et al, op cit p 55.
[1] Code of Practice C, op cit para 3.6.
[2] Baxter and Koffman, op cit.
[3] Code of Practice C, op cit paras 3.6–3.14.
[4] Ibid Note 3G. See Brown et al, op cit p 62.

appropriate adult may not arrive for several hours, by which time there is a major disincentive to further delay whilst waiting for a lawyer. The police know this, and sometimes exaggerate the likely delay in order to discourage requests for legal advice.[5]

Vulnerable suspects are by no means rare. In the most recent study, 17% of suspects were juveniles, and in some stations the percentage is far higher.[6] Whilst suspects with other vulnerabilities may appear to be few and far between, they are not always easy to identify. People with learning disabilities or other educational or social disadvantages often try to hide these problems, and thus learn to appear confident and capable.[7] Gudjonsson et al found that, in a sample of 156 adult detainees, the police only called responsible adults in 4% of cases. Yet the clinical psychologists in the research team identified 15% of the detainees as vulnerable after an interview of 10–15 minutes, and a further 5% after more extensive tests.[8] Clearly at present only a minority of vulnerable suspects secure the help they need from responsible adults, and even with the best will in the world substantial numbers will always be missed in the absence of duty psychologists in all busy stations. Even then, to dichotomise 'vulnerable' and 'normal' people in this way is unrealistic: when in police detention, most of us would be vulnerable to some extent, but often in unpredictable ways. The legal recognition of vulnerability raises major questions about detention, coercion and voluntariness, which we shall explore in due course.

There is no evidence that custody officers deliberately keep appropriate adults away from vulnerable suspects, but difficulties remain. Social workers have dual 'welfare' and 'control' roles, and since they have to work closely with the police they cannot be expected to act as the suspect's advocate. And many parents, in particular those with no experience of the police, misunderstand what is happening, fail to realise how an apparently innocent series of questions and answers can be incriminating and are as intimidated as are their children.[9] There is therefore often more of an illusion of protection than the reality. Thus Dixon et al say that some parents

[5] A Sanders and L Bridges, 'Access to Legal Advice and Police Malpractice' [1990] Crim LR 494; Brown et al, op cit pp 31–34.

[6] Brown et al, op cit p 70.

[7] Examples include the 'Tottenham Three' case (*Re Raghip, Silcott and Braithwaite* (1991) Times, 9 December) and the 'Cardiff Three' case (*Re Paris, Abdullahi and Miller* (1992) Times, 24 December).

[8] G Gudjonsson, I Clare, S Rutter and J Pearse, Persons at Risk during Interviews in Police Custody: the Identification of Vulnerabilities (Royal Commission on Criminal Justice Research Study no 12) (HMSO, 1993).

[9] Brown et al, op cit p 72.

'are notoriously keen to help the police in obtaining confessions from their children. In one incident a mother promised to "get my fist round his lug" (which she later did . . . much to the approval of the investigating officers).'[10]

This partly reflects the contradictions in Code of Practice C about the role of the appropriate adult, which is, inter alia, 'to advise' and 'to facilitate communication'.[11] It may be proper to advise a suspect to remain silent (especially if no lawyer is present) but this cannot be said to facilitate communication. Hence not only parents, but also professional social workers, are left not understanding their proper role. The police do not help here, often failing even to try to explain to suspects and appropriate adults what is expected of them, despite the stipulation in Code of Practice C that they do so.[12]

(d) Police powers[13]

Custody officers have to decide whether the offence for which the person was arrested was a 'serious arrestable offence' or not. Serious arrestable offences are defined in s 116 of PACE and include murder, treason, rape, and various firearms offences.[14] Other arrestable offences can also be regarded as serious if their commission has led, or is intended to lead, to one of various consequences. These include serious harm to any person or serious financial gain to any person.[15] Serious harm or serious loss is defined as 'if, having regard to all the circumstances, it is serious for the person who suffers it.'[16] Thus a very poor person stealing a small amount might be regarded as making a substantial financial gain, where this would not be true if a rich person stole the same amount. And a relatively minor theft from a very poor person could be a serious arrestable offence, while the same value theft from a rich person would not be. Thus in *McIvor*[17] and *Smith*[18] thefts from a Hunt of 28 dogs worth £800, and from a shop of goods worth £916 respectively, were not regarded as serious arrestable offences. The

---

[10] Dixon et al, op cit p 119.
[11] Code of Practice C, op cit para 11.16.
[12] Ibid paras 2.12 and 11.16. See Brown et al, op cit p 72.
[13] Again, there will be no attempt here to provide comprehensive coverage of police powers. See, for a detailed discussion, V Bevan and K Lidstone, *The Investigation of Crime* (Butterworths, 1991).
[14] See Sch 5 of PACE for a full list.
[15] PACE, s 116.
[16] PACE, s 116(7).
[17] [1987] Crim LR 409.
[18] [1987] Crim LR 579.

relativistic definition of 'serious arrestable offence' provides enormous scope for subjective interpretation. We shall see later what the consequences are of an offence being defined by a custody officer as 'serious'.

Now that the purpose of arrest and detention is recognised to be to facilitate interrogation, PACE has introduced a new regime for interrogation aimed at eliminating the abuses which used sometimes to occur. The police may interrogate several times in any period of detention, subject to the rights of the suspect outlined above. But they may normally only do so in a room equipped for this purpose with tape recording facilities, in the presence of an appropriate adult (where the suspect is 'vulnerable') and in the presence of a legal advisor (if requested by the suspect). It is the responsibility of the custody officer to ensure that all these conditions are met. The custody officer also has to decide whether to seek authorisation for further periods of detention and whether to allow other powers (such as intimate and non-intimate searches, house searches, identification parades, final charge or custody following charge) to be exercised.

The police have even more powers in relation to suspects arrested under the prevention of terrorism legislation. These suspects have fewer rights than do 'normal' suspects, even though they are put under particularly great pressure as a result of the crimes of which they are suspected. Some powers in respect of these suspects are difficult to reconcile with international human rights standards.[19]

(e)   Police bail

Suspects who have no action taken against them or who are immediately cautioned (ie officially warned) are released unconditionally from detention. In all other cases, custody officers have to decide whether or not to grant bail. Bail may be granted if the police wish to make further inquiries or to consider whether or not to charge, in which case the suspect is given a date and time to return to the station.[20] This is common in some forces in relation to juvenile suspects, where the choice between prosecution, caution and no action at all is often considered by a multi-agency juvenile bureau.[1]

The main time when bail is considered is after suspects are charged with criminal offences.[2] The custody officer must order release, in most cases, unless certain conditions are satisfied, namely

---

[19]   See B Dickson, 'The Prevention of Terrorism Acts' in C Walker and K Starmer (eds), *Justice in Error* (Blackstone, 1993).
[20]   PACE, s 34(5).
[1]   Discussed more fully in ch 5, below.
[2]   PACE, s 38; Magistrates' Court Act 1980, s 43, as amended by PACE, s 47.

(a) if the suspects's name and address cannot be ascertained;
(b) if the suspect is regarded as unlikely to appear in court to answer the charge;
(c) if interference with witnesses or further investigation is likely; or
(d) if it is thought that the suspect would commit an offence if released.

If one of these conditions is satisfied, the custody officer may keep the suspect in custody until the next magistrates' court hearing.

These provisions echo the general arrest conditions in s 25.[3] Most of them require custody officers to predict what might happen if the suspect is released. These predictions are based on what they are told by the arresting or investigating officers and what little may be known about a suspect's previous record of appearing at court, offending on bail and so forth. It is impossible for suspects to prove that they would not do something wrong if released. Essentially, decisions are taken quickly on the basis of inadequate information. Although this is done by independent custody officers, whose job is to protect suspects from the possible partisanship of arresting officers, most of the information used will come from those very officers. Moreover, assessment of the quality of the information on which decision making is based is almost impossible.

The decision to grant or withhold bail after charge is almost entirely one for the police. One reason why many suspects may be denied bail is that the police often want conditions attached to bail—for instance, that the suspect not contact a particular witness. Conditions can be attached by a court[4] but not by the police. The Criminal Justice and Public Order Bill contains provisions to give the police this power, which may reduce the numbers held in custody by them. The drawback is that this change in the law will give the police considerable power to control the movements of released suspects. Most suspects are more concerned about securing bail than they are about being charged.[5] Not only is a night in the cells unpleasant, but it makes it more difficult to secure court bail, which, in turn, might reduce the chances of securing acquittal or a non-custodial sentence.[6] This makes bail an important bargaining counter, particularly in relation to confessions.[7] Legal

---

[3] See ch 3, section 3(b) above.
[4] See ch 6, section 4(a), below, where the principles regarding bail are discussed fully.
[5] A Sanders, L Bridges, A Mulvaney and G Crozier, Advice and Assistance at Police Stations and the 24 Hour Duty Solicitor Scheme (Lord Chancellor's Department, 1989) pp 72–73.
[6] R Morgan and S Jones, 'Bail or Jail?' in E Stockdale and S Casale (eds), *Criminal Justice Under Stress* (Blackstone, 1992).
[7] See section 5 below, in particular section 5(h), and the extract from an informal interview quoted there.

advisors can make representations about bail to the police, but few are present when the decision is made.[8] Giving the police the power to make conditions will provide them with a new stack of bargaining chips.

3.   DETENTION WITHOUT CHARGE

(a)   'Helping the police with their inquiries'

According to s 29 of PACE, anyone who is at a police station voluntarily (ie not there under arrest):

'(a) shall be entitled to leave at will unless he is placed under arrest;
 (b) shall be informed at once that he is under arrest if a decision is taken by a constable to prevent him leaving at will.'

This is at first sight an odd provision for all it is saying is that if someone is not under arrest—that is, not deprived of their liberty—then they are not to be deprived of their liberty. This appears to be tautologous, and can only be understood in its historical context.

Historically the police have been reluctant to arrest suspects against whom they had not enough evidence to allow them to lay charges immediately. Bevan and Lidstone point out that before 1964 a suspect normally had to be charged immediately following arrest and could not be interrogated first.[9] Arrest marked the end of the investigation, and its purpose was to enable the suspect to be brought to court. The solution for the police who needed extra evidence through, for instance, interrogation was to put people in a situation where they could be interrogated without formally arresting them. Even then, the fiction that the police did not interrogate was still maintained, through the mechanism of the 'voluntary statement' of confession. This might mean detaining someone at their home or another place, or in the police station. There were numerous court cases concerned with whether someone could be detained without being 'arrested'. The limbo in which such people were placed was known as 'helping the police with their inquiries', generally understood to mean people who were involuntarily detained but not formally arrested. A revision to the Judges Rules in 1964 made it easier for the police to interrogate following arrest but it was still common for suspects to 'help the police with their inquiries'. Section 29 is designed to make it absolutely clear that this limbo is no longer allowed.

[8]   See section 4, below.
[9]   Op cit pp 215–218.

Taken on its own, s 29 appears to be an inhibitory rule providing more due process for suspects than had existed hitherto. However, we need to see how far it has really affected police practices, and how the other provisions of PACE affect detention before charge. McKenzie et al looked at three different police force areas, and found that in two of those areas there were indeed very few people in the police station voluntarily who were under suspicion by the police. In the other area, however, about a third of all suspects were there as 'volunteers'—ie they were there 'helping the police with their inquiries'.[10] In a quarter of the police forces surveyed by McKenzie et al, there were formal arrangements for dealing with 'voluntary' attenders. Contrary to the words of s 29, 'voluntary' attenders are not generally free to leave. As a police inspector told McKenzie at al:

'The problem is whether the people actually believe they can leave. I think about fifty per cent of them are convinced that they wouldn't be allowed to and the truth is they wouldn't.'[11]

That the police are guided more by their crime control 'needs' than by the due process values in the law is indicated by a Scottish study showing that after pre-charge detention of only six hours was introduced in Scotland, one third of all suspects (and in one area, over half) were 'volunteers' in 1981–84.[12] So when the police wish to process suspects as 'voluntary attenders', it appears that s 29 has little inhibitory effect. This renders it largely presentational, giving the appearance of due process whilst not affecting police behaviour in practice. That s 29 is not flouted more often is due to the fact that the 24-hour detention time limit which applies for most offences (see next section) is usually more than adequate for police purposes.

(b) Time limits for detention

Under s 41(1) of PACE, if the offence is not a serious arrestable offence then the suspect may be detained without charge for up to 24 hours after the 'relevant time'. For serious arrestable offences, s 42(1) provides that detention may be for up to 36 hours initially. The 'relevant time' is usually the time of arrival at the police station, but not for 'volunteers',

---

[10] I McKenzie, R Morgan and R Reiner, 'Helping the Police with their Enquiries' [1990] Crim LR 22.

[11] Ibid p 32.

[12] J Curran and J Carnie, Detention or Voluntary Attendance ?: Police Use of Detention under section 2 of the Criminal Justice (Scotland) Act 1980 (Scottish Office) (HMSO, 1986).

for whom it is the time of arrest.[13] It is this provision that gives the police the incentive to maintain the 'helping with inquiries' fiction that McKenzie et al discovered. As a detective sergeant told the researchers: '. . . it's convenient because you set the time and . . . it avoids the time clock consideration. If arrest is necessary later, it doesn't count.'[14]

Detention has to be reviewed periodically. Firstly, a senior officer independent of the investigation (usually the custody officer) must review the detention 'not later than 6 hours after the detention was first authorised'.[15] The second review must be 'not later than 9 hours after the first' and subsequent reviews must be at intervals of not more than nine hours.[16] To extend detention beyond 24 hours (in the case of serious arrestable offences) the review must be conducted by an officer of superintendent rank or above. Reviews may be postponed but only under exceptional circumstances and for as short a time as is practicable. The reviewing officer may only authorise continued detention if the original purpose of detention still holds good and if the investigation is being conducted 'diligently and expeditiously'.[17] The reviewing officer must take note of any representations against continued detention which the suspect may make.[18] In reality, though:

'the review procedure tends to be routinised and insubstantial, at least in its early stages; the opportunity to make representations can often consist merely of an inspector asking the suspect, "All right mate?" through the hatch in the cell door.'[19]

Indeed, reviews may take place over the telephone if the review officer is not at the station.[20] Rather than this being exceptional, as was doubtless intended, Dixon et al found this to be common. Moreover, custody record entries often failed to note this use of the telephone, giving the impression that the review was carried out in the normal way. Frequently, they say, 'the inspector's role is purely presentational',[1] which could be said of the rules on reviews as a whole.

If the police wish to continue the detention beyond 36 hours (in the case of serious arrestable offences) this is possible, up to a maximum of

---

[13] Unusual circumstances can affect the operation of these rules, making it an extremely complicated area of law. See Bevan and Lidstone, op cit pp 308–313.
[14] Op cit p 31.
[15] PACE, s 40(3)(a).
[16] PACE, s 40(3)(b)–(c).
[17] PACE, s 42(1)(c).
[18] PACE, s 40(12)–(14).
[19] D Dixon, K Bottomley, C Coleman, M Gill and D Wall, 'Safeguarding the Rights of Suspects in Police Custody' (1990) 1 Policing and Society 115, at pp 130–131.
[20] Code of Practice C, op cit Note 15C.
[1] Dixon et al, op cit at 131.

a further 60 hours.[2] The same criteria apply as above, but authorisation must be by an officer of the rank of superintendent or above, and the police must apply to a magistrates' court for a 'warrant of further detention'.[3] This application must generally be made before the 36-hour period has expired but, in exceptional circumstances, there is some leeway. The criteria on which magistrates decide whether or not to grant such a warrant are broadly similar to the criteria which the superintendent must apply under s 42 in deciding whether to authorise continued detention in the first place. If the police still wish to detain a suspect without charge after the period of further detention has expired, they may apply to a magistrate again for an extension of the warrant for further detention. Such an extension may be granted by a magistrate under s 44 as long as that extension is neither exceeds 36 hours nor ends later than 96 hours after the initial 'relevant time'.[4] This means that the police may apply for, and secure, two warrants of further detention following the initial 36-hour detention. But 96 hours is the overall maximum permissible length of detention without charge.

It is rare for the police to request these warrants. In 1990, for instance, there were only 405 applications. When warrants are requested they are invariably granted (only four were refused in 1990). This is to be expected, since the magistrates apply the same criteria as the police and on the basis of information which the police provide. While the suspect will usually be legally represented, there are few grounds on which defence arguments can be made for release. For instance, if there is little evidence against a suspect, this would scarcely ever justify release since the point of the extended detention is precisely to secure more evidence.

The fact that detention beyond 24 hours is rare does not necessarily mean that the safeguards are adequate. The police usually have no reason to detain suspects once they consider that they have obtained full information from the suspect concerning the alleged offence. To detain any further would be inefficient. Occasionally, though, the police may wish to prolong detention, regardless of evidential or other legal considerations (as where they are seeking information on other suspects). The detention provisions, and the way in which legal duties are carried out by senior police officers, gives them the scope to do almost as they see fit in those few cases of such importance to them.

Whether the offence is a serious arrestable offence or not the suspect must be released when either the period of detention expires or when detention is no longer necessary because the original reason for

---

[2] PACE, ss 42–43.
[3] PACE, s 43.
[4] PACE, s 44(3).

detention no longer applies. Release is either unconditional, on bail to return to the police station pending further inquiries or (having been charged) on bail to appear in court. The only circumstances in which the suspect would not be released would be if he or she was charged and kept in custody pending the earliest available court hearing.[5] Suspects who are released because the time limit has been reached cannot be rearrested without warrant for the same offence unless new evidence is uncovered after release.[6]

When suspects are released on bail to return to the police station, further inquiries will have been made in the meantime. If those inquiries produce more evidence, the police are entitled to 'start the clock' where it had previously been 'stopped'. If they do not, the police should not (in principle) have any further cause to detain the suspect. However, PACE provides that the clock may be started again from the place it had reached at the time of release, even if further inquiries produced no new evidence.[7]

One of the purposes of this part of PACE was to shorten the length of detention, in the interests both of suspects and police efficiency. Because there were no proper records prior to PACE it is difficult to know whether PACE has succeeded in this objective or not. However, studies by Maguire, Bottomley at al and Brown enable us to make some estimates. Maguire found that the average length of detention following the introduction of PACE was three to six hours for suspects who were charged and two to five hours for suspects who were not charged. Within these broad figures, however, individual offences differed greatly: the average for shoplifting was two and a half hours, while the average for robbery and burglary was 16 hours. Maguire concludes that PACE has probably led to longer detention lengths for people who would otherwise have been kept in for very short periods but quite possibly shorter periods of detention for those who would otherwise have been kept in for long periods of time.[8] The other research is broadly consistent with Maguire's findings, and so it seems that the overwhelming majority of arrestees are held for less than nine hours, and over half for less than six hours.[9] In very few cases is the 24-hour limit a problem, and so in serious cases the extra time is rarely needed

---

[5]   The question of police bail is discussed in section 2(e) above.

[6]   PACE, s 41(9).

[7]   PACE, s 47(5)–(6).

[8]   M Maguire, 'Effects of the PACE provisions on Detention and Questioning' (1988) 28 BJ Crim 19.

[9]   D Brown, Detention at the Police Station under the Police and Criminal Evidence Act 1984 (Home Office Research Study no 104) (HMSO, 1989). Also see K Bottomley, C Coleman, D Dixon, M Gill and D Wall, 'The Detention of Suspects in Police Custody' (1991) 31 BJ Crim 347.

either. The reason for these changed lengths of detention is partly because the police now avoid long periods of detention. Unless the offence is a 'serious arrestable', the 24 hour limit is absolute, and even the periodic reviews may concentrate investigating officers' minds. But few people are held for only a brief period partly because of the length of time it takes to complete the paperwork and partly because of the greater numbers seeking legal advice.

Detention of less than six hours in most cases appears not to be excessive. However, the subjective experience of suspects is rather different. Sanders et al found that the most important factor affecting suspects' decisions whether to ask for legal advice was the likely length of detention.[10] Being held overnight, in particular, was regarded with horror. Moreover, the fact that length of detention (up to 24 hours) is in the hands of the police leads suspects to believe that the police 'can do anything they want. They can keep you in overnight if they want'[11]. The significance of detention lengths is not so much the actual detention length but the threat created by the 24 hour limit. The subjective experience of 'only' six hours detention and of the threat of longer detention is not something which legislators or judges are ever likely to have endured.

(c) The purpose of detention

Now that we have examined the mechanisms for authorising and reviewing detention, we need to examine the criteria used to decide whether or not detention should be authorised or continued. Under s 37 of PACE, it is the custody officer's duty to:

'(1)... determine whether he has before him sufficient evidence to charge that person with the offence for which he was arrested and may detain him at the police station for such period as is necessary to enable him to do so.

(2) If the custody officer determines that he does not have such evidence before him the person arrested shall be released either on bail or without bail, unless the custody officer has reasonable grounds for believing that his detention without being charged is necessary to secure or preserve evidence relating to an offence for which he is under arrest or to obtain such evidence by questioning him.

---

[10] A Sanders, L Bridges, A Mulvaney and G Crozier, Advice and Assistance at Police Stations and the 24 Hour Duty Solicitor Scheme (Lord Chancellor's Department, 1989); D Brown, T Ellis and K Larcombe, Changing the Code: Police Detention under the Revised PACE Codes of Practice (Home Office Research Study no 129 (HMSO, 1992) also found this to be suspects' most frequently expressed concern.

[11] Sanders et al, op cit p 77.

(3) If the custody officer has reasonable grounds for so believing he may authorise the person arrested to be kept in police detention.'

These provisions broadly follow the Philips Commission's recommendations and embody its 'necessity principle'. We saw in the chapter on arrest that the Philips Commission believed that many suspects who were arrested and charged could be reported and summonsed instead. It wished to ensure that arrests which led to detention would only be made when necessary. Thus, the Commission stated: 'We do seek to alter the practice whereby the inevitable sequence on the creation of reasonable suspicion is arrest, followed by being taken to the station.'[12] The introduction of a necessity principle into detention logically followed the necessity principle in arrest.

The government, however, only followed the recommendation in relation to detention, producing the strange situation that the police may arrest even when it is not necessary for them to do so but may only detain when it is necessary to do so, except in those (fairly rare) cases when people are to be charged immediately. At least half of all arrested suspects are detained for questioning.[13] In these cases, if the arrests were on reasonable grounds but unnecessary, arrest will be lawful but detention following the arrest would not be lawful. This puts the police, and the custody officer in particular, into a difficult position. For s 37(2) provides that persons who are arrested shall be released unless it is regarded as necessary 'to secure or preserve evidence . . . or to obtain such evidence by questioning.' The presumption in s 37 is that detention should not be authorised, and only if this presumption can be rebutted should detention be authorised. As the then Home Secretary, Douglas Hurd, said in Parliament in 1984, the question is whether 'this detention was necessary—not desirable, convenient or a good idea but necessary.'[14]

The scenario envisaged here—of large numbers of perfectly lawful arrests being negatived by custody officers refusing to authorise detention—is not a likely scenario, nor does it correspond with reality. In every relevant piece of research, virtually all arresting officers were successful in having their suspects detained. Many of the custody officers interviewed by McConville et al expressed surprise that the detention decision could be anything other than automatic. Thus one, when pressed on whether he would ever refuse to authorise detention, replied: 'Probably not in practice, no'. Another said:

---

[12] Royal Commission on Criminal Procedure, Report (Cmnd 8092-1) (HMSO, 1981) para 3.75.
[13] Brown et al, op cit p 90.
[14] HC Official Report, SC E, 16 February 1984, col 1229.

'Often the bloke's remonstrating saying "Not me, it wasn't me. I haven't done it, you've got the wrong man", but of course I have to take the policeman's word, so I accept him on what the policeman tells me.'[15]

As Dixon et al comment after finding not one refusal of detention in their research, 'reception into custody has become an essentially routinised process'.[16] Most custody officers simply write out the words of s 37 and some have even asked for a rubber stamp with these words already on it.[17]

We have seen that the function and place of arrest in relation to investigation has changed over time: whereas at one time arrests came at the end of an investigation and were the inevitable prelude to prosecution, arrest has gradually moved nearer to the beginning of the investigation. Arrest can be, and often is, on the basis of reasonable suspicion, and since that will not suffice to prosecute, the law now envisages that the police will frequently need to get more evidence in order to prosecute.[18] This development occurred gradually and along with this, of course, came the limbo of 'helping the police with their inquiries'. Section 37 of PACE formalises the process by recognising that suspects will be detained without charge following arrest when there is insufficient evidence to prosecute and that the main purpose of this detention is to secure that evidence. This reinforces the decision in *Holgate-Mohammed v Duke*,[19] where the House of Lords ruled that the greater likelihood of confession if a suspect was held at a police station was a legitimate reason for detention, and is entirely consistent with the crime control model. It is, however, entirely inconsistent with the due process presumption in s 37 against detention. Securing evidence through interrogation is rarely necessary, but it is considerably more convenient for the police than securing evidence in most other ways. As investigation is envisaged usually as taking place during detention, the authorisation of detention must be the norm. The presumption against detention in s 37 is thus entirely presentational since it goes against the crime control grain of the rest of the law and practice in this area.

---

[15] M McConville, A Sanders and R Leng, *The Case for the Prosecution* (Routledge, 1991) p 44.

[16] D Dixon, K Bottomley, C Coleman, M Gill and D Wall, 'Safeguarding the Rights of Suspects in Police Custody' (1990) 1 Policing and Society 115 at 130.

[17] I McKenzie, R Morgan and R Reiner, 'Helping the Police with their Enquiries' [1990] Crim LR at 24.

[18] This is in fact the reality: M McConville, Corroboration and Confessions. The Impact of a Rule that no Conviction can be Sustained on the Basis of Confession Evidence Alone (Royal Commission on Criminal Justice Research Study no 13) (HMSO, 1993).

[19] [1984] AC 437, discussed in ch 3, section 5.

It seems then that—rather than the police carrying out the law as made by Parliament—Parliament makes laws aimed at legitimising existing police practice (as happened in successive revisions of the Judges' Rules). What was once part of a judicial process (arrest followed by the prosecution decision) is now part of an Executive process. Not only does this mean that the police make initial decisions relating to detention (as we have seen, up to 36 hours without judicial authority) but in nearly half of all cases this detention is not followed by any judicial proceedings.[20] The Royal Commission on Criminal Justice (Runciman Commission) appeared to be aware of this situation but simply recommended that proper figures be kept.[1] On the fundamental issues of the basis for authorisation of detention, voluntary attendance and reviews of detention, the Runciman Commission was silent.

4.   THE RIGHT TO LEGAL ADVICE

Prior to PACE, access to legal advice was governed by the Judges' Rules. The preamble to the Rules stated that it was an established principle that a suspected person should be able to consult privately with a solicitor provided that it caused the police no unreasonable 'hinderance'. This principle was not easy to operate in practice. Firstly, the Judges' Rules were not 'law' in the sense of being common law or statute. No specific enforcement power was provided, so all that a suspect who was denied access to legal advice could do was to ask for the evidence obtained as a result to be excluded from trial, if there was one. The second problem was the proviso in the Rules which allowed denial of access if it would be likely to cause 'unreasonable hinderance'. What was or was not reasonable was never clearly established. Thirdly, as confirmed by the Fisher inquiry into the 'Confait Affair', many suspects (including the wrongly convicted youths in that case) did not know they had such a right. Elsewhere in the Judges Rules, one of the 'administrative directions' placed an obligation on the police to inform suspects of this right, but in the Fisher inquiry many police officers claimed not to know about this. Fisher quotes a deputy assistant commissioner of the Metropolitan Police saying that 'it has never been recognised by the police . . . as a

---

[20]   McConville et al, op cit p 104, found that only 58% of detained adults and 35% of detained juveniles were prosecuted. Since that study was carried out, in the late 1980s, the caution rate has continued to rise, leading to even smaller proportions being prosecuted in the 1990s (see ch 5).

[1]   Royal Commission on Criminal Justice, Report (Cm 2263) (HMSO, 1993) p 30.

duty to tell a prisoner . . . that he has the right to consult a solicitor'.[2]

Thus, few suspects were informed by officers of this right, fewer tried to exercise it and fewer still had their requests granted. There are no reliable estimates of the proportion of suspects who used to secure legal advice, but in Softley's study of four police stations, around 9% sought advice and around 7% actually secured it.[3] Even these figures are artificially high, for in one of these police stations the police were told (for the purposes of the research) that they had to inform all suspects of their right to a solicitor, whereas in the other three stations they were not so directed. In the station in which suspects were routinely informed of their rights, the numbers requesting and securing access were considerably higher than in the others. As one would expect, being told one's rights is vital. The Philips Commission recognised this. Its recommendations, which aimed to make the right to advice truly available to all, were implemented by the government in PACE.

(a) The right to advice under PACE

Section 58 of PACE states the right of access in the clearest possible terms:

'(1) A person arrested . . . shall be entitled, if he so requests, to consult a solicitor privately at any time.
. . .

(4) If a person makes such a request, he must be permitted to consult a solicitor as soon as is practicable except to the extent that delay is permitted by this section.
. . .

(6) Delay in compliance with a request is only permitted—
  (a) in the case of a person who is in police detention for a serious arrestable offence; and
  (b) if an officer of at least the rank of superintendent authorises it.'

This differs in a number of important respects from the formulation which used to exist in the Judges' Rules. The fact that this is a statutory provision makes it unequivocal, although as we shall see there is still no

---

[2] Sir H Fisher, Report of an Inquiry into the Circumstances leading to the Trial of Three Persons on Charges arising out of the Death of Maxwell Confait and the Fire at 27 Doggett Road, London SE6 (HCP 90) (HMSO, 1977). It is now generally acknowledged by the police 'establishment' that the Judges' Rules were frequently broken by the police. See the speech by Sir John Woodcock (Chief Inspector of Constabulary), quoted in M Zander, 'Ethics and Criminal Investigation by the Police' (unpublished manuscript).

[3] P Softley, Police Interrogation: An Observational Study in Four Police Stations (Royal Commission on Criminal Procedure Research Study no 4) (HMSO, 1981).

enforcement mechanism and no remedy available to suspects who are denied this right. Secondly, the exception provided in sub-s 6 to the right to advice is reasonably tightly drawn. Thirdly, even this exception does not allow advice to be refused but merely delayed. All suspects must be permitted, if they wish, to consult a solicitor within 36 hours (the period beyond which suspects cannot be held without the authorisation of a magistrate).[4] Section 58 applies only to arrested persons, thus excluding 'volunteers'. We have seen that many volunteers are in fact suspects and as in need of legal advice as arrested detainees. Since 'volunteers' are, technically, free to go, however, they are free to do as they please in any lawful way, including insisting on seeing a lawyer. Should the police prevent them from doing so, they would then be deemed to be under arrest.

The 'right to consult a solicitor privately at any time' is a powerful one. It means that there is a right to see a solicitor in person and not be overheard. Suspects who initially decline a solicitor can demand one later, even in the middle of an interview. And suspects can require that the solicitor be present in the interview and may consult with that solicitor (publicly or privately) during it.[5] There are obvious potential difficulties here. One is that the interview might be unduly delayed while waiting for a solicitor. If the consequences would be truly serious (bearing in mind the 24-hour limit in most cases) an officer of the rank of superintendent or above may authorise the interview in the solicitor's absence.[6] If a lawyer's advice and assistance in the interview is such that the police are 'unable properly to put questions to the suspect', the lawyer can be required to leave, but only if authorised by a superintendent, and an opportunity must be given to the suspect to be represented by a replacement lawyer.[7]

Delaying access

Section 58(8) of PACE provides that:

'. . . an officer may only authorise delay where he has reasonable grounds for believing that the exercise of the right . . .
  (a) will lead to interference with or harm to evidence . . .; or
  (b) will lead to the alerting of other persons suspected of having committed such an offence . . .; or
  (c) will hinder the recovery of any property obtained as a result of such an offence.'[8]

---

[4] PACE, s 58(5).
[5] Code of Practice C, op cit para 6.8.
[6] Ibid para 6.6.
[7] Ibid paras 6.9 and 6.10.
[8] Section 58(8A) also provides for delay in relation to certain offences relating to drugs.

In the first few years of the operation of PACE, it was not clear, when a suspect was being held for a serious arrestable offence, how broad these delaying powers were. In *Re Walters*,[9] for instance, the defendant was suspected of a drugs offence and access was delayed because the police feared that co-conspirators might be alerted by using a solicitor as an innocent agent. Deciding that only manifestly unreasonable decisions should be interfered with by the courts, the delay was endorsed by the Divisional Court.

However, in *Samuel*[10] the situation changed. The defendant (D) asked for a solicitor, but access was delayed on the grounds that he had been arrested for a serious arrestable offence and that witnesses or evidence could be interfered with if D saw a solicitor. The police had no particular reason to fear this, but stated that it was possible. By the time D saw his solicitor, he had purportedly confessed. The concerns of the police about D seeing a solicitor in this case were particularly unfortunate, because the solicitor concerned had recently been appointed a Crown Court Recorder and imputations of dishonesty or incompetence would have been extremely hard to substantiate. The Court of Appeal took an unsympathetic view of the police's argument and held that in order to justify delay under s 58 the police would have to demonstrate some reason to believe that, in the particular case, access could lead to one of the specified consequences. The Court of Appeal went on to note that if, as in this case, the solicitor was a duty solicitor (ie not known to the suspect) this would be virtually impossible for the police to prove, since neither the police nor the suspect would know who that individual was until such time as he or she arrived at the police station. The Court of Appeal therefore held that the delay of access was unlawful.[11]

As we observed earlier in this chapter, 'serious arrestable offence' is a vague term which gave rise to great fear, prior to the enactment of PACE, that it would be abused. Cases like *Walters* gave some substance to this fear, but *Samuel* and the cases which followed it reversed that trend. In 1987, delay was authorised in around 1% of all cases (that is, in around half of all serious arrestable offences),[12] but in more recent research, conducted in 1990–91, delay was authorised in only one case

---

[9] [1987] Crim LR 577.

[10] [1988] 2 All ER 135.

[11] In *Alladice* (1988) 87 Cr App Rep 380 the (differently constituted) Court of Appeal regarded itself as bound by *Samuel* but was rather more sympathetic to the police. This led them to a different view of the consequences following on from unlawful delay of access: see ch 9, section 4(b), below.

[12] D Brown, Detention at the Police Station under the Police and Criminal Evidence Act 1984 (Home Office Research Study no 104) (HMSO, 1989) p 68.

out of over 10,000.[13] We shall see later on that the problem now is not formal delay of access but the informal delay which results from the police bending or breaking the rules.

Notification of the right to advice

As we saw before, not all suspects know their rights. Code of Practice C is intended to deal with this:

'3.1   When a person is brought to a police station under arrest or is arrested at the police station having attended there voluntarily the custody officer must inform him clearly of the following rights and of the fact that they are continuing rights . . .

(i)   The right to have someone informed of his arrest . . .

(ii)   The right to consult privately with a solicitor . . . and that the fact that independent legal advice is available free of charge; and

(iii)   The right to consult this and the other codes of practice.

3.2   The custody officer must give the person a written notice setting out the above three rights . . . The notice must also the explain the arrangements for obtaining legal advice . . .'

This should ensure that arrested suspects are told their rights (including that legal advice is free) orally and in a written form. But there are two important loopholes here. Firstly, volunteers need not usually be told their rights, despite the many suspects persuaded to 'help with inquiries'. Secondly, the obligation begins only when the suspect is brought to the police station. Suspects who are arrested a long way from the place of the alleged crime are therefore in police custody for a long time, whilst being transported to the relevant police station, before they are informed of their rights other than the right to silence. This should not matter, since interviewing is prohibited before arrival at the station (discussed later). But illegal interviewing sometimes occurs anyway, and there is no prohibition on letting suspects incriminate themselves voluntarily—if that is an appropriate way of describing the actions of suspects in police custody. Thus in *Khan*[14] the defendant was arrested in Wales and driven to Birmingham by the police who alleged that he voluntarily confessed in the car.

The procedure to be adopted on arrival at the station is as follows.

---

13   D Brown, T Ellis and K Larcombe, Changing the Code: Police Detention under the Revised PACE Codes of Practice (Home Office Research Study no 129) (HMSO, 1992) p 68.

14   (1990) unreported, CA. Discussed in T Kaye, 'Unsafe and Unsatisfactory?' Report of the Independent Inquiry into the Working Practices of the West Midlands Police Serious Crime Squad (Civil Liberties Trust, 1991).

After authorising detention, custody officers must tell suspects of their rights. They will be asked specifically whether they want to consult a solicitor. If so, a solicitor must be contacted as soon as possible. Every step in this process must be recorded on the custody record. For this set of protections to work it is essential that the police operate the system in good faith, and that a solicitor be readily available.

The 24-hour duty solicitor scheme

It is one thing to provide suspects with a right to advice but delivering the advice is another matter entirely. Solicitors are obviously not available around the clock and many suspects are arrested at night, weekends or other awkward times. Before PACE this was a major problem. In Softley's study, around one-quarter of all suspects who requested advice did not get any. This was sometimes because the police refused to let them see a solicitor, but often a solicitor simply could not be found. There was a clear need to provide some form of scheme which secured access within a reasonable amount of time for the sake of both the suspect and the police so that unreasonable delay was not caused. This was bound to cost a lot of money. To the government's credit, it undertook to provide such money as was required.

Suspects requesting legal advice may choose to speak to their 'own' lawyer (if any) or may choose from a list of local lawyers which the police provide. In either case the custody officer will phone the lawyer and ask him or her to speak to the suspect on the phone or to come to the station. If the suspect does not favour either of these alternatives, or if the chosen solicitor is unavailable, a duty solicitor can be requested. The country is divided into a number of legal aid regions, within each of which are several areas. Each area has, or should have, a duty solicitor scheme.[15]

When a duty solicitor is requested, the custody sergeant will not phone a solicitor directly. Instead, a telephone referral service is contacted. The service informs a duty solicitor of the suspect's request for legal advice. Local schemes are organised by local Law Societies, but there is no obligation on solicitors to participate. The result is still a (very) few areas not covered by schemes, some areas where schemes have collapsed and others where there are too few solicitors on the scheme. Consequently, duty solicitors cannot always get to the police station quickly, and sometimes fail to get there at all.[16] All police

---

[15] These were originally established under s 59 of PACE. See now the Legal Aid Board Duty Solicitor Arrangements 1992.

[16] A Sanders, L Bridges, A Mulvaney and G Crozier, Advice and Assistance at Police Stations and the 24 Hour Duty Solicitor Scheme, (Lord Chancellor's Department, 1989).

station work, whether done on a private or duty solicitor basis, is paid for by the state on an hourly basis at no cost to the suspect.

(b)   The takeup of advice by suspects

Solicitors who are able and willing will phone the police station and speak to the suspect or come directly to the station or do both. But of those suspects who request advice, only around three-quarters actually secure it. This proportion has remained fairly constant despite a significant increase in the request rate after a revised code of practice came into operation in 1991:[17]

Table 4.1: Request and consultation rates 1988–91

	Request rate %	Consultation rate %
1988	25	19
1990	24	18
1991	32	25

Within these general figures, there are considerable variations. For instance, advice is sought more often for serious than for minor offences, and advice is sought and received in over half of all cases involving offences tried in the Crown Court.[18] This is understandable, unlike the great variations which persist between different police stations.[19]

Despite the general increase, only a minority of suspects exercise their right to advice, and fewer still actually secure it. This seems difficult to understand at first sight. Nearly all are in the police station involuntarily. Most will be frightened or apprehensive, unsure of their rights and worried about how long they will be detained. Many perceive the police to be 'against' them—as of course they are in an adversarial system. Against this intimidating backcloth they are being offered something for nothing: a lawyer, whose sole job whilst in the

---

[17] 1988 figures from Sanders et al, op cit; 1990 and 1991 figures from Brown et al, op cit. Note that Brown's figures cited here are of his general custody record survey; his smaller study of 'observed' cases show much higher rates of request (33% and 41% in 1990 and 1991, respectively).

[18] Royal Commission on Criminal Justice, Report (Cm 2263) (HMSO, 1993) p 35.

[19] Brown et al, op cit.

station will be to help that suspect, at precisely nil cost. Yet the response of the majority is to say 'no thanks'.

In the earliest study of PACE, Maguire observed that some suspects have a predisposition to seek advice while others do not, and some are very much easier to influence than are others.[20] Suspects arrested for trivial offences like drunkenness are entitled to advice but they correctly perceive that it would be of little use to them. There is a low elasticity of demand among these suspects. Other suspects who reject the idea of legal advice include those who are confident that they can handle the situation and, at the opposite end of the spectrum, fatalistic suspects who believe that nothing can help them at all. Needless to say, neither the confidence nor the fatalism are always justified. Some suspects simply trust the police to deal with them so fairly that they see no need for advice or help from anyone else, which will again be true only some of the time and, of course, begs the question of what is 'fair' in an adversary system.[1]

As we saw earlier, the most important issue for many suspects is getting out of the station as soon as possible. These suspects refuse advice only because it might delay their departure. One-half of all suspects refusing advice would have requested it had a solicitor been in the station.[2] Some suspects plan ahead by leaving messages with parents or friends that a solicitor is to be secured if they are not home by a certain time.[3] These suspects make strategic decisions based on their past experience with police and solicitors. Sometimes their experiences with solicitors are so unsatisfactory that this is why they are reluctant to request them. Others have a low opinion of duty solicitors in particular, and so would see only their own solicitor, preferring to see no one rather than the duty solicitor.

Some suspects have an inflexible elasticity of demand because they always want a solicitor. Many of these are likely to be charged with serious offences, have long records or believe that a solicitor can do them no harm and may well do them some good. These suspects demand solicitors in almost any circumstances, and would do so even if the police did not have to inform them of their rights and to arrange advice for them.

Between these two groups, Maguire argued, there is a large group of suspects with a very high elasticity of demand. Often accused of

---

[20] M Maguire, 'Effects of the PACE Provisions on Detention and Questioning' (1988) 28 BJ Crim 19.

[1] This is all discussed more fully by A Sanders and L Bridges, 'The Right to Legal Advice' in C Walker and K Starmer (eds), *Justice in Error* (Blackstone, 1993); and D Brown et al, op cit pp 36–38.

[2] Brown et al, op cit p 53.

[3] Sanders et al, op cit.

moderately serious crimes such as shoplifting, car theft, handling stolen goods, burglary and deception, their decision whether or not to seek advice is influenced by a large number of factors, including the attitudes and practices of the police and the availability and likely quality of the advice.

(c)   The attitudes and practices of the police

Many suspects learn about their rights for the first time when told them by the custody officer. Others may know some of their rights but not crucial details (such as advice being free). Others may be afraid to ask for a lawyer. It follows that the way the police inform suspects of their rights—whether the choice is put as a 'question expecting the answer yes or the answer no'[4]—could be an important influence upon them. Sanders et al observed the reception of suspects into custody in ten police stations and concluded that the police utilise 'ploys' to dissuade suspects from seeking advice in over 40% of all cases. Table 4.2 shows the great range of ploys used.[5]

It is likely that ploys are even more extensively used than this study detected, since, in this context, the presence of an observer inevitably affects the process being observed. In one example given by Sanders et al, two juveniles suspected of shoplifting from Mothercare were being processed by a custody officer. When the researcher walked into the custody area, he heard and saw the custody officer reading out the suspects' rights in an incomprehensible manner. The custody officer looked up, saw the researcher and said, 'Are you the chap from Mothercare?'. The researcher replied, 'No, I am the chap from Birmingham University', whereupon the custody officer went bright red, stopped, and started reading out the suspects rights very slowly and clearly from the beginning.[6]

Reading rights quickly and incomprehensibly and/or incompletely is the most frequently used ploy. In the somewhat contradictory words of a police officer:

'Now, under PACE, you read them their rights as quickly as you can—hit them with it so quick they can't take it in—say "sign here, here and here" and there you are: nothing has changed. We all know that, though you wouldn't get any policeman to admit it to you.'[7]

Comments such as 'you'll have to wait in the cells until a solicitor

---

[4] Maguire, op cit p 31.
[5] Source: Sanders et al, op cit p 59.
[6] Sanders et al, p 63.
[7] Ibid p 58.

Table 4.2: Types of Ploy

Ploy	Frequency (principal ploy only)	
	No	%
1. Rights told too quickly/incomprehensibly/ incompletely	142	42.9
2. Suspect query answered unhelpfully/incorrectly	5	1.5
3. Inability of suspect to name own solicitor	2	0.6
4. 'It's not a very serious charge'	1	0.3
5. 'You'll have to wait in the cells until the solicitor gets here'	13	3.9
6. 'You don't have to make your mind up now. You can have one later if you want to'	27	8.2
7. 'You're only going to be here a short time'	25	7.6
8. 'You're only here to be charged/interviewed'	14	4.2
9. (To juvenile) 'You'll have to [or 'do you want to'] wait until an adult gets here'	18	5.4
10. (To adult) '[Juvenile] has said he doesn't want one'	8	2.4
11. Combination of 9 and 10	4	1.2
12. 'We won't be able to get a solicitor at this time/ none of them will come out/he won't be in his office'	6	1.8
13. 'You don't need one for this type of offence'	2	0.6
14. 'Sign here, here and here' (no information given)	7	2.1
15. 'You don't have to have one'	4	1.2
16. 'You're being transferred to another station— wait until you get there'	6	1.8
17. Custody officer interprets indecision/silence as refusal	9	2.7
18. 'You're not going to be interviewed/charged'	1	0.3
19. 'You can go and see a solicitor when you get out/ at court'	9	2.7
20. 'You're (probably) going to get bail'	6	1.8
21. Gives suspects *Solicitors' Directory* or list of solicitors without explanation/assistance	3	0.9
22. Other	19	5.7
TOTAL	331	100.0

gets here' are a dire threat to those suspects for whom length of detention is a greater concern than whether or not they are charged. Whilst
the warning is true it is also incomplete: it ignores the fact that most
suspects are put in the cells until they are interrogated anyway.
Juveniles are particularly badly affected by ploys, it often being
(wrongly) suggested to them that a request for legal advice should not
be made until their parents (or other 'appropriate adult') arrive; but
their parents, when they do arrive, are then told (correctly, but
disingenuously) that the suspect did not request a solicitor when
arrested. The more recent study of Brown et al shows that the police
are still very reluctant to act on requests for advice by juveniles,
despite the clear statements of the latter's rights in Code of
Practice C.[8]

It is difficult to establish a causal link between the use of police
ploys and actual requests for advice by suspects. Sanders et al found
that there was little correlation between the two but this may have
been because the police use these ploys primarily against those suspects
whom they thought would ask for a solicitor anyway, or for whom they
particularly did not want a solicitor involved. Brown et al considers the
lack of correlation to be evidence that custody officers are not deliberately trying to obstruct suspects. They argue that:

'. . . over-speedy and unclear expositions of rights may have occurred
simply because custody officers were all too familiar with what they
were saying and failed to appreciate that to some suspects the information was new and unfamiliar . . .'[9]

Similarly, Morgan et al found 'active discouragement, leading questions, or incomplete statement of rights' in 'only' about 14% of cases.
In the rest, they say, rights were presented 'reasonably', but that 'few
suspects are in a "reasonable" frame of mind at the time. There is
usually no attempt to make sure the statement has been understood.'[10]

Thus Brown et al found (after the revised Code of Practice was
introduced) that although the overwhelming majority of suspects
recalled being informed of their rights in general, little over half were
aware that advice would be free, and even fewer were aware that they
could consult an independent solicitor in private.[11] Consistent with
this, Clare and Gudjonsson found that only 40% of suspects could

---

[8] Op cit p 62.
[9] Brown et al, op cit p 29.
[10] R Morgan, R Reiner and I McKenzie, Police Powers and Policy: A Study of the Work
of Custody Officers (report to ESRC) (unpublished).
[11] Op cit pp 37–42.

fully understand the written notice of rights provided to them.[12] The police go through the motions of providing thoroughly due process-based rights to advice, but insufficient attention has been paid to ensuring that the message gets through to the vulnerable, the anxious and the less intelligent, who need them most. And it carries on, in part, because so few suspects realise that their rights are being inadequately communicated to them. Only 8% of suspects interviewed by Brown et al thought they misunderstood what the police told them, even though many more than this were unaware of important details.

Whether instances of the police playing down the value of legal advice can fairly be characterised as 'ploys' remains a matter of debate. Some police manoeuvres are more clear-cut, however. The notification provisions of Code of Practice C were breached, in the opinion of Brown's observers, in 16% of the cases observed prior to the revision of the PACE Codes of Practice in 1991, and in 26% of the cases observed after that revision. Moreover, Brown et al found that, even after the changes to Code of Practice C, sometimes no information at all was provided. Occasionally, suspects were simply asked if they wanted a solicitor.[13]

Whether or not advice was originally requested, the police are supposed to remind suspects of their right to legal advice at the time of each review of detention and at the start of the interview.[14] This was not so under the original version of Code of Practice C, and although the police usually now do this they fail to do so in around one quarter of all cases.[15] Only about 15% of requests for advice come after being officially reminded.[16] That the police do not encourage late requests is evident from the following extract from the transcript of a trial:[17]

Q: (Defence Counsel): 'At the end of that interview you offered the opportunity to have a lawyer?'

A: (Officer): 'That is correct.'

Q: 'Why did you not do that at the beginning?'

---

[12] I Clare and G Gudjonsson, Devising and Piloting an Experimental Version of the 'Notice to Detained Persons' (Royal Commission on Criminal Justice, Research Study no 7) (HMSO, 1993).

[13] D Brown, T Ellis and K Larcombe, Changing the Code: Police Detention under the Revised PACE Codes of Practice (Home Office Research Study no 129) (HMSO, 1992) p 31. About 7–8% of suspects were warned about the likely delay if they requested a lawyer (though Brown et al do not interpret this as a 'ploy'): ibid p 42.

[14] Code of Practice C, op cit paras 15.3 and 11.2.

[15] Brown et al, op cit pp 27–29.

[16] Ibid p 50.

[17] Letter from the trial judge, Judge Sanders—no relation—published at [1989] Crim LR 763.

A: 'Because he had already been offered the opportunity to have a solicitor. If he wanted a solicitor he was welcome to have one but I am not going to encourage it.'

Q: 'You did not offer him one for that reason?'

A: 'No, not at the beginning of the interview.'

Q: 'You suspected that if he did get a solicitor he would be advised to say nothing?'

A: 'Yes.'

Q: 'Which is why he was not offered one?'

A: 'Yes.'

It is clear that, whether by accident or design, many officers discourage recourse to legal advice much of the time. But it is equally clear that many suspects—those with relatively inelastic demand—increasingly persevere with their requests. The police usually accept this, and the request rate is consequently rising. However in some cases—presumably where the police are particularly keen to interrogate the suspect without a lawyer present—the police go to great lengths to block access. The first tactic is to employ numerous ploys.[18] The second is to trick suspects into signing the custody record in the wrong place. This was officially acknowledged as a problem to the extent that para 3.5 of the revised Code of Practice C incorporates a specific injunction against this:

'the person shall be asked to sign on the custody record to signify whether or not he wants legal advice at this point. The custody officer is responsible for ensuring that the person signs the custody record in the correct place to give effect to his decision.'

Another abuse stems from the fact that after advice is requested it is up to the police to make the call. Sometimes the police do not call the lawyer at all, which is clearly unlawful. Sometimes the call is delayed, allowing time to persuade suspects to withdraw their requests for advice, to be interrogated before the lawyer arrives, or to be informally interviewed.[19] Dixon et al comment that solicitors frequently complain that on arrival at the station they are often 'informed by officers that the suspect has changed his mind, agreed to talk to them, and confessed.'[20] The suspicion is that the police play a large part in this volte face. Unfortunately, custody records give no reason for failure to secure

[18] Sanders et al, op cit p 57, found that in these cases the request rate is noticeably lower than average.

[19] A Sanders and L Bridges, 'Access to Legal Advice and Police Malpractice' [1990] Crim LR 494.

[20] D Dixon, K Bottomley, C Coleman, M Gill and D Wall, 'Safeguarding the Rights of Suspects in Police Custody' (1990) 1 Policing and Society 115 at 128.

advice in one quarter of all such cases, thus making it difficult to account for the gap between the numbers requesting advice and those actually securing it.[1]

It would appear that giving the police the job of 'triggering' legal advice is a major obstacle to the success of the scheme. Thus it has been suggested that the scheme be modified to allow solicitors to be in the police station round the clock. This would be difficult and expensive to organise, but would almost certainly increase the advice rate. Alternatively, s 58 might be amended so that advice would be provided unless actively refused. This would at least ensure that all the confused suspects who currently do not secure advice would do so. The Runciman Commission recommended none of these solutions. Apart from some minor changes, it recommended that even suspects who refuse advice 'should then be given the opportunity of speaking to a duty solicitor on the telephone.'[2] But suspects are already entitled to do this. Runciman presumably has it in mind that suspects who refuse advice be asked again. In view of who will be doing the asking, this is unlikely to make any difference. Moreover, this proposal makes assumptions about the value of telephone advice which we shall see are unwarranted. If the police really want to help suspects, they could at present suggest that they speak to a solicitor on the phone. No delay would be incurred and the suspect would have nothing to lose. That this happens only rarely cannot be a mere oversight. The Runciman Commission could have taken this further, recommending that all suspects should automatically be put into telephone contact with a duty solicitor in order to discuss the question of legal advice. The only losers, apart from crime control adherents, would be the Treasury.

(d)   The attitudes and practices of the legal profession

It would be misleading to give the impression that all, or even most, of the problems of securing legal advice in police stations are the fault of the police. Many suspects do not want legal advice because of their experiences with duty solicitors or even with lawyers in general. Delivering legal services to suspects in police custody has many difficulties.

Unavailability

We have seen that around a quarter of suspects who request advice do not get any. This is sometimes due to cancellation of requests because

---

[1]   Brown et al, op cit p 61.
[2]   Report, op cit p 36.

suspects do not want to wait any longer for advice to be provided. Although half of all contacts with solicitors are made within 30 minutes, and three-quarters within one hour,[3] in some cases an able and willing solicitor simply cannot be located at all. This is bound to happen when suspects want to speak to their own solicitors, but it should not happen when a duty solicitor is requested. The problem is that 'duty solicitor' schemes do not always require someone to be on duty.

There are three types of duty solicitor scheme: rota, panel or mixed rota/panel. In a rota scheme, there will always be one or more solicitors on duty, who are paid a retainer for this purpose and who are obliged to provide advice. In a panel scheme, no one is so obliged, but panel membership is an indication of a general willingness to advise. In a mixed system, a solicitor is on duty part of the time. Panel and mixed systems are generally located in small towns where there is relatively little demand. However, because of the difficulty of recruiting solicitors, sometimes there are panel schemes where there should be rotas, or only one solicitor on duty where there should be two or three.

If solicitors are overstretched, the service to suspects may suffer in quality and quantity. Regarding quantity, even duty solicitors were unavailable 20% of the time in the early days of the scheme. By 1991, the overall contact rate with solicitors was 87%, and for duty solicitors the rate was around 95%.[4] Some areas, probably where duty solicitor schemes are particularly stretched, have great trouble putting suspects in contact with solicitors. One station in Brown et al's study had a consultation rate in relation to requests below 50% in 1990 and just 66% in 1991.

Solicitor or clerk

Of those suspects who do secure advice, a large number do not see a solicitor at all, but a solicitor's clerk. This was so in around 30% of cases observed by Sanders et al, the proportion being rather higher for 'own' solicitors (50%) than for duty solicitors (16%). Since that research was conducted, the proportion of cases in which 'paralegals' are used in 'own' solicitor cases seems to have risen to 75%.[5]

---

[3] Brown et al, op cit p 62.

[4] Brown et al, op cit pp 59–60. Note that consultations only occurred in 90% of all cases in which contact was made—often because, by that time, the suspect had already been dealt with.

[5] M McConville and J Hodgson, Custodial Legal Advice and the Right to Silence (Royal Commission on Criminal Justice Research Study no 16) (HMSO, 1993) p 17. Also see M McConville, J Hodgson, L Bridges and A Pavlovic, *Standing Accused* (OUP, 1994). Brown et al, op cit, found much lower figures, but their reliability is doubted by McConville and Hodgson.

There is nothing wrong with the use of paralegals who are properly trained in the art of advising suspects in police custody. However, McConville and Hodgson found that many are ex-police officers who are assumed to know how to do this work, and some are clerical staff with little legal knowledge at all. A professional approach would 'grade' work according to its seriousness and complexity, allowing only the most experienced paralegals to make a judgment on this and to handle the most important cases. This approach is comparatively rare. In most firms, whoever is available does the work, solicitors avoiding it wherever possible. According to McConville and Hodgson, 'In the majority of firms it is never contemplated that solicitors will attend police stations on a routine basis.'[6] This, they say, is because solicitors are paid more for court work, and because police station work is regarded as low grade work. The few firms in which solicitors do regularly attend the station are those firms which (rightly) see the station as the crucial place where the case is, or is not, made. Although this was not the most financially advantageous approach to adopt, none of these solicitors claimed to be suffering unduly.

The result is that many suspects are simply advised badly or not at all. In one case, McConville and Hodgson report the paralegal as having asked the researcher on the way to the station what constituted arson. When she did not say, he remarked, 'Oh well, maybe the police will tell us.'[7] Some paralegals may be knowledgable, but their low status enables the police to undermine them. McConville and Hodgson report the police sneeringly referring to one advisor as the suspect's 'secretary'.[8] Others, ex-police officers in particular (over one quarter of all paralegal advisors), are not imbued with due process ideals, and see their job as being to help the police as much as the suspect.

There is no limit to the extent to which solicitors may use unqualified staff, unless they are acting as a duty solicitor. Most duty solicitor schemes do not allow their use at all, while those that do require training, formal admittance to the scheme and initial screening over the phone by a solicitor member of the scheme. There is abuse of this, however, with some duty solicitors using paralegals when they are not authorised to do so, and screening sometimes not taking place.[9]

If it is thought appropriate that paralegals should be properly trained, and their use regulated, when acting for duty solicitors, this

---

[6] McConville and Hodgson, op cit p 18.
[7] Ibid p 33.
[8] Ibid p 32.
[9] A Sanders, L Bridges, A Mulvaney and G Crozier, Advice and Assistance at Police Stations and the 24 Hour Duty Solicitor Scheme (Lord Chancellor's Department, 1989) p 95.

must surely be equally appropriate when they act for 'own' solicitors. By the same logic, if unqualified staff must satisfy certain basic levels of competence, should not the same be required of qualified staff? The Law Society is now organising training courses and training packs for new solicitors and paralegals, and this is a small but important step in the right direction.

Advice in person or over the telephone

Between a quarter and a third of all advice is only over the phone alone.[10] There is considerable variation, however, as duty solicitors are less willing to attend the station than are 'own' solicitors, some stations are geographically less convenient than others for solicitors and advisors are more likely to attend the station for serious offences than for minor ones. Telephone advice is not necessarily inappropriate. The offence may be trivial and guilt not in doubt; the suspect may want advice on one specific thing only; the police may want to know something discrete and straightforward before, for instance, release on bail. Sometimes it will be clearly inappropriate; where, for instance:

(a) the suspect is disputing, or unclear about, the allegations;
(b) the offence is serious;
(c) the suspect is vulnerable;
(d) detention is likely to be lengthy; or
(e) there may have been malpractice.

Solicitors are professionals who ought to be able to judge these matters. They have official guidance to assist them and, when in doubt, they should go to the station. Moreover, once at the station they should stay, in all but exceptional cases, for any interview that might take place.[11]

In reality, solicitors are often guided by considerations other than the needs of the suspect, and much telephone advice is unsatisfactory. Advice is sometimes given to remain silent, for instance. Although this tells suspects their rights, it does not actually help them to remain silent in the face of vigorous questioning. Sanders et al found that solicitors were wanted for many things other than the simple provision of legal advice—to witness what went on, to act as emotional supports, to secure bail, and to take action over alleged malpractice. As the legislation acknowledges, access to a solicitor is to provide not just advice but also assistance. Little assistance can be provided over the telephone.

---

[10] Since Brown et al's 1990–91 research revealed slightly more phone advice than Sanders et al's 1988 research, it is possible that it is increasing in frequency.

[11] Law Society, *Advising a Suspect in the Police Station* (1991).

Just as the police fail to adhere, in many cases, to their code of practice, so solicitors fail to adhere to theirs. Around 14% of all suspects in 1988 saw a legal advisor in person. Of all interrogated suspects, about 22% saw a legal advisor in person, but only about 14% had a legal advisor with them in the interrogation, because many solicitors who attend the station do not attend the interrogation.[12] In 1991, only 13% of interrogations were attended, even though 31 per cent of all interrogated suspects saw a legal advisor in person.[13] In other words, the rise in legal advice did not lead to a rise in interrogations attended.[14]

Duty solicitors give telephone advice far more often than do 'own' solicitors even though most duty solicitors are 'own' solicitors in some contexts and vice versa. It seems that the type of service given depends as much on the status of the client as the nature of the case, although solicitors deny this.[15] Many solicitors argue that, even if telephone advice is sometimes given inappropriately, this is all that can be expected of an under-remunerated profession under pressure.[16]

The result is that many suspects might as well not receive any advice for all the use their lawyer is to them. Many suspects will not be frank with an often unknown voice on the phone: they may not trust the person, and in any case the police listen to the conversation. As one suspect told Sanders et al: 'If you met him face to face you could talk'. Another, asked if she would have the same solicitor again, replied 'We've not really had him have we? For all I know it might not have been a solicitor!'[17] Cases were seen where suspects who told the solicitor that they had been assaulted were left to languish in the cells for half the weekend, and where suspects were told on the phone 'not to say anything' in the interview when it must have been known that for most suspects this advice would be impossible to follow.[18] As we have seen, many suspects are vulnerable (but not recognised as such) and many more are less than fully rational as a result of their predicament. That most of these people need the support of someone whose job it is to look after their interests is incontrovertible.

---

[12] Sanders et al, op cit, ch 6.

[13] Brown et al, op cit Table 6.5.

[14] These figures should be borne in mind when evaluating the 'right of silence' debate in so far as the 'abolitionists' argue that access to a solicitor is such a protection for suspects that the right of silence is no longer necessary. See A Sanders, 'Rights, Remedies, and the PACE Act' [1988] Crim LR 802.

[15] Sanders et al, op cit ch 6.

[16] The 'pressure' argument is supported by Brown et al, op cit p 88, but rejected by McConville et al, op cit (1994), who point out that some firms, albeit a minority, provide a very good service without noticeable financial hardship.

[17] Sanders et al, op cit pp 119–120.

[18] Sanders et al, op cit pp 117–126.

This has been recognised to some extent by the Legal Aid Board, which tightened up its rules following concern at the findings of Sanders et al. The 1991 scheme, which came into operation at the same time as the revised Code of Practice C, requires duty solicitors to attend the station in certain circumstances, in particular when there is an interrogation. Failure to attend must be explained. Despite these changes in the law, there is reason to doubt that lawyers have modified their behaviour. In the first six months of the operation of the new rules, the average legal aid bill per suspect increased by less than the rise in the rate of solicitors' remuneration (which also took effect in 1991).[19] This suggests that solicitors were doing less for each suspect, rather than more, as Brown's figures for attendance at interrogation in 1991, cited earlier, confirm. The quantity of advice has risen, but the quality has not. This is perhaps not surprising. Firstly, the rules require attendance at the station, not at the interrogation, and so many solicitors leave before it begins. Secondly, the rules apply only to duty, and not to 'own', solicitors. None of this stopped mass protests by solicitors and even some 'duty solicitor strikes', producing less stringent rules than were originally proposed.[20]

An adversarial system?

In an adversarial system, solicitors would be expected to advise and assist suspects in the police station to the best of their abilities, regardless of how difficult this might make it for the police to secure evidence sufficient to prosecute. In a due process system, we would expect to find protections for suspects detained against their will, and would expect legal advisors to help suspects to use these protections. Thus in Britain there are rules which aim to prevent oppressive interrogation and allow suspects to stay silent, which solicitors should use to their clients' advantage. The reality, however, is not so straightforward.

All the research into the work of legal advisors since PACE was introduced has found that legal advisors actually do very little when they attend interrogations, and frequently see their task as facilitating the process, rather than protecting the rights of their clients.[1] Baldwin, for example, looked at 182 interviews in which there were legal representatives. In two-thirds of them, the advisor said precisely nothing, in 8.8%, the role adopted was that of '3rd interviewer' and in only 7.7%

---

[19] A Sanders and L Bridges, 'The Right to Legal Advice' in C Walker and K Starmer (eds), *Justice in Error* (Blackstone, 1993) and D Brown et al, op cit p 52.
[20] Ibid.
[1] See Brown et al, op cit p 89, and McConville and Hodgson, op cit. See also, for further examples, Sanders and Bridges, op cit, (1993) 51 and D Dixon, 'Common Sense, Legal Advice, and the Right of Silence' [1991] PL 233 at 242.

did the advisor 'push the suspect's interests'.[2] Baldwin describes most legal advisors as 'essentially passive'. However, Roberts points out that this does not mean that they fail to do their job in most cases:

'. . . if the police interviewer was behaving professionally and the suspect did not need assistance, intervention on the part of the solicitor would be quite unnecessary.'[3]

Without matching the behaviour of the police and of the solicitor against Code of Practice C and the Law Society guidance, we cannot know whether non-intervention was justified or not. None the less, the research findings of McConville and Hodgson support all the previous findings. They comment:

'We found no evidence of "black sheep" or of practices by advisors which, from the police perspective, could be fairly criticised . . . On the other hand, there is plenty of evidence that advisors are complicit in overly harsh interrogation strategies and fail to protect clients from improper, inappropriate and irrelevant—but potentially damaging—questions.'[4]

They describe the role adopted by most advisors as that of a 'watching brief', involving very little advocacy at all, and often very little knowledge of their client's case other than that which is provided to them by the police.

When legal advisors do act adversarially, it occasions surprise from the police. A police officer told McConville et al that one '. . . solicitor sort of sat there frowning at me not very unbiased at all'. But as another said: 'I quite enjoy it now when they have a solicitor present. They have a word with the defendant, then they have a word with you. They tell you what he is going to say.'[5]

The response of legal advisors to police questioning of their clients can be crucial, as the 'Cardiff Three' case shows.[6] In this case, three men were convicted of killing a woman after one 'confessed'. He challenged the confession in court, but the trial judge ruled it admissible. The tapes of interrogation were played to the Court of Appeal, which condemned them as contrary to Code of Practice C, quashed the convictions and criticised the defendant's lawyer for sitting through these

---

[2] J Baldwin, The Role of Legal Representatives at the Police Station (Royal Commission on Criminal Justice Research Study no 3) (HMSO, 1993) Table 1.
[3] D Roberts, 'Questioning the Suspect: the Solicitor's Role' [1993] Crim LR 369.
[4] Op cit p 171.
[5] Unpublished field notes.
[6] Re Miller, Paris, Abdullahi (1992) Times, 24 December. The case is briefly discussed by the Runciman Commission: Royal Commission on Criminal Justice, Report (Cm 2263) (HMSO, 1993) pp 58 and 62.

interrogations without objecting. Whilst this is just one case, it is illustrative of many others.

The problem is that, contrary to one's intuition, adversarialism is not a natural stance for most defence lawyers, particularly those who spend a lot of time advising suspects. To such lawyers, the police station is the workplace and the importance of maintaining good relations with work colleagues (ie the police) is an important consideration. Dixon quotes a solicitor who says:

'You've got to do the best for your client, but you've still got to live with the system many years on. So . . . most solicitors do their best for their clients, but they also . . . won't generally upset the police.'[7]

Solicitors square this circle by saying that silence, for instance, is rarely as advantageous as telling the truth, or that in order to get information from the police they need to give something back. Junior or unqualified staff are, of course, less likely to be adversarial in the face of police hostility, and fear losing business for their firm if they are particularly adversarial. But even Roberts, the author of the Law Society guidance, is not sure what the role of the advisor should be: 'Interviews run better if the solicitor is able to establish a working relationship with the interviewer based on mutual respect.'[8] Better for whom? And at what cost are those working relationships purchased? Advisors are in a position of role conflict on potentially hostile territory. No wonder many solicitors seek to avoid this work. And, given the nature of most custodial legal advice, it is not surprising that the police are less hostile to the provision of advice than they used to be, even though advice rates have risen. The police know that advice rarely gets in the way of their carrying out their adversarial role. Yet the response of the Runciman Commission to all this evidence—which it did not challenge—was simply to call for more and better training of solicitors and paralegals, and for more monitoring.[9] As Baldwin, author of some of the research on which this recommendation was based, comments, this 'looks at best superficial'.[10] Runciman even endorsed the Law Society guidance which, we have seen, creates the ambiguous role which turns adversarialism on its head. Clearly the Runciman Commission failed to understand that lawyers' behaviour has little to do with education and training, but everything to do with the structural position of legal advisors in police stations.

---

[7] Dixon, op cit p 239. Also see Baldwin, op cit Table 1.
[8] Roberts, op cit p 370.
[9] Report, op cit pp 35–39.
[10] J Baldwin, 'Power and Police Interviews' (1993) 143 NLJ 1194 at 1195.

(e) Legal advice in the station: assistance for whom?

Why are Code of Practice C, the Law Society guidance and the Legal Aid Board's Duty Solicitor Rules all so ineffective ? There are at least three reasons. Firstly, even though it is not in the interests of police officers or solicitors to adhere to these rules, enforcement of them is largely done by those same officers and solicitors. In fact, most solicitors provide such a poor service to their clients (especially when acting in their duty solicitor capacities) that it is difficult to see why the police are as concerned to obstruct access as they are.

Most solicitors only do this work when it is profitable for them to do so. A number of disputes have occurred between solicitors and the Legal Aid Board over rates of pay and required standards of service.[11] In an attempt to ensure that adequate standards are maintained, there is a regional network of committees to oversee local schemes and a national duty solicitor committee of the Legal Aid Board to oversee and regulate the operation of the scheme as a whole. Solicitors who breach the scheme—who, for instance, are unavailable when on duty, fail to give advice at the station when they should, or use paralegals when they should not do so—can be suspended or expelled from it.[12] However, this regulation only applies to duty solicitors, a lot of rule breaking is undiscovered (suspects either do not know they should receive a better service, do not know to whom to complain or are fatalistic about the chances of anything being done about it) and local and regional committees are reluctant to discipline their members. Professional self-regulation is always problematic. And although these committees take these matters relatively seriously in principle, they fear that schemes—often already undersubscribed—will collapse if more pressure is applied to solicitors who are already overcommitted. Disciplinary action is therefore rare and lenient.

Secondly, there is the context. The police station is police territory. When the whole purpose of due process rights is to protect suspects from the police, to make the police the main gatekeepers to these rights is plainly illogical. The counter-argument would be that the purpose of the custody officer as an independent officer is precisely to stand between suspects, on the one hand, and investigating officers, on the other. Since custody officers have no specific interest in any one case, the custody officer will protect suspects by full enforcement of the rights in Code of Practice C, even if investigating officers object. This, however, relies on the rather formalistic distinction between a custody officer's duty and an investigating officer's duty. It does not take into account the shared out-

---

[11] See Sanders and Bridges, op cit (1993).
[12] Sanders et al, op cit ch 8.

look of different police officers. It also does not take into account the fact that an officer who wishes to secure the co-operation of fellow officers one day will not wish to 'get in their way' by acting out the custody officer role to perfection another day. Both custody officers and solicitors have to get on with other police officers in the latter's territory. 'Independent' operation under these conditions is hardly conceivable.

Thirdly, there are the rules themselves: PACE Code of Practice C and the Duty Solicitor Rules. The former allow much less scope than before for rule bending, the result being more rule breaking (but also probably less flouting of the spirit of the rules overall). These are, therefore, partly inhibitory rules with presentational elements. The Duty Solicitor Rules have also been tightened up, but not to the extent of the PACE Code of Practice. They are routinely deviated from in both letter and spirit. Both sets of rules allow proper legal advice and assistance to be denied to suspects who do not demand all to which they are, often unknown to them, entitled.

Suspects need protecting from police, lawyers and themselves. Voluntarism—consent—is completely misplaced when dealing with an intrinsically coercive situation. Just as it is nonsense to argue that most confessions are voluntary, the same is true of decisions about advice. Some suspects are asked by lawyers on the phone whether they want them to come to the station, when the whole point about suspects in detention is that they cannot be assumed to be able to make rational or informed decisions for themselves. The rules at present are operated contrary to the interests of suspects because their interests and the interests of the gatekeepers diverge. To make the rules work it would be necessary to install gatekeepers with the same interests as suspects, perhaps by paying solicitors or trained paralegals specifically for effective police station work and no other. The Runciman Commission could have made recommendations on these lines but did not do so. Commenting on the greater power of the police as compared to suspects, Baldwin says that Runciman's recommendations

'do little, if anything, to modify this power base. It will be surprising if, in consequence, there is much change in existing police practice. The Commission's view seems to be that the status quo represents the best way forward.'[13]

In reality, the most significant power differential is between the police and the legal profession, on the one hand, and the suspect, on the other. But it is true to say that that differential, and the practices which flow from it, will be largely unchanged by the Runciman Commission's complacency.

[13] J Baldwin, 'Power and Police Interviews', op cit at 1197.

5. POLICE INTERROGATION

(a) Introduction: why interrogate?

In the introduction to this chapter, we discussed the way in which the right of silence is part of the basic due process notion of the presumption of innocence and of the responsibility of the prosecution to prove its own case. Due process models further require that proof be proved by the prosecution beyond reasonable doubt. It follows that, to secure acquittal, suspects or defendants are not required to give evidence of innocence or to answer the case for the prosecution (unless, of course, that case proves guilt beyond reasonable doubt). By the same token, the police should not expect to be able to rely on the confessions of suspects, except where made voluntarily. Instead, they should secure independent evidence to prove their case. Even then a pure due process system would be sceptical about police methods of extracting purportedly voluntary confessions. We have seen that 'voluntariness' and 'consent' are meaningless in situations where all the choices available to suspects are unpleasant.

This due process position used to underpin the law firmly, and police interrogation was all but ruled out, at least in theory. The preface (by a judge) to one of the earliest guides to the police said that when an officer

'has a person in custody for a crime, it is wrong to question such person touching the crime of which he is accused ... There is, however, no objection to a constable listening to any mere voluntary statement which a prisoner desires to make ... Never act unfairly to a prisoner by coaxing him by word or conduct to divulge anything. If you do, you will assuredly be severely handled at the trial, and it is not unlikely your evidence will be disbelieved.'[14]

This position was reflected in the original version of the Judges Rules in 1912, although they did allow the police to invite suspects to make voluntary statements. Persons making voluntary statements were not to be 'cross-examined' and only questions aimed at 'removing ambiguity' were to be asked. As the Judges Rules were transformed over the years, however, police interrogation was less frowned upon. The final formulation of the Judges Rules (in force from 1964 until

---

[14] Preface to Vincent's Police Code (1882). Reproduced in Royal Commission on Criminal Procedure, The Investigation and Prosecution of Criminal Offences in England and Wales: The Law and Procedure (Cmnd 8092–1) (HMSO, 1981) app 13, pp 162–163. This position was confirmed in *R v Knight and Thayre* (1905) 20 Cox CC 711.

their replacement by PACE) no longer purported to discourage interrogation but merely to regulate its methods.

PACE and Code of Practice C (Note 1B) maintains the general rule that no one need talk to the police, but that the police may none the less interrogate suspects in order to persuade them to talk. One might think from this that few people would answer questions. However, this would be to ignore the pressures on people to speak when interrogated. It will be recalled that in *Holgate-Mohammed v Duke*[15] the police acknowledged that the reason they arrested the suspect and took her to the police station, rather than interviewing her at home, was precisely because people are more likely to confess when interrogated under conditions of involuntary detention.

It is not possible to estimate the frequency of self-incriminating statements with any accuracy.[16] However, research has found confessions and incriminating statements in around 60% of all cases where there is an interrogation, and in around 80% of guilty pleas.[17] Maguire and Norris comment that confession evidence 'forms the central plank of a high proportion of cases',[18] and McConville and Hodgson state that 'the principal investigative strategy of the police is the interrogation'.[19]

The police have come to rely on police station interrogation in order to secure confessions and convictions. McConville and Baldwin suggest a number of additional functions of interrogation.[20] Firstly, confession evidence may not be the only way of securing conviction, but it is the easiest method. A clear and credible confession often eliminates the need to secure extra evidence (for example, from witnesses or by forensic analysis of blood or semen samples), enabling more cases to be cleared up more quickly than would otherwise be so. Secondly, in the course of interrogation the police often secure valuable information unrelated to the offence in question, such as suspects' other possible offences. And so McConville and Baldwin found that 21% of all guilty pleaders gave information on their other offences. Suspects may also give information about their associates (7% of guilty pleaders in McConville and Baldwin's study did so).

---

15 [1984] 1 All ER 1054 discussed in ch 3, section 5.
16 No official figures are collected, so estimates are based on research studies with different sampling methods. Also it is not always clear what is, or is not, incriminating.
17 M McConville and J Baldwin, Courts, Prosecution and Conviction (OUP, 1981) ch 6; McConville et al, op cit (1993), p 61; and J Baldwin, 'Police Interview Techniques: Establishing Truth or Proof?' (1993) 33 BJ Crim 325, Table 2.
18 M Maguire and C Norris, The Conduct and Supervision of Criminal Investigations (Royal Commission on Criminal Justice Research Study no 5) (HMSO, 1992).
19 M McConville and J Hodgson, Custodial Legal Advice and the Right to Silence (Royal Commission on Criminal Justice Research Study no 16) (HMSO, 1993) p 111.
20 Op cit ch 8.

Information about past or planned crimes in which the suspect is not involved, or general 'criminal intelligence', is also often provided.[1] This is often part of a 'deal', the information being exchanged for bail, lesser charges, no prosecution at all or, of course, money. As Banton pointed out in 1964,[2] and Hobbs more recently,[3] every suspect is a potential informant. Just as stop-search is used in a crime control or even a repressive fashion to facilitate the broadest policing role, so this is true also of interrogation. A few of the police officers interviewed by McConville et al claimed that the restrictions imposed by PACE prevented deals being done, but most said that they had found ways of continuing as before. As one said in relation to access to solicitors: 'You can't make deals with the solicitor present but you can when he's not there. It needs watching that, but you can still do it.'[4]

According to one CID officer, suspects are often keen to open negotiations: 'They [suspects] always want to deal. When they're arrested they're immediately in the game of damage limitation.'[5] Many are as keen as the police on excluding third parties from such negotiations. On one of the few occasions when Sanders et al were denied access to an interrogation, the suspect pointed out, somewhat melodramatically, that he would be 'a dead man' if anyone except the officer was present at what was to ensue.[6] Deals are rarely struck 'cold'. Good bargaining is based on a trusting relationship, a hallmark of good policing. These relationships are built and maintained through policing at every level— on the street, in the station, in court—preventing legal regulation from neatly demarcating separate steps of the process.

The way in which most offences are constructed also encourages interrogation. Most non-Road Traffic Act criminal offences in England require evidence of *mens rea* (intent or recklessness) in order to convict the defendant. Assault is only a crime if a person is hurt intentionally or recklessly as distinct from someone stumbling or being careless and hurting the victim accidentally. Theft is not theft if another's goods are taken accidentally. But how are the police to prove that an item was taken or a person injured deliberately rather than accidentally? Sometimes there will be objective evidence of intent, such as the egging on of someone to do the crime or a written plan, but this is rare. Evidence of intent can best

---

[1] M McConville, A Sanders and R Leng, *The Case for the Prosecution* (Routledge, 1991) ch 4 and Maguire and Norris, op cit chs 5 and 7.

[2] M Banton, *The Policeman in the Community* (Tavistock, 1964).

[3] D Hobbs, *Doing the Business* (OUP, 1988).

[4] McConville et al, op cit (1991) p 62.

[5] Quoted by Maguire and Norris, op cit p 47.

[6] A Sanders, L Bridges, A Mulvaney and G Crozier, Advice and Assistance at Police Stations and the 24 Hour Duty Solicitor Scheme (Lord Chancellor's Department, 1989).

be obtained by the statement of the person doing the crime. Much police interrogation is geared not to establishing the objective facts—who took the articles or injured the victim, about which there is often no dispute—but what the person intended by his or her actions.[7] It follows that, if guilt could be secured by reference to objective facts alone, the pressure on the police to interrogate would be reduced.

(b)   When interrogation may occur

Under s 30(1) of PACE, where a person is arrested for an offence 'he shall be taken to a police station by a constable as soon as practicable after the arrest'. As so often with criminal justice, the phrase 'as soon as practicable' is of prime importance. Section 30(10) provides that:

'nothing in sub-section (1) shall prevent a constable delaying taking a person who has been arrested to a police station if the presence of that person elsewhere is necessary in order to carry out such investigations as it is reasonable to carry out immediately.'

Thus although generally speaking, people who are arrested must be taken to a police station at once, checked in by the custody officer and interrogated only after that, situations are envisaged where police officers can justifiably delay taking suspects to a police station.

Why does this matter? There are dilemmas here which do not involve the clash of due process and crime control principles, but which create problems for due process itself. The conveyance of arrested persons to a station immediately is desirable on due process grounds for several reasons. Firstly, it enables custody officers to decide whether or not arrests are justified and whether suspects are particularly vulnerable. Secondly, it allows as little time to elapse as possible after arrest before suspects have the opportunity to exercise their rights under ss 56 and 58 to consult a lawyer and to have their arrest made known to a relative or friend. Thirdly, it prevents police officers holding suspects incommunicado against their will, thus minimising the opportunity for interrogation in uncontrolled conditions and prior to securing legal advice. In *Kerawalla*[8] the defendant was arrested in a hotel room and questioned there without being allowed to exercise his ss 56 and 58 rights. The Court of Appeal held that they were not applicable to persons detained at premises other than a police station.[9]

---

[7]   R Evans, The Conduct of Police Interviews with Juveniles (Royal Commission on Criminal Justice, Research Study no 8) (HMSO, 1993) and McConville et al, op cit, ch 4.

[8]   [1991] Crim LR 451.

[9]   This decision has been rightly criticised as unnecessarily restrictive: 'Commentary on *Kerawalla*' [1991] Crim LR 453.

On the other hand, we saw in chapter 3, above, that it is undesirable to encourage peremptory arrest on bare reasonable suspicion if the suspect has a exonerating story. If the story can be checked by, for instance, going to the suspects' home to check documents,[10] to a shop where the suspect says he bought allegedly stolen goods[11] or to a place of work where an alibi could be confirmed, this must be better for the suspect than being held in custody while these investigations are made. Then there are suspects who feel, and often are, under less pressure if interrogated somewhere they feel comfortable, such as at home or in the office of their solicitor.[12]

The only way out of this dilemma would be for the police to arrest less often even when they have reasonable suspicion, as the Philips Commission advocated. Its preference was for the suspect to be reported for summons instead, and investigations continued without the suspect being in custody. This would not solve the problem of whether to allow questioning on the street, and it would not be practical in anywhere near all cases, but it would sometimes help. However we have seen that the government completely rejected this approach, that PACE actually extended arrest powers (allowing arrest for non-arrestable offences in certain circumstances) and the Runciman Commission did not even consider the issue.

The result in s 30 is a messy compromise. Its imprecision provides an opportunity for the operation of crime control working rules in relation to interrogation. So, despite its due process credentials, it is primarily an enabling rule. It enables the police to insist on immediate police station interrogation except when they determine that some other course of action is preferable. The suspect has no say in the matter. This enables the police to lengthen the time between arrest and police station detention, exacerbating another problem. If the police interrogate in the period between arrest and arrival at the station, or if information is voluntarily given, should the police and courts be able to use the information? A due process approach would say 'no', especially if the reason for the delay was in order to extract information under these conditions, ie without the protections which apply at the police station. But a crime control approach—concerned only with the truth of what the suspect told the police—would accept the information if it was reliable.

Section 30(10) does not in itself give permission to officers to interrogate other than in a police station. However, if suspects make incriminating statements to the police en route to a police station or

---

[10] As in *McCarrick v Oxford* [1983] RTR 117, discussed in ch 3, section 5.

[11] As in *Madden's* case, also discussed in ch 3, section 5.

[12] A good example is *Holgate-Mohammed v Duke*, above.

some other place envisaged in s 30(10) (such as the suspect's home or place of work) the fact that that person is not taken to the police station immediately does not necessarily invalidate the information given. This gives the police an incentive to seek a confession prior to arrival at the police station. An attempt is made to deal with the problem in para.11.1 of Code of Practice C: 'Following a decision to arrest a suspect he must not be interviewed about the relevant offence except at a police station . . .' The paragraph then goes on to provide for exceptions where the consequence would otherwise be likely to lead to interference with evidence or lead to persons not yet arrested being alerted. Paragraph 11.1 also states that interviewing in such circumstances should cease once the risk has been averted. But crime control concerns are none the less prioritised over due process by these exceptions, opening up the prospect of informal interviewing (to be discussed later).

(c)   When interrogation must end

Paragraph 11.4 of Code of Practice C provides:

'As soon as a police officer who is making enquiries . . . believes that a prosecution should be brought against him and that there is sufficient evidence for it to succeed, he should ask the person if he has anything further to say . . . the officer shall without delay cease to question him about that offence.'

This broadly continues the old common law which provided that once an officer believed that someone should be prosecuted and that there is sufficient evidence, it would be unfair to continue the interrogation.[13] Paragraph 11.4 also implies that suspects cannot be interrogated about a particular offence after being charged with that offence. This is confirmed (with some minor exceptions) in paragraph 16.5: 'Questions relating to an offence may not be put to a person after he has been charged with that offence or informed that he may be prosecuted for it . . .'

The police have a duty to divert offenders from prosecution where appropriate. It may therefore be important to get evidence of, for instance, the suspect's emotional state. This is addressed by the provision that questioning need end only when the officer 'believes that a prosecution should be brought'. But s 37(7) simply provides that:

'. . . if the custody officer determines that he has before him sufficient

---

[13]   Also see s 37(7) and para 16.1, which provide that once there is sufficient evidence to charge, the suspect should be charged or released: either way, further interrogation is precluded.

evidence to charge the person arrested with the offence for which he was arrested, the person arrested—
(a) shall be charged; or
(b) shall be released without charge . . .'

If evidence relating to diversion has not been secured, it would appear that it should not be secured through further questioning. In practice, the police interrogate routinely in any case where *mens rea* is required, even though they will often have sufficient evidence already, but rarely attempt to secure evidence relevant to diversion.[14] As the police are anxious to secure an admission to the *mens rea* element of the crime, one can understand why they would not wish to prompt the suspect into claiming emotional instability, depression or dependency on tranquillisers. The last thing they want to hear is 'I was so upset that I didn't know what I was doing.'

The Runciman Commission was concerned that currently the police 'are precluded too soon from following up potentially productive lines of inquiry' and that 'police officers may now be tempted to prolong questioning beyond the point at which there is sufficient evidence to charge.'[15] It recommended that the questioning of suspects after charge be permissible. This is a pure crime control response, whereby it is assumed that there must be good reasons for the police breaking the rules. So, rather than ensuring that the police are brought into line with the rules, Runciman recommended that the rules be brought into line with police practices.

There are good reasons for restricting police questioning, both before and after charge, which were not even mentioned by Runciman. At present, the police are obliged to release or charge unless detention is necessary in order to obtain further evidence.[16] Paragraph 11.4 of Code of Practice C means that once sufficient evidence is secured, further detention cannot be necessary. Without a cutoff point, the police would be allowed to carry out indeterminate interrogations because they would always be able to claim that further information might be forthcoming, but only under conditions of involuntary detention. If, say, a suspect was arrested at 1 am and made incriminating statements soon afterwards, under para 11.4 he or she would have to be released or held for court later that morning. Without it, there would be nothing to stop the police interrogating for eight hours or more and even holding the suspect over until the next day. On Runciman's proposals, anyone who was charged soon after court ended (say at 2 pm) would be at risk

---

[14] McConville et al, op cit (1991).
[15] Report, op cit p 17.
[16] See above, section 3(c).

of being interrogated (with breaks) for 18 hours after charge until court the following day. Since, as we saw earlier, police interrogation serves broader purposes than just securing evidence of the offence for which a suspect was arrested, this is by no means fanciful. We know that deals and bargaining are of central importance. Suspects faced with these prospects would be in a considerably worse bargaining position than they are now.

(d)   What is a police 'interview'?

So far we have assumed that it is clear when something is, or is not, an 'interview'.[17] In fact this is not so. Drawing a clear line between an interview and a discussion or conversation can be very difficult. Yet it is vital to do so, for s 30 of PACE and Code of Practice C, para 11.1, are only concerned with 'interviews'. If a mere 'conversation' takes place between a suspect and an officer, this is not regulated by s 30 or para 11.1, regardless of whether it produces useful information for the police.

In *Absolam*,[18] the defendant was arrested for suspected drugs offences. He was questioned in the charge room and allegedly gave incriminating answers. Only then was he read his rights and cautioned. A record of the questions and his answers was made but not shown to him. If this was an 'interview', then what happened was unlawful because it took place before the suspect was read his rights and before he had had the opportunity to seek legal advice. If it was not an interview, then it was not unlawful and those protections were not applicable. The Court of Appeal held that this was an interview.[19] This might be taken to suggest, in a due process fashion, that any questioning would amount to an interview. For if questioning is not regarded as interviewing then the protections in PACE and the Code of Practice could be routinely circumvented by the police. However, much police questioning begins as simple information seeking from possible witnesses who may or may not become suspects. It would be neither possible nor desirable to provide all the protections—and the coercion of police station custody—of Code of Practice C and PACE before the police were allowed to talk to them. It is therefore essential for the law to provide that, up to a certain point, question and answer sessions between police and citizens shall not be regarded as interviews for the

---

[17]   We use the terms 'interview' and 'interrogation' interchangeably.

[18]   [1988] Crim LR 748.

[19]   Similarly, conversations in *Oransaye* [1993] Crim LR 772 (questioning at the custody officer's desk) and in *Goddard* [1994] Crim LR 46 (questioning prior to being taken to the police station) were held to be interviews.

purposes of PACE. The question is at what stage questions and answers should become formal interviews and at what stage 'civilians' should become 'suspects'.

Bevan and Lidstone are surely right to argue that all post-arrest conversations about the suspected offence should be regarded as interviews because an arrested person is, by definition, a suspect.[20] But, as they concede, the problem is drawing a line in relation to questioning before arrest. Code of Practice C attempts to draw a line in Note 11A:

'An interview is the questioning of a person regarding his involvement or suspected involvement in a criminal offence or offences. Questioning a person only to obtain information or his explanation of the facts or in the ordinary course of the officer's duties does not constitute an interview for the purpose of this Code. Neither does questioning which is confined to the proper and effective conduct of the search.'

The courts appear to be adopting a number of different ways of distinguishing these two types of questioning.[1] For some time it looked as though formal interviews were being defined as conversations which took place in police stations and that informal conversations (not controlled by PACE and the Code of Practice) were any discussions which took place outside police stations.[2] Allowing the place of the discussion to determine its legal status makes little sense. Many genuine witnesses give evidence to the police in police stations and attend police stations to, for instance, identify possible criminals. Such witnesses do not need the protection of PACE and Code of Practice C. Further, if the place of the conversation is to determine whether the protection of PACE and the Code of Practice is provided, the ability of the police to determine where the conversation takes place will distort what happens. The simple result would be that, rather than interviewing suspects inside police stations, the police would simply do more interviews outside.

Another approach is to examine the intention of the officers in question. But as Field points out, it is easy for officers to claim that it was their intention merely to seek information when in fact it was not.[3] The courts have been rather gullible in this respect. In *Maguire*[4] two

---

[20] Op cit p 436. This appeared to be the basis of the decision in *Goddard*, above.

[1] Including at least one which dismissed Note 11A as unhelpful. See S Field, 'Defining Interviews under PACE' (1993) 13 LS 254. It is open to the courts to ignore Note 11A, for—like the other Notes in the Code of Practice—it is an aid to interpretation and not part of the Code of Practice itself.

[2] See for example, *Maguire* [1989] Crim LR 815 and *Younis* [1990] Crim LR 425.

[3] Op cit pp 259–261.

[4] [1989] Crim LR 815.

youths, seen pushing open the door of a flat, were told on the way to the police car, 'You've both been caught. Now tell us the truth . . . It's for your own good.' This was held not to be an interview. Similarly, in *Pullen*,[5] the court believed that officers visited the defendant's cell 'with the object of relaxing him and . . . restoring some of his dignity', thus holding that only a conversation took place.[6] It is arguable, in any event, that whether someone needs protection depends on the objective evidence against them and on the nature of the discussion, rather than on the intention of the police.[7]

This seems to have been recognised in *Weekes*.[8] Here the Court of Appeal said that an 'understandable enquiry' became an 'interview' when the suspect started making admissions. But by this time, of course, it is too late if the purpose of defining a conversation as an 'interview' is to prevent admissions being made without due process protections. This will be a helpful ruling only if it means that whatever was said as a result of 'understandable enquiries' became unusable as a result of the exchange's transformation into an 'interview'.[9] Some cases, such as *Younis*[10] where the conversation took place in a police car, have been decided on the basis that an exchange is not an interview if it is initiated by the suspect. This could only be relevant if the whole discussion was on the lines initiated by the suspect, which was not so in *Younis*.

There is no obvious way of distinguishing 'conversations' and pre-arrest 'interviews'. This was recognised by the Runciman Commission, which recommended that the 'apparent confusion' in Note 11A 'be clarified'.[11] This, however, implies that the issue is merely technical, when in fact the definition should be formulated in accordance with whatever principles are being promoted in this area of law. The problem is illustrated by *Marsh*:[12] police officers investigating a burglary asked the defendant (D) about some wraps of paper which they found. This produced evidence of D's involvement in drugs offences, which was held to be admissible because there had been no reason to suspect D of involvement in criminal activity. However, the questioning clearly did also seek information about an offence. Note 11A does not solve this problem because it draws an unrealistic distinction between

---

5   [1991] Crim LR 457.
6   Note, however, *Hunt* [1992] Crim LR 582, where the court was more sceptical.
7   See *Sparks* [1991] Crim LR 128.
8   [1993] Crim LR 211.
9   See H Fenwick, 'Confessions, Recording Rules, and Miscarriages of Justice: A Mistaken Emphasis?' [1993] Crim LR 174.
10   [1990] Crim LR 425. Similar cases are discussed by Field, op cit at 261–263.
11   Report, op cit p 27. The Commission did not attempt such a clarification itself.
12   [1991] Crim LR 455.

questioning someone about his or her 'involvement' in an alleged offence and seeking 'information' about an offence. Since all questioning is done with a view to securing incriminating statements, should the person being questioned be guilty, all questioning could be regarded as constituting an interview, and hence not lawful except in the police station; but this would not be regarded by people who could exonerate themselves on the spot, let alone by the police, as desirable.

Police-citizen encounters away from the police station are usually characterised by their low visibility. This means that what went on (who initiated the conversation, what was being sought by it, what the intentions of the officers were and so forth) is only the officers' word against the suspect's. The whole point of PACE and Code of Practice C regulating formal 'interviews' was to eradicate this problem by being able to verify what was said and done objectively. It is precisely this objective verification which the police seek to avoid by so often trying to ensure that their discussions are not classified as interviews.

Field rightly concludes that, no matter how the wording of Code of Practice C is altered, the problems discussed here will remain while the incentives to bargain and deal remain.[13] Equally, the incentive to secure, through informal questioning, confession evidence which can be used in court will still be there for as long as the rules of evidence allow it.[14] Maguire and Norris report that the utility of evidence in court is a major factor influencing whether police officers go out of their way to secure such evidence.[15] PACE, largely through s 30(1) and Code of Practice C, para 11.1, sought to protect suspects by moving interrogation into what was thought to be the controlled environment of the police station. The police responded by increasingly questioning 'informally', and Code of Practice C, Note 11A, is an attempt to control this. This can be seen as a partially successful attempt to impose inhibitory due process rules on a body wedded to crime control-based working rules. However, it is not self-evident that suspects are protected by this wholesale movement of interviewing into the police station. As we have seen, detention is experienced by most suspects as inherently coercive, producing pressures to say and do things, in order to secure release, which they would not normally do. Protection from unregulated police activity is increased in this way, but so is the pressure created by allowing lengthy police detention. This has major implications for the impact of interrogation techniques and the right of silence, but first we need to look more closely at the nature of interrogation.

---

[13] Op cit at 263.
[14] See ch 9 on remedies for discussion of the exclusion of unlawfully obtained evidence.
[15] Op cit p 46.

(e)   Regulating interviews

We have seen that, until the latter half of the twentieth century, compulsory custodial interviewing was greatly restricted. Involuntary detention and interrogation, particularly when not judicially authorised, was seen to undermine the right of silence and to be alien to the due process ideal. Consequently the Judges' Rules required that interviews be carried out in ways that were not 'oppressive' or otherwise liable to produce involuntary or unreliable confessions (as where, for example, 'inducements' to confess were offered). Confession evidence which was secured in breach of these rules was unusable in court.[16] This all remains true under PACE and Code of Practice C, but the legal understanding of what we mean by these concepts has changed.

The Code of Practice provides for interrogation to take place under reasonable conditions, specifying adequate breaks for rest and refreshment (paras 12.2 and 12.7), adequate physical conditions (paras 12.4 and 12.5) and allowing the presence of a legal advisor (if requested). The purpose of all this is in part humanitarian but also to ensure that interrogations are conducted fairly, are not oppressive and that confessions or other information secured is reliable and thus usable in court. However, acceptable methods of questioning are not specified and the number of interviews and their length is not regulated. Interviewing may take place over the 24-hour period (or longer, for serious arrestable offences) of compulsory detention, which would have been regarded as oppressive per se a century ago.[17] Code of Practice C (para.11.3) simply says:

'No police officer may try to obtain answers to questions or to elicit a statement by the use of oppression or shall indicate, except in answer to a direct question, what action will be taken on the part of the police if the person being interviewed answers questions, makes a statement or refuses to do either.'

Contrast this with the earlier position. In 1882, it was unfair even to 'coax' a confession out of a suspect.[18] Now the police can question any way they like, as long as they offer no inducements and are not oppressive or unfair. Let us examine the relevant concepts in turn.

---

[16] Judges' Rules 1964, principle (e). See Royal Commission on Criminal Procedure, Law and Procedure, op cit p 154.

[17] It is true that 100 years ago suspects had no rights to legal advice and so forth. But these rights are not exercised by the majority of suspects: see section 4 above.

[18] See section 5(a) above.

Inducements

Paragraph 11.3 implicitly prohibits the offering of 'inducements', such as bail or non-prosecution.[19] The problem with this is that 'deals' and 'bargains' are central to police-suspect relationships, and what is a deal other than an agreement that each side will accept the inducements offered by the other? As Dixon points out, interrogation is often as a much a process of negotiation (over bail, charges and information about other offences and other suspects, etc) as confrontation.[20] Paragraph 11.3 has not changed this, and so it is merely presentational. The gap between the law and reality could hardly be greater than it is here. The ban on inducements reflects a fear that people offered inducements may say whatever they think the police want to hear, regardless of whether or not it is true. The fear is entirely justified, but it cannot be simply legislated away. The only way to inhibit inducements to confess substantially would be to reduce or eliminate the value of confessions to the police.

'Fairness'

This is not mentioned in Code of Practice C, but it arises because s 78 allows any evidence to be excluded at trial (at the discretion of the judge) if it is obtained 'unfairly'. Examples arising out of the conduct of the interrogation include lies and deception (*Mason*[1]), failure to record suspects' statements contemporaneously (*Canale*[2]) and questioning juveniles without an appropriate adult (*Fogah*[3]). There are also countless other situations outside the interrogation in which s 78 has been invoked, such as *Samuel*[4] (denial of the right to a solicitor) and *Absolam*[5] (failure to advise of the right to legal advice). No modern case, however, has ever regarded 'coaxing' as unfair.

'Oppression'

This is only partially defined. Section 76(8) states that oppression 'includes torture, inhuman or degrading treatment, and the use or

---

19 See *Northam* (1967) 52 Cr App Rep 97 and *Howden-Simpson* [1991] Crim LR 49 (discussed in ch 9, section 4), where the inducement was not to interview the choirboys for whom the suspect was responsible.

20 D Dixon, 'Common Sense, Legal Advice, and the Right of Silence' [1991] PL 233.

1 [1988] 1 WLR 139.

2 [1990] 2 All ER 187.

3 [1989] Crim LR 141.

4 [1988] QB 615.

5 (1988) 88 Cr App Rep 332.

threat of violence (whether or not amounting to torture).' In *Fulling*,[6] the defendant made incriminating statements after being told that her lover had been having an affair with the occupant of the next cell. The Court of Appeal adopted the dictionary definition of oppression, which is:

'Exercise of authority or power in a burdensome, harsh, or wrongful manner, unjust or cruel treatment of subjects, inferiors etc; the imposition of unreasonable or unjust burdens.'

This extremely wide definition was qualified with the view that this would normally have to include an 'impropriety' by the police. The courts do not view all 'improprieties' as oppressive.[7] Presumably this is why the police were held not to have acted 'oppressively' in this case, for the trick played on Fulling was undoubtedly 'cruel', although perhaps not what one would normally think of as oppressive. The recourse to the dictionary definition by Lord Lane CJ in *Fulling* was essentially rhetorical, and the courts have still to clarify what is meant in law by oppression. Is a breach of Code of Practice C a necessary pre-condition for conduct to be considered as possibly oppressive? Probably not. Although neither lying to nor hectoring the suspect is a breach of Code of Practice C, it has been held oppressive to do both.[8]

It is also unclear whether the test is the intention of the officers or the effect on the suspect.[9] The uncertainties involved here, say Bevan and Lidstone, have led to cases which should have been decided under PACE, s 76 being decided under s 78 (the 'unfairness' provision). Overlap between s 76(2)(a) which deals with oppression and s 76(2)(b), which deals with conduct liable to lead to unreliable confession evidence (which also constitutes grounds for excluding the confession evidence in court), has added to the confusion. This might not matter in practical terms,[10] but it is of symbolic importance. Characterisation of police behaviour as 'unfair' by a court is something the police can shrug off, but if more police behaviour were labelled 'oppressive' the police might become more inhibited. As it is, even after years of experience of the 'PACE regime', cases still arise of clear oppression: in the 'Cardiff Three' case[11] a young man with learning difficulties was subjected to 14 hours of interrogation, over no less than 19 separate interrogations,

---

6   [1987] QB 426.
7   In *Davison* [1988] Crim LR 442, for instance (as in many other cases), unlawful denial of access to a solicitor was held not to be oppressive.
8   *Beales* [1991] Crim LR 118.
9   See ch 9, section 4, below.
10   But note that whereas exclusion of 'unfairly' obtained evidence at trial is discretionary, evidence obtained contrary to s 76 must be excluded: see ch 9, below.
11   *Re Miller, Paris, Abdullahi* (1992) Times, 24 December.

held over a four-day period, much of which was extremely aggressive. After 300 denials (and 13 hours of interrogation) he eventually 'confessed'. As the Court of Appeal put it, 'The officers made it clear to Mr Miller that they would go on interviewing him until he agreed with the version of events they required.'[12] He, and two associates, were convicted of murder. When the Court of Appeal judges began hearing the interrogation tapes, they stopped the case and allowed the appeal of all three men on the grounds of oppression before they reached the end, so shocked were they at the behaviour of the police.

'Voluntariness'

The Phillips Commission regarded everything which took place in police custody as being 'involuntary', for anything which a suspect might do voluntarily would not require compulsory detention in the first place. If the job of the police is to persuade people to speak when they do not wish to speak, to regard their speaking as 'voluntary' is a nonsense. Philips regarded itself as faced with the choice between banning custodial interrogation (the due process option) or abandoning the voluntariness principle (the crime control option). It chose the latter. Perhaps regarding this logic as unpalatable, the government retained the voluntariness principle in the form of the caution (that no one need say anything unless they wish to do so) but did not state the principle explicitly anywhere in PACE or Code of Practice C.

Despite the right of silence, Code of Practice C (Note 1B) stipulates that police officers have the right to put questions to all suspects, whether or not they have expressed their intention to remain silent:

'when a police officer is trying to discover whether, or by whom, an offence has been committed he is entitled to question any person from whom he thinks useful information can be obtained, subject to the restrictions imposed by this code. A person's declaration that he is unwilling to reply does not alter this entitlement.'

The law allows the police to persuade suspects to speak when they do not wish to do so, subject to the limits we have just discussed. This ambivalence in the law between the due process principles of the right of silence and voluntariness and the crime control principle of allowing the police latitude in how much pressure they may bring to bear on suspects creates uncertainty about the limits of police interrogation on which the law is largely silent. The main safeguard is supposed to be the presence of a legal advisor.

---

[12]   See (1992) Guardian, 17 December.

Access to legal advice

We have seen that the right to legal advice is a continuing one, which is sometimes used by the police as a ploy to discourage suspects from requesting advice straight away. But being able to request a solicitor when an interview is about to take place, or even during one, is particularly important, as the Code of Practice C (para.11.1) acknowledges:

'Immediately prior to the commencement or re-commencement of any interview at a police station or other authorised place of detention, the interviewing officer should remind the suspect of his entitlement to free legal advice.'

Not only may suspects not be interviewed if they ask for solicitors who have yet to arrive,[13] but also interviews must stop when suspects request a solicitor. As always, these provisions rely on the police informing suspects of a right which is designed to protect them against those very same police officers.[14]

These provisions are subject to exceptions in special circumstances.[15] Interviews may take place even if legal advice has been requested but not yet received if the general delaying conditions apply.[16] If these provisions do not apply, the interview may none the less take place if an officer of the rank of superintendent or above has reasonable grounds for believing that delay will involve risk of harm to persons or serious loss or damage to property, or if waiting for a lawyer could lead to 'unreasonable delay to the process of investigation'. An Inspector may authorise interviewing if no legal advisor can be found at all. Interviews may take place even when these conditions do not apply when suspects who had requested advice change their minds. In these circumstances, suspects must give their agreement, in writing or on tape, to being interviewed without legal advice and an officer of the rank of inspector or above must agree to this.

Given the rights of suspects to be accompanied by legal advisors, why is police interrogation still a problem? Firstly, interrogation in the absence of a legal advisor is only invalid if the above provisions are not complied with. We have seen that only a small proportion of suspects who are interviewed by the police are accompanied (around 14%). Even though many more secure advice of some kind, this does not wrest control of the interrogation from the police. The police can rarely delay access lawfully, and now rarely try, but many suspects do not

---

[13] Code of Practice C, op cit para 6.6. See discussion in section 4(a) above.
[14] See section 4(c) above.
[15] Code of Practice C, op cit para 6.6.
[16] PACE, s 58. See section 4(a) above.

seek, or appear to change their minds about, lawyers. This is partly because of police ploys and partly because of the legal profession itself; and many solicitors often simply decline to attend interviews.

Secondly, many legal advisors are supine in the face of oppressive interrogation, as in the 'Cardiff Three' case and the more general research discussed earlier.[17] However, it has to be recognised that, even if legal advisors are minded to intervene, police interrogation is controlled by the police, as in the following example:

Sol: '. . . the second clarification is the wallet.'
DC: 'We're not on trial here; we're asking the questions, not you; we don't have to clarify anything.'
Sol: 'I am entitled as any defence solicitor would be to ask for clarification—you don't need to give it, officer.'
DC: 'We're not clarifying things here, we're not on trial. You can ask these things later when it comes to court.'[18]

This illustrates a key problem for the argument that legal advice could be a safeguard if the police and legal profession changed their ways. Legal advisors can only intervene to prevent interrogation methods which fail to conform to the standards discussed above. But we saw that none of the key concepts is clear. Not only does this give the police considerable leeway, but it would produce uncertainty in the mind of the most assertive solicitor, let alone the average unqualified clerk. Moreover, whilst the distinction between 'interviews' and 'conversations' remains, legal advisors will continue to be excluded from informal 'conversations' which may be as important as formal interviews. It is to interrogation methods, and then informal questioning, to which we now turn.

(f)   Police interrogation practices

Police interviews with suspects are not usually simple chats. By definition they are adversarial. Some suspects are simply happy to tell the police everything they know, but few take this view since it gains them nothing and can lose them a lot. In the main, then, the interview is about negotiating release of information (in exchange for something

---

17   M McConville and J Hodgson, Custodial Legal Advice and the Right to Silence (Royal Commission on Criminal Justice, Research Study no 16) (HMSO, 1993) and J Baldwin, The Role of Legal Representatives at the Police Station (Royal Commission on Criminal Justice, Research Study no 3) (HMSO, 1993).
18   McConville and Hodgson, op cit p 127. The authors note that the solicitor made no further attempt to interrupt the interrogation. Other examples are provided by J Baldwin, 'Police Interview Techniques: Establishing Truth or Proof?' (1993) 33 BJ Crim 325.

worth gaining) and/or attempting to persuade suspects to provide information which they do not want to provide. Whatever the situation, police strategy is first directed to establishing control.[19] The police control where, when and how interrogations take place, what is asked, what information is given to suspects, and what is said to suspects or solicitors outside the interrogation. This keeps suspects on the defensive, nervous, less able to exercise their normal powers of judgment, and unsure of the applicability of any rights of which they may have knowledge.

This was recognised by the American Supreme Court in the famous *Miranda* ruling, saying that 'the very fact of custodial interrogation exerts a heavy toll on individual liberty and trades on the weaknesses of individuals.'[20] This is illustrated by a study conducted by Griffiths and Ayres of well-educated students who had been told their rights, had consulted lawyers, and had been warned of imminent interrogation.[1] Despite these favourable conditions, many talked to their interrogators despite initial declarations of their unwillingness to do so. Driver concludes his summary of the police science and social science literature on interrogation by describing all interrogation as inherently coercive and incapable of being equally balanced between police and suspect.[2] The imbalance is exacerbated by the use of interrogation 'tactics', as catalogued below.

Use of custodial conditions

Interrogation is nearly always on territory chosen by the police. This enables them to control suspects. The manipulation of custodial conditions is particularly important. Since this, along with several other tactics, was first identified by Irving,[3] several other researchers have endorsed his findings. Just being held for interview is a 'frightener',[4] and suspects are usually placed in the cells for a while prior to interview to 'soften them up' even if there is nothing to prevent the interview going ahead immediately.[5] Isolation, assertion of authority and control over details such as precise times of drinks, breaks and so forth are all important. In the interrogation itself police authority is crucial, eg '*I'll*

---

[19] B Irving, Police Interrogation: A Study of Current Practice (Royal Commission on Criminal Procedure, Research Paper no 2) (HMSO, 1980).

[20] *Miranda v Arizona* 384 US 458 (1966).

[1] J Griffiths and R Ayres, 'A postscript to the Miranda Project: Interrogation of Draft Protestors' (1967) 77 Yale LJ 300.

[2] E Driver, 'Confessions and the Social Psychology of Coercion' (1968) 82 Har LR 42.

[3] Op cit.

[4] Evans, op cit p 25.

[5] Sanders et al, op cit (1989).

decide when the interview finishes', and '. . . don't think we'll just let it go just because in one interview you make no replies—we're just starting.'[6] Recalcitrant suspects are often returned to the cells as a warning of how they will have to spend the rest of their 24 hour detention—a severe threat in view of the feelings of most suspects about detention.[7] Thus Softley found that occasionally a confession was produced almost immediately on return to the cells.[8]

Police discretion

This is when the police allude (overtly or in a veiled manner) to their discretion in relation to bail, the level and number of charges to be preferred, other suspects to be investigated and so forth. Co-operation (or not) will influence the way that discretion is exercised. Examples include the police saying threateningly to a legal representative, in the presence of the suspect, 'We'll have to see about bail if he's not talking',[9] and the police telling a legal representative that they would not charge his client if he confessed.[10] The interviews from one police station looked at by Baldwin contained a spate of inducements to confess on the promise that the offences would merely be 'taken into consideration' (TICd).[11]

Provision of expert knowledge

This is where the police play on their specialist knowledge of the legal system to suggest what the effect will be of their co-operation or otherwise on the attitude of the court, likely sentence, the chance of receiving expert help, and so forth. In the 'Cardiff Three' case, one of the suspects attempted to retract earlier incriminating statements he had made, and was immediately told that 'you're looking at a life sentence if this goes wrong'. He thereupon continued to confess.[12]

---

[6] Both examples taken from McConville and Hodgson, op cit p 126.
[7] Sanders et al, op cit (1989).
[8] P Softley, Police Interrogation: An Observational Study in Four Police Stations (Royal Commission on Criminal Procedure Research Study no 4) (HMSO, 1981).
[9] McConville and Hodgson, op cit p 121. See also the extract from an informal interview quoted in section 5(h) below.
[10] Ibid p 122.
[11] Baldwin, 'Police Interview Techniques: Establishing Truth or Proof?', op cit pp 348–349. Offences taken into consideration are put before the court in abbreviated form at a normal hearing for some other offence. 'TICs' may influence sentencing, but the advantage to the defendant is that it allows the slate to be wiped clean. See also the extract from an informal interview in section 5(h) below.
[12] Extract of interview as broadcast by the BBC programme 'Panorama' on 24 February 1992.

Consequences of confession

Persuasive interviewers can lead suspects to believe that confession will make them appear to be more worthy people and that non-co-operation is socially, emotionally and practically undesirable. For example, 'What's your girlfriend to think about you?',[13] and 'sometimes you have to stand up like a man . . .'[14]

No decision to be made

While the other tactics attempt to force suspects to make a decision, this tactic suggests that there is no decision to make. The suspect is led to understand (whether erroneously or not) that the police have sufficient evidence anyway, so that there is no point in non-co-operation, eg 'We've had a complaint saying you were there ... There are five people to say you were there.'[15]

Now is the time to explain

This implies to suspects who divulge only a little information that failure to explain fully will lead to unspecified harmful consequences. For example, 'It's only fair to tell you that it's in your own interests and to your benefit to give your version of events.'[16]

Accusation or abuse

Examples include: 'Why are they [witnesses] lying? . . . I asked for a reason—there isn't one—why?' and 'You, young man, are a liar basically . . .'[17] This was the tactic used (along with the infamous 'Mr Nice and Mr Nasty' Mutt and Jeff routine) in the Cardiff Three case. According to the Lord Chief Justice:

'Miller was bullied and hectored. The officers . . . were not so much questioning him as shouting at him what they wanted him to say . . . It is impossible to convey on the printed page the pace, force, and menace of the officer's delivery.'[18]

The printed page is certainly no substitute for hearing the tapes, but one extract serves well enough to illustrate the hectoring

[13]   McConville and Hodgson, op cit p 123.
[14]   Ibid p 124.
[15]   Ibid p 125.
[16]   Ibid p 129.
[17]   Ibid p 128.
[18]   (1992) Guardian, 17 December.

that Miller endured when he tried to deny involvement in murder:

Police: 'How you could sit there and say that. You've been in that
             room—seen that girl there, in the state that she was in. And
             you're supposed to have had all this wonderful care for her.
             Seen her damned head hang off, and her arms cut, and
             stabbed to death, and you sit there and tell us that you
             know nothing at all about it, nothing at all about it.
Suspect: 'I wasn't there.'
Police: 'How you can ever . . .'
Suspect: 'I wasn't there.'
Police: 'I just don't know how you can sit there.'[19]

Despite the high profile of this case, because three men were wrongly
jailed for murder, the interrogation techniques employed in it may not
have been unusual. Baldwin also provides examples. At one point in a
series of very aggressive interviews of a juvenile for murder, for
instance, the officer—in an uncanny echo of 'Cardiff Three'—said:

'You can sit here, looking at the floor, crying and crying, but I am not
going to walk out of that door; you are not going to leave here until I
hear it from your own lips. Do you understand ? Did you murder that
boy ?'[20]

These were not idle threats. Custodial interrogation lasted three
days.

The effectiveness of tactics

Some tactics will be more effective than others. According to
McConville and Hodgson, the most common tactics are (in order of frequency of use) 'no decision to make', 'accusation/abuse' and
'consequences'. With any one suspect, however, it may be difficult to
guess what will be effective. It is not surprising to find that in the majority of cases more than one tactic is used. Presumably as one tactic does
not work, the police move on to another. Even then, tactics are thought
to fail to elicit confessions as often as they succeed,[1] or even most of the
time.[2] Police interrogation in general is described in most research
reports as often ineffective, clumsy, rambling, repetitious and hit and
miss.[3] Only rarely (usually when a there is an immediate confession) is

---

[19] 'Panorama', above.
[20] Baldwin, Police Interview Techniques: Establishing Truth or Proof?, op cit p 347.
[1] Evans, op cit pp 44–46.
[2] Baldwin, Police Interview Techniques: Establishing Truth or Proof?, op cit.
[3] See eg ibid and S Moston and T Engelberg, 'Police Questioning Techniques in Tape
     Recorded Interviews with Criminal Suspects' (1993) 3 Policing and Society p 223.

no tactic used.[4] Effectiveness may also be affected by the presence or absence of lawyers and appropriate adults, whether the interview is being recorded or not, and so forth.

The vulnerability of the suspect is crucial. The essence of interrogation tactics is to locate a particular vulnerability and exploit it. In a sense all suspects are vulnerable, however. Twenty-four hours provides a lot of time to explore the vulnerabilities of the psyche. Indeed, Evans comments of juveniles that 'The very fact that juveniles are arrested and detained for questioning by the police may render them psychologically vulnerable.'[5] Not surprisingly, tactics are most used where there is no ready confession and where the other evidence is weak or lacking in a crucial respect, such as intention.[6] From the crime control perspective, tactics are crucial in securing vital information that would be otherwise unobtainable or obtainable only at considerable expense. From the due process perspective, tactics are to be condemned both because they excessively infringe and abuse the liberty of the individual and because they are likely to elicit self-incriminating statements in cases where suspects are factually innocent.

The legality of tactics

The 'police discretion' tactic clearly involves inducements. As such it is unlawful, as it was prior to PACE. Code of Practice C and PACE should have made the rules more inhibitory: there is para 11.3 of the Code (prohibiting oppression and inducements), the more frequent use of legal representatives and requirements to record everything said and done. Irving and McKenzie did indeed find compliance with Code of Practice C in a later study,[7] but McConville and Hodgson, albeit in a small number of cases, did not.[8] It is possible that the police were less inhibited in front of McConville and Hodgson than in front of Irving and McKenzie because PACE was still new and untried when the latter did their research, but by the time the former did theirs (1991–92) the police felt more confident about bending the rules.

---

4   McConville and Hodgson, op cit Table 7.1.
5   R Evans, The Conduct of Police Interviews with Juveniles (Royal Commission on Criminal Justice, Research Study no 8) (HMSO, 1992) p 26.
6   Ibid p 31.
7   B Irving and I McKenzie, Police Interrogation: The Effects of the Police and Criminal Evidence Act 1984 (The Police Foundation, 1989).
8   Op cit. Note that they only observed cases in which there was a legal advisor present. If the legal representatives do inhibit the police, one would expect more breaches of Code of Practice C and PACE in cases not observed by them, especially as the presence of the researchers themselves could also have exerted an inhibitory influence.

As to the other tactics, their legality is difficult to assess. 'Use of custodial conditions' and 'accusation and abuse', in their most extreme manifestations, could be oppressive and thus unlawful.[9] But the other tactics would not be unlawful unless the claims about, for instance, other evidence were blatant lies or deceptions.[10]

The failure of Parliament to specify, in the law, the acceptable outer boundaries of the most important aspect of interrogations—the way they are carried out—is precisely what the police need to enable them to follow their crime control informal working rules and to inhibit legal advisors from intervening in interrogations. Revealingly, the chief constable of South Wales said that, although he did not support oppressive interviewing, two High Court judges had allowed the 'Cardiff Three' confession evidence and 'a full debate on what constituted oppressive questioning was now needed.'[11] Similarly, in a murder case where the trial judge refused to accept alleged confessions secured after the police wrongly told the defendant that they had identification evidence and 'pounded him with sexual allegations' the head of CID for the force concerned said 'It is a matter of interpretation as to what is oppressive . . . It is rather difficult to establish the truth by pussyfooting about.'[12]

The police seek confessions and other information as efficiently as possible, under circumstances which the Philips Commission regarded as extinguishing voluntariness, and which earlier commentators would have regarded as oppressive per se. This is allowed by the silence in the law. It is therefore impossible to estimate how frequently unlawful tactics are used. Evans, however, comments that if, as he found in some cases:

'oppressive and persuasive tactics are used with juveniles, many of whom have committed minor offences, then this may be taken as an indication of their routine use in police interviews. The problem remains as to what constitutes "legitimate persuasion" and whether its use can be justified with groups, such as juveniles, who may be thought to be "at risk" by virtue of their age.'[13]

The use of persuasive tactics against vulnerable suspects—and all suspects are vulnerable in some circumstances—can only be

---

[9] *Fulling* [1987] QB 426 and the 'Cardiff Three' case, above.
[10] *Mason* [1988] 1 WLR 139.
[11] (1992) Guardian, 17 December.
[12] (1993) Guardian, 22 November.
[13] Op cit p 46. A similar point is made in relation to adult interviews by J Baldwin, 'Power and Police Interviews' (1993) 143 NLJ 1194. Like that of Evans, this research was commissioned by the Runciman Commission.

permissible under the law if a narrow interpretation of 'oppression', 'voluntary' and 'inducement' is used. Whether one regards their use as good in the interests of efficiency or bad as being harmful to due process standards depends on one's priorities. What ought to be common ground is that if the current situation is to be tolerated the pretence that 'involuntariness', oppression and inducements are generally unlawful should be dropped. Standards for the conduct of interrogations should then be prescribed. These would not eliminate oppression, but they would at least set limits to it and provide a yardstick for legal advisors.

These conclusions emerge in part from research commissioned by the two Royal Commissions. They were understood by the Philips Commission, and formed part of the analytical basis for its recommendations.[14] This was not true of the Runciman Commission, which stated that in interviews there is

'. . . an over-ready assumption on the part of some interviewing officers of the suspect's guilt and on occasion the exertion of undue pressure amounting to bullying or harassment . . . They entered the interview room with their minds made up and treated the suspect's explanation with unjustified scepticism.'[15]

But the whole point of most interviews is to exert pressure. This is not out of a desire to humiliate suspects or 'fit them up'. It is a product, as one would expect in a crime control system, of a belief in the suspects' guilt and of resource and legal constraints which put a premium on confession evidence. The use of terms like 'unjustified' and 'an over-ready assumption' is indicative of a failure to understand the nature of police interrogation. The report devotes little more than a page to interrogation, and none to the legality or otherwise of police interrogation techniques. The result was an endorsement of Home Office interviewing policy[16] and an emphasis on the need to inculcate those skills 'which are most likely to elicit the truth while at the same time ensuring that they are exercised within a clearly defined code of ethical conduct.'[17] There is no recognition that eliciting the truth and behaving ethically will often be mutually exclusive, or that eliciting the truth in most cases entails tactics which elicit untruths in others.

---

[14] In particular, the recommendation that arrest, and hence detention, be used less often. As we saw above, section 3, this was only partially implemented in PACE.

[15] Report, op cit p 12.

[16] Home Office circulars 22/1992 and 7/1993.

[17] Report, op cit p 13.

(g)   Recording of interviews

One of the most problematic aspects of the interrogation process over the years has been the accurate recording of it. Without knowing what was said and done, by both police officers and suspects, it is impossible to know what pressure was placed on suspects to confess or even whether they confessed at all. Prior to PACE, questions and answers were rarely tape recorded. Confessions (or, more rarely, denials) came in one of two forms. Firstly, 'verbals'. This was a police officer's account of the suspect's voluntary verbal statement, usually written down some time after it was made. Secondly, 'voluntary' written statements, written either by the suspect or, at the suspect's dictation, by a police officer. Both came to be challenged increasingly frequently. 'Verbals' were often said not to reflect accurately what suspects really said, and were sometimes alleged to be complete fabrications.[18] Similarly, voluntary written statements were often said to have been the work of the officers themselves. In an infamous scandal of the 1960s, Sgt Challenor and several colleagues were eventually successfully prosecuted for these practices (and many instances of corruption and brutality) when it was found that statements made by suspects he had arrested all used the same improbable phrases such as 'travelling in a northerly direction' and 'it's a fair cop guv, it was me wot done it'.[19]

Inaccuracy—commonly known as 'gilding the lily'[20] took three forms. Firstly, there was alteration of the words used to create a different impression, either deliberately or inadvertently. As Lord Devlin put it in 1960, when he was a High Court judge, many statements use '. . . the stately language of the police station where, for example, people never eat but partake of refreshment and never quarrel but indulge in altercations.'[1] Police officers, like everyone else, have imperfect recall, and mistakes are made when conversations are reconstructed at a later time, especially when the purpose of the reconstruction is to prove a point.[2]

Secondly, there was the incomplete recording of what was said. It was common to only write down what suspects said 'when they start telling the truth', ie when they agreed with the allegations being put to them.[3]

---

[18]   The Royal Commissions of 1929 and 1962, as well as the Philips Commission, were concerned about 'verbals'. See B Cox, *Civil Liberties in Britain* (Penguin, 1975) ch 4.

[19]   Cox, op cit.

[20]   Kaye, op cit.

[1]   P Devlin, *Criminal Prosecution in England* (OUP, 1960) p 39.

[2]   G Stephenson, 'Should Collaborative Testimony be Permitted in Courts of Law?' [1990] Crim LR 302.

[3]   A Sanders, 'Constructing the Case for the Prosecution' (1987) 14 Journal of Law and Society 229.

As we know, police tactics can lead suspects to 'confess' against their will, and this is difficult to challenge if previous denials are not recorded. Thirdly, there is complete fabrication, as in at least some of Sgt Challenor's cases. In the 'Confait Affair', allegedly voluntary statements were either written by the police entirely or consisted of words put into the suspects' mouths by the police.

The Philips Commission realised the dangers of all these forms of inaccuracy. It did not believe that all, or even most, alleged statements were false. But some were, as even some police officers admit.[4] The problem was in distinguishing the false from the true. In keeping with its general philosophy of keeping records of police-suspect encounters, the Philips Commission recommended that all exchanges be accurately written down so that the question of fabricated confessions did not arise. So, when PACE was introduced, Code of Practice C (para 11.5) required 'an accurate record' of interrogation to be made either 'during the course of the interview' (and to be a 'verbatim record') or, if this was not practicable, 'an account of the interview which adequately and accurately summarises it'.

There were several problems with this. For the police, the laborious writing down of everything everyone said slowed the interview, gave suspects time to think, and inhibited the establishment of rapport. This was probably why Irving and McKenzie found that police use of tactics decreased immediately after PACE,[5] and why the police in general found (or believed) PACE to hamper them.[6] Also, just as before, what was written down might not be accurate or complete. The only difference was that the police would have to claim that it was written contemporaneously instead of afterwards. This became apparent, many years after the event, in the 'Birmingham Six', 'Guildford Four', and 'Tottenham Three' cases. Although the investigations were pre-PACE, the police claimed that they had written notes of interrogations contemporaneously (and the convictions in all these cases were largely based on this), but later scientific evidence proved this not to be so.[7] Finally, there is the problem of what happens outside the interrogation and when it is not 'practicable' to record contemporaneously. Because

---

[4] See McConville et al, op cit (1991) pp 84–87. In the wake of the sensational miscarriages of justice which came to light in the late 1980s, many senior officers admitted that 'noble cause' corruption had occurred but claimed that PACE had put a stop to it. See R Reiner, 'Policing and the Police' in M Maguire et al (eds) *Oxford Handbook of Criminology* (OUP, 1994) p 731.

[5] Op cit.

[6] M Maguire, 'Effects of the PACE Provisions on Detention and Questioning' (1988) 28 BJ Crim 19.

[7] See J Rozenberg, 'Miscarriages of Justice' in E Stockdale and S Casale (eds), *Criminal Justice Under Stress* (Blackstone, 1992).

of the difficulties in establishing rapport while writing everything down, not wanting everything said and done to be recorded, not wanting a legal advisor present, and so forth, this problem grew in magnitude.[8]

It took little insight to recognise the cogency of these criticisms. Well before the Philips Commission reported, many eminent figures were asking for the routine tape recording of interrogations.[9] This was initially resisted by the police, a classic police response being that 'It would wreck the way we do interviews . . . You'd always say things like "Don't fuck me about" but you couldn't on tape which would be in front of a judge and jury really.'[10] However, following the introduction of a new Code of Practice on Tape Recording in 1988 (Code of Practice E), the police adapted rapidly, and tape recording is now usual.[11] Quick-fire question and answer has returned, allowing the re-emergence of most of the old tactics. It is more difficult for the police to record proceedings selectively, and impossible for them to fabricate recordings, but the third problem—interrogation outside the interview room—remains.[12] Moston and Stephenson comment that it is rare to see general conversation appearing on taped interviews, even though conversation between suspect and interviewer at some point is usual. This, they say: '. . . confirms the inadequacy of tape recording inside the police station as a wholly adequate record of all relevant verbal exchanges between suspect and interviewer.'[13]

The requirements of the PACE Codes of Practice are now as follows: except where not practical, the interview should take place in an interview room (Code of Practice C, para 4); that room should have tamper-proof tape recording facilities, and once the interview begins everything said by all parties must be tape recorded, although again there is an 'if practicable' escape clause (Code of Practice E, para 3.3) and an exception in relation to persons suspected of involvement in terrorism or espionage (Code of Practice E, para 3.2). As Fenwick notes,

[8] All these problems of writing down what was, or was not, said apply particularly to informal interviewing, which is discussed later.

[9] See especially G Williams, 'The Authentication of Statements to the Police' [1979] Crim LR 6.

[10] M McConville, A Sanders and R Leng, *The Case for the Prosecution* (Routledge, 1991) p 60.

[11] From 1 January 1992, tape recording became mandatory, except in exceptional circumstances, for all indictable and either way cases.

[12] This is why video taping of interrogation, with which there have been several experiments, is of no substantial help. See M McConville, 'Videotaping interrogations' [1992] Crim LR 532.

[13] S Moston and G Stephenson, The Questioning and Interviewing of Suspects Outside the Police Station (Royal Commission on Criminal Justice Research Study no 22) (HMSO, 1993) p 36.

there is no good reason to exclude such cases, and every reason to include them since so many miscarriage of justice cases have concerned disputed confessions in terrorism cases.[14] Generally, a copy (which can be provided to the suspect) as well as a master copy will be made.

If no tape recording is made, everything said and done must be written down accurately and fully, whether or not the interview takes place at a police station (Code of Practice C, para 11.5(a)). Under para 11.5(c), this must be done during the course of the interview:

'unless in the investigating officer's view this would not be practicable or would interfere with the conduct of the interview, and must constitute either a verbatim record of what has been said or, failing this, an account of the interview which adequately and accurately summarises it.'

Paragraph 11.7 provides that 'if an interview record is not made in the course of the interview it must be made as soon as practicable after its completion'. Further, 'unless it is impracticable the person interviewed shall be given the opportunity to read the interview record and sign it as correct or to indicate the respect in which he considers it inaccurate' (para 11.10).

This is to ensure that what actually was said is written down and that nothing that was not said is not written down. It is also to ensure that suspects who agree that everything that has been written down fairly and accurately indicate that that is so. If a solicitor is present and the suspect so indicates then of course it is almost impossible to challenge the accuracy of the written record, thus reducing the number of cases where there is doubt about what was said. There are three problems. Firstly, even though suspects may sign what is written down this does not mean that what was written down was accurate, for people frequently fail to read documents which they sign. This is not a problem in the majority of formal interviews now that they are tape recorded.

Secondly, although what is written down (or tape recorded) may be accurate, it may none the less be unreliable when suspects are induced to confess, are subjected to oppressive pressure or have words put into their mouths. Again, neither tape recording nor legal advice are panaceas. Not only do these things sometimes happen on tape and with a lawyer present,[15] but they also happen before or between interviews.[16] It is true that 'A written record should also be made of any comments made by a suspected person, including unsolicited comments, which are

---

[14] H Fenwick, 'Confessions, Recording Rules, and Miscarriages of Justice: A Mistaken Emphasis?' [1993] Crim LR 174.

[15] As in the 'Cardiff Three' and other cases discussed earlier.

[16] See section 5(h), below, and McConville, op cit (1992).

outside the context of an interview but which might be relevant to the offence' (Code of Practice C, para 11.13). But it need not be written at the time, and it need only be provided to the suspect for verification and signing 'where practicable'. If these comments were made as a result of unlawful pressure, the full exchange is not likely to be fully recorded by the police and, as with pre-PACE verbals, what was said (and why) often becomes simply a matter of who is believed.

The third problem is that these provisions are not mandatory: they all have 'if practicable' escape clauses. The net result is that interviews outside the station are hardly ever contemporaneously recorded. Moston and Stephenson found that the police admitted to failing to do this in nearly two-thirds of all such interviews, and suspects were asked to check the record in little over one quarter of such cases.[17]

When alleged confessions are not contemporaneously recorded the opportunities for dispute about what was really said are legion. The situation is back where it was in the days of Sgt Challenor's 'verbals' and 'voluntary' statements. Thus in *Khan*,[18] for instance, one interview took place in the police car from Wales back to Birmingham, and one took place later in the police station. The defendant was alleged to have confessed to robbery during the journey, but he denied the offence in the police station and also denied making the earlier alleged confession. The police claimed that they took contemporaneous notes of the interview in the car (which were not shown to Khan at the time). This was accepted at trial at first instance, and he was convicted. It later became clear that the police officers did not write the notes in the car, casting doubt on whether he really did confess, and so his conviction was quashed on appeal. Another example is *Dunn*.[19] The defendant was interviewed with his legal advisor present and denied criminal activity. At the end, while reading through the interview notes, the police claimed that he confessed. The police said that they wrote down this alleged confession, but they did not show the questions and answers to the suspect or to his legal advisor. The court none the less allowed the alleged confession to be used as evidence, as did the Court of Appeal, even though these were clear breaches of Code of Practice C.

These examples show that even when the police are proved to have broken these provisions of Code of Practice C for no good reason, the evidence secured as a result may still be accepted, sometimes with disastrous results for the suspect. They also illustrate the wide scope the

---

[17] Op cit.
[18] (1990) unreported, CA. Discussed by Kaye, op cit.
[19] (1990) 91 Cr App Rep 237. Discussed in J Hodgson, 'Tipping the Scales of Justice' [1992] Crim LR 854. There are many other examples, such as *Canale* [1990] 2 All ER 187.

police have for breaking them, and the opportunities thus provided simply to fabricate confessions and/or impose unlawful pressure on suspects to confess. For every instance where fabrication is proved there must be a dozen where it is alleged. As *Dunn* and *Khan* show, it is often impossible to establish who is telling the truth. Sometimes—and we will never know how often—the courts get it wrong. At other times, of course, the police fabricate confessions by people who really are guilty, but it is usually impossible to tell in which cases this is true.[20] These problems, and these mistakes, will continue for as long as confession evidence secured in the absence of an independent party remains admissible in court.

(h)   Informal interviewing

An interview is 'informal' if, instead of taking place in a police station interview room, it is done in the street, in the car, at the custody officer's desk or in the cells; or if proper cautions and rights are not provided and if the proceedings are not recorded; or if it is simply a neutral attempt to elicit information. There are many reasons why the police question suspects informally, including the fact that it is uncontrolled and unsupervised, no time clock is running, no legal advisor will be present and there are no independent witnesses or checks on the tactics used to elicit incriminating material. But informal interviews are also sometimes initiated by suspects too, who wish to 'deal' confidentially. This makes it hard to disprove police claims that informal discussions began at the behest of the suspect as said in, for instance, *Younis* and *Khan*.[1] The important point about informal interrogations is that, like all interrogations, they are encounters which the police set out to control. When the police choose to interrogate informally, it is because the constraints on formal interrogation which we have discussed in this section would limit their control. Informal interrogations subvert the PACE framework of rules designed to protect the suspect. In an attempt to control informal interviewing, PACE and Code of Practice C provide that 'interviews' may only take place outside police stations and police station interview rooms in exceptional circumstances. As with so many due process rules, these rules go against the grain of policing and, indeed, of normal social interaction: now that formal interviewing is restricted by regulations and protections for the

---

[20]   Even if it were possible to establish that a fabricated confession had been attributed to a person who was in fact guilty, the due process adherent would still argue for an acquittal. The need to uphold the integrity of the criminal process would be seen as more important than the securing of convictions in these cases.

[1]   Above.

suspect it is not surprising that informal questioning has become common. Our concern in this section is to assess the legality and frequency of these 'off the record' encounters.

The most obvious place to interview informally is in the car on the way to the station. As a CID officer said to Maguire and Norris, 'You can't just sit in the car in silence.'[2] Talking is not, in itself, unlawful and it need not amount to an interview but, even without the ever-present prospect of a deal, it would be unnatural for conversation not to turn to the reason for the arrest. Suspect-initiated conversations, we saw earlier, are common and not different in principle from police-initiated conversations.[3] Both may easily become attempts to elicit relevant information. Maguire and Norris quote another officer who said that he 'would not be doing his job'[4] if he did not talk to prisoners, thus echoing the officer who told McConville et al that 'no policeman who did his job is going to say no' if a suspect wanted to talk 'off the record'.[5]

The longer the journey, the more likely it will be that informal interviewing develops out of conversation, whether intended or not. Thus whether or not the defendant in *Khan*[6] really did make admissions in the car, it was predictable that conversation would turn to his alleged offence on a long journey from Wales to Birmingham. Some journeys, however, are unnecessarily lengthened by taking the 'scenic route'. This is a route which lasts as long as it takes to secure the admissions desired, and is clearly unlawful.[7] McConville and Morrel found that when experiments began with the tape recording of interviews in Scotland in the early 1980s, journey times to police stations got significantly longer: interrogations which could no longer take place without scrutiny in police stations simply took place in police cars instead.[8] That this still happens is confirmed by Maguire and Norris. They were, however, unable to estimate the extent of informal interviewing either in its lawful or unlawful forms.[9]

An attempt was made to estimate frequency by Brown et al and by Moston and Stephenson.[10] In both studies, police officers making the arrests in the cases being researched were asked whether they asked

[2] M Maguire and C Norris, The Conduct and Supervision of Criminal Investigations (Royal Commission on Criminal Justice Research Study no 5) (HMSO, 1992) p 46.

[3] Notwithstanding the view of the Court of Appeal in, for instance, *Younis*, above.

[4] Op cit p 46.

[5] Op cit p 58.

[6] Above.

[7] PACE, 30(1), requires transfer to a police station as soon as reasonably practicable.

[8] M McConville and P Morrell, 'Recording the Interrogation: Have the Police got it Taped?' [1983] Crim LR 158.

[9] Op cit p 46.

[10] Both op cit.

suspects questions before arrival at the police station. In Brown's study, 19% said they did before the revised Code of Practice C was introduced, and 10% afterwards. In a further 19% and 16% of cases respectively, the police said that unsolicited comments were made by the suspects.[11] Much, and possibly most, of this questioning, it seems, amounts to 'interviewing',[12] and a large minority of these suspects made admissions or incriminating statements. Moston and Stephenson asked police officers to complete questionnaires about the questioning and interviewing of suspects outside the station. The questionnaires quoted Note 11A in order to assist officers in distinguishing the two. Questioning was reported in 31% of all cases, and interviewing in 8.1% (in over half of which there was initial questioning too). One quarter of the latter were police car interviews. Officers were also asked about interviewing inside the station; in less than 1% of cases were informal police station interviews reported. Full confessions were secured in over 40% of informal interviews, and damaging statements in a further one third. These are much higher rates than are usual for custodial interviewing. Is it that suspects prepared to talk under these circumstances are natural 'confessors'? Is it that the police can be more effective when not restricted? Or are the police simply reporting more of those cases where there clearly was interviewing (because of the recorded statements of the suspects) than those where it could be hidden? In neither study were the police asked whether the questioning or interviewing was lawful in terms of Code of Practice C, para 11.1.

Both studies are methodologically flawed to such an extent that their reliability is highly questionable. Firstly, neither were studies of informal interviewing, but were studies of police claims about informal interviewing. The police might be expected to be less than honest about this, and they were. Moston and Stephenson asked the police about non-offence related conversation. Such conversation is, of course, perfectly proper, yet in one-third of cases it was claimed that no conversation took place at all. The researchers comment:

'These figures are of interest, if only for the fact that police officers often claim to make what are colloquially called "deaf and dumb" arrests . . . This appears to be merely a convenient fiction, at least in a significant proportion of cases.'[13]

Similarly, Brown reports an instance where:

'CID officers were overheard discussing what had been said to them by

---

[11] Op cit p 81.
[12] See ibid Table 6.3.
[13] Op cit p 24.

the suspect in the car on the way to the station, but recorded on the form that no questions had been asked or unsolicited comments made.'[14]

If the police lie (or fail to record the truth) some of the time how can we be confident that they do not do so much of the time? Suspects could have been asked about this issue but they were not. This is puzzling, especially in relation to Brown's study, where suspects were asked about other aspects of the research on, for instance, legal advice. Secondly, the police were asked by Moston and Stephenson separately about 'questioning' and 'interviewing'. This is a distinction which has even defeated the Court of Appeal, so to draw conclusions from questionnaires making this distinction is worthless. Finally, neither study asked about informal interviewing inside the station. Officers were given an implicit opportunity to report this, but the low rate (less than 1%) could have been as much because they were not asked about it directly as because it happened rarely. Despite all this, a considerable amount of informal questioning, albeit perhaps rather less after Code of Practice C was revised in 1991 than before,[15] is admitted by the police.

Informal interviewing in the police station has also been found to be prevalent. Dixon et al, for instance, found 53% of officers admitting always or often 'clarifying' suspects' accounts before beginning the 'proper' interview.[16] Only 28% said they did so rarely or never. Officers say that pre-interview interviewing is important to establish a rapport, as might be expected given the importance of relationships and dealing. Thus McConville et al were told that 'I'd never go cold into an interview. I'd always have a run over first with the person, do an informal chat without taking notes.'[17] This is particularly important for the police if the suspect wants a solicitor. Some custody officers, another officer told McConville et al:

'will just bend a little bit, if you want a quick word with [suspects] to see, you know, if somebody wants a solicitor and you haven't had a chance to chat and don't want him to have a solicitor yet.'[18]

The co-operation of the custody officer in allowing 'off the record' access to suspects is not essential, however, since informal interviews

---

[14] Op cit p 84.

[15] See Code of Practice C, para 11.5, discussed in subsection (g), above, on the recording of interviews.

[16] D Dixon, K Bottomley, C Coleman, M Gill and D Wall, 'Safeguarding the Rights of Suspects in Police Custody' (1990) 1 Policing and Society 115.

[17] Op cit (1991) p 59.

[18] Ibid p 58. Examples are also given by A Sanders and L Bridges, 'Access to Legal Advice and Police Malpractice' [1990] Crim LR 494.

can take place immediately prior to the tape recorded session. As an officer told Evans and Ferguson, 'I like to have a little chat to get things straight before I switch on the tape.'[19] This is, of course, completely unlawful, yet apparently frequent if we can judge by the number of times interviews appear to be 'little more than an attempt to validate what has already been rehearsed'.[20]

Cell visits are also prevalent. Sanders and Bridges, for instance, discuss a case where a CID officer admitted going to the cell of a suspect who refused to confess and secured a confession by being nice to him.[1] According to the custody record, the suspect had asked to see the officer. In the police area researched by Dixon et al, these visits are recorded as 'welfare visits', showing that custody officers allow custody records to be doctored to hide the truth.[2] As well as cell visits, informal interviews also occur at the end of the 'official' interrogation, as when a detective inspector joined other officers and proceeded to threaten the suspect in an 'unpleasant, hectoring and abusive tone'.[3] In this case, microphones installed for the purpose of a TV documentary recorded the informal interview, providing us with an insight into the behaviour of police officers when they believe themselves to be 'off the record'. The defendant had been arrested on suspicion of several burglaries but denied involvement in any of them. Once the police tape recorder was switched off, the detective inspector slipped into 'informal' mode:

DI: '. . . I've told you what I'm gonna do. I ain't bullshitting you, I'm gonna charge you with six [offences]. If you want six fucking charges, you can have six charges—your barrister ain't got much of a fucking argument at the end of the day. I don't really want to charge you with six fucking charges: I'd rather charge you with a couple and you can have four TICs. You can rip the fucking TICs up once you get to court—I don't really give a shit. Do you understand what I am saying?'
Suspect: 'Mmm.'
. . .

DI: 'Now bullshit aside now, that's the deal I can offer. Quite simply you fucking take it or leave it. You know what's going to happen if you fucking leave it. I mean you ain't going to fucking lose nothing, you don't lose anything by saying "OK, I'll fucking take that."'
Another detective: 'Plus the fact that you've got a couple of charges,

[19] R Evans and T Ferguson, Comparing Different Juvenile Cautioning Systems in One Police Force Area (Report to the Home Office Research and Planning Unit)(1991).
[20] J Baldwin, 'Police Interview Techniques: Establishing Truth or Proof?' (1993) 33 BJ Crim 325 at 347.
[1] Op cit (1990).
[2] Dixon et al, op cit.
[3] McConville, op cit (1992) p 542.

court in the morning, def the breach of curfew, "he's got two charges of burglary, he's helped us out." We won't oppose bail. Otherwise we get six charges, "he didn't wanna fucking know" and remand in custody.'
. . .

DI: 'As I say, we'd lay it on heavy or we come off fucking light, it's a matter for you. The most important thing is you've got a fucking decision to make. You're either going to have six fucking charges or you're going to have two and the only fucking way you're having two is you start fucking talking to us.'[4]

None of this exchange was discoverable from the official taped record of the formal interrogation, and the custody officer knew nothing about the informal interview. The detective inspector's presence in the interview was not recorded on the custody sheet, and the custody officer made this note in the custody record: 'PACE codes of practice complied with.'[5] Records are rarely made of informal interrogations which, officially, simply do not happen.[6]

Informal interviewing inside the station is usually a blatant breach of PACE and Code of Practice C, for it can rarely be impractical to turn an informal chat into a formal interview if one is already inside a police station. It often occurs between interviews precisely because the suspect in question does not want to talk. Since the aim of the informal chat is to change the minds of suspects, the dangers of coercion or unlawful inducements—precisely the dangers which the formal interviewing regime of PACE is ostensibly designed to combat—are obvious. Despite this, the products of these interviews are usable as evidence in court even when there is no independent verification of what was said and how what was allegedly said was obtained.

The wrongful conviction and jailing of Khan is an example of what can happen not only when crime control practices are followed, but also when legal rules—in this case, the rule that information freely volunteered may be written down and used—contain crime control values. Research has failed to provide reliable estimates of how frequent informal interviewing really is, whether unlawful or not. And we will never know how often alleged confessions made under these conditions are fabricated by the police. Yet every research project on interrogation carried out since PACE was introduced, with one exception,[7] has found

---

[4] We have used only a relatively small, but representative, part of these officers' attempt to trigger a confession. The entire exchange is quoted by McConville, op cit pp 542–543.

[5] Ibid pp 544–545.

[6] They are usually officially acknowledged only when a confession is made or alleged by the police. An example is *Dunn* (1990) 91 Cr App Rep 237.

[7] B Irving and I McKenzie, Police Interrogation: The Effects of the Police and Criminal Evidence Act 1984 (The Police Foundation, 1989).

that it exists,[8] and many of the infamous miscarriages of the 1990–93 period involved fabricated confessions.

Even to consider making incriminating statements, whether spontaneously made in an informal setting or secured through informal interviewing, inadmissible as evidence would require a major change of attitude by government. But if the rules are to be tightened up they should be formulated with social reality in mind. If legal rules are formulated without taking account of actual police practices, they are likely to be more presentational than inhibitory. Informal interviewing will never be eradicated. As Moston and Stephenson themselves say:

'One central process, namely the general process of questioning and discussion leading to arrest, remains concealed from view, submerged in secrecy and obfuscation.'[9]

All that can be done is to refuse to accept its products as evidence in court. The Runciman Commission, however, simply accepted that there was a considerable amount of questioning outside the station, and did not discuss informal interviewing inside the station.

Although the Runciman Commission recommended that informal interviewing be reduced by encouraging police officers to use portable tape recorders 'because any breach of the code by police officers may be tape recorded',[10] it also commented that 'many witnesses suggested to us that spontaneous remarks uttered on arrest are often the most truthful. We agree.'[11] No evidence or reasoning was given for their agreement with this suggestion. This attitude is likely to encourage police officers to provoke spontaneity on the part of arrestees or, at least, to claim that remarks were spontaneously made. The conclusion flowing from this is that courts should continue to accept evidence provided in such exchanges, whether tape recorded or not, otherwise 'some reliable confessions might be lost.'[12] The absence of concern that some unreliable confessions might also be lost betrays the crime control thinking of Runciman and its reluctance to impose inhibitory rules on the police.

(i)   False confessions

False confessions were one of the motors driving the Philips Commission and PACE. Although the Confait Affair was the cause

---

[8] This includes writers such as Dixon et al, op cit, who distance themselves from the most harsh critics of the police.

[9] Op cit p 43.

[10] Report, op cit p 28.

[11] Ibid p 61.

[12] Ibid p 61.

celebre of the 1970s, other cases included that of Errol Madden,[13] who was accused of stealing a model car, and a man who 'confessed' to stealing money from his employer.[14] The claims in both cases that the confessions were false and made because of pressure from the police were verified by the fact that both the model car and the money turned out not to be stolen at all. The PACE framework of contemporaneous recording and interviewing in the station, together with the outlawing of oppressive treatment, was developed in order to prevent such cases. In the event, as we know from cases like the 'Cardiff Three'[15] and the 'Tottenham Three',[16] the new laws made little difference.

Usually, it is unclear whether confessions made under pressure are false or not. It is generally more difficult to establish conclusively that someone is innocent than to prove that they are guilty. But cases like *Madden* and the 'Confait Affair' illustrate that the police presumption of guilt, which leads them to apply intense pressure to confess, is sometimes demonstrably and wholly unfounded. One such case in the post-PACE era is that of David Blythe. He was arrested in 1987 for murder. He was questioned for hours without legal advice and 'confessed'. He was charged and kept in prison awaiting trial for 11 months. Shortly before the trial was due to commence, someone else was arrested for the murder about whose guilt there was no doubt at all. The prosecution dropped the case against Blythe. The police accepted that he was completely innocent, yet something had happened when he was in custody to make him 'confess'.[17]

From the due process perspective, however, protections for suspects are justified in themselves and should not be dependent on whether or not oppressive behaviour or inducements really do lead to false confessions. On the other hand, since all systems have some false confessions and some wrongful convictions (see discussion in chapter 1, above) the fact that there are some false confessions does not automatically mean that the system must be changed. For while the due process adherent will want to minimise the incidence of false confessions (and minimise the reliance of the system on them) knowing that the result will be the conviction of fewer guilty people, the crime control adherent will wish to maintain the processes which produce false confessions as long as they produce even greater numbers of reliable confessions and expeditious convictions.

In discussing false confessions we need to distinguish between

---

[13] Discussed in ch 3, section 5.
[14] B Cox, *Civil Liberties in Britain* (Penguin, 1975) p 177.
[15] *Re Paris, Abdullahi and Miller* (1992) Times, 24 December.
[16] *Re Raghip, Silcott and Braithwaite* (1991) Times, 9 December.
[17] (1988) Guardian, 2 February.

innocent people who confess 'voluntarily'; people whose innocence or otherwise is unknown who 'confess' through coercion; and people, again whose innocence is unknown, who allegedly confess but who in fact do not. The last category concerns fabricated confessions, and was discussed earlier. There are a number of reasons why people who are, or may be, innocent confess.[18]

'Coerced-compliant' confessions

Here the suspect knows that the confession is false, but is prepared to confess to escape pressure. This pressure will sometimes be oppressive interrogation tactics, or sometimes just the experience of custody and interrogation. This was what apparently happened in the 'Confait Affair' and probably in the 'Cardiff Three' case and several of the other infamous miscarriage cases. Many of these cases involved vulnerable suspects, but people with average IQ and normal personality characteristics are also vulnerable to tactics of this type, as in a false murder confession discussed by Gudjonsson and Mackeith.[19] These confessions can also arise from strong inducements.

'Coerced-internalised' confessions

Here, suspects begin to doubt their own memory. They temporarily believe in their own guilt because of disorientation. Carol Richardson, one of the 'Guildford Four' (imprisoned for terrorist offences for 14 years before having their convictions quashed), reported this experience after being told of the alleged confession of a fellow suspect.[20] In establishing control, interrogators frequently try to throw suspects off balance, creating the continual danger that the suspect will be completely unbalanced.

'Coerced-passive' confession

Here interrogation leads suspects to 'admit' to committing an offence without necessarily adopting or even understanding the substance of this admission. Given the extent to which interrogations centre on repetitious accusations, the pressure simply to agree is enormous. In one case discussed by McConville et al, it was accepted that the suspect

---

[18] The first two categories which follow were developed by G Gudjonsson. See his *The Psychology of Interrogations, Confessions, and Testimony* (Wiley, 1992).

[19] G Gudjonsson and J Mackeith, 'A Proven Case of False Confession: Psychological Aspects of the Coerced-compliant Type' (1990) 30 Med Sci Law 187.

[20] G Stephenson, *The Psychology of Criminal Justice* (Blackwell, 1992) p 127.

broke a car windscreen in the course of an argument. The question was, why?

'Did you intend to smash the windscreen?'
'No.'
'So you just swung your hand out in a reckless manner?'
'Yes, that's it, just arguing . . . Just arguing, reckless, it wasn't intentional to break it.'[1]

In other examples, suspects agreed that they 'stole' goods simply because they took them (not necessarily with intent permanently to deprive the owner), without understanding the legal implications of the term.

Interrogative suggestibility

This involves suspects receiving messages in ways which affect 'their subsequent behaviourial response'.[2] This can occur in all three of the confession types discussed above. 'Vulnerable' suspects are particularly susceptible. Stefan Kiszko had a mental age of 12, and was jailed for life in 1976 for murdering a schoolgirl. He had been interrogated repeatedly, and eventually 'confessed' after his sixth interrogation. In 1992, his conviction was quashed after it was found that the semen on the victim's body could not have been his. This evidence was available at the time of the trial but was not revealed. Kiszko died, aged 41, less than two years after his release. A family friend commented, 'After being released, Stefan could not rouse himself and never recovered from what happened . . . He could not face the world.'[3]

Vulnerable people now have the additional protection during interrogation of an 'appropriate adult'. But as we have seen, the police often fail to identify vulnerable suspects. This was so in the 'Tottenham Three'[4] case, and lower profile examples include *Brine*[5] and *Miller*.[6] In the first two of these cases, confessions were rejected by the Court of Appeal because of the vulnerability of the defendants, but this was not the result in *Miller*. Further, neither appropriate adults nor legal advice prevents the police from placing on suspects the kinds of pressures faced by Kiszko. Indeed, the point of many police tactics is to identify

---

1 Op cit (1991) p 70.
2 G Gudjonsson and N Clark, 'Suggestibility in Police Interrogation: a Social Psychological Model' (1986) 1 Soc Behav 83.
3 (1993) Guardian, 24 December.
4 *Re Raghip, Silcott and Braithwaite* (1991) Times, 9 December.
5 [1992] Crim LR 122, discussed in ch 9, section 4(b), below.
6 [1986] 1 WLR 1191, discussed in ch 9, section 4(a), below.

and exploit vulnerabilities in 'ordinary' people. As the Runciman Commission said:

'... under certain circumstances individuals may confess to crimes they have not committed ... it is more likely that they will do so in interviews conducted in police custody even when proper safeguards apply.'[7]

The dangers of interrogative suggestibility are enhanced by the types of question commonly asked. If interrogations were primarily fact finding, questions would generally be of an open kind ('what did you see?', 'what did you do?') where there would be few dangers of false confessions, if only because the criminal alone would be able to provide the correct details. It may be true, as Evans argues, that most interrogations are like this.[8] In Evans' study, most suspects readily confessed. The important question is what happens in interrogations where suspects do not readily confess? McConville and Hodgson argue that the questions then turn to admission seeking. The most important question forms of this type which they identify are, firstly, leading questions. These seek particular answers by foreclosing others (for example, 'You went down there to get the stuff and assaulted her, didn't you?').[9] Secondly, there are statement questions (such as, 'You did it. You went there. There is no sign of entry, no force; whoever did it, did it by key.'); thirdly, there are legal closure questions ('So you stole the goods?'); fourthly, there are questions seeking the adoption of police opinions ('You are not innocent, you know what goes on.'). Finally, there are accusatory questions.[10]

In the process of 'asking' these questions, the police sometimes let information slip which suspects may incorporate into their answers.[11] And sometimes as the police ask for detail, and the innocent suspect gets it wrong, the suspect is contradicted until, by chance, the correct answer is produced. But in many cases the police seek little more than

---

[7] Report, op cit p 64.
[8] R Evans, The Conduct of Police Interviews with Juveniles (Royal Commission on Criminal Justice Research Study no 8) (HMSO, 1993). Note, however, that his study was of juveniles and, as he recognises, many formal interrogations were preceded by informal interrogations the content of which he was unaware.
[9] M McConville and J Hodgson, Custodial Legal Advice and the Right to Silence (Royal Commission on Criminal Justice Research Study no 16) (HMSO, 1993) p 137.
[10] For an illustration, see the extract from the 'Cardiff Three' interviews, quoted in section 5(g) above.
[11] 'Would I be right in saying that it was cakes and chocolate?': see J Baldwin, 'Police Interview Techniques: Establishing Truth or Proof?' (1993) BJ Crim 325 at 341. This occurred in the 'Cardiff Three', case, above (the police 'fed' Miller with the idea that the reason he could not 'remember' being present at the murder was that he was under the influence of drugs at the time) as did numerous instances of all the admission-seeking questions detailed in the text.

'yes' and 'no' answers, particularly when the purpose of the interrogation is primarily to demonstrate a 'guilty mind'.[12] Thus Baldwin comments that:

'Officers can be seen in many of these examples preoccupied with establishing relevant "points to prove", albeit tackling the question mechanically and inexpertly, almost regardless of the suspects' responses.'[13]

What many researchers, including Baldwin,[14] have described as inadequate interview technique is, in reality, entirely adequate for the purposes of the police. It is the establishment of proof, regardless of truth. The same is true of hectoring, accusatorial questioning. Much of the time it is (as far as it is possible to judge) within the law, and it is consistent with the adversarial role of the police. Yet the Runciman Commission stated that: 'In our view the safeguards under PACE against false confessions are comprehensive and, while not foolproof, are substantially sound.'[15]

To say that the police should minimise false confessions by not interrogating in these ways is too simplistic. These ways are the only ways by which people who are reluctant to confess will do so. It is not possible, certainly on the basis of current knowledge and expertise, to reduce false confessions without reducing true ones. Only Runciman's failure to analyse adequately the nature of interrogation could lead them to conclude that the police might be trained to develop interviewing techniques which were not aggressive and adversarial. The radical solution to such entrenched police practices is not to have custodial interrogation, or at least not to rely on it so heavily. This raises the question of corroboration.

(j)   Corroboration

At present it is possible, and common, to convict on confession evidence alone. As with other evidence there is no need for independent evidence of guilt (corroboration). This reflects a crime control approach: that the police would not be prosecuting if they had no reliable belief in guilt, and that court proceedings exist in most cases merely to approve this prior determination of guilt. Adherents of this approach argue that there is usually other evidence of guilt anyway

---

[12]   See eg Evans, op cit (1993) p 38.

[13]   'Police Interview Techniques', op cit (1993) p 340.

[14]   'A stubborn refusal to listen to a suspect's explanation (or even to allow a suspect to advance an explanation) is a critical failing . . .' ibid p 344.

[15]   Report, op cit p 57.

(for example, the defendant's criminal record) which cannot be revealed in court because of the rules of evidence, and that there is no need to verify uncorroborated evidence because innocent suspects can present evidence of their innocence if they wish. This means that the occasional examples of false and fabricated confessions which do occur are nearly always exposed for what they are, and wrongful convictions are rare. The few that do slip through the net are usually corrected eventually, and they are a small price to pay for the greater number of convictions, and more effective use of resources, which conviction on uncorroborated confession evidence allows.[16]

Due process advocates of a corroboration rule are sceptical about police motives and ability, and sceptical about the value of inadmissible evidence. For the due process adherent, corroboration would have several advantages. Firstly, it would reduce the number of evidentially weak prosecutions, either because cases prosecuted at present would not be prosecuted or because the police would secure corroborative evidence in weak cases, thereby strengthening them. Secondly, it would make convictions more certain and reliable. Although there might be fewer cases prosecuted, there would be less chance of cases being 'lost' and thus the overall level of convictions might be little changed. And there would certainly be fewer questionable convictions. Thirdly, it would shift the emphasis in police investigation away from interrogation to other sources of evidence. The incentive to secure interrogations through coercion or to fabricate confessions would be reduced.

In England and Wales at present, the police frequently fail to interview witnesses to crimes, to secure identification evidence and to do scientific tests on fingerprints blood, hair samples and so forth. In one study, reasonable steps (not including scientific tests) were taken to secure additional evidence in around 80% of the cases, but available sources were, for no apparent reason, not checked in over 10%. In most of the rest, investigation stopped after a confession was obtained because a guilty plea was anticipated.[17] It is not that further investigation was impossible in most of these cases, but that it was simply unnecessary to go through these costly and time-consuming processes when the law allows conviction on confession evidence alone.

It is very difficult to predict what the exact consequences would be of a corroboration rule. Scotland has one, about which there appears to be little dissatisfaction, but it is in a weak form which does not require

16   The same arguments are applicable to other forms of contestable evidence, such as identification evidence. See Stephenson, op cit (1992).
17   M McConville, Corroboration and Confessions: The Impact of a Rule Requiring that no Conviction can be Sustained on the Basis of Confession Evidence alone (Royal Commission on Criminal Justice Research Study no 13) (HMSO, 1993) Table 5.1.

truly independent evidence.[18] Many different types of corroboration rule are conceivable, all of which would have different effects.[19] However, McConville found that at present, in most prosecution cases, where there is a confession there is also admissible independent evidence.[20] A Home Office study carried out for the Runciman Commission found even fewer cases dependent on confession evidence alone.[1] What of the remainder, which would have fallen foul of a corroboration rule ? McConville found that in many of them independent evidence existed which could have been produced at court, and in many others it may have been possible to collect such evidence. About one third of the confession-only cases (about 3% of all prosecuted cases in which the police had interrogated) could not have satisfied a corroboration requirement. In some of these cases, this was because the confessions were so uncertain that they were incapable of being substantiated by reliable evidence. They ended in acquittal anyway. The others, which did end in conviction, would probably not have survived a corroboration rule (sometimes deservedly, given the dubious circumstances of the confessions) but were not particularly serious offences.

As McConville concludes, even the most stringent corroboration rule would affect relatively few cases and lead to few extra acquittals. However, the majority of the Runciman Commission (which was split on the issue) was concerned that the small percentage of cases which would be affected would amount to a large number in absolute terms, and that such a rule 'would not by itself prevent miscarriages of justice resulting from fabricated confessions and the production of supporting evidence obtained by improper means.'[2] It was worried that a corroboration rule would lead to too many guilty defendants walking free, whilst offering negligible protection to the innocent. It was also concerned that the benefits to be derived from such a rule, if any, did not justify the cost of requiring the police to conduct more thorough investigations. Runciman recommended, instead, that judges give a 'corroboration warning' to juries. This would represent a timid step in the direction of due process but the government has not acted on this recommendation.

Runciman's reasoning is flawed. Firstly, it amounts to saying that a

---

18 Sheriff I Macphail, 'Safeguards in the Scottish Criminal Justice System' [1992] Crim LR 144 at 148–152.

19 See McConville, op cit (1993) pp 50–58; R Pattenden, 'Should Confessions be Corroborated?' (1991) 107 LQR 319.

20 This was true of 86.6% of the cases in his study: op cit (1993) p 61.

1 Royal Commission on Criminal Justice, Report, op cit p 65.

2 Report, op cit p 65. For general discussion, see I Dennis, 'Miscarriages of Justice and the Law of Confessions' [1993] PL 291 and J Jackson, 'RCCJ: The Evidence Recommendations' [1993] Crim LR 817.

valid reason for not having a safeguard is that it might be abused by the police. If that was a valid argument, we might as well do away with all safeguards for suspects, for, as we have seen, they are all abused to a lesser or greater degree. The real question is whether a safeguard would offer significant benefits to suspects, and this involves assessing the likelihood that it would be abused. It is one thing for police officers to coerce suspects into confessing or to 'gild the lily' and another deliberately to frame suspects. If, as the research suggests, police officers are often not aware of the pressures under which they place many suspects, there is no reason to believe that in many false confession cases the police would invent supporting evidence, as Runciman seems to be suggesting.[3] It follows that there are good reasons for thinking that a corroboration rule would offer significant protection.

Secondly, there seems to be an inconsistency is saying that, under a corroboration rule, the police would frame the innocent but let the guilty walk free. If anything, one would imagine that it would be easier to frame the guilty, since there are likely to be more raw materials to work with in constructing a prosecution case if a person is actually guilty. If the police did set out to frame any suspects in such a crude fashion, the innocent would suffer no more than the guilty, and probably less so. The other side of the coin is that the innocent would stand to gain more from a corroboration rule than would the guilty, since it would be easier to corroborate a true confession than a false one. It is in this light that one must place Runciman's anxiety over the resource implications of corroboration. The main purpose of a corroboration rule would be to protect the victims of false and fabricated confessions. We know that there are such cases, we know that currently some such cases end in conviction and lengthy prison sentences, and that only luck leads to the eventual release of some (but who could say all?) of the defendants involved. No one would suggest that these cases form more than a tiny percentage of the hundreds of thousands of cases prosecuted each year. There may be only a few, perhaps a few dozen, each year. But if a corroboration rule led to the non-prosecution or the acquittal of at least some of these few then, to the due process adherent, that rule would be worth its weight in gold. One can only conclude that the majority of the Runciman Commission were not due process adherents. It was open to them to make a value choice in favour of crime control, and they did so. That was their privilege. But we were entitled to expect

---

[3] Undoubtedly, however, there is some risk of the police breaking the rules to this extent. In some of the cases dealt with by Challenor (see section 5(g), above), suspects were 'fitted up' (evidence was planted on their person or property) and identification parades 'fixed' (witnesses were given cues regarding who to pick out). This still appears to happen from time to time in the post-PACE era: see eg the *Darvell* case (1992) unreported, CA.

a better argued case and a clearer articulation and defence of those values from a body set up in the wake of a string of spectacular miscarriages of justice.

6. THE RIGHT OF SILENCE

The right of silence occurs at three stages in the criminal process. Firstly, there is a right to silence on the streets. People need not speak to police officers if they are stopped and questioned, whether or not s 1 stop-search powers are being exercised.[4] Silence is not obstruction, although refusal to answer questions could be if accompanied by abuse.[5] Further, under para 10.1 of Code of Practice C, suspects must be told that they need not answer questions:

'A person whom there are grounds to suspect of an offence must be cautioned before any questions about it (or further questions if it is his answers to previous questions that provide grounds for suspicion) are put to him for the purpose of obtaining evidence . . .'

The caution takes the following form: 'You do not have to say anything unless you wish to do so, but what you say may be given in evidence' (para 10.4).

When a person is questioned on the streets, he need not be cautioned if he or she is not suspected of an offence or if the questioning is carried out as part of the exercise of stop-search powers (para.10.1). Otherwise, suspects must be cautioned, whether arrested or not. On arrest, suspects must be cautioned unless this is impracticable because of the condition or behaviour of the suspect or unless the suspect had been cautioned immediately before arrest.

The second stage where the right of silence may be exercised is in the police station, which we shall deal with in this chapter, and finally there is the right to silence in court, looked at in chapter 8.

(a) What is the right of silence ?

It is over the right of silence—otherwise known as the privilege against self-incrimination—that due process and crime control principles clash most fundamentally. For the due process adherent, it is up to the prosecution to find its own evidence. For the adherent to crime control, only the guilty have something to hide. Innocent people have nothing to fear by assisting the prosecution, and have much to gain. As Bentham put it,

---

[4] For stop-search powers, see ch 2, above.
[5] *Ricketts v Cox* (1981) 74 Cr App Rep 298 and *Green v DPP* [1991] Crim LR 782.

'Innocence claims the right of speaking, as guilt invokes the privilege of silence.'[6] The common law adopted the classic due process position. It was ostensibly enshrined in the Judges' Rules in 1912 and in PACE Code of Practice C by the requirement to caution suspects 'before any questions . . . are put to him' (para 10.1). Thus suspects who are cautioned on or before arrest must be cautioned again at the start of any and every interrogation.

Certain consequences are generally thought to flow from this: firstly, that suspects should not suffer because they are exercising their rights. Yet, as we have seen, the main ground for continued detention under s 37 of PACE is to obtain evidence by questioning. Suspects who refuse to speak can therefore be held until they do so, subject to the time limits. It might be thought that these are grim consequences. Lengthy detention, particularly overnight, is the most feared consequence of arrest for most suspects.[7] The modern crime control response, however, seems to be that:

'. . . all citizens may be required to submit to detention and questioning when the conditions set out in the PACE Act are fulfilled. Thus, where the silent suspect is further detained he is simply fulfilling this general social duty rather than suffering punishment for silence.'[8]

The fact that silent suspects end up fulfilling a more onerous 'social duty' than do suspects who confess is, however, inescapable.

Secondly, it might be thought that suspects wishing to exercise their right to silence would not be pressured to change their minds. However, not only can silence lengthen detention, but in the words of Code of Practice C:

'This code does not affect the principle that all citizens have a duty to help police officers to prevent crime and discover offenders. This is a civic rather than a legal duty; but when a police officer is trying to discover when or by whom an offence has been committed he is entitled to question any person for whom he thinks useful information can be obtained, subject to the restrictions imposed by this code. A person's declaration that he is unwilling to reply does not alter this entitlement' (Note 1B).

Thus, in one of McConville and Hodgson's examples, the police

---

6   Quoted by S Greer, 'The Right to Silence: A Review of the Current Debate' (1990) 53 MLR 719.
7   A Sanders and L Bridges, 'Access to Legal Advice and Police Malpractice' [1990] Crim LR 494.
8   R Leng, The Right to Silence in Police Interrogation: A Study of some of the Issues Underlying the Debate (Royal Commission on Criminal Justice Research Study no 13) (HMSO, 1993).

response to a suspect exercising the right to silence was laced with quiet menace: 'Don't rely on anyone else and don't think we'll just let it go because in one interview you make no replies—we're just starting.'[9]

We have seen that questions aimed at persuading suspects to confess were once unlawful. Now, a variety of tactics are permissible,[10] and many other, impermissible, tactics are commonly employed. In another of McConville and Hodgson's examples, the police repeatedly try to find out where the suspect bought a 'dodgy' car, but he cannot or will not say. Eventually his advisor intervenes:

Clerk: 'I think [my client] has given an explanation and you're putting the same question again and again.'
Officer 1: 'We're giving him ample opportunity to explain the events and we're not satisfied with the answers.'
Officer 2: 'We'll go over it again.'[11]

For suspects without a solicitor present, the situation is even worse. Sanders et al report a case where a woman was advised on the phone to remain silent. She informed the police of this, who said (entirely properly) that she would none the less be questioned. Despite her distress she was interrogated and 'confessed'. None of this would have been allowed in 1912 when detention for questioning was unlawful. The result now is false confessions as in Kiszko and the 'Confait Affair'.

Thirdly, exercising silence would normally be thought not to be evidence of guilt. Code of Practice C says that 'no adverse inferences from this silence may be drawn at any trial that takes place' (Note 10D).[12] In reality, juries and magistrates can, and probably do, draw adverse inferences from silence. Although prosecutors are not allowed to suggest to them that they do so,[13] in 80% of all Crown Court trials where defendants are silent under police questioning this becomes known to the jury.[14] Again, the reality of the right of silence is much closer to the crime control model than it might first appear. Under government proposals at the time of writing, the system would move even further towards the crime control model (see below).

[9]   M McConville and J Hodgson, Custodial Legal Advice and the Right to Silence (Royal Commission on Criminal Justice Research Study no 16) (HMSO, 1993) p 124.
[10] *Holgate-Mohammed v Duke* [1984] AC 437.
[11] McConville and Hodgson, op cit p 186.
[12] The Note suggests that the police need only explain this to suspects who appear 'unclear about [the caution's] significance'. This is very strange, since its significance is not even clear to the courts (see further ch 8, section 4(a), below).
[13] See further discussion in ch 8, section 4(a), below and S Easton, *The Right to Silence* (Avebury, 1991) pp 9–17.
[14] M Zander and P Henderson, Crown Court Study (Royal Commission on Criminal Justice Research Study no 19) (HMSO, 1993).

(b) The extent of use of the right

Over half of all suspects who are interrogated either fully confess or make incriminating statements to the police: 60% in one pre-PACE study,[15] and 54% and 75% respectively in two post-PACE studies.[16] This supports the general belief among researchers that PACE has led to only a small or non-existent drop in confessions.[17] Around one-third of all suspects deny, with some sort of explanation, the offence(s) of which they are suspected. It appears that few suspects exercise the right of silence, but no proper figures are kept and estimates from research vary wildly. The few pre-PACE studies estimated that around 4% of suspects were silent, while post-PACE studies indicate anything from less than 3% to 16%.[18]

Exactly how many suspects exercise this right depends on how one defines it. The problem is that there is no agreement on what is meant by 'silence'. Leng argues that silence is not exercised when, despite initial denials or refusals to speak, suspects eventually answer questions; when suspects refuse to answer questions which are substantially the same as earlier questions which were answered; and when questions which are irrelevant to suspects' involvement in alleged offences (questions about friends and acquaintances, for example) are not answered. The corollary of this, however, is that he does regard suspects who answer some, but not all, relevant questions to be exercising their right of silence. A more difficult matter concerns the disclosure of facts or arguments which suspects subsequently use in their defence in court. Leng argues that failure to disclose facts not known to the prosecution (for example, that stolen goods were bought in good faith) should be regarded as silence, but failure to disclose legal arguments of which the prosecution should have been aware (such as that a screwdriver was not being carried for use as an offensive weapon) should not.

Leng analysed the data from McConville at al's post-PACE study on the above basis and calculated that the right to silence was exercised in 4.5% of all interrogation cases. The Runciman Commission estimated a higher rate of exercise of the right, but the basis of this estimate is not set out.[19] Silence is more frequent when suspects have legal advice, especially when the advisor is present at the interview. Whether people

[15] P Softley, Police Interrogation: An Observational Study in Four Police Stations (Royal Commission on Criminal Procedure Research Study no 4) (HMSO, 1981).

[16] Sanders et al, op cit and Evans, op cit (1993). Note though that Evans' was a study of juveniles only, where confession rates are higher.

[17] S Moston, G Stephenson and T Williamson, 'The Effects of Case Characteristics on Suspect Behaviour During Police Questioning' (1992) 32 BJ Crim 33.

[18] Leng, op cit pp 10–15.

[19] Report, op cit p 53.

are silent because of legal assistance, or are determined to seek assistance because they wish to remain silent, is not known.[20] However, McConville and Hodgson found few cases of suspects remaining silent because this was what they had been told by their advisors.[1] When silence was advised it was most often because advisors felt that they had insufficient information about the case and when they felt that suspects might wrongly incriminate themselves.

Concern is often expressed by senior police officers that professional criminals and persons suspected of serious offences exercise silence disproportionately often and thus escape prosecution or, if charged, conviction. There is next to nothing in the research to support this view. Moston and Williamson found little association between silence and the seriousness of the charge or court verdict.[2] Leng also found that in only a tiny percentage of non-prosecuted cases and acquittals was silence exercised, and that these negative outcomes rarely seemed to be a product of silence anyway.[3] Few 'ambush' defences (ie defences based on 'facts' not known to the police and not disclosed in interview) were mounted in court, and none successfully. In some cases, successful defences were based on defences suspects attempted to raise in interviews but to which the police refused to listen. Leng concluded that there were as many cases where the police could have acted on what suspects told them, or attempted to tell them, as where suspects refused to tell them material things.

(c)   Should the right be retained ?

The pros and cons of the right of silence are hotly debated. The most recent history of this debate begins in 1972 with the report of the Criminal Law Revision Committee (CLRC) on Evidence. The CLRC recommended abolition of the rule that no inference of guilt should be drawn from silence. This proved to be extremely controversial, and the report was never implemented. The matter was reconsidered by the Philips Commission, which considered the merits of adopting compromise solutions which would erode the right in some respects but not destroy it absolutely. It decided that, to be practical, the right would either have to be retained in its entirety or abolished in its entirety.[4] The

---

[20] See Sanders et al, op cit ch 7.
[1] Op cit.
[2] S Moston and T Williamson, 'The Extent of Silence in Police Stations' in S Greer and R Morgan (eds), *The Right to Silence Debate: Proceedings of a Conference at the University of Bristol in March 1990* (University of Bristol, 1990).
[3] Op cit.
[4] Note, however, that the law has long been equivocal on the extent of the right of silence: see ch 8, below.

Commission was unwilling to erode due process to the extent of absolute abolition, and so it recommended retention.[5] This was accepted by the government, which produced PACE and Code of Practice C in the form we now have them. Then in 1987 the matter was raised again by the Home Secretary following complaints by the police that their conviction rate was being halved. Even the Lord Chief Justice joined in on the side of the police.[6] The Home Secretary announced in May 1988 that he intended to modify the right of silence and announced a Home Office working party to make recommendations. This led to a change in the law in Northern Ireland in 1989, but proposals for England were deferred pending the report of the Runciman Commission as a result of the Guildford Four and Birmingham Six cases.[7]

Various arguments for abolition were put to Runciman:

(a) proper police interviewing seeks the truth and this is impossible if suspects refuse to answer questions;
(b) the need to prove *mens rea* elements places pressure on the police to secure confessions which would be alleviated if the court could draw inferences about guilt from silence;
(c) suspects mount 'ambush' defences;
(d) it is experienced criminals, not vulnerable suspects, who benefit from the right;
(e) the right of silence was necessary when suspects lacked proper safeguards, but now that PACE and Code of Practice C requires tape recording, regulates custodial treatment and provides for legal advice to be given where requested this is no longer true and the system is now unbalanced.[8]

These arguments can be met by evidence that:

(a) the current pressures on suspects leading to false confessions and misleading incriminating statements would be increased if suspects feared that they would suffer in court;
(b) the pressure on the police to seek confessions is self-imposed because of their reluctance to seek independent evidence and that they are not interested in neutral fact seeking;
(c) ambush defences are rare; and
(d) the safeguards in PACE and Code of Practice C are weak and used by a minority of suspects.

[5] Royal Commission on Criminal Procedure, Report (Cmnd 8092) (HSMO, 1981) pp 80–91.
[6] *Alladice* (1988) 87 Cr App Rep 380.
[7] These events are chronicled by Greer, op cit.
[8] Report, op cit pp 80–91.

Further, when defences are disclosed to the police their natural reaction, in an adversarial system, is to attempt to neutralise those defences. In the 'Confait Affair', the defendants' alibi was neutralised by 'adjusting' the time of death.[9] In the case of the Taylor sisters, an alibi witness was arrested at dawn and told that she would face a charge of conspiracy to murder if she did not change her story.[10]

Indeed, the Philips Commission (and PACE and Code of Practice C) was established to secure a 'balance' which included the right of silence, on one side, and increased powers to arrest, detain, stop-search and so forth, on the other. The government was satisfied with this 'balance' when it enacted these changes. The only thing that happened subsequently to 'upset' the balance was that many more suspects than previously (albeit a minority) actually began to exercise these rights.

The Runciman Commission was split on whether to recommend that adverse inferences be drawn from silence. But the majority agreed with the Philips Commission that:

'It might put strong (and additional) psychological pressure upon some suspects . . . This in our view might well increase the risk of innocent people . . . making damaging statements.'[11]

The majority of the Runciman Commission also thought that erosion of the right of silence would have little effect on experienced criminals, whose conviction rate would therefore not be substantially increased. The Runciman Commission's views on silence at trial were rather different, as chapter 8 will discuss. Despite yet another authoritative rejection of changes to the right of silence, the government has made provision in the Criminal Justice and Public Order Bill to abolish it for all practical purposes.

The Runciman Commission uses an 'instrumental retentionist'[12] argument: little would be gained and much might be lost by abolition or change. Whilst we agree with this, the problem with it is that it gives ground to the crime control approach. If it were found that the innocent could be better protected than at present, and that those believed to be guilty were increasingly using silence to escape conviction, the argument would swing the other way. Would this matter, if the innocent were protected ? 'Symbolic retentionists'[13] would say yes. It is true, they argue, that silence can obstruct the prosecution but this is the

---

[9] This, and the failure to disclose the adjustment to the defence, was the main ground for the convictions being quashed.

[10] (1993) Observer, 13 June.

[11] Royal Commission on Criminal Justice, Report, op cit p 55, quoting Royal Commission on Criminal Procedure, Report, op cit para 4.50.

[12] See Greer, op cit.

[13] Ibid.

whole point of due process. State power is great enough without increasing it further. The right of silence proclaims an ideology of innocence until proven guilty which is all the more necessary in the face of practices which proclaim an ideology of guilty until proven innocent.

Retentionists argue that the right also has valuable side effects, or would have if suspects were not pressured so often into not exercising it. Firstly, it should lead to less emphasis on confessions and more on independent evidence. Secondly, it gives suspects a bargaining tool to secure immediate disclosure from police, although the Runciman Commission's recommendation[14] that the police be obliged to inform legal advisors of the evidence against their clients would, if acted upon, reduce the impact of this argument. As things stand at present, the police exercise silence when they wish and to the extent that they wish, so why should suspects not also do so? Thirdly, abolition would encourage the police to arrest on 'fishing expeditions' (ie without reasonable suspicion) even more than now. They would be able to throw accusations, for which there might be little evidence, at suspects and silence would corroborate evidence which would otherwise be inadequate for conviction.

Thus abolition could have more of an impact on earlier stages of the criminal process (arrest) than on interrogation. McConville and Hodgson point to the increased use of arrest over the last 20 years or so. They argue that the traditional relationship between suspicion and arrest has, in many cases, been reversed:

'Instead of reasonable suspicion giving rise to an arrest, in these cases arrest occurs first, often without a suspicion which can be said to be reasonable. The result of this is that ensuing procedures relating to detention and interrogation, instead of being underpinned by legal justification, are used in order to prop up an otherwise precipitate and unlawful arrest.'[15]

In many cases where this happens, the interrogation collapses and the suspect is released. Abolition of the right of silence could lead, in some of these cases, to suspects being convicted on the basis, in part, of their failure to answer groundless accusations; and in others to their being intimidated (by the prospect of an adverse inference) into incriminating themselves, perhaps misleadingly.

[14] Report, op cit p 36.
[15] Op cit p 198.

7. REMEDIES

The treatment of suspects in the police station is central to criminal justice. This is agreed by adherents of due process and crime control alike. For the latter, the police station is where important evidence can be secured. This is precisely what worries due process adherents. Few would argue with the Runciman Commission that 'The protection of suspects from unfair or unreasonable pressure is just as important to the criminal justice system as the thoroughness with which the police carry out their investigations.'[16]

The more important something is—in this case, a set of rights—the better those rights are usually protected. This is especially true when those rights are threatened or undermined. We have seen that the right to legal advice is often undermined, as are the rights to information, to a telephone call and not to be treated oppressively. These rights are ostensibly inhibitory rules, created with the intention of inhibiting the police from following crime control norms. The main way English law has of protecting rights is by providing a remedy to compensate for their denial, thus deterring future misconduct. Thus one can sue for damages for breach of contract, trespass to one's land, loss of reputation and so forth. What remedies are there for breach of one's rights in the police station?

The Criminal Justice Act 1988 introduced the crime of 'torture' (s 134). This would only apply in the most extreme, and almost unimaginable, circumstances. The tort of unlawful imprisonment is available for suspects detained unlawfully (whether initially or at some point up to or after expiry of the relevant time limit). Unless the time limit is breached or the suspect is held contrary to Code of Practice C, para 11.4 (when sufficient evidence is obtained for prosecution), the only opportunities to sue are if the arrest was not on reasonable grounds (the problems here are discussed in chapter 3) or if detention was not 'necessary'. Since detention is always authorised, and in a 'rubber stamp' manner, one might have thought that many suspects would sue. In fact, there appear to be no reported cases challenging the initial decision to detain. The police are universally assumed to have the right to do this.

What about the other rights? Denial of a solicitor is not breach of contract; nor is it a tort or a crime. PACE provided a right in s 58 but no remedy for its breach.[17] The same is true of breach of all of the Code of

---

[16] Report, op cit p 25.
[17] The tort of 'breach of statutory duty' is a theoretical but not a practical possibility. Its application here is not certain and there are no reported cases. See A Sanders, 'Rights, Remedies, and the Police and Criminal Evidence Act' [1988] Crim LR 802.

Practice C rules—on being informed of one's rights, contemporaneous recording, interviewing in the police station, not being held incommunicado and so forth. The importance of the protection of suspects can be gauged by the fact that there are better remedies available for damage to reputation and trespass on one's land. All suspects can do is to either make an official complaint or seek to have evidence obtained in consequence of the breach of their rights excluded from trial. These are applicable to breach of other police powers, too, and will be discussed in chapter 9. At this point we can simply note that these procedures have a limited deterrent effect on the police, making the rules as much presentational as inhibitory.

8.   CONCLUSION

PACE and its associated codes of practice created a legal framework which deliberately shifted suspect-focused police investigation into the police station. In this respect, and in the detailed rules provided, the change followed an established trend rather than producing a radical break with the past. As McConville and Baldwin said in 1982, before PACE was even drafted:

'. . . the really crucial exchanges in the criminal process have shifted from courts into police interrogation rooms. It is these exchanges that, in a majority of cases, colour what happens at later stages in the criminal process. Indeed they often determine the outcome of cases at trial.'[18]

Detention and questioning post-arrest and pre-charge had become more common throughout this century, especially after 1964. Section 37 and ss 41–44 of PACE set time limits beyond which detention could not extend, explicitly allowing detention pre-charge up to these limits. Not only do these provisions allow the police to detain for questioning, but s 30 almost obliges them to detain if they wish to question, as do increasingly tighter definitions of 'interview'. Under s 37 of PACE, detention is challengeable only if it is not 'necessary', this being as presentational as any of the rules we have yet seen. Even the 'helping with inquiries' limbo, which these provisions were expected to end, still continues when this is convenient to the police.

All the rights which used to be provided by the Judges' Rules are now provided by PACE and Code of Practice C. Of the few additions, the most important are the provision of an appropriate adult to juveniles

---

[18]   M McConville and J Baldwin, 'The Role of Interrogation in Crime Discovery and Conviction' (1982) 22 BJ Crim 165 at 174.

and vulnerable suspects, the majority of the latter being missed by the police and thus denied this protection; the provision of the duty solicitor scheme and detailed information about it, many suspects not in fact being properly informed and most not taking advantage of it; and the almost absolute right to have a legal advisor present at interview, which is none the less not secured by most of those who seek it. The fact that these and the other rights and protections discussed in this chapter have statutory backing has made little difference to either police willingness to make them work or to suspects' capacity to enforce them in the law courts. Police interrogation is more subtle than it used to be and now is rarely directly intimidatory. However, the law allows pressure to be placed on suspects to not exercise their right of silence, without defining how much pressure is lawful, and few indeed are silent. When solicitors are present they rarely act to prevent intense police pressure. When they do protest, the police, entirely lawfully, remind them that they, the police, are in control. Interrogations are tape recorded, but when they want more freedom the police interrogate 'informally'. Interrogation, despite recent police claims to the contrary, is usually adversarial rather than fact finding.

This summary of police station practice sounds far more like Packer's crime control model than his due process model. How is this possible? Firstly, there is police rule breaking. This does occur, and suspects can call on few remedies to deter or punish it. But crime control practices are also a result of laws which, sometimes directly and sometimes through vagueness, are both enabling and legitimising of police norms. Perhaps most important of all, however, is that it is an unintended consequence of a policy designed to help suspects. In chapter 3, we saw that the police can arrest on reasonable suspicion without following up suspects' exculpatory stories. Indeed, s 30 and the rules on interrogation would make it difficult for the police to follow up defences extensively without first taking suspects into custody. Although intended to protect suspects, the effect of this is to allow the police to follow crime control norms. In this chapter, we have seen that the same is true in interrogation. The police are often uninterested in suspects' exculpatory claims and, indeed, sometimes try to suppress them. This they are allowed to do; it is difficult to imagine anything different. All the police can be expected to do is to carry out their adversarial role on crime control lines, because to act as neutral fact finders would be a negation of what being the police is all about. Restricting the police to interviewing in the police station and nowhere else could only be regarded as a due process protection if the context of detention was governed by due process standards. The reality is that, since the police station is 'police territory', it cannot be wrested from police control. Hence the due process safeguards for suspects in the police station are much weaker than they appear, and manifestly fail to 'balance' the powers of the police. For crime control laws tolerate unrestricted questioning, the use of police evidence of what was said in evidence and convictions based on that evidence even when it is contested and uncorroborated.

The police are no more impartial seekers after truth now than they ever were and it is difficult to imagine them being so in the future. As McBarnet argued in relation to the pre-PACE law, the fact that the police act as they do is not surprising, for the law, for the most part, enables them to act in this way.[19] It is the rhetoric of due process which is out of step. However, McBarnet's sweeping characterisation of all law as crime control in content is not accurate, certainly in the post-PACE world.[20] But the laws which are due process-oriented do not hinder the police unduly, for they are reasonably easy to evade or break when the police 'need' to do so.

Neither Royal Commission appeared to accept either that the system should operate in this way (thus rejecting the crime control rhetoric of the police) or that it does so (thus rejecting the due process proposals of the critics). They preferred to believe that the police are capable of both being adversarial and impartial even with unco-operative suspects. The contradictions involved reach their peak in the person of the custody officer. Without police rule breaking, there would be no need to have custody officers. But custody officers are police officers. If suspects need protection from the police, then by what logic can custody officers be expected to provide that protection? The Runciman Commission recognised, to some extent, the failures of custody officers demonstrated in this chapter such as allowing cell visits by officers, rubber stamping detention, failing to provide clear information about rights and adopting ploys to avoid suspects receiving legal advice. Their performance, they say: '. . . still leaves something to be desired . . . It may also be unrealistic to expect a police officer to take an independent view of a case investigated by colleagues.'[1]

After considering the poor performance of custody officers, the Runciman Commission then discussed (very briefly) whether another body could do the job of the custody officer. They decided that all the pressures on them would also be on a replacement body without that body even having the authority, vis-à-vis the police, of a custody officer. This was a due process/crime control cross-roads. The Runciman

---

[19] D McBarnet, *Conviction* (MacMillan, 1983).

[20] Neither is it true to imply, as she does, that criminal justice rhetoric is all due process: M McConville, A Sanders and R Leng, *The Case for the Prosecution* (Routledge, 1991) ch 9.

[1] Report, op cit p 31.

Commission could either allow things to go on, more or less as now (with minor enhancement to the custody officer role) and accept the coercive nature of police station detention; or it could take police investigation out of the police station. It chose the former.[2]

Once it is decided, as the Runciman Commission did, that the police station should be the focus of investigation, and that (by rejecting a corroboration rule) confession evidence alone could form the sole basis for conviction, the crime control framework is accepted, and the room for due process is fundamentally circumscribed. This makes the arguments about the right of silence rather futile. There is not, in any meaningful sense, a right of silence in England and Wales. Suspects need not speak, but the police can do a lot to persuade them otherwise and silent suspects suffer many adverse consequences (far more adverse than the police suffer when breaking rules designed to protect suspects). The 'right of silence' is not meaningful, because institutionalised coercion is allowed by the law. Under these conditions, many confessions are bound to be false and a great number must be put in doubt. Those who can and do exercise the right to silence tend to have more experience of the system, and may be less likely to be innocent than those who do not. This only calls into question the right to silence if one adopts the crime control perspective. From the due process perspective it is the *power to interrogate* which should be questioned. Subjection to involuntary interrogation during involuntary, lengthy and partially indeterminate detention is inconsistent with the presumption of innocence, in the real sense that the innocent can be made to appear to be guilty.

But a pure due process system is not on the cards, and might not be in society's interest. What should be considered seriously is a shift towards due process so as to reduce coerced and false confessions, despite a continued power to interrogate. One possibility is to try to counter-balance police power effectively, as would be expected in a fully adversarial system. This means not making the rights of suspects dependent on custody officers, but making them either automatic or guaranteed by a genuine third party. Independent lawyers working in police stations might be a solution. Unlike most legal aid lawyers at present, however, they would need to attend all interrogations and possess an adversarial ethos. If they were based in law centres rotating with other law centre lawyers, they might not get 'captured' by the police ethos. The law could provide that no interrogation would be valid unless a lawyer was present. Where a suspect wishes to impart confidential information to the police, this could be done informally but

2 Ibid pp 31–34.

without the evidence being directly usable in court. Even these limited moves towards due process are inconceivable at present. Far from reducing the pressures on suspects in these ways, the government, by abolishing the right of silence, is determined to increase them yet further.

Chapter 5

Prosecutions

1. INTRODUCTION

Before police forces were established in 1829 and for some years thereafter, neither local nor central government accepted responsibility for
day-to-day law enforcement. Prosecutions could be initiated by anyone.
Suspects were generally prosecuted, if at all, by the victim.

Police powers of arrest, search and interrogation were originally no
greater than those of ordinary citizens. Similarly, no special prosecution
powers were provided. If the police, or anyone else, wished to prosecute, they had to 'lay an information' before the local magistrates. If the
latter were satisfied that there was sufficient evidence they would issue
a warrant for the suspect's arrest or a summons to appear in court.[1]
Prosecution decisions were judicially controlled. As police forces and
police powers gradually grew throughout the nineteenth and twentieth
centuries, victims gradually came to expect the police to initiate and
conduct prosecutions for them. Extra arrest powers were provided to
the police and they developed the practice of 'charging' suspects, whereunder they took suspects before the magistrates without laying an
information in advance. The police thus began to take control of prosecution decisions away from the magistrates, but no specific
prosecution powers or responsibilities were conferred on the police.
Private prosecution remained the model on which police prosecutions
were based, and the right of private prosecution has remained to this
day.[2]

In the absence of specific laws to regulate their prosecutions, the
police evolved their own system. They prosecuted most of their own
cases in the magistrates' courts, some forces allocating specific officers to
undertake this task. For Crown Court cases, they instructed solicitors

[1] See ch 3, section 3(a) and ch 4, above.
[2] See A Sanders, 'Arrest, Charge and Prosecution' (1986) 6 LS 257.

who then instructed barristers.[3] Most forces used just a few local firms of solicitors, whom they also began to use for the more difficult magistrates' court cases. Gradually, and particularly in the 1960s and 1970s, the larger police forces began to employ their own solicitors, there being dozens of lawyers in the largest prosecuting solicitors departments.[4] Under the traditional solicitor-client relationship, solicitors had to carry out the instructions of the police whatever they themselves thought of the prosecution.[5] Many prosecuting solicitors were unhappy about this subordinate relationship and made this clear in their evidence to the Royal Commission on Criminal Procedure (Philips Commission). If the police insisted on prosecuting in pursuance of their crime control goals, there was little or nothing the prosecutor could do about it.[6]

These arrangements for prosecution had already come under fire in the 'Confait Affair', where the prosecutor was found to have been either unable, or unwilling, to act independently. Fisher believed this was a contributory factor in the wrongful convictions in that unhappy episode.[7] The Philips Commission proposed an independent prosecution service which would take over cases which the police had decided to prosecute. If the prosecutor did not agree with the police, the case could be dropped, the charges changed, or more evidence sought.[8] The government accepted the main thrust of the Commission's proposals.[9] The result was the establishment of the Crown Prosecution Service (CPS) by the Prosecution of Offences Act 1985.

The head of the CPS was to be the Director of Public Prosecutions (DPP). The DPP was first established in 1879 with the function of advising the police on criminal matters and handling particularly important cases. At the time of the establishment of the CPS, the Office of the DPP (which comprised around 70 lawyers) handled murders, other very

---

[3] See J Sigler, 'Public Prosecution in England and Wales' [1974] Crim LR 642 on the use of barristers, and for a general account of the system up to that time.

[4] M Weatheritt, The Prosecution System: Survey of Prosecuting Solicitors' Departments (Royal Commission on Criminal Procedure, Research Study no 11) (HMSO, 1980).

[5] See Sigler, op cit and Royal Commission on Criminal Procedure, The Investigation of Criminal Offences in England and Wales: The Law and Procedure (Cmnd 8092–1) (HMSO, 1991) pp 49–52.

[6] Royal Commission on Criminal Procedure, Report (Cmnd 8092) (HMSO, 1981) para 6.27.

[7] See Report of an Inquiry into the Circumstances leading to the Trial of Three Persons on Charges arising out of the Death of Maxwell Confait and the Fire at 27 Doggett Road, London SE6 (HCP 90) (HMSO, 1977).

[8] Report, op cit ch 7.

[9] Apart from rejecting Philips' recommended local control of prosecutors by enhanced police authorities. See the Home Office White Paper, An Independent Prosecution Service for England and Wales (Cmnd 9074) (HMSO, 1983).

serious cases, and prosecutions of police officers.[10] The jump to a national service, with an initial establishment of over 1,500 lawyers, was sudden, and severe organisational problems were created, including, in the early days, chronic understaffing.[11]

Despite the national identity of the CPS, prosecutors are still based locally, the CPS being organised into branches, each branch serving the police area to which it corresponds.[12] The direct effect on police procedures of the 1985 Act has been small, for the police remain entitled to make prosecution decisions in the same ways as previously. Indeed, decisions not to prosecute remain a matter for the police alone. Only when the case comes to court has control been relinquished. This was the first time since 1829 that the police lost an element of power, except in so far as PACE can be seen in this way.

2. DISCRETION

When the police are interviewing suspects, they have to stop doing so when they believe that 'a prosecution should be brought' and that 'there is sufficient evidence'.[13] This does not require them to prosecute. As with stop-search and arrest powers, the police have discretion in determining whether or not to initiate a prosecution. When the police do not prosecute they may delay their decision (either releasing the suspect on bail to return at a later date or reporting the suspect with a view to a summons), they may release the suspect with a caution (which means, in this context, a warning) or they may take no further action (NFA) at all.

The police have many different reasons for deciding not to prosecute: sometimes there is insufficient evidence, some cases are too trivial, sometimes there will be particularly extenuating circumstances, and sometimes immunity from prosecution is exchanged for information about other offences and other offenders.[14] Our next step, then, is to see what controls there are on these decisions and how effective as inhibitory rules they are. We will be particularly concerned with the extent to which the CPS has injected due process norms into police prosecution processes.

---

[10] See Sigler, op cit and RCCP, Law and Procedure, op cit paras 155–161.

[11] See J Rozenberg, *The Case for the Crown* (Equation, 1987).

[12] The CPS was initially organised into 31 areas which, in most cases, built on existing prosecuting solicitors' departments for each police force. The number of areas, each subdivided into branches, has since been reduced to 13.

[13] PACE Code of Practice C, para 11.4.

[14] See ch 4, section 5.

(a)   'Legality' and 'opportunity'

It is usual to describe prosecution systems as falling into one of two types. The first is the 'legality system'. This is common among European countries of the inquisitorial type, such as Germany. Under the legality principle, the police must report all offences to the prosecutor, who must prosecute. In principle, there is no discretion, although the police sometimes screen out cases where there is no evidence.[15] Common law countries, on the other hand, such as Britain and the United States, tend to have 'opportunity systems' in which there is complete discretion. The opportunity principle is perhaps best encapsulated by a former Attorney General, Lord Shawcross:

'It has never been the rule in this country—I hope it never will be—that suspected criminal offences must automatically be the subject of prosecution. Indeed the very first Regulations under which the Director of Public Prosecutions worked provided that he should . . . prosecute "wherever it appears that the effects or the circumstances of its commission are of such character that a prosecution in respect thereof is required in the public interest." That is still the dominant consideration.'[16]

Opportunity and legality systems are clearly diametrically opposed principles. Legal systems do not, in reality, divide so neatly. Some (like Italy) are in a state of transition, while others (like France) combine elements of both.[17] Even among systems which apparently conform to one or the other, the differences in practice are not so great as one might think. We shall see that, in practice, police discretion in England and Wales is usually exercised, in relation to adults at any rate, in favour of prosecuting. This is true of all legal systems based on the expediency or opportunity principle.

On the other hand, even in the most rigid legality-based systems discretion is exercised more and more frequently. This is usually a product of specific provisions, especially for juveniles, in the laws of those countries. As in Britain, juveniles, old offenders and motoring offences tend to be given special consideration, and ordinary adults are increasingly diverted from prosecution in other countries.[18] In Sweden, for example, prosecution will often be waived if a fine only would be

---

[15] See L Leigh and L Zedner, A Report on the Administration of Criminal Justice in France and Germany (Royal Commission on Criminal Justice Research Study no 1) (HMSO, 1992) pp 28–30.

[16] Quoted approvingly in the Attorney General's guidelines for prosecution, which apply to the police, and in the CPS Code for Crown Prosecutors.

[17] Leigh and Zedner, op cit.

[18] See ibid.

the likely consequence of prosecution. This means that many small shoplifting cases and possession of soft drugs cases are not prosecuted.[19]

It can be seen that there is a large degree of convergence between the two systems. In Britain, where discretion is theoretically total, most cases are prosecuted, and in a legality system, where there is theoretically no discretion available, a similar, or perhaps even greater, number of cases are not prosecuted. Despite this convergence, there are still important differences. Because diversion in a legality system is an exception to a general rule, non-prosecution decisions are relatively strictly controlled even if they are greater in number than in systems like that in England and Wales. The conditions under which those exceptions can be made are generally specified in the laws of those countries, and diversion decisions are usually made by prosecutors. In order to encourage consistency and adherence to official policy, there are relatively small numbers of senior decision makers.

In England and Wales, by contrast, discretion is not closely controlled. Neither the basis for the exercise of discretion nor the level of decision-maker is consistent throughout the system. As a result of the process of historical evolution discussed above, rather than through the establishment of any clear principles, neither prosecution nor non-prosecution is the legal responsibility of any one part of the police force. Another important difference is that, in major crimes, prosecutors (in Germany) or examining magistrates (in France) play an important part in the early stages of the investigation and prosecution process. These people are impartial, in theory at least, in a way that police forces are not and could never be. In Britain, where there is no equivalent of these officials, the prosecution system is the same no matter how serious the offence.

(b) 'Constabulary independence'

One consequence of the 'opportunity principle' is that no one has the authority to tell the police, or indeed other law enforcement agencies such as the Inland Revenue and Customs and Excise, either to prosecute or not to prosecute a particular case in the United Kingdom. The discretion of law enforcement agencies is near absolute. This is the doctrine of 'constabulary independence'. In *Arrowsmith v Jenkins*,[20] the defendant (D) spoke for 30 minutes at a public meeting which obstructed a highway. She was arrested for this offence and was

---

[19] See A Sanders, 'Diverting Offenders from Prosecution: Can we Learn from other Countries?' (1986) 150 JP 614.
[20] [1963] 2 QB 561.

convicted. She appealed on the basis that many meetings had been held in that place previously and that in the past the police had not prosecuted anyone for a criminal offence. D in effect asked 'Why pick on me?' The court's answer on appeal was: 'That, of course, has nothing to do with this court. The sole question here is whether the defendant had contravened section 121(1) of the Highways Act 1959.'[1] In other words, the Divisional Court declined to question the way in which police discretion had been exercised in previous cases, in this particular case, and, therefore, the overall pattern of prosecutions. Similarly, in *R v Inland Revenue Commissioner, ex p Mead*[2] the applicants, who were being prosecuted for tax offences, objected on the grounds that similar offenders were not being prosecuted. It was held that it was not necessarily wrong for apparently similar cases to be dealt with differently.

Limits have, in principle, none the less been set to the doctrine of constabulary independence. In *R v Metropolitan Police Comr, ex p Blackburn*[3] the policy of the Metropolitan Police at that time not to prosecute certain establishments for illegal gambling was challenged. The police altered their policy in the course of the case, so there was no need to decide against them. Lord Denning nonetheless made a more general statement which was therefore obiter (ie not binding on future courts):

'There are some policy decisions with which, I think, the court in a case can if necessary interfere. Suppose a Chief Constable were to issue a directive to his men that no person should be prosecuted for stealing any goods less than £100 in value. I should have thought that the court could countermand it. He would be failing in his duty to enforce the law.'[4]

Edmund-Davies LJ similarly stated that 'the law enforcement officers of this country certainly owe a legal duty to the public to perform those functions which are the *raison d'etre* of their existence.'[5] Both judges were referring to general prosecution policy decisions and not to decisions about individual cases. Thus in *R v Chief Constable of Devon and Cornwall, ex p CEGB*,[6] the police refused to remove protesters from a field. The CEGB claimed that the protesters' behaviour was conduct liable to cause a breach of the peace. It asked the court to state that there is a duty on the police to enforce the law in such cases (and, if necessary, to prosecute) citing Denning's remarks in *Blackburn*. But

[1]   Ibid at 566, per Lord Parker CJ.
[2]   [1993] 1 All ER 772.
[3]   [1968] 2 QB 118.
[4]   Ibid at 136.
[5]   Ibid at 149.
[6]   [1981] 3 All ER 826.

the court refused to see the police inaction as a part of a general policy even though it did stem from their general community policing strategy.[7] The court regarded this as an individual case which could not, therefore, come within *Blackburn*.

To date, it appears that no one has successfully challenged negative decisions not to prosecute under the obiter in *Blackburn* and it will doubtless be very difficult to do so in the future.[8] The same is true of positive decisions to prosecute. In two recent cases, prosecution decisions have been held to be reviewable by the courts. This was something of a breakthrough, although in neither case was the decision itself actually overturned. In *R v Chief Constable of the Kent Constabulary, ex p L*,[9] it was claimed that the prosecution of two juveniles was unreasonable because one should have been cautioned and the other would have been cautioned had she admitted the offence. The other was *Mead*,[10] where it was held that different decisions taken in relation to similar cases were acceptable as long as the same prosecution policy was applied to all of them. As Hilson says,

'. . . while not questioning the policy *of* selective prosecution, he [Stuart-Smith LJ] did stress that any decision should be in accordance with the policy *for* selecting prosecution.'[11]

As with wrongful arrest claims, decisions have to be *Wednesbury*-unreasonable to be successfully challenged.[12] This is extremely difficult to demonstrate, and courts will not substitute their own judgment for that of the enforcement body in question. As was said by Watkins LJ in the *Kent Constabulary* case, the decisions to prosecute could equally have been decisions not to prosecute. But that was not the point. Although a prosecution decision is reviewable, since it involves the exercise of discretion 'in practice it is rarely likely to be successfully reviewed.'[13] Indeed, Popplewell J in *Mead* even doubted whether positive decisions to prosecute were reviewable in principle. The doctrine of constabulary independence, which applies to all enforcement agencies and not just the police, is virtually impregnable.

The consequence is almost complete autonomy for law enforcement

---

[7] See discussion of community policing in ch 2, section 1(a), above.

[8] *R v MPC, ex p Blackburn (No 3)* [1973] QB 241 concerned the non-prosecution of pornography offences. The court clearly believed the material in question to be criminally obscene, but the plaintiff still failed. For discussion of this and other cases, see P Osborne, 'Judicial Review of Prosecutors' Discretion' (1992) 43 NILQ 178.

[9] [1993] 1 All ER 756.

[10] Above.

[11] C Hilson, 'Discretion to Prosecute and Judicial Review' [1993] Crim LR 739 at 742.

[12] See ch 3, section 5.

[13] Above at 770.

bodies in all enforcement and prosecution decisions. This protects them from interference from individuals and from local and central government. The doctrine of independence might have been appropriate in the days when the police were not the sole law enforcement agency for most victims of crime. But now that it is manifestly the job of the police to enforce the law, we have to ask whether the police should be the sole judges of when arrest and prosecution is, and is not, appropriate. No one is advocating political decisions about individual cases, but accountability for prosecution policies is entirely compatible with the rule of law. Indeed, Jefferson and Grimshaw argue that this is essential in a modern democracy.[14] The doctrine of constabulary independence also ignores the role increasingly played in prosecution and caution processes by social services and multi-agency bureaus.[15]

At present, police cautioning policies and the CPS Code for Crown Prosecutors are published but are vague. The police and CPS have more detailed guidelines for their own use which are not published. Against the argument for more openness, Hilson argues that if police and CPS prosecution policies—eg not to prosecute shoplifting of goods worth less than £1, or speeding offences where the limit is exceeded by less than 10 mph—became publicly available then this would be a green light to everyone to break the law up to these limits.[16] He argues that other agencies, such as the Inland Revenue, are able to publish their detailed policies without this happening because they have other ways of securing compliance. Given the level of tax evasion, this is debatable.[17] In so far as he is right, however, it would not be unreasonable to allow alternative sanctions to be operated by the police or, preferably, the CPS.[18] One such example would be the 'prosecutor fine' used in Scotland. This is used in minor cases as an alternative to prosecution. Although this type of scheme is not without its adverse implications for due process, it would encourage prosecution policies to be both open and generous to suspects, without undermining whatever deterrent effect the law might have.

There appear to be three broad legal principles restraining the police and other prosecution agencies from following their informal crime control norms. Firstly, prosecutions must not be made in bad faith. If they are, the court may hold it to be an abuse of process and dismiss the

---

[14] T Jefferson and R Grimshaw, *Controlling the Constable: Police Accountability in England and Wales* (Muller, 1984). See ch 3, section 6, for a brief discussion of these issues in relation to the policing of industrial disputes and of domestic violence.

[15] S Uglow, A Dart, A Bottomley and C Hale, 'Cautioning Juveniles—Multi-Agency Impotence' [1992] Crim LR 632.

[16] Op cit pp 743–747.

[17] D Cook, *Rich Law, Poor Law* (Open University Press, 1989).

[18] See A Sanders, 'The Limits to Diversion from Prosecution' (1988) 28 BJ Crim 513.

case.[19] It may also be possible to sue for malicious prosecution, this being the only available tortious remedy for wrongful prosecution decisions. However, prosecution must be malicious in the sense that false information is deliberately provided and the prosecution must have been resolved in the defendant's favour (either through acquittal or discontinuance).[20] Here again we see the application of the crime control principle that the end justifies the means. No matter how malicious a prosecution might have been, a person would have no remedy if found guilty in the criminal courts.

Decisions not to prosecute which are taken in bad faith (eg for personal reasons) are, of course, not reviewable in these ways. There is no such thing as an action for malicious non-prosecution. A second principle, though, which applies to all prosecution decisions, positive or negative, is that they must not be *Wednesbury*-unreasonable. An example would be prosecuting a case where there was no prima facie evidence (ie where there would be insufficient evidence to convict even if the defence gave no evidence on its own behalf). Finally, prosecution decisions must be taken only after consideration and application of a consistent policy. How far the police are actually inhibited from following crime control norms by these principles will be the subject of the next two sections, after which non-police agencies will briefly be examined.

3. EVIDENTIAL SUFFICIENCY

(a) Deciding there is insufficient evidence

It is a requirement for prosecution that there be an offence 'known to the law'.[1] This is, however, not quite as obvious as it might seem when we remember that, under s 24 of PACE, arrest is allowed if an offence 'is about to be committed' or if an offence is 'reasonably suspected'. Since the former can fall short of an attempt, and the latter can fall short of an actual offence, arrests can be lawful even when no offences have been committed. Someone might be arrested for assault after punching someone when in fact it was a friendly fight, or taking someone's umbrella when in fact it turned out to be their own.

If such offences are reported to the police before the suspected offender is arrested, the police will fill out a 'crime report form'. This is for official Home Office statistical purposes and also forms part of the

---

[19] See Hilson, op cit and cases cited therein.
[20] See H Levenson and F Fairweather, *Police Powers* (Legal Action Group, 1990) ch 13.
[1] Code for Crown Prosecutors, para 4.

prosecution file if the suspected offender is arrested and prosecuted. If, however, the police decide that there was no breach of the criminal law, the offence needs to be 'no-crimed', ie it has to be 'unrecorded' by amending the crime report form. This can actually happen quite a lot. Bottomley and Coleman found in 1972 that 33% of alleged cycle thefts were 'no-crimed', as were 11% of other thefts and 15% of assaults.[2]

The police frequently decide that they have insufficient evidence to prosecute even if there has been, or they believe there to have been, a crime. Many of those arrested turn out to be the 'wrong suspect'. This occurs routinely when the police trawl large suspect populations in major crime enquiries, but also happens in more minor cases, such as drugs raids where people are arrested indiscriminately. McConville et al report such a case where the officer said that: 'It was only after the interview that it was clear that he had nothing to do with the question-able property in the house, the drugs or the credit cards . . .'[3]

McConville et al also refer to cases where the police act on 'infor-mation received' which turns out to be mistaken.[4] Sometimes the police believe that they have the right suspect, but still have insufficient evidence. Sometimes the evidence cannot be secured, but in other cases the police decide that it is not worth investing the time and trouble to pursue the matter further. On occasion, further action could reveal matters which the police would rather conceal, such as a case where, as a police inspector put it, prosecution 'might prove embarrassing to the police' because of racist language used during the arrest.[5] In yet other cases, non-prosecution is the price of a 'deal'. And, of course, there are cases like 'domestics' in which the police have little interest anyway. 'Domestics' are classic examples of this kind, but there are many other situations where victims of violence are seen as 'undeserv-ing' or 'unreliable'.[6]

Thus, large numbers of suspects are released from detention with no further action being taken (NFA). McConville et al found that around one-quarter of all arrests ended in NFA.[7] Although this might seem surprising, it must be remembered that even arrests made on the basis of 'reasonable suspicion' usually require the collection of more evidence

[2] See now A Bottomley and C Coleman, *Understanding Crime Rates* (Saxon House, 1981).
[3] M McConville, A Sanders and R Leng, *The Case for the Prosecution* (Routledge, 1991) p 108.
[4] Ibid pp 29–30.
[5] Ibid p 111.
[6] A Sanders, 'Personal Violence and Public Order' (1988) 16 IJ Soc Law 359 and C Clarkson, A Cretney, G Davis and J Shephard, 'Assaults: The Relationship between Seriousness, Criminalisation and Punishment' [1994] Crim LR 4.
[7] Op cit p 104, Table 10. There are no official figures on this point.

before they become prosecutable, and little over half of all suspects make incriminating statements. Not only does arrest involve a significant curtailment of liberty, but it happens to many people who are legally innocent.

There is nothing new in the police NFAing cases, but the scale has changed in recent years. Thus, Steer found an NFA rate of only 8.3% in 1974.[8] There have been two changes since then. Firstly, as a result of the Philips Commission finding large numbers of weak cases being prosecuted,[9] the DPP's criteria for prosecution were adopted in what became the Attorney General's guidelines for prosecution (now incorporated into the Code for Crown Prosecutors). The police previously used the 'prima facie case' test, but now are supposed to use a 'realistic prospect of conviction' test. Under this test, conviction has to be more likely than acquittal, unlike the prima facie case test where the chances of conviction might be remote.

The new test does not require a belief in the innocence of a defendant in order for a case to be dropped, nor a belief in guilt for a case to be proceeded with; thus it has come under criticism. Williams argues that allegedly corrupt police officers are frequently not prosecuted because it is feared that juries will not accept the word of private citizens, especially if they have criminal records, against that of police officers. Similarly, the application of the test can mean that sophisticated fraudsters are not prosecuted on the ground that it would be difficult to get a jury to understand and convict on the complicated evidence involved.[10] To the extent that prosecutors act on such beliefs about juries,[11] we can see that the application of the same test to people of different status leads to different results, allowing high status defendants to avoid prosecution.[12] Williams argues that the test should not be whether a jury is likely to convict, but whether it ought to convict, given the admissible evidence available to the prosecutor. It is bad enough, he says, that someone believed to be guilty gets acquitted, but to spare them the anguish of the trial too is overgenerous.

The 'realistic prospect' test creates a tougher threshold for the police to surmount than did the old prima facie test. It would be expected that this change would lead to fewer cases being prosecuted (and a higher success rate at court). One might have hoped for fewer

[8] D Steer, Uncovering Crime: The Police Role (Royal Commission on Criminal Procedure Research Study no 7) (HMSO, 1980) Table 4.

[9] Royal Commission on Criminal Procedure, Report (Cmnd 8092) (HMSO, 1981) pp 130–131.

[10] G Williams, 'Letting off the Guilty and Prosecuting the Innocent' [1985] Crim LR 115.

[11] Little is known about the actual behaviour of juries and their reasons for acquittal: see ch 8, section 5, below.

[12] For discussion of this point in the context of arrest, see ch 3, section 4(c).

weak arrests, but instead there appear to be more arrests without prosecution. This has been facilitated by another development in the law: PACE. For s 37 allows suspects to be detained precisely in order to secure sufficient evidence to prosecute. Release without charge is explicitly recognised as a legitimate outcome should that evidence not be produced.

Allowing the police to arrest, collect evidence and weed out cases which they decide do not warrant judicial proceedings is a classic 'let the experts decide' crime control strategy. The due process objections to it are that the process involves considerable infringement on the freedom of those released, as well as prosecuted, by the police, who are not even terribly good at 'weeding'. The problem is not just gardening ability, however. Whether a case is NFAd or not depends not just on police evaluations of evidential strength and offence seriousness. It also depends on how much the police want to prosecute a particular case and a particular individual, and that is shaped by the police's working rules.

(b)　Police working rules and the custody officer

We have already seen that arrests can be used as a resource in street policing. Sometimes the arrest suffices to impose police authority, rendering prosecution unnecessary. Usually, though, prosecution will be a natural follow-through. A police officer justified one prosecution to McConville et al by pointing out that, 'We can't have people going round pushing police officers when they feel like it.'[13] The street working rules examined in chapters 2 and 3 therefore continue to have force in the shaping of prosecution decisions, even when the evidence is weak. The need to uphold order and authority is particularly important, especially when a complaint has been made against the officer,[14] or when the latter is assaulted.[15] A little over half of all arrested adults, and around one-third of all arrested juveniles, are charged.[16] While some arrests which are made without reasonable suspicion are NFAd, many are not.

Conversely, where there is no dimension of public order involved in an incident, the police may see little point in prosecuting from their perspective. This is a particular problem in cases of domestic violence where alleged violence is reported by a woman and a crime

---

[13]　Op cit.
[14]　See A Sanders, 'Prosecution Decisions and the Attorney General's Guidelines' [1985] Crim LR 19; and McConville et al, op cit.
[15]　Clarkson et al, op cit.
[16]　McConville et al, op cit p 104, Table 10.

report is filled in.[17] Susan Edwards, in her study in London in the late 1980s, found that in one area 25 out of 36 domestic assaults were no-crimed and, in another, 23 out of 25 were no-crimed.[18] No other type of assault or other type of crime was no-crimed as much. Can this really be because so many errors were made? This is unlikely. In a case from a different study, the victim and suspect were separated. The suspect assaulted the victim, causing bruising. There was a dispute about who hit who first, but prosecution was recommended because it was thought by a police inspector that the victim used 'reasonable force to evict a trespasser'. The incident was no-crimed, however, on the grounds that it was a 'domestic situation in which the injuries were trivial . . . Three days for the complainant to make up her mind about proceedings . . . Injury sustained is really only a common assault'.[19] In reality, 'actual bodily harm' (bruising) was caused. Trivial injuries do not deter the prosecution of other cases in other circumstances, particularly where public order or authority is threatened.[20]

The Philips Commission was anxious to reduce the number of arrests and the number of weak cases prosecuted. Since arresting officers will often have strong reasons for prosecuting, it was obvious that the imposition of objective standards would be impossible without the decision to prosecute being made by someone independent. The Philips Commission resolved to remedy this through the 'arrest only when necessary' principle, the 'realistic prospect of conviction' test, the custody officer and the CPS. Under its proposals, in most cases in which the police wanted to prosecute, they would have had to report the suspect. The suspect would then have been considered for summons by a senior officer on the basis of a written file of evidence.

This is the system used for road traffic offences, most non-arrestable offences and a minority of minor arrestable thefts and assaults. Decisions take longer than with arrest and charge but they are based on a detached consideration of the evidence, and the coercive process of arrest is avoided. However, as we observed in chapter 3, the 'arrest only when necessary' principle was not applied in PACE to arrestable offences.[1] The result has been that a much larger proportion of cases are processed by way of arrest and charge than the Philips Commission

---

[17] Although it will be recalled again from chapter 3, section 4(b), that the majority of calls to alleged incidents of domestic violence—and other types of violence—lead to no police action at all.

[18] S Edwards, *Policing Domestic Violence* (Sage, 1989).

[19] Sanders 'Personal Violence and Public Order', op cit.

[20] Ibid; McConville et al, op cit and Clarkson et al, op cit.

[1] See section 3(c).

envisaged. Indeed, it seems that a higher proportion of all prosecutions are by way of arrest and charge now than was so in 1981.[2]

The safeguard offered by the Philips Commission for arrest and charge cases (and enacted in PACE) was to replace the charge sergeant with the supposedly more independent custody officer. The problem with decisions taken by charge sergeants was that they were based only on the report of the arresting officer(s) together, perhaps, with that of the interviewing officer (often the same officer). Decisions usually had to be immediate, were based on what the officer(s) said was the evidence and in the presence of those officers. This all made dispassionate decision making virtually impossible. Thus, the Prosecuting Solicitors' Society commented:

'the view of the charge sergeant ... must therefore be gained from what he is told by the investigating officer. As an independent check this must be almost without value.'[3]

The defect in this part of the Philips Commission's strategy is that custody officers are in exactly the same social, occupational and structural position as were the old charge sergeants. Chapter 4 showed that, in relation to the rights of suspects, the custody officer is no more independent than charge sergeants used to be. The same is true in relation to decisions to charge. One custody officer told McConville et al: 'I would go along with what the arresting officers have to say.' Another, when asked whether he had put questions to an arresting officer or the suspect to form his own view of an incident, replied: 'Not at all. I accept that [the officer's] got no cause to be telling lies and the [suspect] has.'[4] It is very rare for custody officers to caution or NFA when arresting officers want to charge, or vice versa. Nothing else can be expected.

Arresting officers can present cases to custody officers in ways that secure the results they want. Officers who want to slip dubious charges past possibly sceptical custody officers can make alleged offences seem particularly serious, or the evidence seem particularly strong. In practice, then, the realistic prospect of conviction test, if in the custody officer's mind at all, is easily overcome. Thus in one of McConville et al's cases there was, in what had been portrayed to the custody officer as a s 47 assault, virtually no injury. The charge had to be reduced in court to the charge of common assault (which would not normally be prosecuted by the police).[5]

[2] McConville et al, op cit pp 38–40.
[3] Evidence to the Philips Commission (1979) para 3.3. This was the message which also emerged from the research of the 1970s and early 1980s. See A Sanders, 'Prosecution Decisions and the Attorney General's Guidelines', op cit.
[4] Op cit p 119.
[5] Op cit p 112.

A further point is that the custody officer operates the same working rules about order, authority and suspiciousness as do all other police officers. In one case discussed by McConville et al, the suspect had no previous convictions and was arrested for drunkenness. The arresting officer said that he had been getting on the custody officer's nerves because he had been 'mouthy', and so was prosecuted for being drunk and disorderly even though he had not actually been disorderly in public. The custody officer said:

'To be perfectly frank you make your decision on what you see in front of you. If he gives you a hard time, say verbally, then you think, "Oh yeah, he's obviously given the PC a hard time on the street and he's obviously of a disorderly nature and therefore we'll send him to court." That's how I decide.'[6]

Like the charge sergeants of pre-PACE days, custody officers take information from arresting/interviewing officers alone, treating their version of events as inherently reliable and the suspect's, if listened to at all, as a tissue of self-interested lies. This dichotomous approach to the nature of truth oversimplifies the sociological reality: a given set of facts can often be interpreted in different ways. But even if the custody officer does wish to hear a suspect's story, the rules on interviewing would make this virtually impossible.[7] Once again, the attempt to secure due process has a paradoxical effect.

(c) Case construction and the CPS

The first task of the CPS, like that of the custody officer, is to ensure that prosecution cases pass the test of evidential sufficiency. How well has this part of the Philips Commission's strategy to sieve weak cases out of the system at an early stage worked? Every case which the police decide should be prosecuted reaches the CPS prior to the first court hearing (although sometimes only immediately before it). The CPS is entitled to drop ('discontinue') the case either immediately or at any time thereafter.[8]

What is the point of the police prosecuting weak cases when the CPS can simply drop them? The answer in part is that when this happens the officers involved can claim that the CPS exercised its judgment poorly. With crime rates continuing to rise, the CPS has become a useful scapegoat for the wider failure of the crime control strategy. In police 'cop culture', the CPS, in dropping cases, is letting the public

---

[6] Op cit pp 113–114.
[7] See ch 4, above.
[8] Prosecution of Offences Act 1985, s 23.

(and the police) down. The CPS has even been dubbed by one wit in blue 'the Criminal Protection Society'. However, the reasons for the police pushing weak cases into the prosecution system run deeper than this.

The 'realistic prospect of conviction' rule is a predictive rule. As Williams observed, it does not relate to the likelihood of guilt but to the likelihood of conviction. It is, in other words, not a rule which asks officers to prosecute cases which are necessarily intrinsically stronger, but cases in which they think they can secure sufficient evidence. This may seem a pedantic distinction, but it is not. The rule encourages the police to strengthen cases which would otherwise be weak. So there may not be fewer prosecutions of weak cases, but simply prosecutions of the same cases in which the evidence has been strengthened. Although this may lead to more forensic investigation, bolstering those cases which would otherwise be likely to fail, it also encourages the stronger construction of cases, whereby weak cases remain weak, but are made to appear strong.

The CPS is in a similar position to that of the custody officer in having to rely on what they are told by police officers who may, and often do, have an interest in the case. The CPS position is not quite so dependent as is that of the custody officer. Firstly, there is no time pressure on the CPS: the suspect is not in the cells awaiting a decision. Secondly, the CPS makes decisions on the basis of written files in which obvious flaws will be more difficult to conceal. On the other hand, the CPS is not a decision taker but a decision confirmer or reverser. It is more difficult to reverse a decision of which one disapproves than it is to refuse to take it in the first place. The result is 'prosecution momentum': the continued prosecution of cases, as a result of inertia, which should never have begun.[9]

The proportion of cases discontinued by the CPS has been rising steadily (13.5% of all cases in 1992–3).[10] Nearly half of these are cases dropped for evidential insufficiency, while in another 17% of dropped cases the prosecution is unable to proceed because, for instance, material witnesses went missing or refused to give evidence.[11] This might suggest that the CPS is doing the job which Philips set out for it. However, between 1985 and 1988 the percentage of cases ending in acquittal rose slightly in the Crown Court (16.7% to 17.6%) but massively in the magistrates' courts (12.5% to 23.8%). Although these figures include cases where no evidence was offered, acquittals following

---

[9]   See A Sanders, 'An Independent Crown Prosecution Service' [1986] Crim LR 27 for cases illustrating this prior to the creation of the CPS.

[10]   Crown Prosecution Service, Annual Report 1992–1993, (HMSO, 1993).

[11]   Crown Prosecution Service, Discontinuance Survey (November 1993) (unpublished).

a full trial rose significantly.[12] This apparent contradiction is explained by McConville and Sanders[13] as follows. First, some cases can be seen to be evidentially weak from the outset, and these were usually dropped. Even then the CPS rarely flexed its muscles independently, as in most of these cases the police themselves—often supervising officers responsible for an area's prosecutions—point these weaknesses out to the CPS. If the CPS did not exist, the police would probably drop most of these cases anyway.

Then there are the cases which appear weak, which the police do not wish to drop and which the CPS do prosecute. Sometimes this is because the police working rules which led to the initial charges embody values shared by the CPS. As one prosecutor told McConville et al, when one suspect gets 'away with it . . . it gets back to the others. You've got to get to know your territory—it's a bit of a policy decision.'[14] At other times there is a good chance of a guilty plea,[15] or the chance of a freak conviction.[16] In many cases, the CPS told the police that the case would be dropped if the defendant pleaded not guilty. In others, McConville et al were told that they (the prosecutors) did not know if the evidence was strong or not but that it did not matter as the defendant was pleading guilty anyway. Why give up the chance of a conviction for the certainty of a 'failure'? A 'realistic prospect of conviction' requires nothing other than a weighing of the odds.

In any group of cases with a realistic prospect of conviction, we would expect some cases to end in acquittal, and some to end in conviction. It is impossible for the CPS to be sure which will fall into which category and so it is not surprising that there is a significant acquittal rate in the criminal courts. This has been recognised for some years.[17] The real issue is whether the CPS is failing to identify cases that do not have a realistic prospect of conviction. In a study for the Runciman Commission, Block et al looked at 100 ordered and directed Crown Court acquittals. At least one-quarter of the acquittals were certainly foreseeable (ie manifestly more likely than not to fail) and another quarter were possibly foreseeable.[18] Similarly, in the Runciman Commission's Crown Court study around 20% of the contested cases were regarded by the barristers and judges involved as 'weak'. Around

---

[12] M McConville and A Sanders, 'Weak Cases and the CPS' (1992) LS Gaz, 12 February, p 24.

[13] On the basis of the official statistics and the findings of McConville et al, op cit.

[14] Quoted by McConville and Sanders, op cit.

[15] See chs 6 and 7.

[16] See ch 8.

[17] See G Mansfield and J Peay, *The Director of Public Prosecutions* (Tavistock, 1987).

[18] B Block, C Corbett, and J Peay, Ordered and Directed Acquittals in the Crown Court (Royal Commission on Criminal Justice Research Study no 15) (HMSO, 1993).

80% of these cases ended in acquittal, but significant numbers ended in conviction.[19] To drop all cases predicted as possible acquittals would therefore lead to convictions as well as acquittals being reduced.[20] Had Block et al looked at 100 convictions, a large number of them would doubtless also have been foreseen as possible acquittals.[1]

The CPS, then, prosecutes many weak cases in the knowledge that they will probably (but not inevitably) fail if they are contested. We suggested that this is done for 'policy' reasons and in the hope of guilty pleas. Unfortunately, the research of Block et al sheds no more light than this on the issue, for they do not appear to have sought the reasons for prosecution in these failed cases.

The above argument does require one important modification. Some acquittals which are predictable will be so at an early stage by, at best, the police alone. This is because they are constructed to appear stronger than they 'really' are. To some extent, a case which is so constructed actually is strong. Facts do not exist in abstract, and who is to say what 'really' happened, or what was in a suspect's mind? Both sides of an adversarial system construct facts, because most facts are not neutral objective entities to be dispassionately evaluated.

When the police construct cases, they seek evidence which will prove their case and avoid or undermine evidence which goes against it. They may do this because they fear that the CPS will not share its view of the importance of prosecuting a particular case. Alternatively, they may do it because they predict that although the CPS will support their decision to prosecute, the chances of success at court if the case is contested would otherwise be slim. A well-constructed case may induce a guilty plea from the defendant, and may even be strong enough to stand up to scrutiny in an adversarial trial.

There is nothing necessarily wrong with case construction. It is a natural part of the adversarial system, and it is a feature of all law enforcement agencies.[2] It would be unobjectionable if the defence had similar resources and approach; but they have neither.[3] Police constructions therefore tend to dominate prosecution and court processes, giving them enormous power in the process of determining guilt and innocence. Let us examine some of the ways in which the police construct cases.

---

[19]   M Zander and P Henderson, Crown Court Study (Royal Commission on Criminal Justice Research Study no 19)(HMSO, 1993) pp 184–185.

[20]   See also the discussion in ch 8, section 1, below.

[1]   McConville et al, op cit ch 8 found that many results were impossible to predict.

[2]   See D Nelken, *The Limits of the Legal Process* (MacMillan, 1983) for a study of case construction by housing officials in relation to harassment cases.

[3]   M McConville, J Hodgson and L Bridges, *Standing Accused* (Clarendon Press, 1994).

Fabrication of evidence

One way of constructing cases is by creating the facts. Occasionally this may be pure fabrication. This is what Sgt Challenor was notorious for,[4] and fabrication has been an element in many of the infamous miscarriage of justice cases. For example, in the 'Guildford Four' case, the police claimed to have taken a contemporaneous note of an interview with one of the defendants, Patrick Armstrong, and then had these typed up. Some 14 years after the interview took place, it was discovered that the typed notes contained deletions and additions, both typed and handwritten. Yet the supposedly contemporaneous handwritten note of the interview corresponded with the amended version of the typed notes. When the Court of Appeal was faced with these facts, it concluded that either the typed notes were a complete fabrication, subsequently copied out by hand so as to appear contemporaneously made, or the police had started with a contemperaneous note, typed it up, amended it to make it more effective as prosecution evidence, and then converted it back to a handwritten note. Either way, the police had lied. This proved vital to the success of the appeal for, as Lord Lane CJ put it, 'If they were prepared to tell this sort of lie, then the whole of their evidence became suspect.' None the less, it took 14 years to demolish this particular police construction.[5]

Interrogation

Usually the process of construction is more subtle, particularly through interrogation. As we saw in chapter 4, most suspects do not confess their crimes in an unprompted manner. Confessions are usually the product of interrogation and part of a sequence of questions and answers, even when they are literally not constructed in officers' notebooks. In this sense, then, all confessions are created by the police (along with the suspect). The facts pointing towards guilt are therefore, in large part, a product of police processes, as in *Madden's* case, the Birmingham Six, the Maguires, the 'Cardiff Three' and so on.

The way the police interrogate is important in constructing cases both in the questions asked and in those not asked. In one case examined by McConville et al, a store detective had asked a suspected shoplifter whether she had forgotten to pay (if she had indeed forgotten to pay, or raised a reasonable doubt about that at court, then she would be entitled to an acquittal on the grounds of no *mens rea*). The police

---

[4] See ch 4, section 5(g), above.
[5] See J Rozenberg, 'Miscarriages of Justice' in E Stockdale and S Casale (eds), *Criminal Justice Under Stress* (Blackstone, 1992) p 94.

decision maker in the case advised the store detective not to ask this sort of question in future.[6] As we have seen, and as this example illustrates, the police are not concerned to discover exonerating facts. The police do not seek all the evidence which might bear on the guilt or innocence of suspects, but only the evidence which will strengthen the case against them.

Summaries of interviews

It is standard for the police to prepare a summary of any tape recorded interview with a suspect. In practice, both defence and prosecution lawyers tend to rely on these summaries in order to save time and money.[7] For many years these particular police constructions have been known to be inaccurate,[8] and they continue to be so.[9] Their inaccuracy is, however, unidirectional. That is, summaries nearly always overstate, and rarely understate, the extent to which a full confession or an incriminating statement was made.[10] Prosecution files are therefore constructed to appear to be stronger than they 'really' are. In the rare event that a tape of interview is listened to or the full transcript read, prosecution momentum will have developed. Sometimes it is only when cases are contested that different versions of the facts emerge. Thus in an offensive weapon case, what was described as a 'truncheon' in the police file turned out to be a decorated rounders bat, a common souvenir from Spain.[11] The pressures on defendants not to contest cases are, however, intense.[12]

Forensic evidence

Even apparently 'hard' scientific facts about times of death, DNA and so forth are susceptible to the processes of case construction. Roberts and Willmore found that scientists sometimes disagreed on the interpretation

---

[6] McConville, Sanders and Leng, op cit p 74.

[7] See J Baldwin and J Bedward, 'Summarising Tape Recordings of Police Interviews' [1991] Crim LR 671 at 672.

[8] See ibid. See also A Sanders, 'Constructing the Case for the Prosecution' (1987) 14 Journal of Law and Society 229 and McConville et al, op cit. A similar problem arises in summary proceedings, where disclosure often takes place by way of a summary of the prosecution case, again prepared by the police: J. Baldwin and A Mulvaney, 'Advance Disclosure in the Magistrates' Courts: How useful are the Prosecution summaries?' [1987] Crim LR 805.

[9] J Baldwin, Preparing the Record of Taped Interview (Royal Commission on Criminal Justice Research Study no 2) (HMSO, 1992).

[10] This point is further discussed in ch 6, section 3(c), below.

[11] McConville et al, op cit pp 116–17.

[12] See chs 6 and 7.

of their findings, that the police sometimes forwarded for examination evidence that might help their case but not that which might undermine it and that some evidential material could be accidentally contaminated by the police or by the laboratory.[13] As they point out, scientists prefer to make clear the limits of their ability to reach black and white conclusions, but the forensic process discourages shades of grey. Perhaps most important of all, forensic examination does not take place in a vacuum: scientists are asked whether particular substances can be identified, or whether a sexual assault could have occurred. This is often unavoidable (any one substance might contain an infinite number of constituents; without knowing what to test for some analyses might never end). The problem lies in the weight to be attributed to the evidence of the prosecution scientist. In the 'Confait Affair' the inability to fix the time of death of Confait accurately allowed the obfuscation of the facts by the prosecution which led to the wrongful conviction of the three defendants.[14] Thus, Roberts and Willmore comment that 'At each stage of the pre-trial process forensic science is utilised by prosecution agencies as a tool for case construction.'[15]

Non-disclosure of evidence

The 'Confait Affair' illustrates another way in which case construction is done. The failure of the police to disclose relevant information can not only make cases appear strong to prosecutors, but actually to be strong in court—often leading, as in that case, to convictions of factually innocent persons.[16] Other wrongful convictions resulting from lack of disclosure include *Virag*[17] and *Judith Ward*.[18] In the latter case, the police hid certain evidence from the prosecution and the defence, and the prosecution hid other evidence from the defence. Government scientists had also deliberately suppressed material unhelpful to the Crown's case, and had created a distorted picture of the forensic evidence. The Court of Appeal laid down strict (although not absolute) rules for disclosure in *Ward*. These rules should lessen the scope for construction by suppression of evidence (although only if the rules are adhered to), but *Ward* represents the high-water mark of the trend towards due process in the law of disclosure. The subsequent case of

---

13 P Roberts and C Willmore, The Role of Forensic Science Evidence in Criminal Proceedings (Royal Commission on Criminal Justice Research Study no 11) (HMSO, 1993).
14 J Rozenberg, *The Case for the Crown* (Equation, 1987).
15 Op cit p 26.
16 This is further discussed in ch 7, section 5(b), below.
17 Unreported. Discussed in Sanders, 'Constructing the Case for the Prosecution', op cit.
18 [1993] 1 WLR 619.

Johnson[19] marks the beginning of a judicial retreat back towards crime control. This retreat was supported by the Runciman Commission which felt that due process-inspired decisions such as *Ward* 'have created burdens for the prosecution that go beyond what is reasonable.'[20] We may, therefore, expect to see fewer rather than more restrictions on the ability of the prosecution to construct cases through non-disclosure in future.

In the light of all these factors, it can be seen that, despite appearances and protestations to the contrary, the CPS is a police-dependent, rather than an independent, institution. This is partly by choice, in so far as the ethos of the two institutions are similar. It is partly a product of the performance indicators—conviction rates, primarily—established as criteria of success for it. Since both the police and the CPS are prosecuting agencies, it could not be expected that either of these conditions be otherwise. Finally, the CPS is almost entirely dependent on the police for its information about cases. Since cases are made up of nothing other than information, cases themselves are police products, and CPS decisions are therefore driven by the police. Above all, it is this structural dependency which empties the CPS duty to ensure that prosecution cases pass the evidential sufficiency test of most of its due process potential.

4. THE PUBLIC INTEREST

The DPP has always been under a duty to prosecute only when this is judged to be in the 'public interest', this principle being embodied in the Code for Crown Prosecutors. The concept of the 'public interest' is, of course, as flexible as any concept can be. What one does or does not perceive as in the public interest will vary according to one's political and social outlook and one's experiences. If most judges are incapable of escaping this subjectivism,[1] why should we expect objectivism of police officers, the DPP, or of her political boss, the Attorney General? Whether or not to prosecute 'political' offences used to be particularly controversial.[2] Obvious examples include offences against the Official Secrets Acts, including the leaking of classified information harmful to ministers but, arguably, not the country, as in the *Ponting* case.[3] Other

---

[19] [1993] Crim LR 689, and accompanying commentary at 690.
[20] Report, op cit p 95.
[1] As J Griffith argues in *Politics of the Judiciary* (Fontana, 1991) ch 9.
[2] J Edwards, *The Attorney General, Politics and the Public Interest* (1984).
[3] C Ponting, *The Right to Know, The Inside Story of the Belgrano Affair* (Sphere, 1985).

examples include killings and wounding by soldiers in Northern Ireland and by mainland police officers, and alleged offences by police officers in general.[4] At least with allegedly biased prosecutions the issues can be aired in public. Allegedly biased decisions not to prosecute are of such low visibility that even speculation is difficult. The majority of cases involving the 'public interest', however, concern the question of cautioning. This apparently benign process attracts little public controversy except in so far as it is perceived by some to be too generous to offenders. The reality is not so straightforward.

(a) Cautioning

Cautioning rates

Cautioning, along with the prosecution of weak cases, was a concern of the Philips Commission.[5] At that time only 4% of adults were cautioned for non-road traffic offences. The cautioning of juveniles was much more extensive (see Table 5.1). This was a result of its encouragement in the Children and Young Persons Act 1969, although the practice had existed for many years before that.[6] The extent of cautioning varied greatly from police force to police force, and it still does, as Table 5.1 shows. Rural Cumbria was always a low caution force and remains so, in contrast with equally rural Devon and Cornwall. But urban South Yorkshire is also a relatively high caution force, as it has always been. Forces do change their policies, however, as is clear from the adult Metropolitan (London) figures.

This was, and is, less a product of the offence profiles of each force and more a product of offender mix (high cautioning forces have more offenders with no criminal record) and police forces pursuing different cautioning policies.[7] It seemed unfair to Philips that whether or not one was prosecuted depended more on where the offence was committed than on what the offence was or who did it. In 1985, the government responded with two sets of caution guidelines (superseding the previous guidelines, issued in 1978), one for adults and one for juveniles, which were intended to promote consistency. In the event, they did not do so.[8] Consequently, new guidelines were issued in 1990, which acknowledged

---

[4] For several examples see S Greer, 'Miscarriages of Criminal Justice Reconsidered' (1994) Modern Law Review 57: 58, at pp 64–65.

[5] Report, op cit paras 6.40–6.41.

[6] J Ditchfield, Police Cautioning (HMSO, 1976).

[7] G Laycock and R Tarling, 'Police Force Cautioning: Policy and Practice (1985) 24 Howard J Crim Justice 81.

[8] R Evans and C Wilkinson, 'Variations in Police Cautioning Policy and Practice in England and Wales' (1990) 29 Howard J Crim Justice 155.

the variations which existed both within and between police forces and exhorted police forces to implement the guidelines consistently.[9] In passing, we might question what the point is of organising police forces on a local basis under local control if local variations are regarded as unacceptable. To put the problem the other way round, what is more important: local control or consistency? It is nigh impossible to achieve both.

Table 5.1: Caution rates (per cent of all those found guilty or cautioned for indictable offences)—selected police force areas[10]

	Juveniles		Adults	
	1978	1992	1978	1992
Cheshire	46	82	1	24
Cumbria	44	74	3	12
Devon/Cornwall	69	86	15	36
Met	46	78	0	30
South Yorks	47	78	9	25
Average	49	78	4	24

Cautioning has been encouraged by government as well as social workers for some years. The ostensible reasons are stated in the 1990 circular:

'There is widespread agreement that the courts should only be used as a last resort, particularly for juveniles and young adults; and that diversion from the courts by means of cautioning or other forms of action may reduce the likelihood of re-offending.'[11]

Prosecution is therefore seen as actually potentially harmful, largely because of its stigmatising effects. It might be thought, on the other

---

[9] Home Office Circular 59/1990 (cautioning of offenders), Annex A.

[10] The figures for 1978 are taken from Table 23.4 of Royal Commission on Criminal Procedure, The Law and Procedure, op cit. The figures are of persons cautioned expressed as a rounded percentage of persons found guilty or cautioned for indictable offences in England and Wales. Juveniles refers to persons aged between 10 and 16 (inclusive) and adults are those aged 17 or over. Figures for 1992 are taken from Criminal Statistics 1992, (HMSO, 1993) Table 5.5. Adults are here classified as 21 or over.

[11] Ibid para 7.

hand, that cautioning erodes the deterrent effect of the law. There is no reliable evidence on this one way or the other.[12]

As Table 5.2 shows, cautioning of both adults and juveniles rose sharply in the 1980s and early 1990s.

Table 5.2: Caution rates (per cent of all found guilty or cautioned for indictable offences)

	Males			Females		
	14–17	17–21	21+	4–17	17–21	21+
1982	38	3	4	65	6	12
1984	45	5	5	71	10	16
1986	55	10	10	80	22	26
1988	60	14	12	80	27	29
1990	69	21	15	86	38	34
1992	73	33	23	90	55	46

(Source: Criminal Statistics, 1992, Table 5.3)

A number of issues fall to be discussed in the light of these trends. Firstly, more cautioning does not necessarily mean more consistent cautioning. Nor does it necessarily mean the right people being cautioned for the right reasons. A more fundamental problem is that of the overall level of prosecution and cautioning. Police prosecution rates remain much higher than those of other law enforcement agencies, such as the Health and Safety Executive and the Inland Revenue. Are there any good reasons for this? Underlying these issues is the most intractable problem of all: the control of prosecution and cautioning.

---

[12] S Keith, 'The Criminal Histories of those Cautioned in 1985 and 1988' (1992) 32 Home Office Research Bulletin 44, examined the conviction rates of young adults cautioned in 1985. She found that they were no more likely to be convicted within two years of being cautioned than young adults who were prosecuted at the age of 19. The overall conviction rates (for offenders of all ages) within two years of being cautioned was about 13%. This might suggest that the deterrent effect of cautioning on further offending is similar to that of prosecution. On the other hand, studies of reconviction rates are not studies of reoffending and so figures of this kind should be used, in the first author's view, with caution. The second author would much prefer not to use them at all for reasons admirably explained by S Box, *Deviance, Reality and Society* (Holt, Rinehart and Winston, 1981).

The framework of cautioning

The pattern of cautioning is affected by the organisational structure within which decision making takes place. The process begins with the investigating officer's opinion regarding what action should be taken in a case. This is communicated to the custody officer in cases where the suspect is arrested. The custody officer must then decide whether to charge, to recommend that the suspect be cautioned by a senior officer immediately or to release the suspect and report to a senior officer to decide whether to recommend caution or summons. Suspects who are not arrested are simply reported. When senior officers consider the cases of juvenile suspects who are reported in either of the above ways, they usually pass the case onto a multi-disciplinary juvenile liaison bureau of some kind which will either recommend a disposition to the police or, occasionally, have the decision delegated to it by the police.[13] In a few areas, there is this type of arrangement for adults (especially young adults aged 17–21) too, but this is rare.[14]

It can be seen that control of adult cautioning is nearly always entirely in the hands of the police. Moreover, investigating officers who favour prosecution against caution can, as with those who favour prosecution against NFA, have the individual charged with little chance of resistance from the custody officer. As with the evidential threshold, just arresting, as distinct from reporting, makes prosecution more likely if that is the wish of the officer. This control is not greatly lessened where juveniles are concerned, as juvenile bureaus are commonly bypassed through arrest and charge.[15] Bureaus are in any case dependent on the police for information and are sometimes pressured into adopting police perspectives.[16] When they refuse to be compliant the police can, and sometimes do, simply override the wishes of the bureau.[17] The *Kent* case arose precisely because the juvenile bureau objected to the police over-riding their recommendation not to prosecute.[18] It seems that, in about 10% of prosecuted

---

[13]   For a description of such a bureau, see S Uglow, A Dart, A Bottomley, and C Hale, 'Cautioning Juveniles—Multi-Agency Impotence' [1992] Crim LR 632.

[14]   For examples, see R Evans, 'Evaluating Young Adult Diversion Schemes in the Metropolitan Police District' [1993] Crim LR 490 and J Dignan, 'Repairing the Damage' (1992) 32 BJ Crim453.

[15]   R Evans and T Ferguson, Comparing Different Juvenile Cautioning Systems in One Police Force Area (Report to the Home Office Research and Planning Unit) (1991).

[16]   McConville et al, op cit pp 137–141 and R Evans, 'Before the Court—Understanding Inter-Agency Consultation with Juveniles and Young Adults' (forthcoming publication).

[17]   Ibid.

[18]   *R v Chief Constable of the Kent Constabulary, ex p L* [1993] 1 All ER 756.

cases going through that particular bureau, the bureau recommended lesser action.[19] Despite this, Evans argues that, without multi-agency bureaus, caution rates for adults will always be considerably lower than for juveniles.[20]

It is now clear from both the Home Office guidelines on cautioning and the Code for Crown Prosecutors that, in every case where there is sufficient evidence, the desirability of prosecution (as against caution or NFA) should be considered rather than assumed. The former Attorney General's statement of the opportunity principle, to the effect that prosecution should only take place if it is in the public interest, appears to create a presumption against prosecution. This contrasts with the decision-making structure described above which gives enormous power to arresting officers to secure the decision they favour.

Cautioning conditions

In considering their decision, the police have to consider, firstly, a series of pre-conditions and, secondly, a series of criteria. There are three pre-conditions to be met in order to caution:

(a) sufficient evidence of the offender's guilt to give a realistic prospect of conviction;
(b) admission of the offence by the offender; and
(c) the informed consent by the offender to being cautioned.[1]

These pre-conditions are intended to ensure that, because a caution is a statement of guilt (which can be cited in court), the offender really is guilty and would be convicted if prosecuted. They are due process safeguards, intended to inhibit the police from cautioning whenever they adjudge a suspect to be guilty but they cannot, or would rather not, collect sufficient evidence to support a prosecution. As a mechanism for protecting innocent suspects from administrative determinations of guilt, the pre-conditions have been found wanting. Earlier guidelines with the same pre-conditions were found to be breached on occasion.[2] Indeed, Sanders found that some cautions were administered precisely because there was insufficient evidence, and sometimes in the absence of consent or an admission.[3] Nor is consent or an admission a safeguard in reality. Young found that juveniles were prepared to admit and consent to almost anything to escape from the

[19] S Uglow et al, op cit.
[20] Evans, 'Evaluating Young Adult Diversion Schemes in the Metropolitan Police District', op cit (1993).
[1] Home Office Circular 59/1990 (cautioning of offenders), Annex B.
[2] Dignan, op cit.
[3] Sanders, The Limits to Diversion from Prosecution', op cit.

'coercive jaws' of the criminal process.[4] Dignan echoes this in relation to adults, observing that offenders were required to 'bargain in the shadow of the law'.[5] In a more recent study, Evans found that 22% of juvenile cautions were in cases where there was no clear admission of guilt (in many, there were in fact denials).[6]

The 1990 Home Office guidelines provide that if one of these pre-conditions is absent prosecution is not inevitable: 'It may be appropriate to take no further action . . .'[7] Again, McConville et al found this to be rare.[8] The fact that senior officers make caution decisions is no safeguard. As in other contexts, the attempt to impose due process standards on the police through rules to be enforced by the police themselves appears doomed to failure. The pre-conditions to cautioning are essentially presentational rules, giving the appearance of due process, but having little or no effect on the police.

Cautioning criteria

If the cautioning pre-conditions are met, there are several criteria for the police to take into account under the 1990 guidelines:

(a) the nature of the offence;
(b) the likely penalty if the offender were to be convicted; and
(c) the offender's age, state of health, previous criminal history and 'attitude towards the offence, including practical expressions of regret'.[9]

The guidelines also suggest that victims should be contacted to ascertain their views, the extent of damage or loss and whether any compensation or reparation has been made. As far as previous criminal history is concerned, as with the 1985 guidelines, previous cautions or even one or two unrelated minor convictions do not preclude cautioning (para 7) although in such circumstances the positive factors have to be stronger. Evans and Wilkinson found that many police forces explicitly developed multiple cautioning as a result of this, even though many police officers and magistrates were unhappy about it.[10]

---

[4] R Young, The Sandwell Mediation and Reparation Scheme (West Midlands Probation Service, 1987).
[5] Op cit p 465.
[6] R Evans, The Conduct of Police Interviews with Juveniles (Royal Commission on Criminal Justice Research Study no 8) (HMSO, 1993) p 41.
[7] Op cit, Annex B.
[8] Op cit.
[9] Annex B, para 3.
[10] R Evans and C Wilkinson, 'Variations in Police Cautioning Policy and Practice in England and Wales'(1990) 29 Howard J Crim Justice 155. New guidelines were issued

The 1990 guidelines supersede the 1985 guidelines but, in essence, they embody the same criteria and policies as before, as do the 1994 guidelines.[11] The main faults of the 1985 guidelines remain, and so it is not surprising that there has been disparity in the past and that the new guidelines are unlikely to end it. For in any one case many of these criteria pull in different directions. An offender may have a serious criminal record but commit a minor offence; or may commit a relatively serious offence but have no previous criminal history. The victim may favour or oppose prosecution, or simply be indifferent.

Guidelines such as these suffer many faults.[12] We mention but three here. Firstly, vagueness: how serious, for instance, is 'serious'? In the *Kent* case, the decision to prosecute was said by the court to be a 'harsh' one, but the seriousness of the offence (assault) made it acceptable.[13] Seriousness is a subjective matter. Secondly, they are manipulable by the police, as we have seen in relation to the views of victims of domestic violence; and cases can be constructed to appear less or more serious.[14] Finally, the cautioning criteria are non-prioritised. In other words, it is impossible to say whether a given decision is right or wrong if an offender 'scores' high on one criteria and low on another. The guidelines explicitly state that the victim's consent is not essential to caution, but no guidance is provided on how far the victim's views should outweigh other criteria. Thus countless pieces of research have found the police justifying non-prosecution of some cases by reference to the views of the victim, but at the same time prosecuting other cases where the victim did not want prosecution.[15]

Rather than the criteria in these guidelines guiding decision making, they end up justifying it. Thus, Evans found that a 'caution consideration chart' given to custody officers to encourage them to caution higher proportions of young adults was known by custody officers as the 'justification to charge sheet'. He comments that 'The most

in Home Office circular 18/1994 on 15 March 1994. Their main purposes are to: limit the use of repeat cautions for all but the most minor offences; to forbid cautions for very serious indictable-only cases (such as rape and attempted murder); and to forbid cautions in all but the most exceptional circumstances in all other indictable-only offences (such as robbery). These guidelines can be expected to produce a small but significant drop in the caution rate from 1994 onwards.

11 For the 1994 position, see n 10, above. A significant change from the 1985 guidelines is the omission of the suspect's 'character' as a relevant consideration.
12 For a longer discussion, see A Ashworth, 'The "Public Interest" Element in Prosecutions' [1987] Crim LR 595.
13 *R v Chief Constable of the Kent Constabulary, ex p L* [1993] 1 All ER 756, discussed above.
14 See Clarkson et al, op cit.
15 See, for example, Sanders, 'Personal Violence and Public Order', op cit; Evans, op cit (1991); Clarkson et al, op cit.

common use of the chart was not as an aid to decision making but as a written justification of a decision that had already been made.'[16] As with the three pre-conditions discussed under the previous subheading, the application of ostensibly inhibitory criteria is given to the very institution which they are supposed to inhibit. Not surprisingly, this renders the criteria presentational. Unfortunately this all seemed to be lost on the Runciman Commission, which did not address itself to the abuses and inconsistencies of the cautioning system and recommended that the police retain their current responsibilities.[17]

(b)   Police working rules and cautioning

We argue above that the cautioning 'rules' do not inhibit the police in any significant fashion. It follows that prosecution decisions must, if decision making is to be other than random and chaotic, be based on the informal working rules used by the police. The official public interest criteria are replaced in practice by the unofficial police interest criteria. These working criteria may, however, lead to three undesirable patterns of decision making: cautioning of those who should be NFAd, cautioning of those who should be prosecuted, and prosecution of those who should be cautioned or NFAd.

There are two types of suspect who are cautioned when they should be NFAd. There are those who, as we have already observed, do not meet the three pre-conditions, and there are those whose offences are so trivial that no action would have normally been taken against them. Caution is supposed to be an alternative to prosecution, not to no action. Yet there is evidence that at least some of the increase in cautioning represents more offenders being drawn into the system. This phenomenon—net widening—is warned against in the 1990 guidelines (para 3) and its existence is undeniable.[18] Indeed, since it has happened with Scottish 'prosecutor fines' as well, it appears to be an endemic feature of all (so-called) alternatives to prosecution.[19]

As far as the police are concerned, cautions are often as useful to them as are prosecutions and (especially in the case of instant cautions)[20] they avoid a considerable amount of paperwork. It makes it

---

[16] R Evans, 'Evaluating Young Adult Diversion Schemes in the Metropolitan Police District' [1993] Crim LR 490 at 494.

[17] Report, op cit p 82.

[18] Ditchfield, op cit; H. Parker, M Casburn and D Turnbull, *Receiving Juvenile Justice* (Basil Blackwell, 1981); Sanders, 'The Limits to Diversion from Prosecution', op cit (1988); Dignan, op cit.

[19] P Duff, 'The Prosecutor Fine and Social Control' (1993) 33 BJ Crim 481.

[20] Where offences are trivial, and the suspects have not been previously prosecuted or cautioned, they may be taken directly by the custody officer to the duty inspector and cautioned on the spot.

worth arresting where it might otherwise not be worthwhile and, of course, where there is insufficient evidence it secures some kind of 'result'. Moreover, if the caution is presented as a favour to the suspect, it provides, or maintains, the basis of a relationship on which future 'deals' can be built. What is certain is that suspects are never given the choice between NFA and caution, even in cases where, if the suspect did not agree to a caution, the police would simply take no further action. Instead, in these cases, the choice is presented to the suspect as either caution or prosecution, and this usually produces the result the police seek. If this is bargaining in the shadow of the law, it must be noted that the nature of the bargains struck will reflect the unequal status of the parties involved.

Cautioning those who should be prosecuted is advantageous for the suspects involved, but not for their victims. It is relatively easy for an officer to secure this result by constructing as trivial cases which are serious.[1] Sometimes the offence is regarded as petty, or sometimes the offence is regarded as 'out of character'. Assessment of character, again as with stop-search and arrest, is fraught with difficulties. Middle class and white people particularly benefit from this.[2] Informers are frequently cautioned rather than prosecuted as part of maintaining a mutually beneficial relationship. It is no accident that control of cautioning remains largely with the investigating officer, for cautioning can be an adjunct of other aspects of policing.

Where policing considerations such as order and authority point the other way, offenders are prosecuted and not cautioned. In one of McConville et al's cases, there was a fight outside a club which was notorious for minor disorder. The arresting officer said that the defendant would normally have been cautioned for his part in the fight but 'the reason he was charged was because we are objecting to the licence at [the club] . . . and the more charges we've got the better'.[3] Kemp et al observe that it is not so much what the victim wants but who the victim is that counts.[4] When business victims demand prosecution, they generally get their way, even where the police have reservations.[5] And just as assessment of character and attitude to the offence can work to the benefit of some groups of people, it works in the opposite direction for those with a 'bad attitude' or 'suspect character'. In one case examined by McConville et al, a youth with previous convictions had picked up a

---

[1] Officers do this all the time to justify not arresting in, for instance, domestic violence cases: see ch 3, section 4, above.
[2] See Fitzgerald, op cit; A. Sanders, 'Class Bias in Prosecutions' (1985) 24 Howard J Crim Justice 76 and McConville et al, op cit p 109.
[3] Op cit p 112.
[4] Op cit.
[5] See the examples cited by McConville et al, op cit pp 113–114.

Mars bar and broken a piece off. Asked why they had charged rather than cautioned, the police described the defendant as a 'toe-rag' who had been suspected of shoplifting on several occasions but never caught.[6]

Research carried out in the 1980s found that very large numbers of cautionable cases were prosecuted.[7] Now that, in the 1990s, caution rates are so much higher, it is likely that many fewer cautionable cases are being prosecuted (although net widening doubtless also accounts for an unquantifiable proportion of the higher numbers cautioned). However, there is no reason to believe that anything has changed in the cases where it is important for the police that a cautionable case be prosecuted. The same working rules that lead to the construction of 'suspiciousness' on the street, for example, still make prosecution more likely than caution for some types of suspect. Thus, the same patterns of race bias which can be observed in street policing seem to operate here.[8] Evans found Afro-Caribbean juveniles to be prosecuted far more often than white juveniles in a study of the Metropolitan Police. He comments that 'this cannot be explained in terms of any differences in offence patterns for different ethnic groups or differences in the proportions of first offenders.'[9] After reviewing several pieces of research carried out throughout the 1970s and 1980s (but not including the above study by Evans), Fitzgerald concludes that: 'Once arrested, Afro-Caribbeans are less likely to be cautioned than whites and may be less likely than Asians to have no further action taken against them.'[10] She does not conclude that direct discrimination is necessarily at work here. However, Afro-Caribbeans are less likely to admit the offence, are likely to be disadvantaged by the application of 'social' criteria (such as domestic circumstances) in an 'ethno-centric' way, and tend to have more previous convictions and cautions (possibly because of earlier biased decisions).

The custody officer is supposed to be a protection here. But as with evidential issues, the custody officer either acts as a rubber stamp or empathises with the arresting officer. Most custody officers, like police officers in general, are against extensive cautioning for adults in particular.[11] One custody officer put it this way:

---

6 Ibid.
7 See eg R Evans, 'Police Cautioning and the Young Adult Offender' [1991] Crim LR 598 and McConville et al, op cit ch 7.
8 See ch 2, section 3(a), and ch 3, section 4(c), above, for related discussion in the context of street policing.
9 R Evans, 'Comparing Young Adult and Juvenile Cautioning in the Metropolitan Police District' [1993] Crim LR 572 at 576.
10 Op cit p 33.
11 Evans 'Comparing Young Adult and Juvenile Cautioning in the Metropolitan Police District', op cit (1993) at 577.

'When someone sits and looks at it in a file coldly the next morning it probably gives them a slightly different picture to what I see—the toe-rag coming in effing and blinding at all and sundry . . . Straight away you think "well yeah, okay, here we go", perhaps an independent would say no, no, NFA.'[12]

However independent a custody officer might wish to be, however, as one told McConville et al, 'I'm dependent completely on what the officer says happened.'[13] As with evidential matters, what the arresting officer does and does not say determines the construction of the case as serious or trivial, and the construction of the suspect either as a public enemy or as a temporarily lapsed paragon.

(c) Case construction and the CPS

One of the functions of the CPS is to exercise control over the 'public interest' dimension of prosecutions, although it cannot, of course, do anything about cases which were cautioned when they should have been NFAd or prosecuted. It can, in principle, ensure that cautionable cases are not prosecuted by discontinuing them. The Code for Crown Prosecutors sets out several 'public interest' criteria which broadly correspond with the criteria in the cautioning guidelines. Prosecutors are enjoined to have regard to such matters as the gravity of the offence, the likely penalty, the age and mental state of the defendant, and the views of the complainant. Thus, a prosecution for breach of the peace of an elderly person suffering from mental disorder would certainly be regarded as not in the public interest. The Code stresses that a prosecutor 'should always apply his mind to the public interest and should strive to ensure that the spirit of the Home Office Cautioning Guidelines is observed.'[14] Given the research showing that, despite higher cautioning rates since the CPS was established, many cautionable cases are still being prosecuted, we would expect the discontinuance of many cases on this basis. Such figures as there are suggest that this may be happening. Discontinuances rose from 9.4% (of all cases completed in the magistrates courts) in 1990–91 to 11.8% in 1991–92 and to 13.5% in 1992–93.[15] This is a considerable rise over the situation in the late 1980s when McConville et al did their

---

[12] McConville et al, op cit p 115.
[13] Ibid p 122.
[14] Para 8. The Code is annexed to the Crown Prosecution Service, Annual Report 1992–1993 (HMSO, 1993).
[15] CPS, Annual Report 1990–1991, (HMSO, 1991) p 11 and CPS, Annual Report 1992–1993, (HMSO, 1993) p 18.

research.[16] Within the general discontinuance figures, it is not possible to ascertain how many are cautionable cases. Home Office research by Moxon and Crisp[17] looked at over 1,000 discontinuances in several different areas in 1990–91. Nearly one-third of the discontinuances were on 'public interest' grounds but, as we shall see, cautionability is not the only 'public interest' criterion. And in only 4% of these cases did the CPS recommend that a caution be substituted (although this was, in part, because discontinuance often took place some time after proceedings were initiated).

When McConville et al did their research, soon after the CPS was established, very few cases were discontinued on grounds of cautionability. They found that, as with evidential sufficiency, there was very little incentive for the CPS to drop cases on this basis and that the CPS and the police had similar outlooks and evaluated cases in much the same way. In one case, where a prosecutor did want to discontinue, the police objected (they sought prosecution for deterrent purposes) and the prosecutor was overruled by his boss. Even lip service was rarely paid to the 'public interest'.[18]

The most important problem for the CPS, however, is that police construction makes it often difficult and sometimes impossible to identify cautionable cases. Factors which could point towards caution or other forms of diversion are not drawn to decision makers' attention in the file, or such facts are not brought out by the police because of failure to ask appropriate questions. Thus in one of McConville et al's cases, the file did not reveal the character of the victim, giving the impression that an assault on him was unprovoked. Some prosecutors recognise this problem, although most of Crisp's respondents appeared to be inappropriately—perhaps even irresponsibly—sanguine.[19] As a Scottish prosecutor told Moody and Tombs 'they (the police) usually don't do it deliberately but they can do it because they decide that the fiscal doesn't want to know that, doesn't need to know that.'[20] And, of course, there is exaggeration. Evans comments that when one gets:

'beneath the legal labels of offences to assess their true seriousness . . .

[16] Op cit.
[17] Discussed by the Royal Commission on Criminal Justice, Report (Cmnd 2263) (HMSO, 1993) pp 76–77, and briefly reported in D Crisp, 'Standardising Prosecutions' (1993) 34 Home Office Research Bulletin 13.
[18] M McConville and A Sanders, 'Fairness and the CPS' (1992) 142 NLJ 120.
[19] Op cit.
[20] S Moody and J Tombs, Prosecution in the Public Interest, (Scottish Academic Press, 1982) pp 47–48. See also L Gelsthorpe and H Giller, 'More Justice for Juveniles' [1990] Crim LR 153 and S Elliman, 'Independent Information for the CPS' (1990) 140 NLJ 812 and 864.

a significant number of "trivial" offences are dealt with by the criminal justice system with legal labels attached that exaggerate their seriousness.'[1]

McConville et al argue that police construction of all these kinds is to be expected and that the CPS attitudes and practices uncovered by them are entrenched features of an agency whose raison d'être is prosecution. As with the police, they argue, if one is concerned with the protection of the interests of suspects, the last place to seek that protection is in an agency with an adversarial relationship with those suspects which, moreover, depends for all of its information on another agency with an adversarial relationship with suspects.

Were they too pessimistic in assuming that the CPS was incapable or unwilling to fulfil its statutory obligations? While the CPS is undoubtedly discontinuing more cautionable cases now than it used to, the issue—as with police cautioning itself—is whether they are discontinuing as often as they should and when they should. It is likely that they are not doing either. In 1988 the VERA Institute conducted an experiment in one court with the co-operation of police, CPS and probation services. Random samples of less serious adult cases were allocated to either an 'experimental' or a 'control' group. Probation officers took the experimental group cases and collected information relevant to cautionability which they passed onto the CPS. Before this intervention, the discontinuance rate in this court on 'public interest' grounds was 1%. This rose to 4% in the control group and 7% in the experimental group. In the month immediately following the intervention the rate fell to 2%.[2] Since then a few additional 'public interest case assessment' (PICA) schemes, as they are known, have been established, with similar results.[3]

PICA schemes show that just sensitising prosecutors to the issue leads to more discontinuances. More important, however, is the fact that the extra information provided by PICA schemes—which the police either do not collect or which they keep from the CPS—enable the CPS to make their own independent decisions. Clearly the independence of the CPS is a chimera without independent sources of information. Until schemes like this become widespread, the CPS will not be able, even if it is willing, to fulfil its statutory obligations.

How, then, is the rise in 'public interest' discontinuances to be

---

[1] R Evans, 'Police Cautioning and the Young Adult Offender' [1991] Crim LR 598 at 605.

[2] C Stone, Public Interest Case Assessment (Inner London Probation Service, 1989).

[3] A Brown and D Crisp, 'Diverting Cases from Prosecution in the Public Interest' (1992) 32 Home Office Research Bulletin 7.

explained? Crisp found that half of them were because a nominal penalty was expected.[4] The Code for Crown Prosecutors requires prosecutors to consider whether a case is too trivial to warrant prosecution:

'particularly where the offence is triable on indictment when Crown Prosecutors should also weigh the likely penalty with the likely length and cost of the proceedings.'[5]

Crisp's findings were mirrored in a more recent, but even less well-reported study.[6] One plausible explanation for the rise in discontinuances would be that, at a time of tight constraints on public expenditure, Crown Prosecutors have become increasingly focused on issues of cost effectiveness in prosecutions. This leaves open the question of whether cautionability on other grounds (such as youth, old age and mental disorder) is being spotted and acted upon as often as it should be.

In the absence of more detailed analyses of CPS practice in the 1990s, the Runciman Commission's judgment that the public interest 'part of the Code is being appropriately applied'[7] seems too hasty. As it is, the Home Office research to which it had access comments that 'prosecutors have no way of knowing what gaps there are in the information they receive'.[8] The Runciman Commission's recommendation that PICA schemes should be expanded 'across the country'[9] suggests that it too, if only it had thought about it, would have realised that the CPS is not applying the Code satisfactorily at present (otherwise there would be no need for PICA schemes). The main failure of the Runciman Commission in this respect, however, is its failure to consider whether the CPS is capable of working as intended, with or without PICA schemes, given the adversarial structure of the criminal justice system.

5. NON-POLICE PROSECUTIONS

Substantial numbers of prosecutions are brought by non-police agencies and even individuals. Health and safety offences are dealt with by the Health and Safety Inspectorate, pollution offences by the various pollution agencies, frauds by various fraud agencies including the Department of Trade and Industry and tax evasion by the Inland Revenue. Because of the British 'opportunity' system, there is no

---

[4] Op cit.
[5] Para 8(i).
[6] Crown Prosecution Service, Discontinuance Survey (1993) pp 6–7.
[7] Report, op cit p 77.
[8] Crisp, op cit p 15.
[9] Report, op cit p 83.

distinction in principle between offences and enforcement dealt with by these agencies, those dealt with by the police and those dealt with by private individuals. This means that each body has developed its own prosecution policies and patterns which are often radically different to those of the police.[10]

Many of the 'suspects' dealt with by these agencies are companies. Their offences ought to be a major concern of policy makers and the public, for some 500 people die at work every year, about 750 people die each year from occupational diseases and there are some 18,000 major work-related injuries annually.[11] The Health and Safety Executive estimates that in most of these incidents the employer was in breach of the Health and Safety at Work etc Act 1974. Thus, most of these incidents give rise to potential criminal, as well as civil, liability. Fraud is equally serious, in a completely different way. Levi estimates that just a few major fraud cases equal in value all the theft and burglary cases prosecuted by the police each year.[12] Doubtless the same is true of tax evasion, where the overwhelming majority of traders' accounts, for instance, understate profits.[13]

(a) Patterns of enforcement

Few non-police agencies possess arrest powers. When they do, it is for offences which are, or could be, enforced also by the police—Customs and Excise (drugs) and the Social Security Inspectorate (benefit fraud) are particularly good examples. With these offences, prosecution patterns and processes are similar to those of the police. But since non-police agencies cannot usually arrest, neither can they charge or detain suspects. Instead they report for summons. Prosecution decisions are always taken in the cold light of day, on the basis of a full written file, by senior officials. In contrast to the police, investigation comes before enforcement action. In these agencies, the decision-making structure produces a propensity not to prosecute.[14] Their prosecution decisions are controlled by the organisation, in contrast to the police, where prosecution decisions are controlled by individual

---

[10] K Lidstone, R Hogg, and F Sutcliffe, Prosecutions by Private Individuals and Non-Police Agencies (Royal Commission on Criminal Procedure Research Study no 10) (HMSO, 1981).

[11] F Pearce and S Tombs, 'Ideology, Hegemony and Empiricism: Compliance Theories of Regulation' (1990) 30 BJ Crim 423 and C Wells, *Corporations and Criminal Responsibility* (Oxford University Press, 1993).

[12] M Levi, The Investigation, Prosecution and Trial of Serious Fraud (Royal Commission on Criminal Justice Research Study no 14, (HMSO, 1993).

[13] D Cook, *Rich Law, Poor Law* (Open University Press, 1989).

[14] See Sanders, 'Class Bias in Prosecutions', op cit.

officers on the ground. Moreover, since these offences usually take place in private rather than in public (drugs and social security fraud again being exceptions) offences are not discovered by patrols or members of the public, and, in the absence of coercive detention, confessions are rare. Offences usually come to light because of accidents or routine inspections, which are sometimes arranged in advance with the 'suspect'.

This means that discovering offending without waiting for accidents to happen is very difficult. The response has been to seek information from the 'suspects' themselves. This requires a very different attitude to that of the police on the streets. The result is the development of 'compliance' modes of working. Rather than treating their suspects as criminals, regulatory agencies seek to maintain continuing relationships with companies, to create 'a friendly working atmosphere',[15] to try to persuade them to comply with the law, and to avoid prosecution wherever possible. Non-police agencies and business criminals 'bargain and bluff' with each other.[16] As with cautioning, this is done 'in the shadow of the law'. The difference here, however, is that the relative bargaining powers are more equal. Indeed, agencies are sometimes in a weaker bargaining position than the companies that they are regulating.[17] Thus Hutter comments that 'officers are to some extent dependent upon the co-operation of the regulated to comply with their demands.'[18]

When agencies discover offences, they usually warn the offenders informally. Enforcement notices (warning letters) are rare; prohibition notices (stopping work until the law is complied with) are rarer still; and prosecution is the last resort. The compliance approach inevitably leads to a reluctance to prosecute. A study of 96 Australian non-police agencies found that, over a three-year period, one-third had launched not one prosecution.[19] In Britain and the United States also, prosecutions by non-police agencies are rare. This is justified on the grounds that most corporations are 'responsible' and not the 'amoral calculators' who would deserve prosecution and take advantage of this 'persuasion first' policy.[20] Companies that do take advantage and hold the law in contempt are slightly more likely to be prosecuted.[1]

---

[15] B Hutter, *The Reasonable Arm of the Law?* (Clarendon, 1988) p 189.
[16] K Hawkins, 'Bargain and Bluff' (1983) 5 L Pol Q 8.
[17] G Richardson, with A Ogus, and P Burroughs, *Policing Pollution: A Study of Regulation and Enforcement* (Clarendon Press, 1983).
[18] Op cit p 188.
[19] Wells, op cit p 27.
[20] Pearce and Tombs, op cit.
[1] W Carson, 'White-Collar Crime and the Enforcement of Factory Legislation' (1970) 10 BJ Crim 383.

Prosecutions are so rare that, in principle, a judicial review invoking the *Blackburn* principle[2] might be thought possible. However, there was no hint of criticism of what the court described as the Inland Revenue's 'selective enforcement' policy in *Mead*.[3]

The aim of the compliance strategy is prevention rather than punishment. Two questions arise: is it justifiable for this pattern to be adopted by non-police agencies but not by the police? And is this an effective method of crime prevention? Effectiveness is a relative matter. How effective would these agencies be if their energies were dissipated by court cases? The answer is dependent on their resources, which are minimal and growing smaller. In the 1980s, the Health and Safety Executive's inspectors, for instance, were reduced in number while the 'law and order' budget rose.[4] The enforcement of 'regulatory' offences is not, it seems, a 'law and order' matter. Questions about the methods of these agencies thus cannot be divorced from political choices about the allocation of resources.

As well as selective enforcement, there is also selective charging. Between 1969 and 1993, 18,151 people have been killed at work. Yet not one company has been convicted of homicide in relation to these deaths.[5] Were the inadequate and unfortunate *Stone and Dobinson*[6] really more culpable than every one of the companies which broke the Health and Safety Act in these cases? Similarly, hundreds of people have died in disasters like the Kings Cross fire of 1987, the Piper Alpha oil rig fire of 1988, the sinking of the 'Marchioness' in 1989 and various train crashes.[7] Again, there have been no prosecutions for manslaughter in any of these incidents, apart from the 'Herald of Free Enterprise' disaster.[8] Although there is usually no deliberate law breaking in these cases (or, at least, no deliberate intention to cause injury) intention is not required for manslaughter charges. These deaths occurred in the course of the perpetrators' attempts to do their legitimate jobs. But that is true also of the many surgeons and anaesthetists who have faced manslaughter charges.[9] The virtual immunity of companies from serious criminal charges is not inevitable in practice (as Dutch experience shows),[10] or in theory.[11]

---

2   See section 2(b), above.
3   This case is also discussed in section 2(b).
4   Wells, op cit p 24.
5   G Slapper, 'Corporate Manslaughter' (1993) 2 Social and Legal Studies 423.
6   *Stone; Dobinson* [1977] 2 All ER 341.
7   Slapper, op cit.
8   *R v P & O Ferries* (1990) 93 Cr App Rep 72.
9   Slapper, op cit.
10 S Field and N Jorg, 'Corporate Liability and Manslaughter: Should we be going Dutch?' [1991] Crim LR 156.
11 Wells, op cit pp 111–113.

(b)   Accounting for different patterns of prosecution

To summarise the above, non-police agencies usually exercise their discretion not to prosecute rather than to prosecute, and their enforcement patterns form the mirror image of those of the police. How do such differences arise and how are they maintained in practice?[12]

The obvious explanation is that coercive methods characteristic of the police are not generally appropriate for people and crimes dealt with by non-police agencies. It is significant that these agencies are usually referred to as 'regulatory', and their law enforcement processes as 'regulation', neutral terms from which stigma and condemnation are removed. Where cause and effect lie here, however, is difficult to say. Does a lack of social stigma lie behind the use of these terms, or do the terms contribute to the lack of stigma? Put this way, one can see that it is not a case of cause and effect at all, but rather of two causes operating on each other in a circular fashion.

One result is that neither the public at large nor traditional text books treat 'regulatory offences' as 'real' crimes (*mala in se*). They are seen, instead, as *mala prohibita*—not things wrong in themselves, but merely things that society requires to be better regulated. It is sometimes said that the behaviour being controlled resembles acceptable business practice and hence is not *mala in se*. However, as Wells points out, this misses the point that it is businesspeople who construct the image of what practices are to be regarded as acceptable in their world. What many men regard as acceptable, by way of rape and violence, is no longer acceptable to the rest of us and nor should it be.[13] Letting criminals decide by what standards they should be judged tells us more about the sources of power in society than about the acceptability or harm of the behaviour in question.

Another reason for the different prosecution policies could be class bias. This explanation might appear to be overly conspiratorial in nature. But class bias—like race bias—can arise indirectly through the application of criteria which bear more heavily on one section of society than another.[14] Thus Hawkins argues that, in the enforcement of 'regulatory' criminal laws, there is a 'need to preserve a fragile balance between the interests of economic activity on the one hand and the public welfare on the other.'[15] It is the unfortunate lot of the poor, the

[12]   There is a sharp debate between researchers who adhere to different positions. See Pearce and Tombs, op cit and the reply by K Hawkins, 'Compliance Strategy, Prosecution Policy, and Aunt Sally: A Comment on Pearce and Tombs' (1990) 30 BJ Crim 444.

[13]   Op cit pp 23–26.

[14]   Sanders, 'Class Bias in Prosecutions', op cit.

[15]   K Hawkins, *Environment and Enforcement* (Oxford University Press, 1984) p 9.

main target group for the police, that their economic activity has increasingly become non-existent through unemployment or replaceable through de-skilling. Credence is given to this explanation by the fact that the only non-police agency 'out of line' is that which deals with social security claimants. Cook found that in 1986–87, for instance, 8,000 supplementary benefit claimants were prosecuted, as compared to 459 tax evaders.[16] This strategy makes sense only in ideological—rather than practical—terms. The ideologies relate to 'deserving' and 'undeserving' groups, to those who pay and those who are paid, and so forth.

A related explanation is 'corporate capture': regulatory agencies become collusive as a result of their dependence on their 'suspects/ clients':

'A captured agency no longer mediates between the interests of the public, which is to be protected through regulation, and the interests of the regulated industry. Instead it uses its discretion to advance the goals of regulation only so far as industry interests permit.'[17]

Underlying both the 'class bias' and the 'corporate capture' explanations is a belief that corporations will act according to capitalist laws of economic behaviour rather than laws of due process or social justice. If forced to comply with laws which make processes uneconomic (or, more realistically, less profitable) firms will simply scale down or move their business. Regulatory agencies which genuinely care about their true clients (the workers) are thus forced into choosing between two unpalatable alternatives: corporate law breaking or reduced economic activity.

The other main reason for different enforcement patterns might be that there are fewer alternatives to prosecution available to the police/CPS than are available to non-police agencies.[18] Some credence is given to this if we consider developments in Scotland in the 1980s. When Moody and Tombs first researched prosecutions, the pattern was similar to the English pattern. By 1991, the non-prosecution rate (including motoring offences) was 47%—a sixfold increase in a decade. Tombs and Moody now argue that this is primarily a consequence of a vastly increased range of alternatives to prosecution, including fixed

---

16 D Cook, *Rich Law, Poor Law* (Open University Press, 1989).
17 N Frank and M Lombness, *Controlling Corporate Illegality* (Anderson, 1988) p 97. This is not always confined to non-police agencies. Police corruption, or even honest 'undercover' work, displays these elements too. see D Hobbs, *Doing the Business* (Oxford University Press, 1988).
18 See Sanders, 'The Limits to Diversion from Prosecution', op cit.

penalties, prosecutor fines and diversion to social work, mediation and so forth.[19]

It might appear that traditional sanctions (fine, probation or prison) are inappropriate for many corporate crimes in particular. But this is certainly not true of non-police offences such as tax evasion where prison might be a very effective deterrent. Also, sentences similar to community service and probation could be devised for companies.[20] Equally important is the fact that diversionary measures could be used more by the police. One example is the well-publicised use in Birmingham's red-light district of letters warning 'kerb crawlers' that their car registrations have been noted and that, if seen in the district again, prosecution will follow. The arrival of the post during the family breakfast was reported to have struck fear into the heart of many a well-heeled Brummie for several weeks thereafter. This sort of thing, with appropriate safeguards, could be extended to many offences.

It appears, then, that progress will require the development of alternatives on Scottish lines, but whether the police or the CPS should be in charge of them is a difficult question. More fundamentally, thought needs to be given to what kinds of offending really are more worthy of prosecution and what kinds of offender are amenable to prosecution and alternatives to it. It is by no means obvious that the current pattern of policies and practices serves the public interest in its widest sense. But without government intervention to alter the economic factors at work, different prosecution policies for regulatory offences could do equal amounts of harm in unanticipated ways.

Finally, what is striking about non-police agencies is one way in which they are like the police: they put their own working rules before legal rules. As Hutter puts it, 'on those occasions when the law is perceived as being discordant with popular, or individual, morality, it is morality rather than the law which takes priority.'[1] The difference is that whereas this works against the interests of suspects in the case of the police, it works in favour of suspects in the case of most non-police agencies.

---

[19] J Tombs and S Moody, 'Alternatives to Prosecution: The Public Interest Redefined' [1993] Crim LR 357. Note, however, that some of these 'alternative' dispositions will have been alternatives to NFA rather than to prosecution.

[20] But see S Box, *Power, Crime, and Mystification* (Tavistock, 1983) pp 67–74, who argues that corporations could be put on probation, given a community service order, and so on.

[1] Op cit p 202.

6. CONCLUSION

One of the paradoxes of the criminal justice system is that the powers which ostensibly exist purely in order to facilitate prosecution are actually subject to more formal regulation than are the powers to prosecute themselves. Yet in reality those facilitative powers—stop-search, arrest and so forth—have much broader purposes and are inadequately regulated, while prosecution is subject to detailed guidelines and the supervision of the CPS and the courts. However, the police manage to reduce or even nullify the impact of external scrutiny by these bodies: by case construction, the use of arrest and immediate charge, and cautioning, where this serves their purposes. The courts themselves, while asserting their theoretical right to review prosecution and non-prosecution decisions, have largely opted out of this in practice. The net result is a pattern of prosecution decisions which harmonise with economic imperatives but which penalise the unfortunate and reward the powerful. The class and race differences created by stop-search and arrest practices are magnified by prosecution processes within the police and by separating police and non-police enforcement and prosecution.

None of this is to deny major changes in the prosecution system in the 1980s and early 1990s. The creation of the CPS has led to more weak and cautionable cases being dropped. The police are cautioning more people who should not be prosecuted. Government guidelines do have some effect. But these rules, guidelines and controls are all only partially inhibitory. When the police want to, they generally do secure cautions or prosecutions in breach of the rules. Little or nothing can be, or is, done about it. If these inhibitory rules are to work when it really matters, they need to be backed up by effective sanctions—otherwise they are almost certain to become 'presentational'. There is no sanction attached to the rules and guidelines discussed in this chapter.

Is prosecution policy about fairness and keeping criminalisation within bounds (due process) or about balancing expediency with police working rules (crime control)? The cautioning movement would suggest the former. We disagree. Cautioning is used for humanitarian reasons, but also in order to increase social control through net widening, to save money where there is little to be lost by not prosecuting, to punish those against whom there is no evidence, to avoid prosecuting those people who could embarrass authority (at the micro (police) level and macro (state) level) and to inject police ideology into the caring professions.

Many argue that cautioning is yet another example of reduced openness in government, with reduced opportunity for public control and scrutiny.[2] As part of other trends noted in this book, control over criminal justice is gradually passing from the judiciary to the police. The result is not just increased police control over the dispersal of stigma, but also increased control over the imposition of penalties. For it used to be common for juvenile offenders, in particular, to be given absolute or conditional discharges on first and sometimes second appearances in court as a 'warning shot'. Now this is rare, for the courts see the caution as that warning shot. Not content with apprehending suspected offenders, the police have become triers of fact, deciders of guilt and innocence and dispensers of penalties. This is why many writers argue against formal cautioning or, at least, against formal cautioning remaining in the hands of the police.[3] Sadly, these debates were not even acknowledged as issues by the Runciman Commission.

Just as the police cannot be expected to protect the rights of suspects, nor can we expect the CPS to do so. We should expect defence lawyers to do so, but while expenditure on the CPS is rising, the legal aid budget is being cut. The issue of summaries of taped interrogations exemplifies the problem. The police and CPS are castigated for producing and accepting these documents. But they have no interest in changing their practices. It should be the defence lawyers who check the accuracy of summaries. But without a remuneration structure that rewards this work, they have no interest either.

Would the CPS have prevented the infamous miscarriages of justice that gave rise to the Runciman Commission ? It seems unlikely, for three reasons. Firstly, the police construct cases to appear to be strong and the job of the CPS is to pursue those cases with vigour. This they do. The fact that the miscarriage of justice cases were miscarriages does not alter the fact that they were sufficiently strong to secure convictions in the first instance. Secondly, the CPS is headed by the DPP. Who prosecuted the 'Birmingham Six', the 'Guildford Four', the youths in the 'Confait Affair' and *Kiszko*? The DPP. Thirdly, miscarriages of justice like the 'Cardiff Three' have continued unabated into the 1990s. The police need prosecutors. The job of the CPS should be to prosecute. To expect any more than this is unrealistic. What is needed above all is strong and committed defence advocacy so as to counter-balance the weighty forces lined up on the other side of the adversarial divide.

---

[2] See eg J Pratt, 'Diversion from the Juvenile Court' (1986) 26 B J Crim 212.

[3] See Sanders, 'The Limits to Diversion from Prosecution' op cit (1988), and writing cited therein. But note the social control implications of informal cautioning by the police too. See A Meehan, 'Internal Police Records and the Control of Juveniles' (1993) 33 BJ Crim 504.

Chapter 6

Summary Justice in the Magistrates' Court

1. INTRODUCTION

In England and Wales, trials are held either in the magistrates' courts or the Crown Court. All criminal prosecutions begin in the former, but the ultimate disposal of a case depends on its classification. Defendants charged with motoring offences (eg, driving whilst disqualified, excess alcohol or lack of due care and attention) or other summary offences (eg common assault, drunk and disorderly or soliciting) will have their case heard in the magistrates' courts. Defendants charged with offences triable only on indictment, such as murder, wounding with intent to cause grievous bodily harm and rape, must be committed to the Crown Court for trial. In between lie a large band of offences which are triable either way, that is, they may be tried either summarily in the magistrates' courts or on indictment in the Crown Court. Examples of 'either way' offences are theft, burglary and assaults causing actual or grievous bodily harm.[1]

The magistrates' court is the workhorse of the system. In 1992, for example, proceedings were begun against about 2.03 million defendants in the magistrates' courts. A quarter of these proceedings were in respect of indictable offences,[2] 46% concerned motoring offences whilst the remaining 30% related to other types of summary offence.[3] Roughly 92,000 defendants (under 5% of the 2.03 million proceeded against) were committed to the Crown Court for trial.[4] Over 80% of those facing either way charges have their case heard in the magistrates' courts.

The 'mode of trial' hearing held in either way cases determines not

---

[1] This threefold classification was introduced by the Criminal Law Act 1977 and re-enacted by ss 17–25 of the Magistrates' Courts Act 1980.
[2] Ie either way offences or offences triable only on indictment.
[3] Criminal Statistics England and Wales 1992 (Cm 2410) p 128, Table 6.4 (HMSO, 1993).
[4] Ibid, p 131, Table 6.4.

just where but how the case should be tried. To try a case summarily in the magistrates' courts is to try it without many of the formalities required by the common law.[5] Some of the most obvious differences between the two tiers of courts concern the personnel who appear in them. Trial by judge and jury takes place only in the Crown Court. The judge, whose formal functions include the determination of any points of law in a case, is a professional lawyer of many years' experience. Some have become full-time judges, whilst others sit on a part-time basis. Questions of fact are left to be determined by a jury made up of 12 lay people, chosen at random (more or less) from the electoral register.[6] The procedure in court and the issues in the case thus have to be rendered comprehensible to 12 complete outsiders who may never have been in court before.

This complex separation of function and mixture of professional expertise and lay involvement in the administration of justice may be contrasted with the position in the magistrates' courts. Questions of both law and fact are there decided upon by a bench of three (sometimes two) lay magistrates, or by a stipendiary (legally qualified) magistrate sitting alone. There are some 78 full-time stipendiary magistrates, based mainly in large urban centres, compared with some 28,000 lay magistrates.[7] The latter rely upon a justices' clerk to advise them on law and procedure. The clerk also plays a key role in administering the business of the court. Since the decision makers in magistrates' courts are insiders, in that they sit regularly in judgment on defendants, proceedings can be conducted swiftly and in a routinised fashion.

The question of who may represent the prosecution and the defence also depends on the level of court. Barristers (lawyers who specialise in advocacy and the drafting of legal advice) may appear at either level to prosecute or defend whereas solicitors (traditionally regarded as the junior branch of the legal profession) have historically lacked rights of audience in the Crown Court, although this is set to change.[8] Skilled advocacy in an adversarial trial can itself increase greatly the length and formality of the proceedings. Crown Prosecutors (whether qualified as barristers or solicitors) may only appear in the magistrates' courts.

---

[5]   See D McBarnet, *Conviction* (MacMillan, 1983) pp 138–143.

[6]   Jury selection procedures are discussed in ch 8.

[7]   There were a further 78 part-time stipendiary magistrates in post on 1 January 1993: Judicial Statistics Annual Report 1992 (Cm 2268) (HMSO, 1993) p 84, Table 9.6.

[8]   An application made to the Lord Chancellor and four designated judges under the Courts and Legal Services Act 1990 to obtain rights of audience was granted in December 1993 in so far as it related to solicitors in private practice. Rights of audience for employed solicitors (which includes those working for the CPS) are still under consideration: (1993) The Lawyer, 14 December.

The summary nature of magistrates' courts justice is reflected, as one might expect from the above description, in lower running costs. It has been estimated that the average cost of proceedings against a person charged with an either way offence in the magistrates' courts is about £210. Leaving aside grave offences (for which lengthy trials may be expected) the average cost of Crown Court proceedings is £1,400 where a guilty plea is entered compared with £12,088 for contested cases.[9] But is there an adequate justification for the difference in treatment meted out to defendants according to how the offence with which they are charged is classified? One argument would be that since the sentencing powers of magistrates are limited to six months' imprisonment or a £2,000 fine, there is less of a need for due process safeguards to apply than in the Crown Court, where a defendant may face life imprisonment on conviction.[10] Another would be that summary offences involve straightforward issues the determination of which do not require other than a straightforward procedure. This is certainly true, for example, of many motoring offences. As nearly half of the magistrates' workload is made up of such offences, observers in these courts might be forgiven for thinking that 'real crime' and courtroom drama were to be found elsewhere. Often, there are no observers, journalists and curious members of the public opting to follow the 'juicier' cases in the Crown Court.

In parentheses we may note that the lack of public scrutiny of these magistrates' courts is particularly helpful for white collar offenders anxious to avoid any damaging publicity. We drew attention in chapter 5 to the presumption against formal action operated by most regulatory agencies. On the rare occasion when white collar criminals are prosecuted, proceedings are virtually always kept in the magistrates' courts and often relegated to a special sitting away from the main work of the day. Thus, even when formal action is taken against business offenders, the visibility of their misdeeds remains low. This helps them play down the seriousness of their actions, and does nothing to challenge the common perception that the crimes they have committed are merely 'technical' in nature.[11]

The ideology of triviality that permeates the magistrates' courts is fuelled by the high proportion of defendants pleading guilty to the charges against them. It is difficult to be precise as to the guilty plea

---

[9] Costs of the Criminal Justice System 1992 (Home Office, 1992) vol 1, pp 15–16.

[10] The law restricting magistrates' sentencing powers is technical and complex. For detailed treatment, see *Blackstone's Criminal Practice* (Blackstone, 1992) pp 1404–1408.

[11] See the discussion by H Croall, 'Mistakes, Accidents and Someone Else's Fault: The Trading Offender in Court' (1988) 15 Journal of Law and Society 293.

rate, as official bodies collect and present the relevant statistical information in different ways.[12] It is clear, however, that the vast majority plead guilty and that very few contest their cases successfully. Thus, the CPS reports that, during the period April 1992 to March 1993, 97.6% of cases proceeding to a hearing resulted in conviction and that 83.6% of the convicted defendants had pleaded guilty.[13] A further 8.1% of cases were proved in the absence of the defendant, thus leaving only 10.4% of cases in which a contested trial took place.

It is tempting, then, to assume that magistrates' courts deal with trivial matters in which the issues are straightforward, defendants willingly accept their guilt and the consequences for defendants of conviction are slight. In truth, however, magistrates are responsible for decisions of far-reaching importance. They decide whether defendants should be released on bail or should lose their liberty pending trial. It is for them, together with their clerks, to determine whether defendants should receive legal aid to assist them with the costs of expert representation. They can direct that either way cases should be heard in the Crown Court, notwithstanding any objections from the defendant. They also have a role to play in supervising the work of other agencies. Before a case proceeds to the Crown Court a committal hearing takes place in which the prosecution have to satisfy the magistrates that there is sufficient evidence fit to be heard at the higher level. And, as we have already seen, the lower courts exercise a measure of supervision over the police in relation to such matters as periods of pre-charge detention of suspects and warrants allowing entry, search and seizure. Finally, they have the ultimate power of depriving convicted defendants of part of their property or part of their liberty. In 1992, magistrates sent 22,000 offenders to prison.[14] If they feel their sentencing powers are inadequate, they can commit defendants convicted of either way offences to the Crown Court for sentence. One way or another, a large proportion of the prison population are there as a result of the decisions of magistrates.

At first sight, the operation of the magistrates' courts appears to be consistent with the crime control model of criminal justice. The high rate of guilty pleas ensures that many of the most important due process protections which might apply in an adversarial system do not come

---

[12] See further J Baldwin and M McConville, 'The New Home Office Figures on Pleas and Acquittals: What Sense do they Make ?' [1978] Crim LR 196.

[13] Crown Prosecution Service, Annual Report for the period April 1992 – March 1993, (HMSO, 1993) p 18.

[14] Criminal Statistics England and Wales 1992 (Cm 2410) p 145, para 7.27 (HMSO, 1993).

into play. Crucially, the prosecution is not obliged to prove its case beyond reasonable doubt before an impartial tribunal. Its evidence is not scrutinised, witnesses are not cross-examined and no question as to the exclusion of evidence (on the grounds that it was obtained oppressively, unfairly or in circumstances that might render it unreliable) can arise. The defendant stands condemned merely as a result of uttering the single word 'guilty' in open court. But is this absence of due process attributable to a free and informed decision by the defendant? Or does the criminal process itself encourage defendants to waive their due process rights by pleading guilty? As the essence of summary justice is a speedy procedure, uncluttered with elaborate judicial rituals, we might expect to encounter antipathy towards due process values in the lower courts. We can examine these questions further by exploring in more detail a number of interrelated issues concerning the operation of justice in the magistrates' courts.

2. LEGAL AID AND LEGAL REPRESENTATION

Legal representation is central to the functioning of the due process model, since it should guarantee that defendants are made aware of their rights and that the remedies available for any abuses of those rights are secured. The principle of equality in the due process model requires that wherever the criminal process affords a theoretical right to legal representation, the means should be made available to enable defendants to exercise that right. To do otherwise would place the poor and those of modest means in an unequal position with the rich.

For suspects detained for questioning in the police station, these due process principles are broadly accepted. As we have seen, the government has provided funds so that all defendants, rich or poor, can have access to a lawyer, regardless of the type of offence with which they are suspected. The machinations of the police combined with the inadequate level of service provided by the legal profession may prevent the scheme from working as effectively as it might, but its formal due process character is none the less incontestable.

This may be contrasted with the position in the magistrates' courts, where legal representation may be characterised as a privilege rather than as a right. There are three types of publicly funded services which fall to be considered: 'green form' advice and assistance, court-based duty solicitor schemes and criminal legal aid.

(a)   The green form scheme

Initial advice may be given by a solicitor under the 'green form' scheme.[15] Bureaucratic control of the operation of the scheme is minimal—all the solicitor needs to do is administer a simple means test.[16] The scheme can be used to cover the cost of preparing a case for court by, for example, taking statements from the defendant and other witnesses. The initial limit of two hours' work can be extended on obtaining authorisation from a legal aid area committee. In practice, the scheme is used by solicitors to cover the costs of an initial interview with a defendant and the making of a full application for legal aid.[17] Less than an hour and a quarter was spent on each criminal green form matter in 1992–3.[18] The main drawbacks of the scheme from a due process perspective are that it does not cover representation in court, it allows solicitors only a limited period of preparation time (subject to the possibility of extensions) and it is means-tested. The means test was tightened significantly with effect from 12 April 1993 and the weekly income limit is now just £61 for a person without dependants.[19]

(b)   Court-based duty solicitor schemes

Those who arrive at court unrepresented may receive advice from a duty solicitor. These schemes, originally operated by the legal profession on a voluntary basis, are now governed by the Legal Aid Act 1988 and regulations made thereunder.[20] Duty solicitors agree to be present at the court on a rota basis. The average number of defendants assisted per solicitor shift was 3.3 in 1992–3 and a total of 226,549 defendants received assistance.[1] No means test is applied, but the scheme is subject to a number of restrictions.[2] A duty solicitor may not provide representation in committal proceedings nor on a not guilty plea, nor, save in

---

[15]   The statutory framework for the scheme is provided by Pt III of the Legal Aid Act 1988. Payment for legal services provided is claimed on a form which is green in colour.

[16]   See further J Baldwin, 'The Green Form: Use or Abuse ?' (1988) 138 NLJ 631.

[17]   For discussion of how solicitors use the green form scheme, see J Baldwin and S Hill, *The Operation of the Green Form Scheme in England and Wales* (Lord Chancellor's Department, 1988) pp 27–28.

[18]   See Legal Aid Board, Annual Reports (1992–93), (HMSO, 1992) p 74.

[19]   For the revised eligibility levels, see (1993) Legal Action, April p 22.

[20]   The origin of these schemes is explored in G Mungham and P Thomas, 'Solicitors and Clients: Altruism or Self-interest?' in R Dingwall and P Lewis (eds), *The Sociology of the Professions* (MacMillan, 1983).

[1]   Legal Aid Board, Annual Reports (1992–93), (HMSO, 1993) p 59 and p 65.

[2]   As laid down in the non-statutory Legal Aid Board Duty Solicitor Arrangements 1990.

exceptional circumstances, may advice or representation be offered to defendants in connection with a non-imprisonable offence. These rules prevent duty solicitors from acting in the most complex or serious proceedings and also in relatively trivial cases. In the former, a grant of full criminal legal aid will usually be forthcoming, whilst in the latter it is apparently thought reasonable for defendants to be left unrepresented in court. Nor may duty solicitors act for a defendant who has already received advice from a duty solicitor on an earlier occasion.[3] This last rule was designed to allay the fears of solicitors that courts might use the existence of a duty solicitor scheme as a reason for refusing the grant of full legal aid and also prevents duty solicitors from mopping up too much legal business.

The overall effect of these schemes has been mixed. Their development in the 1970s undoubtedly represented, in formal terms, a move towards greater due process in the summary courts. A duty solicitor could not be expected, however, to do more than argue a case for bail, or make a speech in mitigation in a straightforward guilty plea case. For more complicated cases, the objective would be to secure an adjournment in order for an application for full legal aid to be made, so that a solicitor could prepare the case properly.[4] One piece of research suggested that a duty solicitor scheme advanced due process values in that more defendants were released on bail and more defendants were granted legal aid.[5] By contrast, other research implied that duty solicitors were providing an inferior level of service compared with solicitors not acting under the scheme in that they more often advised defendants to plead guilty at their first appearance in court. The reasons for this were complex, but the researchers concluded that, 'our evidence suggests that when dealing with their "established" clients, as opposed to what are often seen as "one-off" duty solicitor cases, solicitors may be less willing to proceed with the matter on the same day.'[6] One experienced duty solicitor has conceded more recently that clients continue to see the service provided as second class.[7] A second-class service,

---

[3] This is subject to the exception that advice and representation may be given to such a defendant who is at risk of imprisonment for failing to pay a fine or to obey an order of the court.

[4] See H Johnston, 'Court Duty Solicitors' (1992) Legal Action May, p 11, for an account of how the scheme works (or should work) in practice.

[5] M King, *The Effects of a Duty Solicitor Scheme: An Assessment of the Impact upon a Magistrates' Court* (Cobden Trust, 1977). More recent research tends to confirm that where duty solicitors are active, more legal aid applications will be made, although the relationship is not a strong one. See R Young, T Moloney and A Sanders, *In the Interests of Justice?* (Legal Aid Board, 1992) paras 4.12–4.13.

[6] L Bridges, J Carter, and S Gorbing, 'The Impact of Duty Solicitor Schemes in Six Magistrates' Courts' (1992) LAG Bull, July, p 12 at p 14.

[7] Johnston, op cit.

however, is generally better than none at all. It seems incontrovertible that courts with duty solicitor schemes will adhere more closely overall to the due process model than those without.[8]

(c)   Criminal legal aid

However one sees duty solicitor schemes, it is clear that they are no substitute for the proper funding of the full costs of preparing and mounting a defence. The most comprehensive form of help available is the criminal legal aid certificate.[9] To obtain a certificate, a defendant must make an application to the magistrates' court. This form of legal aid is subject both to a means test and a merits test. The proportion of the population eligible for criminal legal aid fell sharply in April 1993 when the means test was brought in line with that applied to income support claimants. The number of legal aid applicants who pass the means test is unlikely to decrease as sharply, however, since so many of those appearing in the magistrates' courts are in receipt of income support. None the less, from a due process standpoint, it is objectionable that anyone in 1993 with an income of more than £45 a week was excluded from the legal aid scheme.[10]

Turning to the merits test, s 21(2) of the Legal Aid Act 1988 provides that legal aid may be granted where it appears desirable 'in the interests of justice' to do so, and s 22 specifies a number of factors which must be taken into account in determining this matter. Some of these criteria concern the seriousness of the consequences to the defendant of a conviction. If a defendant is facing loss of liberty, livelihood or reputation, more favourable consideration should be given to granting legal aid.[11] The remaining criteria concern the inability of the defendant adequately to conduct a case in person. Thus a grant of legal aid is more likely (at least in theory) if the case requires the tracing and interviewing of witnesses, consideration of a substantial question of law or expert cross-examination, or if the defendant has inadequate knowledge of

---

[8]   The Legal Aid Board has taken steps aimed at improving the selection and training of duty solicitors. See E Cape, 'The New Duty Solicitor Arrangements' (1991) Legal Action, March, p 21.

[9]   Criminal legal aid is governed by Pt V of the Legal Aid Act 1988.

[10]   This figure applies to those without dependants. For full details of eligibility levels, see (1993) Legal Action, April, p 22.

[11]   In certain 'loss of liberty' situations, the defendant must be granted legal aid: where the person is applying for bail having been kept in custody following a remand hearing at which they were unrepresented (s 21(3)(c), Legal Aid Act 1988), where the person is before the court for sentencing only and is to be kept in custody whilst inquiries or reports are prepared (s 21(3)(d)) and where youths are to be sentenced to custody (s 2, Criminal Justice Act 1982).

English or suffers from some mental or physical disability. One final factor to be taken into account is whether it is in the interests of another that the accused be represented. This covers situations where it might lead to difficulties if the accused had to cross-examine witnesses in person, such as in child abuse cases. This is an area in which more due process for the accused can lead to better protection for victims.

These criteria are not exclusive—other factors may be taken into account.[12] Furthermore, s 21(7) of the 1988 Act stipulates that where a doubt arises as to whether legal aid should be granted to a person, 'the doubt shall be resolved in that person's favour'. On the other hand, the mere fact that the circumstances of a case fall squarely within one or more of the statutory criteria does not mean that a grant of legal aid must follow. The Divisional Court in a series of cases has made it plain that those taking decisions on legal aid have a very wide discretion when applying the interests of justice test.[13] Thus, save where the legislature has provided otherwise, no charge of any offence can be regarded as so serious that it leads to an automatic grant of legal aid.[14] Similarly, a legal aid application may be refused notwithstanding that the case involves difficult points of fact or law or that there is a need for expert cross-examination.[15]

The merits test was last fully reviewed in 1966 by the Widgery Committee who decisively rejected the due process equality principle in the following terms:

'It might be held that wherever there is a right to legal representation, the State has a duty, as a kind of social insurance, to provide it for anyone who cannot afford to provide it himself. We do not accept this view; legal representation cannot be said to be a necessary condition for the effective defence of every criminal charge. We had also to bear in mind the practical consideration that there is a limit both to the number of practitioners who can provide legal assistance and to the funds that the State can reasonably be expected to make available. Our conclusions therefore were . . . that the object of the system should be to secure that injustice does not arise through an accused person being

---

[12] This is implicit in the wording of the section, and was acknowledged in *R v Liverpool City Magistrates, ex p McGhee* [1993] Crim LR 609.

[13] See, in particular, *R v Macclesfield Justices, ex p Greenhalgh* (1979) 144 JP 142; *R v Cambridge Crown Court, ex p Hagi* (1979) 144 JP 145 and *R v Havering Juvenile Court, ex p Buckley* (LEXIS 554 1983).

[14] See *R v Highgate Justices, ex p Lewis* (1977) 142 JP 78. The legislature has singled out murder alone as a charge warranting an automatic grant of legal aid: s 21(3)(a) of the Legal Aid Act 1988.

[15] See *R v Cambridge Crown Court, ex p Hagi* (1979) 144 JP 145 and *R v Stratford Magistrates Court, ex p Gorman* (LEXIS 687 1989).

prevented by lack of means from bringing effectively before the court matters which may constitute a defence to the charge or mitigate the gravity of the offence.'[16]

Much, then, relies on the correct identification of those cases where injustice would arise if legal aid was refused. This raises the issue of the degree of care exercised in legal aid decision making.

Applications for legal aid may be made orally in open court, or, as happens much more frequently, to the justices' clerk or other designated court officer on a standard form. This form is divided into sections relating to each of the statutory criteria in turn and is generally completed by a legal adviser acting under the 'green form' scheme described above. Research by Young et al into the determination of legal aid applications found that these forms were frequently completed by unqualified staff using standard wording which often exaggerated the case for granting legal aid.[17] In turn, court clerks were found to give little weight to the statutory criteria but applied a crude rule of thumb in determining an application. Defendants perceived to be charged with a 'serious' offence would almost automatically be granted legal aid, whereas those charged with a 'trivial' offence would similarly be refused. In the middle lay a grey area, which differed from court to court, wherein the chances of obtaining legal aid would depend on how well the legal aid application was argued.[18] Accidents of geography might therefore have a crucial bearing on whether an application would be granted; some of the courts studied granted virtually all applications, whereas others would refuse as many as one in four of those received. Such a rough and ready process does not inspire confidence that the need for legal representation is being correctly identified.

Whilst variation in grant rates between magistrates' courts is directly attributable to the somewhat idiosyncratic legal aid policies pursued by court clerks, at root the problem lies in the law itself. In allowing court clerks discretion in deciding which defendants should receive legal aid, the law condones the subversion of adversarial procedures. An adversarial system cannot work properly if there is an inequality of resources available to the prosecution and the defence. At the time of the Widgery Report, police officers often prosecuted in person, but all prosecutions today are conducted by legally qualified Crown Prosecutors. The case for making a grant of legal aid automatic has thus become all the

---

16 Report of the Departmental Committee on Legal Aid in Criminal Proceedings (Cmnd 2934) (HMSO, 1966) para 56. This document will be referred to hereafter as the Widgery Report.

17 Young, Moloney and Sanders, op cit at pp 62–86.

18 Ibid pp 25–39. See also R Young, 'The Merits of Legal Aid in the Magistrates' Court' [1993] Crim LR 336.

stronger.[19] The arguments against this advanced by the Widgery Committee are unconvincing. Market forces will ensure that an increased demand for legal services will be met by an increased supply of lawyers willing to do the work. The argument concerning resources appears to be a one-sided one; the government has readily provided the funds to ensure that the prosecution is legally represented in every case, however 'trivial' or 'straightforward' it might be. And, because of the way cases are constructed by the prosecution to appear strong on paper,[20] it cannot safely be predicted in advance which cases might lead to injustice if representation was not provided. The whole point of legal representation is to allow hidden aspects of the case to emerge, to render problematic the prosecution version of events and to raise questions about the integrity of the procedures followed. It is impossible to estimate the proportion of cases in which legal aid is currently refused (or not applied for) that would benefit from legal representation. The proportion may be small. But if the system is to give priority to acquitting the innocent and other due process values, the argument for making legal aid much more widely available is hard to resist.

Some important due process protections which have been built into the decision-making process should be mentioned. An application which has been refused can be renewed to the court or clerk at any time. On a renewal, a court clerk cannot refuse an application a second time, but must either grant it or refer it to the court for determination. The court retains the full power to grant or refuse. This enables the defence to have the application put before a different decision maker, although, since the magistrates are used to relying on the advice of their clerk (who will be present in court when the application is renewed) the value of this 'second bite of the cherry' is not as great as it might be. Of greater importance is the right, introduced in 1982, to have a refusal of legal aid reviewed by an area committee of the Legal Aid Board. In 1992–3, area committees, made up of practising solicitors and barristers, granted 52.7% of reviewed applications.[1] The power to review exists only if the refusal was on merits (rather than on means) and the applicant is charged with an indictable or either-way offence.[2] This

---

19 Forbes J in *R v Havering Justices, ex p Buckley* (LEXIS 554 1983) noted that the fact that the prosecution was legally represented was something that magistrates could properly take into account, while stressing that it did not follow that such representation meant that a bench was bound to grant legal aid.

20 See M McConville, A Sanders and R Leng, *The Case for the Prosecution* (Routledge, 1991).

1 Legal Aid Board Annual Reports (1992–93), (HMSO, 1993) p 64.

2 Since the power to review exists only on a first refusal by the court or clerk, applicants would be well advised to seek a review by an area committee prior to renewing an application to the court.

provides an illustration of how defendants charged with summary offences are afforded less due process safeguards.

(d) The rise and fall of legal aid

The introduction of a right of appeal to an area committee (alongside other developments such as duty solicitor schemes) has undoubtedly contributed to an enormous rise in the proportion of defendants who are legally represented in the magistrates' court.[3] In 1964, the overall ratio of grants of legal aid to the total number of defendants proceeded against on indictable matters was only one to nine.[4] By 1990, for every 100 defendants charged with indictable offences in the magistrates' courts, 105.4 legal aid certificates were issued, indicating that legal aid was being granted for at least some summary matters as well as for the great majority of indictable cases.[5]

The explosion in legal representation has been mirrored in the mounting cost of criminal legal aid. The rise has been particularly steep in recent years. In the space of the four years between 1987–88 and 1991–92, the cost of legal aid associated with criminal proceedings in the magistrates' courts (including green form advice, police station and court duty solicitor schemes and full legal aid) almost doubled from 150 million pounds to 286 million pounds.[6] It is this that prompted the government to slash eligibility for green form advice and legal aid. Rates of remuneration for solicitors have also come under attack. In the White Paper which led to the Legal Aid Act 1988, the government declared that it did not consider that rates for legally aided work should match those applied in the private sector.[7] The 1988 Act duly failed to incorporate the long-standing principle that legal aid work should attract reasonable remuneration.[8] The culmination of the government's efforts to control legal aid expenditure came in June 1993 with the introduction of a new system of payment whereunder solicitors receive a fixed fee to cover much of the work involved in a case.[9]

The Law Society has argued that rates of remuneration are now so

---

[3] For a detailed analysis, see L Bridges, 'The Professionalisation of Criminal Justice' (1992) Legal Action, August, p 7.

[4] Ibid.

[5] See Young, Moloney and Sanders, op cit, pp 9–10.

[6] See Legal Aid Board, Annual Reports (1991–92), (HMSO, 1992) p 3. The report for 1992–93 (p 3) shows costs stabilising at 287 million pounds.

[7] Legal Aid in England and Wales: A New Framework (Cm 118) (Lord Chancellor's Department, 1987) para 48.

[8] See s 39(3) of the Legal Aid Act 1974. This aspect of the Parliamentary debate on the Legal Aid Act 1988 is reviewed in D Matheson, *Legal Aid: The New Framework* (Butterworths, 1988) pp 101–104.

[9] See L Bridges, 'The Fixed Fees Battle' (1992) Legal Action November, p 7.

low that legal aid work has become uneconomic and that many firms are giving up criminal legal aid work altogether.[10] If true, defendants might find it increasingly difficult to secure representation. On closer analysis, it seems, however, that firms pulling out of this area tend to be those which did relatively little legal aid work in any case; there is no clear evidence that the total number of lawyers undertaking criminal work in the magistrates' court has declined.[11] On the other hand, after several years of rapid expansion of duty solicitor schemes, the number of courts without schemes rose for the first time (from 16 to 23) in 1992–93.[12] Whether this represents a statistical blip or the start of a trend caused by solicitors pulling out of duty solicitor work in the magistrates' courts remains to be seen. If it proves to be the latter, an important due process safety net for the unrepresented defendant will have begun to unravel. Remuneration is also a vital issue for the handful of firms of scientific experts who conduct forensic work for the defence. In Roberts and Willmore's study for the Royal Commission on Criminal Justice (Runciman Commission) defence experts

'pointed out that criminal legal aid work was not nearly as lucrative as civil litigation and that the ponderous and arbitrary means of payment made legal aid work an ever less attractive proposition.'[13]

If the squeeze on legal aid remuneration continues, the danger must be that the pool of defence lawyers and experts will shrink such that defendants will face a restricted choice of representatives. In the worst scenario, some may be unable to find anyone willing to take on their case.

(e) The quality of defence work under legal aid

A more important issue than the numbers of solicitors working in the magistrates' courts is the quality of service provided. Criminal legal aid rates have fallen far below the rates charged to privately paying

---

[10] For a sceptical response, see P Thompson, 'Have you Really given up Legal Aid?' LS Gaz, 6 July, p 21.

[11] See Bridges, 'The Professionalisation of Criminal Justice', op cit.

[12] Legal Aid Board, Annual Reports (1992–93) (HMSO, 1993) p 65.

[13] P Roberts and C Willmore, The Role of Forensic Science Evidence in Criminal Proceedings (Royal Commission on Criminal Justice Research Study no 11) (HMSO, 1993) p 73. To the Runciman Commission, it was 'unacceptable that, where scientific work is commissioned by the defence in a case, either the solicitor or the scientist is left unpaid for long periods (sometimes for a year or more)' Report, op cit p 155. See also R Stockdale and C Walker, 'Forensic Evidence', in C Walker and K Starmer (eds), *Justice in Error* (Blackstone, 1993) pp 88–90.

customers,[14] and this raises the question of whether defence work has become a second-rate service. An obvious point is that the low paid (and thus low status) nature of legal aid work may deter the best of newly qualified lawyers (and forensic scientists) from specialising in criminal defence. It also leads to experienced criminal practitioners seeking to achieve greater financial security and status by switching to more lucrative types of legal activity such as corporate and commercial work.[15] These are only general tendencies of course but it would be surprising if criminal lawyers as a group were as highly qualified and experienced as those operating in private practice.

The majority of solicitors' offices undertaking criminal defence work do not specialise in this area and are responsible for as little as one court appearance every three and a half weeks. As Bridges observes, standards may slip in such offices more through lack of practice than through the pressures of handling a high caseload.[16] At the other end of the scale, a small minority of offices do a disproportionately large amount of defence work. The organisation of these specialist criminal practices is a key determinant of the quality of defence work.[17] The essential point here is that solicitors are businesspeople. Either they make a profit (or at least break even) or they go out of business. Many solicitors claim that the only way to make legal aid pay is to handle large numbers of cases in a streamlined and bureaucratic fashion. Profits can be maximised by the routine allocation of legally aided work to unqualified staff. As we have already seen, the use of such staff to attend at police stations is extensive and the quality of service provided is often dismal.[18] Unqualified staff are also widely employed in carrying out initial interviews with defendants and applying for legal aid.[19] Research by McConville, Hodgson and Bridges has revealed that 75% of those interviewing clients in prison are not trained lawyers but trainees, legal executives and former police officers recruited for that

---

14 According to (1993) The Lawyer, 27 July, legal aid rates are up to 40% below the rates applied by solicitors to private clients.

15 See R Smith, 'Resolving the Legal Aid Crisis' (1991) LS Gaz, 27 February, p 17. This is true also of defence experts: Roberts and Willmore, op cit p 74.

16 'The Professionalisation of Criminal Justice', op cit at 9.

17 See the excellent analysis of legal aid practices by M King, *The Framework of Criminal Justice* (Croom Helm, 1981) pp 68–75, and the empirical study by M McConville, J Hodgson and L Bridges, *Standing Accused* (Clarendon Press, 1994).

18 See A Sanders, L Bridges, A Mulvaney and G Crozier, Advice and Assistance at Police Stations and The 24 Hour Duty Solicitor Scheme (Lord Chancellor's Department, 1989) pp 81–151 and M McConville and J Hodgson, Custodial Legal Advice and the Right to Silence (Royal Commission on Criminal Justice Research Study no 16) (HMSO, 1993).

19 See McConville, Hodgson and Bridges, op cit, and Young, Moloney and Sanders, op cit pp 81–86.

purpose.[20] The defendant will often meet a solicitor only on the morning of the court hearing. Where a solicitor briefs a barrister (or a solicitor advocate) to handle the case, the defendant becomes one step further removed from his or her legal representative.[1] The ideal of a close client-lawyer relationship in which the lawyer conducts the case in person from the police station right through to the courts is only rarely realised in practice.

A further problem is that a legal aid certificate may not cover all the work that a solicitor thinks is necessary in preparing the defence. In assessing claims for payment for legal services not covered by a fixed fee, the Legal Aid Board is supposed to 'allow a reasonable amount in respect of all work actually and reasonably done.'[2] In practice this means that solicitors often find themselves wrangling with Board officials over the correct level of payment to be made, or, indeed, over whether any payment at all should be forthcoming. Some solicitors have simply stopped carrying out certain preparatory steps in their cases, such as tracing and interviewing witnesses, for fear that they will not receive payment for such work.[3]

One way around this problem is to apply for prior authority to incur specified costs.[4] For example, if the defence wishes to obtain an expert report, they may first apply to the Legal Aid Board for authority to incur the additional expenditure involved. The delay and bureaucracy involved in this process (which can result in the defendant spending a further period remanded in custody) appears to deter solicitors from making applications for prior authority except in serious cases or where the need for an expert report is manifest.[5] None the less, in 1992–93 3,550 applications for prior authority (16.9% of all made) were refused.[6] If the application is refused, the costs involved in obtaining an expert report might still be allowed when the final bill is submitted for scrutiny, but, having received a shot across the bows, it is unlikely that

---

[20] Op cit. See (1993) The Lawyer, 7 September.

[1] Solicitor-advocates (specialising, like barristers, in advocacy) are attracting an increasing market share of magistrates' courts work due to the fact that they are more economic to 'brief' than barristers and operate more flexible working practices: (1994) Guardian, 7 January. The distinctive problems presented by the divided legal profession and the organisation of the Bar are explored in detail in the next chapter.

[2] Legal Aid in Criminal and Care Proceedings (Costs) Regulations 1989, reg 4.

[3] See Young, Moloney and Sanders, op cit pp 75–76 for instance.

[4] Under reg 54 of the Legal Aid in Criminal and Care Proceedings (General) Regulations 1989.

[5] P Roberts and C Willmore, The Role of Forensic Science Evidence in Criminal Proceedings (Royal Commission on Criminal Justice Research Study no 11) (HMSO, 1993) pp 78–81.

[6] Legal Aid Board, Annual Reports (1992–93) (HMSO, 1993) p 64.

a solicitor will take that risk.[7] Applications which are granted are nearly always limited to a specific sum, and if the need arises to exceed this sum further bureaucratic obstacles must be overcome. No such external controls apply to the police when they are conducting an investigation (although they may sometimes be deterred from commissioning expert reports by the cost involved).[8]

This unequal treatment of the prosecution and defence should be seen in the light of the revelations in cases such as the 'Birmingham Six',[9] *Maguire*[10] and *Ward*[11] that scientists acting for the police had misled the courts as to the reliability of the results they had obtained from forensic samples.[12] Steventon's study for the Runciman Commission demonstrated a continuing need for scrutiny of prosecution expert evidence—38% of defence lawyers who had obtained an independent analysis of DNA evidence found that the conclusions drawn by the expert differed from that drawn by the prosecution experts.[13] A broader Runciman Commission study of the use of forensic science evidence in run of the mill cases stressed the need to regard all scientific evidence with caution.[14]

The levels of remuneration obtained under legal aid, together with the way in which bills are assessed, combine to produce a situation in which lawyers aim to spend as little time as possible on a case. Once standard procedures have been developed for unqualified staff to follow, it becomes almost inevitable that cases will be prepared in a standardised manner. The introduction of fixed fees will only reinforce existing bad practice. Under a fixed fees system, lawyers receive the same payment for a category of case whether they spend one hour or two hours preparing it. Only where cases can be presented as sufficiently complex to justify a higher level fee within a category will there be a financial incentive to do more than the bare minimum of preparation. This in itself makes it more likely that no attempt will be made to explore weaknesses in the prosecution case or possible defences to the

---

[7] A similar dilemma for the defence concerns the costs of an expert attending at court, for which no prior authority can be granted. The costs may not be allowed, if allowed may be reduced, and payment may not be forthcoming for several months. See B Steventon, The Ability to Challenge DNA Evidence (Royal Commission on Criminal Justice Research Study no 9) (HMSO, 1993) p 28.

[8] For discussion of police decision making in this respect, see Roberts and Willmore, op cit pp 14–18.

[9] (1991) 93 Cr App Rep 287 at 295–300.

[10] (1992) 94 Cr App Rep 133 at 147–8.

[11] (1993) 96 Cr App Rep 1 at pp 45–52.

[12] For a discussion of these cases, see J Rozenberg, 'Miscarriages of Justice' in E Stockdale, and S Casale (eds), *Criminal Justice Under Stress* (Blackstone, 1992).

[13] Op cit p 42.

[14] Roberts and Willmore, op cit p 143.

charge. It follows that, in terms of standardising cases to maximise profitability, defendants who can be persuaded to plead guilty hold a special attraction.[15] In its essentials, the legal aid scheme has the effect of nudging defence lawyers into a crime control mode of operation.

(f) The Runciman Commission, franchising and the limits of reform

The Runciman Commission recognised that current trends in the legal aid scheme threaten to undermine due process protections for the suspect in the magistrates' courts. It recommended that fixed fees be kept under review 'to ensure their adequacy in attracting sufficient numbers of competent solicitors, properly trained to perform this very necessary work'.[16] Its solution to the problems caused by the need to apply for prior authority for commissioning forensic science tests was to recommend the laying down of clear rules as to what defence solicitors could commission by way of expert reports without waiting for approval from the Legal Aid Board.[17] It did not, however, tackle the thornier question of what those rules should be, nor did it express any clear view on whether the rules needed to be more generous to the defence. A weaker stance still was adopted on eligibility. The Runciman Commission said that it would be very seriously concerned if government policy was 'to have the effect of increasing the number of defendants who have no legal representation, particularly in the Crown Court'.[18] No attempt was made to justify making this distinction between the magistrates' courts and the Crown Court and no formal recommendation on eligibility was made. It seems unlikely that the government will be stopped in its cost-cutting tracks by such a limp response.

As regards the question of standards, the Runciman Commission welcomed a new Law Society guide to the preparation of cases in the magistrates' courts.[19] It also supported the monitoring of solicitors' files that will be undertaken by the Legal Aid Board as part of its franchising initiative.[20] The Board plans to offer preferential payment terms to firms operating franchises and may also grant them delegated powers (such as granting green form extensions and emergency legal aid certificates). In return the franchisees must meet specified standards

---

[15] More principled ways of maintaining profitability are set out in A Edwards, Standard Fees in the Magistrates' Court—a Survival Guide (Law Society, 1993).
[16] Royal Commission on Criminal Justice, Report (Cm 2263) (HMSO, 1993) p 118.
[17] Ibid p 118 and 155.
[18] Ibid p 117.
[19] See *Magistrates' Courts Guide* (Law Society, 1993).
[20] Report, op cit p 118.

relating to such matters as case management, recruitment, training and supervision of staff, and client care.[1] Franchising is as much about controlling costs as raising standards, however. Thus, the Board has indicated that refusals to grant a franchise may be based solely on the ground that an applicant's average costs are higher than the norm.[2] This is not objectionable in itself, since the Board is seeking to guarantee a consistently competent standard of legal aid work at a value for money price rather than merely engaging in a crude drive to reduce costs.[3] Those who wish to offer a higher level of service (or who are simply inefficient) would still be able to operate a legal aid service as a non-franchised firm.

It has now become clear, however, that the government has its own agenda on franchising. Unlike the Board, it wishes to see exclusive franchises being granted following a process of competitive tendering.[4] This would entail a reduction in the choice of solicitors open to defendants and would exert pressure on firms seeking franchises to cut costs and standards to the bone. It would be a relatively small step from this to create a salaried public defender system. It might seem that such a system, by removing the profit motive from defence work, would lead to improved standards. For this to be achieved, however, the salaried service would need to be set appropriate aims and given proper funding. The development of public defender systems in the United States does not bode well in this respect.[5] The poor will always be dependent on the state to fund their defence regardless of whether legal services are based on private sector provision or a salaried defender model. Either way, the state tends to draw the purse strings much tighter in relation to defence work that it does in sponsoring prosecutions.

As the Runciman Commission pointed out, criminal legal aid makes up only 5% of the overall total expenditure on the criminal justice system.[6] Legal aid costs are dwarfed by the estimated 4,837 million pounds spent on the police in 1990–91.[7] The experience on both sides of the Atlantic suggests that the state is more interested in efficient crime control than in expensive adversarial due process. There is a political dimension to this preference. Whereas cuts in spending on the police

[1]   Franchising: The Next Steps, (Legal Aid Board, 1992) pp 2–3.
[2]   Legal Aid Board, Annual Reports (1992-93) p 22, (HMSO, 1993).
[3]   See Legal Aid Board Annual Reports (1992–93) p 21, and A Sherr and R Moorhead, 'Transaction Criteria: Back to the Future' (1993) Legal Action, April, p 7.
[4]   See 'Franchising: a New Agenda' (1993) Legal Action, April, pp 3-4.
[5]   See eg M McConville and C Mirsky, 'The State, the Legal Profession, and the Defence of the Poor' (1988) 15 Journal of Law and Society 342.
[6]   Report, op cit p 70.
[7]   Costs of the Criminal Justice System (Home Office, 1992) p 11. This figure includes the cost of the Forensic Science Service.

and prosecution services might be perceived as an indication that the government had gone 'soft' on crime, the due process rights of suspects present an easier target for cuts. Put crudely, there are more votes in crime control than in due process. The implications for adversarial justice, particularly in the magistrates' courts, are obvious.

3. PRE-TRIAL NEGOTIATION

Our discussion of the legal aid scheme might suggest that the system would work in its intended adversarial manner if only the state would provide the necessary funds to the defence. But properly funded legal aid is not a sufficient condition for more due process. Even where defence lawyers are involved in a case, they spend more time negotiating away defendants' rights than they do in upholding them. The law itself shapes these exchanges and in this section we focus in particular on the extent to which the legal system encourages guilty pleas.

(a) Pressures on defendants to plead guilty

The pressure to plead guilty is made up of two crucial variables: firstly, the perceived likelihood of conviction and, secondly, the differential between the penalty likely to be imposed on a plea of guilty and that which would follow one of not guilty. As regards the latter aspect, there are three important ways in which the legal system holds out the prospect of a lighter sentence to those pleading guilty.

The sentence discount principle

The most naked attempt to persuade defendants to plead guilty lies in the sentencing principle established by the appellate courts that defendants pleading guilty should receive a lighter sentence than those convicted after a contested trial.[8] This principle, while of major importance in the Crown Court, has historically been of little significance in the lower criminal courts. The sentencing guidelines issued by the Magistrates' Association as late as 1989 made no mention of the effect of a guilty plea, and magistrates have publicly questioned the relevance of such a plea to sentence.[9] Research has shown that magistrates pay little attention to legal principle when sentencing, preferring to rely on

---

[8] The case law is discussed in detail in ch 7.
[9] See the discussion by M Wasik and A Turner, 'Sentencing Guidelines for the Magistrates' Courts' [1993] Crim LR 345 at 355.

their own intuitive sense of the right outcome.[10] One such study conducted in the early 1980s found that two-thirds of the 129 magistrates interviewed regarded a plea of guilty as of minor or no significance in mitigation.[11] The position may now be changing, however. The 1993 version of the Magistrates' Association sentencing guidelines state that 'a timely guilty plea may be regarded as a mitigating factor for which a sentencing discount of approximately one-third might be given.'[12] This carries the implication that, when faced with cases in which there has not been a 'timely' guilty plea magistrates should increase these presumptive sentences. The language used in the guidelines, however, hardly amounts to a ringing endorsement of the discount principle and it remains to be seen whether magistrates' sentencing behaviour will be affected.

Sentencing powers and sentencing practice

The organisation of the legal system provides a more subtle form of pressure on defendants to plead guilty. As Heberling notes, 'the basic strategy in English guilty plea representation lies in keeping trial of the case at the magistrates' court level.'[13] The advantage to the defence of having the trial heard in the magistrates' court is that the sentencing powers of the magistrates are limited. Regardless of the statutory maxima prescribed for offences, the maximum penalty which magistrates can impose on summary conviction for an offence triable either way is usually six months' imprisonment and/or a fine of £5,000 (an aggregate of one year and/or £2,000 per offence on conviction of two or more offences).[14] Similarly, the maximum penalty for a summary offence is set at six months' imprisonment or that prescribed by the statute creating the offence, whichever is the less.[15]

But even leaving aside the fact that magistrates' sentencing powers are limited, a de facto sentence discount can be achieved by having a case disposed of at the lower level. This is due to the fact that magistrates on average sentence more leniently than do Crown Court judges.

---

[10] See R Tarling, Sentencing Practice in Magistrates' Courts (Home Office Research Study no 56) (HMSO, 1979) p 43; H Parker, M Sumner and G Jarvis, *Unmasking the Magistrates* (Open University Press, 1989) p 84 and R Henham, *Sentencing Principles and Magistrates' Sentencing Behaviour* (Avebury, 1990) p 181.

[11] Henham, op cit p 133.

[12] The Magistrates' Association, Sentencing Guidelines, p 3, issued September 1993.

[13] J Heberling, 'Plea Negotiation in England' in J Baldwin and A Bottomley (eds), *Criminal Justice: Selected Readings* (Martin Robertson, 1978) p 97.

[14] The maximum fine was increased to £5,000 when s 17(2)(c) of the Criminal Justice Act 1991 came into effect.

[15] Magistrates' Courts Act 1980, s 31(1).

Clear evidence that this was so was first produced by Hedderman and Moxon in a Home Office study of mode of trial decisions and sentencing published in 1992. To ensure that like was compared with like the researchers identified cases dealt with in the magistrates' courts that matched those where the defendant had elected to go to the Crown Court as regards the features that could be expected to affect sentence. This exercise revealed that:

'. . . custody was used almost three times as often and sentences were, on average, about two and a half times longer in elected cases than in comparable cases at magistrates' courts. In other words, the Crown Court imposes more than seven times as much custody as do magistrates' courts for cases having similar characteristics.'[16]

How though does a guilty plea help to ensure that a case is kept in the magistrates' courts? To understand this, we need to examine the practice of charge bargaining (which in itself forms a separate form of pressure to plead guilty) and relate this to the classification of offences and mode of trial decisions.

Charge bargaining

Charge bargaining typically involves the defendant agreeing to plead guilty in exchange for the prosecution proceeding on a less serious charge. For example, theft may be substituted for the original charge of burglary, or assault with intent replaced by simple assault. The law places little constraint on the ability of prosecutors to charge bargain. Under the Prosecution of Offences Act 1985 Crown prosecutors have the power to make additions, deletions or alterations to the charges, and can terminate proceedings altogether. Even on the day of the trial itself the prosecutor can secure the dismissal of the case by offering no evidence. Furthermore, in stressing 'the resource advantages both to the Service and the courts generally' of charge bargaining, the Code for Crown Prosecutors (para 11) makes it clear that such deals are not merely tolerated but encouraged and expected.

The 'advantage' of a charge bargain to the defendant is two fold. Firstly, a more lenient sentence can be expected since the court will sentence on the basis that the defendant committed a less serious form of offence than that with which he or she was originally charged. Secondly, the bargain may mean that the case can be kept in the magistrates' courts where, as we have seen, sentences are generally lighter than those imposed in the Crown Court. If an accused is charged with

---

[16] C Hedderman and D Moxon, Magistrates' Court or Crown Court? Mode of Trial Decisions and Sentencing (Home Office Research Study, no 125) (HMSO, 1992) p 37.

an either way offence originally, it may be possible to persuade the prosecution to substitute a summary charge. A summary trial is then guaranteed. If, on the other hand, the accused is facing a charge of an offence triable only on indictment, an agreement could be made that the prosecution will substitute an either way charge in return for a plea of guilty. This makes it possible for the case to be heard in the magistrates' courts. A mode of trial decision then needs to be made to determine whether the case will be heard by the magistrates or instead committed to the Crown Court for trial.

The procedure to be applied at a mode of trial hearing is prescribed by the Magistrates' Courts Act 1980. At this hearing, the prosecution and the defence are invited to make representations in turn about whether the offence is more suitable for summary trial or trial on indictment. Following on from this, the magistrates must determine whether, having regard to the criteria set out in the 1980 Act, the case is serious enough to justify trial on indictment.[17] If they conclude that it is, then the case will be committed to the Crown Court irrespective of the accused's wishes. If the magistrates decide that summary trial is appropriate, the court explains this to the accused and also the accused may either consent to a summary trial or opt for trial by jury. The choice, in this circumstance, is the accused's alone. Riley and Vennard, in a study conducted by the Home Office, found that magistrates' mode of trial decisions were in line with prosecution preferences in 96% of cases.[18] Whatever the reasons for the correlation between the views of prosecutors and magistrates,[19] there will clearly seem to the defence to be much to gain by persuading the prosecution not to press for Crown Court trial. One way of achieving this is to suggest that the defendant might plead guilty if the case is dealt with summarily.

In less serious cases or cases in which the prosecution evidence is weak, a prosecutor may offer a greater concession to the defence than merely a reduction in charges. One possibility is for the defendant to agree to be bound over in exchange for the dropping of all criminal charges.[20] Crown prosecutors may also be prepared to drop a case if the defendant signs a waiver relinquishing ownership of property which prompted a prosecution, such as an offensive weapon or a shotgun held in contravention of licensing laws. One thing a prosecutor may not do is hold out a promise of a particular sentence. In the English system, the sentence is a matter for the judge, not the prosecutor, and the latter

---

[17] See s 19 of the Magistrates' Courts Act 1980 for a list of the factors to be taken into account by magistrates when taking their decision.

[18] D Riley and J Vennard, Triable-either-way cases: Crown Court or Magistrates' Court? (Home Office Research Study, no 98) (HMSO, 1988).

[19] For discussion see Moxon and Hedderman, op cit pp 14–15.

[20] See J Baldwin, *Pre-Trial Justice* (Basil Blackwell, 1985) pp 79–85.

never recommends a particular sentence on a charge being proved.[1] Any sentence bargaining must accordingly take place between the defence lawyer and the judge. As we shall see in the next chapter, sentence bargaining is frowned upon by the senior judiciary and it is unheard of in the magistrates' courts.

(b) The regulation of pre-trial negotiation

The law's encouragement of guilty pleas is difficult, if not impossible, to reconcile with adversarial principle and the priority supposedly given to acquitting the innocent in legal rhetoric. It is a distinguishing feature of an adversarial system based on due process values that defendants are not obliged to prove their innocence. From this stems their right to remain silent and to be free of any obligation to assist the prosecution. This provides an important protection against the misuse of power by the state, since it reduces the possibility of successful prosecutions based on vague accusations, flimsy evidence or mere supposition. Through being forced to prove its case beyond reasonable doubt in open court, the state is obliged to proceed carefully, collecting substantial evidence through lawful means. Charge bargaining and allied practices undermine this due process protection by encouraging defendants to convict themselves through a guilty plea. Prosecutions on flimsy evidence which would have failed if tested in open court may therefore achieve a conviction. This, in turn, greatly increases the possibility that factually innocent defendants will be convicted. Inducements (by way of reduced charges and lower sentences) to plead guilty also appear inconsistent with the currently fashionable penal philosophy that sentences should be proportionate to the gravity of the offence committed. How has the legal system attempted to manage this gap between due process rhetoric and crime control reality?

One method has been to employ language which glosses over awkward contradictions. A good example is that part of the code for Crown Prosecutors (para 11) which deals with charge bargaining:

'The over-riding consideration will be to ensure that the court is never left in the position of being unable to pass a proper sentence consistent with the gravity of the defendant's actions . . . Administrative convenience in the form of a rapid guilty plea should not take precedence over the interests of justice, but where the court is able to deal adequately with an offender on the basis of a plea which represents a criminal involvement not inconsistent with the alleged facts, the resource advantages both to the Service and the courts generally will be an important consideration.'

---

[1] See the comments of Scarman LJ in *Atkinson* (1978) 67 Cr App Rep 200.

This passage illustrates well the tension between principles of justice and the encouragement of pre-trial negotiation. For how can a court pass a sentence 'consistent with the gravity of the defendant's actions' if the prosecution accepts a plea of guilty to a charge which represents a degree of conduct less serious than that originally alleged? The slippery use of language is exemplified by the encouragement given to prosecutors to accept a plea 'which represents a criminal involvement not inconsistent with the alleged facts'. Presumably the double negative was used because of the difficulty involved in suggesting that a charge bargain might involve the case proceeding on a basis which was consistent with the alleged facts. These passages could only make sense if the original charge overstated what the defendant had done, in which case it would be wrong to extract a guilty plea as the price for reducing the charge. A charge bargain involves the prosecution transforming the nature of the allegation, so that a different legal label can be affixed to the case. Burglary becomes theft, wounding with intent to cause grievous bodily harm becomes simple wounding and so on. This is possible because, when cases are disposed of by way of guilty pleas, it is the lawyers rather than the courts who effectively construct truth and determine guilt and innocence.

This supplanting of the courts' role has not gone unchallenged. That magistrates must not deal summarily with serious cases was stressed, for example, in *Justices of Bodmin, ex p McEwen*.[2] The prosecution and defence had persuaded the justices to agree to a reduction in charge from wounding with intent to do grievous bodily harm to unlawful wounding so that the case could be tried summarily. The defendant had stabbed a fellow soldier in the back with a bayonet. As Lord Goddard CJ observed:

'Here is a case in which a man's life has been seriously imperilled and if he had died, this applicant, the accused, would have been charged with murder . . . For justices to exercise jurisdiction . . . by treating a case of this sort as nothing more than common assault is a most extraordinary state of affairs.'[3]

In *Coe*,[4] a case involving high value property offences, Lord Parker CJ reaffirmed this approach:

'No doubt it is convenient in the interests of expedition, and possibly in order to obtain a plea of guilty, for the prosecution to invite the magistrates' court to deal with indictable offences summarily. But there is

---

[2]   [1947] KB 321.
[3]   Ibid at 324.
[4]   [1968] 1 WLR 1950.

something more involved than convenience and expedition. Above all there is the proper administration of justice to be considered, questions such as the protection of society and the stamping out of this sort of criminal enterprise if it is possible . . . [The prosecution] should only invite summary trial in cases where the power in the magistrates' court to administer punishment is sufficient.'[5]

New mode of trial guidelines issued by the Court of Appeal in October 1990 state that the magistrates' court should never make its decision on the grounds of convenience or expedition. Yet these guidelines also signal a softening of approach by the courts since they at the same time encourage a presumption in favour of summary trial:

'In general, except where otherwise stated, either way offences should be tried summarily unless the court considers that the particular case has one or more of the features set out below *and* that its sentencing powers are insufficient.'[6]

The guidelines go on to list the aggravating features for a number of commonly occurring offences (burglary, theft, criminal damage and so on). If none of these is present, then magistrates are, in effect, exhorted to try the case summarily even though they consider their sentencing powers to be inadequate. The Code for Crown Prosecutors represent an even more marked departure from the position staked out in *Coe*: it advises that representations to the court at mode of trial hearings should focus on those matters to which the court is obliged to have regard under the Magistrates' Courts Act 1980, but adds:

'The prosecutor may also have regard to such factors as delay in the administration of justice, the additional cost and possible effects on witnesses of having the case heard in the Crown Court.'

This gives official endorsement to prosecutors taking into account both convenience and expedition when making representations to magistrates on mode of trial. There thus appears to be a drift towards crime control values in this part of the criminal process.

This is not to say that there was ever a golden age of due process, for it emerges from cases such as *Coe*[7] that attempts to regulate pre-trial negotiation have stemmed from concern that criminals should receive their just deserts. Little anxiety is evident that charge bargains and allied practices might result in the innocent pleading guilty or the undermining of the adversarial system.

---

[5] Ibid at 1953. See also *King's Lynn Justices, ex p Carter* [1969] 1 QB 488.
[6] *Practice Note (Mode of Trial: Guidelines)* [1990] 1 WLR 1439.
[7] Above.

(c)   Lawyer behaviour: manoeuvring, negotiating and pre-trial reviews

It might be thought that defence lawyers could be relied upon to ensure that innocent persons do not succumb to the kinds of pressures discussed above by pleading guilty, and that prosecutors would only seek guilty pleas in cases where the evidence of guilt was very strong. To assess these possibilities we need to examine the behaviour of lawyers.

An immediate difficulty is that, by definition, pre-trial manoeuvring and negotiation is not subject to public scrutiny. Lawyers freely admit, however, that wheeling and dealing is an integral part of their trade, and last-minute negotiations can be observed taking place on a daily basis in court buildings.[8] In the early 1980s, a dozen or so magistrates' courts experimented with a more systematic approach to these negotiations. Pre-trial reviews were introduced for cases likely to be contested. Meetings between the opposing lawyers would be arranged by court clerks who would also be in attendance to make a note of any deals done. This formalisation of pre-trial negotiating allowed researchers to study more easily the types of exchange that occur between prosecutors and defence solicitors.

Before examining the research evidence, it is important to understand the importance of the disclosure of evidence to pre-trial bargaining. Since an adversarial system can only function properly if there is at least rough equivalence in the resources available to the defence and prosecution, it follows that the fruits of the police investigation should be disclosed to the defence regardless of whether or not they favour the prosecution. Moreover, fairness to the accused (who is presumed innocent) requires that the prosecution case is disclosed so that a defence may be prepared. As we shall explore in the next chapter, these principles are broadly accepted in the Crown Court, but only gained a firm foothold in the magistrates' courts as recently as 1985.

In theory, this meant that a key variable in a defendant's decision on plea, the strength of the prosecution case, was unknown. Similarly, there was (and remains) no requirement that the defence disclose its case. The prosecution would, therefore, be unsure as to the strength of its own case and whether it might be worth cutting its losses by striking a deal with the defence. In practice, informal exchanges between prosecution and defence solicitors enabled information to be traded and bargains to be struck. Pre-trial reviews encouraged the more routine

---

[8] This includes youth courts: see H Parker, M Casburn and D Turnbull, *Receiving Juvenile Justice* (Basil Blackwell, 1981) pp 50–55.

disclosure of evidence, partly in order to enable the issues in dispute to be clarified, but also in order to facilitate case settlement.

A study of pre-trial reviews conducted by Baldwin discovered that defence solicitors were willing to trade information and favours with prosecutors.[9] A summary of this research concluded that:

'. . . the criminal courts, at least the lower courts, are based to a much greater extent on compromise and accommodation then on combat and confrontation. Few of these lawyers could be said to relish the thought of fighting cases in court if some acceptable "arrangement" of pleas seemed a possibility . . . Although the textbooks may be written on the assumption that adversarial attitudes will prevail, many solicitors have developed their own practices in which case settlement on an amicable basis is strongly favoured.'[10]

That defence lawyers were prepared to disclose routinely details of their clients' cases is indicative of their lack of concern for basic tenets concerning the rights of suspects supposedly central to English justice. It is, after all, for the prosecution to prove its case and it is not for the defence to assist in that process. In the magistrates' courts, however, defence solicitors appear more concerned to 'play fair' with the prosecution.

The dynamics of pre-trial negotiations should have been altered by the introduction of rules in 1985 directing the prosecution to provide advance disclosure in at least summary form for cases triable either way that were to be heard in the magistrates' courts.[11] Although this development appeared to remove much of the incentive for defence solicitors to disclose details of their cases, the study by Baldwin suggested that no such incentive was needed. It is true that some courts have abandoned or placed less emphasis upon pre-trial reviews, but many more courts have taken their place. A survey by Mulcahy, Brownlee and Walker in the early 1990s found that of 218 respondent courts, 43 operated a formal pre-trial review system. A further 30 magistrates' courts conducted such reviews on an ad hoc basis, whilst 21 other courts were considering introducing this mechanism.[12]

Opinions differ as to the value of pre-trial reviews, although the consensus in this country appears to be that they offer gains in terms of

---

[9] J Baldwin, *Pre-Trial Justice* (Basil Blackwell, 1985). For a summary of the Nottingham research, see J Baldwin, 'Pre-Trial Settlement in the Magistrates' Courts' (1985) 24 Howard J Crim Justice 108.

[10] J Baldwin and F Feeney, 'Defence Disclosure in the Magistrates' Courts' (1986) 49 MLR p 593 at 604–605.

[11] Magistrates' Courts (Advance Information) Rules, SI 1985/601.

[12] A Mulcahy, I Brownlee and C Walker, 'An Evaluation of Pre-Trial Reviews in Leeds and Bradford Magistrates' Courts' (1993) 33 Home Office Research Bulletin 10.

procedural efficiency.[13] According to Baldwin, issues of real importance were resolved at nearly half of the reviews he recorded,[14] and Mulcahy et al argue that their data show that pre-trial reviews are cost effective. The important question, however, is whether a practice which appears to undermine the adversarial system of justice so much is defensible in principle. Baldwin argues that bargaining is endemic in the magistrates' courts and will take place whether or not pre-trial reviews are held. This leads him to the conclusion that:

'Though there are dangers in the extreme informality and flexibility of some of the arrangements that have been adopted, the pre-trial review at least provides a forum which is open to outside scrutiny, and the furtive business of plea negotiation in court corridors is replaced by discussions which are at once more ordered and more seemly.'[15]

If plea-trial reviews are to be accepted as the lesser of two unavoidable evils, what does outside scrutiny reveal? Baldwin, found that:

'the participants aimed to ensure that deals and compromises about charges tallied with the gravity of the offence as revealed in the evidence . . . the present writer did not observe a single case in which a bargain could fairly be described as improper.'[16]

One flaw in this argument is that the material on which the parties base their negotiations is at best partial and at worst thoroughly misleading. From May 1985, it became standard practice to disclose the prosecution case in summary form in either way cases.[17] A study of 200 such summaries (which were prepared by police officers) found that about half did not provide a satisfactory precis of the prosecution's evidence and in about one-third of all cases the summary was inaccurate or misleading.[18] As the authors of the study noted, 'it is too often the prosecution's version of events (sometimes embellished by a certain amount of wishful thinking) that is represented in the summary'.[19] A further study by Baldwin for the Runciman Commission demonstrated that the problem persists: most summaries of police interviews were

[13] For a short review of the American literature see Baldwin, *Pre-Trial Justice*, op cit pp 6–10.
[14] Ibid p 40.
[15] Ibid pp 164–165.
[16] Ibid p 97.
[17] See J Baldwin and A Mulvaney, 'Advance Disclosure in Magistrates' Courts: The Workings of Section 48' (1987) 151 JP 409 and, by the same authors, 'Advance Disclosure in the Magistrates' Courts: Two Cheers for Section 48' [1987] Crim LR 315.
[18] J Baldwin and A Mulvaney, 'Advance Disclosure in the Magistrates' Courts: How Useful are the Prosecution Summaries?', [1987] Crim LR 805 at 808.
[19] Ibid p 813.

found to be unreliable and/or partial. The study indicates that the problem is not soluble by technical means or better training, which is not surprising if one sees the police as following their own working rules in an adversarial manner.[20]

The CPS has placed less emphasis on case summaries in the last few years and introduced a system of disclosure of all witness statements in either way cases.[1] This provides defence solicitors with useful additional material. It is important to remember, however, that there is still no statutory obligation placed upon prosecutors to disclose any evidence at all on a summary charge. This is despite there being no good reason for the different treatment of this category of case.[2] But even when fuller disclosure of the prosecution case is made, a misleading impression may be given of the likelihood of conviction. There may be failures by the police, by forensic experts and by Crown prosecutors to comply with the obligation of disclosure in respect of material helpful to the defence.[3] Furthermore, as we saw in chapter 5, police interviewing techniques result in statements of evidence being stripped of possible ambiguities and exculpatory statements by suspects. In the impartial setting of the courtroom, where evidence is given on oath and is subject to cross-examination, the case may take on a very different complexion. One obvious due process objection to pre-trial bargaining is thus that the lawyers are not negotiating on the basis of 'evidence' at all, since the summaries and statements in the prosecution file are merely indications (or rather, one-sided versions) of what witnesses will say in court.

A system which encourages charge bargains not only allows the prosecution to secure convictions in weak cases that would not have stood up in court but may also lead to an increase in the number of such weak cases being prosecuted. Where a high guilty plea rate is achieved through such inducements there is little need for the prosecuting authorities to ensure that only properly prepared cases are brought to trial. It is interesting to note that when one United States jurisdiction 'banned' various forms of plea bargaining one effect was that prosecutors refused to proceed with weak cases and this, in turn, forced the

---

[20] J Baldwin, Preparing the Record of Taped Interview (Royal Commission on Criminal Justice Research Study no. 2) (HMSO, 1992).

[1] The new practice is based on a recommendation of the Working Group on Pre-Trial Issues, which reported in November 1990.

[2] See generally CJ Emmins, 'Why No Advance Information for Summary Offences' [1987] Crim LR 608.

[3] Many miscarriages of justice, such as the 'Birmingham Six', the 'Guildford Four', *Maguire* and *Ward*, have arisen as a result, in full or part, of failure to disclose relevant evidence. See P O'Connor, 'Prosecution Disclosure: Principle, Practice and Justice' in C Walker and K Starmer (eds), *Justice in Error* (Blackstone, 1993).

police to investigate crimes more carefully and thoroughly from the outset.[4] From this perspective, charge bargains are per se improper.

Of course, prosecutors are directed by the Code to discontinue cases in which the evidence is weak and this provides a theoretical safeguard for defendants. However, the due process model warns us that the prosecutor cannot be trusted to screen out weak cases any more than the police can.[5] The research by McConville et al provides empirical grounds for such distrust. They found that Crown prosecutors, for a variety of reasons, rarely take the initiative in dropping cases. As they explain:

'Dropping cases on grounds of weakness will antagonize the police and may lose a successful conviction, since, as all participants in the system understand, the great majority of cases, weak or strong, are disposed of by guilty pleas. If, on the other hand, there is a weakness in the case which the defence intends to exploit, a decision to drop it, or amend the charges or drop charges in return for a bind over, may always be made once the defence have signalled their intent to contest the case . . .'[6]

Their sample produced cases in which prosecutors had continued with weak cases in order to persuade defendants to withdraw complaints against the police,[7] or to secure a bind over,[8] or on the basis that the case would be dropped if the defendant pleaded not guilty.[9] They conclude that 'what the CPS seek is not a plea to what they can *prove*, but to what they can bluff or "arm-twist" defendants into.'[10]

Where it appears that such cases are to be contested, prosecutors are likely to seek some form of compromise, and in this they often see defence solicitors as their allies rather than their opponents. A good example is provided by the following exchange at a pre-trial review recorded by Baldwin:

Prosecuting solicitor: 'If Mr Hill will be bound over, everything else will be dismissed.'
Defence solicitor: 'That sounds reasonable, though I can't guarantee it. If he doesn't agree, I'd like to reconstitute the PTR.'

---

[4] T W Carns and J Kruse, 'A Re-Evaluation of Alaska's Plea Bargaining Ban' (1981) Alaska LR 8:27.
[5] H Packer, *The Limits of the Criminal Sanction* (Stanford University Press, 1969) p 207.
[6] M McConville, A Sanders and R Leng, *The Case for the Prosecution* (Routledge, 1991) p 146.
[7] Ibid at p 144.
[8] Ibid p 159. See also L Christian, 'Restriction without Conviction' in B Fine and R Millar (eds), *Policing the Miners' Strike* (Lawrence & Wishart, 1985) pp 132–133.
[9] McConville, Sanders and Leng, op cit p 158.
[10] Ibid p 166.

Prosecuting solicitor: 'I think I can tell you that no evidence will be offered even if he is not bound over. I think I ought to tell you that.'

Defence solicitor: 'Are you saying you're offering no evidence.'

Prosecuting solicitor: 'I would like a bind over in this case. And I'm asking you to go to your client and have a genuine interview with him, Peter, and ask him.'

Defence solicitor: 'OK. I'll have a genuine interview with him.'

Prosecuting solicitor: 'And say, "The prosecution are asking you to be bound over", will you?'

Defence solicitor: 'You're not saying to me that I can't tell my client, "Look, they've indicated to me that, even if you're not bound over, they're going to offer no evidence"?'

Prosecuting solicitor: 'No. You can tell him that, obviously, but I leave it to you as the way you do it.'

Defence solicitor: 'OK.'

Prosecuting solicitor: 'I don't like the look of this chap at all, quite frankly, because there are some awful offences being committed. He and his mates have been involved with knives and axes but *we can't identify who exactly is responsible*. And he's the only one charged with any offence.[11] [emphasis added]

The extent to which defence lawyers are prepared at pre-trial reviews to assist the prosecution by disclosing details of their clients' defence and by engaging in plea negotiation suggests that their commitment to adversarial due process is, at best, tenuous. Some writers have gone so far as to argue that 'defence lawyers opt into the Crime Control system. This is because they are *part of*, rather than challengers to, the apparatus of criminal justice.'[12] On this analysis, the common professional training and class culture that defence lawyers share with Crown prosecutors is stressed, as is their shared allegiance to the court and its demand for efficiency in the administration of 'justice'. That defence lawyers may regard continuing relationships with prosecutors and court staff as overriding loyalty to defendants is well recognised.[13] Yet the rhetorical position of the defence lawyer as the champion of the defendant makes it easy for lawyers to persuade their clients to plead guilty. All lawyers need do is convince defendants that they will be convicted if they plead not guilty, and that there is a material advantage to be gained by pleading guilty. The legal system ensures that such advantages are there for the taking whilst prosecution disclosure provides the defence lawyer with ample material on which to base advice

---

[11] J Baldwin, *Pre-Trial Justice* (Basil Blackwell, 1985) pp 81–82.

[12] McConville, Sanders and Leng, op cit p 167.

[13] See, for example, Baldwin, *Pre-Trial Justice*, op cit pp 89–90.

to defendants that their best interests lie in pleading guilty. Consider, for example, another of the interchanges recorded by Baldwin:

Defence solicitor (at the outset of the pre-trial review): 'I want some ammunition . . . What we want is really, if you could supply it, some information about whether to lean on [the defendant]. Have you got lots of nice verbals?'
Prosecuting solicitor: 'Right—I don't know about particularly nice verbals.'
[He then reads out the statements of two police officer witnesses and gives the defence solicitor a copy of the defendant's statement to the police.]
Prosecuting solicitor: 'I think that should give you some of the necessary information to go back to him . . . Do you think you've now got sufficient to get a plea?'
Defence solicitor: 'Yes.'
Prosecuting solicitor: 'Great! Another all-day not guilty bites the dust.'[14]

Baldwin may be right to argue that pre-trial reviews are preferable to less visible forms of bargaining.[15] Their use has allowed researchers to learn a good deal more about the behaviour of lawyers in the lower courts. But what has been learnt should make us wary of concluding that pre-trial bargaining is conducted according to principles of propriety and fairness. From a crime control perspective, it is possible to argue that prosecution and defence lawyers are simply acting in a realistic and pragmatic fashion and doing the public a service in helping to maintain a high rate of conviction at a relatively low cost. Most prosecutions brought by the police are, after all, undoubtedly fully justified and, for summary offences in particular, the defendant's guilt can rarely be seriously in doubt.

From a due process point of view, however, one might argue that it is incumbent on defence lawyers to take seriously such ideals as the presumption of innocence and the right of silence. These are important protections, not just for the minority of defendants who are in fact innocent, but also against the entrenchment of practices that encourage the state to exercise prosecutorial power in an unconstrained manner. Any form of pre-trial bargaining aimed at short-circuiting the court process results in an undermining of these protections. From this

---

[14] Ibid p 88.
[15] As against this, one might argue that pre-trial reviews create an expectation that lawyers should negotiate (even where one or both sides may be reluctant to do so) whereas informal bargaining relies on the parties initiating the bargaining process themselves. For an illustration of the normative pressure to deal exerted by the pretrial review, see ibid pp 42–44.

perspective, pre-trial reviews may be the lesser of two evils, but they remain an evil.

Is it possible to regulate pre-trial negotiation so as to protect the defendant's interests adequately?[16] Baldwin argues that with adequate provision for the disclosure of the prosecution case and other safeguards (such as giving defendants a right to attend) pre-trial reviews need represent 'no affront to basic values enshrined in English criminal procedure'.[17] We have suggested that even full disclosure of all prosecution cases (including those for summary offences) would not necessarily work to the advantage of the defendant. Furthermore, the inhibiting effect of having defendants present during pre-trial reviews is likely only to displace the main bargaining encounters into less visible settings.[18] Whilst it is possible that the CPS may achieve higher standards of case screening in future, it would make little sense in an adversarial system to rely upon prosecutorial propriety as a sufficient safeguard for defendants. To achieve any real progress would seem to require, at the very least, the transformation of the ideology and culture of defence lawyers. This might be achieved, for example, by setting up 'criminal defence centres' to promote and support principled and truly adversarial criminal defence services.[19] Whether such a transformation is possible without wider cultural and structural changes in the legal system and in society itself remains an open question.

4. MAGISTRATES' COURTS JUSTICE

We have seen that the important processes leading up to a court appearance are permeated with crime control values and mechanisms. None the less, one might expect that the claims of due process would jostle for greater attention at the judicial stage of the proceedings and that the personnel staffing the courts might seek to protect the primacy of formal adjudicative methods of fact finding. We will examine these possibilities whilst exploring three important topics: bail; the role of justices' clerks; and the quality of magistrates' justice.

---

[16] For a general discussion, see D Galligan, 'Regulating Pre-Trial Decisions' in I Dennis (ed), *Criminal Law and Justice* (Sweet & Maxwell, 1987).

[17] Baldwin, *Pre-Trial Justice*, op cit p 168.

[18] As was observed to happen at the Leeds Magistrates' Court by Baldwin, ibid pp 111–112.

[19] See the proposals to this effect in McConville, Hodgson and Bridges, *Standing Accused* (Clarendon Press, 1994) and in the report of the Howard League for Penal Reform Working Party on Criminal Justice Administration, The Dynamics of Justice (Howard League, 1993).

(a)   Pre-trial imprisonment: summons, bail, or jail?

Should defendants awaiting trial (or sentencing) be imprisoned? Imprisonment without trial has three obvious attractions for adherents to the crime control model: firstly, it secures the attendance of defendants at court; secondly, it impairs the ability of defendants to interfere with prosecution witnesses; and, thirdly, it prevents defendants from committing further offences whilst awaiting trial. That imprisoned defendants might not have committed any offence in the first place hardly arises due to the factual presumption of guilt at work in this model. Contrast this with the due process model. The normative presumption of innocence is antithetical to pre-trial custody.[20] If the system is serious about prioritising the acquittal of the innocent and guarding against abuses of state power, then defendants should retain their freedom wherever possible. A policy of pre-trial imprisonment may result in an undermining of the defendant's ability or willingness to contest the case and unwarranted or excessive punishment. Punishment will be unwarranted for innocent persons and this is so regardless of whether they are ultimately acquitted or convicted on a guilty plea entered under pressure. It will be excessive for those who are guilty but who face charges which would normally attract a non-custodial or short custodial penalty.

To this the crime control adherent can retort that it is all to the good that defendants' willingness and ability to contest cases is undermined by pre-trial detention. The vast majority of defendants are factually guilty and it would put an intolerable strain on the system if they all contested that fact. Moreover, the correct conclusion to draw from the argument that pre-trial detention may involve punishment which exceeds that likely to be imposed by a court on conviction is that sentencers are too lenient. As Packer puts it, 'For many such persons, a short period spent in jail awaiting trial is not only a useful reminder that crime does not pay but also the only reminder they are likely to get.'[1] The model nevertheless accepts that it would be counter-productive to crime control to overload police cells and the prison system with minor offenders. It maintains, however, that any limits to pre-trial detention should be governed by this consideration of crime control efficiency, rather than by any abstract notion of a right to pre-trial liberty.

An examination of the law and practice of pre-trial imprisonment in

---

[20] Especially as custodial remands can be for such long periods. The average time spent remanded in custody for all untried prisoners (including those committed to the Crown Court) in 1990 was ten weeks: Evidence of the Lord Chancellor's Department to Runciman Royal Commission on Criminal Justice, (November 1991) p 3, para 1.9.

[1] Op cit p 212.

England and Wales suggests that both due process and crime control values are influential, but that the latter have the upper hand. The position as regards minor offenders in the magistrates' courts is that they will usually be summonsed to appear on a particular date and no further restriction on their liberty is imposed. For more serious offenders, the courts typically proceed by way of a series of remand hearings. The purpose of these hearings is to determine what degree of liberty defendants should be permitted to retain pending trial. Defendants may either be remanded in custody or remanded on bail. Since 1991 magistrates have been empowered to remand defendants for extended periods in custody of up to 28 days in duration.[2]

About 65% of persons proceeded against at magistrates' courts in 1992 were summonsed and about 90% of the remainder were bailed rather than remanded in custody. Nearly 49,000 persons were remanded in custody by magistrates in that year.[3] Thus, although the proportion of defendants who are remanded in custody is small, the numbers involved are large and remand prisoners have contributed greatly to prison overcrowding in recent years.[4] Conditions for defendants held on remand are amongst the worst that exist within the prison system—in one institution prisoners have spent 18.5 hours a day in small cells lacking integral sanitation. Remand prisoners have played an active role in the sporadic outbreaks of rioting that have left some establishments (most notably Strangeways in April 1990) in smouldering ruins.[5]

What values does the law relating to bail display? Section 4(1) of the Bail Act 1976 provides that a defendant 'shall be granted bail except as provided in Schedule 1 to this Act'.[6] This creates a due process presumption in favour of bail (a right to bail) although the strength of that presumption depends on the nature of the exceptions set out in Sch 1. For defendants charged with non-imprisonable (ie very trivial) offences, bail need not be granted if there has been a previous failure to answer bail and the court believes that there would be a further failure to appear on this occasion. The apparent restrictiveness of this test is misleading, because such defendants would generally be proceeded against by way of summons.

[2] Magistrates' Courts (Remand in Custody) Order 1991, SI 1991/2667.

[3] Criminal Statistics for England and Wales 1992 (Cm 2410) (HMSO, 1993) p 183. This document stresses that all of the official figures on bail should be treated as estimates due to the poor quality of the data.

[4] See R Morgan and S Jones, 'Bail or Jail?' in E Stockdale and S Casale (eds), *Criminal Justice Under Stress* (Blackstone, 1992) pp 36–38.

[5] See ibid pp 49–54.

[6] For an excellent account of the genesis and (limited) impact of the Bail Act 1976, see M King, *The Framework of Criminal Justice* (Croom Helm, 1981) pp 130–37.

For defendants charged with imprisonable offences, the grounds for refusing bail are much wider.[7] Bail need not be granted if the court is satisfied that there are 'substantial grounds' for believing that the defendant, if released on bail, would either fail to appear, commit an offence or interfere with witnesses or otherwise obstruct the course of justice. Nor need bail be granted if a court is satisfied that the defendant has previously failed to answer bail for the offence or ought to be kept in custody for his or her own good, or where there has been insufficient time to obtain enough information about the person for the court. In determining whether there are substantial grounds for believing that a defendant would fail to appear, commit an offence or obstruct the course of justice, Sch 1 of the Bail Act 1976 provides that the court is to have regard to, firstly, the nature and seriousness of the offence; secondly, the character, previous convictions, associations and community ties of the person; thirdly, the person's record in regard to any previous grant of bail; and finally, the strength of the evidence against the person.[8]

The due process model would object to most of the grounds for detention laid down in the 1976 Act, although the strength of the objection would depend on how discriminating the courts were in making use of them. We will examine here the three main grounds for refusing bail.

Obstructing the course of justice

To detain someone because they might interfere with a prosecution witness is manifestly unsatisfactory, since it penalises the defendant for a supposed disposition. In any case, other ways of reducing the risk of interference can be employed, such as offering police protection to particularly vulnerable witnesses or making bail conditional on the defendant keeping well away from such persons.[9] It would only be proper to confine someone on this ground if there is evidence that a defendant granted bail has made an attempt to obstruct the course of justice.

Committing an offence

A similar objection lies against the ground that the defendant will commit an offence if released. Under this ground too, someone may be

---

[7] Bail Act 1976, Sch 1, Pt 1, paras 2–6.
[8] Ibid para 9.
[9] Clause 38 of the Criminal Justice and Public Order Bill will create new offences of intimidating or harming witnesses and jurors, but, far from this being part of a due process strategy of encouraging a higher bail rate, other clauses in the Bill (discussed in the text) will make remands in custody more likely.

deprived of liberty because of a supposed disposition. The objection is stronger here, however, since a prediction that someone will commit an offence if released rests on the assumption that the defendant committed the offence with which he or she is currently charged. The law thus allows a factual presumption of guilt to override the normative presumption of innocence.

The issue of 'dangerousness' as a ground for detaining persons not yet convicted of crime, or for extending (perhaps indefinitely) the period of detention for those who have been convicted, has been much debated in the context of sentencing and parole, and a similar dilemma applies to the bail decision.[10] The due process model would not argue that the defendants' interests should in every case be overriding. It would seem an affront to common sense to say that a suspected serial killer or pathological rapist should automatically be released on bail. But if the fear of 'further' offending is to be a ground for restraining someone, then there need to be strong due process safeguards. In particular, proper standards are needed to determine who may be presumed sufficiently dangerous to warrant a departure from the normative position that no one should be imprisoned until convicted. By allowing this ground to be applied in all offences which are merely imprisonable (rather than ones in which long terms of imprisonment are likely or virtually certain), and on the basis of little hard information, the Bail Act singularly fails this test.

Failure to answer bail

To detain defendants because of a fear that they might not attend voluntarily to answer the charges against them has greater merit, since the presumption of pre-trial liberty would quickly fall into disrepute if defendants absconded in large numbers. This fear should be properly grounded, however, and much depends on how magistrates make their predictions as to who is likely to abscond if granted bail and what level of risk they are prepared to tolerate. The factors that they are required to take account of, such as the seriousness of the offence and previous bail record, while clearly bearing on the risk of a defendant absconding, are open to wide interpretation. For bail decision making to conform to the due process model would require three things: the provision of high quality information to the court; consistent and principled decision making; and the use of mechanisms to achieve attendance short of detention wherever possible.

---

[10] For a discussion of the 'dangerousness debate' as it relates to sentencing, see A Ashworth, *Sentencing and Criminal Justice* (Weidenfeld and Nicolson, 1992) pp 64–66. On parole, see M Maguire, 'Parole' in Stockdale and Casale, op cit.

Taking the last requirement first, section 6 of the 1976 Act makes it an offence punishable by imprisonment and/or a fine to fail to answer to bail without reasonable cause. This threat should be enough to guarantee the attendance of the great majority of those facing less serious charges. In addition, s 3(6) allows for persons to be released on bail subject to such conditions as appear to the court to be necessary to secure that the defendant surrenders to the court at the appropriate time, does not commit an offence on bail or obstruct the course of justice and is available for the purpose of enabling a court report to be prepared to assist in sentencing. Defendants released on conditional bail typically have to report to the police at periodic intervals, or must reside at a specified address (such as a bail hostel) or must keep away from certain places or people.[11] The government has sought to encourage a greater use of conditional bail for defendants thought to pose too great a risk if released unconditionally. Thus more places have been provided in bail hostels and publicity has been given to other forms of supervised accommodation available to magistrates.[12] In addition, the Criminal Justice and Public Order Bill will allow the police to attach conditions to bail. A breach of a condition of bail is not an offence, although it may lead to defendants being brought back before the court for reconsideration of their remand status.[13]

There are two main difficulties with bail conditions. One is that they may impose excessive restrictions on a defendant's liberty. This is particularly so as one of the grounds for imposing a condition is to neutralise the fear that a defendant will commit an offence (any offence) if bailed. The breadth and vagueness of many criminal laws entails that highly restrictive conditions may lawfully be imposed. Thus in *R v Mansfield Justices, ex p Sharkey,*[14] the Divisional Court upheld the legality of a condition that defendants facing charges arising out of picketing did not take part in any further demonstration connected with the trade dispute between striking miners and the National Coal Board. The court's reasoning was that those attempting to prevent miners going to work by force of numbers and threats of violence would have been guilty of at least the public order offence of threatening behaviour. Anyone attending such a demonstration must be regarded as knowingly taking part in that threatening behaviour. To guard against the risk of the defendants committing offences on bail, it was, therefore,

11   See further B Block, 'Bail Conditions: Neither Logical Nor Lawful' (1990) 154 JP 83, and the trenchant reply at 230.
12   See Home Office circular 25/1988. There are currently some 1,800 such places available for remanded defendants, and there are plans to provide an additional 800 places by April 1995: HC Deb, 6th Series, vol 204, cols 813–814 25 February 1992.
13   Bail Act 1976, s 7(3).
14   [1985] 1 All ER 193.

necessary to prevent them from picketing. Percy-Smith and Hillyard have argued that the widespread policy of imposing this form of conditional bail on striking miners was motivated by a desire not to control crime, but to hamper legitimate protest.[15] Whatever the truth of the matter, it is clear that when laws are drawn in broad crime control terms there is the potential for them to be used in a repressive manner for political reasons.[16]

The second difficulty with bail conditions is that they might be imposed on defendants who would otherwise have received unconditional bail, rather than those who were genuinely at risk of a custodial remand. The evidence on this point is somewhat unsatisfactory and equivocal in nature although it seems that some 'net widening' has taken place.[17] Careful monitoring of this problem is called for in the light of the government's plans to allow conditions to be attached to police bail.

We turn now to the due process requirement of bail decisions being taken on the basis of high quality information. The structure of the Act appears to require bail to be granted unless there is clear evidence to substantiate a belief that one of the evils envisaged by Sch 1 will occur if the defendant is released. But as White observes, in practice, 'a defendant has an uphill struggle to establish reasons why he or she should be released when the Crown Prosecution Service raises objections to the right to bail.'[18] In recognition of this, recent years have witnessed the introduction of bail information schemes in over 100 courts.[19] These schemes involve the probation service providing verified information to the CPS in cases where the police have indicated an objection to bail. It appears that such schemes have proved successful in persuading prosecutors and magistrates to adopt a more liberal attitude to the grant of bail.[20] The

---

[15] J Percy-Smith and P Hillyard, 'Miners in the Arms of the Law: A Statistical Analysis' (1985) 12 Journal of Law and Society 345. See to like effect N Blake, 'Picketing, Justice and the Law' in B Fine and R Millar (eds), *Policing the Miners' Strike* (Lawrence & Wishart, 1985).

[16] See our earlier discussion of this in the context of stop-search powers in ch 2.

[17] Consider eg the debate concerning whether bail hostels are being used to accommodate persons who would otherwise have been remanded in custody: K White and S Brody, 'The Use of Bail Hostels' [1980] Crim LR 420; J Pratt and K Bray, 'Bail Hostels—Alternatives to Custody ?' (1985) 25 BJ Crim 160; and H Lewis and G Mair, Bail and Probation Work II: the use of London Probation Bail Hostels for Bailees (Home Office Research and Planning Unit Paper no 50) (Home Office, 1989).

[18] Op cit p 81 expressing a widely held view: see eg Bottoms and McClean, op cit p 196, and M King, *Bail or Custody* (Cobden Trust, 1971) p 94.

[19] HC Deb, 6th Series, vol 204, col 813, 25 February 1992. Thirteen local prisons or remand centres operate schemes to help prisoners denied bail mount a further application: ibid.

[20] See C Fiddes and C Lloyd, 'Assessing the Impact of Bail Information Schemes' (1990) 29 Home Office Research Bulletin 23 and C Lloyd, Bail Information Schemes: Practice and Effect (Home Office Research and Planning Unit Paper no 69) (Home Office, 1992).

great majority of courts currently operate without bail information schemes, however, and so most magistrates have little on which to base their decisions.

Police or prosecution objections to bail are not invariably upheld by magistrates, although unconditional bail is unlikely to be granted in such circumstances.[1] None the less, the minority of cases in which defendants are released against the wishes of the police may cause the latter great concern and there is thus the potential for friction between the police and the courts.[2] Indeed, the police often voice complaints that too many defendants are released on bail and in recent years have highlighted the 'growing problem' of 'bail bandits', ie offending by persons on bail.[3] The research evidence tends to suggest that in fact there has been little change in the rate of known offending on bail over the last decade or so.[4] That around 10% of those bailed are known to commit an offence may none the less be regarded in some quarters as unacceptable, and the government in early 1992 announced a number of proposals aimed at tackling 'bail banditry'.[5] One product was the Bail (Amendment) Act 1993, which gives the prosecution for the first time the right to appeal against a grant of bail. An appeal lies to a judge in chambers where the defendant stands charged with a crime carrying at least five years' imprisonment.[6] A defendant must be remanded in custody pending the outcome of the appeal. This gives the prosecution the power, in effect, to override a judicial decision to release on bail which can be seen as 'a potentially dangerous departure from constitutional principle.'[7] The government has gone one step further in the Criminal Justice and Public Order Bill: cl 21 states that anybody charged with an indictable offence committed whilst already on bail,

---

1 See M Zander, 'Operation of the Bail Act in London Magistrates' Courts' (1979) 129 NLJ 108; M J Doherty and R East, 'Bail Decisions in Magistrates' Courts' (1985) 25 BJ Crim 251 at 256 and A Hucklesby, 'Unnecessary Legislative Changes' (1993) 143 NLJ 233.

2 See Doherty and East, op cit at 257–258, where it is noted that amongst the 27 cases in which bail had been granted despite police objections there were six in which the defendant faced at least a charge of rape or inflicting actual or grievous bodily harm.

3 See the articles in (1991) Pol Rev, 19 July and 6 September, which summarise the results of studies carried out by the Avon and Somerset and Northumbria police, respectively. For a critique, see A Hucklesby, 'The Problem with Bail Bandits' (1992) 142 NLJ 558.

4 See P F Henderson and T Nichols, 'Offending While on Bail' (1992) 32 Home Office Research Bulletin 23.

5 See HC Deb, 6th Series, vol 204, col 813, 25 February 1992. This episode in criminal justice policy making is described by Morgan and Jones, op cit at 41–44.

6 Additional offences expressly included by the Act are those of taking a conveyance without authority and aggravated vehicle taking ('joyriding'), ss 12 and 12A of the Theft Act 1968 respectively.

7 See the comment by A Samuels (1993) Magistrate, November, 183.

'need not be granted bail', thus introducing another exception to the ever-diminishing 'right to bail.'

In addition to the problem of one in ten defendants offending on bail, about 7.7% of those bailed by magistrates' courts in 1992 failed to appear.[8] Such bare statistics must be treated with caution. For example, statistics on absconding may overstate the problem in that there may be good reasons why defendants fail to appear at court. Statistics on offending on bail may understate the problem, in that much offending on bail may remain undetected, or may overstate it in that they take no account of the possible triviality of the offences in question or the fact that increasing delays in prosecuting cases are likely to lead to an increased offending on bail rate.[9] That people abscond or offend on bail is not necessarily a sign that the remand decision was wrong.

Similarly, it is difficult to quantify the number of defendants who are wrongly denied bail. Morgan and Jones have estimated that the proportion of untried prisoners subsequently acquitted or not proceeded against is around 14–15%. They point out that the fact that persons denied bail are not subsequently convicted may be testimony to the fairness of the courts.[10] In other words, adjudicators seem able in at least some cases to overcome the prejudicial effect created by the sight of an accused being brought up from the cells under the courtroom. Similarly, the high proportionate use of non-custodial sentences for those denied bail and subsequently convicted does not prove that the remand decision was incorrect.[11] Defendants may, for example, have been remanded for their own protection or because it was feared that they would not answer to bail.[12]

On the other hand, there are enormous disparities in the rates at which different courts refuse bail which cannot be explained by differences in caseload.[13] Moreover, bail information schemes have confirmed that many remands in custody are unwarranted and that the standard of decision making can be improved.[14] As is so often the

---

[8] Criminal Statistics for England and Wales 1992 (Cm 2410) (HMSO, 1993) p 193, Table 8.11.

[9] On the latter point, see Hucklesby, op cit (1992) at 560.

[10] Morgan and Jones, op cit pp 38–39.

[11] Ibid p 39. It is there estimated at least a third of males and over a half of females remanded in custody are subsequently given non-custodial sentences.

[12] On this, see the letters from two judges, [1993] Crim LR 324.

[13] See M Winfield, Lacking Conviction: the Remand System in England and Wales (Prison Reform Trust, 1984) and B Gibson, 'Why Bournemouth?—The Home Office Remand Figures' (1987) JP, 15 August 520.

[14] The original experiment from which these schemes developed showed that the increase in granting bail resulting from the provision of better information on defendants did not result in an increase in the failure rate, whether measured as offending on bail, breach of bail conditions or non-attendance at court. See C Stone, Bail Information for the Crown Prosecution Service (VERA Institute of Justice, 1988).

case in the criminal process, certain groups suffer more than others as a result of the law, allowing a large element of discretion to those taking decisions. Hood, for example, found that black defendants had a greater likelihood of being remanded in custody than white defendants, even when all factors legally relevant to the bail decision were taken into account.[15] The framework created by the Bail Act clearly does little to prevent bad, arbitrary or even racist decision making.[16]

The complexity of the Bail Act's provisions and the importance of what is at stake might lead one to think that bail hearings are painstaking affairs. A visit to the local magistrates' court would quickly disabuse an observer of that notion. Bail decision making is speedy. In Zander's study of London courts, the amount of time spent discussing whether defendants should retain their liberty was five minutes or less in 86% of the 261 remand cases observed.[17] The lack of police objections to bail in most cases means that the courts simply apply the statutory presumption of bail without engaging in any lengthy debate. In 70% of the hearings observed by Doherty and East, for example, the possibility of a remand in custody was never raised.[18] But even where the issue of bail is brought alive by police objections, proceedings are rapid. As many as 60% of such decisions in Zander's study were reached within five minutes.[19] Another indication that bail decision making is cursory, if not slipshod, is that in at least some courts defendants have been convicted of the non-existent offence of breaching bail conditions.[20] Magistrate courts' were castigated in the Woolf Report on prison disturbances for giving insufficient status to the bail decision.[1]

Doherty and East identify the main reason for the speed with which bail decisions are taken as being the heavy workload of the magistrates' courts. The participants in the proceedings are all well known to each

---

[15]   R Hood, *Race and Sentencing* (Clarendon Press, 1992) pp 146–149.

[16]   Compare this with the situation applying in countries which have fundamental rights enshrined in constitutional charters. See eg N Padfield, 'The Right to Bail: a Canadian Perspective' [1993] Crim LR 510.

[17]   M Zander, 'Operation of the Bail Act in London Magistrates' Courts' (1979) 129 NLJ 108.

[18]   MJ Doherty and R East, 'Bail Decisions in Magistrates' Courts' (1985) 25 BJ Crim 251 at 257.

[19]   Zander, op cit.

[20]   See N Cameron, 'Bail Act 1976: Two Inconsistencies and an Imaginary Offence' (1980) 130 NLJ 382.

[1]   See Prison Disturbances April 1990, Report of an Inquiry by The Rt Hon Lord Justice Woolf (Parts I and II) and His Honour Judge Stephen Tumim (Part II) (Cm 1456) (HMSO, 1991): 'All too often, remands are dealt with hurriedly before the real business of the day. They can be dealt with by a single Magistrate or two Magistrates rather than a full Court. They can be dealt with hurriedly on a Saturday morning' (para 10.80).

other and are aware that they are expected to assist in the speedy disposal of business.

'In these circumstances it is probably inevitable that a camaraderie develops between the participants, and this no doubt partially explain why so few of the hearings attended were markedly adversarial in character ... In a situation where there is an expectation that cases are dealt with quickly, often in a non-adversarial fashion, it is perhaps not surprising that only limited information of a low quality is made to the courts.'[2]

Brink and Stone found that in court after court one-half to three-quarters of the defendants remanded in custody at their first appearance had not sought bail.[3] This was because lawyers were advising clients not to apply for bail in case it was refused and no subsequent applications were allowed to be made. Although section 4(2) of the Bail Act 1976 imposes a duty on magistrates' courts to consider the issue of bail whenever defendants appear before them, a number of courts were refusing to hear renewed bail applications unless circumstances had changed since the original application was made. The reasoning behind this—that the decision of an earlier court should be followed—was subsequently upheld by the Divisional Court in the *Nottingham Justices* case.[4] Section 154 of the Criminal Justice Act 1988 now provides that, once a defendant has been refused bail, any argument may be used to support an application at the next remand hearing whether or not it has been used previously. Thereafter 'the court need not hear arguments as to fact or law which it has heard previously'. This should mean that lawyers will feel able to make a full bail application at the outset of the case, although a reluctance to apply may still obtain with regard to the second application since courts often interpret s 154 as a licence to hear a maximum of two applications.[5]

Further risks identified by Brink and Stone in applying for bail at first appearance concerned the interests of solicitors rather than clients. Some solicitors believed that they would not receive any payment under the legal aid scheme for making a weak bail application and argued that it was not in the public interest that legal aid be provided for such

---

[2] Doherty and East, op cit p 263.
[3] B Brink and C Stone, 'Defendants who Do not Ask for Bail' [1988] Crim LR 152.
[4] *R v Nottingham Justices, ex p Davies* [1980] 2 All ER 775.
[5] Evidence is emerging that many advocates, magistrates and court clerks are continuing to close their minds to the possibility of a renewed bail application: See M Hinchcliffe, 'Beating the Bail Bandits', (1992) LS Gaz 1 July 19 at 20; N Corre, 'Three Frequent Questions on the Bail Act' [1989] Crim LR 493 at 496–497; and the letter, (1991) JP 771. See also *R v Blyth Juvenile Court, ex p G* [1991] Crim LR 693 and *R v Dover and East Kent Justices, ex p Dean* [1992] Crim LR 33.

applications. More commonly, solicitors said that they would not act for defendants until a legal aid application had been approved, but this might not be until after the first, second or even third remand hearing had taken place. Solicitors were also worried about losing credibility with the court by making weak applications, thereby damaging their chances of winning bail for more deserving clients. As Brink and Stone rightly comment:

'Such an attitude is hardly unique to criminal solicitors in this country, but wherever it is found it is generally regarded as a corruption of the adversary system of justice. Lawyers, as officers of the court, have an obligation to serve the cause of justice, but in an adversary system justice is served by the strongest possible arguments being put in every case.'[6]

The findings of this study are all the more striking given that it focused on solicitors who were identified by the London Criminal Courts Solicitors' Association as 'highly qualified, experienced and respected.'[7] The conclusion must be that the law and the courts' practices are only part of the explanation for the lack of due process at bail hearings. A further factor is that many defence solicitors voluntarily adopt an extreme crime control position in respect of 'undeserving' clients and, by doing so, undermine adversarial justice.

What remedies and controls are built into the law of bail ? Court clerks are obliged, by virtue of s 5, to record a court's reasons for refusing bail or imposing or varying conditions. In addition, the defendant must be informed as to the reasons for any refusal of bail. These requirements are supposed to ensure that magistrates keep within the terms of the Act. But as White has observed:

'it would be a poor clerk who could not formulate a reason falling within the terms of the Act and it would be a foolish magistrate who insisted on recording a personal prejudice as the reason for the decision.'[8]

An appeal against a refusal of bail may be made to the Crown Court under a procedure introduced in 1983, and solicitors enjoy a right of audience for this purpose.[9] Unrepresented defendants of limited means are at a distinct disadvantage here because, although this step lies within the scope of an existing legal aid certificate, legal aid may not be granted solely for the purpose of a bail application. For those not on

---

6 Brink and Stone, op cit p 162.
7 Ibid p 153, 3.
8 R C White, *The Administration of Justice* (Blackwell, 1985) p 84.
9 Criminal Justice Act 1982, s 60.

legal aid, the Official Solicitor—a government lawyer whose duties include safeguarding the rights of prisoners—may act. An alternative procedure is to apply to a High Court judge in chambers.[10] Oral argument is presented by a barrister. Legal aid is theoretically available but the Legal Aid Board would require compelling reasons why a defendant should be given access to the High Court in preference to the (cheaper) Crown Court. One such reason would be the need to challenge the conditions attached to a grant of bail, since these cannot be contested in the Crown Court. Again, the Official Solicitor may act for those denied legal aid, although for most defendants such a safety net provides cold comfort. Under the Official Solicitor procedure, a paper application is simply forwarded to the judge and there is no oral argument. The success rate for Official Solicitor applications in 1980 was 9%, compared with 69% for those privately represented.[11] Generally, it seems that lawyers are wary of making use of these various appeal procedures, on the ground that an unsuccessful outcome might prejudice any subsequent attempt to persuade magistrates to reconsider the question of bail.[12]

The crime control presumption of guilt pervades nearly every discussion about bail and this undoubtedly works to the disadvantage of many defendants. Their rights are regularly given insufficient weight by both magistrates and defence lawyers. At the political level, the suspicion must be that such initiatives as bail information schemes are motivated more by the need to avoid expensive custodial remands than by a concern for defendants' rights. Similarly, whilst successive governments have employed tough crime control rhetoric, they have usually been careful to avoid legislative reform which might reduce the rate at which bail is granted.[13] The requirement, introduced by s 153 of the Criminal Justice Act 1988, that magistrates give reasons for granting bail in murder, rape and manslaughter cases provides a good example of this.[14] This statutory amendment came about because of concerns that bail was being granted in cases where the public had a right to be protected. It represents a watered down version of a clause promoted by a

---

[10] Criminal Justice Act 1982, s 22.
[11] Official Report HC written answers, 6th Series, vol 13, cols 274–275, 23 November 1981. See also N Bases and M Smith, 'A Study of Bail Applications Through the Official Solicitor to the Judge in Chambers' [1976] Crim LR 541.
[12] See A Hall, 'Bail: Appeals' (1984) LAG Bull December 145.
[13] This is a high risk strategy, as tough crime control rhetoric may be just as effective in increasing the remand in custody rate as any legislative reform—see (1993) Guardian, 9 September.
[14] Note that the only lawful reason that can be given for granting bail in such a case would seem to be that none of the statutory exceptions to the presumption of bail applies.

backbench MP which would have required courts to give reasons for overruling police objections to bail for defendants charged with any indictable offence.[15] By substituting its own amendment the government ensured that the need to give reasons for granting bail would arise in few cases. If the original clause had stood it might have been taken by magistrates as a signal that they should refuse bail more often for run of the mill offences, with all that that implies for exacerbating the control problems in an already overcrowded prison system.

As we suggested at the outset, efforts to increase the bail rate for less serious offenders are consistent with the due process model's concern for the liberty of the individual, but also with the crime control model's interest in the efficient use of resources. We would argue that it is the latter concern which has been dominant at the political level, notwithstanding the rhetorical devices occasionally used to disguise this. It would be naive to expect major shifts towards due process in the law and practice of bail in such a climate. Indeed, the government now seems set on introducing measures which will increase remands in custody, such as denying bail to those charged with murder, rape or manslaughter who have a previous conviction for any of these offences,[16] and setting aside the presumption in favour of bail for those who have offended whilst already on bail.[17]

The current Home Secretary, Michael Howard, has broken with his Conservative predecessors by pursuing hardline policies on law and order. The prison population has risen sharply as a result.[18] Concern with the efficient use of resources has been superseded, for the time being, with a cruder crime control policy of deterrence which could be designed to revive the government's popularity amongst the electorate.

(b)   Justices' clerks—liberal bureaucrats ?

Justices' clerks fulfil many functions in the magistrates' courts. They are responsible for training magistrates and they are also responsible for advising them on law and procedure either in court or when a bench retires to consider its verdict, and on sentencing.[19] Through pursuing a more or less conscious policy on the determination of legal aid

---

[15] See J N Spencer, 'Questions of Bail' (1988) 152 JP 244.

[16] Criminal Justice and Public Order Bill, cl 20. In the case of a previous conviction for manslaughter, the person must have received a custodial sentence.

[17] Ibid cl 21, discussed above.

[18] The prison population soared over a ten-month period in 1993 from 41,000 in February to 47,338 in November. On 24 November 1993, the Home Secretary responded to the growing overcrowding crisis by announcing plans to fund an extra 2,000 prison places: (1993) Guardian, 25 November.

[19] This latter aspect of their role is covered by a *Practice Direction* [1981] 2 All ER 831.

applications, they can influence the level of legal representation. They are meant to assist unrepresented defendants in court. Finally, they indirectly affect the conduct of proceedings in court through their role in managing the court's business. Thus, they may encourage pre-trial reviews as means of reducing delays in processing cases or they may adopt aggressive listing policies designed to dispose of as many cases in a single sitting of the court as possible. It is important to examine the behaviour of justices' clerks as they carry out these tasks. In particular, are they influenced by, and do they seek to advance, due process or crime control values?

As noted above, court clerks have a fairly rough and ready approach to granting legal aid applications. The research by Young et al showed that some court clerks had a positive due process attitude towards legal representation whilst others were much less inclined to see the value of granting legal aid, particularly for guilty plea cases and for defendants charged with summary offences.[20] One common argument amongst the more restrictive court clerks was that, save in cases of particular difficulty or complexity, either a duty solicitor or they themselves could adequately protect a defendant's interests.

One study has suggested that court clerks distinctly prefer defendants to be represented by duty solicitors rather than by solicitors acting under a legal aid certificate.[1] The advantage to court clerks of directing legal work towards duty solicitors is that cases may be disposed of more expeditiously than if a legal aid certificate is granted. Duty solicitors can only act on the day, whereas legally aided solicitors might seek adjournments in order to prepare a case more thoroughly. As one clerk interviewed by Young, Moloney and Sanders put it in explaining his reasons for refusing a particular application:

'I think this is a duty solicitor job myself. I think with a bit of sensible advice that would be a plea. So, because in real terms the duty solicitor would get him to plead, we would refuse that one. I'm doing these from a practical point of view you realise.'[2]

This is a typical crime control line of thinking. The clerk is making a decision that the defendant is guilty based on scanty information. Because he has faith in his ability to distinguish between the clearly guilty and the possibly innocent, he decides to refuse legal aid, knowing that his decision is likely to produce the very result that he considers the correct one. There is little difference in nature between this and the

---

[20] Op cit: see especially pp 34–39.
[1] H Astor, 'The Unrepresented Defendant Revisited: A Consideration of the Role of the Clerk in Magistrates' Courts' (1986) 13 Journal of Law and Society, 225 at 234.
[2] Op cit p 53.

way in which the police set out to construct evidence against suspects. In both instances, a preference is being expressed for informal administrative fact-finding procedures over court-based adversarial proceedings as a means of disposing of the case.

The role of the clerk in assisting unrepresented defendants has been examined by Darbyshire and Astor in separate studies. Darbyshire found that some clerks were helpful and patient whilst others were brusque and intimidating.[3] Astor also noted varying standards of help on offer from clerks but made the important point that the 'allegiance of the clerks was ultimately not to the defendants, but to the rules—their insistence was that the court be run "properly", not necessarily that the defendant understood what was going on.'[4] She argues that court clerks have a genuine interest in due process, since as the magistrates' courts' legal advisors they must ensure that the legitimacy of the court is not called into question. At the same time, she acknowledges, they have a strong bureaucratic interest in efficiency and saving court time. She accordingly follows Bottoms and McLean in arguing that the model of the criminal justice process which most accurately described the values 'typically held by humane and enlightened clerks to the justices'[5] was neither crime control nor due process, but the liberal bureaucratic model. Since this model has gained some currency in the literature of criminal justice, it is worth pausing for a moment to consider whether it provides a more useful tool of analysis than Packer's models.[6]

According to Bottoms and McClean, the liberal bureaucratic model differs from crime control in that the need for justice to be done and seen to be done is accepted as ultimately overriding the importance of repressing criminal conduct. Priority must be given to protecting the innocent and the importance of formal adjudicative procedures is recognised. Thus far, this sounds like a fair account of the due process model. Bottoms and McClean argue, however, that the liberal bureaucrat has a strong interest in the efficient throughput of cases. Thus, due process protections must be limited. As they put it:

'If it were not so, then the whole system of criminal justice, with its ultimate value to the community in the form of liberal and humane crime control, would collapse. Moreover, it is right to build in sanctions to

---

[3]   See P Darbyshire, *The Magistrates' Clerk* (Barry Rose, 1984). Her research findings are outlined in 'The Role of the Magistrates' Clerk in Summary Proceedings' (1980) 144 JP 186, 201, 219, and 233.

[4]   Op cit p 232.

[5]   A E Bottoms and J D McClean, *Defendants in the Criminal Process* (Routledge & Kegan Paul, 1976) p 228.

[6]   Packer's crime control and due process models are discussed at length in ch 1.

deter those who might otherwise use their "Due Process" rights frivolously, or to "try it on"; an administrative system at State expense should not exist for this kind of time-wasting.'[7]

They go on to note how the pressures on defendants to elect summary trial—in particular, the fear of a heavier sentence at the Crown Court—and the pressures on defendants to plead guilty all help to smooth the administrative operation of the system. They conclude that:

'despite the superficially apparent similarity of the value-systems underlying the Liberal Bureaucratic and Due Process Models, in practice the Liberal Bureaucratic Model offers much stronger support to the aims of the Crime Control Model than the Due Process Model.'[8]

We would contend that Bottoms and McClean's arguments are inherently contradictory and are based on a misunderstanding of Packer's models. It seems odd to claim that 'humane and enlightened' court clerks are genuinely concerned about protecting the innocent and upholding formal adjudicative procedures, at the same time as suggesting that they support rules and sanctions designed to deter defendants from exercising their due process rights. Such rules and sanctions are, after all, quintessential to the crime control model. That magistrates' court procedures do not conform exactly to the crime control model is insufficient justification to construct some new model of supposedly greater explanatory power. The essential point to grasp here is that the crime control model is not meant to be descriptive. Rather it represents one end of a spectrum of possible criminal justice systems, at the other end of which lies the due process model. By setting up these two opposing models, Packer hoped to illuminate the competing claims and tensions within criminal justice.

By contrast, the so-called liberal bureaucratic model is simply a factual description of the operation of the courts. This description reveals that court procedures display elements of the due process model in that contested trials do occur (albeit rarely), legal aid is (sometimes) available, court clerks will (on occasion) assist unrepresented defendants and so forth. However, the predominance of guilty plea cases, and the pressures on defendants to refrain from pushing the available due process levers, means that the magistrates' courts correspond much more closely to the crime control model than its polar opposite.

To return to Astor's work, while she is undoubtedly correct in suggesting that court clerks are anxious to see the rules followed, what is overlooked is that these rules themselves often display crime control

---

[7] Op cit p 229.
[8] Ibid p 232.

values. A denial of due process can accordingly be achieved without breaking the rules and without any undermining of the court's legitimacy. Thus, the discretion given to court clerks in determining legal aid applications means that they can, by refusing legal aid, deliver defendants into the arms of duty solicitors, knowing that this will aid efficiency and make a guilty plea more likely.

Another illustration is provided by the court clerk's role at the pre-trial stage. As the business managers of the magistrates' courts, clerks played a leading role in developing pre-trial reviews. Clerks attending these reviews will, if negotiations between the lawyers run into difficulty, actively encourage defence disclosure and case settlement.[9] They have shown similar enthusiasm for wheeling and dealing in more informal settings, such as immediately prior to a formal court hearing.[10] This behaviour is hardly consistent with the liberal bureaucrat's supposed concern for justice to be done and to be seen to be done.[11] It is, however, consistent with the law. For whilst no law requires justices' clerks to promote out of court settlements, neither does any law prohibit them from adopting this as an administrative objective.

On current trends, we might expect justices' clerks to develop an even keener interest in crime control strategies. As part of a government drive to improve efficiency, from 1992–93 the funds made available to magistrates' courts will depend, in part, on the throughput of cases.[12] Cases handled will be allocated a number of points based on the seriousness of the offence. The higher the points scored overall, the higher a court's grant will be. Significantly, the points value of a case is not affected by whether it is disposed of by a guilty plea or following a full trial lasting several hours or days. Put bluntly, it will pay justices' clerks to encourage guilty pleas wherever possible.[13] It will pay them in a literal sense too, since their pay is to be related to 'performance' under the new scheme. The Police and Magistrates' Courts Bill, introduced to Parliament in late 1993, has a number of clauses designed to strengthen the government's control over justices' clerks[14] and the pressures on

---

9 See eg J Baldwin, *Pre-Trial Justice* (Basil Blackwell, 1985) p 43 and J Baldwin and A Mulvaney, *Pre-Trial Settlement of Criminal Cases in Magistrates' Courts* (University of Birmingham, 1987) p 15.

10 See Parker et al, op cit pp 50–55.

11 See Bottoms and McLean, op cit p 229.

12 A New Framework for Local Justice (Cm 1829) (1992).

13 For an outline of the debate concerning the management of magistrates' courts, see Zander, op cit pp 19–24.

14 Eg cl 69 makes their appointment subject to the Lord Chancellor's approval and cl 70 gives the Lord Chancellor power to specify standard terms to be included in their contracts of employment (such as that they should be for a fixed term). At the time of writing, the government had run into difficulties with these proposals.

them to achieve 'efficiency' are likely to intensify over the next few years.

(c) Fairness in the magistrates' courts

Defendants do not expect justice to be done in the magistrates' court. Typically, they regard the Crown Court as fairer and more thorough in its approach and offering a better chance of acquittal. By contrast, magistrates' courts are seen as amateurish and pro-police, but speedier and offering the prospect of a more lenient sentence.[15] There is evidence to suggest that their perceptions are accurate.[16] Vennard's study of contested cases in the magistrates' courts found that there was a tendency for magistrates to accept the accuracy of police eye witness evidence and their interpretation of events as against the defendant's denial of the alleged conduct or a claim that the act did not constitute a crime. Even where defendants' credibility was not directly impugned and there was no confession the majority of cases ended in conviction.[17] A further study by Vennard concluded that for contested either way cases, the chances of acquittal were substantially higher in the Crown Court (57%) than in the magistrates' courts (30%).[18]

There are a number of possible explanations for the higher acquittal rate in the Crown Court. The first is simply numerical. At the Crown Court, the prosecution has to convince at least ten out of the 12 jurors that the defendant is guilty.[19] In the magistrates' court, it is enough to convince two out of the three lay magistrates, or even just one stipendiary magistrate.

A second explanatory factor concerns the social composition of the magistracy and juries respectively. Whereas juries are drawn from a reasonably representative cross-section of society,[20] study after study has shown that magistrates are pre-dominantly white, middle aged and

---

[15] See Bottoms and McLean, op cit pp 87–100; J Gregory, Crown Court or Magistrates' Court?, (Office of Population Censuses and Surveys) (HMSO, 1976) and D Riley and J Vennard, Triable-Either-Way Cases: Crown Court or Magistrates' Court?, (Home Office Research Study, no 98) (HMSO, 1988) pp 16–18.

[16] For the evidence on sentencing patterns, see section 3(a), above.

[17] J Vennard, Contested Trials in Magistrates' Courts (Home Office Research Study no 71) (HMSO, 1981) p 21.

[18] J Vennard, 'The Outcome of Contested Trials' in D Moxon (ed), *Managing Criminal Justice* (HMSO, 1985). A Ashworth, 'Plea, Venue and Discontinuance' [1993] Crim LR 830, who does not cite the 1981 study by Vennard (op cit), argues for caution in interpreting this finding (at 833).

[19] Until 1967 the jury's decision had to be unanimous. Now, under the Criminal Justice Act 1967, s 13(3), the court is not supposed to consider the possibility of a majority verdict until at least two hours have elapsed since the jury retired.

[20] For jury selection procedures, which are themselves far from perfect, see ch 8.

middle class.[1] Such people may have an undue respect for and trust in authority. There may be a lack of understanding on the bench as to why a defendant might refuse to answer police questions or might dissemble or make a false confession. Magistrates may have standards of behaviour which are unrepresentative of the wider community and this may be of importance in applying the law. For example, in property offences the test for whether an action is dishonest is whether ordinary people would regard the act as dishonest and whether the defendant was aware that the act would be so regarded.[2] But magistrates are not representative of ordinary people. Juries are less susceptible to these forms of unconscious class bias.

A third factor is that juries come fresh to the criminal courts, hear one or more cases, then leave again to return to their normal occupations. Magistrates, by contrast, hear hundreds of cases each year, so may become 'case-hardened'. The vast majority of those appearing before them plead guilty, cases are generally disposed of quickly and magistrates may find it difficult in this atmosphere to treat each case on its individual merits. Particular problems may be faced by unrepresented defendants. The work of Carlen suggests that magistrates (and their clerks) have a greater interest in maintaining social control in their courtrooms than in giving free rein to defendants to challenge authority by contesting the prosecution version of events or by raising awkward questions about behind the scenes negotiations regarding bail, plea or whatever.[3]

Finally, the procedures in the lower courts place defendants at a distinct disadvantage. As we have commented above, the prosecution need not disclose its case to defendants charged with summary offences and legal aid is less freely available than in the Crown Court. Magistrates, unlike jurors, are privy to much inadmissible evidence. This is because the admissibility of evidence is a question of law which can be decided by the judge in the absence of the jury in the Crown Court. Magistrates, by contrast, determine both questions of fact and law. Even if they decide, for example, that a disputed confession is inadmissible, they may still be prejudiced by the knowledge that an alleged confession exists. There is also some evidence that justices' clerks may occasionally, whether in private or in whispers, transmit opinions, prejudices and hearsay information to magistrates.[4] Magistrates' courts are also

[1]　See eg J Baldwin, 'The Social Composition of the Magistracy' (1976) 16 BJ Crim 171 and M King and C May, *Black Magistrates* (Cobden Trust, 1985).

[2]　*Ghosh* [1982] 2 All ER 689.

[3]　P Carlen, 'Remedial Routines for the Maintenance of Control in Magistrates' Courts' (1974) 1 BJ Law & Society 101 and P Carlen, *Magistrates' Justice* (Martin Robertson, 1976).

[4]　See H McLaughlin, 'Court Clerks: Advisers or Decision-Makers' (1990) 30 BJ Crim 358 at 364.

less accountable in that their proceedings are not recorded in full. If the defence wish to appeal on a point of law to the Divisional Court the magistrates draw up a statement of the facts, the cases cited and their decision. This gives justices' clerks ample opportunity to cover their tracks.[5]

Not surprisingly, then, studies of mode of trial decisions by defendants show that elections for Crown Court trial are strongly associated with intended plea. Riley and Vennard found that defendants who expressed an initial intention to contest the charges against them were twice as likely to elect trial at the Crown Court than were those who intended pleading guilty.[6] A more sophisticated study by Hedderman and Moxon confirmed that plea was central to the mode of trial decision. The perception that the Crown Court offered a fairer hearing even influenced some defendants who were not planning to contest their cases and just over a quarter of those electing Crown Court trial did so intending to plead guilty.[7] Hedderman and Moxon also discovered that a majority of defendants who elected Crown Court trial (including some of those who intended to plead guilty), together with over a third of the solicitors interviewed, were apparently labouring under the false impression that Crown Court judges imposed lighter sentences than magistrates.[8]

Many defendants facing either way charges are committed to the Crown Court for trial at the direction of the magistrates. In the Hedderman and Moxon sample of either way cases tried in the Crown Court, 59% had been sent for trial as a result of magistrates declining jurisdiction. Interviews with these defendants revealed that nearly three quarters would have preferred to have been dealt with at a magistrates' court—usually in the expectation that a lighter sentence might thereby be achieved. The greater prospect of acquittal was the strongest factor for the minority who said they would have elected Crown Court trial if the magistrates had given them a choice in the matter.[9] Hedderman and Moxon also pointed out that where the magistrates had declined jurisdiction, well over half of the defendants concerned received sentences

---

[5] For fuller discussion see I A Heaton-Armstrong, 'The Verdict of the Court . . . and its Clerk?' (1986) 150 JP pp 340 at 343, 357–359.

[6] Riley and Vennard, op cit pp 17–18.

[7] C Hedderman and D Moxon, Magistrates' Court or Crown Court? Mode of Trial Decisions and Sentencing (Home Office Research Study, no 125) (HMSO, 1992) p 23.

[8] Ibid p 20. This finding departs from the pattern found by other studies. Whether this should be taken as evidence of a widespread misconception of recent origin about sentencing patterns or simply attributed to some methodological flaw in the study is not clear. See further L Bridges, 'The Right to Jury Trial—How the Royal Commission Got it Wrong' (1993) 143 NLJ 1542.

[9] Hedderman and Moxon, op cit p 21.

that could have been imposed by the lower courts.[10] They concluded that there was greater scope for magistrates to regard cases as suitable for summary trial.

The proportion of either way cases committed to the Crown Court has grown in recent years and this has led to increased costs for the courts, the CPS, the probation service, the legal aid fund and the prison system. It has also been a major factor in fuelling prison overcrowding, both because defendants remanded in custody have longer to wait if committed to the Crown Court,[11] and because Crown Court judges make much more use of custodial sentences than do magistrates.[12] In response, various attempts have been made to restrict the flow of cases committed from the magistrates' courts. The crudest way of achieving this is simply to remove the right of defendants to elect jury trial by reclassifying either way offences as summary only. Thus, s 15 of the Criminal Law Act 1977 made a number of public order offences and drink-driving offences purely summary. The Criminal Justice Act 1988 (ss 37 and 39) reclassified the offences of taking a motor vehicle, driving whilst disqualified and common assault as summary offences. A more subtle approach has been to encourage magistrates to accept jurisdiction in a higher proportion of cases, most notably through the new mode of trial guidelines, discussed above.[13]

None of this, however, was enough for the Runciman Commission which believed that current procedures are wasteful of resources in view of Hedderman and Moxon's finding that whilst the majority of those electing Crown Court trial did so in the expectation of a fairer trial, the great majority of them (82%) ended up pleading guilty anyway. It recommended that defendants should no longer enjoy the right to elect trial by jury. In either way cases where the prosecution and defence could not agree on the appropriate venue for trial, the decision should be left to the magistrates alone. Its declared motive for making this controversial recommendation was that the savings produced by keeping more cases in the magistrates' courts 'would enable more resources to be devoted to ensuring that the more serious cases going to the Crown Court are not only better prepared but more quickly heard.'[14] The cynic might reply that any resources saved might just as easily be devoted to funding tax cuts or reducing the national deficit.

---

[10] Ibid p vi.
[11] See Morgan and Jones, op cit at 38.
[12] See Hedderman and Moxon, op cit p 37.
[13] There are also plans to produce a leaflet informing defendants that magistrates' courts are less likely to impose custodial sentences than the Crown Court: (1993) The Lawyer, 14 September.
[14] Royal Commission on Criminal Justice, Report (Cm 2263) (HMSO, 1993) p 88.

But even if we could be sure that any savings were applied to improve the quality of justice in the Crown Court, the strategy of allocating more cases to the magistrates' courts remains questionable. The Runciman Commission was well aware of the evidence that the chances of acquittal are better for defendants in the Crown Court, but did not attach great importance to this:

'We do not think that defendants should be able to choose their court of trial solely on the basis that they think that they will get a fairer hearing at one level than the other. Magistrates' courts conduct over 93 per cent of all criminal cases and should be trusted to try cases fairly.'[15]

Since the Runciman Commission failed to commission any research on magistrates' courts (despite the fact that they conduct over 93% of all criminal cases) it is unclear why we should trust magistrates to try cases fairly. The evidence which we have examined suggests that we should not. The Runciman Commission overlooked the fact that Hedderman and Moxon's study was of convicted defendants only and that, since just under half of those pleading not guilty in the Crown Court are eventually acquitted, their figures significantly understate the number of defendants who maintain not guilty pleas following election.[16] None the less, it is clearly the case that substantial numbers of defendants do change their plea to guilty following committal. This, however, leads to a second criticism of the Runciman Commission. Instead of regarding extensive plea changing as a puzzling phenomenon to be explored, it took the view that 'the facts speak for themselves'[17] and that there was self-evidently a waste of resources that ought to be eliminated. But unless we understand why plea changing occurs, we cannot rationally decide what the appropriate response is. For all the Runciman Commission knew, the defendants in these cases might have been bullied into pleading guilty. If that were so, then the correct response would be to encourage defendants to stand firm with their plea of not guilty, rather than to abolish their right to jury trial. (We will explore this issue in more detail in the next chapter.) Finally, one might criticise the Runciman Commission for concentrating its fire on the wrong target. Since most either way cases are committed at the direction of magistrates rather than on an election by a defendant, why did not the Runciman Commission simply recommend that in either

[15] Ibid.
[16] Hedderman and Moxon, op cit p 11. A point made also by Bridges, 'The Right to Jury Trial—How the Royal Commission Got it Wrong', op cit.
[17] Here, we are quoting Michael Zander, a member of the Royal Commission, giving a presentation at the British Criminology Conference held in Cardiff on 29 July 1993.

way cases it should be solely the right of the defendant to choose the venue for trial? There is no need to erode further the due process right of defendants charged with either way offences to elect trial by jury in order to relieve pressure on the Crown Court.[18]

5. CONCLUSION

It is no exaggeration to say that magistrates' courts are crime control courts overlaid with a thin layer of due process icing. At every twist and turn in the process, defendants are saddled with handicaps which undermine their willingness or ability to stand on their rights in court. Some are denied legal aid, some are denied bail and a majority do not receive proper assistance and advice from their legal advisers. Some will not receive advance disclosure of the prosecution case and many more will receive inadequate or misleading disclosure. Many will be told that longer delays and a higher sentence can be expected if they elect trial by jury but that the prospects of acquittal before the magistrates are bleak. Many will already know this from previous experience. Some will be offered tempting oven-ready deals prepared by prosecutors and served up by legal advisers. For defendants, the process must seem like an obstacle course which presents formidable impediments to them continuing to maintain their innocence. Some will end up pleading guilty to crimes they did not commit, and others will plead guilty to crimes that the prosecution could not have proved beyond reasonable doubt.

These miscarriages of justice are not the stuff of headline news. The possibility that innocent people will plead guilty is even now little recognised and excites little concern. Appreciation of the role that more due process could play in protecting us against the abuse of police and prosecutorial power is very limited, but this is to be expected. For it tends to be marginalised groups (black people, the unemployed and the poor) who suffer most from whatever abuse of power takes place. It is easy for the rest of us to turn a blind eye to this as we gratefully focus instead on the high conviction rate that our courts achieve in seeking to repress crime on our behalf.

---

[18] An alternative suggestion is that magistrates should lose the power to commit cases to the Crown Court for sentence, 'a step which could lead many more defendants voluntarily to elect for a magistrates' court trial': Legal Action Group, Preventing Miscarriages of Justice (LAG Education and Service Trust Ltd, 1993) p 5. See also Ashworth, 'Plea, Venue and Discontinuance', op cit at 833–835.

Chapter 7

Guilty Pleas in the Crown Court

1. INTRODUCTION

The Crown Court is a unitary court which sits at around 90 centres throughout England and Wales. It is a court with all the trappings of due process: trial by jury; a professional judge to ensure fair play; expert representation provided by an independent Bar; and virtually automatic grant of legal aid. Around two-thirds of all Crown Court defendants (69% in 1992)[1] give up their right to trial by jury. Either they plead guilty to all charges or plead guilty to some and have pleas of not guilty to others accepted by the court without a jury being sworn in to hear the case.[2] Some defendants intend from the outset to plead guilty and others change their minds about pleading not guilty well in advance of their trial. However, around a third of all defendants make a last minute decision to plead guilty either on or shortly before the day of trial.[3] These late changes of plea cause the trial to collapse or 'crack'.[4] The defendants involved in these cases have resisted all the temptations and pressures to plead guilty until the very last moment, only for their resolve to crumble at the door of the court.

The high rate of guilty pleas in the Crown Court raises an important question. Why is it that the great majority of those defendants who are presented directly with the chance to exercise the supposedly fundamental right of trial by jury choose not to do so? What influences this choice? It was argued in the previous chapter that the twin determinants

---

[1] Judicial Statistics 1992 (Lord Chancellor's Department) (Cm 2268) (HMSO, 1993) p 61, Table 6.7.

[2] Note that the official statistics classify a case as disposed of by a guilty plea only if guilty pleas are entered by all co-defendants (if any): ibid p 57.

[3] See *The Efficient Disposal of Business in the Crown Court* (General Council of the Bar, 1992) app IV.

[4] M Zander and P Henderson, The Crown Court study (Royal Commission on Criminal Justice, Research Study no 19) p 95, found that 26% of all cases 'cracked'.

of a decision regarding plea in the magistrates' courts are the perceived likelihood of conviction and the possibility of obtaining a lighter sentence by pleading guilty. Interviews conducted by Hedderman and Moxon with 282 convicted defendants indicated that this applies equally to the Crown Court: 'it seems that decisions to plead guilty were largely based on a realistic assessment of the chances of acquittal, and the potential benefits in terms of sentence severity.'[5] The researchers do not explain how they formed the view that the assessments made by defendants were realistic although they do point to the crucial influence of legal advice in decisions regarding pleas. Thus, for example, of those who changed their pleas, only one respondent said that this decision had been entirely his own. The rest said that they had been advised by their solicitor or barrister to plead guilty.[6]

In the Crown Court, just as in the magistrates' court, the law provides substantial benefits to those pleading guilty. One possibility is that a bargain may be struck with the prosecution whereby charges are reduced in return for the entry of a guilty plea.[7] In the Hedderman and Moxon sample, 29% claimed to have pleaded guilty as a result of a charge bargain and the authors found plenty of evidence consistent with these claims.[8] The other main advantage of pleading guilty on which defence lawyers can proffer advice is the reduction in sentence which can be obtained by pleading guilty. This influenced 65% of those pleading guilty in the Hedderman and Moxon study. A study of Crown Court cases conducted by Zander and Henderson for the Royal Commission on Criminal Justice (Runciman Commission) also pointed to the importance of sentence reduction in decisions to plead guilty.[9]

Legal advice on the prospect of conviction and the benefits of pleading guilty is not given in a vacuum. It is shaped by the information lawyers receive from other participants within the criminal process, in particular prosecutors and judges. Throughout this chapter we draw

---

[5] C Hedderman and D Moxon, Magistrates' Court or Crown Court? Mode of Trial Decisions and Sentencing (Home Office Research Study, no 125) (HMSO, 1992).

[6] See also Zander and Henderson, op cit p 97.

[7] Charge bargaining is also discussed in section 3 of ch 6.

[8] This was particularly so where the offence charged fell within the Offences Against the Person Act 1861. For example, across the five Crown Court centres studied, between 20% and 37% of the s 47 offences of causing actual bodily harm had originally been charged as s 20 offences of causing grievous bodily harm. Similarly, between one half and three quarters of the s 20 cases had originally been charged as more serious s 18 offences, where an intention to inflict grievous bodily harm must be proved: op cit p 10.

[9] Op cit p 146. Note that this study relied on questionnaires being returned by defendants, lawyers and other participants in Crown Court proceedings. As the response rate for defendants was only 19%, the study's findings on the views of defendants must be treated with great caution.

attention to the personnel involved in plea bargaining in the Crown Court. Whereas the key negotiators in the magistrates' courts were observed to be defence solicitors and Crown Prosecutors, in the Crown Court it is barristers (or 'counsel') who take centre stage. The role of the professional judiciary must also be examined since, unlike the mainly lay magistracy, Crown Court judges are active players in the business of managing the criminal workload. In the next section we explore charge bargaining at this higher level in the court hierarchy. We then examine the sentencing principle that a guilty plea should be treated as a mitigating circumstance and the closely related matter of sentence bargaining between judges and defence counsel.

2. CHARGE BARGAINING IN THE CROWN COURT

It was only in the 1970s that charge bargaining in the Crown Court began to be explored by researchers. In one of the first studies, McCabe and Purves examined the cases of 112 defendants who changed their plea to guilty at a late stage, 64 of whom were involved in some form of charge bargain.[10] The study emphasised the crucial role of lawyers in such decisions and was critical of the process involved:

'. . . it seems fair to say that in most, if not all, cases [a change of plea] followed after the defendant received "certain good advice" from his legal representatives. This is especially the case with late or last-minute changes of plea where counsel, after reviewing his brief and assessing the evidence, speaks urgently to solicitor and defendant in a conference held, in all too many cases, immediately before the trial is due to start . . . A feature of nearly all cases of plea-changing is the speed and urgency with which conferences, discussions and negotiations are conducted . . . it gives rise to an impression that critical negotiations are conducted with furtiveness and without full consideration of matters such as the background of the defendant, the details of the offence, and the explanation to the defendant of his rights.'[11]

Somewhat paradoxically, McCabe and Purves were convinced that no substantial injustice resulted from such plea bargaining, arguing, on the basis of their scrutiny of the prosecution papers, that 'changes of plea are the result of a realistic and practical approach adopted by police, defence and prosecution lawyers, judges, and often, the defendants themselves.'[12] For the researchers, informal negotiated justice

---

[10] S McCabe and R Purves, *By-passing the Jury* (Blackwell, 1972).
[11] Ibid pp 9–10.
[12] Ibid p 26.

was seen as producing much the same end product as would have an expensive and contrived contest in open court. This is the position taken in the crime control model within which there is scepticism concerning the value of such courtroom rituals as a means of establishing the truth. Thus the authors argued that charge bargain cases

'are generally disposed of after informal negotiations between lawyers of both sides acting not so as to impress and confound a jury by rhetoric, innuendo, suggestion, intimidation and manipulation of the rules of evidence and procedure, but in order to reach as expeditious and as economical an agreement as possible after an abandonment of pretence, a concentration on practical calculation, and an open confrontation with hard facts and real probabilities.'[13]

Since McCabe and Purves did not talk to defendants as part of their study, their conclusion that changes of plea were based on a realistic and independent assessment by defendants of their bargaining position (rather than simply relying on the advice of their legal representatives) requires further consideration. Two further studies in the 1970s which were based largely on interviews with defendants help us build up a more accurate picture of the charge bargaining process. Bottoms and McClean found that most late plea changers were advised to plead guilty by their lawyers, and that few welcomed this advice. As they explained:

'. . . these defendants have for many weeks expected to plead not guilty. This intention has been supported by their solicitor—after all, a trained professional. Then, out of nowhere appears a barrister, usually on the morning of the trial, strongly suggesting a change of plea. It is hardly surprising if defendants acquiesce, faced with this predicament; it is also hardly surprising if some of them subsequently resent having acquiesced to last-minute pressure.'[14]

Exactly the same point was made by Baldwin and McConville in their study of late plea changers, one of whom is quoted below:

'I was pleading not guilty all the way through—I was so adamant in my own mind that I'd be found not guilty. I didn't decide to plead guilty. It was decided for me from what the barrister said to me. He said, "This is going to drag on for days because they [the prosecution] won't drop these other offences. If you plead guilty to one, they'll drop these other offences. If you continue to plead not guilty, you'll only antagonise the judge." He said he'd go and see the judge, something which I don't

---

13   Ibid pp 27–29.
14   A Bottoms and J McClean, *Defendants in the Criminal Process* (Routledge and Kegan Paul, 1976) p 130.

readily agree with. He said "My job is wheeling and dealing" and he went to see the judge and said "He's told me that we'll knock so many offences off and you'll get done for one." What could I do? I'd been told that the judge had made his findings even before I went into court. The barrister told me even what the judge was going to do [i.e. impose a fine].'[15]

These later studies revealed that legal advice was crucial in persuading defendants to plead guilty. That the cracked trial is a barrister-centred phenomenon has been more recently confirmed by Bredar:

'This is a drama that usually unfolds in the corridors outside of court, in the barristers' robing rooms, and in the court cells. What generally happens is that prosecuting and defending counsel compare views on the strengths and weaknesses of their respective cases, and, in an indirect way, discuss what it would take from each side to get the case to "crack". Counsel come to a unified view about what would be an appropriate settlement of the matter, and generally that involves dismissal of one or more charges outstanding against the defendant, and guilty pleas to all the remaining charges, or to amended charges . . . Defending counsel discusses the option with his client and instructing solicitors, with an eye towards gaining acceptance.'[16]

In view of this, it is important to examine in more detail the respective roles played by defence and prosecution counsel.

(a) The role of the defence barrister

The organisation of the legal profession into two distinct branches, solicitors and barristers, has an important bearing on charge bargaining. In most cases, a solicitor representing a defendant must hand over the conduct of the case in the Crown Court to a member of the Bar. A defence barrister, on reading the brief prepared by the solicitor, may take a different view of the prospect of winning a case. Indeed, one of the advantages claimed for the split profession is that a barrister, with no direct relationship with the client, is able to be more objective about the prospects of winning a case in court. The introduction of a barrister into the case following committal to the Crown Court may thus lead to a change of plea being advised.[17]

---

[15] J Baldwin and M McConville, *Negotiated Justice* (Martin Robertson, 1977) p 31.
[16] J Bredar, 'Moving Up the Day of Reckoning: Strategies for Attacking the "Cracked Trials" Problem' [1992] Crim LR 153 at 155.
[17] See further J Morison and P Leith, *The Barrister's World* (OUP, 1992) pp 67–69.

It is unlikely that a defence solicitor will dissent from counsel's opinion. The barrister, after all, is the acknowledged expert in the Crown Court arena. Furthermore, as we have seen, most defence solicitors operating in the magistrates' courts seem more interested in settling than contesting cases.[18] It is true that it is because of their advice that many defendants decide to elect trial by jury and plead not guilty. But this may not reflect any genuine commitment to adversarial due process values. Solicitors may have made tactical use of a not guilty plea to strengthen a defendant's bargaining position vis-à-vis the prosecution, to increase the chances of legal aid being granted and so on. In many instances, particularly where conferences are held on the day of the trial, the solicitor will not even be present when counsel advises a client to plead guilty, having sent one of the firm's clerks instead.[19] Ultimately, the high rate of guilty pleas and late plea changing by defendants indicates that many defence solicitors (and their representatives at court) are happy to allow barristers to fulfil their hired gun role of settling cases.[20]

Barristers are self-employed but group together in chambers, sharing office overheads and paying a percentage of their fees to a barristers' clerk. The latter is a pivotal figure whose functions include attracting work from solicitors, allocating briefs within chambers in cases where the solicitor has not specified a particular barrister and negotiating the brief fee. Barristers tend to accept too much work in the expectation that many cases will be settled out of court.[1] This, in itself, provides them with an incentive to try and settle cases through negotiation. But barristers may not wish to achieve a settlement until the day of trial. Under the legal aid scheme the fee chargeable for a straightforward guilty plea case is much smaller than the trial fee obtainable if a case cracks at the last moment.[2] According to Bredar, barristers deny deliberately avoiding early settlement but admit

'that their attention naturally is more focused on their cases which are at the trial (and thus more remunerative) stage, knowing that their cases which are at the earlier, plea review stage will ripen with time.'[3]

---

[18] See section 3(c) of ch 6, above.

[19] See Baldwin and McConville, *Negotiated Justice* (Martin Robertson, 1977) pp 46 and 55. The Crown Court study noted the significant involvement of unqualified staff in Crown Court work, and that 18% of defence respondents had become involved in the case as late as the day before or on the day of the trial itself: Zander and Henderson, op cit pp 194–195.

[20] Morison and Leith, op cit pp 67–69.

[1] Ibid p 64.

[2] See Sch 2 of the Legal Aid in Criminal and Care Proceedings (Costs) Regulations 1989 as amended by the Legal Aid in Criminal and Care Proceedings (Costs) (Amendment) Regulations 1992, (SI 1992/592), in respect of work done on or after April 1992.

[3] Bredar, op cit at 157. See to like effect J Plotnikoff and R Woolfson, *From Committal to Trial: Delay at the Crown Court* (Law Society, 1993) pp 62–65.

By the same token, if a trial fee can be obtained by persuading a client to make a last minute decision to plead guilty, there is little financial incentive to fight a case. As one barrister interviewed by Morison and Leith put it, 'some barristers . . . take the view that if they get paid the same for doing a plea as for doing a trial they will accept . . . the plea and go home by 11.00 o'clock in the morning.'[4]

If, as often happens, barristers find that they cannot conduct a case at all due to pressure of work, then briefs have to be returned to solicitors and another barrister found to handle the case. This happens in nearly half of all contested cases.[5] As barristers are self-employed, a returned brief represents lost income. Barristers who are double-booked commonly wait until the last possible moment before returning a brief. As one barrister has put it, 'You say to yourself, "Well, if something happens to the other case I'll be able to do this one, whereas if I pass it now and something happens to the other case next week I'll be unemployed." '[6] The problem is compounded by the intermediary role played by the barristers' clerks, since they have a direct financial interest in keeping a brief within their chambers. One practising barrister has revealed that often:

'. . . barristers' clerks . . . hang on to a brief even when they know well in advance that the barrister originally instructed will be committed elsewhere. The clerk's aim is to keep the brief within chambers by only informing the solicitor of the difficulty at the eleventh hour, so that he will have no time to try and brief someone else, and will more easily settle for a substitute from the same set of chambers. Often this will be a barrister whom the solicitor does not know, and who is a person of less experience; furthermore because the switch is not made until the last moment the substitute has little time in which to prepare a brief.'[7]

It is thus not surprising that in contested cases a third of defence barristers say that they receive the brief on the day before the hearing or on the day itself.[8] In consequence, barristers commonly arrive at court ill-prepared and ill-disposed to fight on a defendant's behalf, and their conferences with defendants are often hurried last-minute affairs.[9]

---

[4] Op cit p 132.
[5] Zander and Henderson, op cit p 32.
[6] J Morison and P Leith, *The Barrister's World* (OUP, 1992) p 64.
[7] J Caplan, 'The Criminal Bar' in R Hazell (ed), *The Bar on Trial* (Quartet, 1978). See also Royal Commission on Criminal Justice; Submission of Evidence by the Crown Prosecution Service, vol.1 'Evidence', pp 177–178.
[8] Zander and Henderson, op cit p 30.
[9] Defence barristers commonly claim that despite the late receipt of instructions they have sufficient time to prepare the case: ibid. This raises the question of what defence barristers regard as 'adequate' preparation.

Defendants do not see their barrister until the day of the trial in over half of all contested and 'cracked' cases.[10]

Most Crown Court work is funded by the state at a relatively low level and standard fees cover most of the cases handled. As in the magistrates' courts, practitioners say that the only way to make criminal work pay is to turn over a high volume of cases in a relatively standardised fashion.[11] There are, of course, some very able barristers who have a genuine commitment to defence work. In addition, barristers of ability may, because of discrimination on the grounds of race, gender or class, find it impossible to break into the more lucrative areas of the Bar and develop a criminal practice almost by default. None the less, it remains true that the most able (as well as the best connected) young barristers will tend to gravitate towards privately funded commercial work, leaving the inexperienced and the less able to eke out a living by settling cases wherever possible so as to be able to move on to the next brief.

Perhaps of equal importance to these organisational factors, however, is the role allotted to defence counsel in the legal system. It is emphatically not the case that barristers are expected to use every resource at their disposal to secure an acquittal for persons accused of crime. The professional duties of defending counsel are set out in the Code of Conduct for the Bar of England and Wales (5th ed). Paragraph 202 states that:

'A practising barrister has an overriding duty to the court to ensure in the public interest that the proper and efficient administration of justice is achieved: he must assist the court in the administration of justice and must not deceive or knowingly or recklessly mislead the court.'

Thus, the barrister owes a duty first and foremost to the court, and should seek to ensure that justice is administered efficiently. A charge bargain represents an efficient disposal of a case, at least in comparison with the costs of a contested trial. But the Code also refers to the proper administration of justice. Paragraph 203 expands on what is meant by this:

'A practising barrister . . . must promote and protect fearlessly and by all proper and lawful means his lay client's best interests and do so without regard to his own interests or to any consequences to himself or to any other person (including his professional client or fellow members of the legal profession) . . .'

While it is the barrister's job to promote the client's best interests,

---

[10] Ibid p 62.
[11] Morison and Leith, op cit pp 43–44.

this is not necessarily to be achieved by fighting the case to the finish. That defence counsel have a duty to impress upon defendants the advantages that may be secured by agreeing to a charge bargain was stressed by Lord Parker CJ in *Hall*.[12] The appellant claimed that he had been pressurised into pleading guilty by his counsel. In dismissing the appeal, Lord Parker had this to say:

'What the Court is looking to see is whether a prisoner in these circumstances has a free choice; the election must be his, the responsibility his, to plead Guilty or Not Guilty. At the same time, it is the clear duty of any counsel representing a client to assist the client to make up his mind by putting forward the pros and cons, if need be in strong language, to impress upon the client what the likely results are of certain courses of conduct.'[13]

In other words, barristers are obliged by law to make plain to defendants the considerable advantages to be gained through pleading guilty as part of a charge bargain. But the fact that a negotiated plea generally coincides with a barrister's self-interest should make us wary of the proposition that a charge bargain will only be struck when that is in the client's best interests.

(b) The role of prosecuting counsel

Since the CPS lacks rights of audience in the higher criminal courts, it is obliged to brief barristers in private practice. A barrister may be defending one day and prosecuting the next. The Bar claims that this arrangement is advantageous, since it puts the conduct of both sides of a criminal case into the hands of professional and independent lawyers with no psychological commitment to either prosecution or defence. As one barrister interviewed by Morison and Leith expressed it:

'We're independent . . . we get papers—defending or prosecuting—we take a totally objective view and if the client is totally up a gum tree or being stupid I can advise him so... By the same token, the prosecution service may be obsessed with the guilt of an individual even though there's bugger all evidence against him and I, by looking at it afresh from an objective standpoint, can advise them to the contrary.'[14]

This suggests that in the higher courts a defendant is better protected from 'unfair' charge bargaining than in the magistrates' courts because prosecuting counsel are not so concerned with achieving 'a

---

12 (1968) 52 Cr App Rep 528.
13 Ibid at 534–535.
14 J Morison and P Leith, *The Barrister's World* (OUP, 1992) p 67.

result'. Whereas a Crown prosecutor might seek to get a result even in a weak case through a charge bargain, a more objective barrister would simply drop the case altogether. Conversely, where a Crown prosecutor might give too much weight to the bureaucratic demand for efficiency and case settlement, prosecuting counsel would follow the path of justice by prosecuting the case in accordance with the evidence.

The claim to objectivity needs to be seen in the light of how prosecuting and defence work is allocated and conducted in practice. Many barristers become typecast as either defenders or prosecutors. The Crown Prosecution Service, for example, maintains a panel of barristers to whom as a matter of course briefs will be sent. These barristers may well become 'prosecution-minded' and in any event would be anxious not to jeopardise an important source of business by ignoring the wishes of their institutional client. According to Bredar, once counsel have reached a 'unified view' of the appropriate settlement of the case:

'Prosecuting counsel then communicates this view to a CPS law clerk or lawyer, cautiously advising in favour of the proposal . . . CPS law clerks, often in consultation with CPS lawyers over the telephone, seem to be the critical decision-makers: ie once they "bless" the arrangement, the trial quickly "cracks".'[15]

This scarcely accords with the official image of the fearless independent barrister projected by the Bar. Prosecuting counsel have much the same financial and practical interest in driving charge bargains as do their defence counterparts. Briefs are passed on by prosecuting counsel in around 60% of contested cases and half of prosecuting barristers receive their brief either on the day before the hearing or on the day itself.[16] One barrister interviewed by Morison and Leith complained that:

'. . . the public purse is very carefully monitored these days . . . most of the cases I do are standard fee cases where you get the same fee for prosecuting whether it's a plea or a trial . . . That is why so many cases go short, because certain members of my profession like to earn as much money for as little effort.'[17]

As with defence barristers, however, it would be misleading to portray a prosecuting barrister engaging in charge bargaining as having

[15] J Bredar, 'Moving Up the Day of Reckoning: Strategies for Attacking the "Cracked Trials" Problem' [1992] Crim LR 153 at 155.

[16] M Zander and P Henderson, The Crown Court study (Royal Commission on Criminal Justice, Research Study no 19) pp 30-32. See also Royal Commission on Criminal Justice, Submission of Evidence by the Crown Prosecution Service, vol 1 'Evidence', p 177, n 66.

[17] J Morison and P Leith, The Barrister's World (OUP, 1992) p 44.

deviated from a legal duty to fight cases. According to the Court of Appeal in *Herbert*,[18] the practice whereby counsel indicated that the Crown would be prepared to accept pleas of guilty to lesser offences than those charged, or to certain only of the charges, had long been accepted as properly part of counsel's duty. This duty involved satisfying the public interest in prosecuting serious wrongdoing while, on the other hand, not necessarily pursuing every charge regardless of the public purse. The decision confirms that charge bargaining is part of a prosecuting barrister's duty, not a deviation from it.

The implications of this discussion of the role of barristers in the Crown Court may now be spelled out. Barristers, whether defending or prosecuting, are expected to bargain over charges. The organisation of the Bar means that such negotiations tend to take place at a late stage between parties predisposed to compromise. The close-knit social world of a local Bar means that the negotiating parties will, in all likelihood, have concluded many similar agreements in the past and that a relationship of trust will have built up between them. This is important, for, as Moody and Tombs noted in their study of charge bargaining in Scotland, the 'degree to which either party is prepared to negotiate with the other depends very much on a mutual exchange of respect and understanding.'[19] Agreement is facilitated by the fact that both sides are bound by the same code of professional ethics and owe a duty to the court to pursue the efficient administration of justice.

The interest in maintaining good relations with other barristers (and with judges seeking to manage a heavy caseload) may come to assume more importance than the interests of an individual defendant who will probably never be encountered again. As Galanter succinctly expresses it: 'Loyalty is often deflected from the one-time client to the forum or opposite party with whom the lawyer has continuing relations.'[20] In this situation, it is both tempting and easy for barristers to convince clients that their best interests lie in pleading guilty when this is not in fact so. The defence barrister's habit of lowering a defendant's expectations while creating a good impression of the legal service being offered is noted by Morison and Leith.[1] As one barrister told them:

'You always give the client the worst prognosis . . . there is not a barrister at the criminal bar who has not learned that lesson by under

---

[18] (1991) 94 Cr App Rep 230.

[19] S Moody and J Tombs, 'Plea Negotiations in Scotland' [1983] Crim LR 297 at 305.

[20] M Galanter, 'Mega-Law and Mega-Lawyering in the Contemporary United States' in R Dingwall and P Lewis (eds), *The Sociology of the Professions* (Macmillan, 1983) p 159.

[1] Op cit p 70.

estimating what the client would get and then getting the shock of his life . . .'[2]

It is in this context that one must place the finding of the Crown Court survey that the great majority of defendants expressed satisfaction with the service provided by their legal representatives.[3] Defence barristers are, after all, skilled advocates and it is no real surprise to find that defendants are persuaded into believing that their interests have been well served. The stark conclusion reached by Moody and Tombs suggests that the defendants' perceptions are often mistaken:

'there are constant factors which must be present if prosecution and defence are to agree. These centre round the notion of trust resulting in a co-alignment of interests and co-operation between traditional adversaries, while the accused, in the vast majority of cases where pleas are negotiated, stands to gain very little in material terms.'[4]

In such a situation, is there not a need for some judicial oversight of the charge bargaining process? The answer is more problematic than one might suppose.

(c)   Judicial supervision of charge bargaining

If anyone could be expected to monitor the propriety of charge bargains, it would surely be the judge. The judiciary's role as professional dispensers of justice would seem to mark them out as especially fitted for this task. According to McCabe and Purves, every one of the charge bargains they identified had been expressly endorsed by the judge.[5] Zander too argues that judicial supervision provides a safeguard in this area, citing in support the 'Yorkshire Ripper' case in 1981.[6] Here, the trial judge refused to endorse the prosecution's acceptance of Peter Sutcliffe's plea of guilty to manslaughter, insisting that the original murder charge be proceeded with.

At one time, the appellate courts required that the charge brought should correspond to the facts alleged. In *Coe*,[7] for instance, the court deprecated charge reduction in the interests of convenience and

---

[2]   Ibid pp 136–137.
[3]   Zander and Henderson, op cit p 67. Note too the erroneous belief of many suspects in the police station that the police inform them of all their rights (see ch 4).
[4]   Op cit at 307.
[5]   Op cit p 29. See also Bredar, op cit at 155.
[6]   M Zander, *Cases and Materials on the English Legal System* (Weidenfeld and Nicolson, 1992) p 293.
[7]   (1969) 53 Cr App Rep 66. This echoed the earlier case of *Soanes* (1948) 32 Cr App Rep 136.

ruled that the overriding consideration must always be the proper administration of justice. This attitude has since been replaced by a recognition of the advantages of charge bargaining and the dangers of judicial involvement. We have already seen that in *Herbert*[8] the Court of Appeal accepted that it was proper for prosecuting counsel to take into account the savings in public expenditure that a charge bargain could achieve. The Court of Appeal in *Grafton*[9] has now decided that the trial judge is powerless to prevent Counsel dropping or reducing any charges except where the latter seeks the seal of judicial approval for a proposed deal. This rule (and its exception) is an incentive for counsel to keep judges out of charge bargaining altogether. Thus, if a case similar to that of Peter Sutcliffe were to go before the courts today, prosecuting counsel would be free to accept a plea of guilty to manslaughter so long as no express sanction was sought from the judge.

Should one classify *Grafton* as laying down a crime control-based enabling rule—allowing counsel to pursue charge bargaining free of judicial interference? Or is it merely a rule which legitimises a long-established practice? The answer depends on how far trial judges had previously ensured that charge bargains were based, as far as they can be, on considerations of justice rather than merely convenience and efficiency.

What is the evidence on this point ? The Peter Sutcliffe case provides an example of due process-inspired judicial control, but there are many other cases which tend to show that trial judges are just as likely to encourage as restrict the practice of charge bargaining. In, for example, *Winterflood*[10] the judge had sent for counsel after four days of the trial and asked if the defendant would plead guilty to handling stolen property if a robbery charge was dropped. The defendant agreed to this but appealed against the sentence imposed. In dismissing the appeal, the Court of Appeal stressed that private discussions before or during a trial were undesirable but that there was no reason why the discussion in this case should not have taken place, in the absence of the jury, in open court. Similarly, in *Llewellyn*[11] the Court of Appeal emphasised that trial judges should not feel inhibited from taking part in pre-trial reviews to discuss such matters as the correct way of proceeding with the charges brought.

The great majority of Crown Court judges are recruited from the ranks of the practising Bar. Many hold part-time appointments only, spending most of their time as barristers rather than judges. Prosecution and defence counsel have little to fear in seeking the approval of a judge

[8]   (1991) 94 Cr App Rep 230.
[9]   (1992) 96 Cr App Rep 156.
[10] [1979] Crim LR 263.
[11] (1978) 67 Cr App Rep 149.

for a charge bargain, since all of the parties involved share a common outlook, all stand to gain from short-circuiting the formal trial process and all are encouraged to enter into negotiations by the Court of Appeal. The appellate courts proclaim that charge bargains should represent a proper, not merely an inexpensive, outcome to a case, but is this mere lip service to the interests of justice ? The point, after all, of these bargains is to circumvent the very safeguards and procedural protections designed to discover the truth and to produce justice. To take just one example, the rationale for the rule that a jury should not be told of an accused's previous convictions is that the prejudicial effect of this knowledge would outweigh any probative value. Yet barristers engaged in charge bargaining act in full knowledge of any previous record that an accused might have. It is easy to see how a presumption of guilt might arise in these circumstances. The judge, whose independence is supposed to protect defendants against improper pressure, is merely an interested spectator (and potential dealer) at the market place of justice.

Charge bargaining has generated an enormous amount of critical literature in the academic journals. Its potential to undermine adversarial due process and to increase the risk that innocent persons will plead guilty is well understood. This makes it all the more remarkable that the report of the Runciman Commission dealt with the subject in a single sentence:

'We see no objection to such discussions, but the earlier they take place the better; consultation between counsel before the trial would often avoid the need for the case to be listed as a contested trial.'[12]

On this subject, as on many others, the Runciman Commission failed to cite any evidence or marshal any supporting arguments to justify its preference for more crime control.[13]

3.   THE SENTENCING DISCOUNT IN ENGLISH LAW

The principle of sentencing, that a discount should generally be given to those pleading guilty, is well established. For example, in the case of

---

[12]   Royal Commission on Criminal Justice, Report (Cm 2263) (HMSO, 1993) p 114. Many of its recommendations were designed to guarantee earlier communication between opposing counsel. For example, a requirement that the defence disclose its case in outline was supported, in part, because this might result in 'an earlier resolution through a plea of guilty' (p 97) and see also pp 101–108 on encouraging 'pre-trial preparation'.

[13]   Note that not one of the 22 research studies funded by the Runciman Commission was on plea bargaining.

Cain Lord Widgery CJ remarked: 'Everyone knows that it is so and there is no doubt about it. Any accused person who does not know about it should know about it. The sooner he knows the better.'[14] It was said in *Boyd* in similarly robust terms that 'the court encourages pleas of guilty by knocking something off the sentence which would have been imposed if there had not been a plea of guilty.'[15]

Baldwin and McConville argued that the sentence discount principle was so important that:

'there is no other single consideration that so pervades the workings of the whole administration of criminal justice or so conditions and directs the nature of the choices open to a defendant.'[16]

This overstates the importance of the sentence discount principle per se. As we have seen, it plays little part in the thinking of magistrates. Moreover, the most effective way of minimising punishment is to keep the case in the magistrates' court. Failing this, the next most effective way is to strike a charge bargain with the prosecution following committal to the Crown Court. This entails pleading guilty of course, so the discount principle should be applied in such cases. But avoidance of the additional punishment that a defendant would have received had the original charge been contested is achieved largely through the substitution of a less serious charge rather than through credit being given by the judge for a guilty plea. Where the prosecution is unwilling to bargain over the charges, however, the main incentive to plead guilty derives squarely from the sentence discount principle.

Parliament has traditionally eschewed any attempt to control and regulate the sentencing function of judges, leaving the principles that govern the sentencing decision to be gradually developed by the Court of Appeal on a case-by-case basis. One consequence of this is that any statement of the law in this area has to recognise the degree of uncertainty or flexibility inherent in the common law. Cases may contradict each other, judgments may be expressed in vague or ambiguous language and complex questions may arise under the doctrine of precedent as to whether a judge is bound by what was said in a previous case. Moreover, judicial decision making is usually focused on the circumstances of the particular case with little regard for broader issues. It is not surprising, therefore, that judicial precedents usually require further refinement or elaboration through later cases. It is thus to a complex

---

[14] [1976] Crim LR 464.
[15] (1980) 2 Cr App Rep (S) 234.
[16] J Baldwin and M McConville, 'The Influence of the Sentencing Discount in Inducing Guilty Pleas' in J Baldwin and A Bottomley (eds), *Criminal Justice: Selected Readings* (Martin Robertson, 1978) p 116.

body of continually developing case law that one must turn in exploring the sentencing principle under discussion.

(a)   The rationale of the principle

Why do the courts seek to encourage guilty pleas? The obvious rationale lies in the time and expense that is saved when an accused agrees to plead guilty.[17] The average hearing time for a contested trial is seven hours, compared with 54 minutes for a guilty plea case.[18] The Home Office has estimated that, leaving aside the most serious offences, the average cost of a contested case in the Crown Court is £12,088 compared with £1,400 for a guilty plea case.[19] The savings involved in encouraging guilty pleas are clearly substantial and have grown as the workload of the Crown Court has increased. Since 1982, the annual number of cases committed to the Crown Court has shown an average growth rate of just over 4%, and reached a total of 100,994 cases in 1992.[20]

An important subsidiary factor is that by pleading guilty the defendant spares any witnesses from having to attend court and from what may be the distressing experience of giving evidence. If, for example, a defendant contests a charge of rape, the complainant will nearly always face lengthy cross-examination about her previous sexual history in an attempt to destroy her credibility as a witness.[1] It is seen as appropriate in such cases to reward a guilty plea.[2] An important affirmation of the Court of Appeal's stance on the sentencing discount has been provided by Lord Taylor CJ in *Buffrey*.[3] In the context of complicated fraud cases, he observed, there were many reasons why a guilty plea should be rewarded with a reduction in sentence length:

---

[17]   Cases in which this was explicitly recognised include *Boyd* (1980) 2 Cr App Rep (S) 234, *Hollington and Emmens* (1985) 7 Cr App Rep (S) 364 and *Buffrey* (1993) 14 Cr App Rep (S) 511.

[18]   Judicial Statistics 1992 (Cm 2268) Lord Chancellor's Department (HMSO, 1993) p 65, Table 6.20.

[19]   Costs of the Criminal Justice System 1992, (Home Office, 1992) vol, p 16. For the most serious offences, such as murder and rape, no comparison is possible as nearly all defendants plead not guilty.

[20]   Judicial Statistics 1992 (Cm 2268) (Lord Chancellor's Department) (HMSO, 1993) pp 56 and 59, Table 6.1.

[1]   For discussion, see J Temkin, 'Sexual History Evidence—the Ravishment of Section 2' [1993] Crim LR 3.

[2]   See *Barnes* (1983) 5 Cr App Rep (S) 368 (where a plea of guilt had spared the victim of an attempted rape from having to give evidence about the incident) and *Sullivan* (1987) 9 Cr App Rep (S) 492. See also *Billam* (1986) 82 Cr App Rep 347 which, in laying down sentencing guidelines for those convicted of rape, incorporated the discount principle on this basis.

[3]   (1992) 14 Cr App Rep (S) 511.

'Some reduction must be made, as frauds of this kind were so complex and took such a long time to unravel, that they became a burden to the criminal justice system. They were costly in time and money, and caused stress to jurors who had to try them, judges who had to try them, and to witnesses and the defendants themselves.'[4]

As the case of *Cain* (above) shows, the courts are keen for a guilty plea to be entered at the earliest opportunity, as that allows the maximum savings for the system to be made. In comparison with straightforward guilty plea cases, late pleas may involve considerable inconvenience and expense for the courts, for witnesses, for jurors and so on. The Court of Appeal has accordingly sought to discourage defendants from changing their pleas at a late stage in the court proceedings. This is illustrated by *Hollington and Emmens*.[5] The defendant was in custody awaiting trial and in order to keep certain privileges allowed to remand prisoners maintaining their innocence he initially entered a plea of not guilty. He changed his plea late in the proceedings. The Court of Appeal noted that such tactical pleas of not guilty caused a considerable waste of resources and continued:

'The sooner it was appreciated that defendants are not going to get full discount for pleas of guilty in these sort of circumstances, the better it will be for the administration of justice.'[6]

The judgment in this case emphasises that a substantial discount can be obtained by those who on arrest admit guilt and co-operate fully with the police (by, for example, providing information on accomplices or by asking for other offences to be 'taken into consideration').[7] A caveat was entered, however, by the court which noted that if an arrested person does not have much in the way of a defence to the charge then he or she cannot expect much by way of a discount for pleading guilty.

What this case demonstrates is that the sentencing discount is not fixed. The value of the guilty plea to the courts gradually reduces as time wears on and the size of the discount reduces correspondingly. The full discount is only to be offered to those with something substantial to offer in return. But *Hollington and Emmens* also shows that it is not

---

[4] Ibid at 515.
[5] (1985) 82 Cr App Rep 281.
[6] Ibid at 285.
[7] Defendants who would have escaped detection but for their voluntary decision to admit guilt are entitled to even more by way of a discount. See *Hoult* [1990] Crim LR 664, in which the Court of Appeal recognised that a defendant who had gone to a police station to give himself up three years after committing a robbery was entitled to a greater than usual discount.

just a question of the timing of the guilty plea. It seems that those facing strong prosecution evidence were presumed by the court to have little option but to plead guilty, and, therefore, that it would be inappropriate to provide them with much of a reward for doing so. For those facing weak prosecution cases who plead guilty a reward is regarded as appropriate. By this means, defendants are not merely rewarded for their noble decisions to own up to their wrongdoing, they are also being induced to waive their right to put the prosecution to proof. The reasoning in *Hollington and Emmens* comes close to saying that the weaker the prosecution case, the more likely it is that the defendant will put the prosecution to proof and the greater the sentencing discount will need to be to induce the defendant to plead guilty.

This departure from due process values is no less marked than that represented by charge bargaining and the objections are similar in both cases.[8] In brief, the sentencing discount, by encouraging defendants to convict themselves through a guilty plea, reduces the effect of the due process principle that the burden of proof rests on the prosecution. The prosecution of cases involving no more than vague allegations and other potential misuses of state prosecutorial power may be left unchecked. Moreover, the high guilty plea rate to which the sentence discount contributes means that there is little incentive for the prosecuting authorities to ensure that only properly prepared cases are brought to trial. The number of weak cases prosecuted is likely to increase, as is the number of innocent persons wrongly convicted.

A further problem is that the discount principle penalises those who stand on their right to put the prosecution to proof. This is an elementary point and yet many would dispute it. The argument put forward by the judiciary and supported by a number of commentators is that those pleading guilty are rewarded for so doing rather than those pleading not guilty being punished for contesting their case.[9] In the case of *Harper*,[10] the trial judge had commented in critical terms on the way in which the defendant, through his counsel, had conducted his case. The Court of Appeal reduced the sentence from five years' to three years' imprisonment. Its reasons were given by Lord Parker CJ:

---

[8] The due process objections to charge bargaining are set out in ch 6, section 3(b), above. Note that the law prohibits the police from offering suspects inducements to confess (see ch 4). Why should different standards be adopted in these two different contexts?

[9] See eg E Stockdale and K Devlin, *Sentencing* (Waterlow, 1987) p 50 and J Sprack in E Stockdale and S Casale (eds), *Criminal Justice Under Stress* at (Blackstone, 1992) p 86.

[10] [1968] 2 QB 108.

'this court feels that there is a real danger . . . that the appellant was being given what was undoubtedly a serious sentence because he had pleaded not guilty and had run his defence in the way indicated by the recorder. This court feels it is quite improper to use language which may convey that an accused is being sentenced because he has pleaded not guilty, or because he has run his defence in a particular way. It is, however, of course proper to give a man a lesser sentence if he has shown genuine remorse, amongst other things by pleading guilty.'[11]

This judgment seems more concerned with the language of sentencing than its substance, for there are no 'standard' sentences for any crime which can function as a baseline below or above which cases with mitigating or aggravating characteristics can be judged. Ashworth et al examined the sentencing practices of two judges and found that neither was aware of his own pattern of sentencing. In one drugs case, for example, the judge said the offence merited 21 months, but that the sentence would only be 15 months because of mitigating factors; in reality his average sentence for the weight of cannabis involved was 12 months. The authors of the study concluded that:

'. . . this lack of self-awareness seemed to stem from the absence of a fixed point from which to make a reduction for mitigating factors . . . when a judge states in court (and himself believes) that he is passing a lower sentence so as to take account of a mitigating factor, he may not actually be making that reduction. The judge may feel that he is being merciful . . . and the offender may believe that he has been fortunate, but the judge's unawareness of his own sentencing practices may mean that none of this is so.'[12]

This is not to say that all sentencing is arbitrary but it is certainly not a mechanical exercise the outcome of which is capable of exact prediction. The Court of Appeal has done little to discourage inconsistency in sentencing. In *Taylor and Rutherford*[13] for example, the defendant appealed against a sentence on the ground that it was longer than that imposed in a similar case.[14] The Court of Appeal rejected the appeal,

---

[11] At 110. The argument that a plea of guilty should be rewarded because it evinces remorse is occasionally referred to by the courts (see also *Turner* [1970] 2 QB 321) but it is unconvincing. The courts have no sure way of distinguishing between guilty pleas motivated by remorse and those entered simply in order to avoid a greater degree of punishment.

[12] A Ashworth, E Genders, G Mansfield, J Peay, and E Player, *Sentencing in the Crown Court* (Occasional Paper no 10) (Oxford Centre for Criminological Research, 1984) p 49.

[13] [1983] Crim LR 693.

[14] *Sequeira* (1982) 4 Cr App Rep (S) 65.

observing that there could be no fixed tariff on any sentencing matter. Previous sentencing decisions were not to be treated as binding precedents, although they could provide guidance on an appropriate sentence. This still begs the question of what is the appropriate sentence and allows such disparities that it is often impossible to clarify 'standard' sentences for particular offences.[15]

To characterise a guilty plea as mitigation rather than a not guilty plea as aggravation is in any case hypocritical. The inescapable consequence of the sentence discount is that a significant price may have to be paid for putting the prosecution to proof, something which the defendants interviewed by Baldwin and McConville well understood:

'. . . it is easy to see why defendants often regard this sort of reasoning as meaningless. As far as we can tell, the sentencing differential is viewed by virtually all defendants as a penalty imposed on those who unsuccessfully contest their case.'[16]

The judges want to have it both ways. They support the operation of a principle derived from crime control considerations of efficiency and expediency while denying that its practical operation undermines the due process right to put the prosecution to proof.

The tension between the requirements of due process and crime control becomes acute in cases involving co-defendants facing identical charges where one pleads guilty and one not guilty. If a discount is given for a plea of guilty in this situation, it will be immediately apparent to all that the defendant pleading not guilty has received a harsher punishment for doing so regardless of what the judge might say. The Court of Appeal has been prepared to sanction difference of treatment in cases where the discount has merely resulted in a shorter custodial sentence for the defendant pleading guilty, but has equivocated where the disparity has been greater. In *Hollyman*,[17] three defendants were convicted on an identical charge. One received three months' immediate imprisonment and the others two months' imprisonment suspended for two years. The Court of Appeal ruled that it was sufficient justification for the different sentences that the latter pleaded guilty whilst the former contested the case. In *Tonks*,[18] by contrast, the Court of Appeal said that such a course of action would leave the imprisoned offender

---

[15] See the discussion by M Wasik, 'Sentencing: A Fresh Look at Aims and Objectives' in E Stockdale and S Casale (eds), *Criminal Justice Under Stress* (Blackstone, 1992).

[16] J Baldwin and M McConville, 'The Influence of the Sentencing Discount in Inducing Guilty Pleas' in J Baldwin and A Bottomley (eds), *Criminal Justice: Selected Readings* (Martin Robertson, 1978) p 119.

[17] (1979) 1 Cr App Rep (S) 289.

[18] [1980] Crim LR 59.

with a legitimate sense of grievance. The irreconcilability of these two decisions shows how equivocal the courts are about applying due process principles strictly.

(b) How large is the sentencing discount?

The appellate courts have been reluctant to specify a standard discount, arguing that sentencing is a subjective exercise which must be tailored to all the circumstances of each individual case.[19] This position has been endorsed in *Buffrey*[20] by Lord Taylor CJ:

'It would be quite wrong for us to suggest that there was any absolute rule as to what the discount should be. Each case must be assessed by the trial judge on its own facts and there will be considerable variance as between one case and another.'[1]

On the other hand, the Court of Appeal has been prepared to allow appeals against sentence on the ground that insufficient discount was given in return for a plea of guilty.[2] This suggests that some convention or standard is operating to produce a discount of between one-quarter and one-third,[3] or even more in special circumstances.[4] The principle that everything depends on the context and circumstances of each individual case was taken to its logical conclusion in *Costen*.[5] Here the Court of Appeal said that the sentencing discount could be withheld altogether if there had been a last-minute tactical change of plea or if the offender had been caught 'red-handed' and there was no possible defence to the charge.[6] However, it is rare to withhold the discount completely. In *Davis*,[7] some bank robbers had been caught 'red-handed'

---

[19] See eg the case of *Williams* [1983] Crim LR 693.

[20] (1992) 14 Cr App Rep (S) 511.

[1] Ibid at 515.

[2] See eg *Skilton and Blackham* (1983) 4 Cr App Rep (S) 339 and *Boyd* (1980) 2 Cr App Rep (S) 234. In *Buffrey* itself, the sentence was reduced on appeal from five years' imprisonment to four years' imprisonment.

[3] See *Williams* [1983] Crim LR 693 and the accompanying commentary at 694.

[4] See *Buffrey*, above, where Lord Taylor CJ acknowledged that in complex cases, where great savings were produced by a guilty plea, it might be proper to award a discount of one-third to late plea changers. It follows that those pleading guilty from the outset in such cases should be rewarded by an even bigger discount.

[5] (1989) 11 Cr App Rep (S) 182.

[6] Following *Morris* (1988) 10 Cr App Rep (S) 216. Two further exceptions to the mitigating effect of a guilty plea were enumerated by Lord Lane CJ: where a long sentence, possibly the maximum sentence, was thought necessary to protect the public (following *Stabler* (1984) 6 Cr App Rep (S) 129) and where, as in *Costen*, the offender had been convicted on a 'specimen' count.

[7] (1980) 2 Cr App Rep (S) 168.

and their subsequent pleas of guilty were accordingly treated as irrelevant to sentencing. On appeal, however, a different view was taken:

'[T]he court bears in mind that these kinds of criminal will do anything at their trial to evade verdicts of guilty. They often do so by making attacks on police officers and by trying to beguile the jury into believing that in some way they have been treated unfairly. Fortunately they seldom succeed, but in the course of failing they waste much public time and money. They should be encouraged, as far as it is possible to encourage criminals, to stop these sort of tactics.'[8]

Because the defendants had chosen not to waste the court's time in this way, a modest discount was allowed, but the fact that this is not always the result of an appeal[9] demonstrates that this area of 'law' is not rule-bound and hence arguably not law as conventionally understood at all. Similarly, there is scant authority as to whether the discount can change the nature as well as the quantum of the sentence.[10] In view of the apparent uncertainty displayed by the relatively small number of Court of Appeal judges about the nature and size of the guilty plea discount, it is not surprising to find even more uncertainty—and hence disparity—among the Crown Court judges sentencing on an everyday basis.[11] The way in which the discount principle is applied in practice has been examined in three separate studies by Hood, Moxon, and Baldwin and McConville.[12] The last of these reports a spectrum of views on the discount principle:

'Some judges regard a reduction of perhaps a quarter or a third of whatever sentence is to be imposed as a fair reward in most cases for a guilty plea; others view any reduction in sentence as being solely conditional upon evidence of contrition on the part of the defendant which is recognised as a fairly exceptional occurrence.'[13]

---

[8] Ibid at 170.

[9] See *Morris* (1988) 10 Cr App Rep (S) 216 and *Stabler* (1984) 6 Cr App Rep (S) 129.

[10] But see *Hollyman* (1979) 1 Cr App Rep (S) 289, discussed above. The case of *Okinikan* (1993) 14 Cr App Rep (S) 453 holds that a plea of guilty in combination with other mitigating factors may make the difference between an immediate prison sentence and a non-custodial disposal, such as a fine or a community service order.

[11] Dissatisfaction with and ignorance of Court of Appeal sentencing principles amongst Crown Court judges is reported by A Ashworth et al, op cit p 49.

[12] R Hood, *Race and Sentencing* (OUP, 1992) p 87; D Moxon, Sentencing Practice in the Crown Court (Home Office Research Study, no 103) (HMSO, 1988) and J Baldwin and M McConville, 'The Influence of the Sentencing Discount in Inducing Guilty Pleas' in J Baldwin and A Bottomley (eds), *Criminal Justice: Selected Readings* (Martin Robertson, 1978) p 119.

[13] Baldwin and McConville, 'The Influence of the Sentencing Discount in Inducing Guilty Pleas', op cit p 119.

However, all three studies suggested that Crown Court sentencing was consistent with the overall pattern of Court of Appeal judgments in a number of respects: firstly, discounts are generally being awarded for pleas of guilty; secondly, as expected, sentence lengths are being affected by guilty pleas; and thirdly, the type of sentence itself is often determined by whether or not someone pleads guilty. This last point is crucial, as the pressure exerted on defendants to plead guilty by the sentencing discount is obviously much greater if the plea can make the difference between a custodial and non-custodial sentence. Although few appellate cases have dealt with the question of whether such a large sentencing differential is justified, this body of research suggests that Crown Court judges grant these large discounts almost as a matter of course.

One aspect of judicial practice is not consistent with the legal position, however. Late plea changers should, in legal theory, be receiving smaller discounts than those who pleaded guilty at an early stage. Yet despite the fact that the latter undoubtedly contributed more to the efficient administration of justice by the timing of their pleas of guilty, they received less of a reward than the late plea changers in both Baldwin and McConville's study and, to a lesser extent, in that conducted by Moxon. This is consistent with a model of bargaining in which last minute concessions are offered by or wrung out of judges when it is clear that the defendant will otherwise stick with a plea of not guilty.

The Runciman Commission supported the sentencing discount principles developed by the Court of Appeal. In particular, it saw value in giving the greatest discounts for those pleading guilty at an early stage, but agreed that judges must retain their discretion to fix the discount according to the circumstances of the individual case.[14] It recommended that the principle that an early plea of guilty merits the largest discount should be more clearly articulated so as to have greater effect. This immediately raises the question: 'effect on whom?'. The Runciman Commission accepted that it would be 'naive to suppose that innocent persons never plead guilty because of the prospect of the sentence discount'[15] but did not seem worried by this. It rejected the possibility that clearer articulation of the discount principle would increase the risk that defendants may plead guilty to offences which they did not commit.[16] No consideration was given to the argument that early pleas of guilty undermine the due process principle that it is for the prosecution to prove guilt.

[14] Royal Commission on Criminal Justice, Report (Cm 2263) (HMSO, 1993) pp 111–112.
[15] Ibid p 110.
[16] Ibid p 112.

Research by Hood discovered that Afro-Caribbeans tend to plead not guilty more frequently than whites and so are more frequently denied the benefit of the sentence discount principle.[17] This highlights the potential of the principle to work grave injustice. Is it acceptable that blacks receive longer custodial sentences than whites simply because they exercise the right to put the prosecution to proof? To the crime control adherent, this pattern of sentencing would be regarded as the product of the need for efficiency, it being mere coincidence that it happens to impinge more on blacks than whites. From the due process perspective, however, it is predictable that blacks would plead not guilty more often than whites, as one would expect them to more often be at the receiving end of abuses of police and prosecutorial power.[18]

The fact that the sentencing discount produces a form of indirect racial discrimination strengthens the due process argument for abandoning (or at least watering down) this principle of sentencing. By contrast, the Runciman Commission reacted to the research evidence by expressing its support for 'the recommendation made by Hood that the policy of offering sentence discounts should be kept under review.'[19] It was somewhat disingenuous of the Runciman Commission to imply that Hood had merely called for this policy to be kept under review. Rather, he considered that:

'it is time to consider all the implications of a policy which favours so strongly those who plead guilty, when ethnic minorities are less willing to forego their right to challenge a prosecution.'[20]

As Ashworth observes, 'the Commission was wrong to procrastinate on such an important issue.'[1] It is difficult to avoid the conclusion that the Runciman Commission here adopted the crime control position of placing greatest weight on the need for efficiency within the criminal process, and turned a myopic eye towards the evidence of the injustice both produced and compounded by the discount principle.

(c)   The communication of the discount to the defendant

Barristers would be failing in their legal duty if they did not advise defendants about the discount. As Lord Parker CJ put it in the leading case of *Turner*:

---

[17] R Hood, *Race and Sentencing* (OUP, 1992) pp 202–203.
[18] The process by which blacks become over-represented within the criminal system begins with the discriminatory exercise of police powers to stop-search: see ch 2.
[19] Report, op cit p 114.
[20] Op cit p 182.
[1] A Ashworth, 'Plea, Venue and Discontinuance' [1993] Crim LR 830 at 838.

'Counsel must be completely free to do what is his duty, namely to give the accused the best advice he can and, if need be, advice in strong terms. This will often include advice that a plea of guilty, showing an element of remorse, is a mitigating factor which may well enable the court to give a lesser sentence than would otherwise be the case.'[2]

Although Lord Parker went on to say that the defendant, 'having considered counsel's advice, must have a complete freedom of choice whether to plead guilty or not guilty',[3] one may question whether such freedom can co-exist with strong advice from counsel to plead guilty.

Baldwin and McConville's study of late plea changers revealed that 40% of defendants had changed their plea simply as a result of pressure exerted by their barristers, in over half of which 'the advice counsel gave was of such a nature that no reasonable person could say that it was fair or proper or that the final decision to plead guilty was made voluntarily.'[4] One defendant interviewed explained:

'My barrister compelled me to plead guilty. He threatened me saying, "You will go to gaol for three years if you plead not guilty, the case will go on for a long time and you will have to pay all the expenses which will come to £400. But if you plead guilty you will just get a fine." He wouldn't listen to what I had to say; he compelled me to plead guilty.'[5]

The large discounts applied by many Crown Court judges thus provide barristers who wish to settle cases with powerful ammunition to fire at defendants. This may seem emotive language but the interviews conducted by Baldwin and McConville justify its use, as a further example shows:

'The barrister then said, "If you're found guilty you will get about 10 or 15 years but if you plead guilty you will get 4 or 5 years." I was really shocked. I was so scared, sweating and nervous and he frightened me with this 10–15 years stuff and saying I had no chance . . . I agreed to plead guilty but it wasn't my decision; I had no choice about it.'[6]

It must be stressed that even defendants represented by barristers of the highest possible integrity will come under pressure to plead guilty. That pressure will not be exerted by the barrister directly, but by a sentencing principle the operation of which effectively undermines due process rights. "Bad" barristers merely exacerbate the problem.

---

[2] [1970] 2 WLR 1093 at 1097.
[3] Ibid.
[4] Op cit p 45.
[5] Ibid p 50.
[6] Ibid pp 49–50.

We have seen that sentencing is an uncertain business, and that the size, nature and even existence of the guilty plea discount is always uncertain. It depends as much upon the judge as on the facts of the case. This makes it difficult for defence lawyers to advise their clients, and can frustrate judges too, whose hints may not be correctly interpreted. Should the law permit judges to indicate to defendants in advance what view they take of the alleged offence in terms of sentencing, and what discount they would be prepared to give if a guilty plea were entered? The advantage of this would be that defendants would know exactly where they stood. The disadvantage would be that the impartiality of the judge would be brought into question by such communications. It might seem as if the judge were seeking to assist the prosecution in obtaining a conviction, thus placing even more pressure on the defendant to plead guilty.

These issues were raised in the case of *Inns*.[7] The judge had sent for counsel before the trial began. There was a dispute as to what had been said in this private discussion but the result was that the defendant had been advised by counsel that if he contested the case against him and lost, an immediate custodial sentence would be imposed. As Lawton LJ, allowing the appeal, put it, 'he crumpled and took the view that contesting the case was not worth the risk.'[8] He pleaded guilty, was convicted and received a conditional discharge. On appeal, his conviction was quashed and a new trial ordered. Lawton LJ stressed in his judgment that:

'. . . the law attaches so much importance to a plea of guilty in open court that no further proof is required of the accused's guilt. When the accused is making a plea of guilty under pressure and threats, he does not make a free plea and the trial starts without there being a proper plea at all. All that follows thereafter is, in our judgment, a nullity.'[9]

This decision appears to be motivated by due process considerations, in that it inhibits judges from exerting pressure on defendants to plead guilty. On the other hand, the discount principle itself exerts such pressure and the advice offered by counsel on this subject can be expressed, according to the case of *Turner*,[10] 'in strong terms' if need be. The courts have sought to resolve this apparent contradiction by holding that strong advice from counsel does not nullify a plea. According to Lord Parker's judgment in *Turner*, any argument that defence counsel went so far in pressing upon a defendant the

---

[7]   (1974) 60 Cr App Rep 231.
[8]   Ibid at 233.
[9]   Ibid.
[10]   [1970] 2 WLR 1093.

advantages of pleading guilty that a free choice of plea was denied is likely to fail: 'The Court would like to say that it is a very extravagant proposition, and one which would only be acceded to in a very extreme case.'[11] The law thus represents an uneasy compromise between due process and crime control values. A concern with due process appears to lie behind the prohibition on trial judges exerting pressure on defendants directly. The influence of the crime control model can be seen in the discount principle itself and in the leeway allowed to counsel in pressing the merits of pleading guilty on a defendant. That such latitude is granted suggests that the decision in *Inns* was motivated more by the need to preserve the appearance of an impartial judiciary than by any real concern with protecting the right of a defendant to put the prosecution to proof.

Turner [1970] remains to this day the leading case regulating what judges may say and do as regards sentencing and the discount principle prior to conviction. Lord Parker ruled that:

'There must be freedom of access between counsel and judge . . . This freedom of access is important because there may be matters calling for communication or discussion, which are of such a nature that counsel cannot in the interests of his client mention them in open court . . . counsel on both sides may wish to discuss with the judge whether it would be proper, in a particular case, for the prosecution to accept a plea to a lesser offence . . .

The judge should, subject to the one exception referred to hereafter, never indicate the sentence which he is minded to impose. A statement that on a plea of guilty he would impose one sentence but that on a conviction following a plea of not guilty he would impose a severer sentence is one which should never be made. This could be taken to be undue pressure on the accused, thus depriving him of that complete freedom of choice which is essential. Such cases, however, are in the experience of the court happily rare. What on occasions does appear to happen however is that a judge will tell counsel that, having read the depositions and the antecedents, he can safely say that on a plea of guilty he will, for instance, make a probation order, something which may be helpful to counsel in advising the accused. The judge in such a case is no doubt careful not to mention what he would do if the accused were convicted following a plea of not guilty. Even so, the accused may well get the impression that the judge is intimating that in that event a severer sentence, maybe a custodial sentence, would result, so that again he may feel under pressure. This accordingly must also not be

---

[11] Ibid at 1096. Only someone completely unaware of the degree of pressure felt by defendants, as discussed above, could regard this as an 'extravagant proposition'.

done. The only exception to this rule is that it should be permissible for a judge to say, if it be the case, that whatever happens, whether the accused pleads guilty or not guilty, the sentence will or will not take a particular form, eg a probation order or a fine, or a custodial sentence.

Finally, where such discussion on sentence has taken place between judge and counsel, counsel for the defence should disclose this to the accused and inform him of what took place.'[12]

Under these '*Turner* rules', judges must not be drawn as to what sentence they have in mind to impose, unless they can say that it will take the same form irrespective of how the defendant decides to plead. This left open the question of whether a judge could indicate that while a particular type of sentence would be imposed irrespective of plea, a discount would be given for a plea of guilty. In other words, could a judge say that the sentence would, for example, definitely be a community service order but that its length would be reduced were the defendant to plead guilty? This point was reviewed in the case of *Cain*.[13] The trial judge had sent for both counsel and opined that the defendant had no defence and if he persisted in a not guilty plea he would get a very severe sentence but a change of plea would make a considerable difference. On being informed of this the defendant pleaded guilty, but appealed against conviction on the ground that he had been denied a free choice of plea. The Court of Appeal accepted that this was so and ordered a retrial. But Lord Widgery muddied the *Turner* waters by observing:

'it was trite to say that a plea of guilty will generally attract a somewhat lighter sentence than a plea of not guilty and a full-dress contest on the issue. Every defendant should know that. What was being condemned was a more precise offer, because the judge was then inviting the defendant to bargain with him. It was not wrong for the judge to state the obvious . . .'[14]

This seemed to allow the judge to refer to the discount principle in general terms so long as no guarantee was given that the discount would be applied in the instant case. Further confusion was caused by *Cain* when Lord Widgery went on to observe that there could be exceptions to the *Turner* rule that where discussions took place between judge and counsel the accused must be informed of what had taken place. Lord Widgery said that if counsel was unfamiliar with the judge's general views on sentencing and wished to obtain guidance as to the sentence the judge had in mind, so that he could properly advise the defendant, he

---

[12]   Ibid at 1097–1098.
[13]   [1976] Crim LR 464.
[14]   Ibid at 465.

need not inform the accused of what had taken place: 'If he had to disclose what the judge had said the confidentiality between judge and counsel would be broken.'[15] This is a remarkable chain of reasoning. It amounts to saying that counsel might justifiably need a precise indication of sentence from a judge in order to advise a client as to his or her best strategy, but must not reveal to the client that the advice is based on a precise indication from the judge. This appears to conflict with the rule in *Turner* which enjoins counsel to give 'best advice' to a client. The confidentiality between judge and counsel is seen as more important than open acknowledgment of judicial involvement in plea bargaining. This preserves the rhetoric of due process and the reality of crime control.

Predictably, the judgment in *Cain* caused puzzlement as to what defence barristers could and could not say to their clients regarding discussions with trial judges. The Court of Appeal took the unusual step of issuing a *Practice Direction*[16] which stated baldly that in so far as *Cain* and *Turner* were inconsistent, *Turner* should prevail. This did not resolve the confusion as it left some doubt as to which parts of the *Cain* decision were inconsistent with *Turner*.[17] The Court of Appeal has responded by reiterating the message of the *Practice Direction* that it is the *Turner* rules which must be followed.[18]

Under the *Turner* rules, a judge can give an indication that, irrespective of plea, a non-custodial sentence will be imposed. There thus remains a considerable incentive for defence counsel to see the judge in private. The only reason a defendant might be unwilling to plead guilty is the fear of receiving an immediate custodial sentence. If a judge can say that, however the defendant pleads, the penalty imposed will be a fine then defence counsel may find it much easier to persuade a client to plead guilty. This, no doubt, is why it was seen as important in *Turner* to leave this option open to the judge.

Yet, by permitting limited discussions to take place about sentencing, the law has opened the door for misunderstandings to arise and for abuse to occur. It seems that many of those operating in the criminal courts have concluded that it is artificial and unrealistic for the law to encourage guilty pleas through the sentence discount whilst simultaneously denying defendants the opportunity to discover exactly what is on offer in the case at hand. In the next section, we argue that both defence counsel and judges have abused their right to meet in private in order to engage in sentence bargaining.

---

[15] Ibid.
[16] [1976] Crim LR 561.
[17] See eg *Bird* (1977) 67 Cr App Rep 203, discussed below.
[18] In *Atkinson* (1978) 67 Cr App Rep 200, for example, the Court of Appeal emphasised that the *Turner* rules still represented the law and that they were not to be regarded as in any way qualified by the decision in *Cain*.

4.   SENTENCE BARGAINING

(a)   Incidence

Negotiations between judges and counsel, in which the former indicate what reduction in sentence an accused might secure by pleading guilty, are contrary to law. The extent to which they take place is, as a corollary, difficult to assess. One indication of the prevalence of sentence bargaining is the frequency with which cases on the matter have been heard by the Court of Appeal. In the late 1970s, for example, the Court of Appeal had continually to reaffirm the *Turner* rules in the face of appeals, 'all too many in number'.[19] Judgment in as many as seven plea bargaining cases was given by the Court of Appeal within the space of a year, with four of them being decided over an eight day period in December 1977.[20]

A further spate of cases in the late 1980s suggests that Crown Court judges have retained their enthusiasm for sentence bargaining.[1] In *Smith*, Russell LJ found it 'disturbing that despite frequent observations made in this Court discouraging unnecessary visits to the judge's room, they appear to continue up and down the country.'[2] This sentiment was echoed by Lord Lane CJ in the subsequent case of *Pitman*. He reflected wearily:

'There is it seems a steady flow of appeals to this court arising from visits by counsel to the judge in his private room. No amount of criticism and no amount of warnings and no amount of exhortation seems to be able to prevent this happening.'[3]

In the reported cases, defence counsel and Crown Court judges seem to be equally implicated in sentence bargaining. Sometimes defence counsel takes the initiative by going to see the judge in private,[4]

---

[19]   *Llewellyn* (1978) 67 Cr App Rep 149 at 151, per Roskill LJ.
[20]   The four being *Howell* [1978] Crim LR 239; *Bird* (1977) 67 Cr App Rep 203; *Atkinson* (1978) 67 Cr App Rep 200, and *Ryan* (1977) 67 Cr App Rep 177. The other three cases were *Grice* (1977) 66 Cr App Rep 167; *Llewellyn* (1978) 67 Cr App Rep 149; and *Eccles* [1978] Crim LR 757.
[1]   See *Cullen* (1984) 81 Cr App Rep 17; *Keily* (1989) 11 Cr App Rep (S) 273; *Smith* [1990] 1 WLR 1311 and *Pitman* [1991] 1 All ER 468.
[2]   [1990] 1 WLR 1311 at 1314.
[3]   [1991] 1 All ER 468 at 470.
[4]   *Turner* [1970] 2 QB 321; *Plimmer* (1975) 61 Cr App Rep 264; *Quartey* (1975) Crim LR 592; *Coward* (1979) 70 Cr App Rep 70; *Ryan* (1977) 67 Cr App Rep 177 and *Smith* [1990] 1 WLR 1311.

but often the judge summons counsel to initiate discussions over sentence.[5]

That sentence bargaining is an endemic and entrenched phenomenon in the Crown Court is further indicated by the evidence given by judges and counsel as part of these appeals. In *Plimmer*,[6] for example, the trial judge revealed that it was his standard practice to indicate what sentence he would give if a guilty plea were entered. In *Grice*[7] the defendant pleaded not guilty to charges of having unlawful sexual intercourse with his adopted daughter. According to the judge himself:

'a "plea bargain" [was] offered, via Grice's defending counsel, that if he wished to plead guilty to the offences, and so spare the girl the ordeal of giving evidence, we would suspend the sentence. In other words, that the sentence of imprisonment would not come into operation providing Grice behaved himself.'[8]

In *Coward*,[9] defence counsel had

'submitted that it was a common practice for members of the Bar defending in criminal cases to ask to see the judge for the purpose of finding out what sort of sentence the judge would pass if there was a plea of guilty.'[10]

Research confirms the impression given by the reported cases that sentence bargaining is rife in the Crown Court. Around one in five of the late plea changers in Baldwin and McConville's study claimed to have given in to pressure by their barristers and accepted a sentence bargain, while in others barristers gave defendants a 'nod and a wink' that the ground had been prepared for a bargain.[11] The Court of Appeal's attempt to inhibit this practice has met with only limited success. Morison and Leith report that in some of the court centres they studied the practice of visiting the judge in private was frowned upon and did not appear to be employed. In others, however, 'it was commonplace

---

[5] *Inns* (1974) 60 Cr App Rep 231; *Cain* [1976] Crim LR 464; *Bird* (1977) 67 Cr App Rep 203; *Atkinson* (1978) 67 Cr App Rep 200 (in this case the discussion took place at a pre-trial review); *Llewellyn* (1978) 67 Cr App Rep 149; *Grice* (1977) 66 Cr App Rep 167; *Eccles* [1978] Crim LR 757; *Winterflood* [1979] Crim LR 263; *Cullen* (1984) 81 Cr App Rep 17; *Keily* (1989) 11 Cr App Rep (S) 273; *James* [1990] Crim LR 815 and *Pitman* [1991] 1 All ER 468. In *Cullen*, the Court of Appeal said 'We disapprove of a judge himself taking the initiative in sending for counsel.'
[6] (1975) 61 Cr App Rep 264.
[7] (1977) 66 Cr App Rep 167.
[8] Ibid at 170.
[9] (1970) 70 Cr App Rep 70.
[10] Ibid at 75–76.
[11] J Baldwin and M McConville, *Negotiated Justice* (Martin Robertson, 1977) pp 29–35.

for counsel to visit the judge's chambers before a case was heard to discuss what was to follow.'[12] The Crown Court survey conducted for the Runciman Commission provides one explanation for this flouting of the law: neither barristers nor trial judges appear to agree with the position adopted in *Turner*. On being asked, 'Do you think that *Turner* should be reformed to permit full and realistic discussion between counsel and the judge about plea and especially sentence?', the vast majority of barristers and two-thirds of the judges answered in the affirmative.[13] All of this suggests that lawyers and judges in the Crown Court, just like the police, habitually follow their own working assumptions rather than adhering to the legal rules.

(b) Case law developments since *Turner*

In recent years the senior judiciary have signalled their determination to stamp out sentence bargaining. Whereas the *Turner* rules stressed the need for freedom of access between counsel and the judge, subsequent case law has tended to emphasise that private out of court meetings should only be held where absolutely necessary.[14] It appears from the cases, however, that the Court of Appeal has been more concerned that private discussions are apt to produce 'embarrassing situations'[15] and 'unseemly disputes'[16] concerning the terms of any deal struck rather than that they violate due process principles of openness and impartiality. The court has repeatedly emphasised that if private discussions do take place, a record must be made of what is said.[17] But this requirement might simply force Crown Court judges to adopt more subtle tactics. Just as the police are able to circumvent the controls that surround formal interviews at the police station, judges may be able to indicate by gestures (a nod and a wink perhaps?) as much as by words

---

[12] J Morison and P Leith, *The Barrister's World* (OUP, 1992) p 135. See also J Plotnikoff and R Woolfson, *From Committal to Trial: Delay at the Crown Court* (Law Society, 1993) pp 67–68.

[13] M Zander and P Henderson, The Crown Court study (Royal Commission on Criminal Justice Research Study no 19) p 145. Fourteen examples of private discussions with the judge are to be found within a sub-sample of 43 cases drawn from this study, for which details are provided in M Zander, 'The "innocent"(?) who plead guilty' (1993) 143 NLJ 85.

[14] See *Plimmer* (1975) 61 Cr App Rep 264; *Grice* (1977) 66 Cr App Rep 167; *Winterflood* [1979] Crim LR 263 and, more generally, *Harper-Taylor; Bakker* [1988] NLJR 80. See also P Curran, 'Discussions in the Judge's Private Room' [1991] Crim LR 79.

[15] Per Ormrod LJ in *Plimmer* (1975) 61 Cr App Rep 264.

[16] *Smith* [1990] 1 WLR 1311.

[17] The need for some record to be made of any discussions regarding sentence was emphasised in *Llewellyn* (1978) 67 Cr App Rep 149; *Cullen* (1984) 81 Cr App Rep 17; *Keily* (1989) 11 Cr App Rep(S) 273 and *Smith* [1990] 1 WLR 1311.

what sentencing deal is on offer. One Crown Court judge told us in an informal conversation that he sometimes transmits coded messages regarding the sentencing discount by calling in counsel to discuss how much longer a trial is expected to last. Morison and Leith comment:

'Knowing which judges to approach and how to interpret their signals is a difficult skill to master which depends on using personal knowledge about particular conditions.'[18]

An example of the problems that this delicate situation produces is provided by the case of *Coward*.[19] Defence counsel had asked the judge if he could give any indication as to sentence if his client changed his plea to guilty as part of a charge bargain agreed with the prosecution.[20] The judge firmly declined to do so. Counsel persisted by saying that he would be in difficulties in advising his client as to what to do and mentioned the possibility that he would have to make an application to have the case transferred to another court. The judge said 'You can trust me.' Defence counsel took this to mean that, upon the entering of an acceptable plea of guilty, a non-custodial sentence would follow. The judge, however, had meant only that defence counsel would have to trust his judgment. In the event, a custodial sentence was imposed prompting yet another appeal.

Another problem is how far discussions with the judge should be confidential. The Court of Appeal has expressed conflicting views on whether defendants should be told of the judge's views,[1] but defence barristers will usually be happy to preserve the confidentiality of a private discussion. By only hinting that a sentence bargain has been struck, they can make a defendant's decision to plead guilty more appeal-proof. To make a decision to plead guilty absolutely appeal-proof, the barrister need only assert that the advice given is based on previous experience of the trial judge's sentencing patterns, rather than on any private discussion relating to the instant case. In either case, the prediction of sentence is likely both to have a powerful effect and to be proven correct. In any event, where barristers have taken the initiative in striking sentence bargains, it is inconceivable that they will advise defendants that their behaviour was unlawful and that an appeal would be worthwhile. The relative isolation of the Crown Court judges from

---

18 J Morison and P Leith, *The Barrister's World* (OUP, 1992) p 135.
19 (1979) 70 Cr App Rep 70.
20 There was no authoritative record of the discussion, but the various recollections were recognised by the Court of Appeal as differing not so much in substance as in emphasis. The details given in the text are drawn from the prosecuting counsel's notes on the basis that it is the most even-handed and plausible account.
 1 Contrast *Turner* [1970] 2 QB 321 and *Bird* (1977) 67 Cr App Rep 203 with *Cain* [1976] Crim LR 464 and *Pitman* [1991] 1 All ER 468.

the Court of Appeal, combined with the low probability of convicted offenders appealing, means that the many barristers and judges disposed to do so can continue to follow their crime control working assumptions with little fear of being brought to account for their actions.

The possibility of regulating or even eradicating sentence bargaining and charge bargaining has been explored by a number of writers,[2] and has been attempted, with some well documented success, in one American jurisdiction.[3] This strategy is now so far removed from the political agenda as not to merit further analysis here; for the Runciman Commission on Criminal Justice recommended that sentence bargaining should be legitimised, by allowing judges to indicate their views on sentencing at an early stage.

The starting point for the Runciman Commission was the due process inspired recognition that 'to face defendants with a choice between what they might get on an immediate plea of guilty and what they might get if found guilty by the jury does amount to unacceptable pressure.'[4] However, the *Turner* rules were regarded as having had the unfortunate effect of inhibiting judges from entering into any discussion about sentencing. The Runciman Commission accordingly recommended that 'judges should be able to indicate the highest sentence that they would impose at that point on the basis of the facts as put to them.'[5] This seems to do no more than give support to the *Turner* rule that judges may indicate what type of sentence a defendant would receive, irrespective of plea. A few sentences further on the Runciman Commission reveals its true intention: 'The judge may give the answer to the question "what would be the maximum sentence if my client were to plead guilty at this stage?" but to no other.'[6] Since the defence will be able to calculate the likely sentence on a not guilty plea by adding a third or a quarter to this maximum, the defendant will be faced with exactly that form of pressure that the Runciman Commission itself regarded as 'unacceptable'. The self-contradictory nature of its reasoning illuminates the poverty of the thinking that lies behind much of the Runciman Commission's work.

---

[2] See D Galligan, 'Regulating Pre-Trial Decisions' in I Dennis (ed), *Criminal Law and Justice* (Sweet & Maxwell, 1987) and A Bottomley, 'Sentencing Reform and the Structuring of Pre-trial Discretion' in M Wasik and K Pease (eds), *Sentencing Reform* (Manchester University Press, 1987).

[3] T W Carns and J Kruse, 'A Re-Evaluation of Alaska's Plea Bargaining Ban' (1991) 8 Alaska LR 27.

[4] Royal Commission on Criminal Justice, Report (Cm 2263) (HMSO, 1993) p 113.

[5] Ibid.

[6] Ibid.

5. THE PROSPECT OF CONVICTION

The advantages to be gained by pleading guilty explain why defendants who think they will be convicted following trial decide to plead guilty. But why do they expect to be found guilty? This expectation may be influenced by information received directly or indirectly from the judge, the prosecution and the defence barrister.

(a) Predictions of conviction from the judge

Nothing is more likely to cause a defendant to abandon a not guilty plea than a trial judge expressing a view that the defendant is guilty, will be found guilty and is wasting the court's time by pleading not guilty. The defendant can hardly expect a fair trial in such circumstances. With the dice so heavily loaded, all the defendant then has to decide is whether to opt for a more lenient sentence by pleading guilty. In other words, there is no longer a meaningful decision to be made.

The Court of Appeal has made it clear that it is improper for a judge to comment on the strength of the prosecution case as a way of persuading the defendant to enter a plea of guilty. A blatant case is *Barnes*, in which the judge harangued the defendant and his barrister:

'I think it right I should tell you in the presence and hearing of your client that I take a very serious view indeed of hopeless cases, without the shadow of a defence, being contested at public expense . . . I am not going to mince matters. It is absolutely outrageous that other people are waiting for their trials because of behaviour like this.'[7]

The Court of Appeal expressed some sympathy with the trial judge's concerns but pointed out that the defendant was simply exercising his right to put the prosecution to proof. The appearance of a fair trial before an impartial judge had been completely destroyed by the trial judge's outburst and the conviction was accordingly quashed. However, the problem persists. Some of Baldwin and McConville's respondents claimed that they had been compelled to plead guilty by the judge, as in the following example:

'The barrister came back from seeing the judge and said, "Well, the judge says we can argue as long as you like but you'll be found guilty anyway." . . . I think I was more forced into it [pleading guilty] than anything, personally. I was flogging a dead horse. I mean the judge had made up his mind before I even walked through the door.'[8]

---

[7] (1970) 55 Cr App Rep 100 at 104–105.
[8] J Baldwin and M McConville, *Negotiated Justice* (Martin Robertson, 1977) p 33.

Some cases reveal an astonishing level of judicial interference into the conduct of a trial supposed to be conducted on adversarial principles of due process. In *Pitman*,[9] for instance (a case of causing death by reckless driving), the judge sent for counsel and indicated that in his view there was no defence to the charge. Defence counsel said that he had advised a plea of not guilty, as it was arguable that recklessness would not be made out by the prosecution. The judge replied pointedly that the defendant's plea was not a matter for counsel to determine.[10]

So long as trial judges continue to engage in sentence bargaining, the likelihood is that they will either volunteer (or become drawn into giving) their views on the likely outcome of the case. And to a defendant offered a sentence discount in return for pleading guilty, it may seem as if the judge has already decided that a conviction is not in doubt and that all that remains to be determined is the appropriate sentence. The Runciman Commission's proposals to introduce a 'plea canvas' in which judges can be asked to indicate the maximum sentence on a guilty plea are likely to exacerbate these problems.

(b)   Information from the prosecution

In order for the defence to assess the prospects of conviction, it is obviously essential they have advance notice of the prosecution case and of any 'unused material' held by prosecution agencies which might help bolster the defence. As noted in the previous chapter, a duty on the prosecution of advance disclosure of its case is more firmly established for trials on indictment than for proceedings in the magistrates' courts, but gaps still remain.[11] For example, if 'unused material' relates to informants or the work of undercover police officers, the prosecution can make an ex parte application to the court for permission not to disclose such material and the defence need not be told that such an application has been made.[12] It follows that defendants may decide to plead guilty in ignorance of evidence withheld (quite lawfully) by the prosecution that would have helped to establish innocence.

A more frequent problem is that the prosecution fails to comply

---

[9]   [1991] 1 All ER 468.

[10]   The obvious retort is that the defendant's plea was not a matter for the judge either. See also *James* [1990] Crim LR 815.

[11]   See P O'Connor, 'Prosecution Disclosure: Principle, Practice and Justice' in C Walker and K Starmer (eds), *Justice in Error* (Blackstone, 1993). This is a lightly revised and updated version of an article carrying the same title, published at [1992] Crim LR 464.

[12]   *Johnson* [1993] Crim LR 689 and accompanying commentary at 690. The Runciman Commission gave their blessing to this decision and recommended that further restrictions on the prosecution's duty to disclose should be introduced: Report, op cit pp 95–96.

with the duty to disclose. A failure to disclose evidence helpful to the defence has lain at the heart of most of the spectacular miscarriages of justice that have come to light in recent years. Such a failure occurred, for example, in all four of the now infamous 'terrorist' trials heard from 1974–6.[13] It is not safe to assume that the framework of suspects' rights introduced by PACE has engendered a new culture of disclosure within prosecution agencies. In July 1992, Michelle and Lisa Taylor were sentenced to life imprisonment for murder. The conviction was subsequently quashed, in part because the police had deliberately suppressed evidence that would have been helpful to the defence.[14]

A failure to disclose evidence should not be seen as an occasional aberration, the understandable product, perhaps, of the pressure the police come under to achieve 'a result' in murder inquiries. The research by McConville, Sanders and Leng shows that the police (post-PACE) habitually construct the case for the prosecution in a way that strips it of any material helpful to the defence.[15] They also show how the police are adept at presenting positive 'facts' in a way that maximises the probability of prosecution and eventual conviction.[16] With certain offences under the Public Order Act 1986, for example, it must be proved that behaviour was 'threatening', 'abusive' or 'insulting' or that others were likely to be caused 'alarm', 'harassment' or 'distress' by such behaviour. These are vague standards, which were found to provide ample scope for case construction:

'In the large number of cases in our sample in which it was alleged that a public order offence was committed in the presence of police officers, the key evidence was supplied by that officer's characterization of the suspect's behaviour and the assessment of its effects on other people. Because the officer anticipates review of the case for evidential sufficiency and having to prove the offence in court, the relevant behaviour of the accused is described in the exact terms of the offence. Generally evidence of this sort is inscrutable short of cross-examination in court.'[17]

There will be no cross-examination, however, if a defendant is persuaded to plead guilty on the strength of the prosecution case as it

---

[13] The 'Guildford Four', 'Birmingham Six', the Maguires and Judith Ward cases. See O'Connor, op cit, for discussion.

[14] (1993) Guardian, 12 June.

[15] M McConville, A Sanders, and R Leng, *The Case for the Prosecution* (Routledge, 1991). See also P O'Connor, op cit pp 110–111.

[16] Forensic scientists are sometimes just as guilty of presenting their findings in a highly misleading fashion—*Ward* (1993) 96 Cr App Rep 1 provides a good example of this.

[17] McConville, Sanders and Leng, op cit p 134.

exists on paper. That case, far from allowing defendants to make a realistic assessment of their prospects of acquittal, paints a systematically distorted portrait of 'the facts' which may mislead a defendant into believing that there is no option but to plead guilty.

(c)   Advice from the defence barrister

It has been argued in this chapter that defence barristers arrive at court predisposed to settle cases for organisational reasons, and that the law provides them with the raw materials with which to fashion a negotiated settlement. A further issue is whether barristers provide proper advice on the prospect of acquittal.[18] Research suggests that some members of the Bar adopt an unduly pessimistic view of the likelihood of acquittal in order to increase the pressure on defendants to plead guilty.

Some barristers in the Baldwin and McConville study were consistently described, by different defendants in different cases, as either good or bad. The latter were 'seen very commonly as hurried, dismissive or in other ways unsatisfactory.'[19]

We saw above how 'bad' barristers may engage in plea bargaining or make use of the sentencing discount principle in order to pressurise defendants into pleading guilty. Many of the quotes we have used from the Baldwin and McConville study illustrate the point that barristers commonly backed up this pressure by stating that the defendant had little or no chance of being acquitted if the trial proceeded. Protestations of innocence were often brushed aside as irrelevant to this question, as in the following example:

'My barrister pleaded guilty for me. I told him that I was innocent but he said I was a bloody nuisance and that nobody would believe me. He said, "The judge and the others will never believe what you say in court; they will always believe the police." '[20]

This advice would clearly be contrary to the *Turner* rules, under which barristers are supposed to tell clients that they must only plead guilty if they accept that they are guilty. That some barristers were prepared to tell clients that they stood no chance of acquittal notwithstanding their claims of innocence stands as a warning that defendants may not receive objective advice as regards the strength of their

[18]   Although we do not deal here with the part played by rules of evidence and procedure to assessments of the prospect of conviction, their importance should not be underestimated. For a detailed analysis along these lines see D McBarnet, *Conviction* (MacMillan, 1983). In ch 8 we will outline some of the main rules of evidence in the context of our discussion of the jury.

[19]   J Baldwin and M McConville, *Negotiated Justice* (Martin Robertson, 1977) p 42.

[20]   Ibid p 53.

position. This is sometimes because barristers are unfamiliar with their briefs, which is still a major problem.[1] There are, however, wide yet consistent variations in guilty plea rates from area to area. Thus, London has had the lowest guilty plea rate in the country for over 20 years, while the Midland and Oxford, and North eastern circuits have had the highest.[2] This suggests that some local Bars may have developed a powerful culture in which the priority given to settling rather than fighting cases is particularly marked. In short, the claim of the Bar that it always puts the interests of its clients first simply beggars belief. It is much more likely that a substantial minority of barristers continue to treat prosecution evidence uncritically, ignore protestations of innocence and advise that the defendant has 'no choice' but to plead guilty.

6.   DO THE INNOCENT PLEAD GUILTY ?

Many people would perhaps be prepared to tolerate charge bargaining, sentence discounts and sentence bargains if the net result was more convictions of the guilty and no corresponding increase in convictions of the innocent. The ends would be sufficiently desirable to render the means acceptable. This half-way house between due process and crime control may appear attractive, but in practice no guarantee can be given that the innocent will not be made to suffer as a result of striking such a compromise. This is despite the ostensible concern of the appellate courts to ensure that the innocent are not induced to plead guilty by charge bargains and the sentencing discount. Thus in the leading case of *Turner*,[3] Lord Parker CJ was at pains to stress that counsel 'of course will emphasize that the accused must not plead guilty unless he has committed the acts constituting the offence charged.'[4]

The difficulty here is that a barrister will not know if a particular client is innocent or not and indeed may be anxious not to find out. Barristers to whom confessions of guilt are made are subject to strict restrictions in how they may conduct a defence. Certain things they may still do, such as challenge the admissibility of prosecution evidence, but, according to the Code of Conduct for the Bar of England and Wales:

---

[1] See M Zander and P Henderson, The Crown Court Study (Royal Commission on Criminal Justice Research Study no 19) pp 30–31.
[2] M Zander, 'What the Annual Statistics Tell Us About Pleas and Acquittals' [1991] Crim LR 252.
[3] [1970] 2 WLR 1093 at 1097.
[4] Ibid at 1097.

'. . . a barrister must not assert as true that which he knows to be false. He must not connive at, much less attempt to substantiate a fraud. He must not set up an affirmative case inconsistent with the confession.'[5]

Advice on charge bargains and the sentencing discount will thus be given to all clients, guilty or not. The court in *Turner* implicitly recognised this in insisting that barristers stress that no one should plead guilty unless they are guilty. There would be no need for such an exhortation if only the guilty were to receive advice on the advantages of pleading guilty. Many innocent persons will thus inevitably face advice from their barristers to the effect that they would derive considerable advantage from pleading guilty.

Having considered the options, the *Turner* rules state that the final choice of plea is the accused's alone. Nothing prevents accused persons from proclaiming innocence to their lawyers yet insisting on entering a guilty plea in court. In such a situation, it might seem as if a defence lawyer would be contributing to a deception of the court, yet there is no due process requirement that the lawyer reveals the accused's true state of mind. Whereas barristers may not assert that defendants are innocent when they believe them to be guilty, they may conduct a case on the basis of a guilty plea while believing the defendant concerned to be innocent. As the Bar's Code of Conduct explains:

'Where a defendant tells his counsel that he did not commit the offence with which [he] is charged but nevertheless insists on pleading guilty to it for reasons of his own, counsel must continue to represent him, but only after he has advised what the consequences will be and that what can be submitted in mitigation can only be on the basis that the client is guilty.'[6]

The criminal justice system appears to be prepared to tolerate some frauds more than others.

The danger that the factually innocent will be induced to plead guilty is exacerbated by the law providing that, the weaker the evidence against a defendant, the greater the discount given for a plea of guilty should be.[7] One would expect that it would be harder for the police to construct strong cases against the innocent than against the guilty. The option of contesting a case should thus be more attractive to the innocent, since they stand a better chance of success before a jury.

---

[5] See paras 3.3 and 3.4. The Code of Conduct is reproduced in *Archbold, Criminal Pleading, Evidence and Practice* (Sweet & Maxwell, 1994) vol 2, p 1739.

[6] See ibid para 2.5.

[7] *Hollington and Emmens* (1985) 82 Cr App Rep 281.

Yet the effect of this aspect of the discount principle is to make that option less attractive to the innocent, since the costs of failure before a jury are, in effect, increased. They have more discount to lose than the guilty in contesting their cases.

To some, it might seem as if the strongest safeguard against miscarriages of justice arising out of plea bargaining and related practices is the axiomatic truth that no innocent person would ever claim guilt. But just as innocent people sometimes 'confess' to the police under interrogation, so too, it seems, (and often in consequence of having 'confessed' at an earlier stage) do innocent people plead guilty. Nearly half of the late plea changers in Baldwin and McConville's study made substantial and credible claims of innocence.[8] According to one:

'The barrister turned round and says, "If I were you, I'd forget my pride. I know you think you're innocent but if you're proved guilty, I think you'll go down—I can't guarantee it but I think you will." Then I said, "I don't want to do bloody time for something I haven't done" . . . in the end, I turned round and said "Well, I'm here for your advice, I'll also accept it." He was very nice—he didn't try to force me, it was just his advice. I mean if you've got somebody like that as your counsel, you're a mug not to take their advice. That's the way I looked upon it, so I pleaded guilty.'[9]

Baldwin and McConville acknowledged that they had no way of telling whether defendants were in fact innocent or not. But in a substantial number of these guilty plea cases, independent assessors judged the evidence against the defendant to be weak.[10] Similarly, the Crown Court study by Zander and Henderson included a number of 'cracked trials' in which the CPS said that, had they gone to trial, the defendant would have stood a 'good' or 'fairly good' chance of acquittal. On an annual basis, this would total over 600 cracked trials where the defendant would have stood a good chance of acquittal and over 2,000 such cases with a fairly good chance of acquittal.[11] Defendants in these cases may not all be factually innocent, of course, but they may well have emerged from a contested trial legally innocent. The Crown Court study also found that 11% of defendants pleading guilty claimed to be innocent,[12] and that 6% of defence barristers were concerned that their

---

[8]   J Baldwin and M McConville, *Negotiated Justice* (Martin Robertson, 1977) pp 62–63.
[9]   Ibid p 66.
[10]   Ibid p 74.
[11]   Zander and Henderson, op cit p 157.
[12]   Ibid p 139. It should be borne in mind that the response rate of defendants was too low to be statistically reliable.

clients had pleaded guilty, despite being innocent—amounting to some 1,400 cases a year.[13]

As we have seen, the Runciman Commission on Criminal Justice recognised that if inducements were offered to defendants to plead guilty, there was a risk that more innocent persons would be convicted. On this issue, as with many others, priority was given to the more effective conviction of the guilty:

'Against the risk that defendants may be tempted to plead guilty to charges of which they are not guilty must be weighed the benefits to the system and to defendants of encouraging those who are in fact guilty to plead guilty. We believe that the system of sentence discounts should remain. But we do see reason to make the system more effective.'[14]

The abandonment of even any rhetorical attachment to the due process principle that priority must be given to acquitting the innocent has been swiftly followed by a further lurch towards more crime control at the political level, as evidenced by the contents of the Criminal Justice and Public Order Bill. Although the Bill has not taken forward the Runciman Commission's plans for a more formalised system of sentence discounts, it contains clauses designed to abolish the defendant's right of silence. The removal of this right will increase the pressure on defendants to enter into the plea bargaining process and increase the risk that innocent persons will plead guilty.

7.   CONCLUSION

The pre-trial processes in the Crown Court exhibit many of the hallmarks of the crime control model. In a system in which all the participants understand that the majority of cases will be disposed of by guilty pleas, attention is naturally focused on case settlement, rather than preparing for a fight in court. The system itself is geared towards the routine production of guilty pleas, as can be seen in the legal aid fee structure, the organisation of the legal profession, the sentence discount principle and so on. The wholesale adoption of crime control ideology by solicitors, barristers and judges up and down the country

---

[13]   Ibid pp 138–139. The weight to be attached to this latter figure in view of the methodological weaknesses of the Crown Court survey has been much debated. M Zander, 'The "innocent"(?) who plead guilty' (1993) 143 NLJ 85 and M McConville and L Bridges, 'Pleading Guilty whilst Maintaining Innocence', (1993) 143 NLJ 160. For further exchanges see (1993) 143 NLJ at 192, 228 and 276.

[14]   Report, op cit p 111. A Ashworth, 'Plea, Venue and Discontinuance' [1993] Crim LR 830 at 837 describes this passage, from the point of view of principle, as the nadir of the Runciman Commission's report.

further oils the conveyor belt moving defendants inexorably towards conviction. It is undeniable that elements within the legal profession remain committed to due process, but they provide the exception to the rule of crime control. That some defendants insist on trial by jury is in some ways the most remarkable feature of the criminal justice process and is a phenomenon that we explore in the next chapter. Here, however, we wish to pause for a moment and consider in more depth the Runciman Commission's strategy aimed at further reducing the number of contested trials in the Crown Court.

As the Runciman Commission was set up in the wake of the freeing of the 'Birmingham Six', it was widely expected that it would focus on the safeguards and reforms needed to protect better against miscarriages of justice. That these expectations proved false is partly attributable to the way in which the government set its terms of reference. These required the Runciman Commission 'to examine the effectiveness of the criminal justice system in England and Wales in securing the conviction of those guilty of criminal offences and the acquittal of those who are innocent, having regard to the efficient use of resources'.[15] It would have been open to the Runciman Commission to reject the implication in these terms of reference that all three of these matters are of equal weight. Instead it embraced this notion wholeheartedly. Thus, for example, it saw 'miscarriages of justice' as comprising both the conviction of the innocent and the acquittal of the guilty.[16] Because it regarded these matters as of equal concern, it saw no problem in recommending changes to the system which would both undermine the adversarial system and substantially increase the likelihood of innocent persons being convicted. For the Runciman Commission, these costs were more than offset by the prospect of convicting more of the guilty at a 'value for money'[17] price. It is this crude cost-benefit analysis that lay behind its proposals to abolish a defendant's right in either way cases to elect trial by jury and to introduce systematic plea bargaining.

To some extent, then, the Runciman Commission has simply made a value choice, expressing a preference for more crime control and less due process. But as we pointed out at the start of this book, empirical evidence should play a central part in informing one's choice of values. The Runciman Commission's arguments for more crime control are, by contrast, often based on little more than opinion and assertion. It commissioned no research on the quality of justice in the magistrates' courts and, by its own admission, largely overlooked their work in disposing of the vast majority of criminal cases.[18] Yet it sought to ensure, through

15 Report, op cit p i.
16 Ibid p 2.
17 See ibid pp 4–5.
18 Ibid p 2.

its attack on the right to trial by jury, that more cases would be heard by magistrates. Similarly, it commissioned no research on plea bargaining, yet proposed that the inhibitory aspects of the *Turner* rules should be abandoned for the sake of greater efficiency.

This is not to say that the Runciman Commission lacked a view of how the system works, but that view appears to have been based on stereotypes and prejudices as much as on hard evidence. Thus, it declares a belief, without any supporting evidence or argument, that clearer articulation of the sentence discount principle would not increase the risks of the innocent pleading guilty.[19] Again, while the Runciman Commission found it 'odd' that most of those electing trial by jury eventually pleaded guilty it was not interested in exploring the reasons for this.[20] It was simply assumed that defendants were wasting everybody's time and money by delaying their pleas of guilty until the last moment. This crime control line of reasoning, that guilty persons will take advantage of due process protections in order to further their own interests and in seeking to avoid their just deserts, is not borne out by research findings on the operation of the criminal process. Late plea changing in the Crown Court is predominantly the product of a system that simultaneously proclaims the right of defendants to call upon the prosecution to prove its case before judge and jury whilst doing its utmost to ensure that the vast majority waive that right. Defendants do not commonly play the system; the system plays with them, their rights and their freedom.

[19] Ibid p 112.
[20] See ibid p 86.

Chapter 8

Trial by Judge and Jury

Of all defendants proceeded against in the criminal courts, just over 1% have their fate determined by a jury. As we have seen, the vast majority of criminal proceedings (over 95%) are concluded in the magistrates' courts.[1] Even of those committed to the Crown Court for trial, only around a third (31% in 1992) plead not guilty.[2] In recent years, just over half of those defendants pleading not guilty to all counts are acquitted.[3] In practice, most such cases are terminated without the jury being required to assess the question of guilt. The judge simply directs or orders the jury to return a verdict of not guilty. In 1992, 55% of acquittals were of this nature.[4]

The pattern of acquittals points to the importance of the trial judge in the Crown Court. Even where it is left to the jury to decide whether the prosecution has proved guilt beyond reasonable doubt, judges often exert a strong influence on the outcome and are far from being the passive impartial referee as depicted in adversarial theory. Trial by jury may be thought of as the cornerstone of English justice, but the title of this chapter more accurately reflects this aspect of the criminal process.

1. DIRECTED AND ORDERED ACQUITTALS— WEAK CASES?

The formal distinction between directed and ordered acquittals is not difficult to grasp, although, as we shall see, the position in practice is

---

[1] See ch 6, section 1, above.
[2] See ch 7, section 1, above.
[3] The figure was 56% in 1992. See Judicial Statistics: Annual Report 1992 (Cm 2268) (Lord Chancellor's Department) (HMSO, 1993) p 61, Table 6.8.
[4] Of defendants acquitted in 1992, 34% were discharged on the order of the judge, 21% were acquitted on the direction of the judge and 45% were acquitted by a jury. Ibid p 57 para 13.

more complex. If the prosecution indicates that it will not be offering evidence at trial, the judge orders the jury to acquit. A directed acquittal, by contrast, occurs on the instigation of the prosecutor, the defence or the judge, after the trial has begun. The proper approach to be taken in deciding whether to direct an acquittal was laid down in *Galbraith* where Lord Lane CJ ruled that:

'Where the judge comes to the conclusion that the prosecution evidence, taken at the highest, is such that a jury properly directed could not properly convict upon it, it is his duty, upon a submission being made, to stop the case.'[5]

The level of directed and ordered acquittals raises the question of whether the prosecution is adequately discharging its duty to review cases continually and to discontinue those in which the evidence is weak.[6] Research for the Royal Commission on Criminal Justice (Runciman Commission) by Block, Corbett and Peay found that nearly half of the directed and ordered acquittals examined were unforeseeable—in just over half of these, either the victim or a witness went missing or refused to testify.[7] Other cases became (unforeseeably) weak for a variety of reasons, such as where changes in the law defining the offence charged meant that the evidence no longer justified the prosecution in proceeding.

In 55% of the cases studied by Block et al, however, the acquittal was considered one which the prosecution either could or should have foreseen. In some instances, the prosecution spotted the weakness only after committal and, lacking the legal power to discontinue, properly sought an ordered acquittal.[8] But in as many as 43% of all the sampled cases the prosecution had failed to spot or act upon weaknesses in the case in a timely fashion, if at all. In 15% of all cases, the weakness was foreseeable even before committal, while in some weak cases the prosecution was prepared to offer evidence at trial, prompting Block et al to comment:

---

[5] [1981] 1 WLR 1039 at 1042.

[6] This duty is contained in the Code for Crown Prosecutors, para 10. The Code is published as an annex to the Crown Prosecution Service Annual Report 1992–1993 (HMSO, 1993).

[7] B Block, C Corbett and J Peay, Ordered and Directed Acquittals in the Crown Court (Royal Commission on Criminal Justice, Research Study no 15) (HMSO, 1993). The results are summarised by the authors in 'Ordered and Directed Acquittals in the Crown Court: A Time of Change?' [1993] Crim LR 95.

[8] Under s 23 of the Prosecution of Offences Act 1985, a Crown Court case can only be discontinued prior to committal by the magistrates' court. The Runciman Commission recommended that the CPS be given the power to discontinue proceedings up to the beginning of a Crown Court trial: Report, (Cm 2263) (HMSO, 1993) p 77.

'it is an indictment of the CPS that these cases were not converted into ordered acquittals by earlier CPS action, or prevented from becoming acquittals at all by even earlier discontinuance.'[9]

This study supports the argument developed in earlier chapters that the prosecution duty to discontinue weak cases does not provide an adequate due process safeguard for defendants.[10] Should one attribute this to unsatisfactory bureaucratic procedures and professional misjudgment, as Block et al appear to do? No doubt this provides one explanatory factor, but other research shows that the prosecution are often fully aware of weaknesses in their case but proceed in the hope that defendants will throw in their hand and plead guilty.[11] If a defendant calls the prosecution's bluff by insisting on trial by jury, one natural response is to drop the case by offering no evidence.

Block et al also noted that around half of the directed acquittals occurred before the end of the prosecution case at the intervention of the judge. There were also cases in which the judge pressurised the prosecution into offering no evidence, by revealing that the result of the case would be a bind over whether or not the prosecution went ahead.[12] In the researchers' view, the seriousness of the offence and the strength of the evidence in many such instances was such that the case should have been left to the jury to decide.

How might one explain the high proportion of acquittals which are ordered or directed by Crown Court judges? One would expect such activity in a system based on due process values, since it suggests that officials, in weeding out weak cases, are giving proper priority to protecting the innocent against wrongful conviction. Some directed and ordered acquittals are undoubtedly attributable to such concerns. Yet against this analysis is the fact that prosecutors knowingly allow flimsy cases to proceed through the system until the point of trial itself and judges appear prepared on occasion to terminate proceedings where the prosecution has a reasonable prospect of success.

From a crime control point of view, jury trial is an expensive charade and a chronically inefficient method by which to repress crime. Every

---

[9]   See the authors' view in 'A Time of Change?', op cit p 101.
[10] See, in particular, ch 5, section 3(c); ch 6, section 3(c) and ch 7, section 2(b), above. See also the discussion by the Royal Commission on Criminal Justice, Report, op cit pp 74–79.
[11] See M McConville, A Sanders and R Leng, *The Case for the Prosecution* (Routledge, 1991) ch 8.
[12] The bind over is best described as a 'suspended fine' and may be imposed on anyone involved in court proceedings, whether found guilty of an offence or not. See A Ashworth, *Sentencing and Criminal Justice* (Weidenfeld and Nicolson, 1992) p 248.

effort is therefore made to short-circuit the trial process by inducing a high guilty plea rate. This leaves open the question of what to do in that small minority of cases in which defendants maintain their innocence. Confidence in the system would be sapped if prosecutions in very serious cases, such as murder, armed robbery and serial rape, were not pursued. But in less serious cases, such as shoplifting, drunken brawls and burglary of commercial premises, the arguments for devoting further precious resources to securing a conviction are weaker, particularly where the defendant has opted for Crown Court trial. As Hedderman and Moxon's study of mode of trial decisions noted:

'some respondents [justices' clerks and magistrates as well as Chief Crown Prosecutors] questioned the logic of allowing defendants the automatic right to take to the Crown Court matters which were so trivial that judges and prosecutors felt they could not sensibly be pursued there.'[13]

Where the prosecution evidence is not overwhelming (or the matter is perceived to be trivial), either the judge or the CPS (or prosecution counsel) may step in to prevent the case continuing. On this analysis, directed and ordered acquittals may be as much a product of crime control as due process concerns.

The study by Block et al raises further questions about the propriety of defence solicitor or counsel advising defendants that, given the 'strength' of the prosecution case, they should plead guilty.[14] The strength of the case on paper will often not be reflected in court should the defence decide to fight. It should be noted, however, that the Block et al study was not one of weak cases per se, but of cases that ended in an ordered or directed acquittal (some of which were in fact strong). It would be erroneous to assume that all weak cases end in such an acquittal, or, indeed, in any sort of acquittal. In the Crown Court study conducted by Zander and Henderson, judges, defence barristers and prosecution barristers agreed that around 20% of all contested cases were based on a weak prosecution case. Although the great majority of these cases ended in acquittal, the respondents reported that between 4–8% ended in conviction.[15] Conversely, strong cases do not always end in conviction—the acquittal rate in such cases was between 21 and 27%, according to barristers and judges.[16]

---

[13] C Hedderman and D Moxon, *Magistrates' Court or Crown Court?* (Home Office Research Study no 125) (HMSO, 1992) p 16. See ch 5, section 4(c), above for discussion of the public interest criteria which prosecutors are meant to apply in deciding whether to drop cases.
[14] See ch 6, section 3(c) and ch 7, section 5(c), above in particular.
[15] M Zander and P Henderson, Crown Court Study (Royal Commission on Criminal Justice, Research Study no 19) (HMSO, 1993) pp 184–185.
[16] Ibid p 185.

This evidence suggests that the outcome of contested cases is often uncertain. This helps explain why the CPS prosecutes so many weak cases. Where the CPS drop a case, a conviction is lost, whereas one which is continued may result in conviction, notwithstanding its apparent weakness.[17] The police know this, and also know that most cases will, in any event, terminate with a guilty plea. To attempt to secure more evidence in order to 'firm up' a prosecution case, or to clarify ambiguous statements made by witnesses, 'would often be, from the police point of view, wasted effort'.[18] McConville et al conclude that:

'Many [not guilty] verdicts, even when judge-directed, were impossible to predict. Indeed, most contests, and many non-contested cases, represent intrinsically ambiguous situations or situations in which the 'facts' were simply incomplete in vital ways. These were cases which the police may have been able to clarify but did not, cases in which clarification was not possible or potentially strong cases which—because of their relative or absolute triviality—the police and/or CPS could not be bothered to fight over . . . The idea that the pattern of acquittals and convictions reflects either real situations "out there" or the product of the obstacle course of Due Process just does not stand up to scrutiny.'[19]

The outcome of cases is highly dependent on the level of preparatory work carried out by the prosecution and the defence. In reality, the defence rarely does more than respond to the prosecution case and it is the level of care and effort that the police commit to a case that is the crucial factor in determining outcome. As earlier chapters have shown, police commitment is more a product of their own informal working rules and assumptions than officially sanctioned criteria such as the seriousness of the case.[20] As a corollary, the minority of Crown Court cases that go before a jury for determination range from the trivial to the very serious, from the evidentially weak to those in which the prosecution appears to hold all the aces. It is important to keep this point in mind when we consider (in sections 4 and 5, below) the various attempts that have been made to evaluate the performance of the jury and whether the acquittal rate by the jury is 'too high'.

2. THE COMPOSITION OF THE JURY

For centuries, eligibility to serve on a jury was tied to a property qualification which served to exclude all but the well-off from pronouncing

---

[17] See McConville, Sanders and Leng, op cit p 160.
[18] Ibid.
[19] Ibid p 171.
[20] See ch 5 in particular.

on the question of guilt. Following the Jury Act 1974 (as amended), a person is eligible for jury service if aged between 18 and 70, included on the electoral register and resident in the United Kingdom for at least five years since the age of 13. Many of those falling within these parameters are none the less ineligible, disqualified or excusable from service. The ineligible include those who might have an undue influence on a jury's deliberations, such as lawyers, judges and the police, and those who are seen as unsuited for a judgmental role, such as nuns, monks and the clergy. The disqualified include anyone who has received a sentence of imprisonment or community service in the preceding 10 years, or anyone placed on probation in the last 5 years. Members of Parliament, the armed services and the medical profession have the right to be excused if summoned, while any person may be excused service if they can show good cause.

Jury trial is the public face of the criminal justice system, the image with which we are all familiar from countless news reports and fictionalised accounts. Some have argued that the jury's symbolic or legitimising function far outweighs its practical significance, in that the great bulk of defendants are dealt with in the magistrates' courts or by way of a guilty plea, and that the elaborate ritual of a Crown Court contested trial distracts our attention from the lack of due process in pre-trial and post-trial procedures.[1] All of this is true. None the less, the jury is a key battleground for the due process and crime control models. This is so because jury trial is employed in the most serious of cases, such as for offences of murder, rape and terrorism. A high rate of guilty verdicts is thus essential to the strategy of effective crime control. The deterrent aim of the system would be undermined if in 'too high' a proportion of these widely publicised cases the defendants were allowed to walk free from the court. Similarly, the very authority of the state might be called into question if juries acquitted too readily, especially in obviously political cases concerning official secrets, terrorist activities and so forth.

A particular problem for crime control adherents is created by the jury's power to acquit in cases where they have no doubt as to the legal guilt of the defendant but consider the prosecution to be oppressive, the law broken to be unjust or the punishment threatened to be excessive.[2] All three factors were probably at work, for example, in the acquittal of

---

[1] See in particular P Darbyshire, 'The Lamp That Shows That Freedom Lives—Is it Worth the Candle ?' [1991] Crim LR 740.

[2] As has occurred in a number of celebrated cases throughout legal history: W Cornish, *The Jury* (Allen Lane, 1968) ch 5; M Freeman, 'The Jury on Trial' [1981] CLP 65 at 90–93 in particular and M Zander, *Cases and Materials on the English Legal System* (Weidenfeld and Nicolson, 1992) pp 460–461. For an elegant defence of such 'jury equity', see P Devlin, 'The Conscience of the Jury' (1991) 107 LQR 398.

Clive Ponting for offences against the Official Secrets Act (leaking papers containing evidence of government duplicity during the Falklands War).[3] The exercise of such 'jury equity' sabotages crime control in the immediate case and may provoke calls for more due process in pre-trial procedures in future. Ways must therefore be found to ensure that juries will both trust the police and prosecution agencies to identify the guilty correctly, and back the use of state power against the particular defendant before them. This problem became critical in the early 1970s with the widening of the jury franchise. Juries were no longer guaranteed to be 'predominantly male, middle-aged, middle-minded and middle-class',[4] and so could not be relied upon to lean instinctively towards upholding the exercise of state authority. As we shall see, efforts to regulate and restrict jury power have intensified over the last 20 years.

The influence of crime control thought can be seen in the long history of attempts to rig the composition of the jury.[5] Selection from the pool of eligible jurors is supposed to be random, so as to produce a jury which is (reasonably) representative of the wider community. As Lord Denning put it in *R v Crown Court at Sheffield, ex p Brownlow*,[6] 'We believe that 12 persons selected at random are likely to be a cross-section of the people as a whole and thus represent the view of the common man.' Cutting against the principle of random selection is the preliminary investigation of potential jurors by the prosecution in some cases. Information obtained by such 'jury vetting' may be used by the prosecution to 'stand by' (ie exclude) jurors before the trial begins.[7] The practice came to light in modern times in the 1978 'ABC trial' of a soldier and two journalists for offences under the Official Secrets Act. As a result of a secret prosecution application to the judge, an 82-member panel from which a jury was to be chosen was vetted for 'loyalty'. Defence objections to this process were strengthened when it was discovered that the prosecution had failed to act on information that two members of the jury so selected had signed the Official Secrets Act and that the foreman was an ex-member of the SAS (Special Air Services regiment). As a result of the public outcry which followed, the Attorney General published the guidelines for the vetting of jury panels which had existed as a 'restricted document' for three years previously.[8] It was

---

[3] C Ponting, *The Right to Know, The Inside Story of the Belgrano Affair* (Sphere, 1985).

[4] P Devlin, *Trial by Jury* (Stevens & Sons, 1956) p 20.

[5] See Freeman, op cit pp 75–76, for examples drawn from the eighteenth and nineteenth centuries.

[6] [1980] QB 530 at 541.

[7] On the right to stand by see J McEldowney, 'Stand by for the Crown—An Historical Analysis' [1979] Crim LR 272.

[8] The guidelines were published: (1978) Times, 11 October.

admitted in Parliament that jury vetting had been going on 'at least since 1948, and probably since a great deal earlier than that.'[9]

In a civil case decided soon after, the Court of Appeal opined that jury vetting was unconstitutional,[10] but when the point arose for decision in a criminal appeal, *Mason*,[11] a differently constituted Court of Appeal upheld the practice of routine Criminal Records Office checks. There would be no objection to this if the purpose of the check was merely to establish whether any juror fell foul of the disqualification provisions in the Juries Act 1974. But the court went on to say that the prosecution could justifiably exclude a juror with a criminal conviction not serious enough to trigger a statutory disqualification.[12]

The Court of Appeal refrained from commenting on jury vetting which went beyond checking criminal records, but the latest redraft of the Attorney General's guidelines state that additional checks may be made with the security services and the police special branch in security and terrorist cases.[13] This is to counter the perceived

'danger that a juror's political beliefs are so biased as to go beyond normally reflecting the broad spectrum of views and interests in the community to reflect the extreme views of sectarian interest or pressure groups to a degree which might interfere with his fair assessment of the facts of the case or lead him to exert improper pressure on his fellow jurors'.[14]

Since 'extreme views' is a term capable of wide interpretation there is clearly scope for abuse here.[15]

Whether jury vetting is widespread or takes place (whether on an authorised basis or not) only in cases which the prosecution regards as particularly important or sensitive is impossible to know. The secrecy surrounding the practice is itself a denial of due process values. A further problem is that the prosecution is placed under no duty to 'stand by' jurors when checks suggest that they might be biased against the defendant. Instead, the guidelines provide that in such a situation:

---

[9] HC Deb 5th Series, vol 958, col 28, 13 November 1978.
[10] *R v Crown Court at Sheffield, ex p Brownlow* [1980] QB 530 at 542 and 545. One can only speculate as to whether the court was influenced by the fact that in this case it was the defence which was seeking to vet the jury.
[11] [1981] QB 881.
[12] The Runciman Commission supported the routine screening of jurors for criminal convictions but failed to tackle the question of whether details of non-disqualifying convictions should be passed to the prosecution: Report, op cit p 133.
[13] The guidelines are reproduced at [1988] 3 All ER 1086.
[14] Ibid para 5.
[15] See eg R East, 'Jury Packing: A Thing of the Past' (1985) 48 MLR 518 at 527–528.

'the defence should be given, at least, an indication of why that potential juror may be inimical to their interests; but because of its nature and source it may not be possible to give the defence more than a general indication.'[16]

This falls a long way short of mandating full disclosure to the defence. Moreover, the Association of Chief Police Officers has recommended that the police should only make checks on behalf of the defence if requested to do so by the Director of Public Prosecutions.[17] Of course, there is no law which stops the defence from vetting a jury panel itself, although it might have difficulty in securing the names sufficiently in advance. The problem is money. Unlike the prosecution, most defendants do not have unlimited resources and the Legal Aid Board would not pay for a vetting exercise. The evidence suggests that the state authorities are more concerned with ensuring a fair hearing for the prosecution than the defendant, the courts and Parliament choosing to turn a blind eye to this erosion of due process.

Other restrictions on the ability of the defence to influence the composition of the jury support this conclusion. The defence have traditionally been allowed to exclude prospective jurors without the need to give any reason. The number of such 'peremptory challenges' allowed was reduced from 20 to seven in 1948 and to three (per defendant) in 1977, before being abolished by s 118 of the Criminal Justice Act 1987. In the White Paper which preceded the 1987 Act, the government accepted that peremptory challenge might be used for proper reasons, such as to adjust the age, sex or race balance on the jury, but contended that the defence sometimes abused the right so as to remove jurors thought to have too much respect for the law.[18] If the system was serious about prioritising the acquittal of the innocent, one might think that the occasional 'abuse' of the right of peremptory challenge would be regarded as a price worth paying for more representative juries. At the very least, one would expect that the right of peremptory challenge in proper circumstances (as described in the White Paper) would be preserved in any reform of the law. Yet despite the timely publication of research showing that peremptory challenges had no discernible impact on the likelihood of acquittal,[19] the government successfully pressed through its plan to abolish this defence right in its

16 [1988] 3 All ER 1086 at para 11.
17 The recommendations are published as an annex to the Attorney General's guidelines: ibid.
18 Criminal Justice, Plans for Legislation (Cmnd 9658) (Home Office, 1986) para 33.
19 See J Vennard and D Riley, 'The Use of Peremptory Challenge and Stand By of Jurors and Their Relationship to Final Outcome' [1988] Crim LR 731.

entirety.[20] By contrast, the government resisted the powerful argument that fairness demanded that the prosecution should simultaneously lose its equivalent right to 'stand by' (ie, exclude) jurors without cause. Instead the Attorney General issued yet more guidelines exhorting, but not requiring, prosecutors to exercise this right more sparingly in future.[1]

The defence continues to share with the prosecution the right to challenge any juror 'for cause', but this is of little practical use, since jurors may not be questioned about their beliefs or background unless counsel knows of facts to justify such questioning.[2] Where the fruits of a prosecution vetting are passed on to the defence, the generality of the information supplied (see above) may not be enough to support a challenge for cause. Usually defence counsel know no more than a juror's name and address.[3]

The defence can form a visual impression as to the racial, class and age balance on the jury, and this raises the question of whether challenges can be made for cause to achieve a more mixed jury. A *Practice Note* issued in 1973 stressed that it would be wrong to allow the exclusion of jurors on such 'general' grounds as race, religion, political beliefs or occupation.[4] The Court of Appeal subsequently followed this up by declaring in *Ford*[5] that a judge had no discretion to discharge a juror in order to secure a racially mixed jury, nor otherwise to influence the overall composition of the jury. For the court, ' "fairness" is achieved by the principle of random selection.'[6] Whereas the government had suggested in its 1987 White Paper that it would be proper to make a peremptory challenge so as to achieve a socially mixed jury, the courts subsequently denied the defence the ability to challenge for cause on just this basis. Again, the fear seems to be that the defence will seek to 'rig' the jury in its favour. Yet little concern is evident that random selection from the available pool of jurors is unlikely to produce a representative jury. Both the young and those from the new Commonwealth are significantly under-represented on the electoral register.[7] Moreover, stratified sampling would be required in order to

---

[20] For fierce criticism, see J Gobert, 'The Peremptory Challenge—An Obituary' [1989] Crim LR 528.

[1] The guidelines are to be found at [1988] 3 All ER 1086.

[2] See *Chandler (No 2)* [1964] 1 All ER 761. For general discussion, see R Buxton, 'Challenging and Discharging Jurors' [1990] Crim LR 225.

[3] Details of occupation were removed from jury lists in 1983 by order of the Lord Chancellor. A challenge for cause would have been difficult to ground on a juror's occupation, but, prior to the Criminal Justice Act 1987, jurors whose occupations suggested a pro-prosecution outlook might have been peremptorily challenged.

[4] [1973] 1 All ER 240.

[5] [1989] 3 All ER 445.

[6] Ibid at 449.

[7] See (1987) The Law Magazine, 30 October, p 20.

ensure a representative jury. The upshot is that an all-white jury may hear a criminal case against a black defendant, even though such a jury might be wholly unrepresentative of the local community.[8] As Bohlander observes:

'As a result there exists . . . the distinct possibility that the different life style, mentality and experience arising from membership of an ethnic minority will not be taken sufficiently into account in trials where members of such a minority are the defendants.'[9]

The Runciman Commission was aware that two-thirds of all jury trials are heard by white juries, and that the area of concern about jury composition most frequently mentioned by defence barristers was racial mix.[10] Its response was to recommend that the judge be allowed to engineer a racially mixed jury (on application from the defendant) but only in cases with 'unusual and special features'. The Runciman Commission illustrated its proposal by continuing:

'a black defendant charged with burglary would be unlikely to succeed in such an application. But black people accused of violence against a member of an extremist organisation who they said had been making racial taunts against them and their friends might well succeed.'[11]

Cases with such features are likely to be rare.

Jury vetting presents a dilemma for the state. It cannot be seen to interfere with the composition of the jury too readily as this will undermine the useful legitimising effect of jury trial on the criminal process as a whole.[12] On the other hand, the desire to influence the outcome of a particular trial is sometimes very strong. The law both reflects this tension and provides for its resolution, by enabling interference to take place on a covert basis. The prosecution may simply stand by a juror without giving any reason and the defence need not be told that jury vetting has taken place. The prosecutions's duties and powers are governed by broadly drawn administrative directions and guidelines, which provide no sanctions for breach. In stark contrast, the defence has to state reasons for challenging jurors, and may not seek to change the

---

[8] For an illustration of the dangers involved, see J Robbins, 'Who said Anything about Law ?' (1990) 140 NLJ 1275.

[9] M Bohlander, ' ". . . By a jury of his peers"—The Issue of Multi-racial Juries in a Poly-ethnic Society' (1992) XIV(1) Liverpool LR 67.

[10] See M Zander and P Henderson, Crown Court Study (Royal Commission on Criminal Justice, Research Study no 19) (HMSO, 1993) p 241.

[11] Royal Commission on Criminal Justice, Report (Cm 2263) (HMSO, 1993) pp 133–134.

[12] P Duff and M Findlay, 'Jury vetting—The Jury under Attack' (1983) 3 LS at 171–173.

overall balance of the jury. Furthermore, its more limited powers are governed by restrictive case law. The different treatment of prosecution and defence by the state authorities (including Parliament, the government and the courts) is revealing as to the dominant values in our political and legal culture.

In parentheses, it should be noted that a more direct assault on the jury cannot be ruled out. Since 1973, defendants in Northern Ireland charged with offences deemed to be terrorist-related are tried by a single judge sitting without a jury.[13] The introduction of these 'Diplock courts' was justified on the grounds that, firstly, the circumstances of that province left jurors exposed to intimidation and, secondly, that jurors were likely to return perverse verdicts borne of partisanship.[14] However, the thrust of the report which proposed these courts was to dismantle a series of procedural rights and safeguards for suspects, so as to ease the path towards a conviction.[15] As no empirical evidence existed to justify the supposed concerns about jury trials, the suspicion must be that the change was in reality part of the strategy to secure more guilty verdicts. The decline in the acquittal rate in juryless trials since 1973 suggests that increasingly case-hardened judges are delivering the goods.[16] The number of cases heard in Diplock courts is small (416 in 1991)[17] but they represent an area of criminal activity in which, for obvious reasons, the state is particularly keen to secure a high conviction rate. In England and Wales, no attempt has yet been made to remove terrorist-related or other very serious kinds of offences from the province of the jury, although the Roskill Committee in 1986 recommended that complex fraud cases might better be heard by a special tribunal.[18]

---

[13] See the Northern Ireland (Emergency Provisions) Act 1973. The criteria and methods for directing cases to single judge courts are rough and ready and have resulted in the diversion of many cases lacking a terrorist connection away from juries: see J Jackson and S Doran, 'Diplock and the Presumption Against Jury Trial: a Critique' [1992] Crim LR 755.

[14] Report of the Commission to consider legal procedures to deal with terrorist activities in Northern Ireland (Cmnd 5185) (HMSO, 1972). The Commission was chaired by Lord Diplock.

[15] See P Hillyard, 'The Normalization of Special Powers: from Northern Ireland to Britain', in P Scraton (ed), *Law, Order and the Authoritarian State* (Open University Press, 1987) pp 285–286.

[16] Ibid p 294. See also B Dickson, 'Northern Ireland's Emergency Legislation—The Wrong Medicine?' [1992] Public Law 592 at 609–610.

[17] See Dickson, op cit at 608, Table 4.

[18] Report of the Departmental Committee on Fraud Trials (HMSO, 1986). The Runciman Commission concluded that, in the absence of research evidence on the workings of jury trials, there was no basis on which to recommend dispensing with juries for complex frauds or other lengthy cases: Report, op cit p 136.

In this context, however, it is as well to remember that while the most serious cases in the criminal calendar remain within the province of the jury, some fairly serious offences (such as assault on a police constable) have been redirected to the magistrates' courts. For, as we have already seen, Parliament has reclassified many previously either way offences as summary only in order to remove them from the province of the jury.[19] The Runciman Commission has proposed that the right of the defendant to elect trial by jury in either-way cases should be abolished.[20] Thus, the threshold of seriousness thought to justify jury trial is constantly being raised. This particular attack on the jury's role seems primarily to be driven by cost cutting but a useful side-effect, from the crime control point of view, is that magistrates are more likely to convict in these cases.[1] This may be particularly important in public order situations where legitimate protest (picketing, anti-racist marches, demonstrations against the poll tax and so forth) spills over (allegedly) into criminal acts. Such threats to public order, like terrorist offences, amount to threats to the authority of the state itself. Usually, the prosecution evidence in such cases consists entirely of police accounts. A not guilty verdict by a jury would, therefore, both call into question the integrity of the police and undermine the moral authority of the state. Small wonder then that the state ensures that the vast majority of public order offences are heard in the magistrates' courts.

3.   THE VERDICT OF THE JURY

Efforts to influence the jury's verdict in the direction of conviction do not necessarily cease on the conclusion of the selection procedures.

(a)   Majority verdicts

For centuries, jury verdicts had to be unanimous, but the Criminal Justice Act 1967 permitted a majority of not less than ten out of 12. This change has been seen by some critics as undermining the requirement that the prosecution proves guilt beyond reasonable doubt. As Freeman puts it:

'If one or two jurymen conscientiously feel strong enough to dissent

---

[19] See ch 6, section 4(c), above.
[20] Ibid.
[1] See ibid. For further discussion see A Sanders, 'The Erosion of Jury Trial' (1980) 5 Holdsworth LR 21.

from the majority view that demonstrates to my satisfaction that there is reasonable doubt as to the guilt of the accused.'[2]

Others have seen majority verdicts as merely a means to prevent extremists blocking convictions: 'it would enable the racist views of a member of an extreme right wing political party to be discounted in the jury's decision making.'[3] The rationale for the 1967 reform was ostensibly to prevent professional criminals escaping conviction by the expedient of bribing or intimidating individual jurors. That this sometimes happens is undeniable. But the question remains of whether the majority verdict is the correct response to that problem.

In answering, one must consider the effect of the change. The introduction of majority verdicts has led to a trebling of the rate at which juries fail to reach unanimity,[4] and about one in eight guilty verdicts are now by majority only.[5] As Freeman explains:

'juries when told by judges that they may consider a non-unanimous verdict simply stop deliberating when they reach the requisite majority. This may save time and money and it may be "convenient" but how relevant should these considerations be? When managerial efficiency becomes the dominant consideration, justice can soon take a back seat.'[6]

Majority verdicts have thus prodded jury trial in the direction of crime control. The argument that this was necessary in order to guard against 'jury nobbling' is similar to that used to deny bail to defendants on the ground that they might otherwise interfere with prosecution witnesses.[7] In both cases, the argument appears to give greater weight to the conviction of the guilty at the expense of the acquittal of the innocent. In both cases, there is a more appropriate response, which is to safeguard the administration of justice by other means, such as more effective protection for witnesses and jurors. The vast majority of trials do not involve professional criminals and so the risk of 'jury nobbling' is low. The solution adopted, allowing (in all cases) the views of one-sixth of the jury to be dismissed as 'unreasonable', appears grossly disproportionate to the supposed problem.

---

[2] M Freeman, 'The Jury on Trial' [1981] CLP 65 at 69.
[3] R White, *The Administration of Justice* (Blackwell, 1991) p 126.
[4] See Freeman, op cit at 70.
[5] It has been seen that 13% of the defendants convicted in 1992 after a plea of not guilty were convicted on a majority verdict by the jury: *Judicial Statistics: Annual Report 1992* (Cm 2268) (Lord Chancellor's Department) (HSMO, 1993) p 62, Table 6.10.
[6] Op cit at 70. See also P Darbyshire, 'Notes of a Lawyer Juror' (1990) 140 NLJ 1264 at 1266.
[7] On bail, see ch 6, section 4(a), above.

The argument that majority verdicts allow the views of extremists to be neutralised is also defective. By definition, people of extreme views are in a minority in the populace at large. Most juries will have no such jurors and so the problem will rarely arise. Moreover, the views of an extremist will seldom have a bearing on the decision-making process: if a white defendant is alleged to have burgled a shop run by white owners, would not the racist be as open-minded as the next person on the question of guilt? The danger of an extremist very occasionally blocking a justifiable conviction (or acquittal) has to be weighed against the overall due process cost of allowing a majority verdict to be returned in any and every criminal case.

In so far as the 'extremist' argument is used to justify majority verdicts, there is a double standard at work. Like the argument for jury vetting, it claims that the random selection principle cannot be trusted in cases where fierce ethnic or political conflicts are involved. There is some truth in this and that is precisely why ethnic minorities demand some black people on juries when racial hostility is an element. Yet this has been rejected by the government and the courts. In short, the argument that random selection is defective is accepted when this serves prosecution interests, but not otherwise.

In Scotland where juries are 15-strong, it is possible to convict on a simple majority of eight jurors voting for a guilty verdict. Although this suggests that Scots law has even less regard for the presumption of innocence than English law, the comparison is misleading. Scotland has other means of safeguarding defendants which have no parallel in England, such as a general requirement of corroboration of prosecution evidence.[8] Moreover, if a Scottish jury cannot achieve the requisite majority for conviction, the defendant is entitled to an acquittal.[9] In England, by contrast, the defendant is acquitted only if at least ten out of 12 jurors vote for a verdict of not guilty. Otherwise, the jury is said to be 'hung' and the prosecution may opt for a retrial. This symmetry with the requirement for a guilty verdict is impossible to reconcile with the presumption of innocence.[10] For whenever between three and nine jurors vote for acquittal, the prosecution has failed to prove guilt and the presumption of innocence would demand that the defendant be acquitted. Instead, the English system allows guilt or innocence to remain an open question pending a retrial. Statistics on this issue are not published as a matter of course although it is known that some 370

---

[8] See generally Sheriff I D Macphail QC, 'Safeguards in the Scottish Criminal Justice System' [1992] Crim LR 144.
[9] In which case the verdict will either be 'not guilty' or 'not proven'. See G Maher, 'Jury verdicts and the Presumption of Innocence' (1983) 3 146.
[10] Ibid at 151.

retrials of hung cases were heard in 1981.[11] Retrials for this reason also seem inconsistent with the principle of double jeopardy—that no one should stand trial on the same charge twice.

(b) The conduct of the trial by the judge

It is well recognised that judges may have a powerful influence on jury verdicts. Historically, juries were commonly told by judges what verdicts to return and, although juries had the right in legal theory to rebel, they seldom did so.[12] The advent of defence lawyers in the eighteenth century broke up this cosy relationship between judge and jury and caused the criminal trial to move much closer to the adversarial ideal of a passive and impartial judge.[13] The judgment by Lord Denning in *Jones v National Coal Board*[14] is generally regarded as the classic statement of the modern position:

'The judge's part in [an adversarial trial] is to hearken to the evidence, only himself asking questions of witnesses when it is necessary to clear up any point that has been overlooked or left obscure; to see that the advocates behave themselves seemly (sic) and keep to the rules laid down by law; to exclude irrelevancies and discourage repetition; to make sure by wise intervention that he follows the points the advocates are making and can assess their worth . . . If he goes beyond this, he drops the mantle of a judge and assumes the robe of an advocate . . .'[15]

Moreover, it is now clear law that a judge may not direct a jury to convict, however strong the prosecution case may be.[16] At one level, that judges may direct an acquittal but not a conviction is evidence that the law on this point reflects the due process view that wrongful convictions are a greater evil than wrongful acquittals. Closer analysis reveals that conviction-minded judges are given ample scope to parade their views and prejudices before the jury.

The judgment in *Jones v National Coal Board* accepts that judges may properly ask some questions and make some interventions, but its

---

11 S Butler, Acquittal Rates (Home Office Research and Planning Unit Paper no 16) (HMSO, 1983) p 7.

12 See J Langbein, 'The Criminal Trial Before Lawyers' (1978) 45 U Ch LR 263.

13 Ibid at 314.

14 [1957] 2 QB 55.

15 Ibid at 64.

16 *DPP v Stonehouse* [1978] AC 55. A possible exception to the principle that a judge may not direct a conviction is where the defence is based on a point of law and the judge rules against the defence on that point: *Hill; Hall* (1988) 89 Cr App Rep 74. This, however, seems irreconcilable with the concept of jury equity.

tone suggests that these should be limited in number and scope. The reality is that the Court of Appeal has allowed judges a large degree of freedom in conducting trials.[17] In *Gunning*,[18] a conviction was quashed where the judge had asked 165 questions compared with 172 from counsel. But in *Matthews*,[19] a conviction was upheld even though it was conceded that the number of judicial interventions and questions were excessive. The judge had asked 524 questions to counsel's 538, but the Court of Appeal concluded that counsel had not been diverted from his own line of questioning. The issue should not be whether such a diversion occurred, however, but whether the degree of intervention from the bench compromised the appearance or substance of judicial impartiality. The appellate courts seem unable or unwilling to grasp this point. The Court of Appeal ruled in *Ptohopoulos*[20] that gross discourtesy to counsel cannot in itself be sufficient to justify quashing a conviction. In *Hircock*,[1] the trial judge had muttered 'Oh God', and groaned and sighed throughout defending counsel's closing speech. One would have thought that such gross discourtesy impinged on the fairness of the trial. The Court of Appeal decided, however, that the judge's behaviour did not reflect any view of the defendant's case, but was simply implicit criticism of the conduct of the case by defence counsel. One cannot help wondering whether the jury appreciated this subtle distinction.

The Runciman Commission advocated that judges should be more interventionist still in conducting trials in order to save time and money and because shorter trials would make it easier for jurors to recall the essential facts.

'Judges must be prepared to intervene as and when necessary to expedite the proceedings, to see that witnesses are treated by counsel as they should be, to curtail prolix or irrelevant questioning, to prevent the jury from being confused or misled, and to order the payment of costs when they have been wastefully or unnecessarily incurred.'[2]

Thus, for example, it wanted judges to prevent witnesses being 'subjected to bullying and intimidatory tactics by counsel or to deliberately and unnecessarily prolonged cross-examination . . .'[3]

---

[17] For a review of the case law, see S Doran, 'Descent to Avernus' (1989) 139 NLJ 1147.
[18] [1980] Crim LR 592.
[19] [1983] Crim LR 683.
[20] [1968] Crim LR 52.
[1] [1969] 1 All ER 47.
[2] Report, op cit p 119.
[3] Ibid p 122.

'We accept that counsel sometimes need to pursue a line of questioning that is distressing or even offensive to the witness. But it is possible to do this in a courteous way, and it is for the judge to ensure that counsel does so.'[4]

It brushed aside the suggestion that such interventions might give the 'impression of bias' and singularly failed to acknowledge the violence that its proposals would do to the adversarial theory of justice which asserts that the production and presentation of evidence must be left to the parties in dispute.[5] This provides another example of the failure of the Runciman Commission to grapple with underlying theories of criminal justice, a failure reflected by the unprincipled nature of its recommendations. Its proposals evince a degree of trust in judicial impartiality which scarcely seems justified on the past track record of the courts. Moreover, the Runciman Commission made no reference to its own Crown Court survey. This found no support from either prosecuting or defence counsel for more robust interventions from the judge. Where judges had intervened in trials, the interruptions favoured the prosecution much more frequently than they did the defence.[6]

This is not just a simple clash between due process and crime control principles, however. Neither model adequately caters for victims and other witnesses.[7] When the conduct of the case is left to defence and prosecution lawyers, victims often suffer. Concern at the treatment of rape victims in court, in particular, leads naturally to the position adopted by the Runciman Commission. It is significant that some lawyers noted for their due process approach now refuse to defend defendants charged with rape precisely because they object to 'consent' defences which involve attacking the character of the alleged victim. None of this is a conclusive argument in favour of the Runciman Commission's recommendations. It is simply a call for the arguments and policy decisions about judicial intervention to be grounded in clear principles so that the consequences of policy changes can be judged in the light of their objectives.

---

[4] Ibid p 121.
[5] See ch 1 for discussion. The Runciman Commission acknowledged at the start of its report that some of its recommendations could 'fairly be interpreted as seeking to move the system in an inquisitorial direction' (Report, op cit p 3) but did not provide a reasoned justification for such a move, either in general terms, or in support of particular recommendations.
[6] M Zander and P Henderson, Crown Court Study (Royal Commission on Criminal Justice, Research Study no 19) (HMSO, 1993) pp 137–138.
[7] See ch 1.

(c) Summing up by the judge

The last word in a contested trial before the jury retires to consider its verdict is always that of the judge. The judge explains the law to the jury and provides them with a summary of the evidence. This gives judges ample scope for attempting to influence the outcome of the trial. The most notorious recent example of such an attempt was in the trial of the 'Birmingham Six', where Bridge J over a three-day summing up skilfully led the jury by the nose to a verdict of guilty.[8] He began by telling the jury that 'however hard a judge tries to be impartial, inevitably his presentation of the evidence is bound to be coloured by his own view.' He then left them in no doubt as to what that view might be.[9] For example, he sought to depict the defence contention that the police had fabricated evidence and lied in court as far-fetched:

'If the defendants are giving you honest and substantially accurate evidence, there is no escape from the fact that the police are involved in a conspiracy to commit a variety of crimes which must be unprecedented in the annals of British criminal history.'

Other defence witnesses were similarly discredited, such as the prison doctor who gave evidence of injuries to the accused and their probable infliction by the police:

'. . . can you believe one single word of what Dr Harwood says ? There are inescapably many perjurers who have given evidence. If Dr Harwood is one of them, is he not the worst?'

Bridge J made this performance appeal-proof, however, by continually reminding the jurors that it was for them, not him, to decide where the truth lay.[10] Where this formalistic incantation is omitted, the Court of Appeal has sometimes intervened. Thus in *Berrada*,[11] the judge observed that the defendant's allegations of police misconduct were 'really monstrous and wicked'. The Court of Appeal rebuked the judge, declaring that her duty was to sum up impartially without seeking to

---

[8] Excerpts from the transcript of the trial are reproduced (with critical commentary) by J Wood in C Walker and K Starmer (eds), *Justice in Error* (Blackstone, 1993) p 159. See also J Jackson, 'Trial Procedures' in ibid p 145, on the summing up in the 'Carl Bridgewater' case.

[9] After the jury convicted, the judge commented that the evidence in the case was the clearest and most overwhelming he had ever heard.

[10] In the third (and successful) appeal by the 'Birmingham Six', the Court of Appeal acknowledged the forceful nature of the summing up by Bridge J, but did not accept that this had vitiated the proceedings. As Lloyd LJ put it, 'the judge also made it clear throughout the summing-up that it was for the jury, and not for him, to determine where the truth lay': *McIlkenny* (1991) 93 Cr App Rep 287 at 293.

[11] (1989) 91 Cr App Rep 131.

inflate evidence by 'sarcastic and extravagant comment'. More temperate language from the judge is all that the law requires, however. The senior judiciary have declared that trial judges are entitled to express their opinions on the facts in robust and confident terms,[12] and may even observe that the defendant's story is a remarkable one.[13]

One danger in giving judges such freedom of manoeuvre is that they are privy to much inadmissible evidence, including the defendant's previous convictions (if any) and may therefore be biased against the defendant.[14] On the other hand, judges sometimes make plain in their summary of the evidence that they think an acquittal the right result, as in the 'Stephen Waldorf' case, in which the two police officers on trial had shot and pistol-whipped an innocent man by mistake.[15] In general, judges simply get case hardened and sceptical about defendants. This is one of the central arguments for employing a jury to decide questions of fact. Extensive judicial intervention introduces into trials the very problem that the use of juries is meant to avoid—prejudice.

The Runciman Commission was adamant that judges should be

'wholly neutral in any comment that they make on the credibility of the evidence . . . it is inappropriate for judges to intrude their own views of whether or not a witness is to be believed.'[16]

Its clear stance on this issue is undermined, however, by the failure to discuss either the extent to which judges do sum up in a biased fashion, or the extent to which case law allows them to do so. Notably, it failed to make any formal recommendation on the matter, which suggests that either it mistakenly believed that the behaviour of trial judges and the law conformed to its view of the ideal or that it thought the issue a trivial one which raised few problems in practice. Yet its own

[12] See per Channell J in *Cohen* (1909) 2 Cr App Rep 197 at 208.
[13] Per Lord Reading CJ in *O'Donnell* (1917) 12 Cr App Rep 219 at 221. See also the speeches by Lord Salmon and Lord Edmund-Davies in *DPP v Stonehouse* [1978] AC 55. The former said, for example, that it would be in order for a judge to sum up to the jury 'in such a way as to make it plain that he considers the accused is guilty and should be convicted' (at 80).
[14] Zander and Henderson, op cit p 135 found that in cases where judges summed up for conviction and where the defendant had a previous record the summation was in line with the evidence as often as it was against the weight of the evidence. On this basis, they argue that judges do not appear to be influenced by knowledge of prior convictions. This is a crude analysis, however. One would need to control for all factors that might lead to a judge summing up for conviction (such as race, class or sex of the defendant, political/media pressures to clamp down on particular crimes and so on) in order to establish whether knowledge of a defendant's previous record played a part.
[15] See (1983) Times, 19 October.
[16] See Report, op cit p 124.

Crown Court study suggested that trial judges commonly display bias. According to prosecutors, in over 1,000 cases in 1992 the judge summed up against the weight of the evidence, while the figure was more than 2,000 (nearly 10% of all cases tried by jury) according to defence barristers. Prosecuting barristers tended to think that where the summing up was against the weight of the evidence, it favoured an acquittal. According to defence barristers, however, in 92% of the cases where the summing up was identified as biased in this sense, the bias was towards conviction.[17] In half of these cases, the jury convicted.[18]

In the United States, an historical distrust of officialdom is reflected in the rule in most state jurisdictions that the judge in a criminal trial must express no opinion on the weight or credibility of the testimony of a witness or on the merits of either side of the case.[19] In some continental jurisdictions the other extreme of the argument may be seen, in that judges are allowed to retire with juries in order to determine the verdict. The evidence suggests that this co-decision model produces a much lower acquittal rate than when matters are left in the hands of the jury alone.[20]

4.   TRIAL: PROCEDURE, EVIDENCE AND LAW

(a)   Procedure and evidence

In an adversarial system, the decision makers are meant to be passive. It is no part of the jury's role to investigate matters for itself away from the courtroom. Jurors can ask questions in court but rarely do so.[1] Any question is meant to be passed in writing to the judge who will then relay it to a witness if appropriate. The artificiality of this procedure undoubtedly deters jurors from a more proactive role in the trial and they receive little encouragement to assert themselves.[2] It follows that

---

[17] Note that this does not mean that prosecution and defence counsel were disagreeing about where the bias lay in particular cases, since they may well have been talking about different cases. Prosecutors will tend to be alive to bias against their interests but not notice when the bias runs in their favour and the same is true of defence lawyers. Zander and Henderson, op cit p 131, presented evidence of the extent of agreement as to which side was favoured in the judge's summation, but did not do this for cases where the summation not only favoured one side or the other, but was against the weight of the evidence.

[18] See Zander and Henderson, op cit pp 135–136.

[19] See D Wolchover, 'Should Judges Sum up on the Facts?' [1989] Crim LR 781.

[20] See R Munday, 'Jury Trial, Continental Style' (1993) 13 LS 204 at 216, in particular.

[1] In the Crown Court study, under half of jurors had wanted to ask a question and less than 20% of this number had actually done so: Zander and Henderson, op cit, p 213.

[2] Nearly a third of jurors in the Crown Court study had not been informed at any stage that they could ask questions: ibid.

juries must reach their verdicts on the material that is placed before them by counsel for the prosecution and defence. This material is itself shaped by the rules of criminal procedure and evidence. This body of law accordingly forms yet another battleground for Packer's two models of the criminal process.

The clarion call for the crime control model was sounded by the then Commissioner of the Metropolitan Police, Sir Robert Mark, in his Dimbleby lecture of 1973. Arguing that the jury acquits an unacceptably high proportion of those whom the police believe to be guilty, Mark pinned the blame on procedural rules and crooked lawyers:

'It is, of course, right that in a serious criminal case the burden of proof should be on the prosecution. But in trying to discharge that burden the prosecution has to act within a complicated framework of rules which were designed to give every advantage to the defence. The prosecution has to give the defence advance notice of the whole of its case, but the accused, unless he wants to raise an alibi, can keep his a secret until the actual trial. When the police interrogate a suspect or charge him they have to keep reminding him that he need not say anything. If he has a criminal record the jury are not ordinarily allowed to know about it . . . The criminal and his lawyers take every advantage of these technical rules . . . Because of its technicality and its uncertainty, the criminal trial has come to be regarded as a game of skill and chance in which the rules are binding on one side only.'[3]

Much of the academic response to Mark was concerned with demonstrating that the acquittal rate by juries was not 'too high',[4] that professional criminals were not frequently escaping justice by exploiting the rules[5] and that there was little evidence to support the 'bent lawyers' thesis.[6] Less attention was paid to whether the rules of criminal

---

[3] R Mark, Minority Verdict (1973 Dimbleby Lecture) (BBC, 1973). The core of the lecture is reproduced in M Zander, *Cases and Materials on the English Legal System* (Weidenfeld and Nicolson, 1992) pp 471–475.

[4] See Zander, op cit pp 475–476 for a standard statistical response in which it is pointed out that most Crown Court defendants plead guilty and that of the 16% found not guilty by the jury in 1990–91 most were acquitted on the order or direction of the judge. But even this is too high if one operates with a presumption of guilt and belief in the integrity and efficiency of the police and prosecution. Regarding whether there is evidence to ground such a belief, see section 1, above.

[5] Limited support for Mark's thesis was provided by J A Mack, 'Full-time Major Criminals and the Courts' (1976) 39 MLR 241, but see the response by A Sanders, 'Does Professional Crime Pay?—A Critical Comment on Mack' (1977) 40 MLR 553. See also J Baldwin and M McConville, *Jury Trials* (Oxford University Press, 1979) pp 110–112.

[6] See Baldwin and McConville, ibid p 118, and, by the same authors, 'Allegations Against Lawyers' [1978] Crim LR 744.

procedure and evidence did indeed unduly favour the defence. Let us examine Mark's three examples of such 'technical' rules.

Advance disclosure of prosecution evidence

Three points may be made here. Firstly, the requirement that the prosecution give notice of its case to the defence is intended to redress an imbalance between the parties to the case. As was noted by Lloyd LJ in the successful 'Birmingham Six' appeal, a

'disadvantage of the adversarial system may be that the parties are not evenly matched in resources . . . But the inequality of resources is ameliorated by the obligation on the part of the prosecution to make available all material which may prove helpful to the defence.'[7]

The resources of the police and prosecution far outweigh those available to the defence. Moreover, the police are involved in the case from the outset, whereas the defence will not begin to operate until a suspect is arrested. In these circumstances, it is not possible for the defence to carry out an adequate independent investigation of an offence. Access to the material collected by the police allows the defence to perform its duty to present the case in the light that most favours the defendant. Thus, advance prosecution disclosure should not be seen as giving an advantage to the defence, but as a means of redressing a structural disadvantage.

The second point is that unless accused persons are told what the allegations against them are, they cannot prepare a defence. The third is that the duty to disclose was by no means as absolute in 1973 as Mark implied, and there remains uncertainty over the exact scope of that duty.[8] The reality is that the police, the CPS and other prosecution agencies often fail to meet its requirements.[9]

The right of silence

Mark correctly acknowledged the inroads made into the right of silence by s 11 of the Criminal Justice Act 1967 which requires alibi defences to be notified to the police in advance of the trial, so that they may be checked. The right has since been further whittled away by rules made under s 81 of PACE requiring the defence to disclose any expert

---

[7] *McIlkenny* (1991) 93 Cr App Rep 287 at 312.

[8] See P O'Connor, 'Prosecution Disclosure: Principle, Practice and Justice' in C Walker and K Starmer (eds), *Justice in Error* (Blackstone, 1993). For the position in the magistrates' courts, see ch 6, section 3(c), above.

[9] See ch 5, section 3(c) and ch 7, section 5(b), above.

evidence it intends to use[10] and, in the context of fraud trials, by the provisions of the Criminal Justice Act 1987 which can be employed to mandate extensive defence disclosure. Further exceptions are to be found in legislation concerning official secrecy, terrorism, drug trafficking and companies.[11]

Another important point is that the extent to which the right of silence is respected by the courts has been much overstated.[12] The Court of Appeal in *Gerard*[13] declined to intervene when a trial judge commented that an accused's silence before charge might appear 'perhaps a little curious' and 'a little odd'. In *Chandler*,[14] the Court of Appeal ruled that where an accused and an accuser were on equal terms it would be in order to invite the jury to consider whether silence in the face of an accusation or question amounted to an acceptance of what had been said. This equal terms doctrine was in accordance with earlier cases such as *Parkes*[15] but the new departure was to assert that suspects might be adjudged as on level or even superior terms vis-à-vis police officers:

'We do not accept that a police officer always has an advantage over someone he is questioning. Everything depends on the circumstances. A young detective questioning a local dignitary in the course of an inquiry into alleged local government corruption may be very much at a disadvantage.'

In *Chandler*, a police officer was held to be on equal terms with a suspect because the latter had his solicitor present during questioning. But the court went on to rule that no adverse comment should be made with regard to an accused's silence in response to any question put after the police had cautioned the suspect. Its reasoning was that it would be wrong to criticise a defendant for remaining silent after being told that there was a right to do just this. This bizarre logic makes the existence of a right dependent on being told about it. It also ignores the possibility that an accused knew of the right anyway, or as in *Chandler* itself may have been told of it by a solicitor. The decision means that suspects who wish to avail themselves of the right of silence prior to caution should avoid having a solicitor present in police interviews, and that police officers who wish to deny suspects the right of silence should delay administering the caution as long as

---

10   Crown Court (Advance Notice of Expert Evidence) Rules SI 1987/716.
11   For discussion, see Zander, op cit pp 131–133.
12   For a full review of the case law, see the four-part article by D Wolchover, (1989) 139 NLJ at 396, 428, 484 and 501.
13   (1948) 32 Cr App Rep 132.
14   [1976] 1 WLR 585.
15   (1976) 64 Cr App Rep 25.

possible.[16] None of this seems consistent with the view of Mark that procedural rules have been developed so as to give every advantage to the defence.

What of the question of principle? Should defendants be obliged to answer police questions and disclose their defence in advance of trial? From a crime control point of view, such an obligation is essential in order to prevent the defence 'ambushing' the prosecution at trial by adducing evidence that the police have had no opportunity to check. Defence disclosure may also aid efficiency by allowing the prosecution to concentrate only on the issues in dispute. In his note of dissent to the report of the Runciman Commission, Zander forcefully sets out the due process objections to such an obligation.[17] The most important is that defence disclosure is inconsistent with the principle that the burden of proof lies upon the prosecution. Where the state has accused the citizen of a crime, why should the latter be under any obligation to assist in the process of prosecution ? As we have stressed repeatedly, the burden of proof plays an important part in protecting the innocent against conviction, and in guarding against the abuse of power by the police and prosecution agencies.

An illustration of the dangers involved in mandating defence disclosure is provided by the Taylor sisters, freed on appeal in 1993 following their conviction the previous year. In that case, a friend had been prepared to act as a witness for the defence until the police got wind of this and 'interviewed' her. On being threatened with a prosecution for conspiracy to murder, she decided not to give evidence at the trial.[18] Another example is the 'Confait Affair'. Here, one of the accused gave the police an alibi for the suspected time of death. The police responded by persuading the pathologist to alter the estimated time of death, thus eliminating the power of the alibi. Contrary to Mark's position, the innocent may have as much to fear from defence disclosure as the guilty.

The majority of the Runciman Commission brushed aside such points of principle in recommending that the defence should be required as part of pre-trial procedure to disclose the general nature of its case to the prosecution.[19] It also paid little heed to research it had itself commissioned on the right to silence which demonstrated that successful

---

[16] See also the case of *Horne* [1990] Crim LR 188, where the equal terms doctrine was applied to silence in response to a victim's accusation made in the presence of police officers. For the position where the defendant declines to give evidence in court, see *Martinez-Tobon* [1994] 1 WLR 388.

[17] Royal Commission on Criminal Justice, Report (Cm 2263) (HSMO, 1993) p 221.

[18] See (1993) Guardian, 12 June.

[19] Report, op cit pp 97–100.

ambush defences are extremely rare.[20] The majority of the Runciman Commission did believe, however, that the right of silence in the face of police questioning should be retained, and that a refusal on the part of the defendant to testify in court should not be capable of corroborating the prosecution's case.[1] The government has chosen to ignore the Runciman Commission's (admittedly half-hearted) support for the right to silence and the Criminal Justice and Public Order Bill includes a series of clauses (cll 27–30) which will virtually abolish that right. The crime control campaign initiated by Mark against the right of silence has finally come to fruition.

The jury's ignorance of the defendant's criminal record

The rationale for the principle that juries should not ordinarily be told of a defendant's previous convictions (or otherwise be informed that the defendant is of bad character) is that the prejudicial impact of this information outweighs its probative value.[2] Whether one sees this rule as unduly favouring the defendant or merely as a necessary safeguard against juries jumping to unwarranted conclusions depends, in part, on a judgment as to how reliable the police are at identifying the probably guilty in the first place. As earlier chapters in this book have shown, the police have a tendency to focus their attention upon 'known criminals'. Statistically, this strategy may be effective in increasing the number of guilty persons detected, but, by giving insufficient attention to independent evidence of guilt, it also increases the risk that innocent people will be drawn into the criminal process. From a due process perspective, this insight would strengthen the argument for keeping the defendant's past record from the jury. Denied this knowledge, the jury is forced to focus on the essential issue—is there sufficient evidence that the defendant committed the offence as charged ?

As Mark himself recognised, this rule is not applied rigidly, and there are a number of exceptions to it. Firstly, where defendants assert that they are of good character,[3] the prosecution may rebut this by introducing evidence of previous convictions. This seems at first sight a reasonable exception: defendants can hardly complain at the unfairness of the jury being told of a past record of theft if they have claimed to be honest and trustworthy. On the other hand, the courts have adopted a broad definition of what counts as asserting good character. For

---

[20] See R Leng, The right to silence in police interrogation: a study of some of the issues underlying the debate (Royal Commission on Criminal Justice, Research Study no 10) (HMSO, 1992).

[1] Report, op cit pp 54–55.

[2] See *Selvey v DPP* [1968] 2 All ER 497.

[3] On which see *Stronach* [1988] Crim LR 48.

example, in *R v Coulman*[4] the defence was held to have led evidence of good character by establishing that the defendant was married, had a family and was in regular employment.[5] Secondly, if the facts alleged are similar to the facts of previous incidents involving the defendant then the jury may be told of the latter. This rule is sometimes expressed as though there need be some 'striking' similarity 'as virtually to rule out coincidence.'[6] But in the leading case of *DPP v P*,[7] the House of Lords ruled that it was not essential to show that the similarities were striking or that the circumstances were unusual. All that was necessary is that in the judge's view the probative force of the evidence of previous misconduct was sufficiently great as to make it just to admit it, notwithstanding that it was prejudicial to the accused. This seems to leave defendants with convictions for a similar offence to that with which they are now charged at considerable risk of having their record put before a jury.[8] In the case of handling stolen goods, the Theft Act 1968 puts the matter beyond doubt. Section 27(3) provides that once the prosecution has adduced evidence that the defendant committed the *actus reus* of the offence (handling) previous convictions for theft or handling are admissible for the purpose of proving *mens rea* (knowledge or belief that the goods were stolen).[9] This all means that juries are invited to find someone guilty on the same crime control basis that underpinned the defendant's initial arrest by the police.[10] The third exception is that where one co-accused gives evidence against another co-accused, the latter can cross-examine the former about his previous convictions.[11]

The fourth exception is also the most controversial. The Criminal Evidence Act 1898, s 1(f), permits the introduction of previous convictions where 'the nature or conduct of the defence is such as to involve imputations on the character of the . . . witnesses for the prosecution.'[12] This 'tit for tat' rule typically comes into play where the defendant

---

[4] (1927) 20 Cr App Rep 106.
[5] See the discussion by D McBarnet, *Conviction* (MacMillan, 1983) pp 112–113.
[6] Zander, op cit p 381.
[7] [1991] 2 AC 447.
[8] For further discussion, see A Zuckerman, 'Similar Fact Evidence: The Unobservable Rule' (1987) 104 LQR 187.
[9] The effect of this rule has been tempered by the due process-inspired decision given in *Herron* [1967] 1 QB 107 that the judge retains a discretion not to admit evidence of previous theft/handling convictions where its prejudicial effect would outweigh its probative value.
[10] See ch 3, section 4(b), above on the importance of 'previous' to arrests.
[11] See further R Munday, 'The Wilder Permutations of s 1(f) of the Criminal Evidence Act 1898' (1987) 7 LS 137.
[12] For guidelines on how judges should exercise their discretion under s 1(f) see *Britzman; Hall* [1983] 1 All ER 69.

alleges that the police have fabricated or planted incriminating evidence. Since such fabrication undoubtedly occurs from time to time, the question arises of whether it can be right to have a rule which will penalise at least some defendants for making wholly justified attacks on the character of police witnesses. The rationale for the rule seems to be that knowledge of a defendant's previous convictions will assist the jury in deciding who is telling the truth, the police or the defendant. But if evidence of past misconduct is generally thought to be too prejudicial, it seems anomalous that it is not so regarded in this situation also. And if previous convictions are meant to be indicative of the defendant's dishonesty, why are they not routinely admitted in evidence in cases such as where the defendant admits taking goods from a store without payment but denies that this was done intentionally?

The impact of this rule of evidence can be seen in Baldwin and McConville's study of late plea changers discussed in the previous chapter. Of their sample, 40% alleged in interview that the police had falsely attributed to them verbal admissions, and a third of those claiming to be innocent made such allegations.[13] But their counsel had almost invariably advised that any challenge to the police evidence would be foolish since it would rebound on them, the police evidence would be preferred anyway and the judge might be sufficiently annoyed by the defence tactics to impose a heavier sentence.[14] At the same time, if no challenge were made conviction was inevitable. Faced with such advice, it is not surprising that these defendants changed their plea to guilty. As one defendant interviewed by Baldwin and McConville put it:

'My barrister kept saying I had no chance and that it would be bad if I fought it in court . . . I said, "No way, I'm not having it; this copper has made up verbals." The barrister said, "If you stick to your plea of not guilty, it seems to me there is going to be some right mud-slinging towards the police. If you do get found guilty, as you will on something, the judge is going to say, "You don't like the police—our blokes—and all these allegations were made to try and cover yourself up for striking this poor [victim]," and you'll get done very heavily." '[15]

Interestingly, this kind of advice was pressed upon defendants with no previous convictions as well as upon recidivists. This suggests that the real rationale for the 'tit for tat' rule is the perceived need to deter attacks on the integrity of the state authorities which might undermine public confidence in the criminal justice system. Where defendants lack

[13] J Baldwin and M McConville, *Negotiated Justice* (Martin Robertson, 1977) p 68.
[14] Ibid p 69.
[15] Ibid p 47.

previous records, it appears that other mechanisms (such as the threat of stiffer sentences) are employed to deter them from challenging the prosecution version of events.

It is important to stress that the battery of controls and safeguards introduced by PACE since the Baldwin and McConville study was conducted have not altered the position in any significant way. It is still open to the prosecution to adduce evidence of an alleged verbal confession.[16] The due process objections to the 'tit for tat' rule—that it increases the risk that the innocent will plead or be found guilty and that it encourages the police to fabricate evidence—should be borne in mind in evaluating Mark's view that the rules of the adversarial 'game' bind and hamper only the prosecution.

Other rules of evidence

We have shown above that Mark's three examples of rules that favour the defence are neither so absolute nor so favourable as he contended. There are many other important procedural and evidential rules that favour the prosecution rather than the defence. For instance, there is no requirement that the prosecution produce evidence to corroborate the evidence of a witness or the confession of an accused. The jury will be warned that it is dangerous to convict on the unsupported statement of certain types of witness (accomplices and complainants in sexual cases) but this neither amounts to requiring corroboration nor precludes a conviction.[17] The law accepts that its own rules can give rise to convictions of an unsatisfactory nature, thus directly negating fundamental due process propositions. Not even a warning is required where the only evidence is an alleged confession, yet, as chapter 4 demonstrated, extreme caution in this area is vital.

Where the evidence against the accused rests substantially on identification evidence the case of *Turnbull*[18] requires that the judge should direct an acquittal if the quality of the evidence is poor, but otherwise should warn the jury of the need for caution before convicting on such evidence. Arguably, these guidelines do not go far enough in protecting accused persons from wrongful conviction, given the inherently unreliable nature of identification evidence and the role such evidence is known to have played in miscarriages of justice.[19] Subsequent decisions

---

[16] See ch 4.
[17] Under the Criminal Justice and Public Order Bill, the judge will no longer be required to give a corroboration warning in these categories, although warnings may still be given if the judge thinks fit.
[18] [1977] QB 224.
[19] See further J Jackson, 'The Insufficiency of Identification Evidence Based on Personal Impression' [1986] Crim LR 203.

have suggested that the '*Turnbull* guidelines' need in any case only be followed where the identification is based on nothing more than a 'fleeting glimpse'.[20]

The rules prohibiting the admission of hearsay evidence (already subject to many exceptions)[1] have been weakened considerably by s 23 of the Criminal Justice Act 1988. This allows first-hand documentary evidence to be admitted if the maker is dead, ill or cannot be located and brought to court, or if the statement is made to a police officer and the maker does not give oral evidence through fear or because the authorities deem it important to keep the witness out of the public arena. This cuts against the traditional emphasis in criminal procedure on the importance of evidence being given orally in open court, so that it may be subject to cross-examination. As Jackson notes, s 23 'has increased the ability of the prosecution to submit dubious documentary evidence against the accused.'[2] The right of police officers to give evidence of what they say defendants told them is itself an exception to the hearsay rule and gives rise to the phenomenon of alleged confessions, perhaps the single biggest cause of miscarriages of justice. Finally, we should recall our discussion in chapter 1, section 1, above, of the numerous instances throughout the criminal law where the burden of proof has been transferred from the shoulders of the state to those of the defendant, thus undermining the presumption of innocence.

The Runciman Commission approach to the law of evidence was somewhat contradictory. On the one hand, it proposed changes which would increase the due process protection of suspects from wrongful conviction. One example is the recommendation that an attack on the character of a witness for the prosecution which is central to the defence should not expose the accused to the risk of cross-examination concerning previous convictions.[3] Thus, if the defence rested on an allegation that the police had fabricated a confession, the police could be accused of having lied, without fear of the 'tit for tat' rule coming into play. Another example is its recommendation that judges should be required to warn juries of the dangers of convicting on the basis of confession evidence alone.[4]

On the other hand, a somewhat larger number of recommendations

---

[20]   See *R v Curry; R v Keeble* [1983] Crim LR 737.

[1]   As Zander, op cit p 392, observes, 'it is a matter of opinion whether the exceptions now prove or disprove the existence of the rule'.

[2]   J Jackson, 'Trial Procedures' in C Walker and K Starmer (eds), *Justice in Error* (Blackstone, 1993) p 139.

[3]   Report, op cit p 127.

[4]   Ibid p 68; a point not taken forward by the Criminal Justice and Public Order Bill.

will, if acted upon, make it easier for the prosecution to secure a conviction. For example, the Runciman Commission wanted the rules on hearsay evidence to be relaxed still further; it recommended that where the accused admits committing the *actus reus* of the crime but denies acting with intent, knowledge or recklessness (as the case may be) previous convictions for a similar offence should be admissible; and, by a majority, it turned its back on the much canvassed proposal that convictions based on confession evidence should not be tolerated in the absence of corroboration.[5] In his review of this aspect of the Runciman Commissions's work, Jackson concludes that 'it is difficult to feel confident that its recommendations do enough to restore faith in the system's ability to avert miscarriages of justice . . .'[6]

(b) Substantive law and the definition of offences

In understanding why juries are so often convinced of guilt beyond reasonable doubt, it is also necessary to look at the structure of substantive criminal law. We can do no more than scratch the surface of this issue here, but the links between criminal law and criminal justice are too important to ignore. We commented in earlier chapters on how the breadth of the criminal law has implications for police powers of arrest and stop and search, and the implications are no less important at the trial stage. The essential point is that the fewer the elements that have to be proved by the prosecution, and the easier the law makes it to prove those elements, the more likely it is that juries will convict. All-encompassing offence definitions are antithetical to due process, since they leave little for the defence to argue about. To be presumed innocent is of little significance if the prosecution can prove guilt with ease. This is precisely what makes such definitions attractive to crime control adherents, since they assist in curtailing inefficient and pointless adversarial trials. Moreover, they may deter defendants from opting for trial in the first place and thus contribute to maintaining a high guilty plea rate.

Many examples of broadly drawn offences could be given. McBarnet has pointed out that crimes such as theft and assault cover a much wider range of behaviour than the lay person generally realises.[7] Under the Theft Act 1968, the *actus reus* of theft is the appropriation of property belonging to another, and any assumption of any one right of the owner amounts to an appropriation.[8] Simply moving property a

---

[5] See ibid pp 127, 126 and 68, respectively.
[6] J Jackson, '(2) The Evidence Recommendations' [1993] Crim LR 817 at 828.
[7] See D McBarnet, *Conviction* (MacMillan, 1983) pp 13–14.
[8] *Morris* [1984] AC 320.

short distance may be such an assumption. Moreover, the House of Lords has held in *Gomez*[9] that it is an appropriation notwithstanding that the owner authorises the taking or moving of property. Thus simply taking down a bottle of whisky from a supermarket shelf amounts to an appropriation and if there is, in addition, evidence of dishonesty and an intention to deprive the supermarket of the whisky permanently, then a conviction for theft could follow. As the only evidence of a defendant's state of mind is likely to be a confession, it seems dangerous to reduce the conduct element of the crime of theft to this minimum level. As we saw in chapter 4, the risk of false confessions is great and it would be more in accordance with due process principles to require that the defendant did some act which was strongly corroborative of his or her criminal purpose (such as concealing the whisky under an overcoat).

General principles of liability further extend the prodigious reach of the criminal law. For example, s 1(1) of the Criminal Attempts Act 1981 makes it an offence to do an act which is more than merely preparatory to the commission of an indictable offence if done with intent to commit such offence. To take our earlier example, merely reaching to pick up the bottle of whisky from the shelf may be classified as a criminal attempt.

The law concerning the mental element in crime is also often broadly drawn, as in the case of '*Caldwell* recklessness'. Prior to the case of *Caldwell*,[10] decisions of the Court of Appeal had established that 'recklessness' (the mental element required in offences such as assault, criminal damage, and one of the variants of manslaughter) meant the state of mind of one who was consciously aware of the risk that an action would bring about certain consequences.[11] In *Caldwell*, a case of criminal damage, the House of Lords held by a narrow majority that the term also encompassed persons who failed to consider whether such a risk existed when that risk would have been obvious to a reasonable person. There are sound policy arguments for extending the scope of recklessness in this way—the moral culpability of someone who cannot be bothered to address his or her mind to the possibility of risk may be no less than one who consciously takes risks but exercises a degree of care in doing so.[12] But while Lord Diplock, speaking for the majority, justified the development of the law on such moral grounds, it is striking that he was much influenced by the supposed difficulties juries would have in distinguishing those who appreciated the risks in

[9]   [1993] 1 All ER 1.
[10]   [1981] 1 All ER 961.
[11]   See, in particular, *Cunningham* [1957] 2 QB 396 and *Stephenson* [1979] QB 695.
[12]   See S Gardner, 'Recklessness Refined' (1993) 109 LQR 21.

their actions and those who did not.[13] In the subsequent case of *Reid*,[14] Lord Keith reiterated this point, arguing that it would be impossible for a juror to be satisfied beyond reasonable doubt that a defendant was aware of a risk, rather than having merely failed to advert to the possibility of risk. 'So logically', he continued, 'if only the first state of mind constituted the relevant mens rea, it would be impossible ever to get a conviction.'[15]

We are dealing here with entirely bogus logic. The appellate courts have so far confined the impact of *Caldwell* to offences of criminal damage, reckless driving[16] and manslaughter,[17] and have refused to extend it to rape,[18] assault[19] and statutorily defined offences against the person which require the act to be performed 'maliciously'.[20] In these latter cases the courts have been perfectly satisfied that juries will be able to draw practical distinctions between the two states of mind referred to by Lord Keith. What is certainly true is that the decision in *Caldwell* extends the ambit of criminal liability so as to make it more likely that juries will convict. For if jurors no longer have to consider whether a defendant did intend or foresee the result of an action, but only whether he or she ought to have foreseen that result, they can simply ask themselves whether they, as reasonable people, would have foreseen it. If so, they will convict. The fact that the defendant did not foresee it becomes irrelevant.[1] As well as increasing the conviction rate, this saves time as it is no longer necessary for the prosecution to adduce evidence of the defendant's state of mind—only the objective circumstances need be put before the jury.[2]

How does the law deal with the alternative situation where the

---

[13] [1981] 1 All ER 961 at 965.

[14] [1992] 3 All ER 673.

[15] Ibid at 674.

[16] *Lawrence* [1982] AC 510. The offences of reckless driving and causing death by reckless driving have since been replaced by s 1 of the Road Traffic Act 1991 (substituting new ss 1 and 2 into the Road Traffic Act 1988) with the offences of dangerous driving and causing death by dangerous driving.

[17] *Seymour* [1983] 2 AC 493.

[18] *Satnam; Kewal* (1983) 78 Cr App Rep 149.

[19] *Spratt* [1990] 1 WLR 1073.

[20] See *Savage* [1991] 4 All ER 698.

[1] Unless the defendant falls into the so-called *Caldwell* gap by claiming that thought was given to the possibility of risk but the erroneous conclusion drawn was that there was no risk. Since the risk is one that would be obvious to a reasonable person, juries are unlikely to accept such a claim: see *Reid* [1992] 3 All ER 673 at 690, per Lord Goff.

[2] Thus in *Lawrence* [1982] AC 510 at 527, Lord Diplock observed that: 'if satisfied that an obvious and serious risk was created by the manner of the defendant's driving, the jury are entitled to infer that he was in one or other of the states of mind required to constitute the offence and will probably do so; but regard must be given to any explanation he gives as to his state of mind which may displace the inference.'

prosecution must establish intent or foresight of risk ? How can the prosecution make the jury sure beyond reasonable doubt of a defendant's state of mind? The defendant, after all, is entitled not to answer questions about this matter. In reality, many defendants do answer police questions designed to elicit evidence of the requisite state of mind.[3] Where there is no confession, some other device must be found if the jury is to be convinced of guilt. The senior judiciary have provided this in an evidential test, repeatedly emphasising that the question of what a reasonable person would have intended or foreseen in identical circumstances is something to be considered by the jury in reaching its verdict. An example is the Court of Appeal decision in a pre-*Caldwell* criminal damage case, *Stephenson*:

'A man is reckless when he carries out [a] deliberate act appreciating that there is a risk that damage to property may result from his act . . . Proof of the requisite state of knowledge in the mind of the defendant will in most cases present little difficulty. The fact that the risk of some damage would have been obvious to anyone in his right mind in the position of the defendant is not conclusive proof of the defendant's knowledge, but it may well be and in many cases doubtless will be a matter which will drive the jury to the conclusion that the defendant himself must have appreciated the risk.'[4]

Trial judges can accordingly reassure juries that the state of a defendant's mind, far from being virtually unknowable in the absence of a confession, can be established from objective circumstances 'in most cases [with] little difficulty.'

Similarly, in crimes where intention has to be proved, the leading case has it that:

'the greater the probability of a consequence the more likely it is that the consequence was foreseen and that if that consequence was foreseen the greater the probability is that that consequence was also intended.'[5]

Apparently, subjective states of mind can, in this way, be proved by referring to objective probabilities. In legal theory, the jury is not obliged to infer that the defendant intended a certain consequence whenever they conclude that that defendant foresaw the consequence as possible, likely, highly probable or whatever.[6] But in practice, although foresight or foreseeability are not the same thing as intention, high

---

[3] See ch 4.
[4] [1979] QB 695 at 703.
[5] *Hancock; Shankland* [1986] AC 455 at 473.
[6] See s 8 of the Criminal Justice Act 1967.

judicial authority has it that 'either may give rise to an irrestible inference of such . . .'[7]

Finally, we may note that the criminal law generally ignores the defendant's motive in defining what counts as a guilty state of mind.[8] Defendants charged with theft of food will not be heard to say in their defence that they were hungry, nor will those who enter a boarded-up building as trespassers, intending to chop up floorboards for firewood, be allowed to defend a charge of burglary by arguing that they were cold and homeless.[9] Juries are enjoined to do justice according to law, but the law incorporates a particular kind of justice which skates over awkward problems arising from gross inequalities in society.[10] In this way too, the issues to be debated at trial are narrowed and the potential for adversarial challenge is reduced.

As we hinted above, the main function of broad offence definitions may not be to produce more verdicts of guilty from the jury but to dissuade defendants from pleading not guilty in the first place. This is also true of offences typically dealt with in the magistrates' courts. The difference is that offences that can only be tried summarily are much more frequently defined in such a way as to make the prosecution's burden of proof easy to bear. An example is the offence under s 139 of the Criminal Justice Act 1988 of having any article which has a blade or is sharply pointed in a public place.[11] The prosecution is not required to prove any mental state at all here, only the objective fact of possession of a sharply pointed article. Section 139(4) provides that it shall be a defence for a person charged with this offence to prove that he or she had good reason or lawful authority for having the article in a public place. Thus, once the objective circumstances have been established by the prosecution, it is for the defence to prove innocence rather than the prosecution to prove guilt. When offences are defined in this way, the presumption of innocence and the right to silence have little content or force. Although the burden of proof is generally more difficult for the prosecution to discharge for matters dealt with in the Crown Court, it is rarely as difficult as due process rhetoric would suggest.

---

[7] *Moloney* [1985] AC 905 at 913, per Lord Hailsham, quoted with approval in *Hancock; Shankland* [1986] AC 455 at 472 by Lord Scarman.

[8] See the discussion by A Norrie, *Crime, Reason and History* (Weidenfeld and Nicolson, 1993) pp 36–47.

[9] It is possible that they would have a defence of duress of circumstances if they could argue that they acted reasonably and proportionately in order to avoid death or serious personal injury (through starvation or exposure): *Martin* [1989] 1 All ER 652.

[10] There is a striking contrast here with non-police agencies. Immunity from prosecution (and hence conviction) for crimes which are a product of the economic facts of life is almost universally accepted. See ch 5, section 5, above, for further discussion.

[11] It is not an offence to have a folding penknife unless the cutting edge of its blade exceeds three inches (s 3).

5.   EVALUATING THE JURY'S PERFORMANCE

It was argued in chapter 6 that magistrates are more likely than jurors to embrace crime control ideology. This is largely because jurors are outsiders, free of the administrative concerns of dealing speedily with a large caseload. Moreover, unlike magistrates, jurors bear no direct responsibility for sentencing and are accordingly less likely to see themselves as instruments for upholding law and order. It is common for jurors who are called for service to be kept hanging around at court for some days before being selected to hear a case. As jury service is statistically a once in lifetime opportunity, it seems unlikely that in such circumstances jurors will in general subscribe to the crime control view that their task is to trust the prosecution evidence and convict without more ado. On the other hand, one must not simply assume that the jury operates according to due process principles. Rather, we must question whether juries in practice set aside their prejudices, seek hard evidence of guilt and apply the appropriate standard of proof.

An immediate problem in evaluating juries is that they are not required to articulate reasons for the conclusions they reach at the end of a case. They deliberate in private and, on their return to the court, merely give a general verdict of 'guilty' or 'not guilty'.[12] Moreover, a stifling and all-embracing concern to protect the secrecy of the jury has prevented any systematic study based on direct observation or recording of its deliberations. For many years, the exact legal position was unclear on this point, although a convention of jury secrecy was maintained. But s 8 of the Contempt of Court Act 1981 made it contempt to 'obtain, disclose or solicit any particulars of statements made, opinions expressed, arguments advanced or votes cast by members of a jury in the course of their deliberation.' It is sometimes said that such a rule is necessary to protect individual jurors from reprisals or to preserve the finality of jury verdicts, although closer analysis suggests that the purpose of s 8 was to 'maintain the authority of particular verdicts, and indeed of jury trial in general, in the eyes of the public.'[13]

Do juries deserve public confidence ? The answer to this can only be equivocal, since the existing studies are either anecdotal or based on the impressions of judges, lawyers and police officers, or on simulations with 'shadow' or 'mock' juries. To this motley collection may now be added the Runciman Commission's Crown Court survey of views on the jury. We will look at each type of evidence in turn.

---

[12]   In the case of a 'guilty' verdict, the jury foreman will be asked to state the number of jurors voting for and against conviction. To avoid 'second-rate acquittals', this question is not put if a 'not guilty' verdict is returned.

[13]   J Jaconelli, 'Some Thoughts on Jury Secrecy' (1990) 10 LS 91 at 99.

(a) General impressions

Individual jurors have published their recollections of their period of service both before and after the Contempt of Court Act 1981. Some have been disillusioned or even dismayed by their experiences, while others have reported broad satisfaction with the jury process.[14] As such experiences are unlikely to be typical, we do not dwell upon them here. The Crown Court survey found that 80% of jurors rated trial by jury as a good or very good system and only 5% rated it as poor or worse.[15] Jurors typically claimed that they had little difficulty in understanding or remembering the evidence, in coping with legalistic language or in following directions on the law from the judge.[16] The judges surveyed thought the jury system was good or very good in terms of 'generally getting a sensible result' in 79% of cases, the prosecution barristers in 82% and defence barristers in 91%. The survey 'found' that 8% of judges rated the system as poor or very poor, compared with 4% of prosecuting barristers and 2% of defence barristers.[17]

(b) Disagreement with juries

A number of studies have sought to go beyond general impressions by examining the more specific question of the extent of disagreement with jury verdicts in particular cases. The important study in the United States by Kalven and Zeisel examined 3,576 trials and found that judges agreed with the decision reached by the jury in 75% of cases.[18] As Stephenson has pointed out, this is not a particularly high level of agreement. On his analysis, the most striking finding of this study is that judges, as well as agreeing with nearly all jury decisions to convict, would also have convicted 57% of the 1,083 persons whom the jury acquitted.[19] Judges attributed the disagreement between themselves and the juries they instructed to a range of factors. In nearly a third of cases, they thought juries had been swayed by their dislike for the law and had exercised jury equity. In 15% of cases, they acquitted, in the judge's view, because either the defendant or defence counsel had made a favourable impression upon them. In 54% of cases, the judge thought that the jury had taken a different approach to the evidence.[20]

[14] See eg the five accounts published in (1990) 140 NLJ 1264–1276.
[15] M Zander and P Henderson, Crown Court Study (Royal Commission on Criminal Justice, Research Study no 19) (HMSO, 1993) p 232.
[16] See ibid pp 206, 208, 212 and 216, respectively.
[17] Ibid pp 172–73.
[18] H Kalven and H Zeisel, *The American Jury* (Little Brown & Co, 1966).
[19] G Stephenson, *The Psychology of Criminal Justice* (Blackwell, 1992) pp 180–181.
[20] Kalven and Zeisel, op cit p 115.

The early English studies that measured the extent of agreement amongst lawyers and police officers with jury verdicts concluded that these groups for the most part had no quarrel with the jury's decision.[1] Very few verdicts were described as perverse in the sense that they were not in accordance with the weight of the evidence. The most substantial study of this type, conducted by Baldwin and McConville in the mid-1970s, painted a more critical picture. Of 370 randomly selected cases heard in one Crown Court centre, 114 ended in acquittal. Of the latter, serious doubts were expressed about the jury's verdict by the judge in 32% of cases, by the police in 44%, by prosecuting solicitors in 26% and by defence solicitors in 10% of cases.[2] Baldwin and McConville defined a 'questionable acquittal' as one where the judge and at least one other respondent thought the acquittal was not justified. They considered whether jury equity explained the high incidence of questionable acquittals (36% of all acquittals), but concluded that it did not. As they put it:

'The number of defendants who seem to us to have been acquitted in questionable circumstances, without any apparent equitable justification save in a handful of cases, suggests that trial by jury is a relatively crude instrument for establishing the truth.'[3]

The proportion of convictions that were questioned was much smaller, but in 15 cases (6% of all convictions) two or more of the parties to the case had serious doubts about the jury's verdict. Whereas the judge had reservations in eight of these cases, it is striking that the police doubted the verdict in all but two instances. The researchers considered that the most likely explanation for these doubtful convictions was that the jury had failed to appreciate the high standard of proof required in criminal cases and that it had lacked comprehension of the issues involved.[4] There was also evidence to suggest that in some of these cases the jury might have been swayed by racial prejudice.[5] This, from a due process point of view, is the flip side of 'jury equity' and it must be taken into account by those who find attractive the idea of a jury following 'its conscience' rather than the law.[6] Overall, the authors concluded that:

---

[1] See S McCabe and R Purves, *The Jury at Work* (Blackwell, 1972) and M Zander, 'Are Too Many Professional Criminals Avoiding Conviction?' (1974) 37 MLR 28. For a critique of such research, see Freeman, op cit pp 85–97.
[2] J Baldwin and M McConville, *Jury Trials* (Oxford University Press, 1979) pp 45–47.
[3] Ibid pp 66–67.
[4] Ibid p 76.
[5] Ibid pp 80–81.
[6] See also J Gordon, 'Juries as Judges of the Law' (1992) 108 LQR 272 at 278.

'the performance of the jury did not always appear to accord with the principle underlying the trial system in England that it is better to acquit those who are probably guilty than to convict any who are possibly innocent. On the contrary, the jury appeared on occasion to be over-ready to acquit those who were probably guilty and insufficiently prepared to protect the possibly innocent.'[7]

Two points need to be made concerning Baldwin and McConville's work. The first is that their methods for assessing questionable jury acquittals is itself highly questionable. Of the four parties to the case whose views they sought, two (prosecuting solicitor and police) are clearly conviction-minded, one (the judge) is, as this chapter has argued, very often pro-conviction, and only one is likely to be pro-acquittal (defence solicitor). Note that whereas defence solicitors had serious doubts about acquittals in 10% of all acquittal cases, the other three groups had such doubts in much larger proportions, ranging from 26% to 44%. By defining a questionable acquittal as one in which the judge and one other party to the case thought the jury's verdict to be wrong, Baldwin and McConville built into their measurements an inherent prosecution bias. That juries were found to be acquittal-prone by the standards of state officials and representatives is not surprising, given the state's commitment to crime control values.

The second point is to ask what meaning to attribute to evidence of disagreement between professionals and lay jurors. If juries always reached verdicts of which judges approved, one might legitimately question the value of having a jury at all. One of the strongest arguments for retaining trial by jury is to avoid leaving the fate of defendants to be determined by professionals, applying professional standards. Thus, Bankowski and Mungham contend that since there is no consensus about what constitutes a 'good' jury decision and the lawyer's view of a case is not the only sensible or rational interpretation, professional disagreement with jury verdicts tells us nothing meaningful about jury competence.[8] Baldwin and McConville attempt to deal with this critique by arguing as follows:

'A verdict is not invalidated simply because the lawyers do not agree with it; equally it is not validated by the mere fact that they approve of

---

[7] Baldwin and McConville, *Jury Trials* op cit p 128. See also Zander and Henderson, op cit pp 162–172, for the reactions of lawyers, police officers and judges to particular jury verdicts. As with Baldwin and McConville, 'problematic' acquittals were found to be more prevalent than problematic convictions.

[8] G Mungham and Z Bankowski, 'The Jury in the Legal System', in P Carlen (ed), *The Sociology of Law* (University of Keele, 1976) p 209. See also M Freeman, 'The Jury on Trial' [1981] CLP 65 at 85–88 and 95–97, in particular.

it. On the other hand, determining whether a verdict accords with the law provides one starting-point for locating the extent of jury departure from legal rules.'[9]

But it does not follow from the fact that lawyers (including judges) disagree with a verdict that the jury has departed from the legal rules. If one accepts that law is not an absolute but must always be interpreted and applied in specific contexts and circumstances, it follows that jurors may take a different view of what the law requires in a particular case to that adopted by lawyers. The institution of the jury represents a policy preference for the process by which this judgment is to be left, ultimately, in the hands of lay people rather than professionals. This injection of a lay element into the administering of justice does not have to be justified on the ground that the jury is more reliable or efficient as a finder of fact than a professional judge. Rather, one can argue that lay involvement is necessary in order to allow jury equity to be exercised (if we think this to be desirable) and also to ensure that law and justice do not become monopolised by professionals.[10] The crime control model advocates that we should trust professional judgment, that we should trust the experts. It is vital, if due process is to retain a foothold, that professional expertise is challenged and laid bare before the community as represented by the 12 individuals on the jury.

(c)   Shadow juries

An obvious difficulty with all studies measuring professional disagreement with verdicts is that they are based on indirect measurements of the jury's work. It is possible that observation of the jury's deliberations would have indicated to Baldwin and McConville a satisfactory explanation (whether of an evidential or equitable nature) for many of the verdicts they classified as questionable.

Direct observation of 'shadow' juries—where 12 people observe or listen to trials in tandem with the real jury and then retire to consider their 'verdict'—have provided some insight into the dynamics of the jury room. All such studies show a fairly high level of correspondence between the verdicts of the real and the shadow juries, suggesting that the latter approach their simulated task in a realistic manner. In a study of 30 cases, McCabe and Purves concluded that:

---

[9]   Baldwin and McConville, *Jury Trials*, op cit p 18.
[10]   See Mungham and Bankowski, op cit, and Freeman, op cit, for extended treatment of this theme.

'The "shadow" juries showed considerable determination in looking for evidence upon which convictions could be based; when it seemed inadequate, they were not prepared to allow their own "hunch" that the defendant was involved in some way in the offence that was charged to stand in the way of an acquittal ... There was little evidence of perversity in the final decisions of these thirty groups. One acquittal only showed that sympathy and impatience with the triviality of the case so influenced the "shadow" jurors' view of the evidence that they refused to convict.'[11]

Another study, also conducted in the early 1970s, concluded to like effect that juries approach the task of determining guilt as a serious responsibility.[12] More recently, McConville has reported on a televised study of five real cases heard by a shadow jury. Striking a decidedly more positive tone than in his earlier work on juries with Baldwin, he writes that:

'Although not dealing with the fate of actual defendants, the shadow jury's deliberations have an authentic ring, marked by fierce debate, acute analysis, common sense, personal experience, stubbornness and occasional whiffs of prejudice ... Overall, the quality and power of the argument within the shadow jury room, and the high level of correspondence between the verdicts of the real and shadow juries, suggests that confidence in the jury is well-placed.'[13]

6. CONCLUSION

Much of the research on the jury should now be regarded as out of date. The impact of PACE and the inception of the CPS on the workings of jury trials has yet to be charted. The weight of the evidence to date suggests, however, that juries do conform much more closely to due process principles than crime control ideology. But since, as demonstrated earlier, it is not the jury, but the judge, who is the central directing figure in a trial, and since judges commonly adopt crime control positions, juries are in reality unlikely to base decisions on anything like a pure due process approach.

This point must be amplified. Juries do not act in a vacuum, nor do they act as finders of the truth.[14] They simply decide a 'case'. The case

---

[11] S McCabe and R Purves, *The Shadow Jury at Work* (Oxford University Penal Research Unit: Blackwell, 1974) p 61.

[12] L Sealy and W Cornish, 'Juries and the Rules of Evidence' [1973] Crim LR 208.

[13] M McConville, 'Shadowing the Jury' (1991) 141 NLJ 1588 at 1588 and 1595.

[14] See Mungham and Bankowski, op cit p 206 and pp 212–213.

that is presented to the jury is shaped by rules of evidence, procedure and substantive law, the presentation skills of opposing counsel, the preparatory work by the police, the influence of the judge and a host of other factors. We have argued throughout this book that all pre-trial and trial processes are imbued, to a greater or lesser degree, with crime control values. No matter how due process oriented juries might be, they cannot be relied upon to spot the crime control workmanship that went into building the case put before them. To expect the jury to deconstruct the case and re-examine it under a due process microscope is simply unrealistic. The fact that every major miscarriage of justice case that has come to light in recent years required a guilty verdict from a jury is evidence of this.

The one recommendation of the Runciman Commission that has received unequivocal support from the academic community is that s 8 of the Contempt of Court Act 1981 should be amended so as to permit proper research into jury decision making.[15] For while the evidence available suggests that juries conform more to due process principles than other components of the criminal justice system, that evidence is neither so satisfactory, nor so unequivocal, as to be conclusive. Such research would, however, have to be clear about what was being tested. As we have argued, testing whether professional lawyers agree with jury verdicts is an inherently unsatisfactory approach to this issue. In our view, an examination of the process by which juries arrive at their verdicts is likely to provide more meaningful insights, providing it is recognised that that process cannot be divorced from the overall context of the criminal justice system.

Moreover, any research should not confine itself to an examination of the workings of the jury. Rather, a comparison should be attempted between different possible modes of trial, including trial by lay magistrates, by a stipendiary magistrate (sitting with or without lay colleagues) and by 'Diplock' courts. For while jury trial may have its faults, the real question is whether other modes of trial are, or could be made to be, any better. Where comparisons have been attempted, they have tended to flatter jury trial. We noted in chapter 6 that research by Vennard suggests that juries approach prosecution evidence with more care than do magistrates.[16] The empirical evidence concerning the gathering and presentation of evidence by the police and the CPS (reviewed in chapters 2–5, above) shows that such circumspection is fully justified. This may convince some of the force of due process arguments, but the committed crime control adherent may still prefer to see priority given

---

[15] See Report, op cit p 2.
[16] See J Vennard, Contested Trials in Magistrates' Courts (Home Office Research Study no 71) (HMSO, 1981) p 21.

to maintaining a high conviction rate at low cost. As we stressed in chapter 1, arguments about the future development of the criminal justice system should be informed by hard facts, but can rarely be resolved by them.

Finally, one should bear in mind that, for the vast majority of defendants, arguments about modes of trial are essentially meaningless. The 'mode of trial' most often employed in this country is the simple guilty plea. The great majority of defendants in both the magistrates' courts and the Crown Court waive their right to put the prosecution to proof by waiving their right to trial. Thus, perhaps the single most important reform of the system would be to require that magistrates and judges should not accept a plea of guilty (and police officers should not caution) without first examining closely the adequacy of the prosecution case. Such a reform could scarcely be effective, however, given the current absence of a cultural commitment to due process amongst legislators, the appeal courts, trial judges, lawyers and the police. From this perspective, the jury's injection of due process into a predominantly crime control system might appear to be little more than a placebo.

Chapter 9

Remedies

1. INTRODUCTION

In criminal justice, as in all other processes, a balance has to be struck between guarding against error and facilitating efficiency. The way that balance is and should be struck has been an important theme of this book. The imposition of controls on the police (such as restrictions on the use of powers, supervision by senior officers and the recording of events) and the provision of rights to suspects and defendants (such as legal aid) are, at least in part, attempts to guard against error. Since these attempts will never be entirely successful, it follows also that error has to be anticipated and procedures have to be established for their identification and correction. It is with these procedures that this chapter is concerned.

The role of remedial procedures in the due process and crime control models is very different. Due process is sceptical about the reliability of administrative fact-finding processes and therefore expects errors to be legion. There must therefore be easy access to appeal procedures. The model accepts that maintaining public confidence in the system is important, but argues that the way to achieve this is for the system to demonstrate its willingness to own up to and correct error. It would be better, of course, to remedy errors at the earliest possible stage, thus removing the need for an appeal. The exclusionary remedy, which operates at the trial stage, can serve this purpose. Errors that affect the reliability of evidence (such as uncorroborated confessions obtained through oppressive interrogations) must be corrected by the trial judge ruling that evidence inadmissible. But even where the evidence obtained unlawfully is shown to be reliable, exclusion must still follow, since only in this way can the system uphold its own integrity and remove the incentive for the police to break the rules. If the collapse of prosecution cases following exclusion adversely affects the morale of the police, the answer lies in their hands, since if they kept to the rules they would not lose convictions in this way. Other remedies must also be provided, however, since exclusionary rules can only affect that small percentage of criminal cases which are both prosecuted and contested, and may, in any case, be ineffective in punishing and deterring the particular police officers responsible for malpractice. Causes of action must therefore be provided to citizens so that they can sue such officers in the civil courts, and disciplinary mechanisms must be set up so that police forces are empowered to investigate wrongdoing and punish or even dismiss officers who break the law. Criminal prosecution may be justified in some cases. A strong system of remedies is bound to impair police efficiency, but this is a price worth paying for upholding the fairness of procedures and the liberty of the individual. Such a system is consistent with this model's close attention to protecting the factually innocent against conviction, even if that means that more factually guilty persons are enabled to evade justice.

The crime control model concedes that errors will occur but not on the scale envisaged by the due process adherent. Trial judges can be relied upon to detect most errors, so the role of appeal procedures is regarded as relatively marginal. These procedures should be made available only to those who can show that a clear error was made at their trial. Moreover, only errors which undermine confidence in the reliability of the evidence put before the court and the accuracy of the finding of guilt require an exclusionary or appellate remedy. It would be intolerable to allow a guilty person to go free because of some technical procedural error. To do so would undermine both police morale and public confidence in the system, whilst having little effect on police practices. By making remedies difficult to operate and available only in narrowly defined circumstances, crime control ensures that only those with genuine grievances will complain. The best way to tackle police malpractice is through disciplinary mechanisms which focus on how to make individual officers more efficient in future. Efficiency is generally best served by requiring police officers to keep to the rules regarding the treatment of suspects. In a crime control system, the primary aim of these rules is not to protect suspects but simply to ensure that any evidence obtained from them is reliable. By keeping to the rules, the police reduce the risk that evidence will be ruled unreliable and thus inadmissible at trial. Some police officers may, because of their lack of faith in the utility of such rules, none the less break them. If any evidence obtained as a result can be verified from other sources, all well and good. If not, the officer concerned may well have lost the opportunity to obtain a confession that would have been regarded as reliable. Officers who are unable to judge accurately when it is rational to break the rules in the search for the truth should be regarded as terminally inefficient and dismissed.

It can be seen that both models accept that errors may be dealt with in many different ways but differ on what the purpose of a remedy should be. In reality, remedies may serve a variety of purposes. The purpose may simply be to correct a wrong decision. This will most obviously include appeal procedures undertaken with the aim of quashing the conviction of an innocent person (see sections 5 and 6, below). This can also be the purpose of excluding evidence obtained wrongfully, as where a confession is extracted through 'oppressive' interrogation. Not allowing the evidence secured in that way to be used might be seen as directly righting the wrong (see section 4, below).[1] The quashing of a conviction or the exclusion of evidence on the grounds of police malpractice may also serve the purpose of deterring or punishing (albeit indirectly) the police. The extent to which the courts regard punishment and deterrence as legitimate considerations (the due process approach) in these contexts will be examined below.

Sometimes the purpose of a remedy is to compensate the subject of the error. This is true of actions in tort in the civil courts, where these are available (see section 2, below). Compensation is generally only awarded to the extent that damage is suffered, although the courts have discretion to award 'punitive' or 'exemplary damages' if they consider that a particular instance of police malpractice merits punishment or needs to be deterred in future. Although compensation for wrongful conviction is provided, this is only where there has been a miscarriage of justice. If a wrongful conviction is quashed as a result of normal appeal procedures, then no compensation is payable.

The most obvious way to punish or deter the police from breaking the law is to prosecute them when they do so. Breaches of the criminal law (for instance, assault, perjury and corruption) are sometimes prosecuted, as happened to three of the detectives accused of fabricating evidence in the 'Guildford Four' case.[2] This is rare, however, the DPP prosecuting in only about 1.5% of the cases of alleged police malpractice referred to her.[3] The evidential and public interest tests we discussed in chapter 5 are applied when processing these cases. The

---

[1] There is also the writ of habeas corpus, which can secure the release of someone held illegally in detention. It is rarely used, partly because the courts have taken to adjourning applications for habeas corpus for 24 hours to give the police time to prepare their case, and by the expiry of 24 hours the police will usually have charged or released the suspect anyway. See H Levenson and F Fairweather, *Police Powers, a Practitioner's Guide* (LAG, 1990) ch 13.

[2] See J Rozenberg, 'Miscarriages of Justice' in E Stockdale and S Casale (eds), *Criminal Justice Under Stress* (Blackstone, 1992). The three detectives were acquitted following their trial in 1993. This does not mean that they were factually innocent, any more than it means that the 'Guildford Four' were factually guilty. It simply means that the prosecution failed to prove the detectives' guilt beyond reasonable doubt.

[3] K Hyder, 'Cause for Complaint' (1990) New Statesman and Society, 12 January.

difficulty of proving a case (where it is usually one citizen's word against that of one or more police officers) weighs heavily against prosecution. From a due process perspective, it is right that police officers are protected from prosecution when the case against them is weak. In so far as non-prosecution follows the application of 'public interest' criteria, one presumes that the need (as defined in the crime control model) to maintain police morale and public confidence in the criminal justice system are the operative factors. Unfortunately, the absence of accountability for prosecution decisions at the level of prosecution policy[4] means that these matters are never openly discussed even in principle, let alone in respect of individual cases. This makes it difficult to assess whether or not decisions not to prosecute police officers are shaped by due process or crime control considerations.

Punishment and deterrence may also be pursued in other ways. One is through the complaints and discipline mechanism (see section 3, below). Here too there is a clash between due process and crime control values. For example, the detective superintendent in charge of the inquiry into the murder of PC Blakelock (which led to the wrongful conviction of the 'Tottenham Three') was put before a disciplinary tribunal by the Police Complaints Authority (PCA). The assistant commissioner of the Metropolitan Police is reported to have urged the PCA to drop proceedings 'on grounds including the damage which substantiation of the allegations would do to force morale.'[5]

In this chapter, then, an attempt is made not just to describe the chief remedies available within the criminal justice system, but to identify where they lie between the polarities of due process and crime control.

2.   CIVIL ACTIONS

(a)   Causes of action

Although PACE defines, and sets limits to, a large number of police powers and rights for suspects, it does not provide specific enforcement mechanisms or civil remedies. As regards the codes of practice, s 67(10) of PACE provides that a failure on the part of a police officer to comply with any of their provisions 'shall not of itself render him liable to any criminal or civil proceedings.' Existing tortious remedies—developed many years ago before police forces and modern investigative techniques were created—have to be applied to the PACE framework of rights and powers, in so far as that is possible. There are a number of possibilities which fall to be examined.

---

[4] See ch 5, section 2, above.
[5] (1990) Guardian, 12 May.

False imprisonment

The tort of false imprisonment applies to unlawful police detention. This would include detention in breach of the 'necessity' rule in s 37 of PACE (see chapter 4, section 3, above) although there are no reported cases on this. However, the courts have decided that unlawful detention conditions do not make the detention itself unlawful.[6] Thus breaches of PACE Code of Practice C, for example, such as denying suspects refreshment or sleep, could not form the basis of this action.

False imprisonment also applies to wrongful arrest.[7] This is because the tort involves the unlawful infliction of bodily restraint.[8] Bodily restraint is the essence of both arrest and police station detention. It is also, of course, the essence of stop-search under PACE, s 1, for, as we argued in chapter 3, stop-search is a form of arrest. It should therefore follow that unlawful stop-search be subject to the tort of false imprisonment, but, once again, there are no reported cases on this. There is, otherwise, no specific civil action available in relation to stop-search.

Trespass

If the police enter property without lawful authority, an action for trespass may follow. This can occur when an arrest warrant is invalid, or in the purported exercising of other police powers, such as search and/or seizure of property (powers to enter property, search the premises and seize certain types of property are provided, in certain circumstances, by PACE, ss 8–22).

Assault and intimidation

Assault and intimidation are further torts which sometimes occur in the course of arrest. Anything in excess of 'reasonable force' to effect an arrest is an assault, and the threat of an unlawful act (for example, unreasonable use of force) is intimidation.[9] This may also occur if the police try to secure a confession through threats.[10]

---

[6] See eg *Williams v Home Office (No 2)* [1981] 1 All ER 1151, and discussion by J Robbilliard and J McEwan, *Police Powers and the Individual* (Blackwell, 1986) p 251.

[7] See eg *Wershof v MPC* [1978] 3 All ER 540.

[8] See Levenson and Fairweather, op cit ch 9.

[9] See eg *Allen v MPC* [1980] Crim LR 441.

[10] Levenson and Fairweather, op cit.

Malicious prosecution

If a prosecution is initiated both without prima facie evidence and maliciously, the defendant may sue for malicious prosecution.

Breach of statutory duty

This cause of action arises where no other remedy is available.[11] However, it is unclear whether this action will lie in respect of all or even any breaches of PACE, and it certainly does not apply to rights found in the codes of practice only (such as the right to be informed of one's rights and the right not to be held incommunicado) since the latter are not statutes. If there have been any attempts to use this tort in relation to PACE, they have not been reported.

Thus, there are a number of possible causes of action, but the dearth of reported cases suggests that they are rarely of much practical use. The main difficulty is establishing a case on the balance of probabilities (the civil standard of proof) when it is usually just one person's word against another's. But there is a broader problem. This is that no civil actions are possible in respect of much of the subject matter of this book.[12] This is particularly true in relation to police detention—the right to legal advice, not to be kept incommunicado, and to be informed of one's rights; and the duties of the police to interrogate fairly,[13] to do so under the formal conditions laid down in Code of Practice C, and to record all questions and answers. These provisions are supposedly the centre piece of the 'balance' struck by the Royal Commission on Criminal Procedure (Philips Commission) which it regarded as a quid pro quo for increasing police powers (regarding stop-search and pre-charge detention, for example). Many now argue that these safeguards are so powerful that the right of silence can no longer be justified and should go. As against this, we should note that the government did not think to provide a remedy for suspects who suffer from the breach of these supposedly fundamental safeguards. Loss of reputation can be compensated by suing for libel. Homeless travellers can be ejected from one's holiday cottage, development land or empty office block and sued for the owner's loss of amenity. But there is no such remedy if one is isolated from a lawyer and induced into a false confession through

---

11   R Clayton and H Tomlinson, *Civil Actions Against the Police* (Sweet and Maxwell, 1987) ch 9.

12   See A Sanders, 'Rights, Remedies and the Police and Criminal Evidence Act' [1988] Crim LR 802.

13   This duty is only implicit, but arises because the courts have a discretion under s 78 of PACE to exclude evidence which would have an adverse effect on the fairness of the proceedings if admitted. See chapter 4, section 5(e), above.

lies or deception. This is also true in relation to the abuse of other police powers not covered in this book, such as those concerning road-blocks and identification parades.

Thus there is simply no civil remedy available in respect of many of the rights provided in PACE and the codes of practice. The inadequate protection of these rights is indicative of a lack of commitment to due process values. But the problem may stem more from a fundamental misunderstanding of how the criminal justice system works than such a lack of commitment. The Royal Commission on Criminal Procedure (Philips Commission) considered that there was no need for new civil or criminal remedies to enforce the rights of suspects. Its view was that the new controls it advocated, such as the custody officer, combined with enhancements to the police complaints system, would provide suffi-cient protection. Closer examination of the system suggests that this is questionable,[14] but—unlike the Royal Commission on Criminal Justice (Runciman Commission)—at least Philips did consider the matter.[15]

(b)   Pursuing civil actions

Having the right to sue does not mean that one is always able to sue. We have suggested that proving one's case is a major hurdle. Another factor is cost. A large proportion of people could not afford the cost of their own lawyers, let alone those hired by the police. Fighting an appeal can be financially crippling and this may deter many, uncertain of their prospects of winning a case, from taking the gamble. Suspects are drawn from the poorest sections of society, so very few indeed can afford to sue. Legal aid is, in principle, available for those who cannot afford to sue. However, the means test has been steadily tightened up in the 1980s and early 1990s, making an ever smaller proportion of the population eligible for legal aid.[16]

There is also a 'merits' test. Legal aid is generally only granted if the action would be worth bringing were it to be privately funded. The issue here is partly one of likelihood of success.[17] It is also one of cost in relation to the likely level of damages.[18] A brief detention for the

---

[14] For discussion of the role of the custody officer, see ch 4, above; for the police com-plaints system, see section 3, below.

[15] Royal Commission on Criminal Procedure, Report (Cmnd 8092) (HMSO, 1981) paras 4.121–4.122.

[16] O Hansen, 'A Future for Legal Aid?' (1992) 19 Journal of Law and Society 85.

[17] An applicant for legal aid must satisfy the Legal Aid Board that there are 'reasonable grounds for taking... proceedings': Legal Aid Act 1988, s 15(2).

[18] Under s 15(3) of the Legal Aid Act 1988, the Legal Aid Board can refuse legal aid if it appears to the Board 'unreasonable' to grant it. The normal criterion is whether the financial benefit to be gained from bringing the action outweighs the cost involved.

purpose of an unlawful stop-search would not attract significant damages even if a claim of assault was upheld, so legal aid would generally not be provided.[19] Some torts can attract significant damages, however. Damages for false imprisonment, malicious prosecution and trespass have occasionally been awarded at the level of several thousand pounds. Levenson and Fairweather give examples of cases where a suspect punched in the street by a police officer was awarded £3,000 compensation, plus £7,500 exemplary damages; for false imprisonment and assault, £2,000 compensation plus £3,000 exemplary damages; and £2,000 (by consent) for unlawful strip-search.[20] Exemplary damages are not awarded if the police are provoked by the plaintiff. Thus in *O'Connor v Hewitson*,[1] the arrested plaintiff was violent and uncooperative. The police hit him once or twice unnecessarily, for which he was awarded only £125. Nor are exemplary damages awarded if the police make a genuine mistake. In *Wershof v MPC*,[2] a solicitor was arrested in a shop. He was put in a 'half-nelson', marched down a crowded street, and detained in the police station for an hour. For assault and false imprisonment he was awarded £1,000. His behaviour, the judge commented, lacked 'discretion' (he forcefully asserted his rights).

Again, the class issue is important. People with reputations and salaries to lose would command relatively high levels of damages, but these people are rarely arrested, let alone wrongly. Wershof was an exception, and had he been an unemployed labourer he would have received far less than £1,000. In one case, a lecturer held incommunicado for 21 hours was awarded £600, perhaps illustrating the modern status of academics.[3] Where the police behave extraordinarily, and exemplary damages are awarded, the sums tend to be much larger, although it is a matter of judgment as to whether they are large enough. In *White v MPC*[4] a middle aged West Indian couple were dragged from their beds at night. They resisted and were violently treated and held in custody, in their night clothes, for several hours. They were charged with assaulting the arresting officers. At trial they were acquitted. They sued the police who, the judge said, 'showed no regard to human dignity' and were 'monstrously wicked'. One was awarded £4,500 and the other £6,500 for assault, false imprisonment

---

[19] The Legal Aid Board has indicated, however, that in cases affecting the applicant's status, reputation or dignity, legal aid might be appropriate even though the financial benefit to be gained by an action would be small.

[20] Op cit p 243.

[1] [1979] Crim LR 46.

[2] [1978] 3 All ER 540.

[3] See the cases discussed by Robbilliard and McEwan, op cit, pp 254–255.

[4] (1982) Guardian, 24 April.

and malicious prosecution. They were also awarded £20,000 each exemplary damages.

Most cases are settled out of court. As one might expect, settlement involves compromise—the plaintiff generally accepts a lower level of damages but avoids the delay involved in pursuing court proceedings and the risk of losing. In 1984, the Metropolitan Police alone paid damages of over £178,000 to 44 claimants (ie an average of just over £4,000 each) of whom 37 settled out of court. By 1988, this bill had nearly doubled, to £357,000.[5] Over the five years 1988–92 inclusive the total paid by the Metropolitan police was £2,623,000—an average of over £500,000 per year.[6] Despite all of the obstacles strewn in the path of those wanting to sue the police, the number of actions continues to grow. It is estimated that around 1,000 civil actions are brought against the police each year.[7]

When civil cases are settled out of court, the remedy has served one of its purposes in that the individual citizen has obtained redress for a wrong. But the opportunity that a public court hearing would have provided for bringing police officers to account is diminished. When police forces settle they make no admission of liability and the shame of a public hearing and adjudication is avoided. The corollary of the high rate of case settlement is that most civil actions do not serve the purposes of punishment and deterrence as effectively as they might. The next question to ask is whether the police complaints system, the other remedy with the potential to put individual police officers on the spot, serves these purposes any better.

3. COMPLAINTS AGAINST THE POLICE

The 1964 Police Act introduced a uniform system for the investigation of complaints against the police. It provided for all complaints to be recorded and investigated by either a senior officer from the force or, where complaints were particularly serious, from a different force. Reports of the investigation went to the deputy chief constable (or, in certain cases, the Police Authority[8]), who decided whether or not there was evidence of:

---

[5] K Williams, 'Suing Policemen' (1989) 139 NLJ 1164.
[6] (1993) Guardian, 15 April.
[7] Williams, op cit.
[8] Each police force is loosely accountable to a police authority currently made up of local magistrates and councillors. The Metropolitan Police Force is an exceptional case, as it is accountable directly to the Home Secretary. See L Lustgarten, *The Governance of Police* (Sweet and Maxwell, 1986).

(a) a criminal offence, in which case the file was sent to the Director of Public Prosecutions, who decided whether or not to prosecute;

(b) a disciplinary offence (including abuse of police power or the rights of suspects), in which case a disciplinary hearing was arranged; or

(c) no offence at all, in which case no action was taken.

The spectacle of the police investigating themselves, deciding whether or not the investigations revealed grounds for complaint, and then (in non-criminal allegations) deciding whether or not the complaint was proven, led to sharp criticism. In response, the Police Act 1976 established a civilian Police Complaints Board (PCB). All procedures remained as before except that where the police decided that there was no evidence for any proceedings, the file was passed onto the Board. In the nine years of its existence (1976–1985), the Board recommended charges in just 210 cases out of around 50,000 (0.42%).[9] Not surprisingly, it failed to enhance public confidence.[10] The opportunity was taken in PACE to modify the system yet again.

The PCB was replaced by the Police Complaints Authority (PCA).[11] Like the PCB, this is a body of the 'great and the good', but some of its members are full-time and it has a substantial staff. As far as the majority of complaints are concerned, the system is almost unchanged. Investigation is by a senior officer who presents the investigation to the appropriate assistant or deputy chief constable. Where no action is proposed, and where the file is not sent to the DPP for consideration of criminal proceedings, the file is passed to the Police Complaints Authority (which can, if it considers it appropriate, send the file to the DPP for possible criminal proceedings or order disciplinary proceedings).[12] The difference lies largely in respect of very serious and relatively minor complaints. The latter may now be dealt with informally, and are discussed below. The former are still investigated by the police, but under the supervision of the PCA.

Serious complaints include allegations of corruption or 'serious arrestable offences'[13] or conduct leading to death or serious injury (which includes most assaults). In such cases, the police must refer the complaint to the Police Complaints Authority to begin with. The police may also refer any other complaints to the Authority if they wish, and

[9] M Maguire and C Corbett, A Study of the Police Complaints System (HMSO, 1991).

[10] For discussion and chronicling of the events of the 1970s and early 1980s see Robbilliard and McEwan, op cit pp 227–233. D Brown, Police Complaints Procedure (Home Office Research Study no 93) (HMSO, 1987) is an interesting survey of complainants' views under the pre-PACE system.

[11] PACE, s 83.

[12] PACE, ss 92, 93.

[13] See, for definition, ch 4, section 2(d), above.

any other conduct by an officer which might be indicative of a serious criminal or disciplinary offence. In addition, the PCA can insist on any complaint being referred to it at any time, even if it does not come into the above categories.[14] Where the Police Complaints Authority is involved in any of these ways, it supervises the investigation, thus introducing—for the first time—an independent element into the complaints investigation process. The way in which the police investigate complaints is, however, still the key to the process.

By the late 1980s, so many serious allegations had been levelled against the police that nearly every force in the country was involved in complaints investigation, either as investigator of another force or as the subject of investigation by another force. In 1989–90, out of the 43 police forces, at least 17 had been investigated by another force, and at least 22 had carried out an investigation. Indeed, at least ten forces had both been investigated and conducted an investigation. Investigations covered such allegations as incompetence (for example, in the Hillsborough tragedy), bribery and corruption, the planting of evidence, assault and the fabrication of confessions.[15]

(a) Investigation of complaints

The Police Complaints Authority neither investigates complaints itself nor has a body of investigators under its own control. 'Supervision' is at a distance, and only applies to a small proportion of complaints (4–5%).[16] This is largely an artefact of limited resources, as reflected in the fact that the PCA declines to supervise 70–80% of the cases referred to it by the police.[17] Even when the infamous West Midlands Police Serious Crime Squad affair erupted, the Authority initially avoided involvement. In one of the early cases, that of Paul Dandy, the police were alleged to have forged a confession. It was not until five months after the prosecution had dropped the charges against him, and following repeated calls for its involvement in the investigation of his complaints against the police, that the PCA expressed an interest.[18] The squad was disbanded over one year later, following the failure of several more of its cases and some barbed judicial criticism.

Having taken this dramatic step, the West Midlands Police chief constable went further by asking the Police Complaints Authority to supervise an investigation into the squad's past activities. At last the

---

[14] PACE, ss 87–89.

[15] See Kaye, op cit app A.

[16] A Hall, 'Police Complaints. Time for a Change?' (1990) Legal Action, August, p 7; Maguire and Corbett, op cit.

[17] Maguire and Corbett, op cit p 12.

[18] See Kaye, op cit, for discussion of this affair in general and Dandy's case in particular.

PCA stirred itself. Dozens of cases, going back several years, were investigated by several officers from West Yorkshire working full-time over several months. Even so, PCA supervision amounted to just one member of the Authority, responsible for many other cases as well, meeting regularly with those officers.[19] Despite well over a dozen convictions being overturned because of rule breaking by members of the squad, there have been no prosecutions. Some disciplinary hearings have been held, however, and a few officers have been dismissed.

Maguire and Corbett studied the operation of the police complaints system in 1986–88. They identified three different ways in which complaints investigation may be 'supervised'. Initially the Police Complaints Authority receives basic documentation (for example, the custody record, if the complainant was arrested) and can decide which officer should investigate (whether from the force being investigated or from an outside force). It will also be given regular progress reports (at least monthly) by investigating officers. Where this is all that supervision involves (and 60% of Maguire and Corbett's sample involved little or no discussion between the PCA and the investigating officer) it can be termed 'passive'.[20] 'Active' supervision entails substantive discussion of the progress of investigations and occasional observation of interviews with witnesses, and comprised around 30% of their sample. In 10% or less was supervision 'directive', in the sense that investigating officers were formally requested to pursue particular lines of inquiry.

The report of the investigation is sent to the Police Complaints Authority, not the police, in the first instance. Frequently the PCA requests more information or further interviews. When the supervising member of the PCA thinks that little more is to be gained from further investigation it accepts the report, which is then transmitted to the police. What action, if any, should follow from the investigation is considered by other PCA members separately. Maguire and Corbett found that at this stage members frequently 'noted a lack of thoroughness' in investigation by which time nothing could be done about it.[1]

This study also found that most complainants whose investigations were supervised by the PCA were dissatisfied with the process, had less faith in the complaints system than before they started and asserted that they had been kept badly informed throughout. This was despite the majority originally feeling more confident when they heard that the PCA would be involved.[2] Although complaints are more often

---

[19] It is estimated that each member of the Authority has a caseload of 50–60 cases: B Loveday (1989), 'Recent Developments in Police Complaints Procedure' Local Government Studies, May/June, p 25.

[20] Op cit p 136.

[1] See ibid p 143.

[2] Ibid pp 147–148.

'successful' when they are supervised by the PCA than when they are not, this could be due simply to the fact that one criterion used in selecting cases for supervision is the likelihood of success.

The judiciary are sometimes critical of the performance of the Police Complaints Authority. In one case, the Court of Appeal quashed two convictions because of what the Lord Chief Justice called the 'tainted evidence' of several police officers. The circumstances of this case were being reviewed as part of a PCA investigation into one particular police station which had been proceeding for two years. The Lord Chief Justice said that 'dynamite' should be put behind the PCA.[3]

Even if all the investigation of all cases were supervised, and if that supervision were not so inadequate, the notion of investigation by the police would still be fundamentally flawed. This is because the Police Complaints Authority (like the PCB before it and, indeed, like the deputy chief constable) is in a similar position to that of the CPS. None of these bodies assesses the facts of the incidents complained of, except in those few cases where supervision is participative. What they assess are reports of the facts, compiled by investigators whose job is to present a case. Since those investigators are police officers, the case they are generally predisposed to present will be that there is insufficient evidence to proceed. For although investigating officers are investigating alleged wrong doing by other officers, much of this wrongdoing is part of everyday policing, is consistent with police working rules and will have been engaged in by themselves and/or their close colleagues. Writing in 1975, Box and Russell argued that the police psychologically neutralise the apparently deviant nature of their rule breaking by using 'techniques of neutralisation' common to all occupational and cultural groups.[4] These techniques include 'condemning the condemners' and 'denying the victim', ie either blaming the complainant or disputing a crucial alleged fact about the complainant's injuries or loss. Such techniques enable the police to shrug off most complaints with a clear conscience.

Complaints investigation, which is akin to case construction in prosecution decisions (see chapter 5), is described by Box and Russell as a process of 'discrediting' based on neutralisation techniques. Just as cases against ordinary suspects can be constructed to justify prosecution, cases against police suspects can be constructed to justify no further action. Arrest and/or prosecution of the complainant is one method of discrediting. The White case, discussed above, involved an attempt to discredit the Whites' complaints of assault by charging them

---

[3] (1993) Guardian, 15 December.
[4] S Box and K Russell, 'The Politics of Discreditability: Disarming Complaints Against the Police' (1975) 23 Soc Rev 315.

with assaulting the arresting officers and resisting arrest.[5] Arrest and/or prosecution transforms the identity of the complainant from 'good citizen' to 'criminal suspect'. This makes denial of the allegations more plausible and provides an explanation for what is claimed to be a false complaint (ie a complaint is said to lend substance to a defendant's claim to be, for instance, 'fitted up'). Previous criminal record, a past record of mental illness and alleged drunkenness are other 'facts' used to discredit complainants.

The result is not just a generally low rate of substantiation, but a particularly low rate for those people whose complaints can be easily discredited. In Box and Russell's sample, 32% had two or more 'discredits' against them. None of their complaints was substantiated. One in ten of those with one discredit, but four in ten of those with no discredits, had their complaints substantiated. One result of this was that working class people had little success (8% of their complaints were substantiated, as against 28% of the complaints of middle class people).[6] It is, of course, possible that drunks, criminals and the mentally ill really do make more false complaints than do other people. But the failure of the complaints mechanism in notorious cases such as *Madden*'s case[7] and the 'Confait Affair'[8] leads one to suspect that, however true this may be in part, the investigative process is intrinsically faulty.

The more recent research by Maguire and Corbett suggests that the advent of the Police Complaints Authority has made little difference to the substance of the investigative process as described by Box and Russell. They detected 'a certain amount of 'stereotyping' by police (including investigating) officers—for instance, a belief that almost all complaints by certain kinds of people are made purely in order to cause trouble for the police, or a tendency to treat complainants as either 'deserving' or 'non-deserving' of serious attention, depending on their background and character.'[9] Investigating officers, in other words, are steeped in 'cop culture' (see chapter 2, section 1, above) and are unable to avoid viewing policing and rule breaking through the eyes of that culture:

'What a police officer may honestly (and perhaps justifiably) regard as

---

[5] For other examples, see A Sanders, 'Prosecution Decisions and the Attorney-General's Guidelines' [1985] Crim LR 4. See also ch 5, section 3(b), above.

[6] Box and Russell, op cit, also discuss other class attributes, such as lower educational levels, which could adversely affect the success of their complaints.

[7] *R v Police Complaints Board, ex p Madden* [1983] 2 All ER 353.

[8] See J Baxter and L Koffman, 'The Confait inheritance—Forgotten Lessons?' [1983] Cambrian LR, 14.

[9] Op cit p 130.

totally "reasonable force" to manoeuvre an intoxicated person quickly and effectively into a police van, may appear to the person—or to bystanders—as totally unreasonable force.'[10]

Sometimes these attitudes are noticed by the Police Complaints Authority, and commented upon adversely, but the PCA can do nothing about this, short of demanding a new investigation.

(b)   Adjudication and discipline

Table 9.1 shows the number of complaints made in 1987–89 and the results of the investigations into them.

Table 9.1: Complaints against the police[11]

	1987	*1988*	*1989*
Number of complainants	13,147	12,523	11,155
Disciplinary charges preferred by the police	135	140	177
Disciplinary charges recommended by PCA	17	32	17
Percentage of complaints resulting in disciplinary charges	1.2%	1.4%	1.7%

There are three points of particular interest. Firstly, the level of complaints is falling. This is sometimes taken to be more of a reflection of a lack of public confidence in the complaints system[12] than a sign that there is increasingly less to complain about.[13] A more cogent explanation is that many complaints are now dealt with by conciliation procedures (discussed below); this reduces the number of formal complaints without there necessarily being less to complain about. Secondly, the percentage of complaints in which there are charges is remarkably low. Thirdly, the impact of the Police Complaints Authority appears to be minimal. It recommends few additional

---

10   M Maguire, 'Complaints against the Police: Where Now?' (Unpublished manuscript).
11   Source: Hall, op cit.
12   Acknowledged even by several different police organisations: Hall, op cit.
13   Attention is often drawn to the parallel rise in civil actions. See eg ibid and Williams, op cit.

charges to those brought by the police themselves, and few more charges than did the old PCB. The number of charges seems particularly low because they are made in little over half of all the cases in which the complaint is substantiated. In the other substantiated complaints, the officer is 'advised' about his behaviour or 'admonished'.[14] Also, the percentages in Table 9.1 do not take into account complaints which are withdrawn or which are made the subject of conciliation procedures. Thus while over 8% of all completed investigations were substantiated in 1989, the substantiation rate for all complaints was just 2.6%.

The complaints can be broken down as follows: 28% are of assault, 21% of incivility, 10% of irregular procedure and 9% each of neglect of duty and oppressive conduct/harassment. Allegations of dishonesty and of unlawful arrest/detention comprise 6% each. Other complaints, such as discrimination, form a very small proportion of the total. The more serious the complaint, the less likely to be successful it is. Thus nine times as many 'neglect of duty' complaints are successful as assault complaints.[15] However, 'dissatisfaction' with the process is not confined to unsuccessful complaints. Maguire and Corbett found that even successful complainants were unhappy at the time taken, the lack of apology and the lack of information provided (for example, about what the investigation found and about disciplinary proceedings). Poor communication is almost as much of a problem as the nature and quality of the investigation and subsequent decisions about disciplinary or criminal proceedings.

There are many reasons for the low rate of substantiation of complaints. Firstly, there is the process of case construction and discrediting, discussed earlier. Secondly, there is the closing of ranks by police officers who might have witnessed the events complained of and the inherent difficulty that people mistreated in police custody have in finding independent witnesses. 'Cop culture', in other words, creates evidential problems.[16] A stark illustration of this is the 'Holloway Road transit case' in which five boys aged 13–16 were brutally beaten by a vanload of police officers. It was established that the attack must have been carried out by officers patrolling in one of three specific police vans, but it was not known which. The police involved broke further criminal laws by covering up the truth. Many of those questioned exercised their right to silence. For over two years, investigation followed investigation, with no charges, because no officer was prepared to 'inform'. Only when immunity was promised to any officer not directly

---

14 Maguire and Corbett, op cit ch 2.
15 Ibid ch 3.
16 See L Lustgarten, *The Governance of Police* (Sweet and Maxwell, 1986).

involved in the assault was the 'wall of silence' breached, leading eventually to the successful prosecution and jailing of five officers.[17] Dramatic though this case is, it is not unique. The 'Manchester case' in March 1985 involved nearly as much unprovoked brutality by police officers, but the identity of the officers could not be established.[18] Of the officers Maguire and Corbett interviewed, 60% 'admitted the existence of something like a "Code of Silence" among junior officers.'[19] As Loveday says, 'Breaking through the "blue curtain" has in practice proved as difficult for the PCA as for its predecessor body, the PCB.'[20]

These problems are exacerbated by the evidential threshold. This is the same standard of proof—beyond reasonable doubt—as is used in criminal proceedings, whereas in every other occupation the civil standard (balance of probabilities) is used in disciplinary proceedings. This has the consequence that officers who are prosecuted and acquitted would be likely to escape if disciplined too. Further protection is provided by the double jeopardy rule, which prevents officers from being charged with disciplinary offences which are 'in substance the same' as criminal offences with which they have been charged and acquitted.[1] On one occasion, an innocent and unarmed man, Steven Waldorf, was mistaken for a dangerous criminal and shot several times by police officers. The officers who shot him were tried for attempted murder and inflicting grievous bodily harm, but were acquitted on the ground that they had acted in self-defence (mistakenly believing themselves to be under attack). This then made it impossible to bring disciplinary charges against them.[2]

The Runciman Commission recommended abolition of both the criminal standard of proof and the double jeopardy rule,[3] and proposals to this effect were included in the Criminal Justice and Public Order

---

[17] The case is discussed by R East, 'Police Brutality—Lessons of the Holloway Road Assault' (1987) 137 NLJ 1010 and by B Hilliard, 'Holloway Road—Unfinished Business' (1987) 137 NLJ 1035.

[18] Loveday, op cit.

[19] Op cit p 71.

[20] Op cit p 29. Individual police officers have occasionally yanked down this curtain and rooted out the misconduct of their colleagues. For example, a detective inspector in the Avon and Somerset force deserves significant credit for uncovering the malpractice by Surrey officers which led to the conviction of the 'Guildford Four'. (She was acting for an inquiry ordered by the Home Office, rather than under the supervision of the PCA.) See J Rozenberg, 'Miscarriages of Justice' in E Stockdale and S Casale, (eds), *Criminal Justice Under Stress* (Blackstone, 1992).

[1] PACE, s 104(1).

[2] M Tregilgas-Davey, 'The Police and Accountability' (1990) 140 NLJ 697. Note, however, that officers who are convicted of criminal offences are automatically guilty of the disciplinary offence of committing a crime: *R v Secretary of State for Home Department, ex p Thornton* [1986] 2 All ER 641. See s 104(2) of PACE.

[3] Royal Commission on Criminal Justice, Report (Cm 2263) (HMSO, 1993) p 48.

Bill. The police have fiercely resisted these proposals and, at the time of writing, it appears that the government has decided to drop these reforms. It appears that some sections of the community are more effective in preserving their procedural rights than are others. Lustgarten has commented that 'The police are a uniquely favoured class of wrongdoers'[4], and it seems that this situation is going to be allowed to continue.

Officers under investigation often take early retirement or resign for 'medical' reasons.[5] This is a form of plea bargain: from the police force's point of view the problem is dealt with easily and speedily, while the officers concerned lose their jobs but protect their record and pension rights. While the difficulties of proof doubtless strengthen the hands of police officers, the attractions of this type of bargain for both sides will never disappear. For the fact is that the police simply do not wish to discipline officers in many cases. This is sometimes because of sympathy with the officers, but more often because of fear of adverse publicity and the cans of worms (57 varieties) which might be opened.

If the police reject proceedings but the Police Complaints Authority insist on them—a rare but occasional event—the Authority may also insist on a disciplinary tribunal instead of the usual disciplinary proceedings conducted by a chief officer alone. The tribunal is chaired by a senior officer of the force which decided against proceedings (flanked by two PCA members) and the 'prosecution' is presented by another member of that force. In successive years, the Police Complaints Authority criticised police forces for presenting cases without 'clarity and vigour' leading cases to fail.[6] Even if the tribunal decides against the officer, the police chairperson or chief officer decides the punishment.[7] This, of course, is also true of the majority of discipline proceedings (which the police themselves decide to hold) where the PCA has no involvement at all. Fitting the punishment of police officers to the offence is a matter for the police alone. That the Police Complaints Authority recommends proceedings in such a small number of cases may be due as much to its structurally weak position as to case construction or complicity with the police. Perhaps the PCA is resigned to the fact that there will often be little point in insisting on proceedings. The situation is illustrated by the 'Tottenham Three' detective superintendent mentioned earlier. In this case, the Metropolitan Police officer who conducted the investigation recommended no action, despite criticism of the detective by the Court of Appeal. The PCA insisted on a

4 Lustgarten, op cit p 153.
5 See Hall, op cit.
6 Quoted by Hall, op cit.
7 PACE, s 94(7).

tribunal. This tribunal will be run by the Metropolitan Police and the level of any punishment will be determined by a police officer.

Examination of the effects on the complaints and discipline process of proceedings in the ordinary courts is revealing. Over the five years 1988–92 inclusive, 80% of the Metropolitan Police officers involved in civil actions where over £10,000 was paid in damages or settlements had no disciplinary action taken against them.[8] The Runciman Commission was concerned that action was frequently not taken in this situation, nor where 'police malpractice has contributed to a miscarriage of justice', nor 'where a prosecution has been dismissed because of a more than technical breach of PACE or its codes and the actions of the police have been publicly criticised by the judge.'[9] Runciman found that the police had no mechanism for noting and acting upon judicial criticism of officers.

(c) Conciliation

One source of dissatisfaction among complainants discovered by Brown[10] was that making a complaint was 'all or nothing' regardless of the seriousness of the incident. Many of them wanted nothing more than an apology and a recognition of how they felt about their treatment by the police. This was catered for by s 85 of PACE which allows the 'informal resolution' (conciliation) of complaints if this is the wish of both chief officer and complainant, and if the matter would be insufficiently serious for it to be dealt with through disciplinary proceedings even if proven. Note that the officer complained of need not consent. Conciliation appears to be popular, being used in over 7,000 cases in 1989 (24% of all complainants).[11] However, although most complainants using it did so voluntarily, some say that they are 'nudged' into it, or even presented with a fait accompli.[12] Conciliation is not the same as an officer being 'advised' or 'admonished', for conciliation involves no formal admission of guilt and is not noted on the officers' records.

The frequency of the use of conciliation is to a large extent an indication of the relatively trivial nature of many complaints. However, different forces interpret the seriousness threshold differently. Some reserve conciliation for incivility, while others also use it for harassment,

(1993) Guardian, 15 April.
Report, op cit p 48.
D Brown, Police Complaints Procedure (Home Office Research Study no 93) (HMSO, 1987).
Maguire and Corbett, op cit.
C Corbett, 'Complaints Against the Police: The New Procedure of Informal Resolution' (1991) 2 Policing and Society 47.

neglect of duty (for example, not providing a party to a car accident with promised details of the other driver) and unlawful disclosure of information, such as informing an employer that an employee was a robbery suspect.[13] Some of these complaints ended with explanations by the police (such as blaming civilian employees for information not being transmitted) and sometimes with simple apologies by the officer. Occasionally the outcome was more dramatic, as where an investigating officer gave the officer complained of what can only be described as a 'roasting' designed to intimidate him.[14] While most complainants were happy with the outcome, some were dissatisfied with it, feeling that the conciliatory spirit was lacking. Some wished to meet the officer complained against, but this was arranged only rarely. When the officer refuses to be conciliatory, the process should be regarded as having failed. This would leave the complainant either to withdraw the complaint or to pursue it formally. In practice, however, these options do not seem to be offered to complainants.

The flaws in the conciliation process make one wary about encouraging its wider use. However, Corbett found that some assault allegations, which are automatically classified as too serious for conciliation, might have been dealt with effectively in this way. In one, for example, the complainant admitted that he had struggled on arrest, and only wanted it acknowledged that the officer was 'a bit out of order'. She concludes that, as it provides a rare opportunity for members of the police force and members of the public to understand each other's behaviour, its advantages outweigh its disadvantages.[15] Its speed and relatively high level of 'success' for the complainant are also important advantages (57% of these complainants were satisfied, compared with 10% whose complaints were fully investigated formally),[16] but this perhaps tells us more about the flaws in the formal procedures than the virtues of conciliation.

(d) Withdrawn complaints

The low level of substantiation of complaints against the police could reflect a high level of bogus complaints as much as unfair investigation processes. Were this so, one would expect most people with a grudge against the police—whether justified or not—to complain wherever possible. If anything, however, the reverse is true. Like the 'hidden

---

[13] Ibid.
[14] Ibid p 54.
[15] Ibid. See also Maguire, op cit, for a discussion of the problem of complaints procedures being, in part, a matter of communication, perception and different experiences.
[16] Maguire and Corbett, op cit Table 7.

figure' of unreported crime, there is a 'hidden figure' of unreported complaints. Tuck and Southgate found, prior to the creation of the Police Complaints Authority, that over 10% of their sample wished to complain, but only 1% actually took steps to do so and none actually completed the process.[17] The 1988 British Crime Survey found that little had changed after the creation of the PCA. 20% of the sample were 'really annoyed' by at least one officer over the previous five years; half of these (ie 10%) wished to complain, and 20% (ie 2%) took steps to do so, but it is not known how many pursued their complaints to a conclusion.[18]

Whatever the merits of a particular complaint, pursuing it is clearly not something done that in general is done lightly.[19] The drop off rate of those who initiate a complaint but fail to complete it is important. Although complainants may complain directly to the Police Complaints Authority, callers are generally advised to contact their local police station—which is, of course, often the location of the incident being complained about. Once there, many are dissuaded from continuing by the police. Those who continue are interviewed by an investigating officer, after which over 40% of complainants withdraw their complaints.

Many of those who persevered with their complaint told Maguire and Corbett that this was despite police pressure to withdraw. Pressure can take the form of inducements (for example, an offer to drop charges), charm (as when apologies or compensation is offered), threat (as where the possibility of charges against the complainant or associates is raised), dissuasion (explaining that success is very unlikely) or moral pressure (asking the complainant to consider the likely impact on the officer's career). Sometimes what is said satisfies complainants, who then withdraw, but most feel pressured into giving up. A higher proportion of assault complaints (60%) are withdrawn than average. Officers do not dispute the fact that they often advise withdrawal but, of course, they generally claim that they do this only where appropriate. Like most police work, interviews between investigating officers and complainants are hidden from view, making what the police do largely unaccountable. Even the thin protection of the PCA is not provided where complaints are withdrawn. For as long as the police remain responsible for complaints investigation, this situation will continue.

---

[17]   M Tuck and P Southgate, Ethnic Minorities Crime and Policing (Home Office Research Study no 70) (HMSO, 1981).

[18]   P Mayhew, D Elliott and L Dowds, The 1988 British Crime Survey (Home Office Research Study no 111) (HMSO, 1989).

[19]   This may be contrasted with the belief of most police officers that most complaints are malicious and/or time-wasting: Maguire and Corbett, op cit ch 5.

Police working rules will continue to dominate the complaints process. The weakness of the legal framework for handing complaints enables the police to continue breaking the PACE rules (for example, denying a suspect access to legal advice) with little fear of being disciplined for doing so. We may therefore conclude that that legal framework is essentially presentational, providing an appearance of due process whilst changing police behaviour very little.[20]

(e) Proposals for reform

Despite several major changes in the system over the past 30 years or so, the complaints system is still unsatisfactory—except as a way of preserving the freedom of the police to follow their own informal norms. This is partly because investigating malpractice by anyone (including criminals) is intrinsically difficult and likely to fail in the majority of cases.[1] It is also because processes requiring articulate argument, polite persistence and so forth favour middle class people. Since most complainants are working class, they are less likely to succeed in their complaints.[2]

Little can be done about the above problems. However, what could be altered are the other most important features of the system: the way it deals with complainants and the investigation of the police by the police.[3] What about 'civilian' investigators or civilian review boards? In some jurisdictions, such as Toronto and several American cities, these solutions appears to be more successful than our own. They are, however, fraught with new difficulties, including obstruction by the police or civilian investigators over identifying with the problems of the police.[4] It is also said that civilians who have not experienced 'the street' could 'not easily tell the difference between an officer "trying honestly to do his job, but perhaps making mistakes", and a truly deviant officer "who should not be in uniform".'[5] None the less, where 'external'

---

[20] These kinds of problems have been observed in many other jurisdictions, and not just in Britain. See A Goldsmith, 'External Review and Self-regulation' in A Goldsmith (ed), *Complaints Against the Police: the Trend to External Review* (OUP, 1991).

[1] See ibid.

[2] Box and Russell, op cit.

[3] It is common for complaints against professions—for example, the legal and medical professions—to be investigated by those professions. Whether this reflects the likely ineffectiveness of external investigators or the power wielded by most professions to protect themselves against outside interference is open to discussion.

[4] For good surveys, see Loveday, op cit and M McMahon, 'Police Accountability: the Situation of Complaints in Toronto' (1988) 12 Contemporary Crises 301. Also see A Goldsmith and S Farson, 'Complaints against the Police in Canada: A New Approach' [1987] Crim LR 615 and Goldsmith (ed), op cit.

[5] Maguire, op cit (quoting police officers).

involvement in investigation is more than merely supervisory, its impact can be considerable.[6]

The Police Complaints Authority has expressed concern about the lack of independence of investigations in relation to assaults.[7] Members of the Authority are frequently dissatisfied with the uncritical acceptance by investigating officers of police statements contradicting those of complainants, with missing evidence and so forth.[8] But they can do nothing about this. Lord Scarman's report into the Brixton 'riots' of the early 1980s stated that 'if public confidence in the complaints procedure is to be achieved, any solution falling short of a system of independent investigation . . . is unlikely to be successful.'[9] This was echoed by both the PCB and the PCA, which recommended that a national specialist team of investigating officers be recruited on a secondment basis.[10]

Major changes to the system, such as civilian investigators or even a body of seconded officers, are not likely. All that is currently being proposed is abolition of the double jeopardy rule and a change to the evidential threshold to make dismissal and other disciplinary action easier. Although this follows concern expressed by the Police Complaints Authority that there is no simple procedure for removing 'unsuitable police officers',[11] it also follows wide-ranging managerialist proposals regarding the police service. Since the proposals would make it easier to dismiss for simple inefficiency, we can say that they are as much inspired by crime control concerns as with the rights of complainants. And, as we have noted, even these relatively modest proposals are foundering in the face of vociferous police opposition.

The treatment of complainants is a separate issue from who investigates. Unlike in a civil case, complainants have no rights in the investigation process, such as to ensure that their witnesses are interviewed. Complainants may attend the disciplinary hearing or tribunal (if there is one) but may not stay for the verdict or punishment (if any) and may never find it out. Some complaints take a year or more to investigate and then a hearing may take as long again. Again, complainants have no right to know the causes of the delay and have no power to question it. Complainants have no right to the investigation file or to know its contents. Indeed, under s 98 of PACE, it is a criminal offence for anything other than a summary of an investigation to be

---

6 Goldsmith, op cit.
7 See eg Police Complaints Authority, Annual Report 1987 (HMSO).
8 Maguire and Corbett, op cit.
9 Sir L Scarman, The Brixton Disorders: 10–12 April 1981 (Cmnd 8427) (HMSO, 1981) para 4.2.
10 Police Complaints Board, Triennial Report (HMSO, 1980), discussed by Reiner, op cit p 235 and Loveday, op cit.
11 Police Complaints Authority, Annual Report 1987 (HMSO).

disclosed except for the purpose of disciplinary or legal proceedings. While this would not preclude a reasonably detailed summary being provided to complainants, instead bland uninformative statements are provided, creating the dissatisfaction noted earlier.[12]

Perhaps the most constructive immediate reforms which can be currently envisaged would be, firstly, to allow complainants access to investigation files for the purposes of civil actions, something which the courts' interpretation of s 98 currently prohibits.[13] Secondly, conciliation procedures could be expanded in order to increase understanding on both sides. This does, however, presuppose that there is common ground to be occupied and that policing really is 'for' the whole community and not against parts of it.[14] Finally, for that minority of truly serious allegations, genuinely independent investigators are needed. None of these should be seen as 'quick-fix' solutions to complex policing and investigatory processes.[15] If anything, their value would lie less in establishing the 'truth' or in securing more 'successes' for complainants than in opening up investigation and police processes to public scrutiny. Such a reform programme may not succeed in making the complaints system conform to due process values, but at least the limitations of the system would become more widely recognised. Less would be claimed for the system and less expected of it.

At present, it is as though the police complaints procedure does not exist for those who set it in motion—complainants—but is essentially an internal matter for the police and the PCA. The complaints procedure has been grafted onto the police disciplinary procedure and the PCA has been grafted onto that. If the current system allows a degree of latitude for police working rules by prioritising morale, efficiency and cost considerations, this is because it is not intended to punish and deter most breaches of the legal rules or to protect suspects and defendants. It is not intended to expose police procedures and practices for the public to see. It is a process which facilitates crime control and not due process. Only when this is grasped can the current system be fully understood and proposals for reform be realistically evaluated.

---

[12] See Maguire and Corbett, op cit and Loveday, op cit. The PCA itself is unhappy about this, to some extent self-imposed, restriction: see its Triennial Review 1985–88, (HC 466) (1988).

[13] The legal position is discussed by M Zander, *The Police and Criminal Evidence Act 1984* (Sweet and Maxwell, 2nd edn, 1990) pp 235–238.

[14] See ch 2, particularly section 5, above, for consideration of this point.

[15] McMahon, op cit.

4.   EXCLUSION OF EVIDENCE[16]

One of the great dilemmas of any system of criminal justice is what to do about evidence obtained in the course of rule breaking by police and other officials. The crime control position is that the only sensible test of evidence is its probative value—ie its reliability. If evidence is obtained wrongly, the officials responsible should be dealt with and the wronged defendant should be compensated, in proceedings designed for those purposes. The remedies and complaints procedures discussed above should therefore compensate, punish and deter. Excluding reliable evidence at trial so that a guilty person walks free merely punishes the innocent public along with (and only in a very indirect sense) the guilty police. The purpose of the criminal trial is to establish guilt or innocence, so legal niceties should not obstruct the search for the truth.

The due process position is that the best way of deterring future breaches of the rules is by preventing the police from benefiting from them. In so far as due process protections have value in themselves as ethical standards, a system which accepts evidence secured in breach of those standards is tainted. If citizens are to respect the law, the criminal justice system has to set an example. The crime control adherent argues that the ends justify the means, while the due process adherent argues that the means themselves must have moral integrity, regardless of what ends are being pursued.

There are a number of problems with both positions. For instance, both make assumptions about the value of all these remedies and controls without a firm factual basis for those assumptions. What discredits the criminal justice system more: ignoring apparently reliable evidence and allowing the apparently guilty to go free, or using illegally obtained evidence and, by doing so, condoning illegal police behaviour which may not be subject to any other sanction? What is the best way of controlling police illegality? Is it the threat of civil or disciplinary sanctions, given what we have said about them earlier in this chapter ? Do not exclusionary rules—as these due process-based rules of evidence are known—operate equally quixotically, 'punishing' police officers only when illegal behaviour occurs in cases with not enough lawfully obtained evidence to support a conviction? And how valuable are exclusionary rules as protections? They provide no comfort for suspects who are not charged or who plead guilty or who may have

---

[16] The literature on this topic is enormous. See, for instance, A Zuckerman, 'Illegally Obtained Evidence—Discretion as a Guardian of Legitimacy' [1987] CLP 55; I Dennis, 'Reconstructing the Law of Criminal Evidence' [1989] CLP 21 and J McEwan, *Evidence and the Adversarial Process* (Blackwell, 1992) pp 172–175.

suffered greatly through having had their home unlawfully searched, being interrogated roughly or being denied access to legal advice.[17]

It is important to draw attention to the common ground shared by crime control and due process models. Few civilised systems would countenance the use of evidence secured through torture, no matter how reliable it might be. Crime control stops short of advocating this. If a minor rule were breached (for example, refreshments to a suspect held in cells being provided 20 minutes late) it would be difficult to argue for all evidence secured thereafter being excluded. Due process would not support such a rule. There are no systems in democratic societies which use absolute inclusionary or exclusionary rules. This means that rules and principles have to be developed which effect some kind of compromise. But whereas due process and crime control adherents can reach some agreement on the outer limits of an exclusionary rule, they are unable to reach consensus on what this compromise should be. The exact compromise will depend on the priorities allocated to the competing claims of truth (ie truth about guilt, since it is the police's rule breaking in furtherance of the case for the prosecution which is in issue) and of moral integrity. As we have argued above, however, the choice to be made should also be informed by an awareness of the limitations of exclusionary rules, and of their interrelationship with other remedies (which may themselves be less effective than appearances would suggest).

Historically, the common law position on exclusion was at the crime control end of the spectrum. In *Sang*[18] (where evidence was obtained by an *agent provocateur*) it was held that judges had no general discretion to exclude evidence simply because of the duplicitous or oppressive way in which it was obtained. However, there were various common law exceptions to this, particularly in relation to confession evidence. This has always been treated differently, because of the peculiar difficulty of reconciling police questioning which produces confessions with the right of silence.[19] The Judges' Rules, which codified the common law, stated that 'it is a fundamental condition of the admissibility in evidence' of a confession that 'it shall have been voluntary' and not secured 'by oppression'.[20] The preamble also stated that non-conformity with the rules (for example, the requirement to caution suspects) 'may render answers and statements liable to be excluded.' Confessions obtained involuntarily, through oppression or through inducements

---

[17] Many of these arguments were canvassed by the Philips Commission: Report, op cit pp 110–118.
[18] [1980] AC 402.
[19] See ch 4, section 5, above.
[20] See ch 4, above, for discussion of these rules.

had therefore to be excluded. Confessions obtained in breach of other of the Judges' Rules could be excluded in certain circumstances.[1] Most non-confession evidence (for example, fingerprints, blood or clothing) would not generally be excluded, however it was obtained.[2]

When PACE was drafted, the government intended largely to re-enact these common law rules. What is now s 76 provides for the exclusion of confession evidence obtained oppressively or in conditions making it likely to be unreliable.[3] And what is now s 82(3) provides that 'Nothing in this Part of this Act shall prejudice any power of a court to exclude evidence . . . at its discretion', allowing the judges to apply the common law as it had been developing. Amendments were put forward, however, which would have introduced a powerful exclusionary rule. As a compromise, the government introduced what is now s 78, allowing judges to exclude—at their discretion—any evidence obtained 'unfairly'.[4] This criterion need not relate to reliability at all. Thus it covers most situations covered by s 82(3), but not all.[5] Section 78 also covers some situations covered by s 76, and many other situations not previously covered by the common law.[6]

Section 78 clearly represents a movement towards due process. The extent of that movement has depended, and will continue to depend, on the way 'unfairness' is interpreted by the judges and how they use their discretion. As in other areas of law we have examined, the judicial role is of utmost importance, and this is equally true in relation to judicial interpretation of s 76. In the following discussion, we will not attempt to suggest that one approach is better than the other, but will simply identify which approach judicial interpretation most consistently draws upon.

---

[1] See generally P Mirfield, *Confessions* (Sweet and Maxwell, 1985).
[2] See eg *Jeffrey v Black* [1978] QB 490, in which evidence of theft, obtained after an unlawful search, was held to be admissible.
[3] There is, significantly, no mention of 'voluntariness'. The Philips Commission drew on research showing that 'voluntariness' was a meaningless concept in the context of involuntary police station detention and recommended that it be abandoned: see ch 4, section 5(e), above.
[4] For the legislative history of s 78 see Zander, op cit pp 199–200.
[5] In *Howden-Simpson* [1991] Crim LR 49, the Court of Appeal ruled that confession evidence obtained through an inducement (not interviewing choristers about the defendant's alleged dishonesty if he confessed) should have been excluded. The Court of Appeal appeared to think that s 82(3) should have been applied by the trial judge, but this is not clear from the report. The trial judge in fact took a decision under s 76 not to exclude. Section 78 might also have provided a base for exclusion. The overlap between these provisions has contributed to a lack of clear jurisprudence on how each should be applied.
[6] See D Birch, 'The PACE Hots Up: Confessions and Confusions Under the 1984 Act' [1989] Crim LR 95.

(a) PACE, s 76: oppression and reliability

Confession evidence cannot be presented in court unless the prosecution proves that it was not obtained:

'(a) by oppression of the person who made it; or
(b) in consequence of anything said or done which was likely, in the circumstances existing at the time, to render [it] unreliable . . .' (s 76(2)).

We saw in chapter 4 that 'oppression' is not defined in PACE or elsewhere. It includes 'torture, inhuman or degrading treatment, and the use or threat of violence . . .' (s 76(8)) but is not confined to such extreme circumstances.[7] In *Fulling*,[8] it was stated, obiter, that oppression must almost necessarily 'entail some impropriety'.[9] However, not all law-breaking, such as denial of access to legal advice, is oppressive. As Zander says, 'It remains to be seen . . . what degree of gravity of police misconduct qualifies as oppression.'[10] Not knowing just what behaviour will, and will not, be excluded under this heading means its value as a deterrent to malpractice is limited. Circumstances 'likely' to render confession evidence 'unreliable' is similarly vague and thus of similarly limited value as a deterrent.

Whilst this section seems to be intended to protect suspects, the focus of the courts in interpreting it has been on examining police intentions rather than the effects of their behaviour on suspects. In *Miller*,[11] a paranoid schizophrenic was questioned at length. This produced hallucinations and delusions, along with a confession. The Court of Appeal held that the fact that the defendant experienced the interrogation as oppressive did not make it so in law, for this was not the intention of the police and would not have been the result in normal circumstances. This was small comfort to Miller. The decision ignored the fact that few suspects experience custodial interrogation as normal, that the application of pressure is a natural police interrogation tactic and that many more suspects are 'vulnerable' than are ever officially recognised as such.[12] However, the 'reliability' rule should cater for such cases, and the Court of Appeal has held on a number of occasions

---

[7] In *Davison* [1988] Crim LR 442, where the police breached many rules and detained the defendant unlawfully, the confession was held by the Crown Court judge to have been obtained by oppression.
[8] [1987] QB 426. The case is more fully discussed in ch 4, section 5(e).
[9] See, similarly, *Heaton* [1993] Crim LR 593.
[10] M Zander, *The Police and Criminal Evidence Act 1984* (Sweet & Maxwell, 2nd edn, 1990) p 191.
[11] [1986] 1 WLR 1191.
[12] See ch 4, section 2(c), above.

that confessions by vulnerable suspects with very low IQs should have been excluded on this basis.[13] Section 77 of PACE requires a special warning to be given to juries if a prosecution case relies wholly or largely on a confession by a 'mentally handicapped' person where the confession is not made in the presence of an independent party. These circumstances should not, of course, ever occur, but Parliament and the courts have had to accept that occur they do.

One problem for which there is no easy solution is what happens when there is a series of interviews which begin oppressively. Should confession evidence from the later interviews be excluded on the grounds that they are 'tainted' by the earlier oppression? The courts have adopted a case-by-case approach here: in *Glaves*,[14] interviews separated by eight days were held to be tainted in this way, as separate interviews were in *Canale*[15] (a s 78 case). However, in *Gillard and Barrett*[16] (another s 78 case) later interviews were held not to be tainted in this way because the earlier improprieties were no longer operative.

Section 76 does not take the due process route as far as happened for a while in the United States. The 'fruit of the poisoned tree' doctrine used in some American cases would mean that evidence obtained as a result of oppressively obtained confessions is no more admissible than the confessions themselves.[17] Section 76(4)(a), however, provides that exclusion does not affect the admissibility 'of any facts discovered as a result of the confession.' Such facts might be the hidden proceeds of a robbery, or blood-stained clothes worn by the suspect at the time of an assault and then discarded. Where suspects are likely to both confess and tell the police where to find evidence of this kind, the exclusionary rule may not deter the police from oppressive questioning.[18]

(b)   PACE, s 78: fairness

Section 78(1) provides that:

'. . . the court may refuse to allow evidence . . . if it appears to the court that, having regard to all the circumstances in which the evidence was obtained, the admission of the evidence would have such an adverse

---

13   See eg *Everett* [1988] Crim LR 826; *Delaney* (1988) 88 Cr App Rep 338; and the 'Tottenham Three' case: *Re Raghip, Silcott and Braithwaite* (1991) Times, 9 December.

14   [1993] Crim LR 685.

15   [1990] 2 All ER 187.

16   [1991] Crim LR 280.

17   There has been a retreat from this doctrine in recent years. See J Driscoll, 'Excluding Illegally Obtained Evidence in the United States' [1987] Crim LR 553 and J McEwan, op cit pp 173–174.

18   Exclusion of the collateral evidence could still be considered under s 78, however.

effect on the fairness of the proceedings that the court ought not to admit it.'

Whereas s 76 applies to confession evidence alone, s 78 applies to all evidence, including confession evidence. Unlike in s 76, the burden of proof in s 78 is on the defence.[19]

The test is one of 'fairness' and if the court is satisfied on this it must then exercise a discretion (unlike s 76 where exclusion is mandatory if the 'oppression' or 'reliability' tests are satisfied). No criteria are provided either for recognising 'unfairness' or to provide guidance on exercising the discretion. All that is clear is that a pure due process 'disciplinary' rule is disallowed, for a court which automatically excluded evidence obtained in breach of legal rules would not be exercising discretion properly; and that a pure crime control 'reliability' principle is also disallowed, for 'unfairness' does not necessarily imply a lack of probative value.

The decision not to adopt a hard and fast rule, combined with the sheer volume of unfair police practices, has resulted in a flood of reported appellate cases on exclusion (44 were reported in the period 1986–90 according to Zander)[20] and a formidable academic literature.[1] Of the 44 cases catalogued by Zander, twenty led to a decision that the evidence should have been excluded. This could be taken as an even-handed approach, but appealed cases are not necessarily representative of all cases. We have little idea of how Crown Court judges exercise their discretion. If Zander's survey of cases proves anything, it is the scope that s 78 provides for confusion and inconsistency of approach.

It is difficult, to put it mildly, to perceive any consistent pattern in the appellate decisions. However, three broad—but conflicting—principles can be discerned. It is possible that, in time, the courts will opt for just one principle. Meanwhile, there is sufficient choice for a court to decide which result it desires and then find a principle and an authority to justify it.

Bad faith

In *Matto v Wolverhampton CC*,[2] the police pursued a speeding driver. He stopped his car on his driveway and the police asked him to take a breath test. He protested that they were on his private property. They replied that if they wrongly arrested him he could sue. He was

---

[19] See the commentary on *Keenan* [1989] Crim LR 720.
[20] See Zander, op cit pp 205–207 for a table showing the issues canvassed and results.
[1] See, as a starting point, the sources cited in ibid p 204.
[2] [1987] RTR 337.

convicted of driving with excess alcohol. It was held on appeal that the evidence of intoxication obtained as a result of the wrongful arrest should have been excluded because of the bad faith of the police. Had the wrongful arrest been an honest mistake, as in a later case,[3] the evidence would have been admissible.[4] In *Alladice*,[5] the police delayed access to legal advice under s 58. They thought that they were entitled to do this but the Court of Appeal decision in *Samuel*[6] intervened, making what they thought was lawful into an unlawful act. The confession evidence secured in the absence of a solicitor was held admissible due, in part, to what the Court of Appeal regarded as their good faith.

Section 78 does not require that there be a breach of the law or of PACE. In *Brine*,[7] the defendant suffered from stress and mental illness. His confession under normal interrogation conditions was thought to be unreliable because of this. The Court of Appeal held that s 78 should be applied even though the police behaviour remained within the law. And in *Mason*,[8] the police deliberately deceived the defendant (D) and his solicitor, saying that they had found D's fingerprints on an item when in fact they had not. D confessed. It was held that the confession should have been excluded, even though the police lies were not characterised as unlawful. However, only rarely is it held that behaviour which does not breach PACE should be excluded. Trickery, for instance, is not regarded as per se unfair. An example is *Maclean and Kosten*.[9] A suspected drugs importer (K) was tricked by customs officers into believing that a drugs courier (C) had been involved in a car accident when transporting drugs. An officer masqueraded as a car salvage operator and thereby successfully trapped K in incriminating circumstances. This subterfuge was ruled by the Court of Appeal to be acceptable.

As with the case law on oppression, the court is looking at the issue of exclusion and fairness from the point of view of the police rather than the defendant. Alladice suffered no less through the police making an honest mistake than he would have done if they had acted out of malice. Good or bad faith is, in any case, difficult to ascertain. With no solicitor present, and no other independent witness, it was the officers' word against that of Alladice. It is also questionable whether good and

---

[3] *Thomas v DPP* (1989) Times, 17 October, where the facts were otherwise similar and the evidence was not excluded.
[4] See also *Quinn* [1990] Crim LR 581.
[5] (1988) 87 Cr App Rep 380.
[6] [1988] QB 615.
[7] [1992] Crim LR 122.
[8] [1987] 3 All ER 481.
[9] [1993] Crim LR 687.

bad faith are meaningful concepts in the context of police interrogation. After all, if suspects do not wish to speak, it is the job of the police to persuade them to do so. Like inducements, 'bad faith' is part of the game.

Most important of all, in *Alladice*, as in many of these cases,[10] the defendant not only disputed the offence, but also disputed making the alleged confession to it. One of the purposes of having a right to a solicitor is to have a witness to the interrogation precisely to avoid such disputes.[11] Unlawful denial of the right to a solicitor deprives suspects of the chance of calling independent evidence to corroborate their claims that they did not make the confessions attributed to them. The most powerful argument for excluding evidence in such circumstances, whatever the motives of the police, is that this is the only way of ensuring that suspects do not suffer from the wrongs done to them by the police.

Protective

Excluding unlawfully obtained evidence under s 78 because otherwise defendants would suffer—ie in order to protect defendants—is the application of the 'protective' principle.[12] It is an attractive principle, for it allows evidence to be excluded where there are serious breaches of propriety but only where the defendant would be prejudiced if the evidence was admitted. The problem is the evaluation of whether or not there would be such prejudice. In *Samuel*,[13] the defendant was thought to have suffered through the admission at trial of illegally obtained evidence. While similar decisions have been made in several other 'access to solicitor' cases,[14] some decisions on this point have gone the other way. In *Alladice*,[15] the Court of Appeal considered that, leaving aside the issue of good faith, the confession was rightly admitted. Its reasoning was that had Alladice seen a solicitor, the solicitor would only have told him of the rights of which he was already aware. No consideration was given to whether Alladice would have been better able to exercise his rights (particularly to silence) had his lawyer been present or, of course, to Alladice's 'right' to have a witness to what he did say to the police. As is clear from chapter 4, knowing one's rights and having the

---

[10] For example, *Samuel*, above. See ch 4, section 5, above, for discussion of interrogation and confession problems.

[11] *Dunn* (1990) 91 Cr App Rep 237.

[12] The phrase was coined by A Ashworth, 'Excluding Evidence as Protecting Rights' [1977] Crim LR 723.

[13] Above.

[14] See eg *Parris* [1989] Crim LR 214.

[15] Above.

resilience to exercise them when under pressure to speak are entirely different things. If the protective principle is to afford any real protection to suspects, the courts must take into account the realities of police interrogation rather than make the glib assumption that knowledge of one's rights puts one on an even par with the police.

The protective principle has formed the basis of many Court of Appeal decisions. It was reiterated in relation to access to legal advice in, for instance, *Dunford*[16] and *Oliphant*.[17] In *Dunn*,[18] it was employed following a failure to take contemporaneous notes in an 'informal interview' conducted after the tape recording of a formal interview ended. It was applied in *Quinn*[19] in relation to improperly obtained identification evidence. And in *Taylor*,[20] it was utilised in relation to breach of the requirement to review the detention of a suspect in the police station at periodic intervals.

Significant breach

Some s 78 cases have held that some breaches of PACE or the codes of practice are so serious that exclusion of evidence is justified regardless of what the intentions of the police or the consequences of that breach might have been. One such case was *Keenan*,[1] where contemporaneous notes were not taken. Others include *Canale*[2] and *Oransaye*,[3] in each of which the police blatantly breached the rules on, among other things, contemporaneous recording,[4] and *Weekes*,[5] where a 'conversation' was said by the Court of Appeal to be an 'interview'. The defendant was a juvenile at the time, so not only did the interview wrongly take place outside the station, but an appropriate adult should have been present.

However, the principle was diluted somewhat in *Walsh*[6] where the Court of Appeal held that it was not enough that there be a substantial breach; there must also be 'such an adverse effect that justice requires the evidence to be excluded'. This seems to be a move towards the protective principle, and suggests that the interests of the defence and

---

[16] (1990) 91 Cr App Rep 150. Discussed by A Sanders, 'Access to a Solicitor and s 78 PACE' (1990) LS Gaz 31 October p 17; J Hodgson, 'Tipping the Scales of Justice: The Suspect's Right to Legal Advice' [1992] Crim LR 854.

[17] [1992] Crim LR 40.

[18] (1990) 91 Cr App Rep 237. Discussed in ch 4, section 5(g), above.

[19] [1990] Crim LR 581.

[20] [1991] Crim LR 541.

[1] [1989] 3 All ER 598.

[2] [1990] 2 All ER 187.

[3] [1993] Crim LR 772.

[4] Doubtless the 'good faith' principle also operated in these cases.

[5] [1993] Crim LR 211. Discussed in ch 4, section 5(d), above.

[6] [1989] Crim LR 822.

prosecution must be weighed and balanced in what can only be a highly subjective exercise. The result is a case like *Dunn*[7] where the failure to record the informal interview was, by any standards, a substantial breach. Despite this breach of Code of Practice C, the Court of Appeal held that the evidence was rightly admitted.[8] The court justified its stance by arguing that the safeguard that contemporaneous recording would have provided was rendered redundant because Dunn's solicitor was present to witness the informal interview. On this reasoning the defence argument for exclusion failed for not satisfying the protective principle either.[9]

The merit of the undiluted 'significant breach' test is that it enables judges to exercise discretion on the basis of the objective significance of the law in question. This is more certain and fairer than the other two tests which require subjective judgments and, in the case of the protective principle, a guess as to what defendants would have done had they been allowed by the police to exercise their rights. However, what is a substantial breach is itself a matter of subjective interpretation. The factors that might be considered in making such a judgment were alluded to in *Marsh*.[10] The officers in this case did not caution the suspect as they did not regard their conversation as an 'interview'. The Court of Appeal held that this was not a substantial breach. LJ Bingham said:

'There has to be a reasonable common-sense approach to the matter such that police officers confronted with unexpected situations, and doing their best to be fair and to comply with the Codes, do not fall foul on some technicality of authority or construction.'[11]

This appears to dilute the substantial breach test by incorporating into it the additional test of whether the police officers acted in good faith. The danger in this approach is that the courts, lacking insight into the realities of police practices, may take too charitable a view of whether police officers in any given case were 'doing their best to be fair and to comply with the Codes.'

---

[7] (1990) 91 Cr App Rep 237. Discussed earlier in this chapter, and in ch 4, section 5(g), above.

[8] 'Contemporaneous recording' cases like this will be of continued relevance, despite tape recording requirements, for as long as alleged confessions made informally are allowed. See ch 4, section 5(h), above.

[9] Had the argument used in *Dunn* that a major purpose of a legal advisor is to act as a witness been accepted in *Alladice* and *Dunford*, the rights of, and protections for, the suspects in those cases would have been regarded as significantly violated. This would have justified exclusion of the evidence in those cases. It seems that the Court of Appeal is being selective about the purposes it attributes to government legislation, as well as the principles it uses in reviewing the application of it by trial judges.

[10] [1991] Crim LR 455.

[11] Quoted in Commentary [1991] Crim LR 456.

One of the major sources of miscarriages of justice concerns confession evidence: what was said and whether what may have been said was true. Adherence to PACE and the codes of practice would not completely eliminate disputes over these issues, but it would substantially reduce the use of 'informal' and therefore unverifiable statements and unlawful pressure. Thus in *Scott*,[12] the defendant allegedly made an incriminating remark after the end of the interview, and so it was not tape recorded. Nor was a note of it taken contemporaneously. He was convicted after the judge allowed it to be used in evidence. The Court of Appeal held that this was a substantial breach and the alleged comment should have been excluded because he had not been given the opportunity to deny making the comment at the time he was alleged to have made it. The application of the substantial breach principle, as in this case, is the most effective way of reducing miscarriages of justice, short of a complete exclusion rule. From a due process perspective, it is to be regretted that the Court of Appeal has allowed this principle to be watered down by conflating it with the 'good faith' and 'protective' principles.

Given the complex nature of exclusion under s 78, the conflicting decisions springing from this statutory source and the resulting torrent of contested cases and appeals, we looked forward to the Runciman Commission's evaluation of this crucial aspect of PACE. Its contribution to this much-debated topic was less than profound, amounting to a single sentence: 'We are satisfied generally with the way in which section 78 has worked in practice and propose no changes to it.'[13] This sits rather oddly with the majority's recommendations on removing the power of the Court of Appeal to quash convictions where malpractice has occurred but the evidence against a defendant is none the less reliable.[14] If the crime control 'reliability principle' is to govern the Court of Appeal's powers to quash convictions, then why not also the trial judge's powers to exclude evidence? As Zander points out in his dissent to the Runciman Commission's report, the stance of the majority risks

'undermining the principle at the heart of section 78 . . . the majority would in effect be encouraging the Court of Appeal to undercut a part of its moral force by saying that the issue of "unfairness" can be ignored where there is sufficient evidence to show that the defendant is actually guilty.'[15]

---

[12] [1991] Crim LR 56.

[13] Report, op cit p 58.

[14] See section 5(c), below.

[15] Ibid pp 234–235. One other member of the Runciman Commission supported Zander in this part of his dissent. There were 11 members of the Runciman Commission in total.

The inadequate and incoherent treatment of s 78 by the Runciman Commission is revealing as to that body's priorities. Whereas pages and pages of its report were devoted to numbingly tedious managerial concerns—how to process cases more cheaply and efficiently—s 78 was afforded the most cursory of nods.

5. APPEALS AGAINST CONVICTION

(a) Introduction

Part of the common ground that exists between the crime control and due process models is that the criminal system's potential for error necessitates some form of appellate review. As we observed in the introduction to this chapter, the two models differ sharply as to the scope of such review. It is important to elaborate on this divergence prior to examining appellate procedures as they operate in this country.

Crime control

The crime control model rests on the assumption that the administrative procedures operated by police and prosecutors reliably screen out the probably innocent at an early stage. That the vast majority of those processed through the system plead guilty is testimony to this essential fact. Where defendants plead not guilty, any remaining doubts about guilt should be resolved by the court of first instance. Thus, as Packer puts it, in the crime control model:

'the role of an appellate review system is highly marginal: it is available to correct those occasional slips in which the trier of fact either makes a plain error about factual guilt or makes so gross a procedural mistake that the reliability of the guilt-determining process is called into question.'[16]

The aim of ensuring certainty and finality within the criminal process would be undermined if convicted persons could delay the imposition of punishment. Appeals should therefore be so discouraged that only those with the clearest grounds for complaint will pursue the matter. No financial assistance should be given to the appellant until the case has been screened and determined to be of sufficient merit. Moreover, as the quote above suggests, the grounds for appeal should be narrow. Only when the appellate tribunal finds that no reasonable trier of fact could have convicted on the evidence presented should a

[16] Packer, op cit p 228.

conviction be quashed. It would not be enough for the appellate court to consider that it would have acquitted or that most juries would have acquitted. Procedural errors, such as breaches of the *Turner* rules on plea bargaining[17] or biased summaries of evidence by trial judges,[18] should likewise not justify the quashing of a conviction unless it is adjudged that, had the error not occurred, an acquittal would have been probable. It would be intolerable to quash the conviction of a probably guilty person on such a technicality. This model therefore focuses exclusively on the accuracy of the determination of guilt by the court of trial.

Due process

Due process, whilst acknowledging the importance of rectifying errors in the determination of factual guilt, places equal stress upon appellate review as a means of upholding the moral integrity of the criminal process. Abuses of official power, whether by the police, prosecutors or trial judges, must be corrected and deterred. Any infringement of the basic rights of an accused person, such as unlawful arrests, oppressive interrogation or the wrongful admission of evidence at trial, should suffice for the quashing of a conviction, regardless of the strength of the evidence against the appellant. Even minor infringements of procedural rules may justify this course if their cumulative effect is significant. As Packer puts it:

'The reversal of a criminal conviction is a small price to pay for an affirmation of proper values and a deterrent example of what will happen when those values are slighted. When an appellate court finds it necessary to castigate the conduct of the police, the prosecutor, or the trial court, but fails to reverse a conviction, it simply breeds disrespect for the very standards it is trying to affirm.'[19]

Moreover, the further elaboration of due process rights depends upon a steady flow of appeals to the higher courts. The raw material for these appeals is plentiful, given this model's assumption that frequent mistakes about factual guilt are made at earlier stages of the process. There must, therefore, be unrestricted access to appellate review. Preliminary screening of appeals to assess their worth should be seen for what it is—a second-rate form of appellate review. Finally, but of fundamental importance, legal aid must be available to underwrite the cost of appealing. If convicted persons are unable to afford legal advice

---

[17] See ch 7, above.
[18] See ch 8, section 3(b), above.
[19] Packer, op cit pp 231–232.

and representation the chances are that they will neither appreciate whether grounds for appeal exist nor be able to present their case effectively.

(b)   Appeals from the magistrates' courts

There are three channels of appellate review for those convicted in the magistrates' courts: a rehearing in the Crown Court, an appeal by way of case stated to the Divisional Court or judicial review.

Rehearings in the Crown Court

The rights of appeal in the English system differ markedly according to whether the defendant was convicted in the magistrates' court or the Crown Court. Partly as a result of historical accident, and partly due to the unsatisfactory nature of summary justice, it is a magistrates' court conviction which is subject to the more extensive form of appellate review.[20] No leave is required for an appeal from this court to the Crown Court, and the appeal takes the form of a complete rehearing of the case before a judge and two or more magistrates.[1] The Royal Commission on Criminal Justice (Runciman Commission) was careful to draw attention to this 'second bite of the cherry' for 'aggrieved defendants' in its report.[2] It did so to pre-empt criticisms of its proposal to increase the proportion of defendants tried in the magistrates' courts by removing the right to elect trial by jury in either way offences.[3] Any unfairness arising in the magistrates' courts could always be put right on appeal. But this form of appellate review is neither so generous nor so effective as the Runciman Commission implied.

To begin with, an appeal against conviction does not lie to the Crown Court if the defendant pleaded guilty in the magistrates' court.[4] This automatically excludes close to 90% of all defendants tried in the lower courts from the appeal system. Many such defendants may be very much aggrieved by the circumstances of the police investigation, the conduct of the prosecution and the behaviour of the magistrates' court itself, yet have felt themselves to have had little option but to

---

[20] See I Scott, 'Criminal Procedure: Appeals to Quarter Sessions' (1970) 134 JP and G Rev 843.

[1] The average hearing time for an appeal is 48 minutes, compared with the seven hours it takes on average to hear a trial on indictment: Judicial Statistics: Annual Report 1992 (Lord Chancellor's Department) (Cm 2268) (HMSO, 1993) p 66, Table 6.20.

[2] Royal Commission on Criminal Justice, Report (Cm 2263) (HMSO, 1993) p 88.

[3] Ibid and see further the discussion in ch 6, section 4(c), above.

[4] Magistrates' Court Act 1980, s 108.

plead guilty.[5] Only if the plea of guilty can be said to have been entered improperly might an appeal lie,[6] but this is where crime control rules of criminal procedure bite. The Court of Appeal insists, for example, that while defendants who plead guilty as a result of a charge bargain may face difficult choices between unpalatable alternatives, that is no ground for arguing that the plea of guilty was not freely made.[7] What amounts to improper pressure on a defendant to plead guilty is obviously much more narrowly defined in a system which operates on crime control lines than one in which due process principles prevail. Not surprisingly, few defendants convicted on a guilty plea have managed to appeal successfully. If it were otherwise, finality, the quality of the criminal process much valued in the crime control model, would be seriously undermined.

Defendants who were legally aided in the magistrates' courts may receive preliminary advice, at public expense, on whether they have grounds for appeal.[8] Those who were not legally aided may receive advice under the 'green form' scheme.[9] In all cases, however, a grant of legal aid for appellate proceedings is subject to the application of a means test and a merits test. Since the wealthy can fund their own appeals, regardless of the merits of the case, the legal aid rules breach the due process equality principle.[10] These rules provide a screening device in all but name for all but the rich.

It is unlikely that those denied legal aid at first instance (ie because their case was seen as not meriting publicly funded legal representation) will receive it for a rehearing. Since only those who pleaded not guilty can appeal to the Crown Court, and since the vast majority of not guilty pleaders charged with either way offences are legally aided in the magistrates' courts, this does not usually present a problem. There are many defendants pleading not guilty who do not receive legal aid, however. This is especially true of those facing summary only charges (such as assaulting a police officer). For them, the costs involved of funding their own appeals will be a major deterrent.

A further crime control deterrent to appeals lies in the wide powers of the Crown Court to vary the decision appealed, remit the matter back to the magistrates with their opinion or make such other order as the court thinks just.[11] It is even open to the Crown Court to impose a

---

[5]   For discussion, see ch 6.
[6]   See *R v Crown Court at Huntingdon, ex p Jordan* [1981] QB 857.
[7]   See the case of *Herbert* (1991) 94 Cr App Rep 230.
[8]   Legal Aid Act 1988, s 19(2).
[9]   See ch 6, section 2(a), above.
[10] See ch 6, section 2, above.
[11] Supreme Court Act 1981, s 48.

more severe sentence than that imposed by the magistrates.[12] The uncertainty of outcome and the possibility of being punished (in effect) for appealing may dissuade the aggrieved defendant from taking matters further, notwithstanding that in reality the Crown Court rarely increases a sentence on an appeal against conviction.[13]

In 1992, 19,765 appeals from magistrates' courts were heard at the Crown Court,[14] of which about two-thirds were appeals against sentence and one-third appeals against conviction.[15] It is sometimes said that, although the number of appeals against conviction appears to be large, the rate of appeals is very low.[16] Thus, in 1992, 993,018 defendants were found guilty in the magistrates' courts according to CPS figures,[17] yet there were only some 6,500 appeals against conviction in that year, giving an appeal rate of 0.65%. But bearing in mind that, of those convicted, only 80,665 pleaded not guilty[18] and thus qualified for an appeal, the true appeal rate is 8%. In other words, around one in twelve of those defendants who are eligible for an appeal opt for a rehearing in the Crown Court. That more do not do so should not be taken as a sign of satisfaction with summary trial procedures. As the James Committee noted, delay, expense, a reluctance to face the ordeal of a rehearing, a wish for finality and the possibility of receiving a stiffer sentence all provide disincentives to appealing.[19] In 1992, the average waiting time from lodging an appeal to the start of the rehearing in the Crown Court was just over two months—a third of defendants waited sixteen weeks or more.[20] For those not sent to prison on conviction in the magistrates' courts—as with well over 95% of those sentenced for indictable offences in 1992[1]—the advantages of appealing may seem slight compared with the disadvantages.

Between a quarter and a third of those who do appeal are successful in having their convictions quashed. Since the great majority of appeals

---

[12] Ibid sub-s (4).

[13] For discussion, see I Scott, 'Appeals to the Crown Court following Summary Conviction' (paper delivered to SPTL Criminal Law Group) (1977) pp 17–19.

[14] See Judicial Statistics, op cit p 59, Table 6.1.

[15] The official statistics do not break down appeals according to whether they were against sentence or conviction. The break down given in the text is based on R White, *The Administration of Justice* (Blackwell, 1991) p 137.

[16] Eg see White, op cit p 137.

[17] Crown Prosecution Service, Annual Report for the Period April 1992—March 1993, (HMSO, 1993) p 18.

[18] Ibid.

[19] Report of the Interdepartmental Committee on The Distribution of Criminal Business between the Crown Court and Magistrates' Courts, (Cmnd 6323) (HMSO, 1975) p 139, Table 7B.

[20] Judicial Statistics, op cit p 65, Table 6.19.

[1] Criminal Statistics: England and Wales 1992 (Cm 2410) (HMSO, 1993) p 139, Table 7B.

assert simply that the original conviction was 'against the weight of the evidence',[2] the number of successful appeals raises further doubts about the quality of justice in the magistrates' courts. It is a pity that the Runciman Commission did not look at magistrates' courts in this way, adopt the James Committee's approach, and fund research on the issue. As it is, we can say little about the adequacy of appellate review by the Crown Court. Nearly all of the literature in this area concerns itself with the more glamorous matter of appeals to the Court of Appeal following trials on indictment.[3] Yet miscarriages of justice are not confined to cases serious enough to find their way to the senior judiciary, but are routinely produced by magistrates' courts up and down the country on a daily basis. More attention to the effectiveness of Crown Court appellate review is surely warranted.

Appeals by way of case stated to the Divisional Court

An appeal lies to the Divisional Court (made up of High Court judges, commonly led by the Lord Chief Justice) where it is claimed that the decision of the magistrates' court was in excess of jurisdiction or wrong in law.[4] Since no record of proceedings is kept in the magistrates' court, the clerk to the justices is required to state the details of the case including the question(s) for determination by the Divisional Court. The court hears only legal argument and no evidence. Under 200 such appeals are heard each year. Leave to appeal is not required, although the justices may refuse to state a case if they consider the application 'frivolous'. The prosecution has the same right to appeal as does the defence, thus providing an exception to the usual rule that the prosecution cannot appeal against an acquittal. The Divisional Court may dispose of the case in various ways, including remitting the case to the magistrates' court with a direction to convict. It appears that the appellate courts do not regard the concept of 'jury equity' as having any application in the magistrates' courts.[5] Magistrates may be dictated to in a way that juries may not.

Judicial review

Applications for judicial review provide an alternative way of mounting a challenge to a magistrates' court decision in the Divisional Court.

---

[2]   Scott, 'Appeals to the Crown Court following Summary Conviction', op cit p 10.

[3]   In M Zander, *Cases and Materials on the English Legal System* (Weidenfeld and Nicolson, 1992), the material on appeals to the Crown Court (scattered throughout the 60-page chapter on appeals) is scarcely enough to fill a single page.

[4]   Magistrates' Courts Act 1980, s 111(1).

[5]   Jury equity was discussed in ch 8, sections 2 and 5, above.

There are somewhat fewer applications for judicial review each year than there are appeals by way of case stated.[6] The purpose of such an action is to obtain a ruling that the proceedings in the lower court were tainted by illegality. For example, where the rules of natural justice have been breached, the Divisional Court may apply the remedy of certiorari to quash the magistrates' decision. Leave to apply must always be obtained and the procedure is open to the prosecution as well as the defence.

At one time, the judicial view seemed to be that the remedy might only be employed to correct defects or irregularities in the trial itself.[7] A broader approach was established in *R v Leyland Justices, ex p Hawthorn*[8] where, following conviction, it emerged that the prosecution had not told the defence of two witnesses whose statements were helpful to the defendant. The prosecutor's omission had prevented the court from giving the defendant a fair trial, so the conviction was quashed. Given the importance of pre-trial procedure in settling the fate of the defendant, this decision represented a significant shift towards due process values.

Subsequent cases suggest, however, that the Divisional Court will not quash a conviction simply because the prosecution failed in its duty to bring all material evidence before the court. Rather that failure must have resulted in an 'unjust or potentially unjust decision'.[9] This is in line with the general stance of the senior judiciary to unlawful police or prosecutor behaviour, since the focus is primarily on the soundness of the conviction rather than the fairness of the procedures followed. This point is best explored in our review below of the way in which the Court of Appeal approaches its work.

(c) Appeals from the Crown Court to the Court of Appeal

There is no right of appeal from the Crown Court to the Court of Appeal, save where the appeal is on a point of law or in the rare case which is certified as suitable for appeal by the trial judge. Normally, leave to appeal must be sought (within 28 days of conviction) from a

---

[6] The two procedures overlap and the Divisional Court in *R v Crown Court at Ipswich, ex p Baldwin* [1981] 1 All ER 596 directed that judicial review should only be used for straightforward applications. Where detailed information from the justices was likely to be needed, the case stated procedure had clear advantages.

[7] See *West Sussex Quarter Sessions, ex p Albert and Maud Johnson Trust Ltd* [1974] QB 24, per Orr LJ.

[8] [1979] 1 All ER 209.

[9] See *R v Liverpool Crown Court, ex p Roberts* [1986] Crim LR 622. For discussion of the case law, see J Spencer, 'Judicial Review of Criminal Proceedings' [1991] Crim LR 259.

single High Court judge, who determines the matter on the papers submitted by the putative appellant. If an application for leave is refused, it may be renewed to the Court of Appeal which will consider the matter at a hearing. If the Court of Appeal decides to grant leave, the full appeal will then be heard. There are thus two preliminary filters operating to weed out supposedly weak appeals. The weakness of an appeal, however, is not so much an objective quality as a reflection of the legal and social processes through which the case is constructed. It is only by examining these processes that one can determine whether the appeal process conforms more closely to crime control than due process ideals.

Legal aid

It is standard for legal aid to be granted to cover representation for Crown Court trials (subject to a means test) and the legal aid order covers the cost of counsel advising on the prospect of a successful appeal. If counsel advises that there are grounds for appeal, then legal aid also covers the professional drafting of these grounds in support of the application to the single judge. If that application is successful, legal aid will be extended to cover the costs of the full appeal. On the other hand, if counsel's initial advice is that there are no grounds for appeal, or if the application to the single judge is unsuccessful, then legal aid is terminated and the appellant must either pay for legal assistance privately or try to pursue an appeal unassisted. Initial advice from counsel that grounds for appeal do not exist can thus operate as an additional filter, since many convicted persons may be deterred from pursuing an appeal if denied access to legal assistance,[10] or may fail in an application to the single judge (or a renewed application to the Court of Appeal) purely because they lacked professional help in preparing the paperwork.[11] Since the rich can afford the legal costs of applications for leave to appeal to single judges and renewed applications to the Court of Appeal, regardless of the strength or weakness of the particular case, the legal aid rules once again breach the due process principle of equality of access to justice.[12]

Another aspect of the appeals process which is shaped by the legal

---

[10] In one study, approximately half of the prisoners who did not appeal gave as one of their reasons the fact that a lawyer had advised them not to appeal: J Plotnikoff and R Woolfson, Information and Advice for Prisoners about Grounds for Appeal and the Appeals Process (Royal Commission on Criminal Justice, Research Study no 18) (HMSO, 1993) p 78.

[11] See the discussion by K Malleson, Review of the Appeal Process (Royal Commission on Criminal Justice, Research Study no 17) (HMSO, 1993) pp 29–30.

[12] For other breaches of this principle, see ch 6, section 2, above.

aid rules is the type and amount of work which lawyers will undertake in preparing appeals. As with legal aid generally, claims made for work done may be reduced or even refused if considered unreasonable. In Plotnikoff and Woolfson's research for the Runciman Commission, between a quarter and a third of solicitors and barristers complained that they had lost money in this way. It was claimed by 20% of solicitors that they no longer bothered to charge for work done in the 28 days following conviction, but this does not necessarily mean that they provided a proper service to clients. Others were clearly offering what they themselves regarded as a sub-standard service in order to stay within the legal aid rules. As Plotnikoff and Woolfson put it:

'Many lawyers talked of a policy on the part of determining officers of reducing claims without reason or explanation and a total lack of understanding of the amount of work involved in properly serving the interests of one's client . . . Despite the obligation to communicate with their client, many solicitors said that the costs of visiting a prison to discuss an appeal were never allowed and some now refused to make such visits for this reason.'[13]

That convicted persons do not always receive adequate legal assistance cannot be attributed solely to the legal aid rules, however, as the next section will demonstrate.

The quality of legal advice

There has long been concern at the quality of advice provided to convicted persons. The Criminal Justice Act 1967 entitled all legally aided defendants to legal advice on whether grounds for appeal existed. Zander's important study in the early 1970s found that as many as one in ten of legally aided prisoners claimed not to have received such advice, and in at least 25% of cases where an appeal had been advised, no help was provided in drafting the grounds.[14] Publication of these findings was followed by a flurry of pamphlets and good practice guides, not to mention a practice note issued by the Lord Chief Justice,[15] all designed to emphasise counsel's obligations of advice and assistance to convicted persons.

Plotnikoff and Woolfson's research established, however, that the

---

13 Op cit p 83.
14 M Zander, 'Legal Advice and Criminal Appeals: A Survey of Prisoners, Prisons and Lawyers' [1972] Crim LR p 132. Strong dissatisfaction amongst defendants with the level of attention received from lawyers following conviction was also detected by A Bottoms and J McClean, *Defendants in the Criminal Process* (Routledge & Kegan Paul, 1976) p 184.
15 [1974] 2 All ER 805.

legal profession is still failing its clients in a number of important respects. Whereas a solicitor is supposed to attend the client in the court cells following conviction, 65% of solicitors indicated that unqualified staff carry out this function. A third of prisoners claimed that the question of an appeal was not discussed with them, as it should have been, immediately after conviction and the majority of these (comprising a quarter of all respondents) stated that they did not receive advice on appealing at any point during the 28 days following conviction. Although counsel should provide a client in the court cells with a written statement on whether grounds for appeal exist, almost 90% of solicitors and barristers said that clients were never given anything in writing during a cell visit.[16] The quality of advice offered was often poor, with solicitors most at fault, in that half of those responding said that they gave the erroneous advice to clients that their sentences might be increased if their appeal was unsuccessful. For whilst the Crown Court can increase a sentence following an appeal from the magistrates' court, the Court of Appeal has no such power. Yet the fear of an increased sentence was a major factor in decisions taken by prisoners convicted in the Crown Court not to appeal.[17] The researchers concluded that there was, amongst the legal profession, 'widespread ignorance both of some aspects of the law on appeals and of the guidelines to good practice on the responsibilities of legal advisers . . .'[18]

A safeguard for convicted persons given a custodial sentence is provided by each prison designating one of its staff as a 'legal aid officer', with responsibility to advise on appeals. In practice, however, this safety net is somewhat threadbare, largely because these prison officers are diverted by other demands on their time. As Plotnikoff and Woolfson conclude:

'These problems are reflected in the fact that only 32 per cent of inmates claimed to have received advice on appeals from the prison and in the widespread ignorance of the appeals process demonstrated by prisoners in their responses.'[19]

Bottoms and McClean report that many of the convicted persons they interviewed saw the appeals process 'as a somewhat remote affair, a lawyer's procedure where they essentially had to rely on the professionals'.[20] A major determinant of the low appeals rate (discussed

---

[16] Plotnikoff and Woolfson, op cit p 73.
[17] Ibid p 82.
[18] Ibid p 115.
[19] Ibid p 118. This does not necessarily mean that prisoners did not receive adequate information and advice, although it does suggest that (in so far as they did) it was not communicated adequately.
[20] Bottoms and McClean, op cit p 178.

below) is that legal advice, when offered at all, is predominantly against appealing. Even where legal representatives consider that there might be merit in an appeal, their overestimation of the risks involved tends to deter all but the most committed of convicted persons from taking any further action.

Delays and the loss of time 'rules'

The incentive to appeal is much reduced for those imprisoned citizens who are due to be released before the appeal can be heard.[1] Delays in hearing cases will therefore be one determinant of the overall level of appeals. In 1990, the typical delay in hearing a case was around four to five months. The time factor is exacerbated by the loss of time 'rule', under which the Court of Appeal may order that time spent appealing will not count towards sentence. This has a greater proportional effect on those serving short sentences. Loss of three months time may mean a doubling of sentence for those sentenced originally to three months' imprisonment, whereas for someone sentenced to life imprisonment the threat of an additional three months is unlikely to have much deterrent effect.

The loss of time rule is a classic crime control device developed by a judiciary anxious to deter people from exercising their rights. In 1966, a change in the law made it easier for convictions to be quashed, resulting in a quadrupling of applications to the Court of Appeal. The Lord Chief Justice responded by announcing that in future single judges hearing applications for leave deemed 'frivolous' could, and should, order loss of time.[2] This warning proved effective: the number of applications was instantly halved and remained at the lower figure of around 6,000 a year for several years. A subsequent affirmation of this judicial policy gave a stern warning to those contemplating an appeal without professional assistance:

'It may be expected that such a [loss of time] direction will normally be made unless the grounds are not only settled and signed by counsel, but also supported by the written opinion of counsel.'[3]

This makes it still more unlikely that convicted persons whose lawyers advise against an appeal (or fail to give any advice at all) will pursue the matter. Denied legal aid, and faced with the potent threat of loss of time, the prospect of launching an appeal is scarcely an enticing

---

[1] Of those deciding not to appeal, 11% gave this as one of their reasons to Plotnikoff and Woolfson, op cit p 104.

[2] *Practice Note* [1970] 1 WLR 663.

[3] *Practice Note* [1980] 1 All ER 555.

one. Even those who are advised that they do have grounds for appeal may be deterred by the loss of time rules. The single judge retains the discretion to make a loss of time order in all cases, regardless of whether they are supported by lawyers or not; and appellants denied leave to appeal by the single judge are warned that on a renewal of the application to the full court the risk of losing time is increased, 'since the appellant' (as the official guidance laconically puts it) 'will have the advantage of the single judge's view of the merits of his case'.[4] Single judges typically are required to determine applications for leave to appeal in batches of six in their spare time, usually in the evening after a day in court.[5] One may question whether it is appropriate that decisions made in this way should carry such ramifications for the application of the rules governing both legal aid and loss of time.

What most lawyers fail to point out to their clients is that loss of time orders are extremely rare and in practice are never made for longer than 28 days.[6] Malleson's examination of 65 renewed applications for leave to appeal (made in 1990 following refusal of leave by the single judge) found that the time loss rules were never mentioned, still less applied. This was so even though some of these applications were obviously regarded by the Court of Appeal as groundless, being described in such terms as 'disgraceful', 'a tissue of lies' or a 'cock and bull story'.[7]

The gap between the formal time loss rules and the practice of the court is not hard to explain. The court is able to have it both ways: its rules are so effective in keeping down its workload that, by almost never applying the rules in individual cases, it can give the appearance of adhering to due process values. This resolution of the conflict between the ideological demands of due process and crime control is highly functional for the criminal system. Indeed, one of the pervasive themes of this book has been to argue that the criminal system deflects criticism by projecting an image of due process whilst, behind the scenes, crime control engineering ensures that the reality is quite different.

Appeal rates in context

Figures supplied to the Runciman Commission revealed that in 1992 14,661 persons were convicted in the Crown Court following a not guilty plea. Two-thirds of the 1,552 persons applying for leave to appeal

---

4   A Guide to Proceedings in the Court of Appeal Criminal Division, (Criminal Appeals Office, 1990) para 9.2.
5   K Malleson, 'Miscarriages of Justice and the Accessibility of the Court of Appeal' [1991] Crim LR 323 at 331.
6   See Plotnikoff and Woolfson, op cit p 79.
7   Malleson, op cit (1993) p 15.

in that year to the single judge had their application rejected. Some 40% persevered by renewing their application to the full Court but, of these, only 12% were successful. In total, 64% of those seeking leave to appeal had their applications refused. Of those reaching the court, 299 (45%) succeeded in their appeal against conviction. The Runciman Commission observed that:

'The overall picture, therefore, is that few defendants seek to appeal against conviction and of those who do, few are granted leave to appeal. But the success rate of those whose appeal reaches the full court is relatively high.[8]

Those who reach the court are not a representative group of appellants, nor are they necessarily the appellants with the strongest cases. As Malleson notes, serious offences attracting long custodial sentences, relatively rare in the Crown Court, are the staple diet of the Court of Appeal.[9] Since more run of the mill cases are allocated to less experienced Crown Court judges (under whom miscarriages of justice might be expected to occur more frequently) it appears that the system operates so as to exclude the majority of potential appeals. As Malleson observes:

'The appeal process can be likened to an obstacle race: only the determined, strong and well prepared will reach the end—and they are likely to be found in the higher reaches of the offence and sentence scale.'[10]

The true function of the various filters within the appeal system is not so much to weed out weak appeals as to deter all but the most committed from challenging their conviction. The strength of this commitment will depend as much on such factors as the availability of legal advice and legal aid, the quality of legal advice, sentence length, and the fear of loss of time, as on the merits of the case or the intensity of grievance nursed.

The grounds for appeal

A further factor dissuading convicted persons from challenging convictions is the restrictive approach of the Court of Appeal to the appeals that come before it. The Court of Appeal operates a quite different form of appellate review to that performed by the Crown Court. Whereas the latter rehears cases tried in the magistrates' courts from scratch, the Court of Appeal's primary role is to review the procedures followed and decision reached in the trial court. The modern grounds

[8] Report, op cit p 163.
[9] Malleson, op cit (1991) p 325.
[10] Ibid p 328.

for appeal were established in 1966 and are now contained in s 2(1) of the Criminal Appeal Act 1968 (as amended by s 44, Criminal Law Act 1977) as follows:

'Except as provided by this Act, the Court of Appeal shall allow an appeal against conviction if they think:

(a) that the [conviction] of the jury should be set aside on the ground that under all the circumstances of the case it is unsafe and unsatisfactory; or

(b) that the judgment of the court of trial should be set aside on the ground of a wrong decision of any question of law; or

(c) that there was a material irregularity in the course of the trial, and in any other case shall dismiss the appeal:

Provided that the court may, notwithstanding that they are of opinion that the point raised in the appeal might be decided in favour of the appellant, dismiss the appeal if they consider that no miscarriage of justice has actually occurred.'[11]

The last sentence sets out what has become known as 'the proviso'—a device which allows the upholding of a conviction even in the face of a material irregularity or a wrong decision on a question of law. Right from the outset, then, it can be seen that the Court of Appeal is discouraged from adopting a pure due process posture in which the integrity of procedural justice must be upheld at all costs. Rather it is prodded into the crime control approach of focusing ultimately on the appellant's factual guilt. But since the proviso merely gives the court the freedom to overlook procedural errors rather than mandating that it shall do so, we must examine how the statutory framework is interpreted in practice.

Prior to 1966, the Court of Appeal refused to overturn the verdict of the jury unless it was one which no reasonable jury could have arrived at. The fact that members of the court thought that they themselves would have returned a different verdict was, according to the judgment in *Hopkins-Husson*, 'no ground for refusing to accept the verdict of the jury, which is the constitutional method of trial in this country.'[12] A new approach was announced in *Cooper*[13] by Lord Widgery CJ.

---

[11] For the sake of completeness we should here mention that a further appeal may lie (with leave) to the House of Lords but only if the Court of Appeal is prepared to certify that a point of law of general public importance is involved. This hurdle is not easy to overcome where the Court of Appeal has reached a factual decision on fresh evidence or made use of a discretionary power as in applying the s 2(1) proviso. (See P Alldridge, 'For the Repeal of the Proviso' [1984] Crim LR 220.) Proceedings in the Crown Court are also subject to judicial review, in the same manner as are proceedings in the magistrates' courts.

[12] (1949) 34 Cr App Rep 47, per Lord Goddard CJ.

[13] [1969] 1 QB 267.

After observing that appeals might now be allowed where the Court considered the jury's verdict unsafe and unsatisfactory, he continued:

'the court must in the end ask itself a subjective question, whether we are content to let the matter stand as it is, or whether there is not some lurking doubt in our minds which makes us wonder whether an injustice has been done.'[14]

In *Cooper*, there was no complaint about the way in which the case had been put in court—it was simply asserted that the jury had come to the wrong verdict. If such an approach was followed with enthusiasm many more appeals might well succeed, but the Court of Appeal has only rarely applied the 'lurking doubt' test. Although its use appears to have increased in recent years, it remains exceptional for a conviction to be quashed on this basis.[15] In this area, the court manifests a concern with proof, not truth. So long as the correct procedures were followed in proving the case against the defendant, it is unlikely that the Court will overturn a verdict on the ground that it may not represent the truth. In its view, the trial is the proper place to conduct an adversarial fight and the main task of the Court of Appeal is simply to ensure that these fights are conducted according to the rules. As Malleson notes, to succeed in the Court of Appeal:

'an appellant needs a good meaty question of law or an obvious failure by the judge to follow an accepted practice or set procedure in relation to the summing up or evidential matters.'[16]

On the other hand, complaints about lying witnesses, charges of bias on the part of the judge or jury, and allegations of incompetence on the part of defence lawyers are rarely entertained. In *Ensor*,[17] it was held that counsel's errors may constitute valid grounds of appeal only in the case of flagrantly incompetent advocacy. Since sub-standard defence lawyering is undoubtedly one of the most potent sources of miscarriages of justice, the reluctance of the court to accept this as a ground of appeal is particularly disturbing.[18] As the Runciman Commission put it in criticising the decision in *Ensor*:

'. . . wrong jury verdicts of guilty may be the result of errors by the lawyers—whether of judgement or of performance—which do not amount to "flagrantly incompetent advocacy". It cannot possibly be

---

[14] Ibid at 271.
[15] Malleson, op cit (1993) p 24.
[16] Malleson, op cit (1991) p 330.
[17] [1989] 1 WLR 497.
[18] See the report by the organisation Justice, Miscarriages of Justice (1989) p 3 and p 51.

right that there should be defendants serving prison sentences for no other reason than that their lawyers made a decision which later turns out to have been mistaken.'[19]

There is the possibility, however, that the court will go beyond merely reviewing the papers relating to the original trial. The court has the power under s 23 of the Criminal Appeal Act 1968 to order the production of any document, exhibit or other thing connected with the proceedings and to order that witnesses attend for examination. Occasionally, making extensive use of these powers, it has gone far beyond reviewing the original conviction and permitted a limited retrial of certain issues.[20] Section 23 also obliges the Court of Appeal to receive fresh evidence if it is satisfied that there is a reasonable explanation for the failure to adduce it during the original trial.[1] In practice, however, the court has been reluctant to step outside its narrow review function by admitting fresh evidence. Here too, the court's priority appears to be other than establishing the truth. Thus, where the failure to adduce evidence at the original trial is attributable to a mistake on the part of the defendant's lawyers, the court rarely permits that evidence, however cogent, to be heard on appeal.

In the infamous 1972 case of Luke Dougherty, a veritable busload of witnesses could have provided the defendant with a cast-iron alibi on a shoplifting charge, but only two were called at trial:[2] one was Dougherty's girlfriend and the other had previous convictions. The jury believed neither and convicted. Dougherty faced a 15-month prison sentence for a crime he plainly did not commit.[3] Leave to appeal was refused by the single judge, who ruled that the fresh evidence from others who went on the same bus trip as Dougherty could not be heard. The Court of Appeal subsequently confirmed that the single judge's stance was correct. It was only when the case was referred back to the Court of Appeal by the Home Secretary that the alibi witnesses were heard and the conviction quashed. But by this time Dougherty had already spent nine months in prison. Malleson's study for the Runciman Commission demonstrated a continuing judicial distaste for

---

[19] Report, op cit p 174.

[20] For discussion and criticism, see P O'Connor, 'The Court of Appeal: Re-Trials and Tribulations' [1990] Crim LR 615 at 619.

[1] Under the terms of s 23, the court can refuse to hear the evidence if satisfied that it would not afford any ground for allowing the appeal or if it would have been inadmissible at the original trial.

[2] The case is discussed at length in ch 2 of the Report of the Departmental Committee on Evidence of Identification in Criminal Cases HCP 338 (1976).

[3] The sentence for shoplifting was six months' imprisonment, and the judge activated a nine-month suspended sentence to run consecutively with this.

fresh evidence. She writes: 'Only in very limited circumstances will such evidence be admitted and if admitted form the basis for a successful appeal.'[4]

The proviso

In one area, the Court of Appeal does prioritise truth over the question of whether the correct procedures were followed. Whenever it applies the proviso to s 2(1) of the Criminal Appeal Act 1968, it acknowledges that a procedural injustice was done to the appellant whilst at the same time expressing its view that the appellant is nevertheless so obviously guilty that the conviction must stand. Roughly 10% of unsuccessful appeals are dismissed on the application of the proviso.[5] The statutory framework, as interpreted by the Court of Appeal, thus seems to have an inbuilt bias towards upholding convictions. It seems that 'truth' is paramount when this can justify upholding a conviction, but 'proof' takes precedence when the 'truth' would point towards overturning a conviction.

An extensive analysis of criminal appeals by Knight demonstrated that the proviso was frequently applied even in cases where there were serious errors at trial.[6] This is not to suggest that the Court of Appeal's use of the proviso amounts to a subversion of due process values as enshrined in the law. Rather, the proviso should be seen for what it is, an enabling rule which allows the court to follow its crime control instincts. For while such a proviso might exist in a due process system, it would allow only minor procedural errors to be overlooked. By contrast, the s 2(1) proviso may be applied even though the Court has found there to be, in the language of s 2(1)(c), a 'material irregularity in the course of the trial'. But the proviso also contains a residual due process element, since its discretionary nature allows the Court to quash convictions even where the evidence of guilt is compelling. Knight's analysis did uncover the occasional case in which a fault was regarded as so serious that a deserved conviction was quashed.[7] A cynic might say that the discretionary nature of the proviso provides a useful safety valve in high profile cases where public unease has been aroused by the manner in which a defendant was tried. Certainly, if the conduct of the trial is so blatantly unfair that it threatens to bring the criminal justice system into disrepute, the court is likely to have little difficulty in declining to apply the proviso.

---

[4] Malleson, op cit (1993) p 11.
[5] Ibid p 12.
[6] M Knight, *Criminal Appeals* (Stevens, 1970) pp 15–21.
[7] Ibid pp 30–37.

Retrials

The final power of the Court of Appeal which merits attention here is that provided by s 7(1) of the Criminal Appeal Act 1968 of ordering a retrial following a decision to allow an appeal. The power used to apply only where an appeal was allowed on the basis of fresh evidence but by s 43 of the Criminal Justice Act 1988 this restriction was removed. Thus, s 7(1) now gives the court an alternative to applying the proviso in cases where, although there has been some error at the trial, the Court concludes that the appellant is probably guilty. It might also encourage the Court to allow more appeals in the first place. If these were the effects of s 7(1), due process values would be advanced. But the subsection might also be used as an alternative to quashing a conviction in cases where the court has concluded that so serious a procedural error occurred at the original trial that the proviso should not be applied. If it were used in the latter way an important opportunity for affirming fundamental due process values would be lost. Section 7(1) merely provides that a retrial may be ordered if 'it appears to the court that the interests of justice so require', but gives no guidance as to whether the definition of those interests should be inspired by due process or crime control values. Again, then, we must examine the actual practice of the court in ordering retrials.

Over time, the Court of Appeal has shown itself reluctant to exercise its power to order retrials in fresh evidence cases. This was partly because of the decision of the House of Lords in *Stafford v DPP*[8] that the task of the Court of Appeal in such cases was to decide whether it thought the verdict unsafe and unsatisfactory rather than open up the question of what a jury might think of the new evidence. In their Lordships' view, there was no point in ordering a retrial, because if the court thought there was no reasonable doubt about the correctness of the verdict (one way or the other) it followed that it would think that a jury would come to the same conclusion. This specious logic has been attacked by Lord Devlin who argues that it implies there is no point in having a jury full stop.[9] The *Stafford* decision has no application to appeals not involving fresh evidence, however, and it seems that the Court of Appeal is more willing to order retrials in such cases. From 1985 to 1990, the number of retrials ordered per annum fluctuated from nought to three, but once the Criminal Justice Act 1988 amendment to s 7 came into force, the number jumped to 13 in 1991 and 23 in 1992.[10]

[8] [1974] AC 878.
[9] P Devlin, *The Judge* (Oxford University Press, 1979) pp 148–176. See also O'Connor, op cit at 618–622.
[10] Malleson, op cit (1993) 25 and Royal Commission on Criminal Justice, Report, op cit p 175.

The judgments of the Court of Appeal so far give little clue as to why retrials are thought appropriate in some cases but not others, but what is clear is that the court sometimes orders retrials even when has been a flagrant breach of due process values at the original trial. An example is the case of King in which the Court denounced the trial judge's summing up for the jury in trenchant language: 'We have read this summing-up with dismay . . . we hope that we never again see a summing-up which is as unfair and unbalanced as this.'[11] Despite the ferocity of its criticism, the court ordered a retrial, thus, in Packer's phrasing, breeding disrespect for the very values it was professing to affirm. For why should the police, the prosecution or the trial judge remain faithful to the dictates of due process if the worse that can happen in the event of infidelity is that the initial adversarial fight is declared void and a rematch ordered?

6. PETITIONS TO THE HOME SECRETARY

For those convicted in the Crown Court, once the normal appeal channels have been exhausted there remains the possibility of the case being referred back to the Court of Appeal by the Home Secretary—using the power provided by s 17 of the Criminal Appeal Act 1968. The powers of the Court of Appeal in relation to referred cases are identical to those it possesses in respect of the normal appeal procedure.[12] On average, the Home Office receives some 700–800 requests each year to reopen cases in this way, but very few references are made as a result of these petitions. The number of references increased in the years 1989–1992, but still amounted to only seven cases per annum.[13] There are a number of interrelated factors behind this low success rate.

Legal aid is not available for the preparation of petitions and, in consequence, many are ill-conceived or poorly presented. Yet petitions need to be detailed and convincingly argued to stand a chance of success. This is partly because they are considered by a small number of legally unqualified civil servants (based in 'C3' within the Home Office) who lack the resources to carry out further investigation and research into particular grievances.[14] Mansfield and Taylor point out that these civil servants may ask the police to re-examine evidence on occasion but that in 'such an instance it seems more likely that the police will try and shore up the case and protect themselves rather than root out any

[11] Quoted in ibid p 26.
[12] See *R v Chard* [1983] 3 All ER 637.
[13] See Royal Commission on Criminal Justice, Report, op cit p 181.
[14] See O'Connor, op cit at 616.

potential miscarriage.'[15] But even were more resources devoted to this activity, the Home Office would not wish to do much more than scrutinise the papers submitted by petitioners. In its view, to do so would amount to interfering with the judicial function. For the same reason, it will only refer cases to the Court of Appeal if there is fresh evidence or some other new consideration of substance that has yet to be put before the court. To do otherwise would amount to the Executive suggesting to the judiciary that the courts had erred when first determining the matter. In addition to the constitutional concern to maintain a separation of powers, the Home Office has potentially conflicting roles, since it is responsible for the police and the maintenance of law and order. Given these factors, it would be naive to expect the Home Secretary to use the s 17 power with enthusiasm.[16]

From the appellants' point of view, the unavailability of legal aid makes it almost essential to enlist the aid of lawyers prepared to act on a voluntary basis and, better still, public figures, bodies or campaigning journalists prepared to fight their corner. How else is fresh evidence to be found when the convicted person remains incarcerated in prison, and how else can the Home Office be persuaded to act in this sensitive area? Luke Dougherty would not have achieved even the limited degree of success that he did were it not for 'Justice' taking up the case on his behalf. A House of Commons select committee noted in 1982 that in practice the 'chances of a petition being ultimately successful might sometimes depend less on its intrinsic merits than on the amount of external support and publicity it was able to attract.'[17] This remains true today. Mansfield and Taylor write that:

'there was an air of inevitability about the release of the *Guildford Four* when, by late 1988, they had the endorsement of such worthies as Cardinal Basil Hume, Archbishop Runcie, two former Home Secretaries (Roy Jenkins and Merlyn Rees) and two former Law Lords (Lords Devlin and Scarman).'[18]

The Court of Appeal attracted notoriety in the 1980s for its evident distaste for the reference procedure. A striking example is provided by the closing remarks of Lord Lane CJ in dismissing the 1988 appeal of the 'Birmingham Six':

---

15   M Mansfield and N Taylor, 'Post-Conviction Procedures' in C Walker and K Starmer (eds), *Justice in Error* (Blackstone, 1993) p 164.

16   See O'Connor, op cit at 182.

17   Home Affairs Committee, Report on Miscarriages of Justice, (HC 421) (1981–82) para 10.

18   Mansfield and Taylor, op cit p 166.

'As has happened before in references by the Home Secretary to this court under section 17 of the Criminal Appeal Act 1968, the longer this hearing has gone on the more convinced this court has become that the verdict of the jury was correct. We have no doubt that these convictions were both safe and satisfactory.'[19]

As Rozenberg puts it: 'Not only was Lord Lane saying Douglas Hurd had been wrong to send this case back to the Court of Appeal, he was suggesting that the Home Office was too ready to refer other hopeless cases.'[20]

Most infamous of all judicial comments was that of Lord Denning MR in terminating the civil action brought by the 'Birmingham Six' for assault against the police:

'If the six men win, it will mean that the police were guilty of perjury, that they were guilty of violence and threats, and the confessions were involuntary and were improperly admitted in evidence and that the convictions were erroneous. That would mean the Home Secretary would either have to recommend that they be pardoned or he would have to remit the case to the Court of Appeal. This is such an appalling vista that every sensible person in the land would say: It cannot be right these actions should go further.'[1]

In Lord Denning's world view, it is evidently more important that the criminal justice system preserve its good name than that possibly innocent persons are given the chance to regain theirs. In his retirement, he continued to criticise those striving to have cases reopened:

'My opinion is that it is more important to uphold public confidence in our system of justice than to allow convicted people—whom the media on their own investigations allege to be innocent—go free.'[2]

The 'Birmingham Six' remained in prison for 11 years after Lord Denning had refused to contemplate the awful possibility that their story might be true, and for three years after Lord Lane dismissed their appeal in 1988. Only after a further reference from the Home Secretary were their convictions finally quashed, by which time they had spent a total of 16 years in prison.

The restrictive approach of the Court of Appeal, combined with the caution shown by the Home Office in dealing with petitions, has led to

[19] Quoted by J Rozenberg, 'Miscarriages of Justice' in E Stockdale and S Casale (eds), *Criminal Justice Under Stress* (Blackstone, 1992) p 104.
[20] Ibid.
[1] *McIlkenny v Chief Constable of the West Midlands* [1980] 2 WLR 689 at 706.
[2] (1988) Times, 31 March.

calls for reform.[3] Many commentators and official reports have argued for the creation of some extra-judicial tribunal or commission to be set up to consider alleged miscarriages of justice, although there is less agreement on the composition and powers of such a body, and on its relationship with the Court of Appeal. Such proposals have been deflected or rejected by successive governments over a period of some 25 years, but new life was breathed into the idea by the Runciman Commission. Its recommendation was that a 'Criminal Cases Review Authority' should be set up to consider alleged miscarriages of justice, to supervise their investigation if further inquiries are needed and to refer appropriate cases back to the Court of Appeal. As with the current reference procedure, the new body would only review Crown Court convictions, not the larger category of miscarriages of justice arising from magistrates' courts trials.[4]

The Runciman Commission has been taken to task by commentators for the conservative nature of its proposal.[5] Some of the main flaws identified are that the Authority would rely on the police to carry out any necessary investigations, that it should not have to disclose the report produced for it by the police, that its decisions should not be subject to appeal or judicial review and that legal aid should not normally be made available during the period in which the Authority is investigating a case. Furthermore, it would lack the power to take cases of its own motion, and, when referring cases to the Court of Appeal, would have no power to make any recommendation as to outcome. Small wonder that Thornton is driven to the conclusion that 'Apart from being independent of the executive, the proposed body looks remarkably like C3.'[6] One may go further and question whether such independence would be more apparent than real, in the light of the Runciman Commission's recommendation that the members of the Authority be appointed by the government. The parallels with the Police Complaints Authority are all too obvious.

The Home Secretary committed himself to setting up a new body to investigate miscarriages of justice in his speech to the Conservative Party conference on 6 October 1993. But a lack of enthusiasm for both the idea and the costs involved is suggested by the omission of this long-awaited reform from the Criminal Justice and Public Order Bill announced later that year. If such a reviewing body is to be set up, it is

---

[3] The debate on this issue is reviewed in M Zander, *Cases and Materials on the English Legal System* (Weidenfeld and Nicolson, 1992) pp 614–622.

[4] Report, op cit pp 180–187.

[5] See, in particular, J Wadham, 'Unravelling Miscarriages of Justice' (1993) 143 NLJ 1650 and P Thornton, 'Miscarriages of Justice: A Lost Opportunity' [1993] Crim LR 926.

[6] Op cit p 929.

important to be aware of its potential limitations—regardless of the exact details concerning its composition, powers and relationship with the courts. Unless provided with generous resources (unlikely in the present financial climate) it will be forced into a sifting process almost as rigorous as that now operated by the Home Secretary. Petitions will depend for their success, as they do now, on being professionally presented and argued. If legal aid is not made freely available (also unlikely) a convicted person's chances of success will, as now, be determined largely by whether they can persuade lawyers or campaigning bodies to act voluntarily on their behalf. One may predict that the reviewing body would deal mainly with high profile cases in which lengthy prison sentences were imposed. Mundane miscarriages of justice will continue to be swept under the carpet.

If the Runciman Commission's blueprint is accepted by the government, much will depend on the Court of Appeal's dealing with references in a more constructive manner and to use its powers more extensively than it has hitherto. There are hopeful signs here. For example, the Runciman Commission were told that of the 38 appellants involved in cases referred back to the Court of Appeal in 1989–91, 37 had their convictions quashed.[7] There is little doubt that the uncovering of a string of sensational miscarriages of justice in the late 1980s and early 1990s amounted to both a cause and an effect of the Court of Appeal's greater willingness in recent years to contemplate 'appalling vistas' of police and prosecution malpractice.[8] The strongly worded judgment in the *Judith Ward*[9] case, in which the Court of Appeal laid down clear rules governing the prosecution duty to disclose, is one example of this. Another example is the decision in *Edwards*[10] in the aftermath of the disbanding of the West Midlands Serious Crimes Squad in 1989 because of mounting allegations that its officers were fabricating evidence. The Court of Appeal here ruled that the prosecution had a duty to disclose a police officer's disciplinary record to the defence. It also said that the defence could put before the jury the fact that any police witnesses in the case had previously been disbelieved by juries in earlier trials.[11] The development of due process principles in cases such as these shows that the judiciary is no longer blind to the possibility of systematic malpractice by the police and prosecution

---

[7] Two of these were ordered to be retried and were subsequently acquitted: see Report, op cit p 181.

[8] See Zander, op cit p 627.

[9] [1993] 1 WLR 619. See chapter 5, section 3(c), above, for discussion.

[10] [1991] 2 All ER 266.

[11] For criticism that the decision does not go far enough in allowing the defence to cast doubt on a police officer's credibility, see R Pattenden, 'Evidence of Previous Malpractice by Police Witnesses and R v Edwards' [1992] Crim LR 549.

agencies. By 1993, however, it appeared as if the pendulum was already beginning to swing back towards crime control, with the Court of Appeal signalling a retreat from the 'Judith Ward rules' on prosecution disclosure.[12]

The major miscarriage of justice cases show why the crime control demand for finality within the criminal process needs to be resisted. The Maguires, for example, had been convicted at trial in 1976 and had failed to have their convictions overturned through the normal appeal channel in 1977. An attempt to have the case referred back to the Court of Appeal foundered in 1987. The Home Office took the view that there was insufficient evidence to cast doubt on the validity of the prosecution's forensic evidence which suggested that the Maguires had handled explosives. The Home Office refused to set up a committee of scientists to reconsider that evidence. But when the 'Guildford Four' were released in 1989, Sir John May was asked by the Home Office to inquire into the circumstances of the convictions of the related Maguires' case. At last, adequate resources were committed to testing theories which might undermine the prosecution case. Sir John May's inquiry duly found that the Maguires need not have handled explosives at all; they could simply have picked up traces of nitroglycerine from drying their hands on a towel. This finding led directly to the quashing of the Maguires' convictions. It also led to the forensic evidence in the 'Birmingham Six' case being scientifically reviewed. The findings this time were even more remarkable. It now appeared that tests which the prosecution had relied upon as demonstrating that the men had handled nitroglycerine were thoroughly unreliable. The 'positive results' could equally well have been attributed to the soap used to wash the laboratory dishes prior to samples being tested or to the fact that the men smoked cigarettes.[13] In other cases, it has been a matter of sheer good luck that evidence of fabricated confessions, in the form of supposedly contemporaneous notes of interview, have not been destroyed or misplaced.

It follows that prosecution cases which appear to the trial court and the Court of Appeal as unshakeable at first, second and even third sight may be merely artful constructions, with no more inherent strength than a house of cards. In the 1988 appeal of the 'Birmingham Six', Lord Lane CJ said that fresh evidence had made the court sure that one of the men had had nitroglycerine on his hand, 'for which there is and can be no innocent explanation.'[14] Three years later, the court was forced to

---

[12] See ch 5, section 3(c), above.

[13] For a fuller account of this sequence of events, see J Rozenberg, 'Miscarriage of Justice' in E Stockdale and S Casale (eds), *Criminal Justice Under Stress* (Blackstone, 1992).

[14] Ibid p 104.

admit that a number of innocent and plausible explanations could be advanced to account for this fresh evidence. In 1988, the court had concluded that they were 'certain' that the superintendent in charge of the inquiry into the pub bombings in Birmingham, who the 'Birmingham Six' accused of fabricating evidence and perjury, had not sought to deceive them. In 1991 the court said, 'On the evidence now before us, Superintendent Reade deceived the court.'[15] There could be few better illustrations of the point that the courts are not dealing in moral certainties and truth but in degrees of proof. An awareness of the realities of case construction by police and prosecution agencies strengthens the argument for always leaving open the possibility of a further challenge to the basis for a conviction.

The Runciman Commission itself exhorted the Court of Appeal to be 'readier to overturn jury verdicts' and be 'more willing to consider arguments that indicate that a jury might have made a mistake.' It also called for the court to be more prepared to admit fresh evidence that might favour the appellant's case, even if it could have been available at the trial.[16] These recommendations are consistent with the due process model in that they acknowledge the likelihood of a high rate of fact-finding error in pre-trial and trial procedures.

But other recommendations on the powers of the Court of Appeal are clearly influenced by crime control arguments. A majority of the Runciman Commission favoured narrowing the grounds on which appeals might be allowed. Under the new scheme, the only question for the Court of Appeal would be whether a conviction was or might be unsafe.[17] Section 2(1) (b) and (c) of the Criminal Appeal Act 1968 would become redundant, and, as a corollary, so would the proviso.[18] The focus of an appeal would be entirely upon the question of guilt or innocence; the fairness of the proceedings would become irrelevant. This would mark a shift towards the crime control model. Thus, the majority recommended that if the court concluded that, despite procedural errors at or before the trial, the conviction was safe, then the appeal must be dismissed.

A minority of three commissioners thought that even obviously

---

[15] Ibid p 106.

[16] Report, op cit p 162, and 170–175.

[17] If deemed unsafe, the conviction would be quashed. If deemed possibly unsafe, a retrial would be ordered wherever practicable: ibid p 168. Where a retrial was impracticable, and the case involved fresh evidence, the court would have to determine the effect of that evidence in accordance with the approach laid down by the House of Lords in *Stafford* (p 175); but if the case involved a technical error (such as a misdirection on the law) a narrow majority of the Runciman Commission thought the court should be obliged to quash the conviction (pp 175–176).

[18] For argument in support of this position, see R Buxton, 'Miscarriages of Justice and the Court of Appeal' (1993) 109 LQR 66.

guilty persons should be afforded a retrial if there was a sufficiently serious error at trial and that, if a retrial was not practicable, the conviction should be quashed.[19] The minority position is stated thus: 'In our view defendants should not be serving prison sentences on the basis of trials that are seriously flawed.'[20] Just two commissioners thought that serious pre-trial irregularities (such as police fabrication of confessions or failures to disclose material helpful to the defence) should lead to the court either ordering a retrial or quashing the conviction, depending on the view it took of the gravity of the error.[1]

The arguments on this last point illustrate well the tension between the due process and crime control models regarding the role of remedies. To quote the report:

'In the view of the majority, even if they believed that quashing the convictions of criminals was an appropriate way of punishing police malpractice, it would be naive to suppose that this would have any practical effect on police behaviour. In any case it cannot in their view be morally right that a person who has been convicted on abundant other evidence and may be a danger to the public should walk free because of what may be a criminal offence by someone else. Such an offence should be separately prosecuted within the system.'[2]

The minority position was set out in the dissenting note appended to the report by Professor Michael Zander. It clearly accepts the due process argument that the criminal system should itself accept the responsibility for upholding the integrity of its own procedures. This was because the majority's approach would weaken the 'role of the Court of Appeal in promoting observance of the complex and crucial network of PACE rules'[3] and because it might encourage serious wrongdoing by police officers.[4] Also, there was a moral issue involved which went beyond such utilitarian concerns:

'The moral foundation of criminal justice requires that if the prosecution has employed foul means the defendant must go free even though he is plainly guilty. Where the integrity of the process is fatally flawed, the conviction should be quashed as an expression of the system's repugnance at the methods used by those acting for the prosecution.'[5]

---

[19] Ibid p 170.
[20] Ibid p 233.
[1] Ibid p 172.
[2] Ibid.
[3] Ibid p 234. For discussion, see section 4(b), above.
[4] Ibid.
[5] Ibid.

It is ironic that this firm statement of principle appears only in the concluding few paragraphs of the note of dissent tucked away at the back of the Runciman Commission's report. It is much to be regretted that the report proper did not commence with an attempt to ground its 352 recommendations on either these or some other principled foundations.

We may now draw out the implications of this discussion of the Court of Appeal's role within the criminal justice system, both in hearing appeals from the Crown Court and in accepting references from the Home Secretary. In one of the earliest studies of the appeals process, Bottoms and McClean highlighted the conflict that exists between fairness and justice, on the one hand, and the demands of efficient administration, on the other. The central issue for them was the status of the appeals process. Was an appeal to be a general right for all defendants, or a special procedure designed to correct the occasional wrong?[6] The history of the Court of Appeal suggests that it is the latter that was intended from the outset. The Court of Appeal was created in 1907 in response to a public outcry over a particular miscarriage of justice, the Adolf Beck case. As Malleson convincingly argues:

'The original purpose of the Court of Criminal Appeal was therefore bound up with the desire of the judiciary to provide a mechanism to sift out and put right such serious and rare cases which generated public concern and brought the Criminal Justice System into disrepute . . . The present design of the system, the limited and narrow powers of the Court and the hazardous path to that institution are not accidental or a mistake but persist because there has never been the will or intention to have a system the size and scope of which is determined by the numbers of miscarriages of justice occurring.'[7]

In other words, our system of appellate review is dominated by crime control considerations. As we have noted, the crime control model is reluctant to concede that its procedures are likely to produce miscarriages of justice. Every acquittal and every successful appeal serves to sap public confidence in the reliability of the system in distinguishing the innocent from the guilty. This undermines the deterrent efficacy of the criminal law and threatens the entire crime control project. But public confidence might drain away altogether if the system failed to right its obvious mistakes in a timely fashion. However, the processes of case construction and evidential constraints (such as the reluctance to admit fresh evidence) ensures that, although errors are legion, few are obvious. Even then, it is only when major public

---

[6] Op cit pp 186–187.
[7] Op cit (1991) p 331.

campaigns are mounted that the public takes an interest in the fate of convicted persons. The Court of Appeal exists to ensure that convictions in such high profile cases are either quashed or given the seal of approval by the senior judiciary. Because miscarriages of justice occurring in more run of the mill cases attract minimal public interest, there is no need to ensure that they are subject to appellate review and much to be said for suppressing appeals.

7. CONCLUSION

In this book, we have tried to show that in criminal justice, as in the rest of life, you cannot have everything. Tradeoffs cannot be avoided. In criminal justice, the main tradeoff is that in the course of catching and convicting more criminals, one will catch and convict more innocent people too. The legal rules reflect the natural ambivalence most of us feel when faced with this uncomfortable reality, but unwillingness to accept this lesson fully has led to many of the rules—those with most due process content—being unworkable. This is not to say that due process-based rules are necessarily unworkable. But they will be whilst we refuse to face up to the nature of the criminal justice system and whilst we continue to demand a maximum apprehension and conviction rate, for the working rules of the law enforcement bureaucracies are not in harmony with those legal rules which are due process-based. And so we have a significant (but unquantifiable) level of rule breaking by law enforcement agencies, some of which leads to wrongful conviction, and much of which leads to unnecessary and unpleasant pre-charge detention. But many legal rules are inspired by crime control ideology, so we also have a significant (and also unquantifiable) level of wrongful conviction which is a product of the police following the legal rules, just as much unpleasant pre-charge detention is perfectly lawful.

In this chapter, we have examined the response of the system to error. One response is the exclusion of evidence obtained through, or in the course of, rule breaking. Exclusionary rules have several potential rationales:

(a) to prevent the conviction of the factually innocent (the reliability rule);
(b) to compensate (the protective principle); and
(c) to punish and deter malpractice (the rules on oppression and inducements, and the 'bad faith' and 'substantial breach' principles).

Due process theorists would advocate all three rationales. Our system is driven much more by the first than the second and third. For the crime control theorist only the first is valid: punishment, compensation and deterrence are all laudable objectives of the system but should be pursued through other mechanisms. Those mechanisms are civil, criminal and disciplinary proceedings. Evaluation of the due process and crime control models and our own system's position between them should depend, in part, on the effectiveness of those alternative mechanisms.

Civil procedures seek mainly to compensate, although punishment and deterrence are secondary rationales. They are necessary because the exclusion of evidence rules caters only for those who are prosecuted and who plead not guilty. Appeal procedures are likewise only available to this small minority group, and there is the additional qualification that one must first be convicted in order to have a right of appeal. Civil actions, by contrast, are available to anyone who has suffered at the hands of the police. However, we saw that the limited number of causes of action, restrictions on legal aid and evidential barriers all limit the possibilities of suing in the civil courts. Civil actions were designed to allow propertied individuals to assert their rights against other individuals, not to remedy criminal injustice.

The complaints and discipline system, like recourse to the civil courts, is in theory open to all. One might think that this system would be geared towards punishing malpractice and deterring it in future. It too, however, was designed for something else—to discipline officers breaking the rules of the police organisation—and this is reflected in the operation of the system. Unlike the other remedies, this one is largely controlled by the police themselves. Complainants find themselves complaining to the police about the police, and initiating a process in which the police investigate the police, the police adjudicate on the police and the police decide on the punishment for the police. That this system is put to police purposes (improving efficiency and defusing and deflecting criticism) rather than being operated for the benefit of complainants is hardly surprising.

Finally, there are appeals against conviction, both immediately after conviction and through the Home Secretary's reference procedure. Here the crime control pursuit of 'truth', regardless of technical procedures, suddenly hits a brick wall. There are time limits, legal aid restrictions, delays, penalties and restrictive rules about fresh evidence. Complaints about incompetent defence lawyers are generally ruled inadmissible, even though we now know both that most defence lawyers offer an incompetent service to their clients and that inadequate defence lawyering is a potent source of injustice. Jury verdicts (but not jury selection procedures) are sacrosanct, so cannot be overturned just because a guilty verdict is against the weight of the evidence. Retrials are possible, in an attempt to get to the 'truth', but are ordered as much to avoid overturning a guilty verdict following a flawed pre-trial or trial process as to allow a dubious conviction to be reviewed. Sometimes, though, when gross malpractice is proved, but there was none the less sufficient reliable evidence on which to convict, the police and prosecution agencies are punished by the Court of Appeal quashing the conviction. But if the Runciman Commission has its way, even this rare example of a due process-based disciplinary practice will fall, with an undercutting effect on the exclusionary principle expressed in s 78 of PACE.

(a) Remedies: common features

One problem common to these various remedies is that of inadequate resources. Remedial procedures exist in order that abuse of power by officials (the police, prosecutors and trial judges) acting for, or in tandem with, the Executive may be checked and redressed. Yet it is the Executive which determines how well resourced these procedures shall be. There is a conflict of interest here. In practice, remedial procedures are starved of the necessary resources. Legal aid is being cut for civil actions, is not available for police complaints and does not get through to convicted people who might have grounds for appeal. Neither the Court of Appeal nor the Police Complaints Authority have the resources needed to assert true independence from the Executive, and the same is increasingly true of defence lawyers. The former two bodies are forced into deterring, sifting out and not acting upon the majority of cases which potentially fall within their jurisdictions, whilst the most important decision most of the latter have to make is the precise level of malpractice at which they will operate. But the problems run deeper, much deeper, than a lack of resources.

None of the remedies we have discussed provides adequate protection for some of the most central 'rights' in the criminal justice system. Rules restricting stop-search, roadblocks and unsuitable identification procedures, and rights, for instance, to a lawyer, to silence, and to be treated with respect when in police custody, are not catered for at all by civil and criminal remedies; equivocally by exclusionary rules; and only half-heartedly by appeal procedures. These rights have no effective remedies. This is troubling for legal theorists of various persuasions.[8] 'Realists' argue that 'real' law is the 'law in action' but there is little action available to remedy abuse of rights. Positivists argue that laws are commands backed by sanctions. A right without a remedy is a command without a sanction. Thus Lawson and Rudden say that 'English lawyers . . . think of legal relations as directly or indirectly giving a specific plaintiff an action against a specific defendant.'[9] And Lawson

---

[8] See ch 2, section 3(a), above, for related discussion of the various theoretical approaches to law.

[9] F Lawson and B Rudden, *Law of Property* (OUP, 1982) p 2.

says that '. . . a wrong which cannot give rise to a remedy is not properly speaking a wrong.'[10]

Whichever school of jurisprudential thought one subscribes to, it seems that the police are barely subject to that old constitutional chestnut, the rule of law. Thus our system of remedies is primarily enabling, legitimising and presentational in relation to police working rules. This is not to say that the police do not fear losing cases or being sued, sacked or prosecuted. But it is to say that they so rarely do lose cases and so rarely are sued, sacked or prosecuted that this fear is slight. In any case, there is so much that the police can do in furtherance of their goals within the rules that there is rarely much need to breach them. In low visibility situations, police officers may none the less break the rules (for efficiency's sake) on a systematic basis, for there is little risk of any sanctions being applied as a result. In higher visibility situations, perhaps where a middle class suspect is being interrogated with a competent solicitor present, the police can simply revert to 'doing it by the book'. This may be relatively inefficient, but it avoids the risk of sanctions, and the rulebook gives plenty of scope for dragging confessions out of people.

All the remedies discussed are individualistic, that is, they all treat alleged wrongs and errors as individual problems arising from individual mistakes. This is inevitable, for this is a book about law and legal processes usually individualise conflict. This may be so even when it seems glaringly obvious that the problems are structural rather than individual. Thus, when the Police Complaints Authority belatedly launched an inquiry into the West Midlands Police Serious Crime Squad, this took the form of pursuing individual malpractices, rather than investigating the squad and its working practices as a whole. But the response need not be individualistic. In *Edwards*,[11] the Court of Appeal has accepted that some police officers break the law on a systematic basis and that defence lawyers should be able to discredit them by referring to their past deeds. Similarly, in *Judith Ward*,[12] the Court of Appeal responded to evidence of the systematic non-disclosure of evidence by the police, government forensic scientists, the Director of Public Prosecutions and prosecuting counsel by laying down, for the first time, a systematic statement of the common law requirements on disclosure. And wide-ranging inquiries into policing, its context and its consequences are possible, as Lord Scarman's inquiry into the Brixton

---

[10] F Lawson, *Remedies of English Law* (OUP, 1980) p 2.

[11] [1991] 2 All ER 266.

[12] [1993] 1 WLR 619. See section 6 of this chapter and ch 5, section 3(c), above for discussion.

disorders of 1981 demonstrates.[13] But the Scarman inquiry was unique, and the government has not repeated the experiment.

It is one thing to point to systemic malpractice by one squad, and another to claim that all police malpractice is, in general, systemic (ie a natural product of the criminal justice system). There are several possible explanations for police malpractice, none of which is mutually exclusive.

(b)   Theories of police malpractice

Firstly, there is the 'rotten apple' theory, beloved of senior police officers and politicians, whereby a few unscrupulous or incompetent officers commit all the wrongs. Such rotten officers will be detected and removed from the barrel before the great mass of law-abiding police officers become infected through contact. This ignores the evidence of widespread rule breaking uncovered by research; the 'code of silence' operated by senior as well as junior officers to cover it up; and the failure to discipline adequately most of those few officers who are found to have broken the rules. If malpractice is a result of rotten apples, they must have infected the barrel as well as its contents.

Secondly, there is the 'technical failure' theory. We all make mistakes, rules are misunderstood, training needs improvement, technology needs development. That there is some truth in this is undeniable. But for it to be generally true we would expect many more even-handed 'errors': as many summaries of interrogation which wrongly suggest that no incriminating statements were made as suggest the opposite; tape recordings and notes of 'conversations' as well as failures to tape record 'interviews'; non-authorisation of detention when it is necessary, as well as authorisation when it is not; police contact with solicitors, friends or family when it was not clear that this was the wish of the suspect, as well as non-contact in these circumstances; and contact with a psychologist or social worker when a suspect might be, but probably is not, vulnerable, as well as non-contact when suspects might not be, but probably are, vulnerable. The 'errors' we detected as we examined each stage of the criminal process in turn can scarcely be described as even-handed.

These two theories are primarily individualistic. The remedies we have discussed are directed at 'the problems' as conceived by these theories. They are individualistic remedies for individualistic problems. They seem to us to be inadequate in the light of the evidence discussed in this book. The final two theories are systemic. Irving and Dunnighan

---

[13] Sir L Scarman, The Brixton Disorders: 10–12 April 1981 (Cmnd 8427) (HMSO, 1981), discussed in ch 2, section 2, above.

apply a systems approach to police work similar to that applied by social psychologists in other fields of work.[14] This approach assumes that humans naturally err and that the best systems are those that accept this as inevitable but which also work on the basis that this is undesirable. Prevention and correction of error should therefore be designed into the system through quality control procedures as with factories and other production systems. Irving and Dunnighan found that the CID has no systems for identifying the sources of error, that training does not direct itself to sources of error, and that there is little, if any, supervision which aims to identify error.[15]

The implications of Irving and Dunnighan's theory are that individualistic remedies will be far less effective as preventative measures than will training and supervision which focuses on error combined with a complete redesign of police structures. But they seem to assume that systemic error in legal terms is also systemic error in terms of the organisation and production of criminal justice. The evidence discussed in this book suggests that this is rarely so. Arrest without reasonable suspicion is often functional for the system, so is unnecessary detention and informal interviews. And the issue goes beyond the police. Prosecutors prosecute in breach of prosecution guidelines, judges engage in plea bargaining and defence lawyers do little by way of defence, even if these things are not always and everywhere the same. Much of this behaviour involves rule breaking but it is all grist to the crime control mill. Systemic rule breaking, on this theory, then, is a product of the lack of fit between due process rules (to the extent that they are due process in content) and crime control roles, objectives and working rules. On this theory, unlike in Irving and Dunnighan's, it is not in the interest of the organisation to discover and correct most rule breaking because rule breaking is, in general, functional for it. This could explain why there are no quality control systems, why complaints procedures 'fail' to uncover malpractice, and why court-based remedies are so inadequate. There are only two ways to eradicate malpractice: either eradicate the whole crime control environment so that roles, objectives and working rules are transformed and infused with due process values (unrealistice in the current political climate) or eradicate the due process rules so that practices are no longer malpractices.

---

[14] B Irving and C Dunnighan, Human Factors in the Quality Control of CID Investigations (Royal Commission on Criminal Justice, Research Study no 21) (HMSO, 1993).

[15] On the inadequacy of supervision, see also the similar conclusions of J Baldwin and T Moloney, Supervision of Police Investigation in Serious Criminal Cases (Royal Commission on Criminal Justice Research Study no 4) (HMSO, 1992) and M Maguire and C Norris, The Conduct and Supervision of Criminal Investigations (Royal Commission on Criminal Justice, Research Study no 5) (HMSO, 1992).

(c) Rhetoric and reality: mananging the gap

Some may see the Criminal Justice and Public Order Bill as part and parcel of the latter strategy. Perhaps that is so. But, for two reasons, we doubt whether such a strategy could ever be pushed so far to justify alarmist talk of a 'police state' or of 'totalitarianism'. Firstly, it would simply be too politically dangerous. Within all the major political parties, there is sufficient attachment to the rhetoric and substance of due process to rule out the possibility of introducing an undiluted and naked system of crime control. The Criminal Justice and Public Order Bill represents a shift towards crime control but the idea of 'balance' between police powers and suspect safeguards has been retained. Thus, for example, there has been no suggestion that the right of detained persons to receive legal advice free of charge should be abolished, despite the considerable cost implications of the duty solicitor scheme.

The second reason is ideological. By arguing that the criminal justice system has become too heavily tipped towards the interests of suspects, the government has chosen to lock itself into the discourse of 'balance' in which more crime control can be justified by reference to bits and pieces of due process. In this sense, rather than in the crude sense implied by McBarnet,[16] due process is for crime control. But it also means that some due process safeguards are sure to be retained, since one cannot create the appearance of due process if there are no such safeguards. It also means that the system will continue to have some due process substance, since otherwise the appearance of due process would soon be dissipated.[17] Such a dissipation would not be functional for the continuing and historical drift towards crime control.

Thus the system will continue to represent a site of struggle and conflict. Many skirmishes will result in victories for due process (as where evidence is excluded on the grounds of unfairness), even some battles may be won (as with the creation of court and police station duty solicitor schemes), but the war will simply continue. Crime control cannot be imposed by force, since its ideological justification is that it increases real freedom and liberty, but nor are we asked to consent to it. Instead we are presented with a picture of a system—neatly balancing

---

[16] D McBarnet, *Conviction* (MacMillan, 1983) p 156: 'The law on criminal procedure in its current form does not so much set a standard of legality from which the police deviate as provide a licence to ignore it. If we bring due process down from the dizzy heights of abstraction and subject it to empirical scrutiny, the conclusion must be that due process is *for* crime control.' This argument assumes that we must characterise rules of procedure as due process even when they serve the goals of crime control. This is mistaken, in our view. Rules of procedure can be either due process- or crime control-inspired, as Packer, op cit, himself pointed out.

[17] In this, we follow E P Thompson, *Whigs and Hunters* (Penguin, 1975) pp 259–265.

due process rights and crime controls powers—which is a gross distortion of reality.

Part of this distortion is achieved by judges and legislators proclaiming the virtues of due process at the same time as they are acting on crime control instincts. For example, the case law on exclusion provides the judges with a wide scope as to which precedents to follow, which tests to apply and which decisions to reach. The open texture of the law means that, and on this point we follow McBarnet, 'judges can both *uphold*, even eulogise, the rhetoric yet simultaneously deny its applicability . . .'[18] Thus in *Fulling*,[19] we saw the Court of Appeal adopt a broad definition of oppression, which clearly covered the case in question, yet the appellant still lost. Similarly, in examining the Court of Appeal's powers, we saw how malpractice by police or prosecution agencies might be condemned but the conviction upheld.

This ideological double-talk reduces the need to provide due process substance within the law, but we hold to our view that some substance there must still be; a complete sham would fool no one. Thus we saw that the Court of Appeal can and sometimes does quash convictions to express its disapproval of police malpractice even though there is reliable evidence of guilt, and some defence lawyers have provided an outstanding service to their clients, often at great emotional and financial cost to themselves.[20] What is lacking is an appreciation of how exceptional these events and people are. Such exceptions to the rule of crime control tend to occur in high profile contexts (as with the dramatic freeing of the 'Birmingham Six'), creating an appearance of far more due process than is really the case.

Above all, however, is the uneven distribution of due process protections across society. At various points in this book, we have seen that disadvantaged sections of society are disproportionately at the receiving end of state power. 'We' are taken in by the ideological self-portrait of criminal justice because we have so little experience of the system and have no incentive to question its operation. It does not threaten 'our' interests, but appears to serve them. Ask most black people and, to a lesser extent, young working class males and they will have a different story to tell. We saw this in relation to dissatisfaction with the police complaints system and this disaffection—bordering on disbelief in the rule of law—can be seen in many other criminal justice contexts.

Since we cannot expect the adoption of either a consistent crime control philosophy and all that goes with it, nor the adoption of the due

---

18 McBarnet, op cit.
19 Above.
20 As when they have joined or spearheaded campaigns to have miscarriage of justice cases referred back to the Home Secretary.

process model and all that that would imply, the prospects for an open, rational and coherent system of justice are bleak in the extreme. So where do we go from here? There are two possibilities, and they are not mutually exclusive. The first is to seek to reduce the amount of error occurring in our predominantly crime control system, by rethinking our approach to remedies. The second is to expose the system to more scrutiny so that we can better understand and debate its inherent problems and the options for change.

(d) Remedies or preventive controls?

We have seen that remedies may serve several different purposes. They can compensate suspects and defendants, punish and discipline police officers and correct and prevent error. To correct and prevent error, the fullest information is needed. To secure this, especially in a low visibility occupation like the police, the co-operation is needed of those who know what is happening. If either of the two individualistic theories (especially the 'rotten apple' theory) are valid, co-operation would be expected: information would be provided by the 'good' officers against the 'bad'. This rarely seems to happen.

If most malpractice cannot be explained individualistically, information and co-operation will not be provided willingly. For everyone will be protected by the silence of the others, and it will be perceived as unfair to punish one person for something that is routine and condoned by senior officers. The protection of colleagues, oneself and one's organisation is a natural response if discovery of malpractice is likely to lead to adverse consequences for those 'found out' or for organisational morale. On the other hand, if information and co-operation are required only to correct and prevent error, with no disciplinary or punitive consequences, co-operation and information are much more likely to be forthcoming. As Irving and Dunnighan say:

'Where systems of discipline . . . exist against operatives, accurate data about system malfunction, human factors phenomena, etc can only be obtained by offering informants generous protection and by keeping the de-briefing procedures as far as possible inside the work group.'[1]

In other words, systems of discipline are incompatible with systems of diagnosis and prevention. Even the brutality of the Holloway Road

---

[1] Op cit p 5.

scandal—which could well have had a 'bad apple' element to it—was opened up only after limited immunity was offered.[2]

Irving and Dunnighan's analysis applies equally to our systemic theory of rule breaking. If it is right, it means that the only way malpractice can be tackled systematically, if at all, whilst retaining a genuine system of remedies (ie which punish and/or compensate), is by having two systems working in parallel: a management information system and a complaints and remedies investigation system, whereby no 'leakage' would be allowed from the former to the latter.[3] At present there is no 'leakage' allowed from complaints investigation to civil actions, although the discipline and criminal prosecution processes do share the same information. It seems that if we want to alter police practices systematically we not only have to accept Irving and Dunnighan's optimistic theory of malpractice, we also have to abandon the idea that complaints files be made available to civil litigants, and agree to keep separate investigations into error from investigations into possible criminal acts by officers. This might be too high a price to pay for the hope of improving police practices in general. If we abandon that goal, we could instead try to make investigation procedures work against a 'wall of silence', but this would be an enormous undertaking. Only one thing is reasonably certain: if we stick with our current messy compromise, we will satisfy few wronged individuals and change few systemic malpractices.

This might seem an unduly negative and cynical conclusion. We seem to be stuck with accepting a crime control culture, where a fairly high level of wrongful convictions are inevitable and many more suspects suffer indignity and deprivation. But our aim in pointing this out is, in our view, constructive. Since those who know our earlier work may find this hard to swallow, we should conclude this book by explaining ourselves.

Scepticism about the way systems work need not be cynical. Irving and Dunnighan's work in effect applies to the police the sceptical model of analysis which sociologists have long applied to all occupations. Their aim, like ours, is to improve the police system, not to undermine

---

[2] A similar problem dogged the Sir John May inquiry into the 'Guildford Four' case. In November 1989, he said he wanted to receive factual evidence, but could not do so until the prosecution of the police officers allegedly involved in malpractice was completed. He thought this would take two or three months. It in fact took four years. See Rozenberg, op cit pp 95–97.

[3] This problem arises in all occupational settings. Academics, for example, are fighting to keep the system of personal appraisal (in which an individual's weaknesses are meant to be identified, discussed and remedied) separate from the system of determining pay and promotion. If they are not kept so separate, the prospects for frank discussion during appraisal are, for obvious reasons, poor.

it. The first step to successful reform is accurate identification of the problem to be addressed. Reforms are doomed to failure if the system they are applied to is not understood in the first place. Thus we seek to raise the level of debate from the rhetorical to the factual and moral, and identify real—not idealised—choices.

Our negative tone might still be criticised, however, on the grounds that the English system is, for all its faults, the best in the world. It is probably true that it is better than most, and undoubtedly true that it is better than some. This is as it should be, as we are still one of the wealthiest societies in the world. We ought to be able to afford the best justice. And if we are as civilised as we would like to think, we should aspire to have the best system. The argument of this book is that the system neither achieves, nor aspires to achieve, such high standards.

Bibliography

J. Alderson, *Policing Freedom* (Macdonald and Evans, 1979).

P. Alldridge, 'For the Repeal of the Proviso' [1984] Crim LR 220.

A. Ashworth, 'Excluding Evidence as Protecting Rights' [1977] Crim LR 723.

A. Ashworth, 'A threadbare principle' [1978] Crim LR 385.

A. Ashworth, 'The "Public Interest" element in Prosecutions' [1987] Crim LR 595.

A. Ashworth, 'Defining Offences Without Harm' in P. Smith (ed) *Criminal Law: Essays in Honour of J.C. Smith* (Butterworths, 1987).

A. Ashworth, 'Public Order and the Principles of English Criminal Law' [1987] Crim LR 153.

A. Ashworth, *Sentencing and Criminal Justice* (Weidenfeld and Nicolson, 1992).

A. Ashworth, 'Plea, Venue and Discontinuance' [1993] Crim LR 830.

A. Ashworth, E. Genders, G. Mansfield, J. Peay, and E. Player, 'Sentencing in the Crown Court', Occasional Paper No 10 (Oxford Centre for Criminological Research, 1984).

H. Astor, 'The Unrepresented Defendant Revisited: a Consideration of the Role of the Clerk in Magistrates' Courts' (1986) 13 Journal of Law and Society 225.

S. Bailey and D. Birch, 'Recent Developments in the Law of Police Powers' [1982] Crim LR 475.

S. Bailey and M. Gunn, *Smith and Bailey on the English Legal System* (Sweet & Maxwell, 1991).

I. Balbus, *The Dialectics of Legal Repression* (Russell Sage, 1973).

J. Baldwin, 'The Social Composition of the Magistracy' (1976) 16 BJ Crim 171.

J. Baldwin, *Pre-Trial Justice* (Basil Blackwell, 1985).

J. Baldwin, 'Pre-Trial Settlement in the Magistrates' Courts' (1985) 24 The Howard Journal 108.

J. Baldwin, 'The green form: use or abuse?' (1988) 138 NLJ 631.

J. Baldwin, 'Preparing the Record of Taped Interview', Royal Commission on Criminal Justice, Research Study No 2 (HMSO, 1992).

J. Baldwin, 'The Role of Legal Representatives at the Police Station', Royal Commission on Criminal Justice, Research Study No 3 (HMSO, 1993).

J. Baldwin, 'Power and Police Interviews' (1993) 143 NLJ 1194.

J. Baldwin, 'Police Interview Techniques: Establishing Truth or Proof?' (1993) 33 BJ Crim 325.

J. Baldwin and J. Bedward, 'Summarising Tape Recordings of Police Interviews' [1991] Crim LR 671.

J. Baldwin and F. Feeney, 'Defence Disclosure in the Magistrates' Courts' (1986) 49 MLR 593.

J. Baldwin and S. Hill, *The Operation of the Green Form Scheme in England and Wales* (Lord Chancellor's Department, 1988).

J. Baldwin and M. McConville, *Negotiated Justice* (Martin Robertson, 1977).

J. Baldwin and M. McConville, 'The new Home Office figures on pleas and acquittals: what sense do they make?' [1978] Crim LR 196.

J. Baldwin and M. McConville, 'The Influence of the Sentencing Discount in Inducing Guilty Pleas', in J. Baldwin and A. Bottomley (eds), *Criminal Justice: Selected Readings* (Martin Robertson, 1978)

J. Baldwin and M. McConville, 'Allegations Against Lawyers' [1978] Crim LR 744.

J. Baldwin and M. McConville, *Jury Trials* (Oxford University Press, 1979).

J. Baldwin and T. Moloney, 'Supervision of Police Investigation in Serious Criminal Cases', Royal Commission on Criminal Justice, Research Study No 4 (HMSO, 1992).

J. Baldwin and A. Mulvaney, 'Advance Disclosure in Magistrates' Courts: the Workings of Section 48' (1987) 151 Justice of the Peace 409.

J. Baldwin and A. Mulvaney, *Pre-Trial Settlement of Criminal Cases in Magistrates' Courts* (University of Birmingham, 1987).

J. Baldwin and A. Mulvaney, 'Advance Disclosure in the Magistrates' Courts: two Cheers for Section 48' [1987] Crim LR 315.

J. Baldwin and A. Mulvaney, 'Advance Disclosure in the Magistrates' Courts: how useful are the prosecution summaries?' [1987] Crim LR 805.

M. Banton, *The Policeman in the Community* (Tavistock, 1964).

N. Bases and M. Smith, 'A Study of Bail Applications Through the Official Solicitor to the Judge in Chambers' [1976] Crim LR 541.

J. Baxter and L. Koffman, 'The Confait inheritance – forgotten lessons?' (1983) Cambrian Law Review, 14.

J. Bell 'The French Pre-Trial System' in C. Walker and K. Starmer (eds), Justice in Error (Blackstone, 1993).

V. Bevan and K. Lidstone, *The Investigation of Crime: A Guide to Police Powers* (Butterworths, 1991).

D. Birch, 'Hunting the Snark: the Elusive Statutory Exception' [1988] Crim LR 221.

D. Birch, 'The PACE Hots Up: Confessions and Confusions under the 1984 Act' [1989] Crim LR 95.

D. Birch, 'Documentary Evidence' [1989] Crim LR 15.

N. Blake, 'Picketing, Justice and the Law', in B. Fine and R. Millar (eds) *Policing the Miners' Strike* (Lawrence & Wishart, 1985).

B. Block, 'Bail Conditions: Neither Logical nor Lawful' (1990) 154 Justice of the Peace 83.

B. Block, C. Corbett, and J. Peay, 'Ordered and Directed Acquittals in the Crown Court' Royal Commission on Criminal Justice, Research Study No 15 (HMSO, 1993).

B. Block, C. Corbett, and J. Peay, 'Ordered and Directed Acquittals in the Crown Court: a Time of Change?' [1993] Crim LR 95.

M. Bohlander, '". . . By a jury of his peers" – The issue of multi-racial juries in a poly-ethnic society' [1992] XIV(1) Liverpool Law Review 67.

A. Bottomley, *Decisions in the Penal Process* (Martin Robertson, 1973).

A. Bottomley, 'Sentencing reform and the structuring of pre-trial discretion', in M. Wasik and K. Pease (eds) *Sentencing Reform* (Manchester University Press, 1987).

A. Bottomley and C. Coleman, *Understanding Crime Rates* (Saxon House, 1981).

A. Bottomley and K. Pease, *Crime and Punishment: Interpreting the Data* (Open University Press, 1986).

A. Bottomley, C. Coleman, D. Dixon, M. Gill and D. Wall, 'The detention of suspects in police custody' (1991) 31 BJ Crim 347.

A. Bottoms and J. McClean, *Defendants in the Criminal Process* (Routledge & Kegan Paul, 1976).

S. Box, *Deviance, Reality and Society* (Holt, Rinehart and Winston, 1981).

S. Box, *Power, Crime and Mystification* (Tavistock, 1983).

S. Box and K. Russell, 'The Politics of Discreditability: Disarming Complaints Against the Police' (1975) 23 Sociological Review 315.

M. Brake and C. Hale, *Public Order and Private Lives* (Routledge, 1992).

J. Bredar, 'Moving Up the Day of Reckoning: strategies for attacking the "cracked trials" problem' [1992] Crim LR 153.

L. Bridges, 'The professionalisation of criminal justice' Legal Action, August 1992, 7.

L. Bridges, 'The fixed fees battle' Legal Action, November 1992, 7.

L. Bridges, 'The right to jury trial – how the Royal Commission got it wrong' (1993) 143 NLJ 1542.

L. Bridges, J. Carter, and S. Gorbing, 'The Impact of Duty Solicitor Schemes in Six Magistrates' Courts', LAG Bulletin, July 1982, 12.

L. Bridges and T. Bunyan, 'Britain's new urban policing strategy – the Police and Criminal Evidence Bill in context' (1983) 10 Journal of Law and Society 85.

B. Brink and C. Stone, 'Defendants who do not ask for Bail' [1988] Crim LR 152.

G. Broadbent, 'Offensive Weapons and the CJA' (1989) 86 LS Gaz, 12 July, 23.

A. Brogden, 'Sus is dead: what about "SaS"?' (1981) 9 New Community 44.

M. Brogden and A. Brogden, 'From Henry III to Liverpool 8' (1984) 12 International Journal of the Sociology of Law 37.

M. Brogden, 'Stopping the People' in J. Baxter and L. Koffman (eds) *Police – The Constitution and the Community* (Professional Books, 1985).

M. Brogden, *On the Mersey Beat* (Oxford University Press, 1991).

A. Brown and D. Crisp, 'Diverting Cases from Prosecution in the Public Interest', (1992) 32 Home Office Research Bulletin 7.

D. Brown, 'Police Complaints Procedure', Home Office Research Study No 93 (HMSO, 1987).

D. Brown, 'Detention at the police station under the Police and Criminal Evidence Act 1984', Home Office Research Study No 104 (HMSO, 1989).

D. Brown, T. Ellis and K. Larcombe, 'Changing the Code: Police detention under the revised PACE Codes of Practice', Home Office Research Study No 129 (HMSO, 1992).

S. Butler, 'Acquittal Rates', Home Office Research and Planning Unit Paper 16 (HMSO, 1983).

R. Buxton, 'Challenging and Discharging Jurors' [1990] Crim LR 225.

R. Buxton, 'Miscarriages of Justice and the Court of Appeal' (1993) 109 LQR 66.

E. Buzawa and C. Buzawa, 'The Impact of Arrest on Domestic Assault' (1993) 36 American Behavioural Scientist 558.

N. Cameron, 'Bail Act 1976: two Inconsistencies and an Imaginary Offence' (1980) 130 NLJ 382.

E. Cape, 'The New Duty Solicitor Arrangements', Legal Action, March 1991, 21.

J. Caplan, 'The Criminal Bar' in R. Hazell (ed) *The Bar on Trial* (Quartet, 1978).

P. Carlen, 'Remedial Routines for the Maintenance of Control in Magistrates' Courts' (1974) 1 BJ Law and Society 101.

P. Carlen, *Magistrates' Justice* (Martin Robertson, 1976).

T. Carns and J. Kruse, 'A Re-Evaluation of Alaska's Plea Bargaining Ban', 8 Alaska Law Review, 27.

W. Carson, 'White Collar Crime and the Enforcement of Factory Legislation' (1970) 10 BJ Crim 383.

E. Cashmore and E. McLaughlin (eds), *Out of Order?* (Routledge 1991).

M. Chatterton, 'Police in Social Control' in J. King (ed) *Control Without Custody* (Cambridge Cropwood Papers, 1976).

L. Christian, 'Restriction without Conviction' in B. Fine and R. Millar (eds) *Policing the Miners' Strike* (Lawrence & Wishart, 1985).

I. Clare and G. Gudjonsson, 'Devising and Piloting an Experimental Version of the "Notice to Detained Persons"', Royal Commission on Criminal Justice, Research Study No 7 (HMSO, 1993).

R. Clarke and M. Hough, 'Crime and Police Effectiveness', Home Office Research Study No 79 (HMSO, 1984).

C. Clarkson, A. Cretney, G. Davis and J. Shepherd, 'Assaults: the relationship between seriousness, criminalisation and punishment' [1994] Crim LR 4.

R. Clayton and H. Tomlinson, *Civil Actions Against the Police* (Sweet and Maxwell, 1987).

R. Clayton and H. Tomlinson, 'Arrest and Reasonable Grounds for Suspicion' (1988) 85 LS Gaz, 7 September, 22.

Commission Justice Penale Et Droits De L'Homme. Rapport Sur La Mise En Etat Des Affaires Penales (1990).

D. Cook, *Rich Law, Poor Law* (Open University Press, 1989).

C. Corbett, 'Complaints Against the Police: The New Procedure of Informal Resolution', 2 (1991) Policing and Society 47.

W. Cornish, *The Jury* (Allen Lane, 1968).

N. Corre, 'Three Frequent Questions on the Bail Act' [1989] Crim LR 493.

R. Cotterrell, *The Politics of Jurisprudence* (Butterworths, 1989).

B. Cox, *Civil liberties in Britain*, chapter 4 (Penguin, 1975).

Criminal Appeals Office, *A Guide to Proceedings in the Court of Appeal Criminal Division* (1990).

D. Crisp, 'Standardising Prosecutions' (1993) 34 Home Office Research Bulletin 13.

H. Croall, 'Mistakes, Accidents and Someone Else's Fault: The Trading Offender in Court' (1988) 15 Journal of Law and Society 293.

Crown Prosecution Service, *Annual Report 1990–1991* (HMSO, 1991).

Crown Prosecution Service, 'Royal Commission on Criminal Justice; Submission of Evidence, vol 1' (undated).

Crown Prosecution Service, *Annual Report 1992–1993* (HMSO, 1993).

Crown Prosecution Service, 'Discontinuance Survey' November 1993 (unpublished).

J. Curran and J. Carnie, *Detention or Voluntary Attendance?: Police use of detention under section 2 of the Criminal Justice (Scotland) Act 1980*, Scottish Office (HMSO, 1986).

P. Curran, 'Discussions in the Judge's Private Room' [1991] Crim LR 79.

M. Damaska, 'Evidentiary barriers to Conviction and Two Models of Criminal Procedure: A Comparative Study', University of Pennsylvania Law Review, 121 (1973) 506.

P. Darbyshire, *The Magistrates' Clerk* (Barry Rose, 1984).

P. Darbyshire, 'The Role of the Magistrates' Clerk in Summary Proceedings' (1980) Justice of the Peace, 186, 201, 219, and 233.

P. Darbyshire, 'Notes of a Lawyer Juror' (1990) 140 NLJ 1264.

P. Darbyshire, 'The Lamp That Shows That Freedom Lives – Is it Worth the Candle?' [1991] Crim LR 740.

I. Dennis, 'Reconstructing the Law of Criminal Evidence' (1989) Current Legal Problems 21.

I. Dennis, 'Miscarriages of Justice and the Law of Confessions' (1993) Public Law 291.

Devlin Committee, 'Report of the Departmental Committee on Evidence of Identification in Criminal Cases', House of Commons Paper 338 (1976).

P. Devlin, *Trial by Jury* (Stevens & Sons, 1956).

P. Devlin, *Criminal prosecution in England* (Oxford University Press, 1960).

P. Devlin, *The Judge* (Oxford University Press, 1979).

P. Devlin, 'The Conscience of the Jury' (1991) 107 LQR 398.

B. Dickson, 'Northern Ireland's Emergency Legislation – The Wrong Medicine?' [1992] Public Law 592.

B. Dickson, 'The Prevention of Terrorism Acts' in C. Walker and K. Starmer (eds) *Justice in Error* (Blackstone, 1993).

J. Dignan, 'Repairing the Damage' (1992) 32 British Journal of Criminology 453.

J. Dine, 'European Community Criminal Law?' [1993] Crim LR 246.

Diplock Commission, 'Report of the Commission to consider legal procedures to deal with terrorist activities in Northern Ireland', Cmnd 5185 (HMSO, 1972).

J. Ditchfield, *Police Cautioning* (HMSO, 1976).

D. Dixon, 'Common Sense, Legal Advice, and the Right of Silence' (1991) Public Law 233.

D. Dixon, A. Bottomley, C. Coleman, M. Gill and D. Wall, 'Reality and Rules in the Construction and Regulation of Police Suspicion', International Journal of the Sociology of Law, 17 (1989) 185.

D. Dixon, C. Coleman and K. Bottomley, 'Consent and the Legal Regulation of Policing' (1990) 17 Journal of Law and Society, 345.

D. Dixon, K. Bottomley, C. Coleman, M. Gill and D. Wall, 'Safeguarding the Rights of Suspects in Police Custody' (1990) 1 Policing and Society 115.

M. J. Doherty and R. East, 'Bail Decisions in Magistrates' Courts' (1985) 25 BJ Crim 251.

S. Doran, 'Descent to Avernus' (1989) 139 NLJ 1147.

J. Driscoll, 'Excluding Illegally Obtained Evidence in the United States' [1987] Crim LR 553.

E. Driver, 'Confessions and the Social Psychology of Coercion' (1968) 82 Harvard Law Review 42.

P. Duff, 'The Prosecutor Fine and Social Control' (1993) 33 BJ Crim 481.

P. Duff and M. Findlay, 'Jury vetting – The jury under attack' (1983) 3 Legal Studies 159.

R. Dworkin, *Taking Rights Seriously* (Duckworth, 1977).

R. East, 'Jury Packing: A Thing of the Past?' (1985) 48 MLR 518.

R. East and P. Thomas, 'Freedom of Movement: Moss and McLachlan' (1985) 12 JLS 77.

R. East, 'Police Brutality – Lessons of the Holloway Road Assault' (1987) 137 NLJ 1010.

S. Easton, *The Right to Silence* (Avebury, 1991).

A. Edwards, *Standard Fees in the Magistrates' Court – a survival guide* (Law Society, 1993).

J. Edwards, *The Attorney General, Politics and the Public Interest* (1984).

S. Edwards, *Policing Domestic Violence* (Sage, 1989).

S. Elliman, 'Independent Information for the CPS' (1990) 140 NLJ 812 and 864.

C. Emmins, 'Why No Advance Information for Summary Offences' [1987] Crim LR 608.

R. Ericson, *Making Crime: A Study of Detective Work* (Butterworths, 1981).

R. Ericson, *Reproducing Order: A Study of Police Patrol Work* (University of Toronto Press, 1982).

R. Evans, 'Police Cautioning and the Young Adult Offender' [1991] Crim LR 598

R. Evans, 'The Conduct of Police Interviews with Juveniles', Royal Commission on Criminal Justice, Research Study No 8 (HMSO, 1993).

R. Evans, 'Evaluating Young Adult Diversion Schemes in the Metropolitan Police District' [1993] Crim LR 490

R. Evans, 'Before the Court – Understanding Inter-Agency Consultation with Juveniles and Young Adults' (forthcoming).

R. Evans and T. Ferguson, 'Comparing Different Juvenile Cautioning Systems in One Police Force Area', Report to the Home Office Research and Planning Unit (1991).

R. Evans, 'Comparing Young Adult and Juvenile Cautioning in the Metropolitan Police District' [1993] Crim LR 572.

R. Evans and C. Wilkinson, 'Variations in Police Cautioning Policy and Practice in England and Wales' (1990) 29 Howard Journal of Criminal Justice 155.

S. Farson, 'Complaints against the Police in Canada: A New Approach' [1987] Crim LR 615

H. Fenwick, 'Confessions, Recording Rules, and Miscarriages of Justice: A Mistaken Emphasis?' [1993] Crim LR 174.

C. Fiddes and C. Lloyd, 'Assessing the impact of bail information schemes' (1990) 29 Home Office Research Bulletin, 23.

S. Field, 'Defining Interviews under PACE' (1993) 13 Legal Studies 254.

S. Field and N. Jorg, 'Corporate Liability and Manslaughter: Should we be going Dutch?',[1991] Crim LR 156.

N. Fielding, *Joining Forces* (Routledge, 1988).

B. Fine and R. Millar (eds) *Policing the Miners' Strike* (Lawrence and Wishart, 1985).

Fisher, H. Sir, 'Report of an Inquiry into the Circumstances leading to the Trial of Three Persons on Charges arising out of the Death of Maxwell Confait and the Fire at 27 Doggett Road, London SE6', HCP 90 (HMSO, 1977).

M. Fitzgerald, 'Ethnic Minorities and the Criminal Justice System', Royal Commission on Criminal Justice, Research Study No 20 (HMSO, 1993).

R. Franey, *Poor Law* (NCCL, 1983).

N. Frank and M. Lombness, *Controlling Corporate Illegality* (Anderson, 1988).

M. Frankel, 'The Search for the Truth: An Umpireal View', University of Pennsylvania Law Review, 123 (1975) 1031.

M. Freeman, 'The Jury on Trial' (1981) Current Legal Problems 65.

L. Fuller, 'The Forms and Limits of Adjudication' (1978) 92 Harvard Law Review, 353.

M. Galanter, 'Mega-Law and Mega-Lawyering in the Contemporary United States' in R. Dingwall and P. Lewis (eds) *The Sociology of the Professions* (Macmillan, 1983).

D. Galligan, 'Regulating Pre-Trial Decisions' in I. Dennis (ed) *Criminal Law and Justice* (Sweet & Maxwell, 1987).

S. Gardner, 'Recklessness refined' (1993) 109 LQR 21.

L. Gelsthorpe and H. Giller, 'More Justice for Juveniles' [1990] Crim LR 153

R. Gemmill and R. Morgan-Giles, 'Arrest, Charge and Summons: Arrest Practice and Resource Implications', Royal Commission on Criminal Procedure, Research Study No 9 (HMSO, 1981).

B. Gibson, 'Why Bournemouth? – The Home Office Remand Figures', Justice of the Peace, August 15, 1987, 520.

J. Gobert, 'The Peremptory Challenge – An Obituary' [1989] Crim LR 528.

A. Goldsmith, 'Taking Police Culture Seriously: Police Discretion and the Limits of the Law' (1990) 1 Policing and Society 91.

A. Goldsmith, 'External review and self-regulation' in A. Goldsmith (ed) *Complaints Against the Police: the Trend to External Review* (Oxford University Press, 1991).

A. Goldsmith (ed) *Complaints Against the Police: the Trend to External Review* (Oxford University Press, 1991).

J. Gordon, 'Juries as Judges of the Law' (1992) 108 LQR 272.

P. Gordon, 'Community Policing: Towards the Local Police State' in (ed) P. Scraton, *Law, Order and the Authoritarian State* (Open University Press, 1987).

S. Grace, C. Lloyd and L.J.F. Smith, 'Rape: from Recording to - Conviction', Research and Planning Unit Paper 71 (Home Office, 1992).

P. Green, *The Enemy Without: Policing and Class Consciousness in the Miners' Strike* (Open University Press, 1990).

S. Greer, 'The Right to Silence: A Review of the Current Debate' (1990) 53 Modern Law Review 719.

J. Gregory, *Crown Court or Magistrates' Court?* Office of Population Censuses and Surveys (HMSO, 1976)

J. Griffiths, *The Politics of the Judiciary* (Fontana, 1991).

J. Griffiths and R. Ayres, 'A postscript to the Miranda Project: Interrogation of Draft Protestors' (1967) 77 Yale Law Journal 300.

G. Gudjonsson, *The Psychology of Interrogations, Confessions, and Testimony* (Wiley, 1992).

G. Gudjonsson, I. Clare, S. Rutter and J. Pearse, 'Persons at risk during interviews in police custody: the identification of vulnerabilities', Royal Commission on Criminal Justice, Research Study No 12 (HMSO 1993).

G. Gudjonsson and N. Clark, 'Suggestibility in police interrogation: a social psychological model', 1 Soc Behav 83.

G. Gudjonsson and J. Mackeith, 'A proven case of false confession: psychological aspects of the coerced-compliant type', 30 (1990) Med Sci Law 187.

A. Hall, 'Bail, Appeals' (1984) LAG Bulletin 145.

A. Hall, 'Police Complaints. Time for a Change?' Legal Action, August 1990, 7.

S. Hall, C. Critcher, T. Jefferson, J. Clarke and B. Roberts, *Policing the Crisis* (Macmillan, 1978).

O. Hansen, 'A Future for legal Aid?' (1992) 19 Journal of Law and Society 85.

H. Hart, *The Concept of Law* (Oxford University Press, 1961).

K. Hawkins, *Bargain and Bluff* (1983) 5 Law and Policy Quarterly 8.

K. Hawkins, *Environment and Enforcement* (Oxford University Press, 1984).

K. Hawkins, 'Compliance Strategy, Prosecution Policy, and Aunt Sally: A Comment on Pearce and Tombs' (1990) 30 BJ Crim 444.

P. Healy, 'Proof and Policy: No Golden Threads' [1987] Crim LR 355.

I. Heaton-Armstrong, 'The Verdict of the Court . . . and its Clerk?', 150 Justice of the Peace 340 and 357.

J. Heberling, 'Plea Negotiation in England' in J. Baldwin and A. Bottomley (eds) *Criminal Justice: Selected Readings* (Martin Robertson, 1978).

C. Hedderman and D. Moxon, 'Magistrates' court or Crown Court? Mode of trial decisions and sentencing', Home Office Research Study No 125 (HMSO, 1992).

P. F. Henderson and T. Nichols, 'Offending while on bail' (1992) Home Office Research Bulletin No 32, 23.

R. Henham, *Sentencing Principles and Magistrates' Sentencing Behaviour* (Avebury, 1990).

B. Hilliard, 'Holloway Road – Unfinished Business' (1987) 137 NLJ 1035.

P. Hillyard, 'The Normalization of Special Powers: from Northern Ireland to Britain' in P. Scraton (ed) *Law, Order and the Authoritarian State* (Open University Press, 1987).

C. Hilson, 'Discretion to Prosecute and Judicial Review' [1993] Crim LR 739.

M. Hinchcliffe, 'Beating the bail bandits', The Law Society's Gazette 1 July 1992, 19.

D. Hobbs, *Doing the Business* (Oxford University Press, 1988).

J. Hodgson, 'Tipping the Scales of Justice: The Suspect's Right to Legal Advice' [1992] Crim LR 854.

J. Hodgson and G. Riche 'A criminal defence for the French?' (1993) 143 NLJ 414.

Home Affairs Committee, 'Report on Miscarriages of Justice' (1981–82 HC 421).

Home Office, 'An Independent Prosecution Service for England and Wales', Cmnd 9074 (HMSO, 1983).

Home Office, 'Criminal Justice, Plans for Legislation', Cmnd 9658 (1986).

Home Office, 'The Cautioning of Offenders', Circular 59/1990, Annex A (1990).

Home Office, 'Report for 1992' (HMSO, Cm 1909).

Home Office, 'Costs of the Criminal Justice System 1992', Vol 1 (Home Office, 1992).

R. Hood, *Race and Sentencing* (Clarendon Press, 1992).

M. Hough and P. Mayhew, 'Taking Account of Crime', Home Office Research Study 111 (HMSO, 1985).

Howard League for Penal Reform Working Party on Criminal Justice Administration, *The Dynamics of Justice* (Howard League, 1993).

A. Hucklesby, 'The problem with bail bandits' (1992) 142 NLJ 558.

A. Hucklesby, 'Unnecessary legislative changes', 143 (1993) NLJ 233.

B. Hutter, *The Reasonable Arm of the Law?* (Oxford University Press, 1988).

K. Hyder, 'Cause for Complaint', New Statesman and Society, 12 January 1990.

B. Irving, 'Police Interrogation: a Study of Current Practice', Royal Commission on Criminal Procedure, Research Paper No 2 (HMSO, 1980).

B. Irving and C. Dunnighan, 'Human Factors in the Quality Control of CID Investigations', Royal Commission on Criminal Justice, Research Study No 21 (HMSO, 1993).

B. Irving and I. McKenzie, *Police Interrogation: the Effects of the Police and Criminal Evidence Act 1984* (The Police Foundation, 1989).

J. Jackson, 'The Insufficiency of Identification Evidence Based on Personal Impression' [1986] Crim LR 203.

J. Jackson, 'RCCJ: The Evidence Recommendations' [1993] Crim LR 817.

J. Jackson, 'Trial Procedures' in C. Walker and K. Starmer (eds) *Justice in Error* (Blackstone, 1993).

J. Jackson and S. Doran, 'Diplock and the Presumption Against Jury Trial: a critique' [1992] Crim LR 755.

J. Jaconelli, 'Some thoughts on jury secrecy' (1990) 10 Legal Studies 91.

James Committee, 'Report of the Interdepartmental Committee on The Distribution of Criminal Business between the Crown Court and Magistrates' Courts', Cmnd 6323 (HMSO, 1975).

T. Jefferson and R. Grimshaw, *Controlling the Constable: Police Accountability in England and Wales* (Muller, 1984).

T. Jefferson, M. Walker and M. Seneviratne in D. Downes (ed) *Unravelling Criminal Justice* (Routledge, 1992).

T. Jefferson and M. Walker, 'Ethnic Minorities in the Criminal Justice System' [1992] Crim LR 83.

C. Johnston, 'Trial by dossier' (1992) 142 NLJ 249.

H. Johnston, 'Court duty solicitors', Legal Action, May 1992, 11

T. Jones, B. McLean, J. Young, *The Islington Crime Survey* (Gower, 1986).

M. Joutsen, *The Role of the Victim of Crime in European Criminal Justice Systems* (Helsinki Institute for Crime Prevention and Control, 1987).

Justice, *Miscarriages of Justice* (1989).

H. Kalven and H. Zeisel, *The American Jury* (Little Brown & Co, 1966).

T. Kaye, *'Unsafe and Unsatisfactory'? Report of the Independent Inquiry into the working practices of the West Midlands Police Serious Crime Squad* (Civil Liberties Trust, 1991).

S. Keith, 'The criminal histories of those cautioned in 1985 and 1988' (1992) 32 Home Office Research Bulletin, 44.

C. Kemp, C. Norris, and N. Fielding, 'Legal Manoeuvres in Police Handling of Disputes' in D. Farrington and S. Walklate (eds) *Offenders and Victims, Theory and Policy* (British Society of Criminology, 1992).

M. King, *Bail or Custody* (Cobden Trust, 1971).

M. King, *The Effects of a Duty Solicitor Scheme: An Assessment of the Impact upon a Magistrates' Court* (Cobden Trust, 1977).

M. King, *The Framework of Criminal Justice* (Croom Helm, 1981).

M. King and C. May, *Black Magistrates* (Cobden Trust, 1985).

M. Knight, *Criminal Appeals* (Stevens, 1970).

J. Langbein, 'The Criminal Trial Before Lawyers' (1978) 45 University of Chicago Law Review, 263.

Law Society, *Advising a Suspect in the Police Station* (1991).

A. Lawson, 'Whither the "General Arrest Conditions"?' [1993] Crim LR 567.

F. Lawson, *Remedies of English Law* (Oxford University Press, 1980).

F. Lawson and B. Rudden, *Law of Property* (Oxford University Press, 1982).

G. Laycock and R. Tarling, 'Police Force Cautioning: Policy and Practice' (1985) 24 Howard Journal of Criminal Justice 81.

Legal Action Group, *Preventing Miscarriages of Justice* (LAG, 1993).

Legal Aid Board, *Franchising: The Next Steps* (1992).

Legal Aid Board, *Annual Reports (1992–93)* (HMSO, 1992).

L. Leigh and L. Zedner, 'A Report on the Administration of Criminal Justice in the Pre-Trial phase in England and Germany', Royal Commission on Criminal Justice, Research Study No 1 (HMSO, 1992).

R. Leng, 'The Right to Silence in Police Interrogation: A Study of Some of the Issues Underlying the Debate', Royal Commission on Criminal Justice, Research Study No 10 (HMSO, 1993).

R. Leng and A. Sanders, 'The CLRC Report on Prostitution' [1983] Crim LR 644.

H. Levenson and F. Fairweather, *Police Powers, a Practitioner's Guide* (LAG, 1990).

M. Levi, 'The Investigation, Prosecution and Trial of Serious Fraud', Royal Commission on Criminal Justice, Research Study No 14 (HMSO, 1993).

H. Lewis and G. Mair, 'Bail and Probation Work II: the use of London Probation Bail Hostels for Bailees', Home Office Research and Planning Unit Paper No 50 (Home Office, 1989).

K. Lidstone, R. Hogg and F. Sutcliffe, 'Prosecutions by Private Individuals and Non-Police Agencies', Royal Commission on Criminal Procedure, Research Study No 10 (HMSO, 1980).

C. Lloyd, 'Bail Information Schemes: Practice and Effect', Home Office Research and Planning Unit Paper No 69 (Home Office, 1992).

Lord Chancellor's Department, 'Legal Aid in England and Wales: A New Framework', Cm 118 (1987).

Lord Chancellor's Department, 'Evidence to Runciman Royal Commission on Criminal Justice', November 1991.

Lord Chancellor's Department, 'A New Framework for Local Justice', Cm 1829 (1992).

B. Loveday, 'Recent Developments in Police Complaints Procedure', Local Government Studies May/June 1989, 25.

L. Lustgarten, *The Governance of Police* (Sweet and Maxwell, 1986).

L. Lustgarten, 'The Police and the Substantive Criminal Law' (1987) 27 BJ Crim 24.

J. A. Mack, 'Full-time Major Criminals and the Courts' (1976) 39 Modern Law Review 241

Sheriff I. Macphail, 'Safeguards in the Scottish Criminal Justice System' [1992] Crim LR 144.

M. Mansfield and N. Taylor, 'Post-Conviction Procedures' in C. Walker and K. Starmer (eds) *Justice in Error* (Blackstone, 1993).

D. McBarnet, *Conviction* (MacMillan, 1983).

S. McCabe and R. Purves, *By-passing the Jury* (Blackwell, 1972).

S. McCabe and R. Purves, *The Jury at Work* (Blackwell, 1972)

S. McCabe and R. Purves, 'The Shadow Jury at Work' (Oxford University Penal Research Unit: Blackwell, 1974).

M. McConville, 'Search of persons and premises: new data from London' [1983] Crim LR 605.

M. McConville, 'Shadowing the jury' (1991) 141 NLJ 1588

M. McConville, 'Videotaping interrogations' [1992] Crim LR 532.

M. McConville, 'Corroboration and Confessions: The Impact of a Rule Requiring that no Conviction can be Sustained on the Basis of

Confession Evidence Alone', Royal Commission on Criminal Justice, Research Study No 13 (HMSO, 1993).

M. McConville and J. Baldwin, *Courts, Prosecution, and Conviction* (1981).

M. McConville and J. Baldwin, 'The Role of Interrogation in Crime Discovery and Conviction' (1982) 22 BJ Crim 165.

M. McConville and L. Bridges, 'Pleading guilty whilst maintaining innocence' (1993) 143 NLJ 160.

M. McConville and J. Hodgson, 'Custodial Legal Advice and the Right to Silence', Royal Commission on Criminal Justice, Research Study No 16 (HMSO, 1993).

M. McConville, J. Hodgson, L. Bridges, and A. Pavlovic, *Standing Accused* (Oxford University Press, 1994).

M. McConville and C. Mirsky, 'The State, the Legal Profession, and the Defence of the Poor' (1988) 15 Journal of Law and Society 342.

M. McConville and P. Morrell, 'Recording the Interrogation: Have the Police got it Taped?' [1983] Crim LR 158.

M. McConville and A. Sanders, 'Weak Cases and the CPS' (1992) Law Society's Gazette 12 February, 24.

M. McConville and A. Sanders, 'Fairness and the CPS' (1992) 142 NLJ 120.

M. McConville, A. Sanders and R. Leng, *The Case for the Prosecution* (Routledge, 1991).

M. McConville and D. Shepherd, *Watching Police, Watching Communities* (Routledge, 1992).

J. McEldowney, 'Stand by for the Crown – An Historical Analysis' [1979] Crim LR 272.

J. McEwan, 'Documentary Hearsay Evidence – Refuge for the Vulnerable Witness' [1989] Crim LR 629.

J. McEwan, *Evidence and the Adversarial Process* (Basil Blackwell, 1992).

I. McKenzie, R. Morgan and R. Reiner, 'Helping the police with their enquiries' [1990] Crim LR 22.

H. McLaughlin, 'Court Clerks: Advisers or Decision-Makers' (1990) 30 BJ Crim 358.

M. McMahon, 'Police Accountability: the Situation of Complaints in Toronto' (1988) 12 Contemporary Crises 301.

Magistrates' Association, *Sentencing Guidelines*, September 1993.

M. Maguire, 'Effects of the PACE provisions on detention and questioning' (1988) 28 British Journal of Criminology 19.

M. Maguire, 'Complaints against the Police: Where Now?' (unpublished manuscript).

M. Maguire and C. Norris, 'The Conduct and Supervision of Criminal Investigations', Royal Commission on Criminal Justice, Research Study No 5 (HMSO, 1992).

M. Maguire, 'Parole' in E. Stockdale and S. Casale (eds) *Criminal Justice Under Stress* (Blackstone, 1992).

M. Maguire and C. Corbett, *A Study of the Police Complaints System* (HMSO, 1991).

G. Maher, 'Jury verdicts and the presumption of innocence' (1983) 3 Legal Studies 146.

K. Malleson, 'Miscarriages of Justice and the Accessibility of the Court of Appeal' [1991] Crim LR 323.

K. Malleson, 'Review of the Appeal Process', Royal Commission on Criminal Justice, Research Study No 17 (HMSO, 1993).

G. Mansfield and J. Peay, *The Director of Public Prosecutions* (Tavistock, 1987).

R. Mark, *Minority Verdict*, The 1973 Dimbleby Lecture (BBC, 1973).

D. Matheson, *Legal Aid: The New Framework* (Butterworths, 1988).

P. Mayhew, D. Elliott and L. Dowds, 'The 1988 British Crime Survey', Home Office Research Study No 111 (HMSO, 1989).

P. Mayhew, N. Maung and C. Mirrlees-Black, 'The 1992 British Crime Survey', Home Office Research Study No 132 (HMSO, 1993).

A. Meehan, 'Internal Police Records and the Control of Juveniles' (1993) 33 BJ Crim 504.

D. Miers, 'The Responsibilities and the Rights of Victims of Crime' (1992) 55 Mod L Rev 482.

P. Mirfield, *Confessions* (Sweet and Maxwell, 1985).

P. Mirfield, 'The Legacy of *Hunt*' [1988] Crim LR 19.

P. Mirfield, 'An Ungrateful Reply' [1988] Crim LR 233.

S. Moody and J. Tombs, 'Plea Negotiations in Scotland' [1983] Crim LR 297.

S. Moody and J. Tombs, *Prosecution in the Public Interest* (Scottish Academic Press, 1982).

R. Morgan, R. Reiner, I. McKenzie, 'Police Powers and Policy: A study of the Work of Custody Officers', Report to ESRC (unpublished).

R. Morgan and S. Jones, 'Bail or Jail?' in E. Stockdale and S. Casale (eds) *Criminal Justice Under Stress* (Blackstone, 1992).

J. Morison and P. Leith, *The Barrister's World* (Oxford University Press, 1992).

R. Morley and A. Mullender, 'Hype or Hope? The Importation of Pro-Arrest Policies and Batterers' Programmes from North America to Britain as Key Measures for Preventing Violence against Women in the Home' (1992) 6 International Journal of Law and the Family 265.

P. Morris and K. Heal, 'Crime Control and the Police', Home Office Research Study No 67 (HMSO, 1981).

S. Moston and T. Engelberg, 'Police Questioning Techniques in Tape Recorded Interviews with Criminal Suspects' (1993) 3 Policing and Society 223.

S. Moston and G. Stephenson, 'The Questioning and Interviewing of Suspects outside the Police Station', Royal Commission on Criminal Justice, Research Study No 22 (HMSO, 1993).

S. Moston, G. Stephenson and T. Williamson, 'The Effects of Case Characteristics on Suspect Behaviour During Police Questioning' (1992) 32 BJ Crim 33.

S. Moston and T. Williamson, 'The Extent of Silence in Police Stations' in S. Greer and R. Morgan (eds) *The Right to Silence Debate: Proceedings of a Conference at the University of Bristol in March 1990* (University of Bristol, 1990).

D. Moxon, 'Sentencing Practice in the Crown Court', Home Office Research Study No 103 (HMSO, 1988).

A. Mulcahy, I. Brownlee and C. Walker, 'An Evaluation of Pre-Trial Reviews in Leeds and Bradford Magistrates' Courts' (1993) 33 Home Office Research Bulletin 10.

R. Munday, 'The Wilder Permutations of s 1(f) of the Criminal Evidence Act 1898' (1987) 7 Legal Studies, 137.

R. Munday, 'Jury trial, continental style' (1993) 13 Legal Studies 204.

G. Mungham and Z. Bankowski, 'The jury in the legal system' in P. Carlen (ed) *The Sociology of Law* (University of Keele, 1976).

G. Mungham and P. Thomas, 'Solicitors and clients: altruism or self-interest?' in R. Dingwall and P. Lewis (eds) *The Sociology of the Professions* (MacMillan, 1983).

D. Nelken, *The Limits of the Legal Process* (MacMillan, 1983).

A. Norrie, *Crime, Reason and History* (Weidenfeld and Nicolson, 1993).

C. Norris, N. Fielding, C. Kemp, J. Fielding, 'Black and Blue: an Analysis of the Influence of Race on Being Stopped by the Police' (1992) 43 BJ Sociology 207.

P. O'Connor, 'The Court of Appeal: Re-Trials and Tribulations' [1990] Crim LR 615.

P. O'Connor, 'Prosecution Disclosure: Principle, Practice and Justice' in C. Walker and K. Starmer (eds) *Justice in Error* (Blackstone, 1993).

P. Osborne, 'Judicial Review of Prosecutors' Discretion' (1992) 43 NILQ 178.

H. Packer, *The Limits of the Criminal Sanction* (Stanford University Press, 1968).

N. Padfield, 'The Right to Bail: a Canadian Perspective' [1993] Crim LR 510.

H. Parker, M. Casburn and D. Turnbull, *Receiving Juvenile Justice* (Basil Blackwell, 1981).

H. Parker, M. Sumner and G. Jarvis, *Unmasking the Magistrates* (Open University Press, 1989).

R. Pattenden, 'Should Confessions be Corroborated?' (1991) 107 LQR 319.

R. Pattenden, 'Evidence of Previous Malpractice by Police Witnesses and *R v Edwards*' [1992] Crim LR 549.

F. Pearce and S. Tombs, 'Ideology, Hegemony and Empiricism: Compliance Theories of Regulation' (1990) 30 BJ Crim 423.

J. Percy-Smith and P. Hillyard, 'Miners in the Arms of the Law: A Statistical Analysis' (1985) 12 Journal of Law and Society, 345.

I. Piliavin and S. Briar 'Police encounters with juveniles' (1964) 70 American Journal of Sociology 206.

J. Plotnikoff and R. Woolfson, *From Committal to Trial: Delay at the Crown Court* (Law Society, 1993).

J. Plotnikoff and R. Woolfson, 'Information and Advice for Prisoners about Grounds for Appeal and the Appeals Process', Royal Commission on Criminal Justice, Research Study No 18 (HMSO, 1993).

Police Complaints Authority, *Annual Report 1987* (HMSO).

Police Complaints Board, *Triennial Report* (HMSO, 1980)

C. Ponting, *The Right to Know, The Inside Story of the Belgrano Affair* (Sphere, 1985).

D. Powis, *The Signs of Crime* (McGraw-Hill, 1977).

J. Pratt, 'Diversion from the Juvenile Court' (1986) 26 British Journal of Criminology 212.

J. Pratt and K. Bray, 'Bail Hostels – Alternatives to Custody?' (1985) 25 BJ Crim 160

R. Reiner, *The Politics of the Police* (Harvester Wheatsheaf, 1992).

R. Reiner and S. Spencer (eds) *Accountable Policing* (IPPR, 1993).

J. Rex, *The Ghetto and the Underclass* (Avebury, 1988).

G. Richardson, with A. Ogus, and P. Burroughs, *Policing Pollution: A Study of Regulation and Enforcement* (Clarendon Press, 1983).

D. Riley and J. Vennard, 'Triable-either-way cases: Crown Court or Magistrates' Court?', Home Office Research Study No 98 (HMSO, 1988).

J. Robbilliard and J. McEwan, *Police Powers and the Individual* (Blackwell, 1986).

J. Robbins, 'Who said anything about law?' (1990) 140 NLJ 1275.

D. Roberts, 'Questioning the Suspect: the Solicitor's Role' [1993] Crim LR 369.

P. Roberts and C. Willmore, 'The Role of Forensic Science Evidence in Criminal Proceedings', Royal Commission on Criminal Justice, Research Study No 11 (HMSO, 1993).

Roskill Committee, 'Report of the Departmental Committee on Fraud Trials,'(HMSO, 1986).

Royal Commission on Criminal Procedure, 'Report', Cmnd 8092 (HMSO, 1981).

Royal Commission on Criminal Procedure, 'The Investigation and Prosecution of Criminal Offences in England and Wales: The Law and Procedure', Cmnd 8092-1 (1981).

Royal Commission on Criminal Justice, 'Report', Cm 2263 (HMSO, 1993).

J. Rozenberg, *The Case for the Crown* (Equation, 1987).

J. Rozenberg, 'Miscarriages of Justice' in E. Stockdale and S. Casale (eds) *Criminal Justice Under Stress* (Blackstone, 1992).

A. Sanders, 'Does Professional Crime Pay? – A Critical Comment on Mack' (1977) 40 Modern Law Review 553.

A. Sanders, 'The Erosion of Jury Trial' (1980) 5 Holdsworth Law Review 21.

A. Sanders, 'Prosecution Decisions and the Attorney-General's Guidelines' [1985] Crim LR 4.

A. Sanders, 'Class Bias in Prosecutions' (1985) 24 Howard Journal of Criminal Justice 76.

A. Sanders, 'An Independent Crown Prosecution Service' [1986] Crim LR 27.

A. Sanders, 'Diverting Offenders from Prosecution: can we learn from other countries?' (1986) 150 JP 614.

A. Sanders, 'Arrest, Charge and Prosecution' (1986) 6 Legal Studies, 257.

A. Sanders, 'Constructing the Case for the Prosecution' (1987) 14 Journal of Law and Society 229.

A. Sanders, 'Personal Violence and Public Order' (1988) 16 International Journal of the Sociology of Law 359.

A. Sanders, 'Rights, Remedies, and the Police and Criminal Evidence Act' [1988] Crim LR 802.

A. Sanders, 'The Limits to Diversion from Prosecution' (1988) 28 BJ Crim 513.

A. Sanders, 'Access to a solicitor and s 78 PACE' Law Soc Gaz 31 October 1990, 17.

A. Sanders and L. Bridges, 'Access to Legal Advice and Police Malpractice' [1990] Crim LR 494.

A. Sanders, L. Bridges, A. Mulvaney and G. Crozier, *Advice and Assistance at Police Stations and the 24 Hour Duty Solicitor Scheme* (Lord Chancellor's Department, 1989).

A. Sanders and L. Bridges, 'The Right to Legal Advice' in C. Walker and K. Starmer (eds) *Justice in Error* (Blackstone, 1993)

Sir L. Scarman, 'The Brixton Disorders: 10–12 April 1981', Cmnd 8427 (HMSO, 1981).

I. Scott, 'Criminal Procedure: Appeals to Quarter Sessions' (1970) 134 Justice of the Peace and Local Government Review 843.

I. Scott, 'Appeals to the Crown Court following Summary Conviction', Paper delivered to SPTL Criminal Law Group (1977).

Seabrook Report, 'The Efficient Disposal of Business in the Crown Court' (General Council of the Bar, 1992).

L. Sealy and W. Cornish, 'Juries and the Rules of Evidence' [1973] Crim LR 208.

J. Shapland and R. Hobbs, 'Policing priorities on the Ground' in R. Morgan and D. Smith (eds) *Coming to Terms with Policing* (Routledge, 1989).

J. Shapland and J. Vagg, *Policing by the Public* (Routledge, 1988).

L. Sherman, 'The Influence of Criminology on Criminal Law: Evaluating Arrests for Misdemeanour Domestic Violence' (1992) 83 Jo Crim Law and Criminology 1.

A. Sherr and R. Moorhead, 'Transaction criteria: back to the future', Legal Action, April 1993, 7.

J. Sigler, 'Public Prosecution in England and Wales' [1974] Crim LR 642.

W. Skogan, 'The Police and Public in England and Wales', Home Office Research Study No 117 (HMSO, 1990).

G. Slapper, 'Corporate Manslaughter' (1993) 2 Social and Legal Studies 423.

D. Smith, 'Origins of Black Hostility to the Police' (1991) 2:1 Policing and Society 6.

D. Smith and J. Gray, *Police and People in London*, vol 4, *The Police in Action*, Policy Studies Institute (Gower, 1983).

R. Smith, 'Resolving the Legal Aid Crisis', Law Society's Gazette, 27 February 1991, 17.

P. Softley, 'Police Interrogation: An Observational Study in Four Police Stations', Royal Commission on Criminal Procedure, Research Study No 4 (HMSO, 1981).

P. Southgate and P. Ekblom, 'Contacts Between Police and Public', Home Office Research Study No 77 (HMSO, 1984).

P. Southgate, 'Police–Public Encounters', Home Office Research Study No 90 (HMSO, 1986).

P. Southgate and D. Crisp, 'Public Satisfaction with Police Services', Home Office Research and Planning Unit Paper 73 (Home Office, 1993).

J. Spencer, 'Questions of Bail' (1988) 152 Justice of the Peace, 244.

J. Spencer, 'Judicial Review of Criminal Proceedings' [1991] Crim LR 259.

J. Sprack 'The Trial Process' in E. Stockdale and S. Casale (eds) *Criminal Justice Under Stress* (Blackstone, 1992).

D. Steer, *Police Cautions* (Blackwell, 1972).

D. Steer, 'Uncovering Crime: The Police Role', Royal Commission on Criminal Procedure, Research Study No 7 (HMSO, 1980).

G. Stephenson, 'Should collaborative testimony be permitted in courts of law?' [1990] Crim LR 302.

P. Stevens and C. Willis, 'Race, Crime and Arrests', Home Office Research Study No 58 (HMSO, 1979).

B. Steventon, 'The Ability to Challenge DNA Evidence', Royal Commission on Criminal Justice, Research Study No 9 (HMSO, 1993).

E. Stockdale and S. Casale (eds) *Criminal Justice Under Stress* (Blackstone, 1992).

E. Stockdale and K. Devlin, *Sentencing* (Waterlow, 1987)

R. Stockdale and C. Walker, 'Forensic Evidence' in C. Walker and K. Starmer (eds) *Justice in Error* (Blackstone, 1993).

C. Stone, *Bail Information for the Crown Prosecution Service* (Vera Institute of Justice, 1988).

C. Stone, *Public Interest Case Assessment* (Inner London Probation Service, 1989).

E. Sward, 'Values, Ideology, and the Evolution of the Adversary System' 64 (1989) Indiana Law Journal 301.

R. Tarling, 'Sentencing Practice in Magistrates' Courts', Home Office Research Study No 56 (HMSO, 1979).

J. Temkin, 'Sexual History Evidence – the Ravishment of Section 2' [1993] Crim LR 3.

E.P. Thompson, *Whigs and Hunters*, pp 259–65 (Penguin, 1975).

P. Thompson, 'Have you really given up legal aid?', Law Society's Gazette, 6 July 1988, 21.

P. Thornton, 'Miscarriages of Justice: A Lost Opportunity' [1993] Crim LR 926.

J. Tombs and S. Moody, 'Alternatives to Prosecution: The Public Interest Redefined' [1993] Crim LR 357.

M. Tregilgas-Davey, 'The Police and Accountability' (1990) 140 NLJ 697.

M. Tuck and P. Southgate, 'Ethnic Minorities, Crime and Policing', Home Office Research Study No 70 (HMSO, 1981).

S. Uglow, A. Dart, A. Bottomley and C. Hale, 'Cautioning Juveniles – Multi-Agency Impotence' [1992] Crim LR 632.

J. Vennard, 'Contested Trials in Magistrates' Courts', Home Office Research Study No 71 (HMSO, 1981).

J. Vennard, 'The Outcome of Contested Trials' in D. Moxon (ed) *Managing Criminal Justice* (HMSO, 1985).

J. Vennard and D. Riley, 'The Use of Peremptory Challenge and Stand By of Jurors and Their Relationship to Final Outcome' [1988] Crim LR 731.

R. Vogler, 'Magistrates and Civil Disorder', LAG Bulletin, 12 November 1982.

J. Wadham, 'Unravelling miscarriages of justice' (1993) 143 NLJ 1650.

R. Walmsley: 'Indecencies Between Males' [1978] Crim LR 400.

M. Wasik, 'Sentencing: a Fresh Look at Aims and Objectives' in E. Stockdale and S. Casale (eds) *Criminal Justice Under Stress* (Blackstone, 1992).

M. Wasik and A. Turner, 'Sentencing Guidelines for the Magistrates' Courts' [1993] Crim LR 345.

M. Weatheritt, 'The Prosecution System: Survey of Prosecuting Solicitors' Departments', Royal Commission on Criminal Procedure, Research Study No 11 (HMSO, 1980).

C. Wells, *Corporations and Criminal Responsibility* (Oxford University Press, 1993).

K. White and S. Brody, 'The Use of Bail Hostels' [1980] Crim LR 420.

R. White, *The Administration of Justice* (Blackwell, 1985).

G. Williams, 'The authentication of statements to the police' [1979] Crim LR 6.

G. Williams, 'Letting off the Guilty and Prosecuting the Innocent' [1985] Crim LR 115.

K. Williams, 'Sueing policemen' (1989) 139 NLJ 1164.

C. Willis, 'The use, effectiveness and impact of police stop and search powers', Home Office Research and Planning Unit Paper 15 (Home Office, 1983).

M. Winfield, *Lacking Conviction: the Remand System in England and Wales* (Prison Reform Trust, 1984).

D. Wolchover, 'Should Judges Sum up on the Facts?' [1989] Crim LR 781.

Woolf Report, 'Prison Disturbances April 1990', Report of an Inquiry by The Rt Hon Lord Justice Woolf (Parts I and II) and His Honour Judge Stephen Tumim (Part II) Cm 1456 (HMSO, 1991).

M. Young, *An Inside Job* (Oxford University Press, 1991).

R. Young, *The Sandwell Mediation and Reparation Scheme* (West Midlands Probation Service, 1987).

R. Young, T. Moloney and A. Sanders, *In the Interests of Justice?* (Legal Aid Board, 1992).

R. Young, 'The Merits of Legal Aid in the Magistrates' Court' [1993] Crim LR 336.

M. Zander, 'Legal Advice and Criminal Appeals: A Survey of Prisoners, Prisons and Lawyers' [1972] Crim LR 132.

M. Zander, 'Are Too Many Professional Criminals Avoiding Conviction?' (1974) 37 Modern Law Review 28.

M. Zander, 'Operation of the Bail Act in London Magistrates' Courts' (1979) 129 NLJ 108.

M. Zander, *The Police and Criminal Evidence Act 1984*, 2nd ed (Sweet and Maxwell, 1990).

M. Zander, 'From inquisitorial to adversarial – the Italian system' (1991) 141 NLJ 678.

M. Zander, 'What the Annual Statistics Tell Us About Pleas and Acquittals' [1991] Crim LR 252.

M. Zander, *Cases and Materials on the English Legal System* (Weidenfeld and Nicolson, 1992).

M. Zander, 'The "innocent" (?) who plead guilty' (1993) 143 NLJ 85.

M. Zander and P. Henderson, 'Crown Court Study', Royal Commission on Criminal Justice, Research Study No 19 (HMSO, 1993).

A. Zuckerman, 'Similar Fact Evidence: The Unobservable Rule' (1987) 104 LQR 187.

A. Zuckerman, 'Illegally Obtained Evidence – Discretion as a Guardian of Legitimacy' (1987) Current Legal Problems 55.

Index